Land Rover Discovery Diesel

Owners Workshop Manual

Martynn Randall

Models covered (5562 - 272)

Discovery 'Series 3' models with 2.7 litre (2720cc) V6 turbo-diesel engines

Does NOT cover petrol engine models
Does NOT cover 'Discovery 4' range introduced May 2009

© Haynes Group Limited 2012

ABCDE
FGHI

A book in the **Haynes Owners Workshop Manual Series**

All rights reserved. No part of this book may be reproduced or transmitted in any form or by any means, electronic or mechanical, including photocopying, recording or by any information storage or retrieval system, without permission in writing from the copyright holder.

ISBN 978 0 85733 983 6

British Library Cataloguing in Publication Data
A catalogue record for this book is available from the British Library.

Printed in India

Haynes Group Limited
Sparkford, Yeovil, Somerset BA22 7JJ, England

Haynes North America, Inc
2801 Townsgate Road, Suite 340, Thousand Oaks, CA 91361

The manufacturer's authorised representative in the EU for product safety is:

HaynesPro BV
Stationsstraat 79 F, 3811MH Amersfoort, The Netherlands
gpsr@haynes.co.uk

Disclaimer

There are risks associated with automotive repairs. The ability to make repairs depends on the individual's skill, experience and proper tools. Individuals should act with due care and acknowledge and assume the risk of performing automotive repairs.

The purpose of this manual is to provide comprehensive, useful and accessible automotive repair information, to help you get the best value from your vehicle. However, this manual is not a substitute for a professional certified technician or mechanic.

This repair manual is produced by a third party and is not associated with an individual vehicle manufacturer. If there is any doubt or discrepancy between this manual and the owner's manual or the factory service manual, please refer to the factory service manual or seek assistance from a professional certified technician or mechanic.

Even though we have prepared this manual with extreme care and every attempt is made to ensure that the information in this manual is correct, neither the publisher nor the author can accept responsibility for loss, damage or injury caused by any errors in, or omissions from, the information given.

Contents

Illegal Copying

It is the policy of the Publisher to actively protect its Copyrights and Trade Marks. Legal action will be taken against anyone who unlawfully copies the cover or contents of this Manual. This includes all forms of unauthorised copying including digital, mechanical, and electronic in any form. Authorisation from the Publisher will only be provided expressly and in writing. Illegal copying will also be reported to the appropriate statutory authorities.

Contents

REPAIRS AND OVERHAUL

The Discovery models covered by this manual were introduced in August 2004. Although a continuation of the long-established Discovery models, the Discovery 3 is a completely new design. In contrast to previous models, it incorporates fully independent front and rear suspension, with fixed final drive units and separate articulated driveshafts. The body is mounted on the separate chassis, and the interior boasts class-leading standards of luxury and occupant protection.

The V6 2.7 litre diesel engine, a joint development between Ford and PSA, incorporates double overhead camshaft cylinder heads, with 4 valves per cylinder, and centrally-mounted electronic fuel injectors. In order to enhance performance and exhaust emissions, the engine is equipped with a large, variable geometry turbocharger, intercooler, exhaust gas recirculation system, and an exhaust particulate filter. 6-speed manual or automatic transmissions were available, with a transfer gearbox to distribute the power to the front and rear final drive units. An ETM (Electronic Torque Managed) rear final drive was available as an option, where the differential could be 'locked' to varying degrees to suit the traction conditions encountered.

Air suspension was fitted to all models, except for the base spec vehicles, where traditional steel coils springs are fitted. The air suspension system allows for ride heights at each wheel to be varied, to suit the driving conditions. Front and rear anti-roll bars are fitted to all models.

A wide range of standard and optional equipment is available within the Discovery range to suit most tastes, including central locking, electric windows, front and rear air conditioning, electric sunroof, anti-lock braking system, electronic brake force distribution, traction control system, hill descent control, satellite navigation, and numerous airbags. The models were available with 5 doors, and 5 or 7 seats.

Provided that regular servicing is carried out in accordance with the manufacturer's recommendations, the Discovery should prove reliable and economical. The engine compartment is well-designed, and most of the items requiring frequent attention are easily accessible.

Your Discovery manual

The aim of this manual is to help you get the best value from your vehicle. It can do so in several ways. It can help you decide what work must be done (even should you choose to get it done by a garage). It will also provide information on routine maintenance and servicing, and give a logical course of action and diagnosis when random faults occur. However, it is hoped that you will use the manual by tackling the work yourself. On simpler jobs it may even be quicker than booking the car into a garage and going there twice, to leave and collect it. Perhaps most important, a lot of money can be saved by avoiding the costs a garage must charge to cover its labour and overheads.

The manual has drawings and descriptions to show the function of the various components so that their layout can be understood. Tasks are described and photographed in a clear step-by-step sequence.

References to the 'left' and 'right' of the vehicle are in the sense of a person in the driver's seat facing forward.

Acknowledgements

Thanks are due to Draper Tools Limited and Auto Service Tools Limited (asttools.co.uk) who provided some of the workshop tools, to Polybush (polybush.co.uk) who supplied suspension bush kits, and to all those people at Sparkford who helped in the production of this manual.

We take great pride in the accuracy of information given in this manual, but vehicle manufacturers make alterations and design changes during the production run of a particular vehicle of which they do not inform us. No liability can be accepted by the authors or publishers for loss, damage or injury caused by any errors in, or omissions from, the information given.

Working on your car can be dangerous. This page shows just some of the potential risks and hazards, with the aim of creating a safety-conscious attitude.

General hazards

Scalding

- Don't remove the radiator or expansion tank cap while the engine is hot.
- Engine oil, transmission fluid or power steering fluid may also be dangerously hot if the engine has recently been running.

Burning

- Beware of burns from the exhaust system and from any part of the engine. Brake discs and drums can also be extremely hot immediately after use.

Crushing

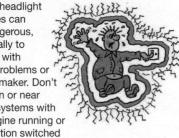

- When working under or near a raised vehicle, always supplement the jack with axle stands, or use drive-on ramps. ***Never venture under a car which is only supported by a jack***.
- Take care if loosening or tightening high-torque nuts when the vehicle is on stands. Initial loosening and final tightening should be done with the wheels on the ground.

Fire

- Fuel is highly flammable; fuel vapour is explosive.
- Don't let fuel spill onto a hot engine.
- Do not smoke or allow naked lights (including pilot lights) anywhere near a vehicle being worked on. Also beware of creating sparks (electrically or by use of tools).
- Fuel vapour is heavier than air, so don't work on the fuel system with the vehicle over an inspection pit.
- Another cause of fire is an electrical overload or short-circuit. Take care when repairing or modifying the vehicle wiring.
- Keep a fire extinguisher handy, of a type suitable for use on fuel and electrical fires.

Electric shock

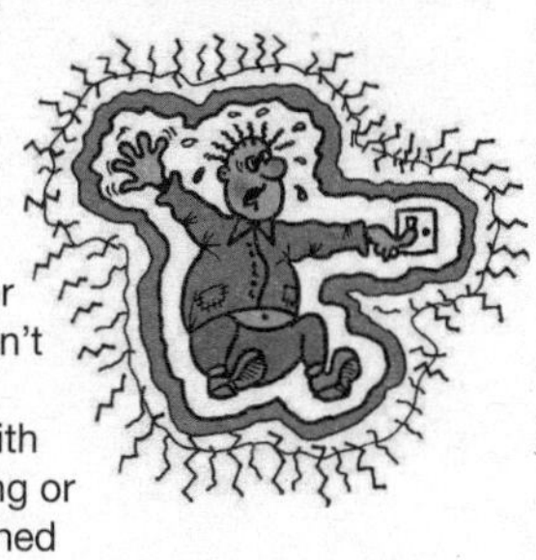

- Ignition HT and Xenon headlight voltages can be dangerous, especially to people with heart problems or a pacemaker. Don't work on or near these systems with the engine running or the ignition switched on.
- Mains voltage is also dangerous. Make sure that any mains-operated equipment is correctly earthed. Mains power points should be protected by a residual current device (RCD) circuit breaker.

Fume or gas intoxication

- Exhaust fumes are poisonous; they can contain carbon monoxide, which is rapidly fatal if inhaled. Never run the engine in a confined space such as a garage with the doors shut.
- Fuel vapour is also poisonous, as are the vapours from some cleaning solvents and paint thinners.

Poisonous or irritant substances

- Avoid skin contact with battery acid and with any fuel, fluid or lubricant, especially antifreeze, brake hydraulic fluid and Diesel fuel. Don't syphon them by mouth. If such a substance is swallowed or gets into the eyes, seek medical advice.
- Prolonged contact with used engine oil can cause skin cancer. Wear gloves or use a barrier cream if necessary. Change out of oil-soaked clothes and do not keep oily rags in your pocket.
- Air conditioning refrigerant forms a poisonous gas if exposed to a naked flame (including a cigarette). It can also cause skin burns on contact.

Asbestos

- Asbestos dust can cause cancer if inhaled or swallowed. Asbestos may be found in gaskets and in brake and clutch linings. When dealing with such components it is safest to assume that they contain asbestos.

Special hazards

Hydrofluoric acid

- This extremely corrosive acid is formed when certain types of synthetic rubber, found in some O-rings, oil seals, fuel hoses etc, are exposed to temperatures above 4000C. The rubber changes into a charred or sticky substance containing the acid. *Once formed, the acid remains dangerous for years. If it gets onto the skin, it may be necessary to amputate the limb concerned*.
- When dealing with a vehicle which has suffered a fire, or with components salvaged from such a vehicle, wear protective gloves and discard them after use.

The battery

- Batteries contain sulphuric acid, which attacks clothing, eyes and skin. Take care when topping-up or carrying the battery.
- The hydrogen gas given off by the battery is highly explosive. Never cause a spark or allow a naked light nearby. Be careful when connecting and disconnecting battery chargers or jump leads.

Air bags

- Air bags can cause injury if they go off accidentally. Take care when removing the steering wheel and trim panels. Special storage instructions may apply.

Diesel injection equipment

- Diesel injection pumps supply fuel at very high pressure. Take care when working on the fuel injectors and fuel pipes.

Warning: Never expose the hands, face or any other part of the body to injector spray; the fuel can penetrate the skin with potentially fatal results.

Remember...

DO

- Do use eye protection when using power tools, and when working under the vehicle.
- Do wear gloves or use barrier cream to protect your hands when necessary.
- Do get someone to check periodically that all is well when working alone on the vehicle.
- Do keep loose clothing and long hair well out of the way of moving mechanical parts.
- Do remove rings, wristwatch etc, before working on the vehicle – especially the electrical system.
- Do ensure that any lifting or jacking equipment has a safe working load rating adequate for the job.

DON'T

- Don't attempt to lift a heavy component which may be beyond your capability – get assistance.
- Don't rush to finish a job, or take unverified short cuts.
- Don't use ill-fitting tools which may slip and cause injury.
- Don't leave tools or parts lying around where someone can trip over them. Mop up oil and fuel spills at once.
- Don't allow children or pets to play in or near a vehicle being worked on.

The following pages are intended to help in dealing with common roadside emergencies and breakdowns. You will find more detailed fault finding information at the back of the manual, and repair information in the main chapters.

If your car won't start and the starter motor doesn't turn

- ☐ Lift the bonnet, release the clips and remove the battery cover. Make sure that the battery terminals are clean and tight.
- ☐ Switch on the headlights and try to start the engine. If the headlights go very dim when you're trying to start, the battery is probably flat. Get out of trouble by jump starting using a friend's car.

If your car won't start even though the starter motor turns as normal

- ☐ Is there fuel in the tank?
- ☐ Is there moisture on electrical components under the bonnet? Switch off the ignition, then wipe off any obvious dampness with a dry cloth. Spray a water-repellent aerosol product (WD-40 or equivalent) on fuel system electrical connectors like those shown in the photos.

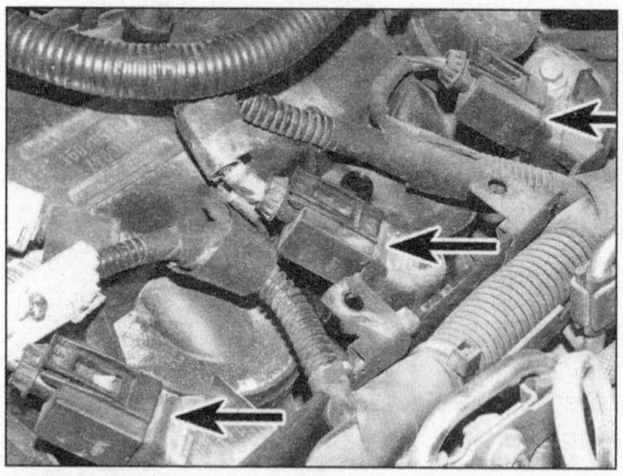

A Check the security of the injector wiring connectors.

B Check the airflow meter wiring connector with the ignition switched off.

C Check the security and condition of the battery terminals.

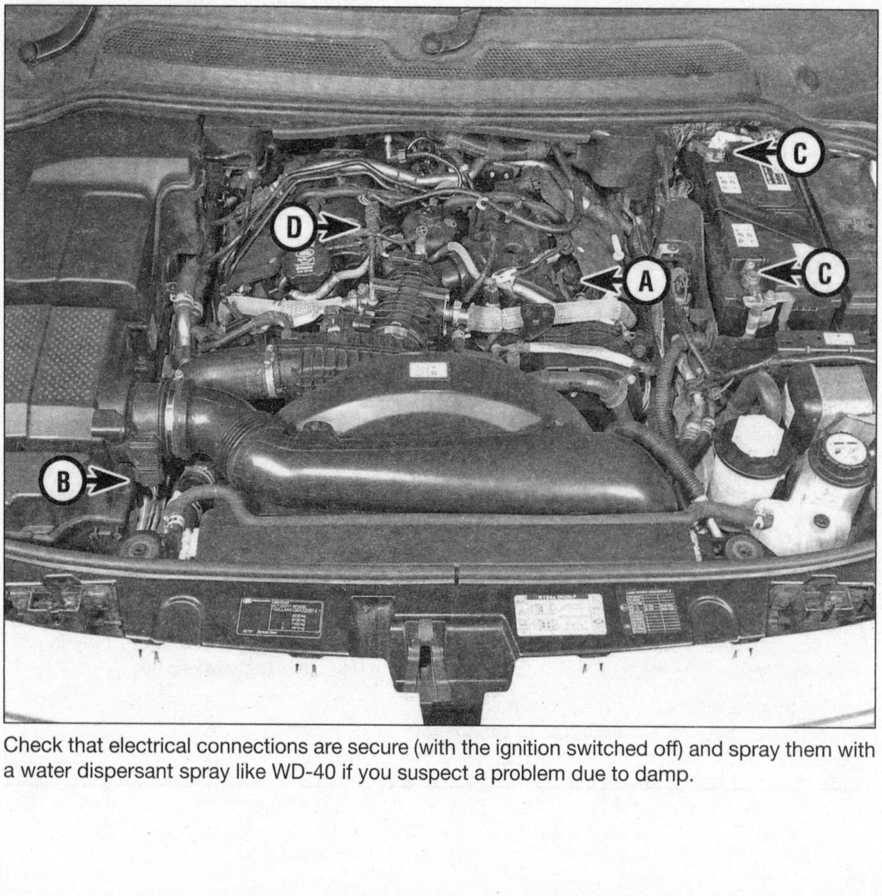

Check that electrical connections are secure (with the ignition switched off) and spray them with a water dispersant spray like WD-40 if you suspect a problem due to damp.

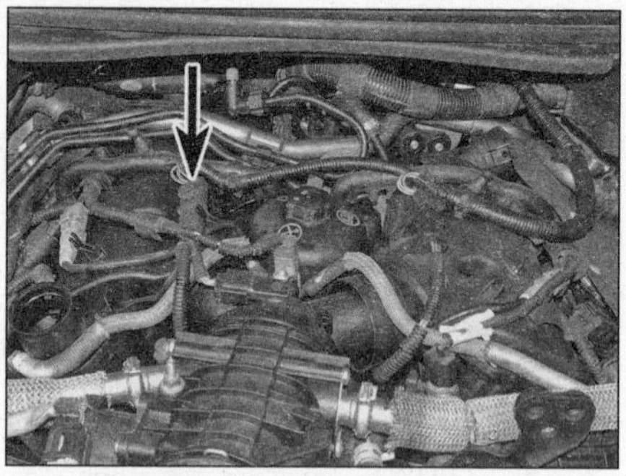

D Check the glow plug connectors.

Jump starting

> **HAYNES HiNT** *Jump starting will get you out of trouble, but you must correct whatever made the battery go flat in the first place. There are three possibilities:*
>
> ***1** The battery has been drained by repeated attempts to start, or by leaving the lights on.*
>
> ***2** The charging system is not working properly (alternator drivebelt slack or broken, alternator wiring fault or alternator itself faulty).*
>
> ***3** The battery itself is at fault (electrolyte low, or battery worn out).*

When jump-starting a car, observe the following precautions:

✓ Before connecting the booster battery, make sure that the ignition is switched off.

Caution: Remove the key in case the central locking engages when the jump leads are connected

✓ Ensure that all electrical equipment (lights, heater, wipers, etc) is switched off.

✓ Take note of any special precautions printed on the battery case.

✓ Make sure that the booster battery is the same voltage as the discharged one in the vehicle.

✓ If the battery is being jump-started from the battery in another vehicle, the two vehicles MUST NOT TOUCH each other.

✓ Make sure that the transmission is in neutral (or PARK, in the case of automatic transmission).

> **HAYNES HiNT** *Budget jump leads can be a false economy, as they often do not pass enough current to start large capacity or diesel engines. They can also get hot.*

1 Release the clips, remove the plastic cover from the flat battery, and connect the red jump lead to the positive terminal. Ensure all electrical consumers are switched off.

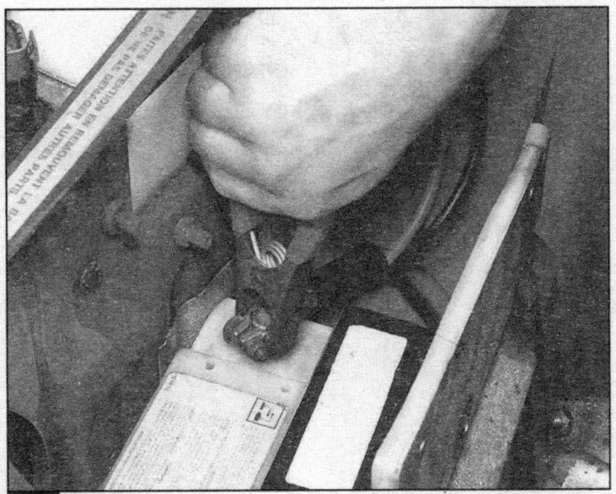

2 Connect the other end of the red lead to the positive (+) terminal of the booster battery.

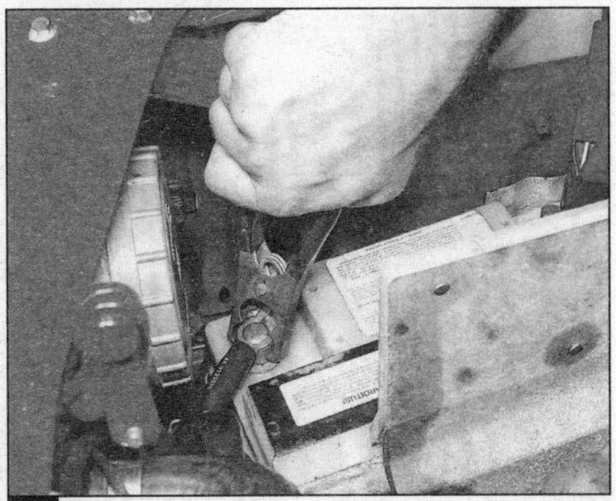

3 Connect one end of the black jump lead to the negative (-) terminal of the booster battery

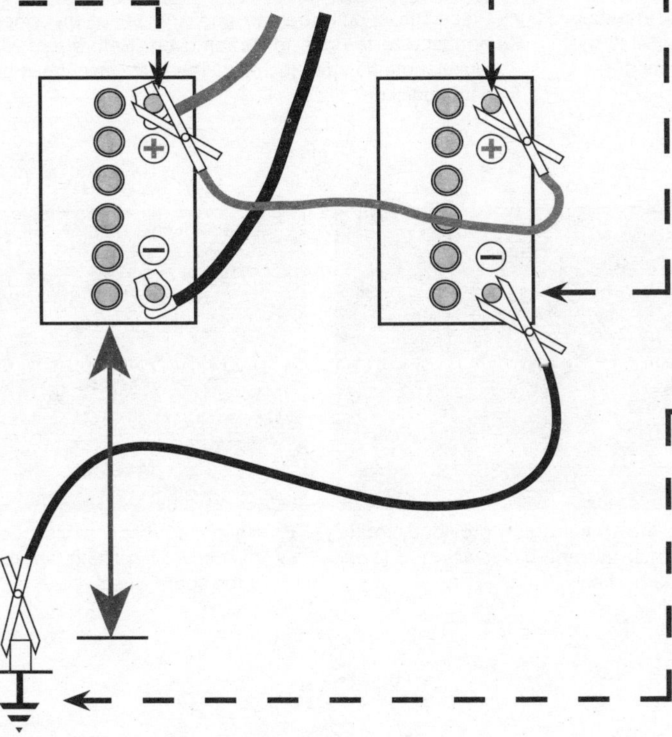

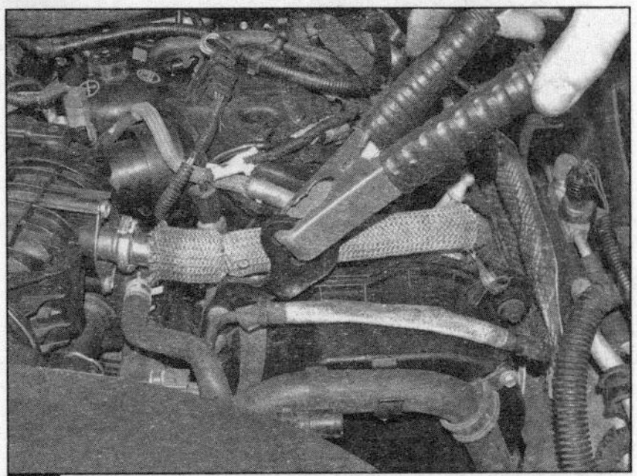

4 Connect the other end of the black jump lead to good earth point (eg, engine mounting bracket) at least 0.5 metre (18") from the battery, fuel and brake pipes on the vehicle to be started

5 Make sure that the jump leads will not come into contact with the fan, drive-belts or other moving parts of the engine.

6 Start the engine using the booster battery and run it at idle speed. Switch on the lights, rear window demister and heater blower motor, then disconnect the jump leads in the reverse order of connection. Turn off the lights etc.

Wheel changing

Warning: Do not change a wheel in a situation where you risk being hit by another vehicle. On busy roads, try to stop in a lay-by or a gateway. Be wary of passing traffic while changing the wheel – it is easy to become distracted by the job in hand.

Preparation

- ☐ When a puncture occurs, stop as soon as it is safe to do so.
- ☐ Park on firm level ground, if possible, and well out of the way of other traffic.
- ☐ Use hazard warning lights if necessary.
- ☐ If you have one, use a warning triangle to alert other drivers of your presence.
- ☐ Apply the handbrake and engage first or reverse gear. On automatic transmissions, ensure the selector lever is in position P (park). On all models, select position L for the transfer box.
- ☐ Chock both sides of the wheel diagonally opposite the one being removed – chocks are located with the tools in the tool bag.
- ☐ If the ground is soft, use a flat piece of wood to spread the load under the foot of the jack.

Changing the wheel

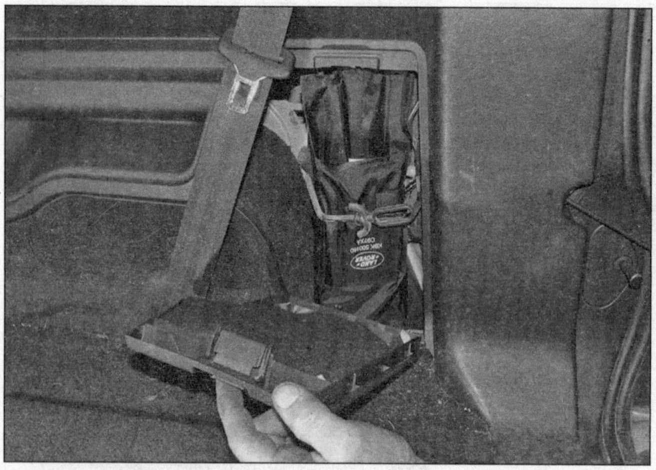

1 The spare wheel is located under the rear of the vehicle. The tools/jack are stored under the luggage compartment floor panel (5-seat models) or behind the right-hand side luggage compartment panel (7-seat models).

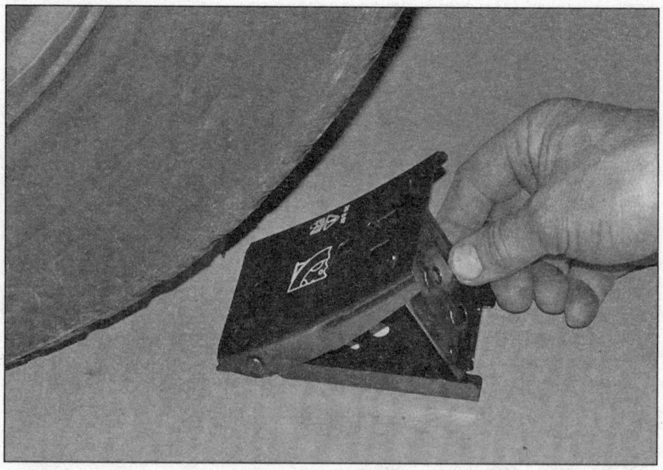

2 Place the chocks behind and in front of the wheel diagonally opposite to the one to be removed. Before removing the spare wheel, note its fitted location. The roadwheel must be fitted in the same position.

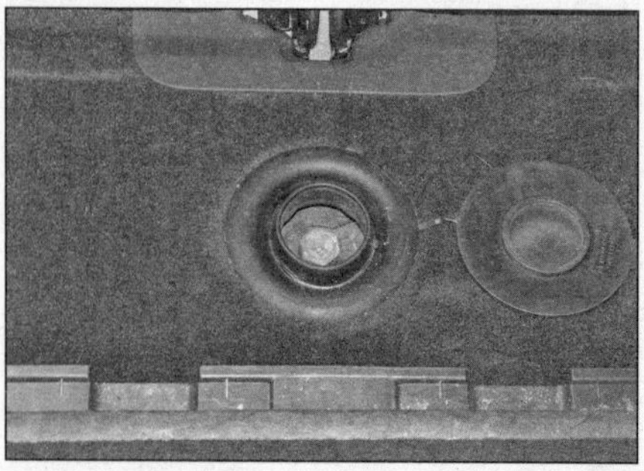

3 Lift the luggage compartment floor panel and remove the jack (5-seat models only), then remove the cover from the luggage compartment floor.

4 Using the wheel brace provided, rotate the winch nut anti-clockwise and lower the spare wheel.

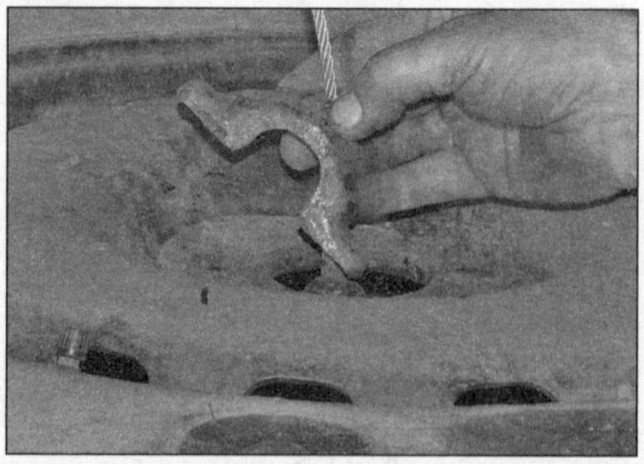

5 When the winch cable becomes slack, manoeuvre the lifting lug from the centre of the spare wheel.

6 On models with air suspension, ensure the suspension is set to the off-road height, then position the jack under the vehicle chassis, so the pin on the jack head is aligned with the corresponding hole. Raise the jack using the 2-piece jack lever and wheel brace, until the pin engages with the hole.

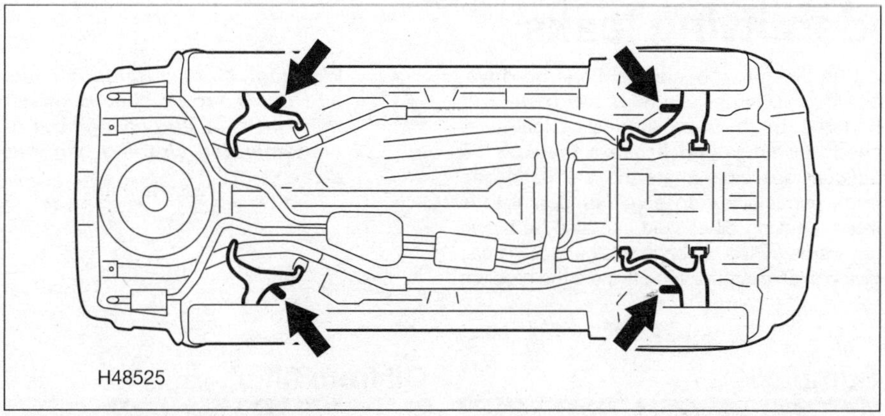

7 On models with steel coil spring suspension, position the jack under the jacking point on the relevant suspension lower arm. Raise the jack so the jack is located securely, but the wheel is still on the ground.

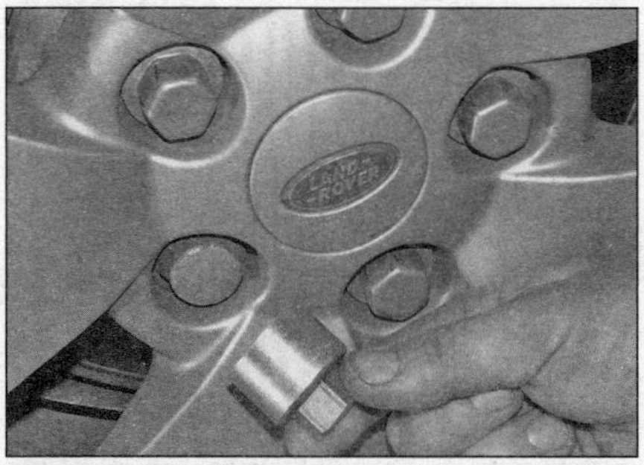

8 Use the wheel brace to slacken the roadwheel nuts half-a-turn. Note that where alloy wheels are fitted, use the locking nut adapter in the tool bag to unscrew the nut. Operate the jack until the wheel is raised clear of the ground. Unscrew the wheel nuts and remove the wheel.

9 Fit the spare wheel and screw on the wheel nuts. Lightly tighten the nuts with the wheel brace then slowly lower the vehicle to the ground. Securely tighten the wheel nuts then refit the wheel trim/hub cap (as applicable). Note that the wheel nuts should be slackened and retightened to the correct torque (140 Nm/103 lbf ft) at the earliest possible opportunity.

Finally...

- ☐ Remove the wheel chocks.
- ☐ Stow the wheel, jack, chocks and tools in the correct locations in the car. The spare wheel winch should be raised until the mechanism 'clutches-out'.
- ☐ Check the tyre pressure on the wheel just fitted. If it is low, or if you don't have a pressure gauge with you, drive slowly to the next garage and inflate the tyre to the correct pressure.
- ☐ Change the transmission to H high-range before driving off.
- ☐ On models with alloy wheels, remove the wheel and apply anti-seize grease to the hub and wheel mating surfaces at the earliest opportunity.
- ☐ Refit the circular centre cap to the stowed wheel to prevent dirt ingress.
- ☐ On models with the temporary 'space-saver' spare wheel, do not exceed 50 mph, and fit a normal wheel as soon as possible.
- ☐ Have the damaged tyre or wheel repaired as soon as possible, or another puncture will leave you stranded.

Towing

When all else fails, you may find yourself having to get a tow home – or of course you may be helping somebody else. Long-distance recovery should only be done by a garage or breakdown service. For shorter distances, DIY towing using another car is easy enough, but observe the following points:

☐ Use a proper tow-rope – they are not expensive. The vehicle being towed must display an ON TOW sign in its rear window.

☐ Always turn the ignition key to the 'on' position when the vehicle is being towed, so that the steering lock is released, and that the direction indicator and brake lights work.

☐ Only attach the tow-rope to the towing eyes provided. The towing eyes are located behind a removable panel in the front and rear bumpers. Rotate the fasteners anti-clockwise 90° and remove the panels.

☐ Attach the towing rope/bar, then turn the ignition switch to position II, then shift the transmission into position N or neutral, as applicable. If the vehicle is suffering a power failure (battery), release the selector lever (automatic transmission only) as described in Chapter 7B.

☐ Turn the ignition to position I (not 0), apply the footbrake and release the parking brake. If required, turn the ignition switch to position II to operate the brake lights or indicators. The vehicle is now ready to be towed.

☐ Note that greater-than-usual pedal pressure will be required to operate the brakes, since the vacuum servo unit is only operational with the engine running. Greater-than-usual steering effort will also be required.

☐ The driver of the car being towed must keep the tow-rope taut at all times to avoid snatching.

☐ Make sure that both drivers know the route before setting off.

☐ Only drive at moderate speeds (up to 30 mph) and keep the distance towed to a minimum (less than 30 miles). Drive smoothly and allow plenty of time for slowing down at junctions.

Identifying leaks

Puddles on the garage floor or drive, or obvious wetness under the bonnet or underneath the car, suggest a leak that needs investigating. It can sometimes be difficult to decide where the leak is coming from, especially if an engine undershield is fitted. Leaking oil or fluid can also be blown rearwards by the passage of air under the car, giving a false impression of where the problem lies.

Warning: Most automotive oils and fluids are poisonous. Wash them off skin, and change out of contaminated clothing, without delay.

HAYNES HiNT *The smell of a fluid leaking from the car may provide a clue to what's leaking. Some fluids are distinctively coloured. It may help to remove the engine undershield, clean the car carefully and to park it over some clean paper overnight as an aid to locating the source of the leak. Remember that some leaks may only occur while the engine is running.*

Sump oil

Engine oil may leak from the drain plug...

Oil from filter

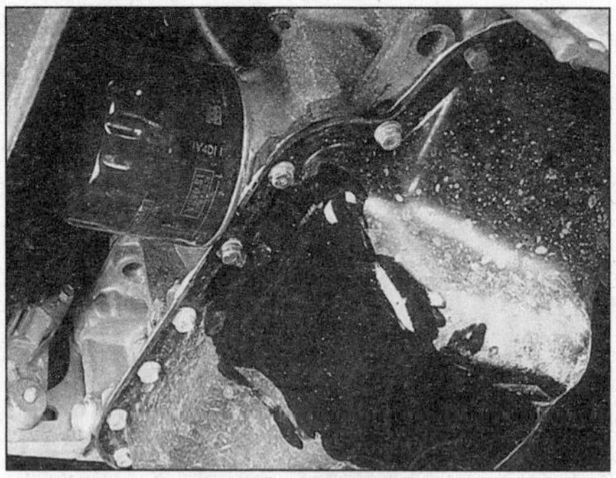

...or from the base of the oil filter.

Gearbox oil

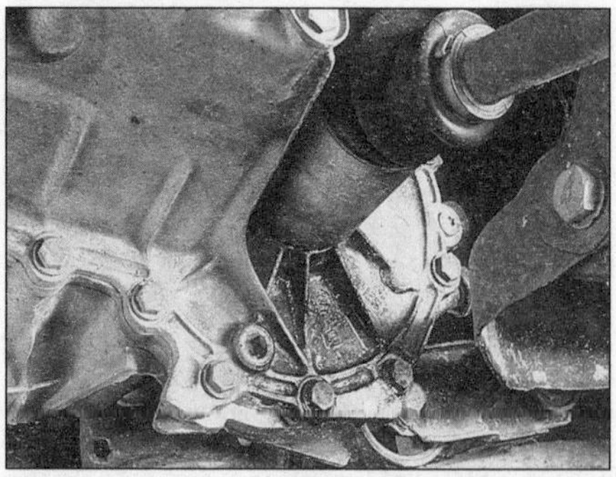

Gearbox oil can leak from the seals at the inboard ends of the driveshafts.

Antifreeze

Leaking antifreeze often leaves a crystalline deposit like this.

Brake fluid

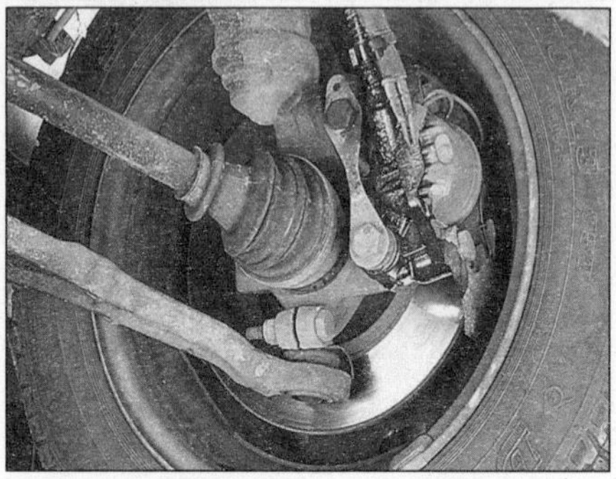

A leak occurring at a wheel is almost certainly brake fluid.

Power steering fluid

Power steering fluid may leak from the pipe connectors on the steering rack.

Introduction

There are some very simple checks which need only take a few minutes to carry out, but which could save you a lot of inconvenience and expense.

These checks require no great skill or special tools, and the small amount of time they take to perform could prove to be very well spent, for example;

☐ Keeping an eye on tyre condition and pressures, will not only help to stop them wearing out prematurely, but could also save your life.

☐ Many breakdowns are caused by electrical problems. Battery-related faults are particularly common, and a quick check on a regular basis will often prevent the majority of these.

☐ If your car develops a brake fluid leak, the first time you might know about it is when your brakes don't work properly. Checking the level regularly will give advance warning of this kind of problem.

☐ If the oil or coolant levels run low, the cost of repairing any engine damage will be far greater than fixing the leak, for example.

Underbonnet check points

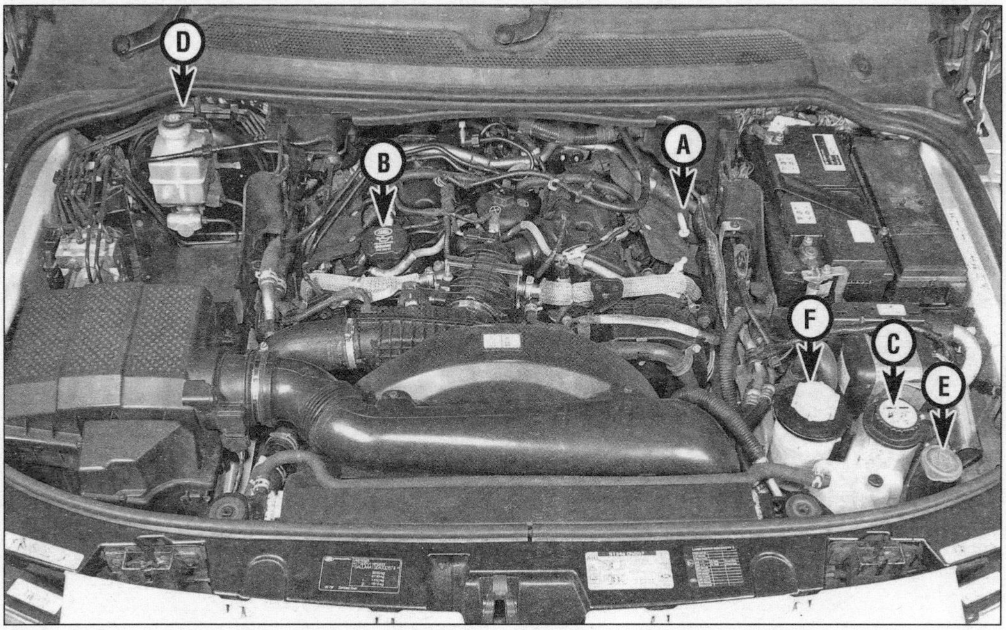

◀ **2.7 litre Discovery 3**

A *Engine oil level dipstick*
B *Engine oil filler cap*
C *Coolant expansion tank*
D *Brake and clutch fluid reservoir*
E *Screen washer fluid reservoir*
F *Power steering fluid reservoir*

Coolant level

Warning: DO NOT attempt to remove the expansion tank pressure cap when the engine is hot, as there is a very great risk of scalding. Do not leave open containers of coolant about, as it is poisonous.

Car care

● With a sealed-type cooling system, adding coolant should not be necessary on a regular basis. If frequent topping-up is required, it is likely there is a leak. Check the radiator, all hoses and joint faces for signs of staining or wetness, and rectify as necessary.

● It is important that antifreeze is used in the cooling system all year round, not just during the winter months. Don't top-up with water alone, as the antifreeze will become too diluted.

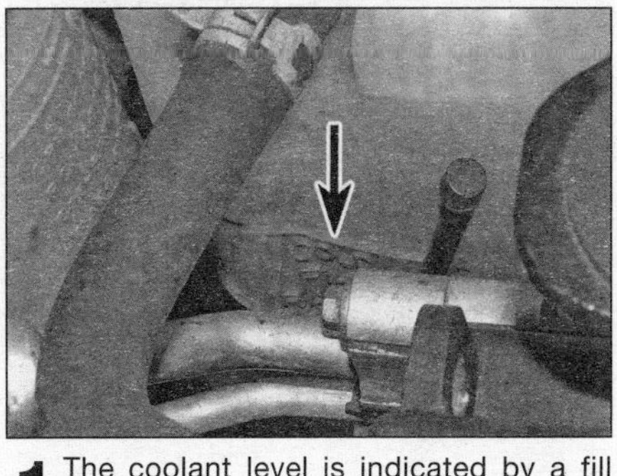

1 The coolant level is indicated by a fill level line on the side of the expansion tank on the left-hand side of the engine compartment.

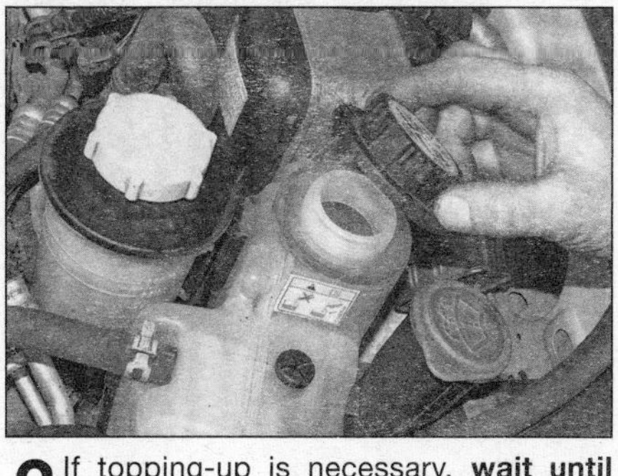

2 If topping-up is necessary, **wait until the engine is cold**. Slowly remove the expansion tank cap, to release any pressure present in the cooling system, and remove it.

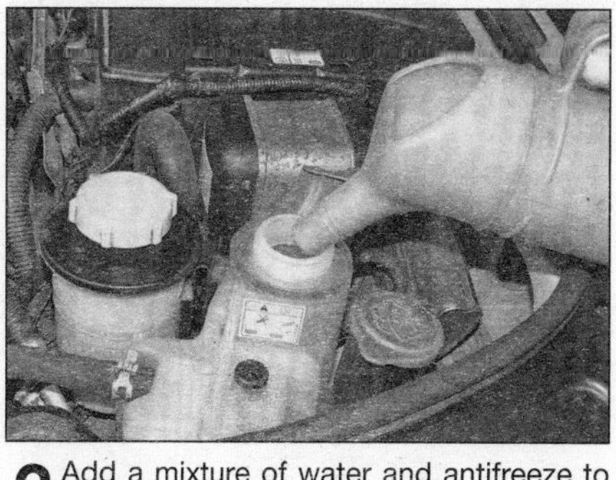

3 Add a mixture of water and antifreeze to the expansion tank until the surface of the coolant is level with the mark on the expansion tank. Refit the cap securely.

Engine oil level

Before you start

✔ Make sure that your car is on level ground.
✔ Check the oil level before the car is driven, or at least 5 minutes after the engine has been switched off.

The correct oil

Modern engines place great demands on their oil. It is very important that the correct oil for your car is used (see *Lubricants and fluids*).

Car care

- If you have to add oil frequently, you should check whether you have any oil leaks. Place some clean paper under the car overnight, and check for stains in the morning. If there are no leaks, the engine may be burning oil, or the oil may only be leaking when the engine is running.
- Always maintain the level between the upper and lower dipstick marks (see photo 3). If the level is too low severe engine damage may occur. Oil seal failure may result if the engine is overfilled by adding too much oil.

HAYNES HiNT ***If the oil is checked immediately after driving the vehicle, some of the oil will remain in the upper engine components, resulting in an inaccurate reading on the dipstick.***

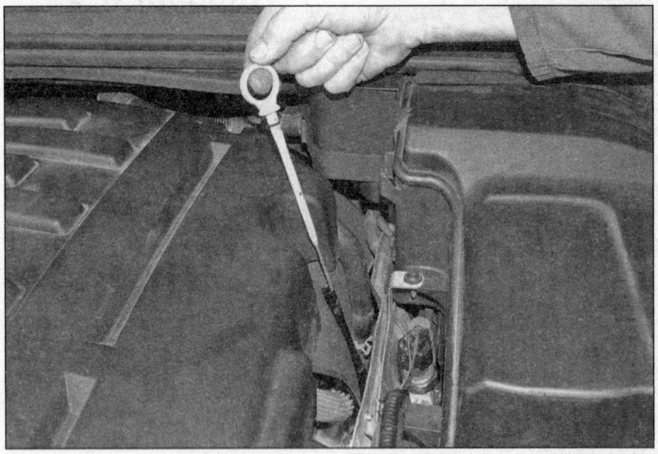

1 The dipstick top is often brightly-coloured for easy identification (see *Underbonnet check points* for exact location). Withdraw the dipstick.

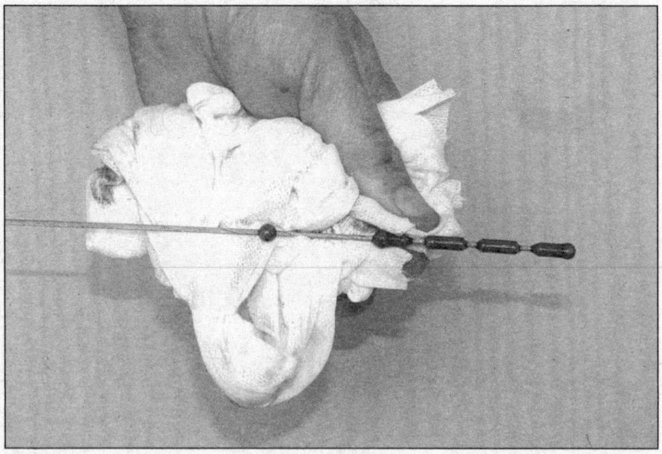

2 Using a clean rag or paper towel remove all oil from the dipstick. Insert the clean dipstick into the tube as far as it will go, then withdraw it again.

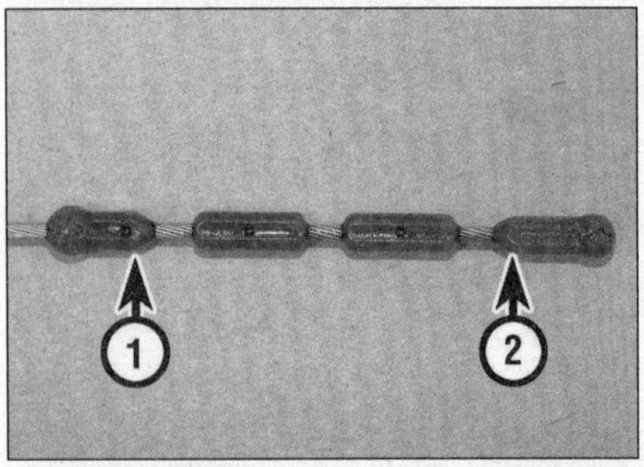

3 Note the oil level on the end of the dipstick, which should be between the upper full mark (1) and low minimum mark (2). Approximately 1.75 litres of oil will raise the level from the lower mark to the upper mark.

4 Oil is added through the filler cap. Unscrew the cap and top-up the level; a funnel may help to reduce spillage.

5 Add the oil slowly, checking the level on the dipstick often. Don't overfill (see *Car care*).

Brake (and clutch) fluid level

Warning:
- ***Brake fluid can harm your eyes and damage painted surfaces, so use extreme caution when handling and pouring it.***
- ***Do not use fluid that has been standing open for some time, as it absorbs moisture from the air, which can cause a dangerous loss of braking effectiveness.***

HAYNES HiNT ***The fluid level in the reservoir will drop slightly as the brake pads wear down, but the fluid level must never be allowed to drop below the MIN mark.***

Before you start

✔ Make sure that your car is on level ground.

Safety first!

- If the reservoir requires repeated topping-up this is an indication of a fluid leak somewhere in the system, which should be investigated immediately.
- If a leak is suspected, the car should not be driven until the braking system has been checked. Never take any risks where brakes are concerned.

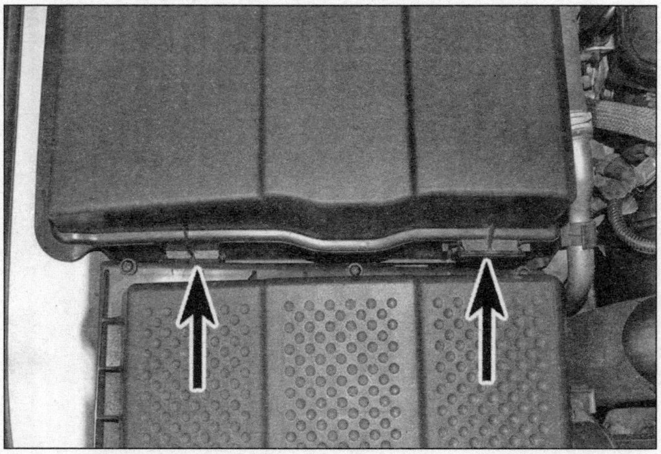

1 Release the clips and remove the plastic cover from the right-hand side of the engine compartment.

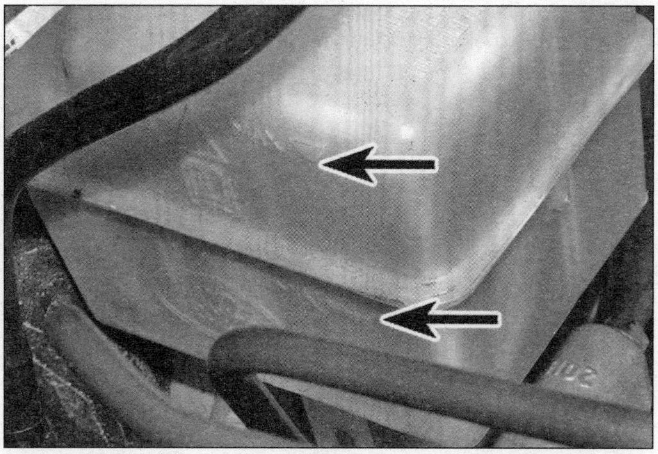

2 The MAX and MIN marks are indicated on the side of the reservoir. The fluid level must be kept between the marks at all times.

3 If topping-up is necessary, first wipe clean the area around the filler cap to prevent dirt entering the hydraulic system.

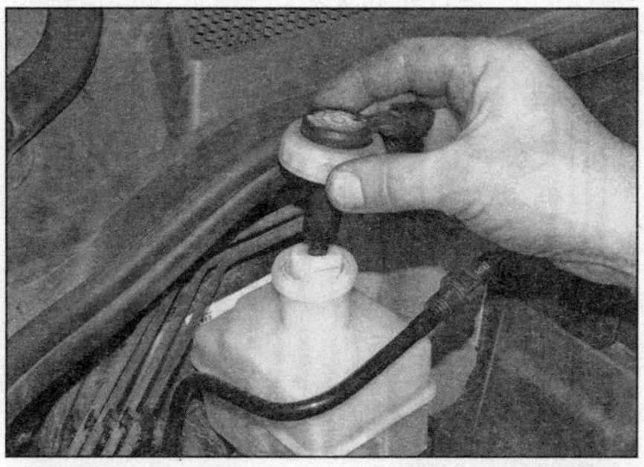

4 Disconnect the level sensor wiring plug, then unscrew the reservoir cap and carefully lift it out of position, taking care not to damage the level switch float. Inspect the reservoir, if the fluid is dirty the hydraulic system should be drained and refilled (see Chapter 1).

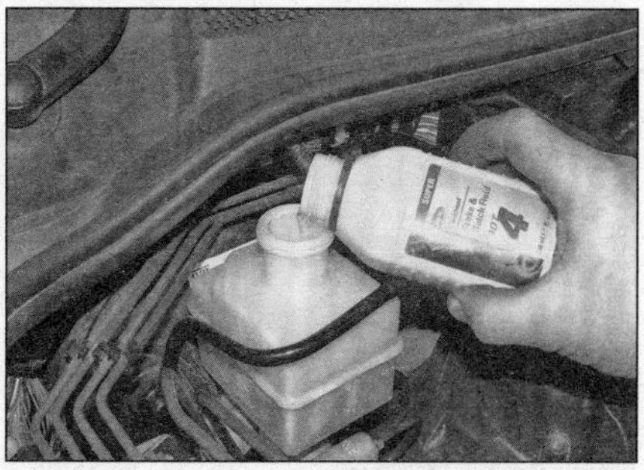

5 Carefully add fluid taking care not to spill it onto the surrounding components. Use only the specified fluid; mixing different types can cause damage to the system. After topping-up to the correct level, securely refit the cap and wipe off any spilt fluid.

Tyre condition and pressure

It is very important that tyres are in good condition, and at the correct pressure - having a tyre failure at any speed is highly dangerous.
Tyre wear is influenced by driving style - harsh braking and acceleration, or fast cornering, will all produce more rapid tyre wear. As a general rule, the front tyres wear out faster than the rears. Interchanging the tyres from front to rear ("rotating" the tyres) may result in more even wear. However, if this is completely effective, you may have the expense of replacing all four tyres at once!
Remove any nails or stones embedded in the tread before they penetrate the tyre to cause deflation. If removal of a nail does reveal that the tyre has been punctured, refit the nail so that its point of penetration is marked. Then immediately change the wheel, and have the tyre repaired by a tyre dealer.
Regularly check the tyres for damage in the form of cuts or bulges, especially in the sidewalls. Periodically remove the wheels, and clean any dirt or mud from the inside and outside surfaces. Examine the wheel rims for signs of rusting, corrosion or other damage. Light alloy wheels are easily damaged by "kerbing" whilst parking; steel wheels may also become dented or buckled. A new wheel is very often the only way to overcome severe damage.
New tyres should be balanced when they are fitted, but it may become necessary to re-balance them as they wear, or if the balance weights fitted to the wheel rim should fall off. Unbalanced tyres will wear more quickly, as will the steering and suspension components. Wheel imbalance is normally signified by vibration, particularly at a certain speed (typically around 50 mph). If this vibration is felt only through the steering, then it is likely that just the front wheels need balancing. If, however, the vibration is felt through the whole car, the rear wheels could be out of balance. Wheel balancing should be carried out by a tyre dealer or garage.

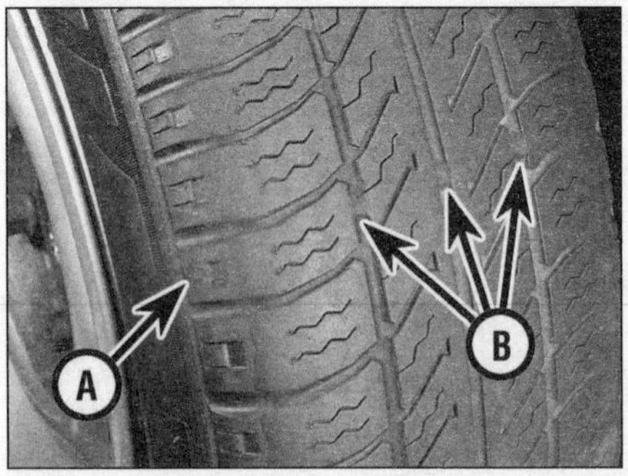

1 ***Tread Depth - visual check***
The original tyres have tread wear safety bands (B), which will appear when the tread depth reaches approximately 1.6 mm. The band positions are indicated by a triangular mark on the tyre sidewall (A).

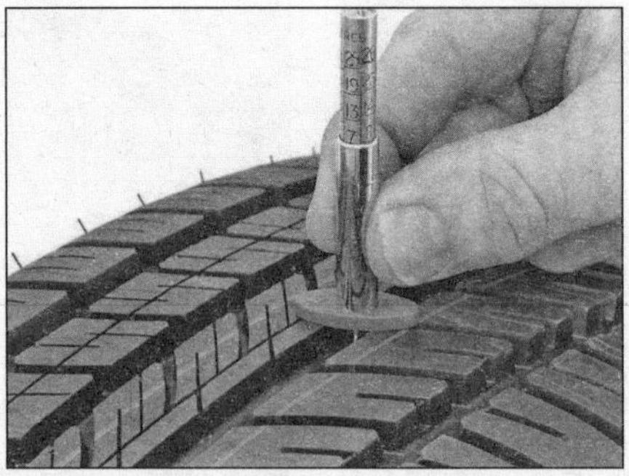

2 ***Tread Depth - manual check***
Alternatively, tread wear can be monitored with a simple, inexpensive device known as a tread depth indicator gauge.

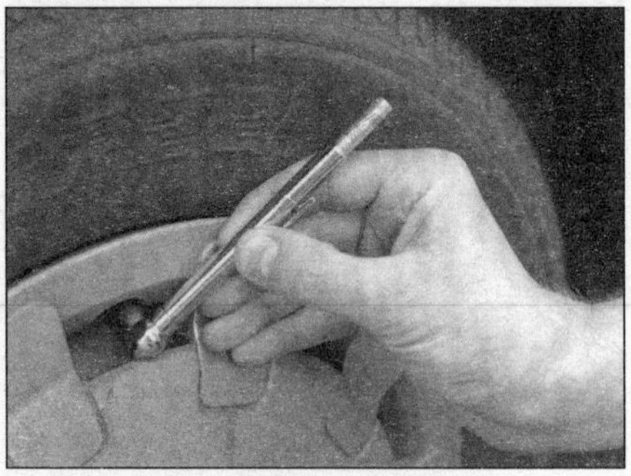

3 ***Tyre Pressure Check***
Check the tyre pressures regularly with the tyres cold. Do not adjust the tyre pressures immediately after the vehicle has been used, or an inaccurate setting will result.

Tyre tread wear patterns

Shoulder Wear

Underinflation (wear on both sides)
Under-inflation will cause overheating of the tyre, because the tyre will flex too much, and the tread will not sit correctly on the road surface. This will cause a loss of grip and excessive wear, not to mention the danger of sudden tyre failure due to heat build-up.
Check and adjust pressures
Incorrect wheel camber (wear on one side)
Repair or renew suspension parts
Hard cornering
Reduce speed!

Centre Wear

Overinflation
Over-inflation will cause rapid wear of the centre part of the tyre tread, coupled with reduced grip, harsher ride, and the danger of shock damage occurring in the tyre casing.
Check and adjust pressures

If you sometimes have to inflate your car's tyres to the higher pressures specified for maximum load or sustained high speed, don't forget to reduce the pressures to normal afterwards.

Uneven Wear

Front tyres may wear unevenly as a result of wheel misalignment. Most tyre dealers and garages can check and adjust the wheel alignment (or "tracking") for a modest charge.
Incorrect camber or castor
Repair or renew suspension parts
Malfunctioning suspension
Repair or renew suspension parts
Unbalanced wheel
Balance tyres
Incorrect toe setting
Adjust front wheel alignment
Note: *The feathered edge of the tread which typifies toe wear is best checked by feel.*

Power steering fluid level

Before you start

✔ Park the vehicle on level ground.
✔ Set the steering wheel straight-ahead.
✔ The engine should be turned off, and the fluid cool.

HAYNES HiNT ***For the check to be accurate, the steering must not be turned while the level is being checked.***

Safety first!

● The need for frequent topping-up indicates a leak, which should be investigated immediately.

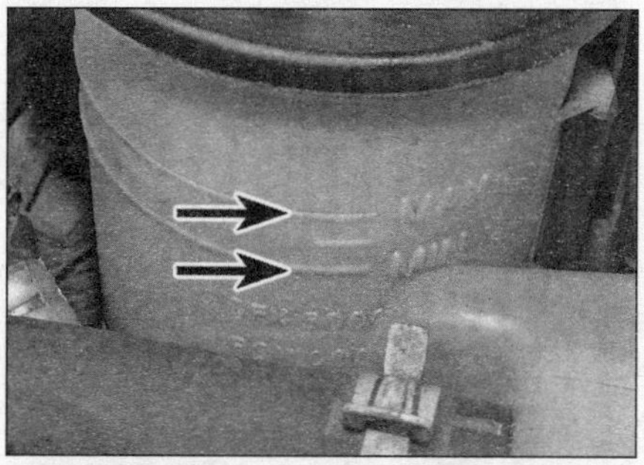

1 The reservoir is located on the left-hand side of the engine compartment. The minimum and maximum levels are indicated by marks on the side of the reservoir. The fluid level should be between MIN and MAX.

2 If topping-up is required, wipe clean the area around the reservoir filler neck(s) and unscrew the filler cap(s) from the reservoir.

3 When topping-up, use the specified type of fluid and do not overfill the reservoir. When the level is correct, securely refit the cap(s).

Screen washer fluid level

● Screenwash additives not only keep the windscreen clean during foul weather, they also prevent the washer system freezing in cold weather – which is when you are likely to need it most. Don't top-up using plain water as the screenwash will become too diluted, and will freeze during cold weather.

Caution: On no account use coolant antifreeze in the washer system – this could discolour or damage paintwork.

1 The screen washer fluid reservoir is located in the front, left-hand corner of the engine compartment. If necessary, remove up the cap.

2 When topping-up, add a screenwash additive in the quantities recommended by the manufacturer.

Battery

Caution: Before carrying out any work on the vehicle battery, read the precautions given in 'Safety first!' at the start of this manual.

✔ Make sure that the battery tray is in good condition, and that the clamp is tight. Corrosion on the tray, retaining clamp and the battery itself can be removed with a solution of water and baking soda. Thoroughly rinse all cleaned areas with water. Any metal parts damaged by corrosion should be covered with a zinc-based primer, then painted.

✔ Periodically (approximately every three months), check the charge condition of the battery, as described in Chapter 5, Section 3.

✔ If the battery is flat, and you need to jump start your vehicle, see *Roadside repairs*.

Warning: Do not disconnect the battery without referring to the instructions given in Chapter 5, Section 4.

Battery corrosion can be kept to a minimum by applying a layer of petroleum jelly to the clamps and terminals after they are reconnected.

1 The battery is located under a cover in the left-hand corner of the engine compartment. Release the clips and remove the cover.

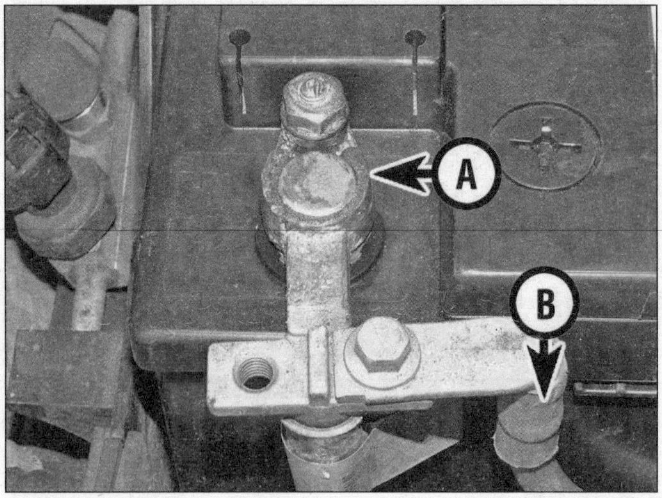

2 Check the tightness of battery clamps (A) to ensure good electrical connections. You should not be able to move them. Also check each cable (B) for cracks and frayed conductors.

3 If corrosion (white, fluffy deposits) is evident, remove the cables from the battery terminals, clean them with a small wire brush, then refit them. Automotive stores sell a tool for cleaning the battery post…

4 …as well as the battery cable clamps.

Electrical systems

✔ Check all external lights and the horn. Refer to Chapter 13, Section 2, for details if any of the circuits are found to be inoperative.

✔ Visually check all accessible wiring connectors, harnesses and retaining clips for security, and for signs of chafing or damage.

HAYNES HiNT ***If you need to check your brake lights and indicators unaided, back up to a wall or garage door and operate the lights. The reflected light should show if they are working properly.***

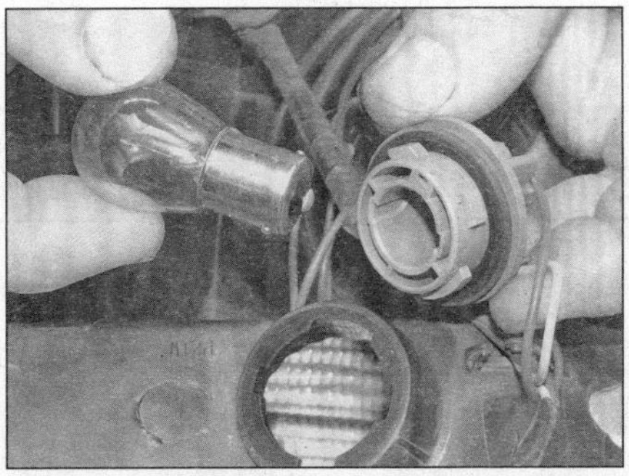

1 If a single indicator light, brake light or headlight has failed, it is likely that a bulb has blown and will need to be renewed. Refer to Chapter 13, Section 5, for details. If both brake lights have failed, it is possible that the switch has failed (see Chapter 10, Section 19).

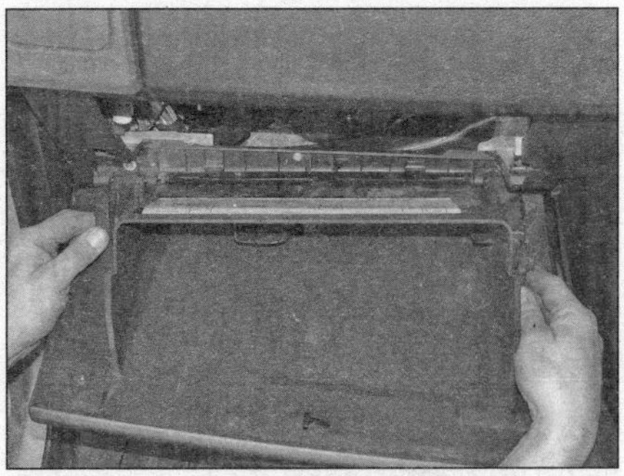

2 If more than one indicator light or tail light has failed check that a fuse has not blown or that there is a fault in the circuit (see Chapter 13, Section 2). Fuses are located behind the passenger's glovebox. Press down/forwards the clips at the top of the support struts and lower the glovebox lid. Details of the circuits protected by the fuses are shown on the card in the fusebox.

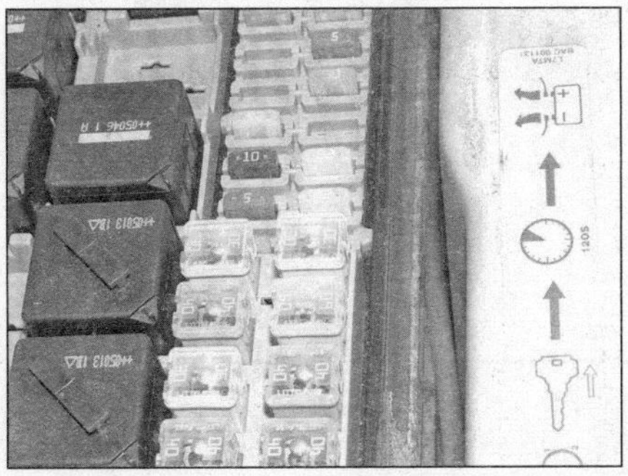

3 Fuses are also located at the left-hand side rear of the engine compartment.

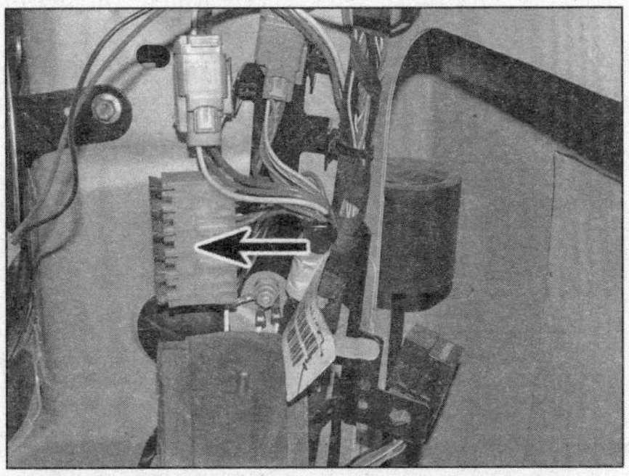

4 Note that a supplementary fusebox is fitted to some models to protect the tow hitch circuits – behind the left-hand side luggage compartment side panel.

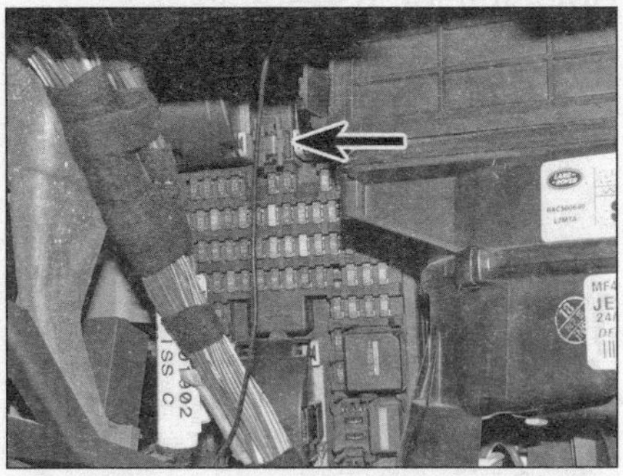

5 To renew a blown fuse, using the tweezers provided, simply pull it out and fit a new fuse of the correct rating. If the fuse blows again, it is important that you find out why – a complete checking procedure is given in Chapter 13, Section 2.

Wiper blades

⚠ ***Check the condition of the wiper blades; if they are cracked or show any signs of deterioration, or if the glass swept area is smeared, renew them. Wiper blades should be renewed annually.***

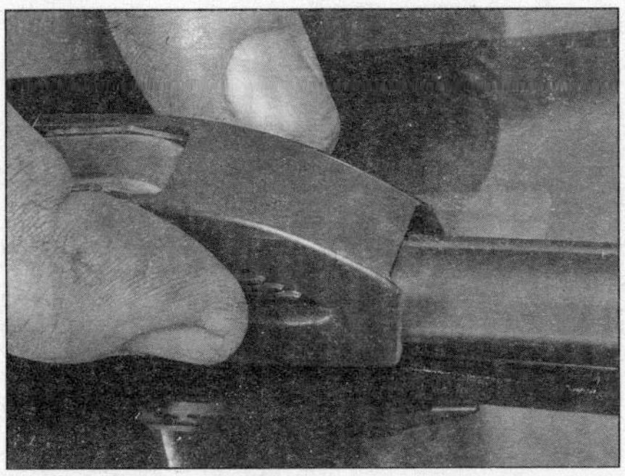

1 To remove a front wiper blade, pull the arm away from the screen, squeeze together the sides and pivot the cover upwards.

2 Press apart the clips and slide the blade from the arm.

3 To remove a rear wiper blade, pull the arm away from the screen, use a screwdriver to depress the tab, and slide the blade from the arm.

Lubricants and fluids

Engine	Multigrade engine oil, viscosity SAE 5W/30 to ACEA B1/B3 Land Rover specification WSS-M2C-913B
Cooling system	Ethylene glycol based antifreeze with OATS corrosion inhibitors
Manual transmission	Castrol MTF BOT338
Automatic transmission	Shell ATF M1375.4
Transfer gearbox	Shell TF 0753
Final drives	
Non-locking	Castrol 75W-90 SAF XO
Locking (ETM)	Castrol SAF Carbon Mod Plus
Braking/clutch system	Hydraulic fluid to DOT 4
Power steering	Texaco 14315 Cold Climate PAS fluid

Tyre pressures

	Front	**Rear**
All tyres at normal operating conditions (up to 4 passengers and luggage):		
Normal roadwheels	2.3 bar (33 psi)	2.5 bar (36 psi)
Spacesaver spare wheel	4.2 bar (61 psi)	4.2 bar (61 psi)
All tyres at gross vehicle weight (fully-loaded):		
Normal roadwheels	2.3 bar (33 psi)	2.9 bar (42 psi)
Spacesaver spare wheel	4.2 bar (61 psi)	4.2 bar (61 psi)

The pressures are also on a label attached to the driver door sill.

Chapter 1
Routine maintenance and servicing

Contents

Degrees of difficulty

Easy, suitable for novice with little experience	**Fairly easy,** suitable for beginner with some experience	**Fairly difficult,** suitable for competent DIY mechanic	**Difficult,** suitable for experienced DIY mechanic	**Very difficult,** suitable for expert DIY or professional

Lubricants and fluids	Refer to *Lubricants and fluids*	

Capacities

Engine oil (including filter)

All engines	5.5 litres	
Difference between upper and lower dipstick markings	1.75 litres	

Cooling system (approximate)

With rear passenger compartment heating:		
With fuel burning heater	13.1 litres	
Without fuel burning heater	12.1 litres	
Without rear compartment heating:		
With fuel burning heater	10.3 litres	
Without fuel burning heater	9.4 litres	

Transmission

Manual transmission (approx.)	1.6 litres	
Automatic transmission:		
Dry fill	9.5 litres	
Fluid renewal	5.0 litres approx.	
Transfer gearbox	1.5 litres	

Front and rear final drives

Front final drive	0.6 litres	
Rear final drive:		
'Open' differential	1.1 litres	
ETM (Electronic Torque Managed) differential	1.5 litres	

Washer fluid reservoir

Windscreen/rear window washer	5.0 litres	

Fuel tank

All models	86.0 litres	

Cooling system

Antifreeze mixture:		
50% antifreeze	Protection down to –48°C	

Note: *Refer to antifreeze manufacturer for latest recommendations.*

Brakes

Friction material minimum thickness:		
Brake pads	3.0 mm	
Parking brake shoes	2.0 mm	

Torque wrench settings	**Nm**	**lbf ft**
Engine oil drain plug	25	18
Engine oil filter cover	25	18
Roadwheel nuts	140	103
Trackrod end nuts (M12 only)	76	56

The maintenance intervals in this manual are provided with the assumption that you, not the dealer, will be carrying out the work. These are the minimum maintenance intervals recommended by the manufacturers for vehicles driven daily under normal operating conditions. If you wish to keep your vehicle in peak condition at all times, you may wish to perform some of these procedures more often. This applies especially if the vehicle is used in particularly hot or dusty climates, or if the vehicle is regularly used for towing. We encourage frequent maintenance because it enhances the efficiency, performance and resale value of your vehicle.

When the vehicle is new, it should be serviced by a dealer service department (or other workshop recognised by the vehicle manufacturer as providing the same standard of service) in order to preserve the warranty. The vehicle manufacturer may reject warranty claims if you are unable to prove that servicing has been carried out as and when specified, using only original equipment parts or parts certified to be of equivalent quality.

Every 250 miles or weekly

- Refer to *Weekly checks*

Every 6000 miles or 6 months, whichever occurs first

Renew the engine oil and filter (Section 3)

Every 12 000 miles or 12 months, whichever occurs first

In addition to the item listed above, carry out the following:

- Check the condition of the brake pads and discs (Section 4)
- Check all pipes and hoses for leaks and condition (Section 5)
- Check the parking brake adjustment (Section 6)
- Check the operation of all door, bonnet and tailgate locks. Lubricate all hinges and locks (including the fuel filler) (Section 7)
- Check the steering and suspension components, including all hydraulic pipes and hoses for leaks and condition (Section 8)
- Check the condition of the auxiliary drivebelt (Section 9)
- Carry out a road test (Section 10)
- Drain the fuel sedimenter (Section 11)
- Check the exhaust system for security and condition (Section 12)
- Rotate the roadwheels to opposite sides of same axle (Section 13)
- Renew the pollen filter (Section 14)
- Check the condition and operation of all seat belts (Section 15)
- Check the condition of the wheel speed sensor harnesses (Section 16)
- Check the antifreeze concentration (Section 17)
- Reset the service interval indicator (Section 18)

Alarm handset battery renewal

There is no requirement to change the alarm handset battery, as the unit is recharged whenever the ignition key is inserted into the ignition switch and the engine started.

Any problems with the handset should be referred to the Land Rover dealer or specialist.

Every 24 000 miles or 2 years, whichever occurs first

In addition to all the items listed above, carry out the following:

- Check the driveshafts and gaiters (Section 19)
- Renew the fuel filter element (Section 20)

Every 48 000 miles or 3 years, whichever occurs first

In addition to all the items listed above, carry out the following:

- Renew the brake fluid (Section 21)
- Renew the air cleaner element (Section 22)

Every 72 000 miles

- Renew the transfer gearbox fluid (Section 23)
- Renew the rear final drive fluid – ETM locking differential only (Section 24)
- Renew the air suspension intake filter (where fitted) (Section 25)

Every 6 years regardless of mileage

- Renew all flexible brake hoses and seals (Section 26)

Every 108 000 miles or 7 years, whichever occurs first

- Renew the auxiliary drivebelt (Section 9)
- Renew the timing belt and tensioner (Section 27)
- Renew the fuel pump drivebelt and tensioner (Section 28)

Every 144 000 or 10 years, whichever occurs first

- Renew the automatic transmission fluid (Section 29)
- Renew the manual transmission oil (Section 30)
- Renew the front and rear final drive fluid (Section 24)
- Renew the coolant (Section 31)

Underbonnet view

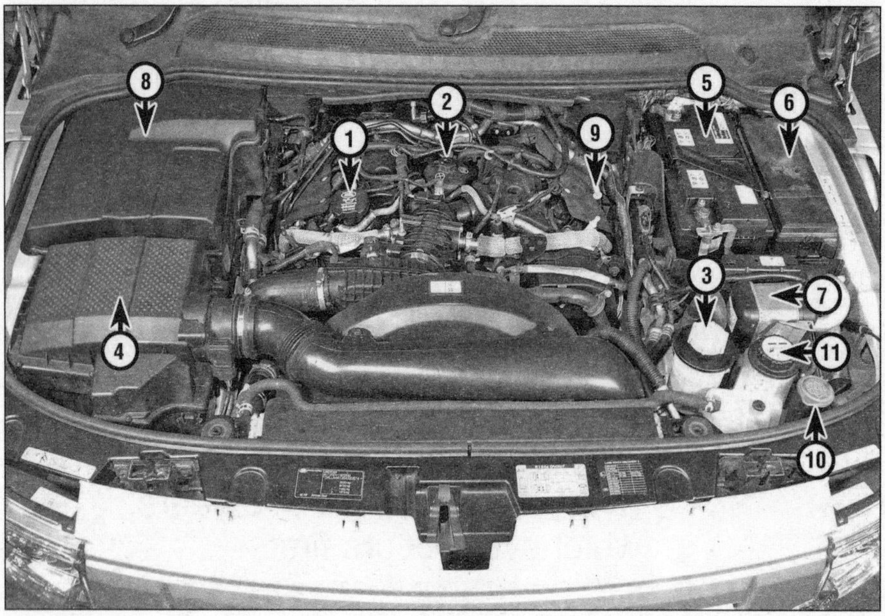

1 Engine oil filler cap
2 Oil filter housing
3 Power steering fluid reservoir
4 Air filter housing
5 Battery
6 Fuse/relay box
7 Fuel burning heater
8 Auxiliary battery cover
9 Engine oil level dipstick
10 Washer fluid reservoir
11 Coolant expansion tank

Front underbody view

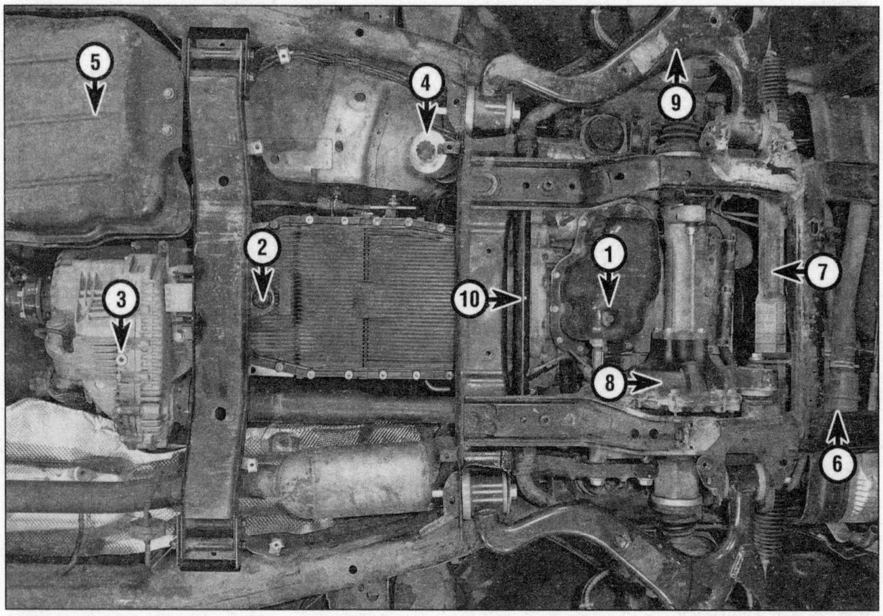

1 Engine oil drain plug
2 Transmission oil drain plug
3 Transfer gearbox drain plug
4 Fuel filter
5 Fuel tank
6 Thermostat housing
7 Steering rack
8 Front final drive
9 Lower suspension arm
10 Anti-roll bar

Rear underbody view

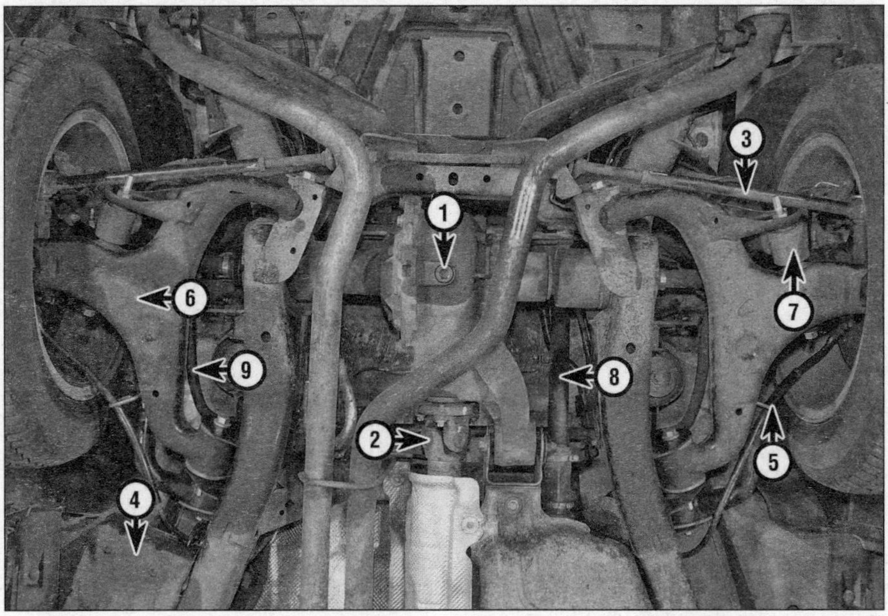

1 Final drive drain plug
2 Propeller shaft universal joint
3 Toe link
4 Air compressor cover
5 Parking brake cable
6 Lower suspension arm
7 Suspension strut
8 Fuel filler hose
9 Rear anti-roll bar

1 General information

1 This Chapter is designed to help the home mechanic maintain his/her vehicle for safety, economy, long life and peak performance.
2 The Chapter contains a master maintenance schedule, followed by Sections dealing specifically with each task in the schedule. Visual checks, adjustments, component renewal and other helpful items are included. Refer to the accompanying illustrations of the engine compartment and the underside of the vehicle for the locations of the various components.
3 Servicing your vehicle in accordance with the Schedule and the following Sections will provide a planned maintenance programme, which should result in a long and reliable service life. This is a comprehensive plan, so maintaining some items but not others at the specified service intervals, will not produce the same results.
4 As you service your vehicle, you will discover that many of the procedures can – and should – be grouped together, because of the particular procedure being performed, or because of the proximity of two otherwise-unrelated components to one another. For example, if the vehicle is raised for any reason, the exhaust can be inspected at the same time as the suspension and steering components.
5 The first step in this maintenance programme is to prepare yourself before the actual work begins. Read through all the Sections relevant to the work to be carried out, then make a list and gather all the parts and tools required. If a problem is encountered, seek advice from a parts specialist, or a dealer service department.

2 Regular maintenance

1 If, from the time the vehicle is new, the routine maintenance schedule is followed closely, and frequent checks are made of fluid levels and high-wear items, as suggested throughout this manual, the engine will be kept in relatively good running condition, and the need for additional work will be minimised.
2 It is possible that there will be times when the engine is running poorly due to the lack of regular maintenance. This is even more likely if a used vehicle, which has not received regular and frequent maintenance checks, is purchased. In such cases, additional work may need to be carried out, outside of the regular maintenance intervals.
3 If engine wear is suspected, a compression test (refer to Chapter 2, Section 2) will provide valuable information regarding the overall performance of the main internal components. Such a test can be used as a basis to decide on the extent of the work to be carried out. If, for example, a compression test indicates serious internal engine wear, conventional maintenance as described in this Chapter will not greatly improve the performance of the engine, and may prove a waste of time and money, unless extensive overhaul work is carried out first.
4 The following series of operations are those most often required to improve the performance of a generally poor-running engine:

Primary operations

a) Clean, inspect and test the battery (See 'Weekly checks').
b) Check all the engine-related fluids (See 'Weekly checks').
c) Check the condition of the air filter, and renew if necessary (Section 22).
d) Check the condition of all hoses, and check for fluid leaks (Section 5).

5 If the above operations do not prove fully effective, carry out the following secondary operations:

Secondary operations

All items listed under *Primary operations*, plus the following:

a) Check the charging system (see Chapter 5, Section 5).
b) Check the fuel system (see Chapter 4A and 4B).

3.3 Pull the engine cover upwards

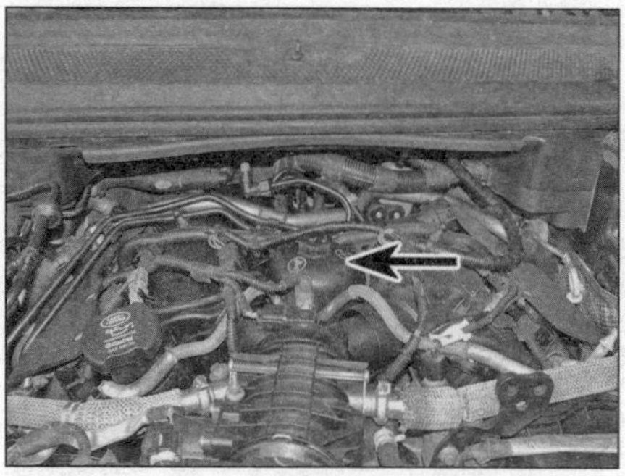

3.4a Unscrew the engine oil filter cover (arrowed) ...

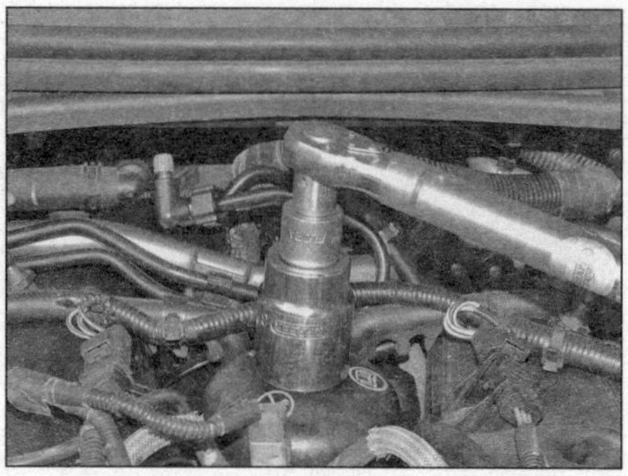

3.4b ... 4 complete revolutions

Every 6000 miles or 6 months

3 Engine oil and filter renewal

HAYNES HiNT ***Frequent oil and filter changes are the most important preventative maintenance procedures that can be undertaken by the DIY owner. As engine oil ages, it becomes diluted and contaminated, which leads to premature engine wear.***

1 Before starting this procedure, gather together all the necessary tools and materials. Also make sure that you have plenty of clean rags and newspapers handy, to mop-up any spills. Ideally, the engine oil should be warm, as it will drain better, and more built-up sludge will be removed with it. Take care, however, not to touch the exhaust or any other hot parts of the engine when working under the vehicle. To avoid any possibility of scalding, and to protect yourself from possible skin irritants and other harmful contaminants in used engine oils, it is advisable to wear rubber gloves when carrying out this work.

2 Access to the underside of the vehicle will be greatly improved if it can be raised on a lift, driven onto ramps, or jacked up and supported on axle stands (see *Jacking and vehicle support*). Whichever method is chosen, make sure that the vehicle remains as level as possible, to enable the oil to drain fully.

3 Remove the engine oil filler cap, then pull the cover upwards from the top of the engine to release the rubber mountings **(see illustration)**

4 Clean the area around the filter cover, then use a socket to unscrew the filter cover 4 complete revolutions to allow the oil to drain **(see illustrations)**.

5 Completely unscrew the filter cover, and pull the element from place. Discard the O-ring seal **(see illustrations)**. Be prepared for fluid spillage.

6 Working underneath the vehicle, undo the retaining bolts and remove the engine undershield **(see illustration)**. Note the locations of the various washers. Take care as the undershield is surprisingly heavy.

7 Clean the drain plug and the area around it, then slacken it using a suitable socket or spanner **(see illustration)**. If possible, try to keep the plug pressed into the sump while unscrewing it by hand the last couple of turns. As the plug releases from the threads, move it away sharply, so that the stream of oil issuing from the sump runs into the container, not up your sleeve.

8 Allow some time for the old oil to drain, noting that it may be necessary to reposition the container as the oil flow slows to a trickle.

9 After all the oil has drained, wipe off the drain plug with a clean rag, and discard the seal – a new seal must be fitted **(see illustration)**. Clean the area around the drain

3.5a Pull the filter element from the cover

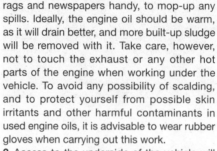

3.5b Renew the O-ring seal (arrowed)

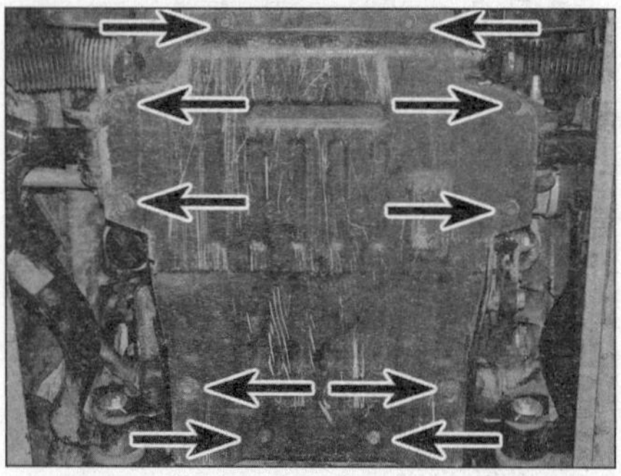

3.6 Engine undershield retaining bolts (arrowed)

3.7 Slacken and remove the engine oil drain plug (arrowed)

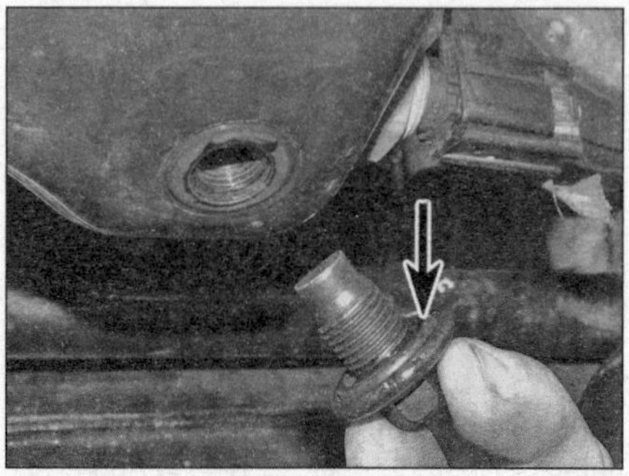

3.9 Renew the drain plug seal (arrowed)

3.10 Align the filter spigot with the hole in the filter housing (arrowed)

3.11 Lubricate the filter cover O-ring seal

plug opening, then fit the seal and tighten the plug to the specified torque setting.

10 Insert the new filter element, ensuring the spigot aligns with the corresponding hole in the filter housing **(see illustration)**.

11 Renew the filter cover O-ring seal, lubricate the seal with clean engine oil, then refit the cover and tighten it to the specified torque **(see illustration)**.

12 Fill the engine with the specified quantity and grade of oil. Pour the oil in slowly, otherwise it may overflow. Check that the oil level is up to the correct level on the dipstick (see *Weekly checks*), then refit and tighten the oil filler cap.

13 Remove the old oil and all tools from under the vehicle, then refit the engine undershield and lower the vehicle to the ground.

14 Refit the engine top cover.

15 Run the engine for a few minutes, and check that there are no leaks.

16 Switch off the engine, and wait a few minutes for the oil to settle in the sump once more. With the new oil circulated and the filter now completely full, recheck the level on the dipstick, and add more oil if necessary.

17 Dispose of the used engine oil responsibly, with reference to *General repair procedures*.

Every 12 000 miles or 12 months

4 Brake pads, discs and calipers check

1 Jack up the vehicle, support securely on axle stands, then remove the roadwheels (see *Jacking and vehicle support*).

2 For a quick check, the thickness of friction material remaining on each pad can be measured through the slot in the caliper body. If any pad is worn to the specified minimum thickness or less, **all four** pads must be renewed (see Chapter 10, Section 4 or 5) **(see illustration)**.

3 For a comprehensive check, the brake pads should be removed and cleaned. This will allow the operation of the caliper to be checked, and the condition of the brake disc itself to be fully examined on both sides (see Chapter 10, Section 6 or 7).

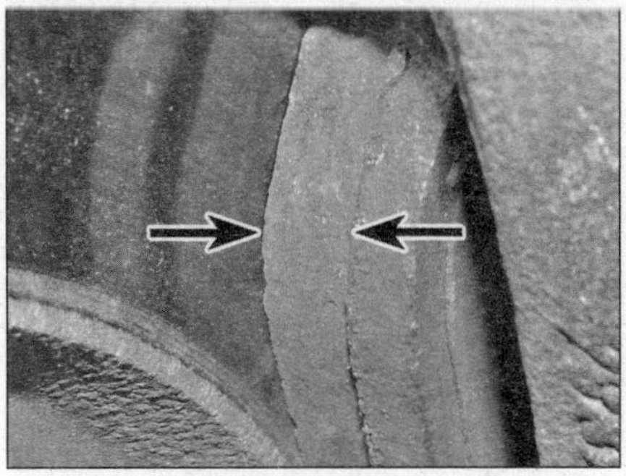

4.2 Check the thickness of the brake pad friction material (arrowed)

4 With the pads removed, check the area around the caliper piston for any signs of fluid leakage. Use a large screwdriver to gently move the pistons back in to the caliper body a little. If it is impossible to move the pistons, the caliper may need overhauling/renewing as described in Chapter 10, Section 8 or 9.

5 Hose and fluid leak check

Note: *Also see Section 8.*

1 Visually inspect the engine joint faces, gaskets and seals for any signs of water or oil leaks. Pay particular attention to the areas around the camshaft covers, cylinder heads, oil filter and sump joint faces. Bear in mind that, over a period of time, some very slight seepage from these areas is to be expected – what you are really looking for is any indication of a serious leak. Should a leak be found, renew the offending gasket or oil seal by referring to the appropriate Chapters in this manual.

2 Also check the security and condition of all the engine-related pipes and hoses. Ensure that all cable-ties or securing clips are in place and in good condition. Clips which are broken or missing can lead to chafing of the hoses, pipes or wiring, which could cause more serious problems in the future.

3 Carefully check the radiator hoses and heater hoses along their entire length. Renew any hose which is cracked, swollen or deteriorated. Cracks will show up better if the hose is squeezed. Pay close attention to the hose clips that secure the hoses to the cooling system components. Hose clips can pinch and puncture hoses, resulting in cooling system leaks.

4 Inspect all the cooling system components (hoses, joint faces etc.) for leaks **(see Haynes Hint)**. Where any problems of this nature are found on system components, renew the component or gasket with reference to Chapter 3.

HAYNES HiNT

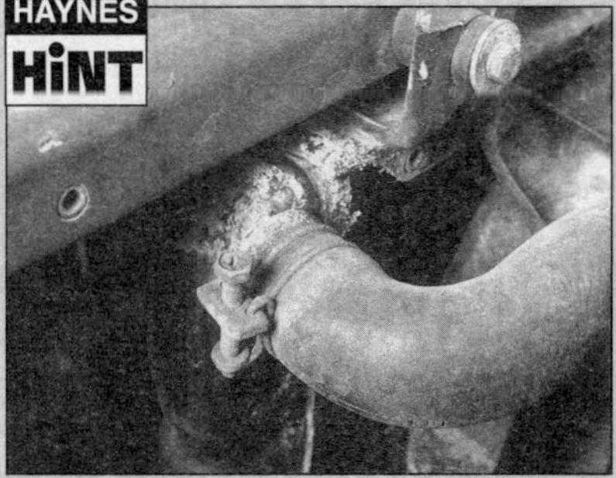

A leak in the cooling system will usually show up as white- or antifreeze coloured deposits on the area adjoining the leak.

5 Where applicable, inspect the automatic transmission fluid cooler hoses for leaks or deterioration.
6 With the car raised, inspect the fuel tank and filler neck for punctures, cracks and other damage. The connection between the filler neck and tank is especially critical. Sometimes a rubber filler neck or connecting hose will leak due to loose retaining clamps or deteriorated rubber.
7 Carefully check all rubber hoses and metal fuel lines leading away from the fuel tank. Check for loose connections, deteriorated hoses, crimped lines, and other damage. Pay particular attention to the vent pipes and hoses, which often loop up around the filler neck and can become blocked or crimped. Follow the lines to the front of the car, carefully inspecting them all the way. Renew damaged sections as necessary.
8 Closely inspect the metal brake pipes which run along the car underbody. If they show signs of excessive corrosion or damage they must be renewed.
9 From within the engine compartment, check the security of all fuel hose attachments and pipe unions, and inspect the fuel hoses and vacuum hoses for kinks, chafing and deterioration.
10 Check the condition of the power steering and air suspension hoses and pipes.

6 Parking brake adjustment

1 The adjustment procedure is described in Chapter 10, Section 8.

7 Hinge and lock check and lubrication

1 Lubricate the hinges of the bonnet, doors and tailgate/liftgate with a light general-purpose oil. Similarly, lubricate all latches, locks and lock strikers. At the same time, check the security and operation of all the locks, adjusting them if necessary (see Chapter 12).
2 Lightly lubricate the bonnet release mechanism and cable with a suitable grease.

8 Steering and suspension component check

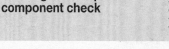

1 Apply the handbrake, then raise the front of the vehicle and securely support it on axle stands (see *Jacking and vehicle support*).
2 Visually inspect the balljoint dust covers for splits, chafing or deterioration. Any damage will cause loss of lubricant, together with dirt and water entry, resulting in rapid deterioration of the balljoints.
3 Where applicable, check the power steering fluid hoses for chafing or deterioration, and the pipe and hose unions for fluid leaks. Also check for signs of fluid leakage under pressure from the steering box, which would indicate failed fluid seals within the steering box assembly.
4 Grasp the roadwheel at the 12 o'clock and 6 o'clock positions, and try to rock it **(see illustration)**. Very slight free play may be felt, but if the movement is appreciable, further investigation is necessary to determine the source. Continue rocking the wheel while an assistant depresses the footbrake. If the movement is now eliminated or significantly reduced, it is likely that the hub bearings are at fault. If the free play is still evident with the footbrake depressed, then there is wear in the suspension joints or mountings.
5 Now grasp the wheel at the 9 o'clock and 3 o'clock positions, and try to rock it as before. Any movement felt now may again be caused by wear in the hub bearings, or the steering track rod and drag link balljoints. If a balljoint is worn, the visual movement will be obvious.
6 Using a large screwdriver or flat bar, check for wear in the suspension mounting bushes by levering between the relevant suspension component and its attachment point. Some movement is to be expected, as the mountings are made of rubber, but excessive wear should be obvious. Also check the condition of any visible rubber bushes, looking for splits, cracks or contamination of the rubber.
7 With the vehicle standing on its wheels, have an assistant turn the steering wheel back and forth. There should be very little, if any, lost movement between the steering wheel and roadwheels. If this is not the case, closely observe the joints and mountings previously described, but in addition, check the steering column universal joints for wear.
8 On models with M12 track rod end locknuts, check the tightness of the nuts, and if necessary, tighten them to the specified torque.

9 Auxiliary drivebelt check and renewal

Check

1 An automatic drivebelt tensioner is fitted, and no checking of the tension is necessary. However, the belt should be inspected for wear and damage and the recommended intervals.
2 The belt should be inspected along its entire length, and if it is found to be worn, frayed or cracked, it should be renewed as a precaution against breakage in service. It is advisable to carry a spare drivebelt of the correct type in the vehicle at all times.

Renewal

3 Remove the cooling fan coupling as described in Chapter 3, Section 5.
4 Using a 3/8" square-drive bar, rotate the belt tensioner pulley arm anti-clockwise to move the tensioner and relieve the tension in the belt **(see illustration)**.

8.4 Grasp the roadwheel at 12 and 6 o'clock positions and try to rock it

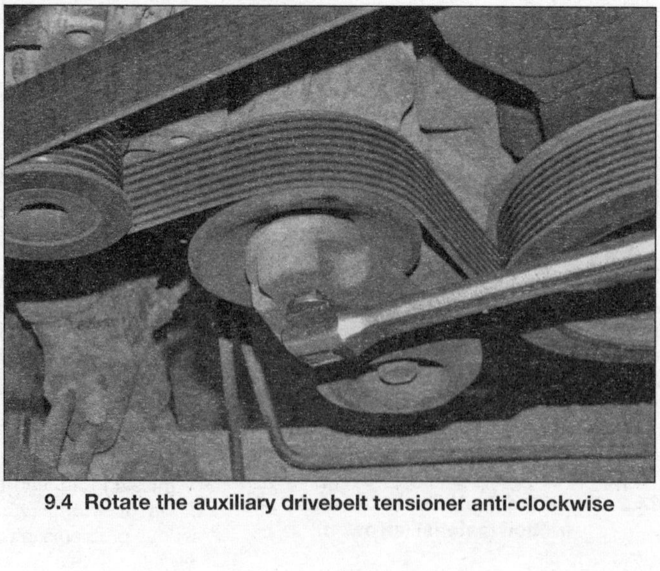

9.4 Rotate the auxiliary drivebelt tensioner anti-clockwise

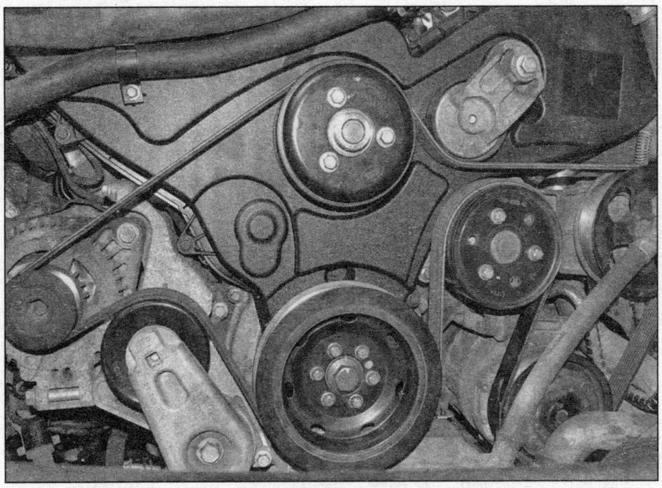

9.7a Auxiliary drivebelt routing

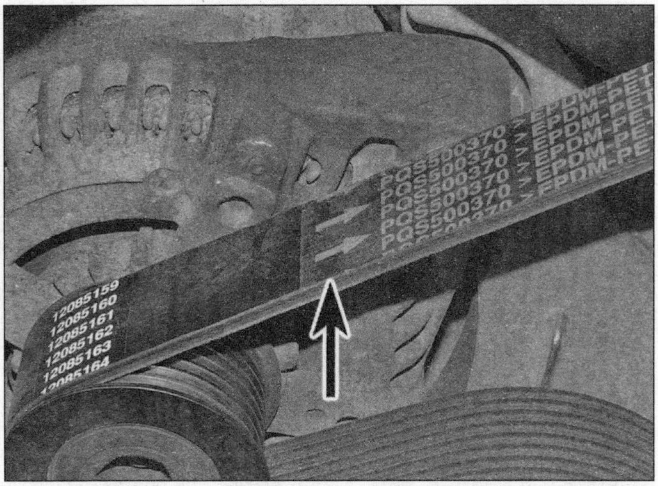

9.7b Observe the direction-of-rotation arrows on the belt

5 Take note of the routing, then slide the belt from the pulleys.

6 If the original belt is to be refitted, mark the running direction to ensure correct refitting.

7 Refitting is a reversal of removal, but ensure that the belt is correctly routed and the direction-of-rotation arrows on the belt are observed **(see illustrations)**.

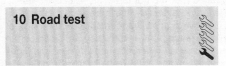

10 Road test

Instruments and electrical equipment

1 Check the operation of all instruments and electrical equipment, including the washers and wipers.

2 Make sure that all instruments read correctly, and switch on all electrical equipment in turn, to check that it functions properly.

Steering and suspension

3 Check for any abnormalities in the steering, suspension, handling or road 'feel'.

4 Drive the vehicle, and check that there are no unusual vibrations or noises.

5 Check that the steering feels positive, with no excessive 'sloppiness', or roughness, and check for any suspension noises when cornering and driving over bumps.

Drivetrain

6 Check the performance of the engine, clutch and propeller shafts.

7 Listen for any unusual noises from the engine, clutch and transmission.

8 Make sure that the engine runs smoothly when idling, and that there is no hesitation when accelerating.

9 Check that the clutch action is smooth and progressive, that the drive is taken up smoothly, and that the pedal travel is not excessive. Also listen for any noises when the clutch pedal is depressed.

10 Check that all gears can be engaged smoothly without noise, and that the gear lever action is not abnormally vague or 'notchy'. This check applies to both the main gearbox and the transfer gearbox.

11 Select LOW range gear, drive the vehicle forwards 3 to 4 vehicle lengths, stop the vehicle and select HIGH range gear – the gears should engage smoothly.

Braking system

12 Make sure that the vehicle does not pull to one side when braking, and that the wheels do not lock when braking hard.

13 Check that there is no vibration through the steering when braking.

14 Check that the handbrake operates correctly without excessive movement of the lever, and that it holds the vehicle stationary on a slope.

15 Test the operation of the brake servo unit as follows. With the engine switched off, depress the footbrake four or five times to exhaust the vacuum. Start the engine, keeping the footbrake depressed. As the engine starts, there should be a noticeable 'give' in the brake pedal as vacuum builds up. Allow the engine to run for at least two minutes, and then switch it off. If the brake pedal is depressed again, it should be possible to detect a hiss from the servo. After about four or five applications, no further hissing should be heard, and the pedal should feel considerably firmer.

11 Fuel sedimenter draining

1 The sedimenter is fitted to the base of the fuel filter, and is designed to remove the larger droplets of water and dirt from the fuel. Apply the handbrake, then raise the front of the vehicle and securely support it on axle stands (see *Jacking and vehicle support*).

2 Undo the bolts and remove the transmission undershield **(see illustration)**.

3 Undo the 3 bolts and remove the fuel filter heat shield (where fitted) **(see illustration)**.

4 Attach a suitable rubber/plastic hose to

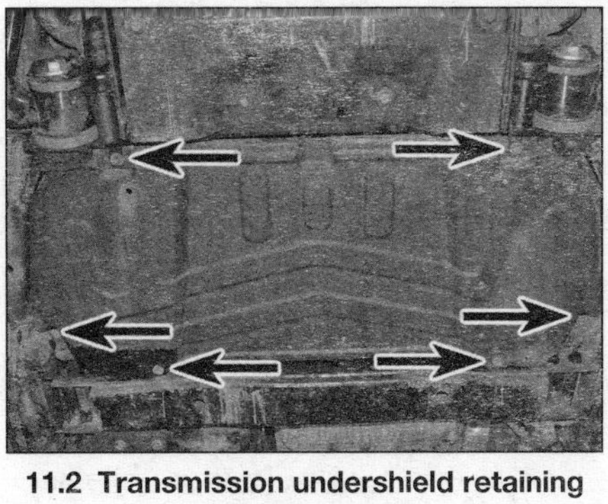

11.2 Transmission undershield retaining bolts (arrowed)

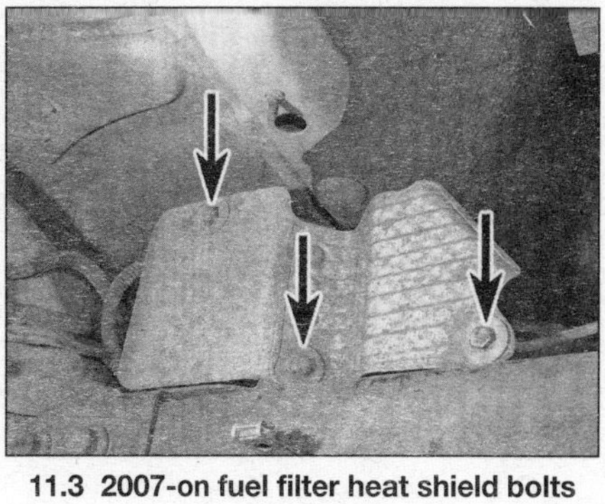

11.3 2007-on fuel filter heat shield bolts (arrowed)

11.4a Attach a hose to the drain port (arrowed) – pre-2007 models ...

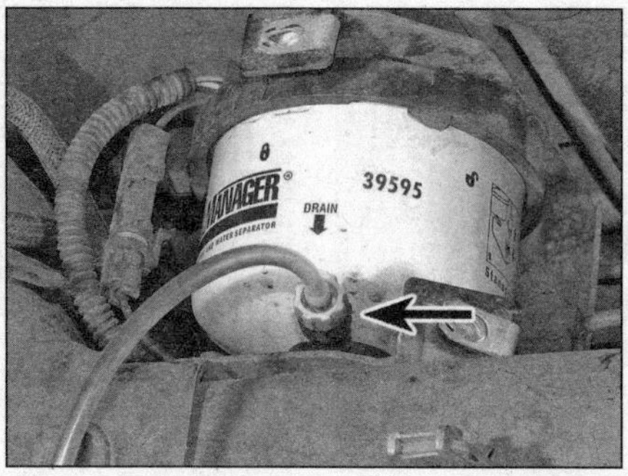

11.4b ... and 2007-on models (arrowed)

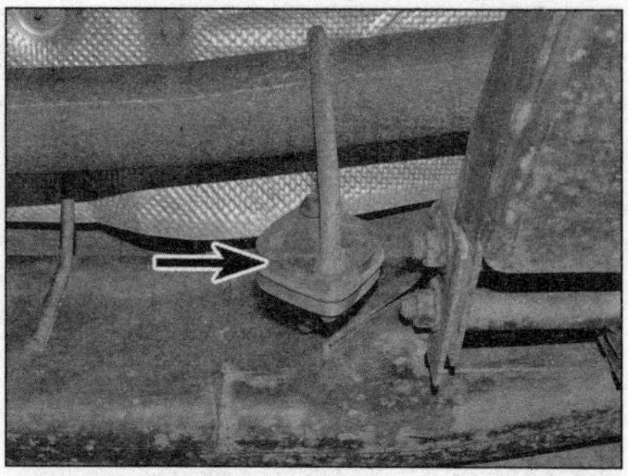

12.3 Check the condition of the exhaust mounting rubbers (arrowed)

the drain port, and place the other end in a container **(see illustration)**.

5 Slacken the drain port 2 complete revolutions to allow the fluid to drain.

6 Turn the ignition switch to position II until approximately 100 ml of fluid is drained. Turn off the ignition.

7 Tighten the drain port securely, and disconnect the hose.

8 The remainder of refitting is a reversal of removal. Start the engine and check for leaks.

12 Exhaust system check

1 With the engine cold (at least an hour after the vehicle has been driven), check the complete exhaust system from the engine to the end of the tailpipe. Ideally, the inspection should be carried out with the vehicle raised (see *Jacking and vehicle support*).

2 Check the exhaust pipes and connections for evidence of leaks, severe corrosion and damage. Make sure that all brackets and mountings are in good condition, and tight. Leakage at any of the joints or in other parts of the system will usually show up as a black sooty stain in the vicinity of the leak..

3 Rattles and other noises can often be traced to the exhaust system, especially the brackets and mountings **(see illustration)**. Try to move the pipes and silencers. If the components can come into contact with the body or suspension parts, secure the system with new mountings. If possible, separate the joints, and twist the pipes as necessary to provide additional clearance.

4 Run the engine at idle speed, then temporarily place a cloth rag over the rear end of the exhaust pipe, and listen for any escape of exhaust gases that would indicate a leak.

5 On completion, where applicable, lower the vehicle to the ground.

13 Wheel/tyre rotation

1 On vehicles with non uni-direction tyres (tyres that are not direction-sensitive – check the tyre sidewall), the roadwheels should be removed, and swapped to the other side of the vehicle, but ensure they are fitted to the same axle. Ensure the hub/wheel mating faces are clean and apply a little anti-seize grease to the faces before fitting the wheels.

14 Pollen filter renewal

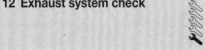

1 Open the passenger's glovebox, press forwards/downwards the tops of the support stays, and lower the glovebox lid **(see illustration)**.

2 Release the clip and remove the pollen filter housing cover **(see illustration)**.

3 Remove the filter from the housing **(see illustration)**.

4 Refitting is a reversal of removal, noting the direction of airflow arrows on the new filter **(see illustration)**.

15 Seat belt check

1 Carefully examine the seat belt webbing for cuts, or any signs of serious fraying or deterioration. If the seat belt is of the retractable type, pull the belt all the way out, and examine the full extent of the webbing.

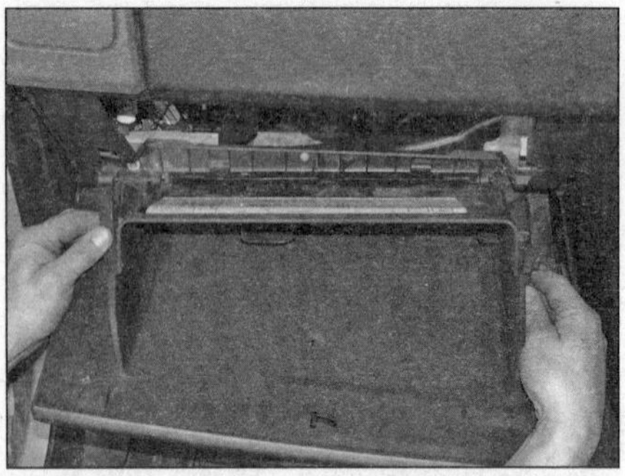

14.1 Press forwards/downwards the tops of the support stays

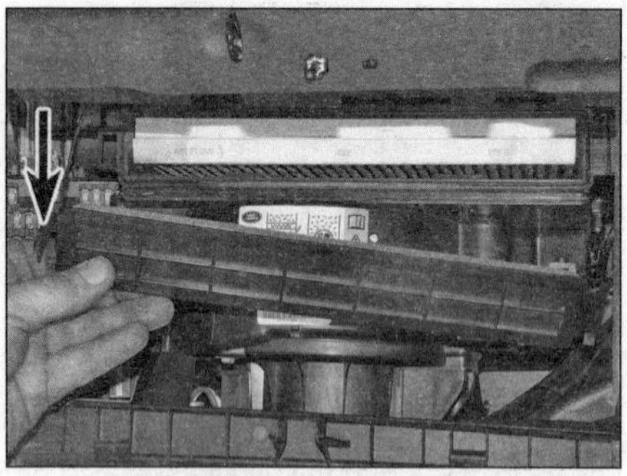

14.2 Release the clip (arrowed) and remove the cover ...

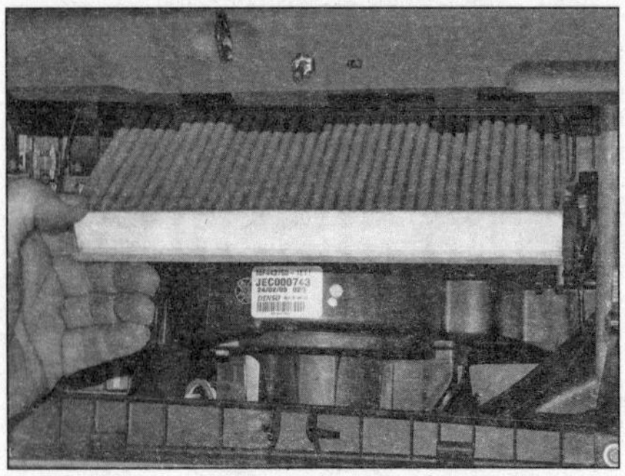

14.3 ... followed by the pollen filter element

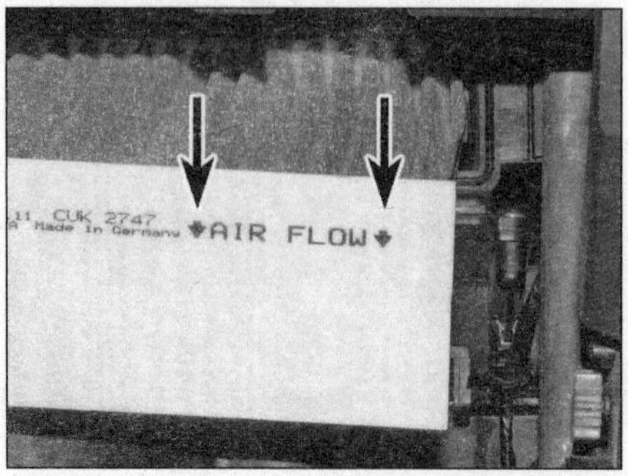

14.4 Note the arrows indicating airflow direction

2 Fasten and unfasten the belt, ensuring that the locking mechanism holds securely, and releases properly when intended. If the belt is of the retractable type, check also that the retracting mechanism operates correctly when the belt is released.
3 Check the security of all seat belt mountings and attachments which are accessible (without removing any trim or other components) from inside the vehicle.
4 Renew any worn components as described in Chapter 12, Section 25.

16 Wheel speed sensor harness check

1 Working underneath the rear of the vehicle, check each sensor harness for chafing and damage, and that they are correctly routed.

17 Coolant check

1 Use a hydrometer to check the strength of the antifreeze. Follow the instructions provided with your hydrometer. The antifreeze strength should be approximately 50%. If it is significantly less than this, drain a little coolant from the radiator (see Section 31), add antifreeze to the coolant expansion tank, then recheck the strength.

18 Service interval indicator reset

Note: *The following procedure applies only to vehicles that are due a scheduled service. If the time or distance covered is outside the programmed parameters of the vehicle (determined by the manufacturer), then manual resetting of the indicator may not be possible. If this is the case, the indicator must be reset using Land Rover diagnostic equipment (T4). Entrust this task to a Land Rover dealer or suitably-equipped repairer.*
1 With the ignition switched off, press and hold the trip reset button.
2 Turn the ignition switch to position II, the message SERVICE will flash for 5 seconds, then be permanently displayed.
3 Release the trip reset button within 10 seconds, the display will change to DIST.
4 Within 10 seconds, press and hold the trip reset button again for at least 6 seconds. The message RST will be displayed for 5 seconds, followed by END.
5 Release the button, wait 10 seconds, and switch the ignition off.

Every 24 000 miles or 2 years

19 Driveshaft and gaiter check

1 With the vehicle raised and securely supported on stands (see *Jacking and vehicle support*), turn the steering onto full lock then slowly rotate the roadwheel. Inspect the condition of the outer constant velocity (CV) joint rubber gaiters while squeezing the gaiters to open out the folds **(see illustration)**. Check for signs of cracking, splits or deterioration of the rubber which may allow the grease to escape and lead to water and grit entry into the joint. Also check the security and condition of the retaining clips. Repeat these checks on the inner CV joints, and the rear driveshaft joints. If any damage or deterioration is found, the gaiters should be renewed as described in Chapter 9, Section 3.
2 At the same time check the general condition of the CV joints themselves by first holding the driveshaft and attempting to rotate the wheel. Repeat this check by holding the inner joint and attempting to rotate the driveshaft. Any appreciable movement indicates wear in the joints, wear in the driveshaft splines or loose driveshaft retaining nut.

20 Fuel filter element renewal

1 Apply the handbrake, then raise the front of the vehicle and securely support it on axle stands (see *Jacking and vehicle support*).
2 Undo the bolts and remove the transmission undershield **(see illustration 11.2)**.
3 Undo the 3 bolts and remove the fuel filter heat shield (where fitted) **(see illustration 11.3)**.

Models up to VIN SALLA000304 (end of 2006 model year)

4 Undo the clamp bolt and release the filter from the mounting bracket **(see illustration)**.
5 Undo the 2 bolts and slide down the filter bracket **(see illustration)**.
6 Clean the area around the fuel pipes on the filter, and note their fitted locations.
7 Depress the release buttons, then disconnect the fuel supply pipe from the tank (yellow connector No. 1) and the fuel tank vent pipe (small blue connector No. 4) from the filter **(see illustration)**. Be prepared for fluid spillage. Plug/cover the openings to prevent contamination. Remove the clip between pipes number 1 and 4.
8 Depress the release buttons, then disconnect the high-pressure pump supply pipe (large blue connector No. 3) and the fuel cooler return pipe (white connector No. 2) from the filter. Plug/cover the openings to prevent contamination.
9 Push the pipes onto the ports on the new filter. Ensure the colours of the connectors match the colours of the discs supplied with

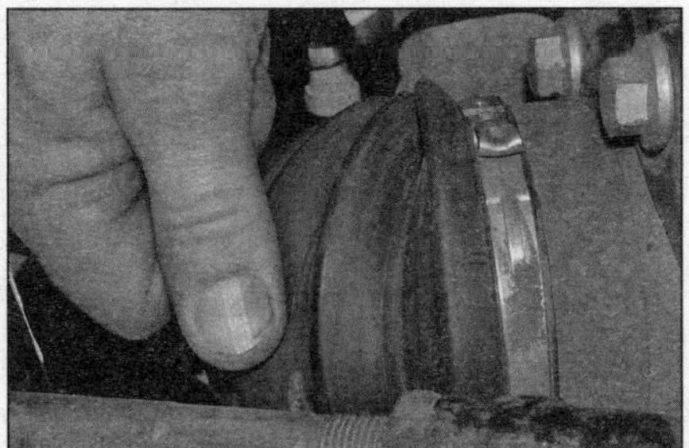

19.1 Check the condition of the driveshaft gaiters

20.4 Undo the bolt (arrowed) each side, then slide the filter and bracket downwards

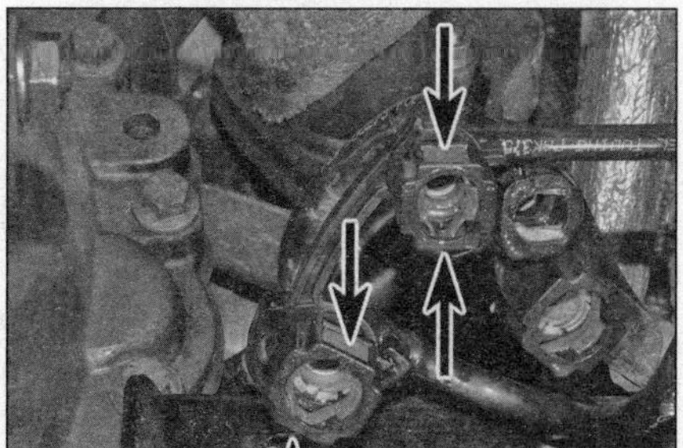

20.7 Depress the release buttons each side of the connectors

20.9a The new filter has coloured discs which correspond the colours of the pipe connectors

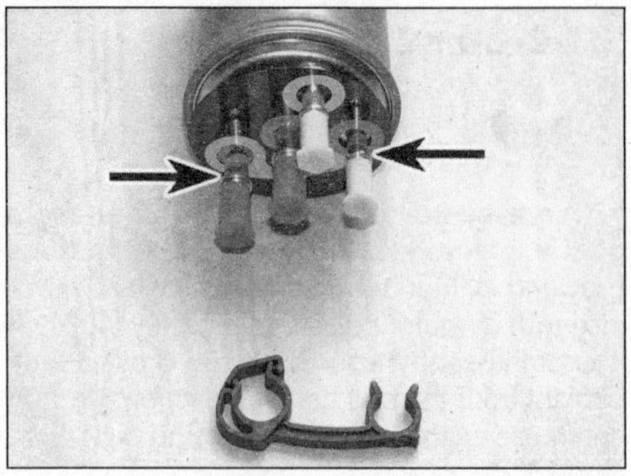

20.9b Fit the retaining clip between the pipes connected to ports 1 and 4 (arrowed)

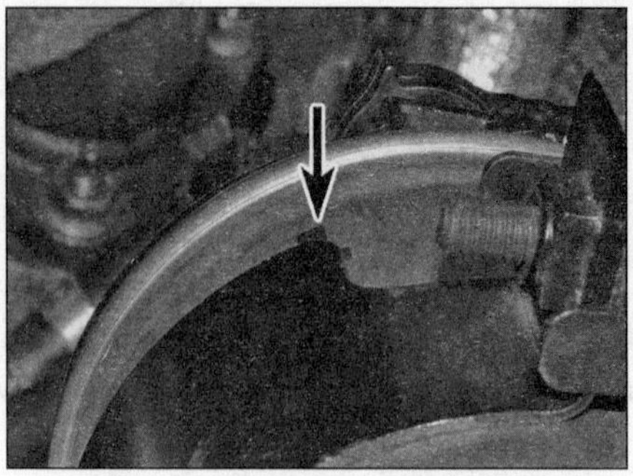

20.11 Align the filter mark with the edge of the clamp (arrowed)

the new filter **(see illustrations)**. Fit new the retaining clip between pipes Nos. 1 and 4. Note that the filter ports are two different diameters to avoid mis-connection.

10 Refit the filter bracket and tighten the retaining bolts securely.

11 Align the mark on the filter with the edge of the clamp, refit the clamp bolt and tighten it securely **(see illustration)**.

Models from VIN SALLA000304 (2007 model year on)

12 Attach a suitable rubber/plastic hose to the drain port, and place the other end in a container **(see illustration 11.4b)**.

13 Slacken the drain port 2 complete revolutions to allow the fluid to drain. Close the port and disconnect the hose.

14 Clean the area around the filter, then disconnect the water-in-fuel sensor wiring plug.

15 Unscrew the filter by hand approximately 90° **(see illustration)**.

16 Unscrew the water-in-fuel sensor from the base of the filter **(see illustrations)**. Discard the O-ring seals.

17 Fit the new O-ring seals to the sensor, aligning the drain port with the mark on the new filter, and tighten the sensor nut securely **(see illustration)**.

18 Thoroughly clean the mating face of the filter head, then position the new filter cartridge into place, aligning the mark on the filter with the inlet pipe on the filter head **(see illustration)**.

19 Now tighten the filter until the lock symbol is aligned with the pointer on the filter head **(see illustration)**.

20 Reconnect the water-in-fuel sensor wiring plug.

All models

21 Refit the heat shield, transmission undershield and lower the vehicle to the ground.

22 Bleed the fuel system as described in Chapter 4A, Section 5.

20.15 Unscrew the filter element (arrowed) approximately 90° anti-clockwise

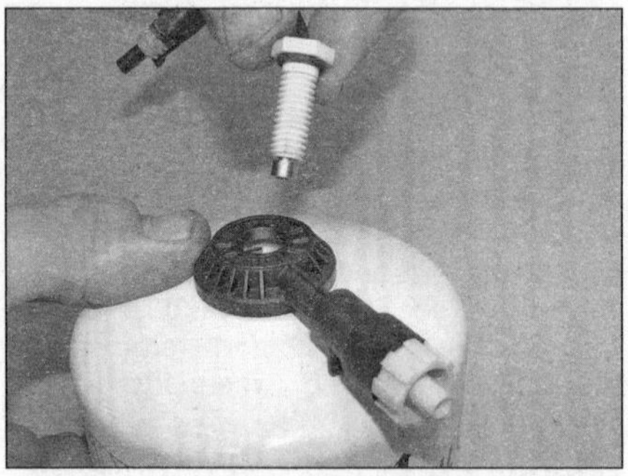

20.16a Unscrew the water-in-fuel sensor, and remove the drain

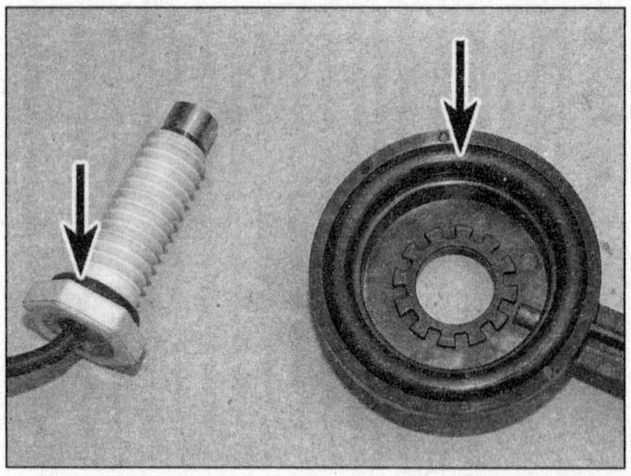

20.16b Renew the O-ring seals (arrowed)

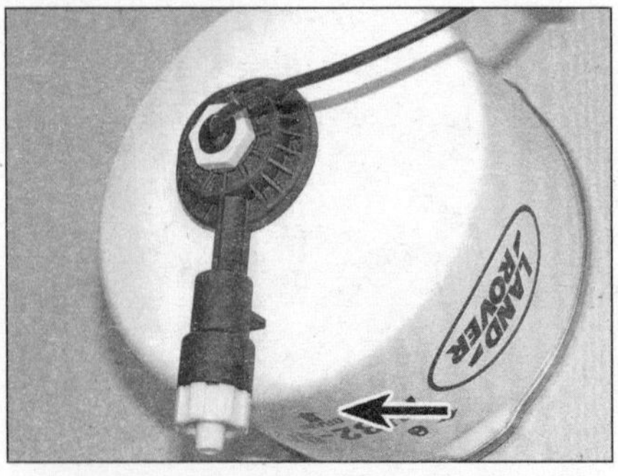

20.17 Align the drain port with the mark (arrowed) on the side of the new filter

20.18 Align the mark (arrowed) with the inlet pipe (arrowed)

20.19 Rotate the filter until the mark (arrowed) aligns with the pointer on the filter head (arrowed)

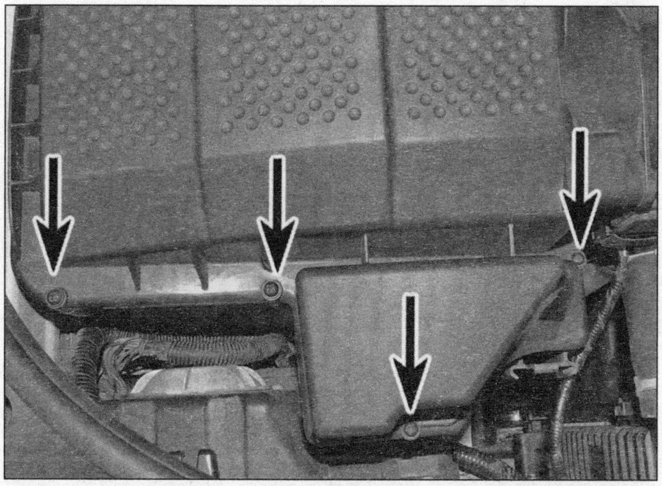

22.1a The air filter cover is secured by 4 screws at the front edge (arrowed) ...

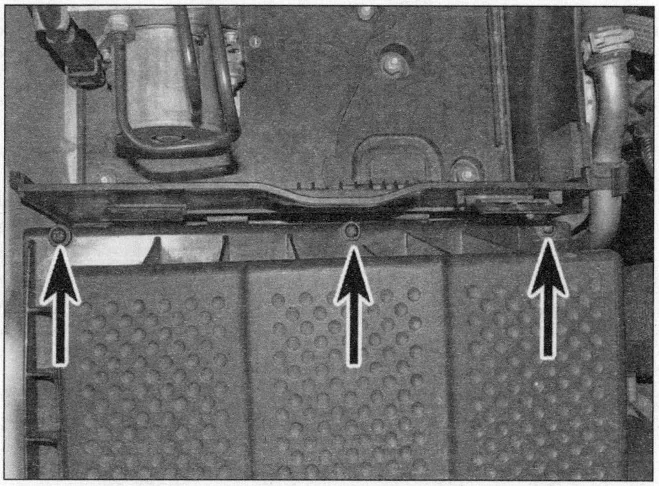

22.1b ... and 3 screws at the rear edge (arrowed)

Every 48 000 miles or 3 years

21 Brake fluid renewal

1 The procedure is similar to that for the bleeding of the hydraulic system as described in Chapter 10, Section 2, except that the brake fluid reservoir should be emptied before starting. Either siphon off the fluid, using a (clean) old battery hydrometer or similar, or open the first bleed screw in the sequence, and pump the fluid from the reservoir. Allowance should be made for all the old fluid to be expelled from the circuit when bleeding each section of the circuit. Used brake fluid is usually much darker in colour than fresh fluid, making it easy to distinguish the two.

22 Air cleaner element renewal

1 Undo the 7 retaining screws and remove the air cleaner housing cover **(see illustrations)**.

2 Lift the old element from place, then remove any debris and clean the inside of the housing and cover.

3 Fit the new element into the housing **(see illustration)**.

4 Refit the cover and securely tighten the retaining screws.

22.3 Fit the new air filter element

Every 72 000 miles

23 Transfer gearbox fluid renewal

Renewal of the transfer gearbox fluid is described in Chapter 7C, Section 4.

24 Final drive fluid renewal

Renewal of the final drive fluid is described in Chapter 9, Section 10.

25 Air suspension intake filter renewal

Renewal of the filter is described in Chapter 11, Section 16.

Every 6 years

26 Braking system hose and seal renewal

1 At this interval, Land Rover recommend that all the brake system rubber seals and flexible rubber hoses are renewed, and the hydraulic system filled with fresh fluid. Refer to Chapter 10 for renewal information.

Every 108 000 miles or 7 years

27 Timing belt and tensioner renewal

Renewal of the timing belt and tensioner is described in Chapter 2, Section 7.

28 Fuel pump drivebelt and tensioner renewal

Renewal of the fuel pump drivebelt and tensioner is described in Chapter 4A, Section 11.

Every 144 000 miles or 10 years

29 Automatic transmission fluid renewal

Renewal of the automatic transmission fluid is described in Chapter 7B, Section 7.

30 Manual gearbox oil renewal

Renewal of the main manual gearbox oil is described in Chapter 7A, Section 4.

31 Coolant renewal

Coolant check

1 Refer to Section 17.

Draining

Warning: Wait until the engine is cold before starting this procedure. Do not allow antifreeze to come in contact with your skin, or with the painted surfaces of the vehicle. Rinse off spills immediately with plenty of water. Never leave antifreeze lying around in an open container, or in a puddle in the driveway or garage floor. Children and pets are attracted by its sweet smell, but antifreeze is fatal if ingested.

2 Raise the front of the vehicle and support it securely on axle stands (see *Jacking and vehicle support*).

3 Set the heater controls to maximum heater output.

4 Undo the oil filler cap, then pull the plastic cover upwards from the top of the engine **(see illustration 3.3)**.

5 Cover the expansion tank with a wad of rag, and slowly turn the cap anti-clockwise to relieve any pressure in the cooling system (a hissing sound will normally be heard). Wait until any pressure remaining in the system is released, then continue to turn the cap until it can be removed.

6 Undo the 4 bolts and remove the access panel beneath the radiator **(see illustration)**.

7 Position a suitable container beneath the thermostat housing. Release the retaining clip, then disconnect the radiator lower coolant hose from the thermostat housing and allow the coolant to drain into the container **(see illustration)**.

8 Once the coolant has stopped draining, reconnect the hose and secure it with the clip.

Models with auxiliary (rear) heating system

9 Remove the spare wheel from under the rear of the vehicle.

10 Position a suitable container beneath the rear heater coolant hoses. Release the retaining clips, then disconnect the hoses and allow the coolant to drain into the container.

11 Once the coolant has stopped draining, reconnect the hoses and secure them with the clips.

Filling

12 Before attempting to fill the cooling system, make sure that all hoses and clips are in good condition, and that the clips are tight. Note that an antifreeze mixture must be used all year round, to prevent corrosion of the alloy engine components.

13 Slacken the bleed screw in the top of the coolant expansion tank, and the bleed screw in front of the left-hand cylinder head cover **(see illustrations)**.

14 Fill the system by slowly pouring the coolant into the expansion tank to prevent airlocks from forming.

15 If the coolant is being renewed, begin by pouring in a couple of litres of water, followed by the correct quantity of antifreeze, then top-up with more water.

16 When air-free coolant emerges, tighten the bleed screws.

17 Top-up the expansion tank to the correct level, then refit the expansion tank cap.

18 Start the engine, run it at 3000 rpm for 1 minute, then allow it to idle for 5 minutes. Repeat this procedure until it reaches normal operating temperature, then stop the engine and allow it to cool.

19 Check for leaks, particularly around disturbed components. Check the coolant level in the expansion tank, and top-up if necessary. Note that the system must be cold before an accurate level is indicated in the expansion tank. If the expansion tank cap is removed while the engine is still warm, cover the cap with a thick cloth. Unscrew the cap slowly, to gradually relieve the system pressure (a hissing sound will normally be heard). Wait until any pressure remaining in the system is released, then continue to turn the cap until it can be removed.

20 Refit the radiator access panel, engine cover and spare wheel (where applicable). Lower the vehicle to the ground.

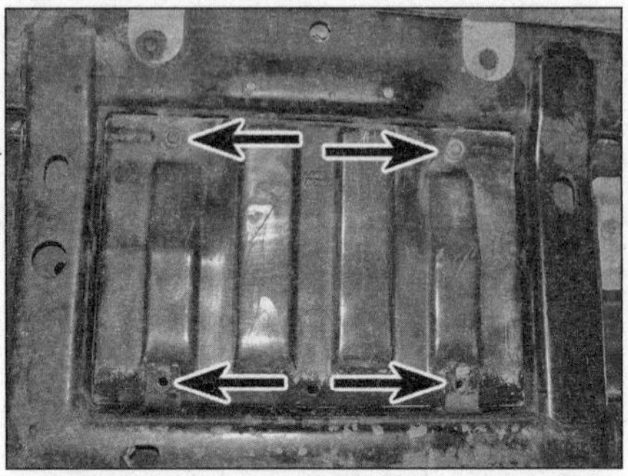

31.6 Undo the bolts (arrowed) and remove the panel beneath the radiator

31.7 Working underneath, release the clamp and disconnect the radiator hose from the thermostat housing (arrowed)

31.13a Slacken the coolant bleed screw on the top of the expansion tank (arrowed) ...

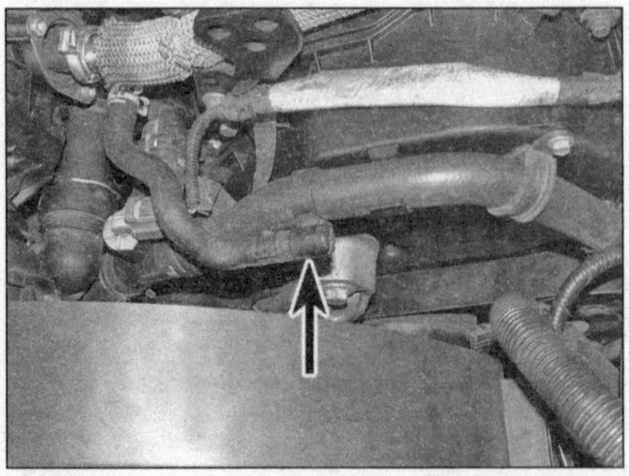

31.13b ... and the bleed screw at the front of the left-hand cylinder head

Chapter 2
Engine in-car repair procedures

Contents

Degrees of difficulty

Easy, suitable for novice with little experience	**Fairly easy,** suitable for beginner with some experience	**Fairly difficult,** suitable for competent DIY mechanic	**Difficult,** suitable for experienced DIY mechanic	**Very difficult,** suitable for expert DIY or professional

Specifications

General

Engine type	Six-cylinder, 60° V-formation, water-cooled. Belt-driven exhaust camshafts linked to the intake camshafts via chains, operating 24 valves via rocker arms and hydraulic clearance adjusters
Bore	81.00 mm
Stroke	88.00 mm
Capacity	2720 cc
Firing order	1-4-2-5-3-6 (No 1 at right-front, No 4 at left-front)
Direction of crankshaft rotation	Clockwise (viewed from timing belt end of engine)
Compression ratio	17.3:1
Maximum power (DIN)	147 kW (197 bhp) @ 4000 rpm
Maximum torque	440 Nm (324 lbft) @ 1900 rpm
Maximum compression pressure difference between cylinders (typical value)	5.0 bars (70 psi)
Weight:	
Manual transmission (inc. clutch)	260 kg
Automatic transmission	235 kg

Cylinder head

Maximum permissible distortion of sealing face (typical value)	0.10 mm

Note: *It is not permissible to recut or renew the valve seats.*

Cylinder head gasket selection

Piston protrusion:	Gasket identification	Gasket thickness
0.541 to 0.590 mm	1 serration	1.12 mm
0.591 to 0.640 mm	2 serrations	1.17 mm
0.641 to 0.690 mm	3 serrations	1.22 mm
0.691 to 0.740 mm	4 serrations	1.27 mm
0.741 to 0.790 mm	5 serrations	1.32 mm

Valves

Valve clearance (intake and exhaust)	Hydraulic adjusters
Valve head diameter:	
Intake	35.0 mm
Exhaust	31.0 mm
Valve stem diameter:	
Intake	5.0 mm
Exhaust	5.0 mm
Maximum valve head deflection – see text:*	
Intake	0.025 to 0.059 mm
Exhaust	0.035 to 0.069 mm

** These are typical values – Land Rover do not specify a value.*

Valve springs

Free length	Not available

Cylinder block

Cylinder rebore oversizes	No oversizes available

Crankshaft

Crankshaft endfloat	0.21 to 0.43 mm

Camshaft

Endfloat	0.065 to 0.185 mm

Lubrication system

Normal oil pressure:	
At idle speed	0.7 bar
At 3500 rpm (hot)	1.9 bar
Oil pump type	Eccentric rotor, driven from crankshaft
Relief valve opening pressure	4.5 bar
Pressure switch opening pressure	0.15 to 0.41 bar

Torque wrench settings

	Nm	lbf ft
Alternator mounting bracket	22	16
Auxiliary drivebelt idler assembly bolt	47	35
Auxiliary drivebelt idler pulley bolt	23	17
Auxiliary drivebelt tensioner bolts:		
M10	47	35
M8	25	18
Camshaft inner bearing cap bolts:		
Stage 1	1	0.7
Stage 2	5	4
Stage 3	10	7
Camshaft front hub bolts (lubricate lightly):*		
Stage 1	80	59
Stage 2	Angle-tighten a further 90°	
Camshaft position sensor bolt	10	7
Camshaft rear sprocket bolt:*		
Stage 1	80	59
Stage 2	Angle-tighten a further 90°	
Camshaft sprocket bolts	23	17
Coolant outlet elbow	10	7
Coolant pump pulley bolts	23	17
Crankshaft position sensor bolt	6	4
Crankshaft pulley bolts	23	17
Crankshaft rear oil seal housing bolts	10	7
Crankshaft sprocket bolt (**do not** lubricate):*		
Stage 1	100	74
Stage 2	Angle-tighten a further 90°	
Cylinder head bolts (**do not** lubricate):*		
Stage 1	20	15
Stage 2	40	30
Stage 3	80	59
Stage 4	Angle-tighten a further 180°	
Cylinder head cover bolts	10	7
EGR valve	10	7
EGR valve inlet tube	10	7

Torque wrench settings

	Nm	lbf ft
Engine breather tube bolt	10	7
Engine-to-transmission bolts	45	33
Engine mountings:		
Mounting bracket-to-mounting nut	90	66
Mounting-to-chassis bolts:*		
Stage 1	45	33
Stage 2	Angle-tighten a further 60°	
Mounting bracket to cylinder block	80	59
Engine undershield bolts	62	46
Exhaust manifold heat shield	10	7
Exhaust manifold nuts	23	17
Front axle crossmember	115	85
Front axle retaining bolt	105	77
Flywheel/driveplate securing bolts:*		
Stage 1	50	37
Stage 2	Angle-tighten a further 45°	
Stage 3	Angle-tighten a further 45°	
Injection pump	23	17
Injection pump sprocket nut	50	37
Knock sensor	25	15
Oil cooler bolts	10	7
Oil filter	25	18
Oil pressure warning light switch	15	11
Oil pump strainer bolts	10	7
Oil pump to cylinder block	10	7
Oil temperature sensor	10	7
Piston cooling/lubrication jets	10	7
Sump drain plug	23	17
Sump extension to engine block:		
Stage 1 Bolts 1 to 5	10	7
Stage 2 Bolts 10 to 14	10	7
Stage 3 Bolts 6 to 9	4	3
Stage 4 Bolts 15 to 18	4	3
Stage 5 Bolts 1 to 5	24	18
Stage 6 Bolts 10 to 14	24	18
Stage 7 Bolts 6 to 9	10	7
Stage 8 Bolts 15 to 18	10	7
Sump pan-to-extension bolts	10	7
Timing belt cover bolts	10	7
Timing belt idler pulley retaining bolt	45	33
Timing belt tensioner retaining bolt*	24	18
Timing chain tensioner retaining bolt	10	7
Vacuum pump:		
Bolts	23	17
Nuts	13	10

* *Do not re-use*

1 General information

General information

This Chapter describes the repair procedures which can reasonably be carried out on the engine while it remains in the vehicle. Traditionally, the engine would be removed to renew the pistons, crankshaft and main bearings. However, removal of these components is not recommended by the manufacturer. Once disassembled, the production tolerances set during manufacture cannot be achieved during reassembly – the act of disassembly will cause the main bearing carrier and cylinder block to distort. If these components are worn/damaged/faulty, a new engine must be fitted – check with your local Land Rover dealer, parts specialist or automotive engineering workshop.

In order to remove the engine, the complete vehicle body must be lifted from the chassis. This can **only** be accomplished using a 2-post powered ramp – not normally available to a DIY repairer. Consequently, although the procedure itself is not technically demanding, we have had to conclude that engine removal and refitting is beyond the scope of this manual. For information, brief guidelines concerning the procedure are provided in Section 18 of this Chapter.

Engine description

The TDV6 is a new engine for Land Rover, not based on any previous design, the result of collaboration between Ford/Jaguar and PSA (Peugeot/Citroën). The engine is a V6 double overhead camshaft, 4 valves per cylinder unit, with direct injection, variable-nozzle turbocharger and intercooler. The engine block is made from compacted graphite iron (CGI), with an aluminium stiffener plate (sump extension) fitted to its base. The cylinder heads are aluminium – no refacing/skimming or the cylinder head is permitted. The cylinders are 'direct' bored into the engine block, then plateau honed – no reboring of the cylinders is possible. Lubrication and cooling of the pistons/gudgeon pins is provided by jets bolted to the base of the cylinder bores.

The double camshafts run directly in the cylinder heads, and are retained by bearing caps. The valves are operated by roller-rocker arms fitted directly below the camshaft lobes.

The roller-rocker arms pivot on hydraulic lash adjusters – no checking or maintenance of the valve clearances is required.

The exhaust camshafts are driven from the crankshaft by a timing belt. The belt is tensioned automatically by a spring-loaded tensioner assembly. A single row chain from each exhaust camshaft drives the corresponding intake camshaft, and a belt from the rear of the left-hand exhaust camshaft drives the high-pressure fuel injection pump.

The eccentric-rotor oil pump is located over the front end of the crankshaft, and driven by a machined flange integral with the crankshaft.

The fillet rolled, forged steel crankshaft is supported on 4 plain bearing shells, with endfloat controlled by thrustwashers integral with each No. 4 main bearing shell.

The connecting rods are attached to the crankshaft by fracture-split big end caps. With this design, the connecting rods are made as one casting, then fractured and split to form the removable big-end cap. This ensures a unique fit between the two components, resulting in greater rigidity and strength. The aluminium pistons have molybdenum coated skirts to reduce friction, and swirl chambers located in the piston crown. The pistons are attached to the connecting rods by gudgeon pins, which are a push-fit in the connecting rod small-end bores. The gudgeon pins are retained by circlips. The pistons are fitted with three piston rings – two compression rings and an oil control ring.

The coolant pump is located on the front face of the cylinder block, and is driven by the auxiliary drive belt.

Operations with engine in vehicle

The following operations can be carried out without having to remove the engine from the vehicle.

- a) *Removal and refitting of the camshaft/rocker shaft/hydraulic lash adjusters.*
- b) *Removal and refitting of the cylinder head.*
- c) *Removal and refitting of the timing belt and sprockets.*
- d) *Removal and refitting of the sump.*
- e) *Removal and refitting of the oil pump.*
- f) *Renewal of the engine mountings.*
- g) *Removal and refitting of the flywheel.*

2 Compression and leakdown tests – description and interpretation

Compression test

Note: *A compression tester specifically designed for diesel engines must be used for this test.*

1 When engine performance is down, or if misfiring occurs which cannot be attributed to the fuel system, a compression test can provide diagnostic clues as to the engine's condition. If the test is performed regularly, it can give warning of trouble before any other symptoms become apparent.

2 A compression tester specifically intended for diesel engines must be used, because of the higher pressures involved. The tester is connected to an adapter which screws into the glow plug hole. It is unlikely to be worthwhile buying such a tester for occasional use, but it may be possible to borrow or hire one – if not, have the test performed by a garage.

3 Unless specific instructions to the contrary are supplied with the tester, observe the following points:

- a) *The battery must be in a good state of charge, the air filter must be clean, and the engine should be at normal operating temperature.*
- b) *All the glow plugs should be removed before starting the test.*

4 There is no need to hold the accelerator pedal down during the test, because the diesel engine air intake is not throttled.

5 The actual compression pressures measured are not so important as the balance between cylinders. Land Rover do not specify compression pressures, but a typical value for the maximum difference between cylinders is given in the Specifications.

6 The cause of poor compression is less easy to establish on a diesel engine than on a petrol one. The effect of introducing oil into the cylinders ('wet' testing) is not conclusive, because there is a risk that the oil will sit in the recess on the piston crown, instead of passing to the rings. However, the following can be used as a rough guide to diagnosis.

7 All cylinders should produce very similar pressures; any difference greater than that specified indicates the existence of a fault. Note that the compression should build up quickly in a healthy engine; low compression on the first stroke, followed by gradually-increasing pressure on successive strokes, indicates worn piston rings. A low compression reading on the first stroke, which does not build up during successive strokes, indicates leaking valves or a blown head gasket (a cracked head could also be the cause). Deposits on the undersides of the valve heads can also cause low compression.

8 A low reading from two adjacent cylinders is almost certainly due to the head gasket having blown between them; the presence of coolant in the engine oil will confirm this.

9 If the compression reading is unusually high, the cylinder head surfaces, valves and pistons are probably coated with carbon deposits. If this is the case, the cylinder head should be removed and decarbonised.

Leakdown test

10 A leakdown test measures the rate at which compressed air fed into the cylinder is lost. It is an alternative to a compression test, and in many ways it is better, since the escaping air provides easy identification of where pressure loss is occurring (piston rings, valves or head gasket).

11 The equipment needed for leakdown testing is unlikely to be available to the home mechanic. If poor compression is suspected, have the test performed by a suitably-equipped garage.

3 Top dead centre (TDC) for No 1 piston – locating

Note: *Suitable tools will be required to lock the flywheel and the camshaft in position during this operation. The Land Rover special tools may be available, alternatively try an automotive tool specialist* ***(see illustration)****.*

1 Top dead centre (TDC) is the highest point in the cylinder that each piston reaches as the crankshaft turns. Each piston reaches TDC at the end of the compression stoke, and again at the end of the exhaust stroke.

2 Remove the starter motor as described in Chapter 5, Section 9.

3 Remove the timing belt cover as described in Section 6.

4 Remove the crankshaft timing alignment hole grommet from the rear of the cylinder block **(see illustration)**.

5 Using a spanner/socket on the crankshaft sprocket, rotate the crankshaft until the holes in the camshaft sprockets align with the corresponding holes in the cylinder heads.

6 Insert the camshaft sprocket alignment tools (303-1126 or equivalent) through the holes in the camshaft sprockets and into the

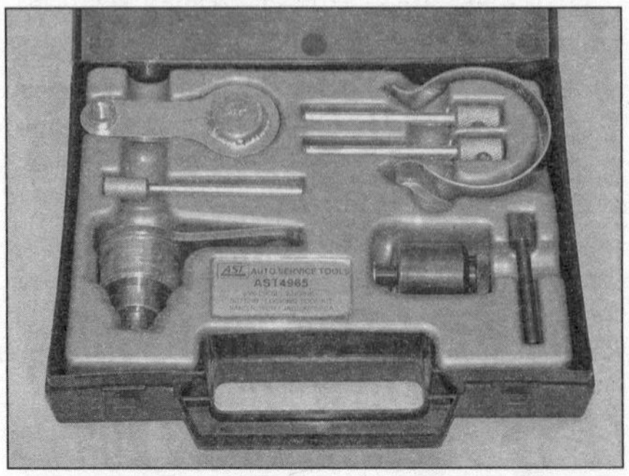

3.0 Special tools like these from Auto Service Tools Limited are needed to lock the engine at TDC

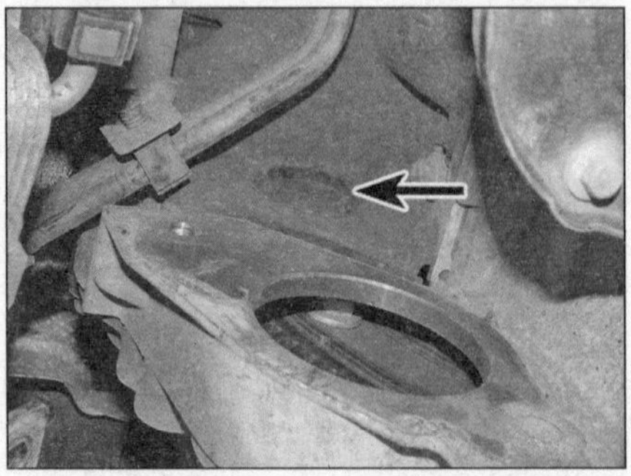

3.4 Remove the grommet (arrowed) from above the starter motor aperture

3.6a Rotate the crankshaft clockwise until the special tools (arrowed) ...

3.6b ... can be inserted through the camshaft sprocket hubs and into the holes in the cylinder heads

cylinder head **(see illustrations)**. Note that it may be necessary to turn the crankshaft forwards or backwards a few degrees in order to fully insert the tools.

7 With the camshaft locked in position, it should now be possible to insert tool No. 303-1116 (manual transmission) or 303-1117 (automatic transmission), or equivalent, through the bellhousing to lock the flywheel/driveplate/crankshaft in position **(see illustrations)**. Note that the tool should be secured using a bolt/nut through the starter motor mounting upper hole.

8 The engine is now locked at TDC for No. 1 cylinder.

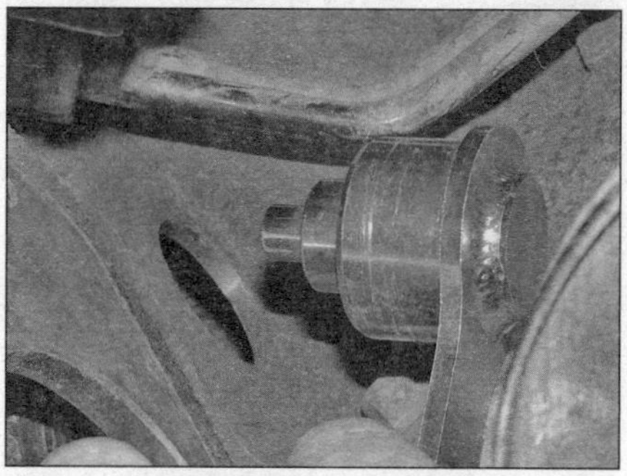

3.7a Insert the locking tool into the holes in the flywheel/driveplate and cylinder block

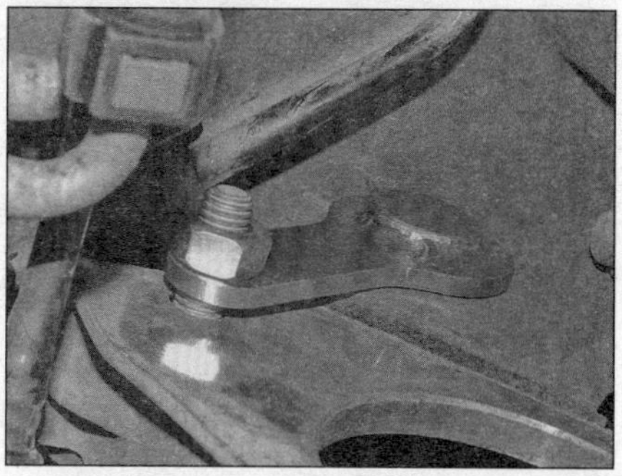

3.7b Lock the tool in place using a nut and bolt through the starter motor upper mounting hole

4 Cylinder head covers – removal and refitting

Removal

1 Disconnect the battery negative lead as described in Chapter 5, Section 4.

2 Remove the air shut-off valve as described in Chapter 4A, Section 9.

Right-hand cover

3 Unclip the glow plug wiring harness, and the knock sensor wiring harness from the cylinder head cover **(see illustration)**.

4 Disconnect the breather hose from the cover **(see illustration)**.

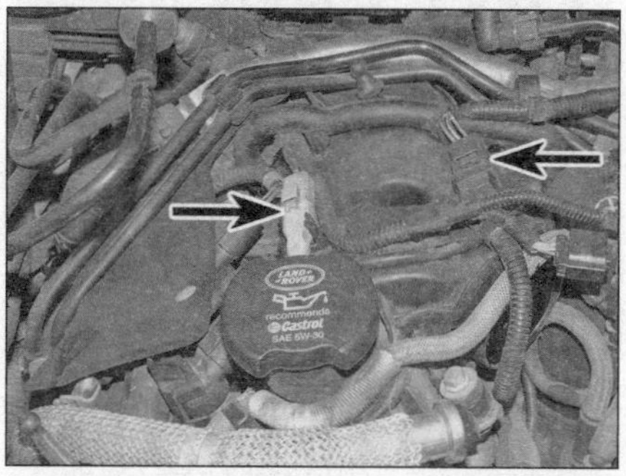

4.3 Unclip the glow plug and knock sensor wiring harnesses (arrowed)

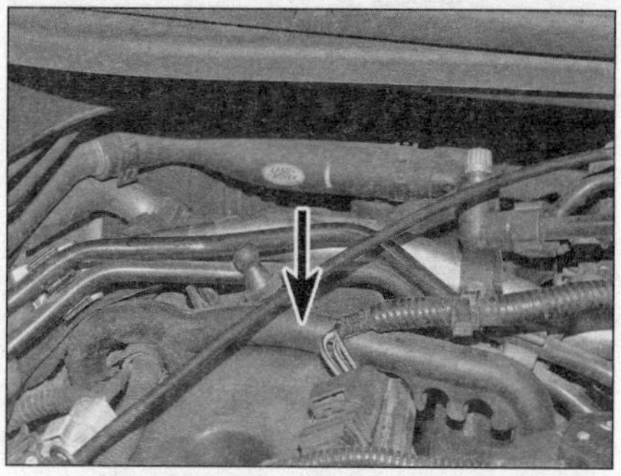

4.4 Disconnect the breather hose (arrowed)

5 Remove the right-hand side fuel injectors as described in Chapter 4A, Section 8.

6 Undo the unions, release the support bracket and remove the high-pressure fuel pipe from the diverter rail to the common rail. Plug/cover the openings to prevent contamination. Discard the fuel pipe – a new one must be fitted.

7 Undo the retaining bolts and remove the common rail **(see illustration)**. Disconnect any wiring plugs as the common rail is withdrawn.

8 Unclip the fuel hoses, then undo the retaining bolt and remove the fuel hose bracket **(see illustration)**.

4.7 Right-hand common rail mounting bolts (arrowed)

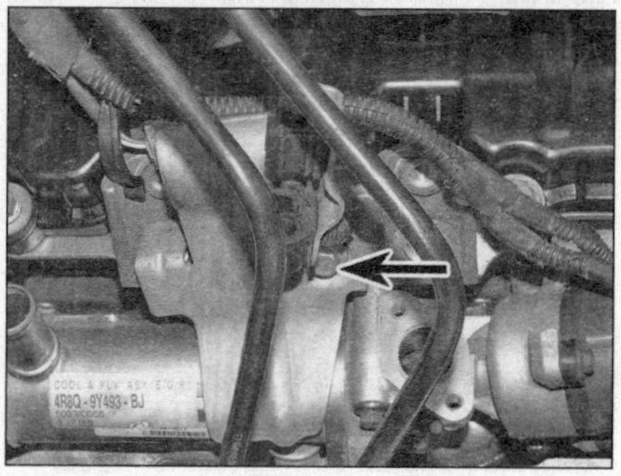

4.8 Undo the bolt (arrowed) and remove the fuel hose bracket

4.10a Engine cover locating studs (arrowed)

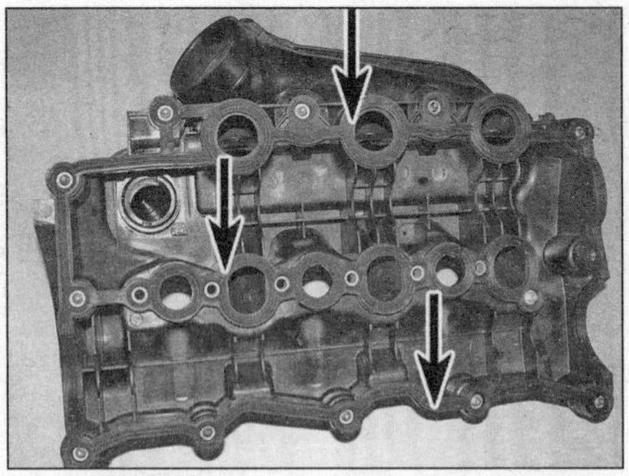

4.10b Check the condition of the gasket (arrowed) ...

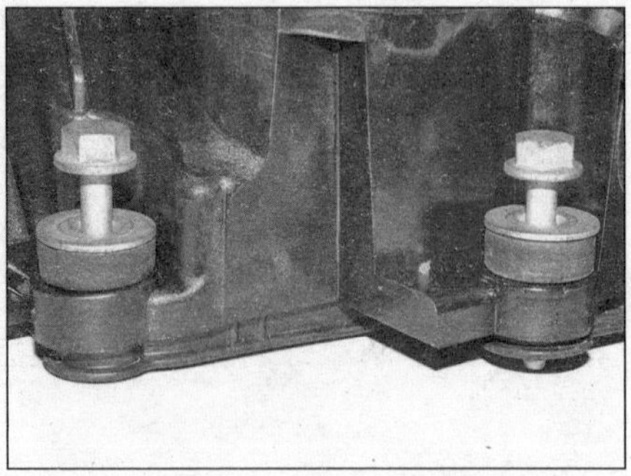

4.10c ... and the sealing washers/spacers

9 Remove the common fuel rail support bracket.

10 Remove the engine cover locating studs, then undo the bolts and remove the cover. Check the condition of the rubber gasket, sealing washers and spacers, and renew as necessary **(see illustrations)**.

Left-hand cover

11 Remove the auxiliary drivebelt as described in Chapter 1, Section 9.

12 Remove the auxiliary drivebelt idler pulley **(see illustrations)**.

13 Disconnect the knock sensor wiring plug, glow plugs wiring plug, and oil pressure sensor wiring plug, then unclip the harnesses from the cylinder head cover **(see illustration)**.

14 Disconnect the breather hose from the cylinder head cover **(see illustration)**.

15 Remove the left-hand side fuel injectors as described in Chapter 4A, Section 8.

16 Undo the unions, release the support bracket and remove the high-pressure fuel pipe from the diverter rail to the common rail **(see illustration)**. Plug/cover the openings to prevent contamination. Discard the fuel pipe – a new one must be fitted.

17 Undo the retaining bolts and remove the common rail **(see illustration)**. Disconnect any wiring plugs as the common rail is withdrawn.

18 Remove the retaining bolts and withdraw

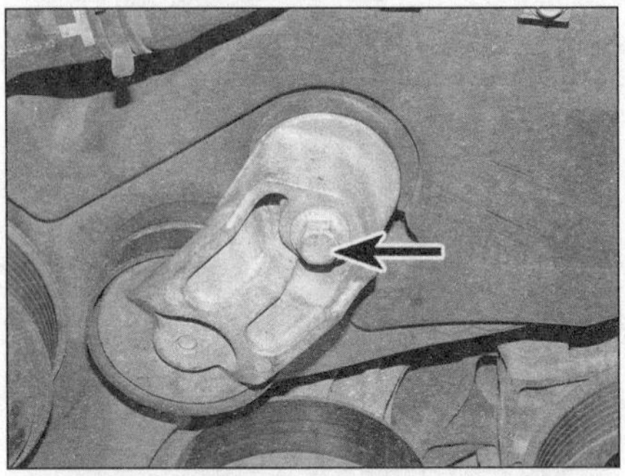

4.12a Undo the bolt (arrowed) and withdraw the auxiliary drivebelt idler pulley

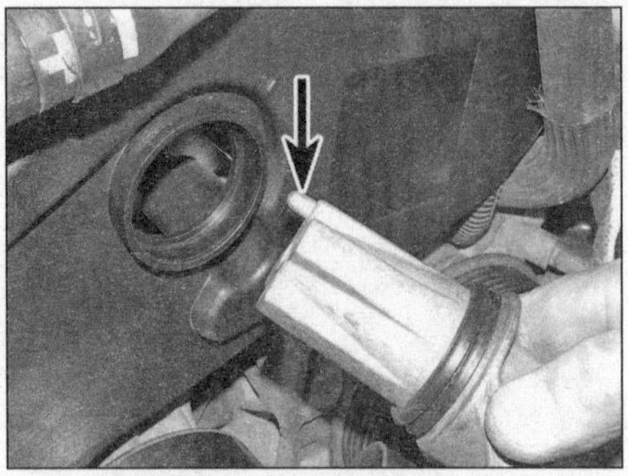

4.12b When refitting, the pin (arrowed) on the end of the pulley assembly ...

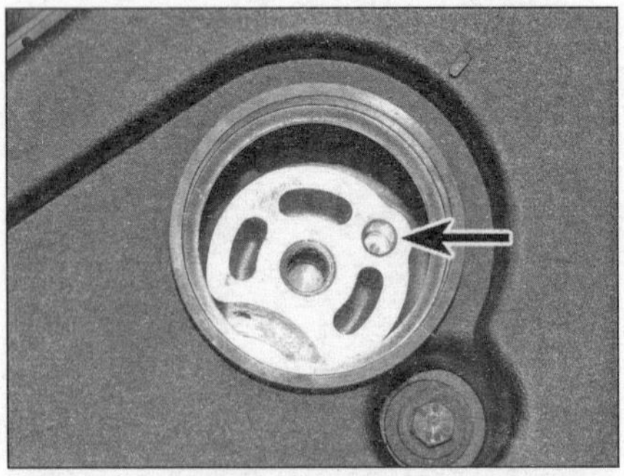

4.12c ... must align with the corresponding hole (arrowed) in the cylinder head

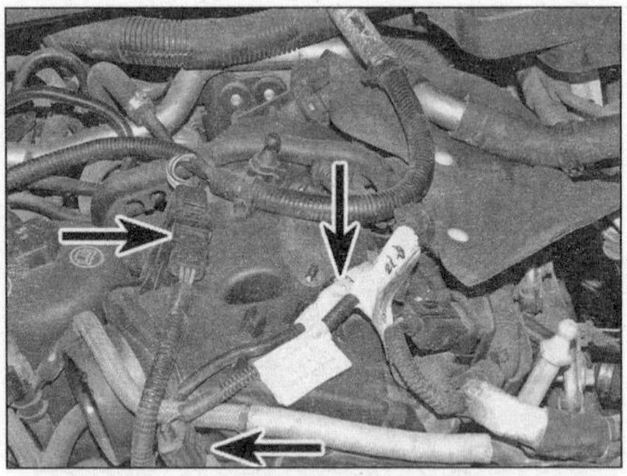

4.13 Disconnect the knock sensor, glow plugs, and oil pressure sensor wiring plugs (arrowed)

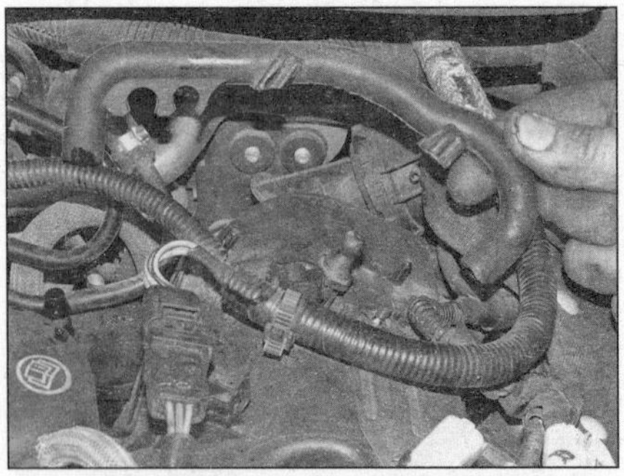

4.14 Disconnect the breather hose

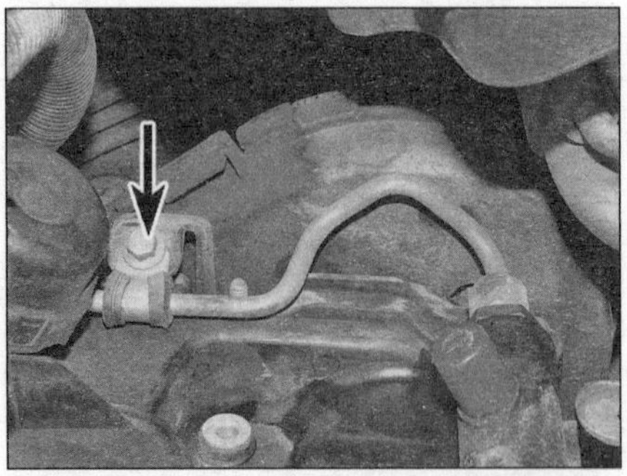

4.16 Remove the pipe from the diverter rail to the common rail. Note the support bracket bolt (arrowed)

4.17 Common rail retaining bolts (arrowed)

4.18 Undo the bolt securing the oil level dipstick guide tube, and the common rail support bracket (arrowed)

4.21 Manoeuvre the cylinder head cover from place

the common rail support bracket **(see illustration)**.

19 Remove the engine cover locating studs.

20 Slacken the 7 timing belt cover bolts and move the cover slightly to access the cylinder head cover bolts.

21 Undo the bolts and remove the cover **(see illustration)**. Check the condition of the rubber gasket, sealing washers and spacers, and renew as necessary **(see illustrations 4.10b and 4.10c)**.

Refitting

22 Commence refitting by thoroughly cleaning the gasket faces of the cover and the cylinder head.

23 Refit the cover(s) and tighten the retaining bolts to the specified torque.

24 The remainder of refitting is a reversal of removal. After starting the engine, check for oil leaks from the covers before venturing out onto the road.

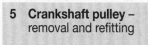

5 Crankshaft pulley – removal and refitting

1 Remove the auxiliary drivebelt as described in Chapter 1, Section 9.

2 Undo the bolts securing the pulley to the crankshaft sprocket **(see illustration)**.

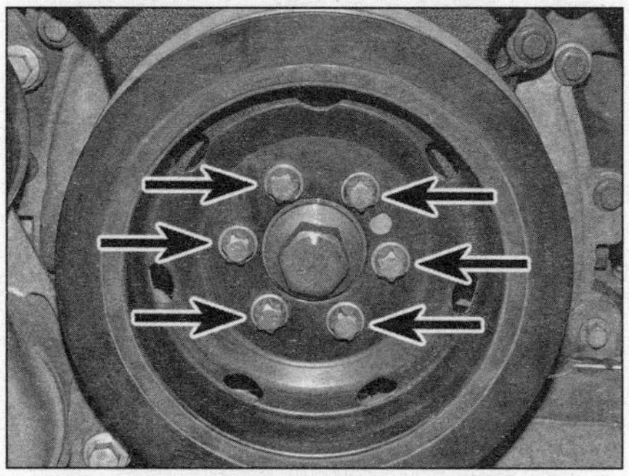

5.2 Undo the damper retaining bolts (arrowed)

3 Refitting is a reversal of removal, bearing in mind the following points:

a) Tighten the pulley bolts to the recommended torque.

b) Refit and tension the auxiliary drivebelt as described in Chapter 1, Section 9.

6 Timing belt cover – removal and refitting

Removal

1 Remove the crankshaft sprocket as described in Section 5.

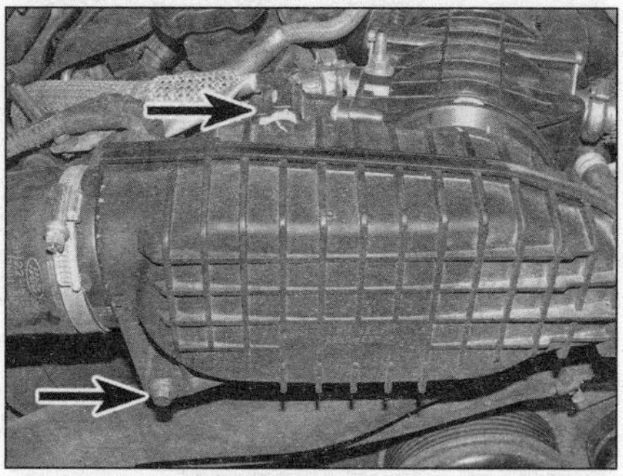

6.3a Disconnect the wiring plug, undo the bolt (arrowed) ...

2 Drain the coolant as described in Chapter 1, Section 31.

3 Undo the retaining bolt, disconnect the wiring plug, release the clip, and remove the throttle body elbow **(see illustrations)**.

4 Release the retaining clip and disconnect the coolant hose from the cylinder head outlet elbow **(see illustration)**.

5 Undo the bolts and remove the throttle body elbow support bracket **(see illustration)**.

6 Undo the screw securing the intake hose to the left-hand side of the shroud, then unclip the hoses beneath, release the clips each

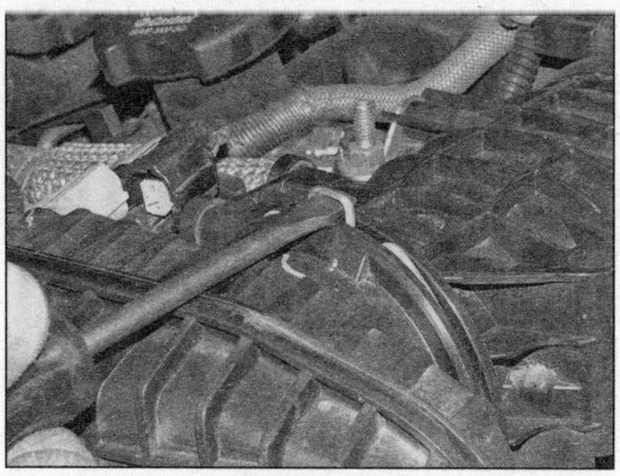

6.3b ... then prise up the clip and remove the throttle body elbow

6.4 Prise out the clip (arrowed) and disconnect the coolant elbow

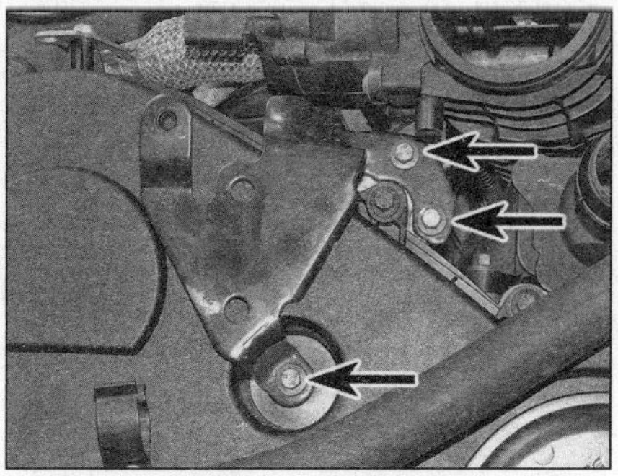

6.5 Throttle body elbow support bracket bolts (arrowed)

6.6a Slide up the connector from the lower shroud

6.6b Release the clip (arrowed) each side ...

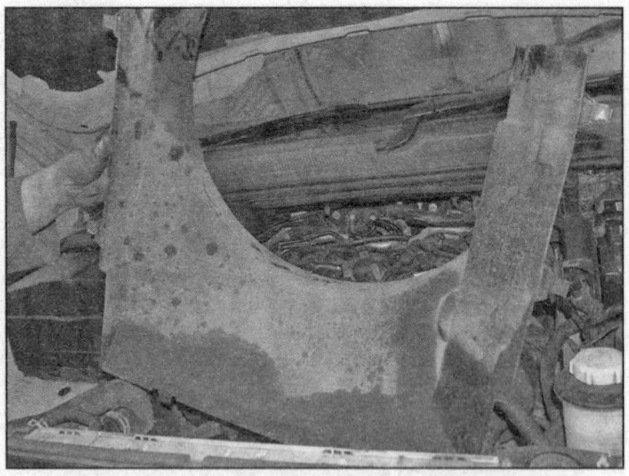

6.6c ... and manoeuvre the shroud upwards

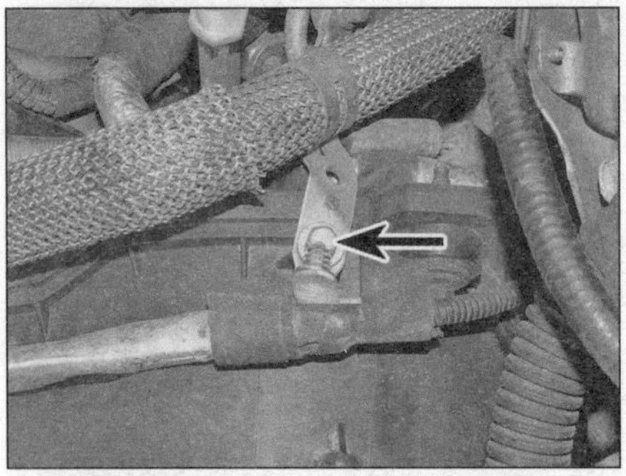

6.8 Undo the bolt (arrowed) securing the EGR pipe brackets each side

6.9 EGR coolant hose clamps and bracket bolt (arrowed)

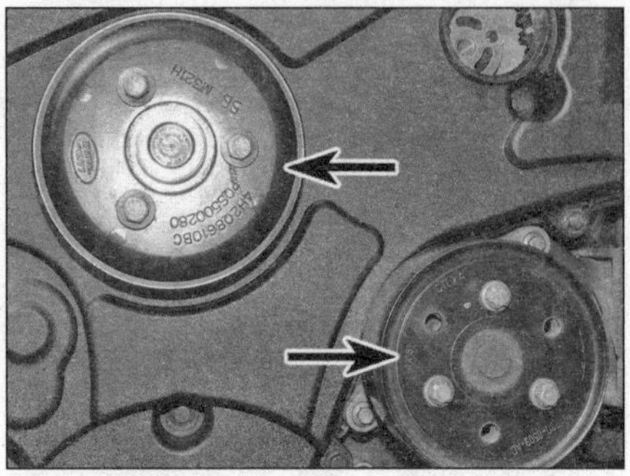

6.10 Coolant pump and fan coupling pulleys (arrowed)

side and slide the cooling fan lower shroud upwards **(see illustrations)**.

7 Undo the bolt and remove the auxiliary belt idler assembly **(see illustrations 4.12a, 4.12b and 4.12c)**.

8 Undo the bolts securing the EGR pipe brackets to the timing belt cover **(see illustration)**.

9 Release the clips and disconnect the right and left-hand EGR coolant inlet hoses from the coolant temperature sensor housing. Undo the bracket bolt, and unclip the hoses from the timing belt cover **(see illustration)**.

10 Undo the retaining bolts and remove the coolant pump and fan coupling pulleys **(see illustration)**.

11 The timing belt cover is secured by 16 bolts. Undo the bolts, release the wiring harness clips, and remove the cover **(see illustration)**.

Refitting

12 Refitting is a reversal of removal, noting the following points:

a) Tighten all fasteners to their specified torque, where given.

b) Refill the cooling system as described in Chapter 1, Section 31.

7 Timing belt and tensioner – removal and refitting

Removal

1 Set the camshafts and crankshaft positions as described in Section 3.

2 Counterhold the sprockets with a suitable tool, and slacken the sprocket's retaining bolts; not the centre hub bolt **(see illustrations)**.

Note: *Do not be tempted to rely on the locking tools to prevent the sprockets from rotating – damage to the tools/engine castings may result.*

HAYNES HiNT ***To make a camshaft sprocket holding tool, obtain two lengths of steel strip about 6 mm thick by 30 mm wide or similar, one 600 mm long, the other 200 mm long (all dimensions are approximate). Bolt the two strips together to form a forked end, leaving the bolt slack so that the shorter strip can pivot freely. At the end of each 'prong' of the fork, secure a bolt with a nut and locknut; these will engage with the cut-outs in the sprocket and should protrude by about 30 mm.***

6.11 Undo the bolts and remove the timing belt cover

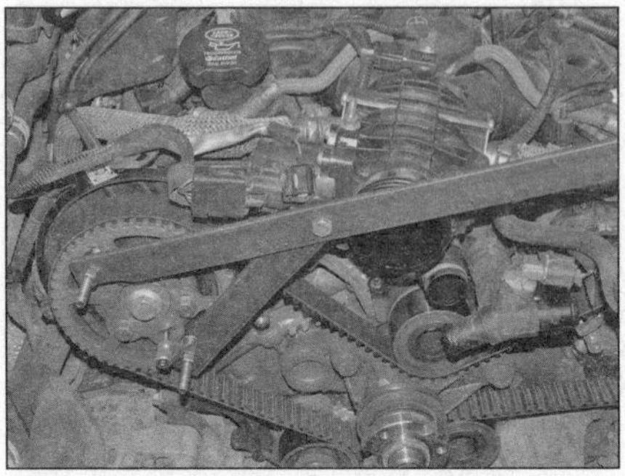

7.2a Using a home-made tool to prevent rotation ...

7.2b ... whilst slackening the camshaft sprocket bolts (arrowed)

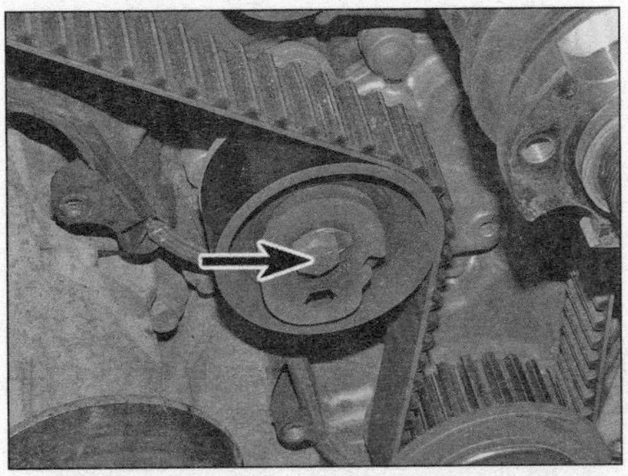

7.3 Timing belt tensioner retaining bolt (arrowed)

7.4 Undo the bolt and remove the upper belt idler sprocket

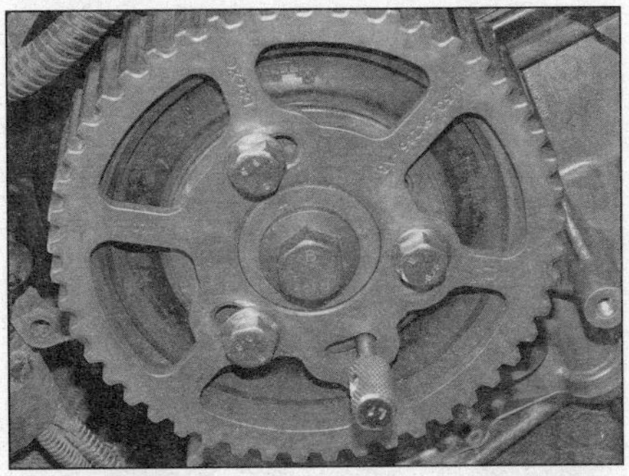

7.7 Rotate the camshaft sprockets fully clockwise to the end of the bolt slots, independently of the camshaft hub

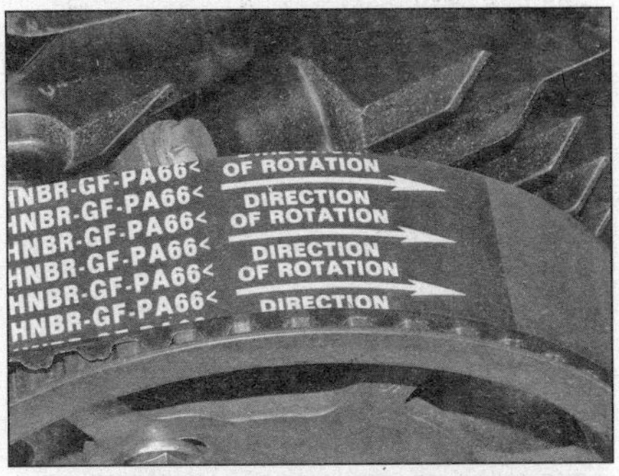

7.9 Fit the new timing belt, observing the direction-of-rotation arrows

3 Undo the retaining bolt and remove the timing belt tensioner **(see illustration)**. Discard the tensioner – a new one must be fitted.

4 Disengage the belt from the sprockets, then undo the bolt and remove the upper timing belt idler sprocket **(see illustration)**. Remove the belt. Land Rover insist that whenever the belt is removed, it must be renewed.

5 Check the old belt for signs of oil contamination. If any is found, trace the source of the oil leak, and rectify it. Wash down the engine timing belt area and all related components, to remove all traces of oil.

Refitting

6 Ensure that the camshaft and crankshaft locking tools are still in place, as described in Section 3.

7 The camshaft sprocket bolts should be slackened sufficiently that they can just be rotated independently of the camshafts. Rotate bolt camshaft sprockets clockwise to the stop **(see illustration)**.

8 Position the new timing belt tensioner, but only finger-tighten the new retaining bolt at this stage.

9 Place the new belt roughly in position, observing the direction of rotation arrows on the belt, then refit the upper idler sprocket and tighten the retaining bolt to the specified torque **(see illustration)**.

10 Fit the new timing belt in the following **anti-clockwise** sequence **(see illustration)**:

a) Crankshaft sprocket.
b) Idler pulley.
c) Left-hand camshaft sprocket.
d) Idler pulley.
e) Right-hand camshaft sprocket.
f) Timing belt tensioner.

Throughout this procedure, ensure the camshaft sprockets remain in their fully-clockwise positions.

11 Rotate the tensioner assembly anti-clockwise until the 'window' is aligned with the groove **(see illustration)**. Tighten the tensioner to the specified torque.

12 Counterhold the camshaft sprockets with a suitable tool **(see illustrations 7.2a and 7.2b)**, and tighten the retaining bolts to the specified torque. **Note:** *Do not be tempted to rely on the locking tools to prevent the sprockets from rotating – damage to the tools/engine castings may result.*

13 Remove the camshaft and crankshaft locking tools, and rotate the crankshaft using a socket on the crankshaft sprocket bolt two full rotations clockwise, until the crankshaft locking tool can be re-inserted.

14 Check that the camshaft locking tools can still be inserted. If not, slacken the tensioner bolt, refit the camshaft tools and repeat the belt fitting/tensioning procedure.

15 With the timing belt correctly fitted, and tensioned, remove the various locking tools.

16 The remainder of refitting is a reversal of removal.

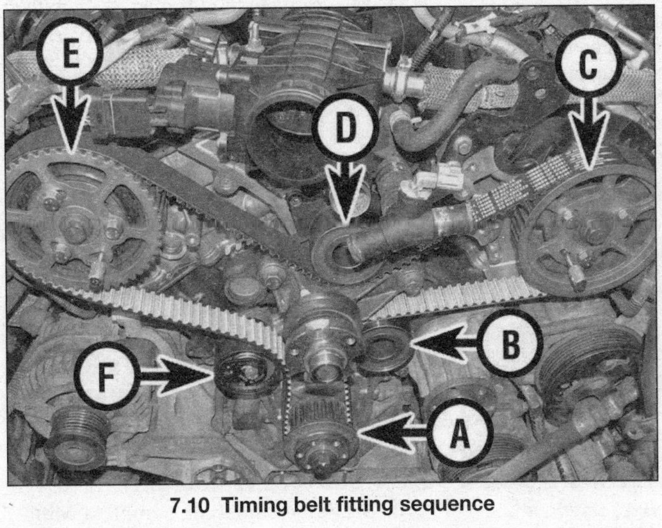

7.10 Timing belt fitting sequence

A Crankshaft sprocket
B Idler pulley
C Left-hand camshaft sprocket
D Idler pulley
E Right-hand camshaft sprocket
F Tensioner

7.11 Use an Allen key to rotate the new tensioner anti-clockwise until the 'window' is aligned with the groove (arrowed)

8 Camshafts, rocker arms and hydraulic adjusters – removal, inspection and refitting

Camshafts

1 Disconnect the battery negative lead as described in Chapter 5, Section 4.
2 Remove the oil filler cap, then pull up and remove the engine top cover **(see illustration)**.
3 Remove the camshaft oil seal(s) as described in Section 12.
4 Remove the relevant cylinder head cover as described in Section 4.

Right-hand camshafts

5 Remove the vacuum pump as described in Chapter 10, Section 20.

Left-hand camshafts

6 Remove the fuel injection pump drivebelt as described in Chapter 4A, Section 11.
7 Remove the camshaft rear oil seal as described in Section 12.
8 Undo the bolts and remove the fuel injection pump belt inner cover **(see illustration)**.

8.2 Pull the engine cover upwards to remove it

8.8 Undo the bolt/stud (arrowed) and remove the pump belt inner cover – shown with the engine removed for clarity

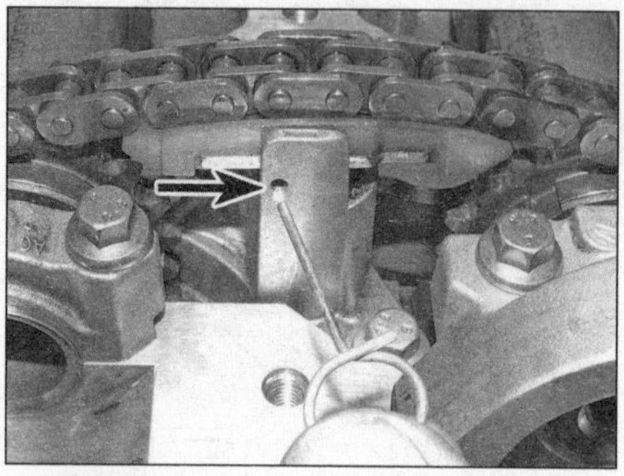

8.9 Press down the chain to compress the tensioner piston, and lock it in place by inserting a 1.5 mm pin/drill bit into the hole in the housing (arrowed)

8.10 The camshaft bearing caps may already be marked (arrowed) – if not, make your own location marks

All camshafts

9 Press down on the secondary timing chain between the two camshafts, to compress the tensioner piston, then lock the piston in this position using a 1.5 mm diameter drill bit or rod **(see illustration)**.
10 Using paint or similar, mark the camshaft bearing caps to indicate their location. It's absolutely essential that they are refitted to their original positions **(see illustration)**.
11 Evenly and progressively, in a diagonal pattern, slacken and remove the 18 bolts securing the camshaft bearing caps. Lift away the bearing caps **(see illustration)**.
12 Undo the bolts securing the secondary timing chain tensioner to the cylinder head, and withdraw it **(see illustration)**.
13 Carefully lift the camshafts, complete with timing chain, from the cylinder head **(see illustration)**.
14 Thoroughly clean all components, and check them for obvious signs of wear or damage. Absolute cleanliness is essential – ensure all oilways and fuel galleries in the cylinder head are free of dirt/debris. Any contamination could cause severe damage to the cylinder head and camshafts.
15 Check the camshaft lobes and bearing journals for any sign of wear or damage. Check the corresponding bearing surfaces in the cylinder head and the camshaft bearing caps. As the bearing caps and cylinder head are matched, any damage/wear to the caps means the cylinder head must be renewed, and *vice-versa*. If in doubt, consult an engine reconditioning specialist.
16 Lay the camshaft in position in the camshaft carrier and check the camshaft endfloat in the carrier. Have the components inspected by an engine reconditioning specialist, who should be able to determine which components require renewal.
17 Liberally coat the camshaft bearing surfaces in the cylinder head with clean engine oil.
18 Fit the timing chain around the camshaft

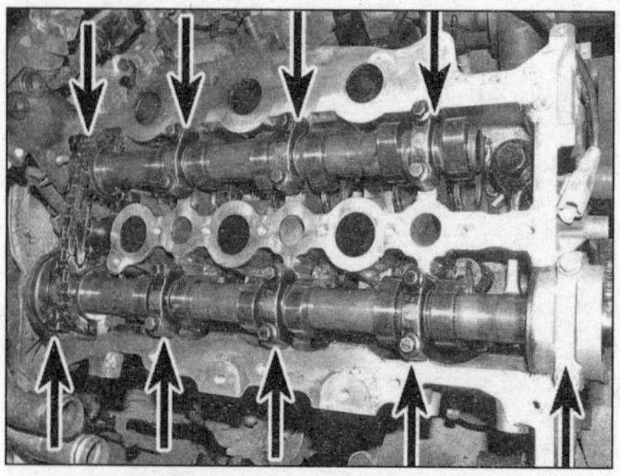

8.11 Gradually and evenly, slacken the bolts and remove the camshaft bearing caps (arrowed) – right-hand camshafts shown

8.12 Undo the secondary timing chain tensioner bolts (arrowed)

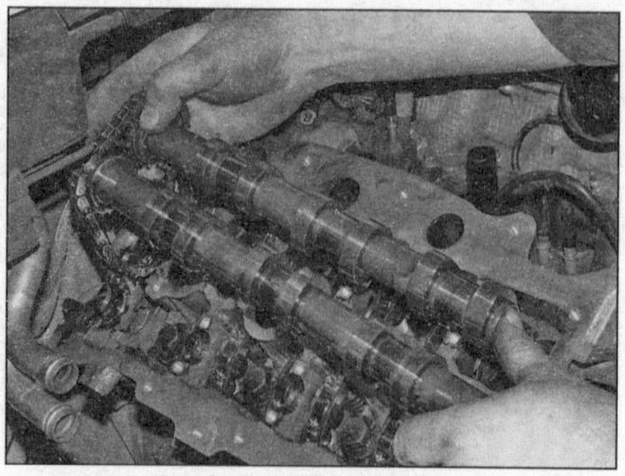

8.13 Lift the camshaft, complete with chain, from the cylinder head

8.18a Fit the chain around the camshaft sprockets ...

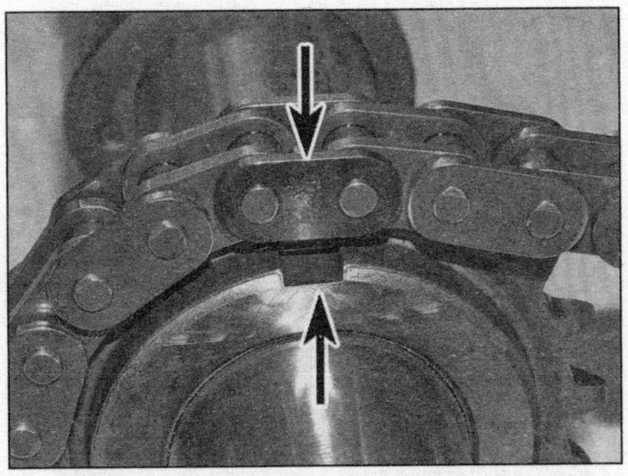

8.18b ... aligning the coloured chain links with the cut-outs on the sprockets (arrowed)

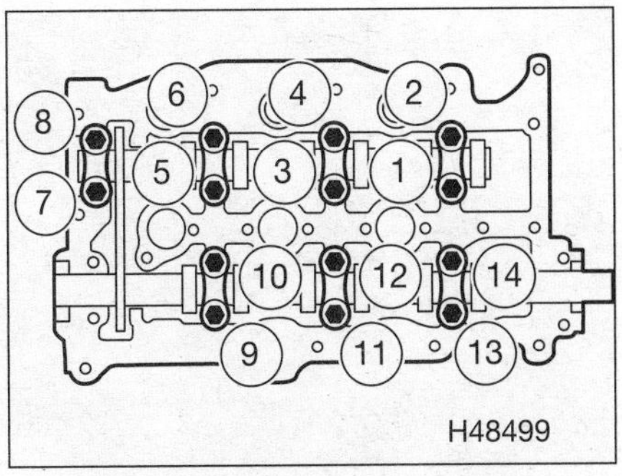

8.22a Camshaft bearing cap bolt tightening sequence – right-hand camshafts

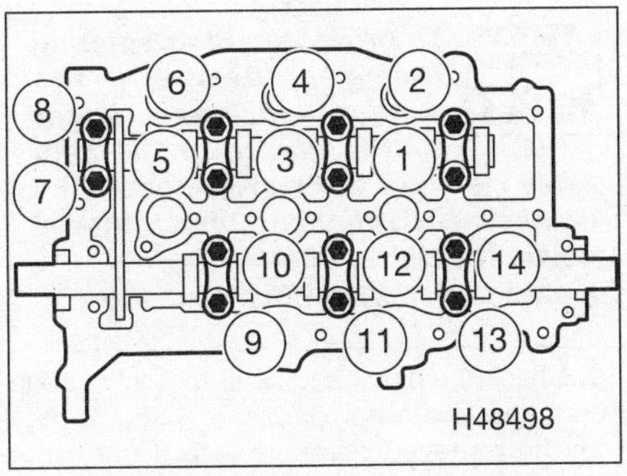

8.22b Camshaft bearing cap bolt tightening sequence – left-hand camshafts

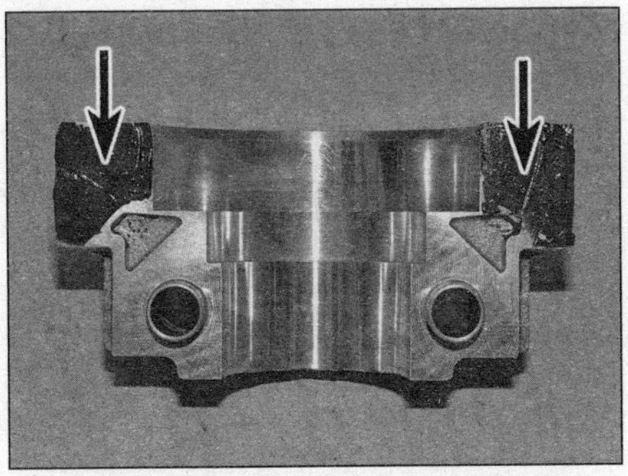

8.23a Apply sealant to the exhaust camshaft end caps ...

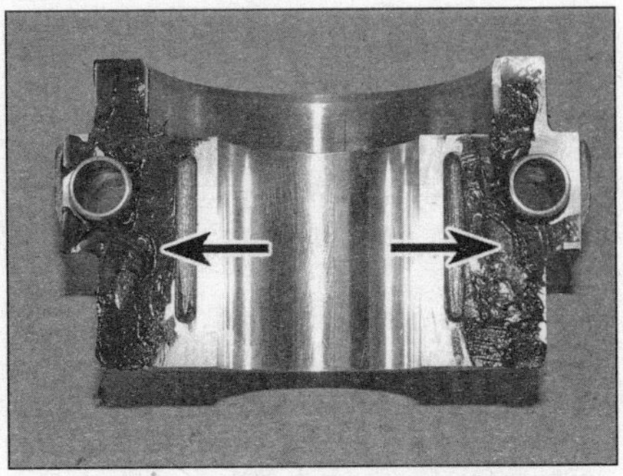

8.23b ... in the areas arrowed

sprockets, aligning the cut-outs on the sprockets with the coloured links on the timing chain **(see illustrations)**.

19 Install the tensioner between the runs of the chain, then lower the camshafts, tensioner and chain assembly into position in the cylinder head.

20 Apply clean engine oil to the camshaft bearing and lobe surfaces.

21 Refit the chain tensioner retaining bolts and tighten them to the specified torque.

22 Refit the bearing caps to their original locations, insert the bolts and gradually tighten them to the specified torque in the sequence shown **(see illustrations)**. **Note:** *Do not refit the exhaust camshaft end bearing caps at this stage.*

23 Apply sealant (Land Rover No. 8510302) to the underside of the remaining exhaust camshaft bearing caps as shown **(see illustrations)**.

24 Refit the remaining camshaft bearing caps, insert the bolts and tighten them to the specified torque in the sequence shown **(see illustration)**.

25 With the bearing caps secured, withdraw the locking pin from the chain tensioner.

26 The remainder of refitting is a reversal of removal.

Rocker arms and adjusters

27 Remove the camshafts as previously described in this Section.

28 Prepare a compartmentalised box, filled with clean engine oil, to store the hydraulic adjusters so that they are kept in their original fitted order. Note that the rocker arms must also be kept in their original order.

29 Withdraw the rocker arms and hydraulic adjusters, and store them in order so that they can be refitted to their original locations – place them in the oil-filled box **(see illustration)**.

30 Check the rollers on the rocker arms are free to rotate with no sign of binding or roughness.

31 Check the hydraulic adjuster bores in the cylinder head for signs of wear or scoring. Check the adjusters themselves for signs of wear or overheating (blueness). Renew as necessary.

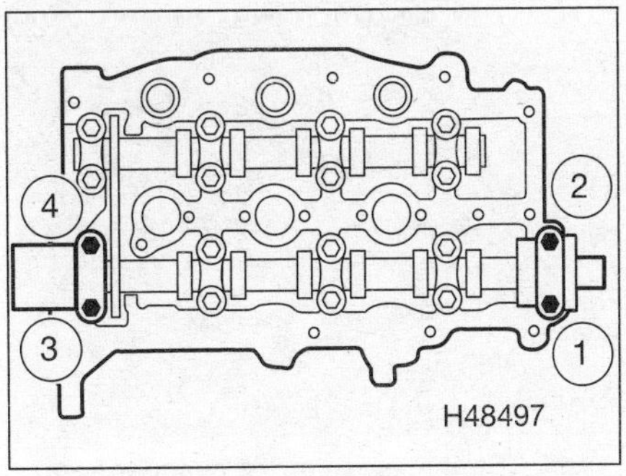

8.24 Camshaft bearing cap bolt tightening sequence

32 Refit the hydraulic adjusters and rockers arms into their original locations in the cylinder head.

33 Refit the camshafts as previously described in this Section.

9 Cylinder heads – removal, inspection, overhaul and refitting

Removal

1 Disconnect the battery negative lead as described in Chapter 5, Section 4, then prise out the strut clips, lift the bonnet to the service position, and engage the hinge straps.

8.29 The rocker arms and hydraulic adjusters are clipped together

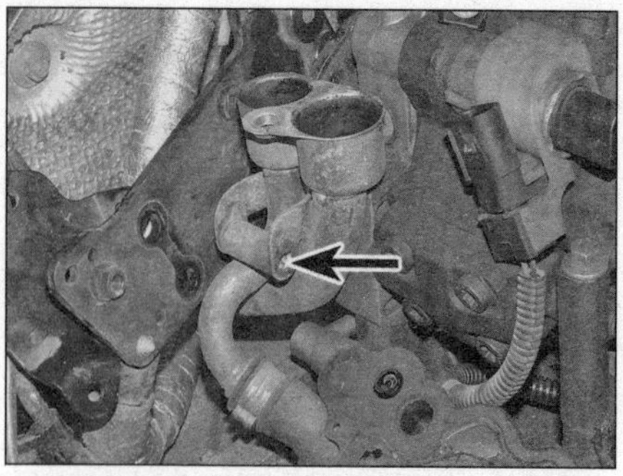

9.4 Remove the bolt (location arrowed) securing the breather tube – shown with the cylinder head removed for clarity

9.5 Remove the support bracket at the rear of the cylinder head

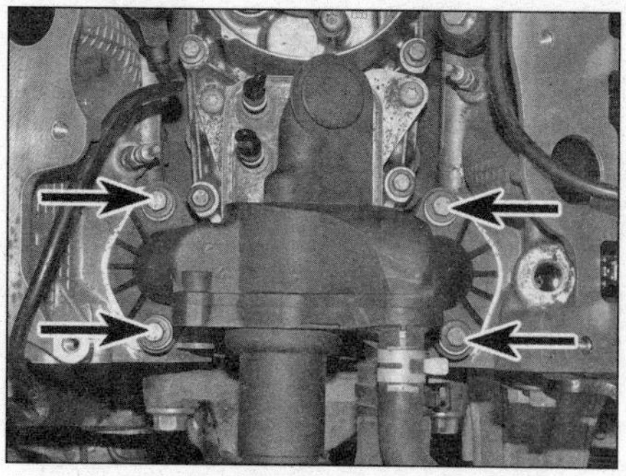

9.8a Coolant elbow retaining bolts (arrowed)

2 Remove the relevant exhaust manifold as described in Chapter 4A, Section 16. If the left-hand cylinder head is to be removed, remove the camshaft rear oil seal as described in Section 12.

3 Remove the relevant camshafts, rockers arms and hydraulic adjusters as described in Section 8.

Right-hand cylinder head

4 Remove the wiring loom bracket from the back of the cylinder head, then undo the bolt securing the engine breather tube **(see illustration)**. Access is extremely limited.

5 Undo the bolts securing the metal support bracket to the rear of the cylinder head **(see illustration)**.

Left-hand cylinder head

6 Disconnect the glow plug wiring harness wiring plugs.

Both cylinder heads

7 Release the coolant bleed hose retaining clip at the front of the left-hand cylinder head.

8 The cylinder head coolant elbow is secured by 4 bolts. Release the clips, disconnect the coolant hoses, undo the bolts and remove the elbow. Discard the O-ring seals – new ones must be fitted **(see illustrations)**.

9 Working from the outside inwards, slacken and remove the cylinder head bolts. Discard the bolts – new ones must be fitted.

10 With the help of an assistant, carefully lift the cylinder head from the cylinder block. If necessary, tap the cylinder head gently with a soft-faced mallet to free it from the block, but **do not** lever at the mating faces. Note that the cylinder head is located on dowels. Lift the cylinder head from the vehicle.

11 Recover the cylinder head gasket. The thickness of the cylinder head gasket is indicated by a series of serrations cut into the front end of the gasket **(see illustration)**. Take a note of the number of serrations before discarding the gasket.

Caution: As the heater plug tips project below the surface of the cylinder head, do not place the head on any work surface without positioning a block at each end to prevent damage.

Inspection

12 The mating faces of the cylinder head and block must be perfectly clean before refitting the head. Use a scraper to remove all traces of gasket and carbon, and also clean the tops of the pistons. Take particular care with the aluminium cylinder head, as the soft metal is damaged easily. Also, make sure that debris is not allowed to enter the oil and water channels – this is particularly important for the oil circuit, as carbon could block the oil supply to the camshaft or crankshaft bearings. Using adhesive tape and paper, seal the water, oil and bolt holes in the cylinder block. Clean the piston crowns in the same way.

HAYNES HiNT ***To prevent carbon entering the gap between the pistons and bores, smear a little grease in the gap. After cleaning the piston, rotate the crankshaft so that the piston moves down the bore, then wipe out the grease and carbon with a cloth rag.***

13 Check the block and head for nicks, deep scratches and other damage. If slight, they may be removed carefully with a file. Note that if the scratches are deep, the head may need to be renewed. Refacing or skimming of the cylinder head is not permitted. If in doubt have the cylinder head inspected by an engine reconditioning specialist.

14 If warpage of a cylinder head is suspected, use a straight-edge and feeler blade to check that the cylinder head surface is not distorted **(see illustration)**. If the specified distortion limit is exceeded, the cylinder head must be renewed – consult a Land Rover dealer for further information.

15 Clean out the bolt holes in the block using a pipe cleaner, or a rag and screwdriver.

Warning: Make sure that all oil is removed, otherwise there is a possibility of the block being cracked by hydraulic pressure when the bolts are tightened.

16 Examine the bolt threads and the threads

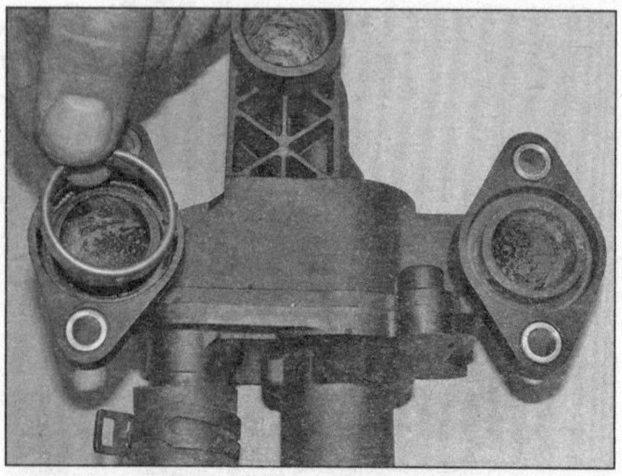

9.8b Renew the coolant elbow O-ring seals

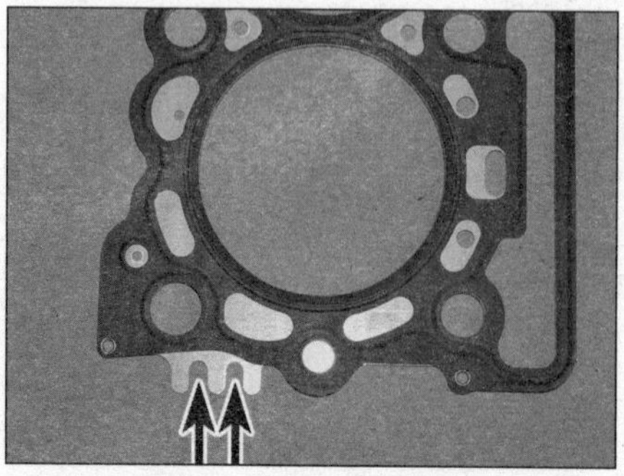

9.11 The thickness of the cylinder head gasket is indicated by the serrations (arrowed) cut into it

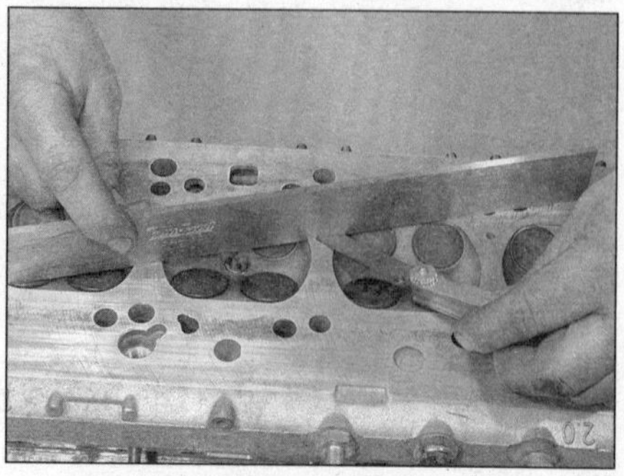

9.14 Check for warpage with a straight-edge and feeler gauges

in the cylinder block for damage. If necessary, use the correct-size tap to chase out the threads in the block, and use a die to clean the threads on the bolts.

Gasket selection

17 Assuming no new main engine components (crankshaft, pistons, connecting rods, main bearings or big-end bearings) have been fitted, use a new gasket the same thickness as the old one. The gasket identification holes are located at the front right-hand side of the gasket **(see illustration 9.11)**. Note that it is permissible to have different grades of gasket between the right-hand and left-hand cylinder banks.

Overhaul

18 To remove a valve, fit a valve spring compressor tool. Ensure that the arms of the compressor tool are securely positioned on the head of the valve and the spring cap **(see illustration)**.

19 Compress the valve spring to relieve the pressure of the spring cap acting on the collets. If the spring cap sticks to the valve stem, support the compressor tool, and give the end a light tap with a soft-faced mallet to help free the spring cap.

20 Extract the two split collets, then slowly release the compressor tool.

21 Remove the spring cap, spring and valve stem oil seal (using long-nosed pliers if necessary). Withdraw the valve from the cylinder head.

22 Repeat the procedure for the remaining valves, keeping all components in strict order, so that they can be refitted in their original positions, unless all the components are to be renewed. If the components are to be kept and used again, place each valve assembly in a labelled polythene bag or a similar small container **(see illustration)**. Note that, as with cylinder numbering, the valves are normally numbered from the timing belt end of the engine.

23 Examine the valve seats in the cylinder head. If the seats are severely pitted, cracked or burned, then the cylinder head may need to be renewed – valve seat recutting or renewal is not permissible on these engines. If only slight pitting is evident, this can be removed by grinding the valve heads and seats together with coarse then fine grinding paste, as described later in this Section.

24 If the valve guides are worn, indicated by a side-to-side motion of the valve, the guides cannot be renewed. To measure the valve stem play in the guide, insert the valve into the relevant guide, with the valve head positioned approximately 10.0 mm from the seat. A square and feeler blade may be used to determine whether the amount of side play of the valve exceeds the specified maximum.

25 Check the camshaft bearing surfaces for wear or damage. If evident, then the cylinder head and camshaft bearing caps must be renewed, as they are matched together.

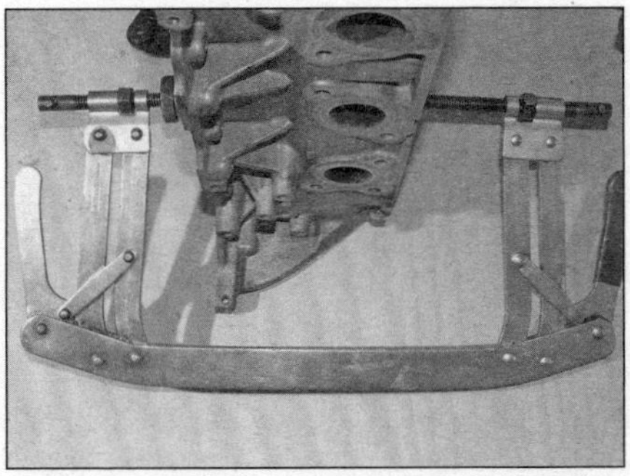

9.18 Position the ends of the compressor on the head of the valve and the spring cap

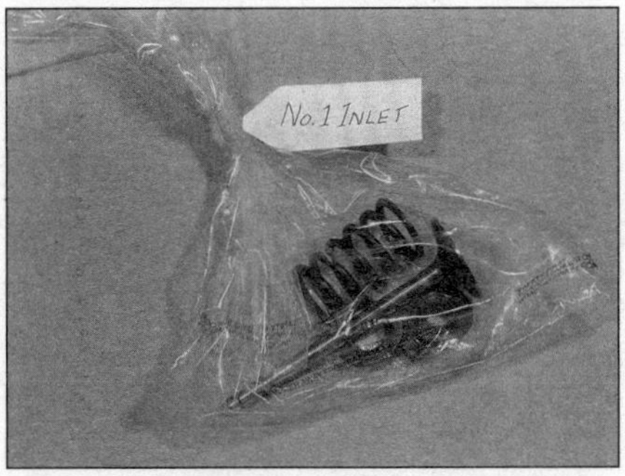

9.22 Place the valve components together in a labelled polythene bag

26 Examine the head of each valve for pitting, burning, cracks and general wear, and check the valve stem for scoring and wear ridges. Rotate the valve, and check for any obvious indication that it is bent. Look for pitting and excessive wear on the end of each valve stem. If the valve appears satisfactory at this stage, measure the valve stem diameter at several points, using a micrometer. Any significant difference in the readings obtained indicates wear of the valve stem **(see illustration)**. Should any of these conditions be apparent, the valve(s) must be renewed.

27 If the valves are in satisfactory condition, they should be ground (lapped) onto their respective seats, to ensure a smooth gas-tight seal.

28 Valve grinding is carried out as follows. Place the cylinder head upside down on a bench, with a block of wood at each end to give clearance for the valve stems.

29 Smear a trace of coarse carborundum paste on the seat face in the cylinder head, and press a suction grinding tool onto the relevant valve head. With a semi-rotary action, grind the valve head to its seat, lifting the valve occasionally to redistribute the grinding paste **(see illustration)**. When a dull, matt, even surface is produced on the faces of both the valve seat and the valve, wipe off the paste and repeat the process with fine carborundum paste. A light spring placed under the valve head will greatly ease this operation. When a smooth unbroken ring of light grey matt finish is produced on both the valve and seat faces, the grinding operation is complete. Carefully clean away every trace of grinding paste, taking great care to leave none in the ports or in the valve guides. Clean the valves and valve seats with a paraffin-soaked rag, then with a clean rag, and finally, if an airline is available, blow the valves, valve guides and cylinder head ports clean.

⚠ ***Warning: Wear eye protection when using compressed air.***

30 Check that all the valve springs are intact. If any one is broken, all should be renewed.

31 Stand each spring on a flat surface, and check it for squareness. If possible, check the free length of each spring against a new one. If a spring is found to be too short, or damaged in any way, renew all the springs as a set. Springs suffer from fatigue, and it is a good idea to renew them, even if they look serviceable.

32 All valve stem oil seals should be renewed as a matter of course.

33 With all the components cleaned, starting at one end of the cylinder head, fit the valve components as follows. If the original components are being refitted, all components must be refitted in their original positions.

34 Lubricate the valve stem oil seal with clean engine oil, then fit the oil seal by pushing it into

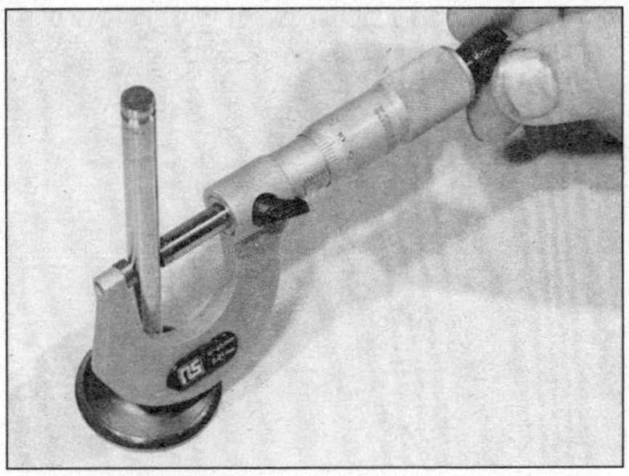

9.26 Measure the diameter of the valve stem with a micrometer

9.29 Grinding-in a valve seat

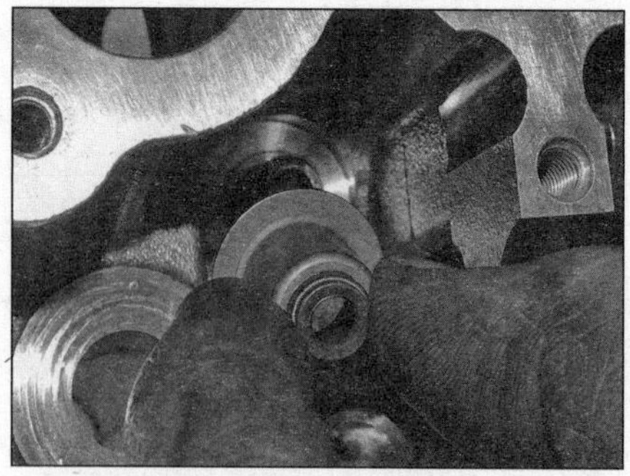

9.34a Position the new seal over the end of the valve guide ...

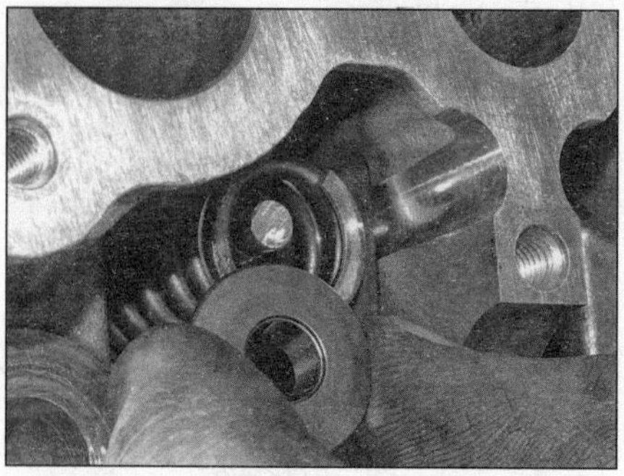

9.36b ... and locate the spring cap

position on the cylinder head using a suitable socket **(see illustrations)**. Ensure that the seal engages correctly over the valve guide.

35 Insert the appropriate valve into its guide (if new valves are being fitted, insert each valve into the location to which it has been ground), ensuring that the valve stem is well-lubricated with clean engine oil. Take care not to damage the valve stem oil seal as the valve is fitted.

36 Fit the valve spring (either way up) and the spring cap **(see illustrations)**. Make sure that the spring cap is correctly located on the top of the spring.

37 Fit the spring compressor tool, and compress the valve spring until the spring cap passes beyond the collet groove in the valve stem.

38 Apply a little grease to the collet groove, then fit the split collets into the grooves, with the narrow ends nearest the valve head **(see illustration)**. The grease should hold them in the grooves.

9.42 Locate the new gasket over the dowels (arrowed) with the word TOP uppermost (arrowed)

9.34b ... and press it into place using a suitable socket

9.38 Fit the spring collets (arrowed) into the grooves on the end of the valve stem

39 Slowly release the compressor tool, ensuring that the collets are not dislodged from the groove. When the compressor is fully released, give the top of the valve assembly a tap with a soft-faced mallet to settle the components.

40 Repeat the procedure for the remaining valves, ensuring that if the original components are being used, they are all refitted in their original positions.

41 Where applicable, refit any brackets, etc, which were removed before dismantling the cylinder head.

Refitting

42 Fit the correct gasket with the word TOP uppermost over the dowels and on to the cylinder block **(see illustration)**.

43 Lower the cylinder head onto the block, and position the head over the two dowels in the engine block.

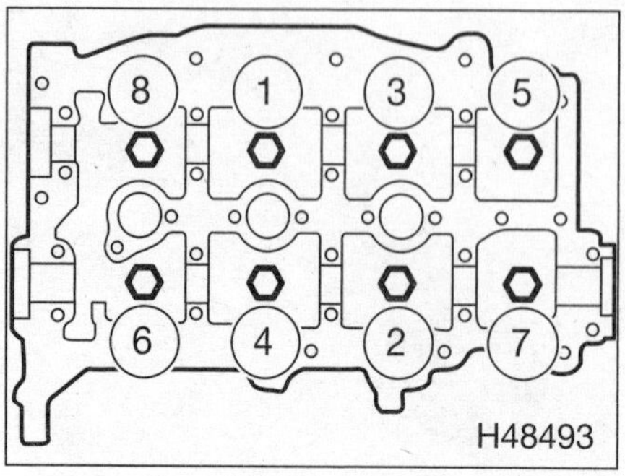

9.44 Cylinder head bolt tightening sequence

9.36a Fit the valve spring ...

44 Fit the new cylinder head bolts (without lubrication), then tighten them in the sequence shown to the Stage 1 torque setting, then in sequence to the Stage 2 setting, then the Stage 3 and Stage 4 settings, then angle-tighten them in turn to the Stage 5 settings as given in the Specifications at the start of this Chapter **(see illustration)**.

45 The remainder of refitting is a reversal of removal, noting the following points:

a) Tighten all fasteners to their specified torque where given.

b) Refill the cooling system as described in Chapter 1, Section 31.

10 Sump – removal and refitting

Sump pan

Removal

1 Disconnect the battery negative lead as described in Chapter 5, Section 4.

2 Remove the oil filler cap, then pull up and remove the engine top cover **(see illustration 8.2)**.

3 Drain the engine oil as described in Chapter 1, Section 3.

4 Disconnect the engine oil temperature sensor wiring plug, and release the wiring harness from the retaining bracket.

5 Undo the retaining bolts and lower the sump pan from place. Discard the gasket **(see illustration)**.

10.5 Undo the bolts and remove the sump pan

10.7 Renew the sump pan gasket

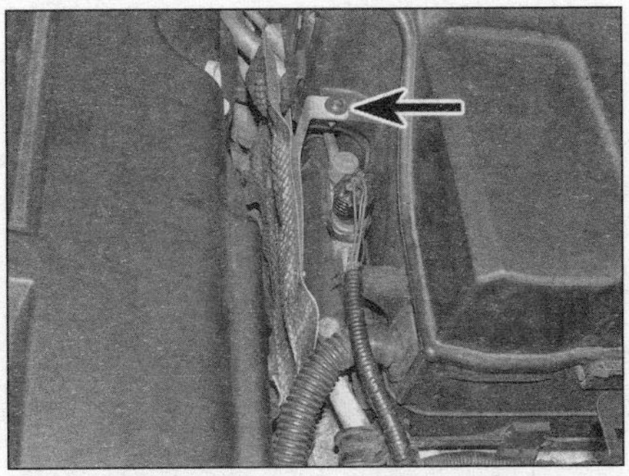

10.12 Undo the bolt (arrowed) and lift out the heat shield

10.13 Move the soundproofing to one side (arrowed)

Refitting

6 Clean all traces of gasket and oil from the mating faces of the sump pan and extension, taking care not to allow debris to enter the engine.

7 Position the new gasket and offer the sump pan into place **(see illustration)**.

8 Evenly and progressively tighten the retaining bolts to their specified torque.

9 The remainder of refitting is a reversal of removal.

Sump extension

Removal

10 Disconnect the battery negative lead as described in Chapter 5, Section 4.

11 Remove the oil filler cap, then pull up and remove the engine top cover **(see illustration 8.2)**.

12 Undo the retaining screw and remove the engine compartment upper heat shield on the left-hand side **(see illustration)**.

13 Move the injector soundproofing to one side **(see illustration)**.

14 Undo the retaining bolt and pull the engine oil level dipstick guide tube from the sump extension. Discard the O-ring seal – a new one must be fitted **(see illustrations)**.

15 Remove the front propshaft described in Chapter 8, Section 2.

16 Remove the sump pan as previously described in this Section.

17 Remove the starter motor as described in Chapter 5, Section 9.

18 Undo the retaining bolt and remove the oil strainer/pick-up assembly **(see illustration)**.

10.14a Engine oil level dipstick guide tube bolt (arrowed)

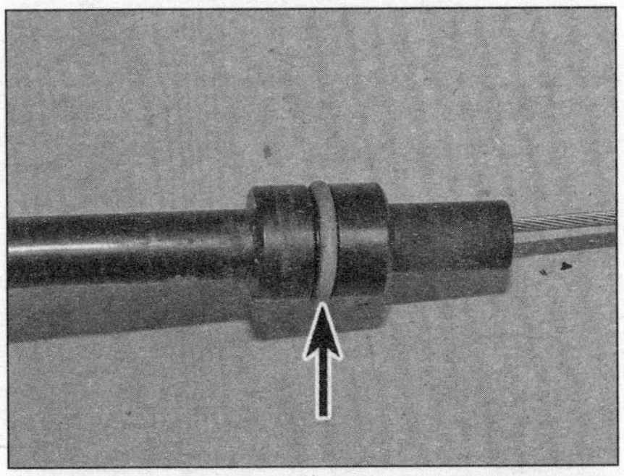

10.14b Renew the guide tube O-ring seal (arrowed)

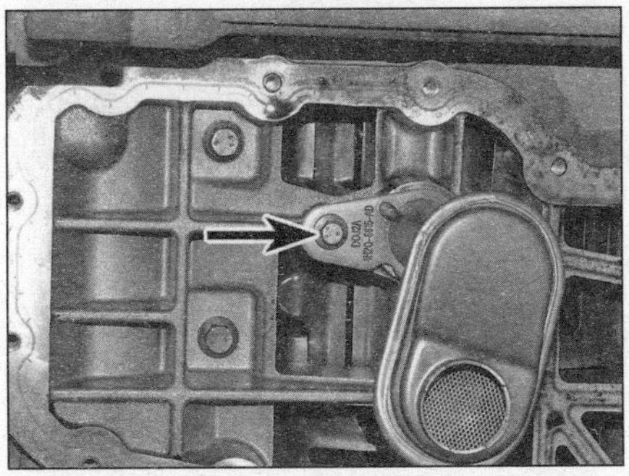

10.18 Oil strainer/pick-up assembly retaining bolt (arrowed)

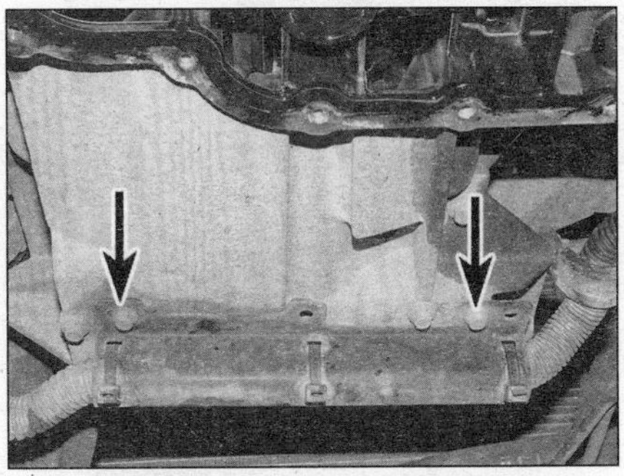

10.19 Undo the cable guide bolts (arrowed) at the front of the sump

Discard the O-ring seal – a new one must be fitted.

19 Remove the bolts securing the battery-to-starter motor cable guide **(see illustration)**.

20 Remove the auxiliary drivebelt tensioner bracket bolt **(see illustration)**.

21 Remove the air conditioning compressor lower mounting bolt.

22 Undo the bolts and remove the turbocharger oil return pipe **(see illustrations)**. Release the wiring harness as the pipe is withdrawn. Discard the gasket and O-ring

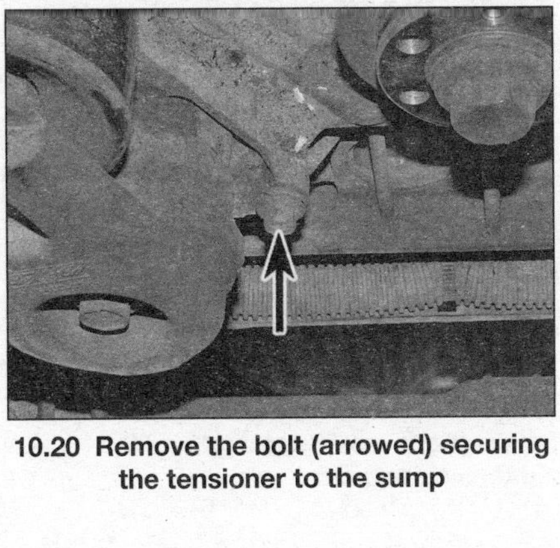

10.20 Remove the bolt (arrowed) securing the tensioner to the sump

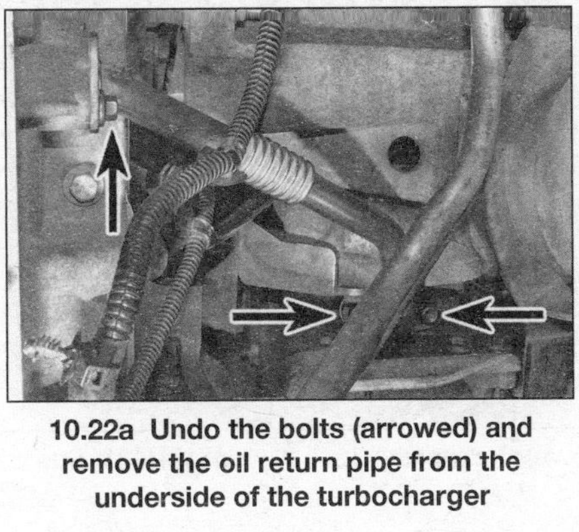

10.22a Undo the bolts (arrowed) and remove the oil return pipe from the underside of the turbocharger

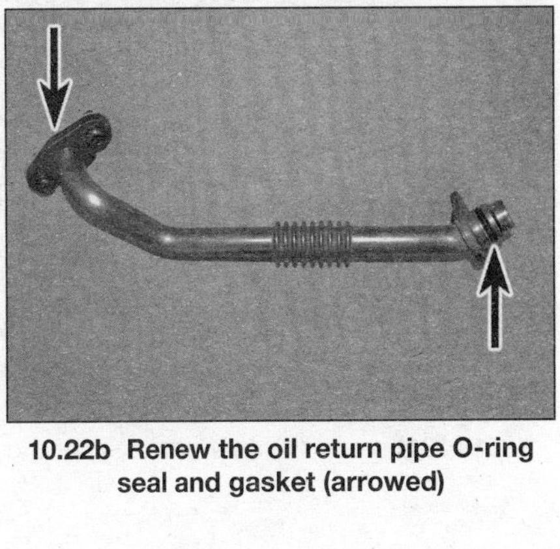

10.22b Renew the oil return pipe O-ring seal and gasket (arrowed)

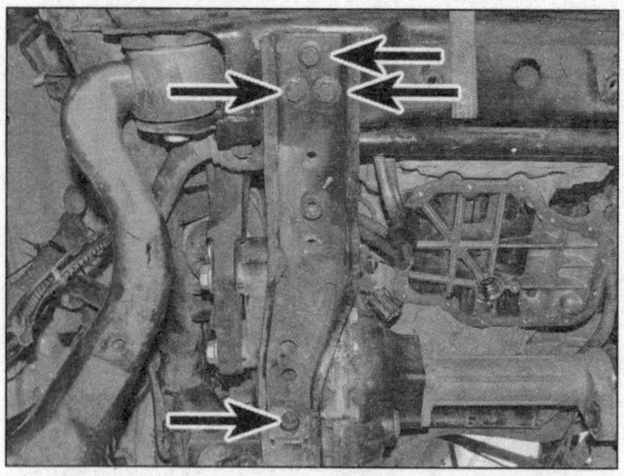

10.25 Front axle crossmember bolts (arrowed)

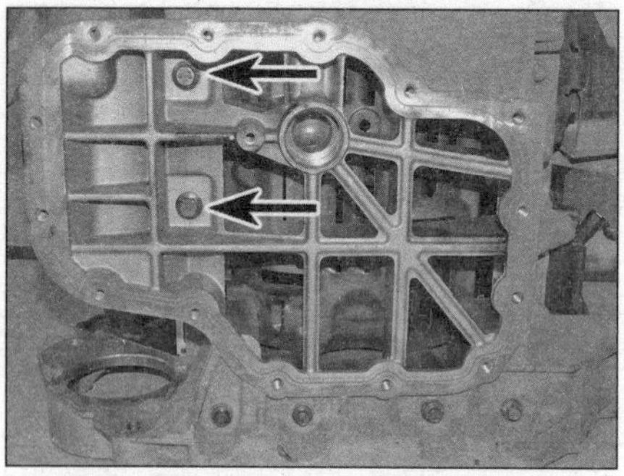

10.28b Note the bolts (arrowed) in the sump pan aperture

seals – new ones must be fitted. Plug/cover the openings to prevent contamination.

23 The turbocharger support bracket is secured by 2 bolts to the cylinder block. Remove the bolts.

24 Undo the 3 lower bolts securing the transmission to the sump extension.

25 Undo the 4 bolts and remove the front axle crossmember **(see illustration)**.

26 Position a workshop jack under the front final drive assembly, and raise the jack head to take the weight.

27 Unscrew and remove the bolt securing the

10.27 Front final drive-to-chassis bolt

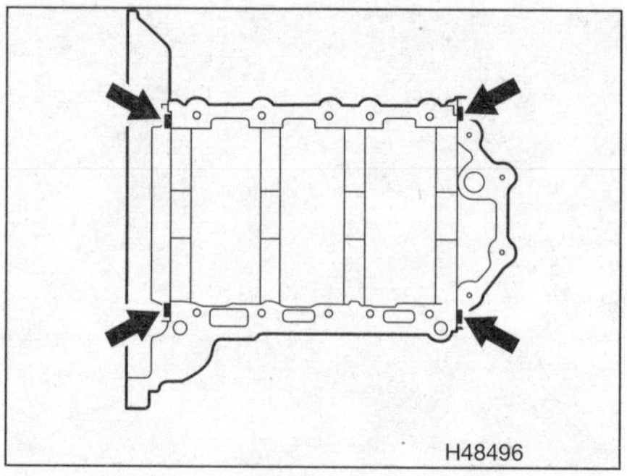

10.31 Apply sealant to the cylinder block as shown

front final drive to the chassis, and carefully lower the final drive a little **(see illustration)**.

28 Undo the retaining bolts and remove the sump extension. Note the fitted positions of the bolts, so they can refitted to their original locations **(see illustrations)**.

29 Recover and discard the gasket.

Refitting

30 Clean all traces of gasket and oil from the mating faces of the engine and the sump extension, taking care not to allow debris to enter the engine.

31 Apply an 8 mm thick bead of sealant (Land

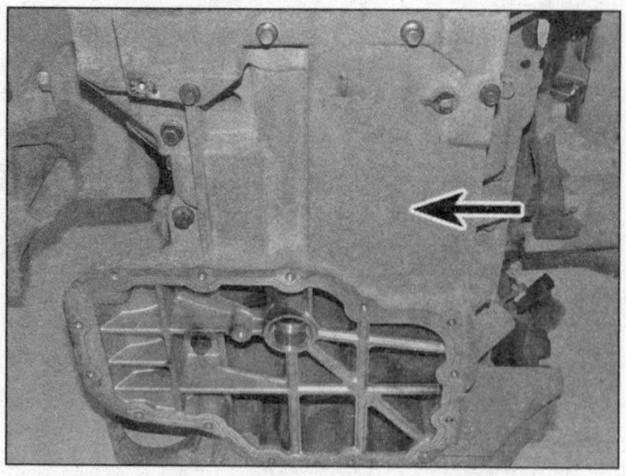

10.28a Undo the bolts and remove the sump extension (arrowed)

Rover WSS-M4G323-A4-RTV or equivalent) to the underside of the engine block as shown **(see illustration)**. Note that the sump must be refitted within 20 minutes of applying the sealant.

32 Position the new gasket, lift the sump extension into place, then loosely fit the securing bolts sufficiently to locate the sump securely on the engine **(see illustration)**.

33 Tighten the sump extension retaining bolts in the sequence given in the Specifications **(see illustration)**.

34 The remainder of refitting is a reversal of removal, noting the following points:

a) *Refit the sump drain plug with a new sealing washer.*
b) *Refill the engine with new oil as described in Chapter 1, Section 3.*
c) *Reconnect the battery negative lead as described in Chapter 5, Section 4.*

11 Oil pump – removal, inspection and refitting

Removal

1 Remove the alternator as described in Chapter 5, Section 6.

10.32 Locate the new gasket over the dowels (arrowed)

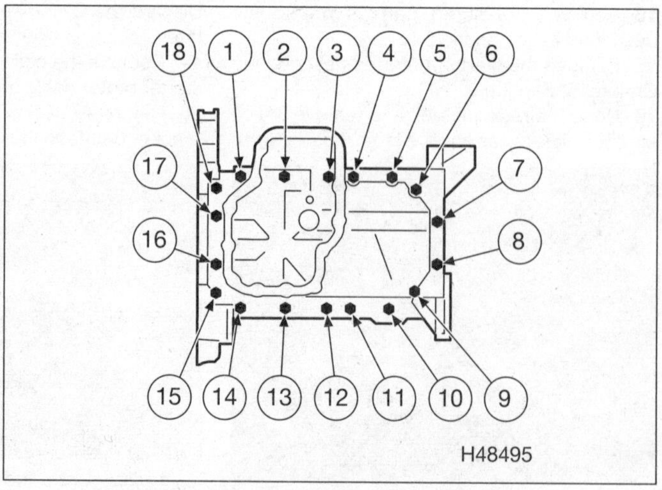

10.33 Sump extension bolts (see Specifications for tightening sequence)

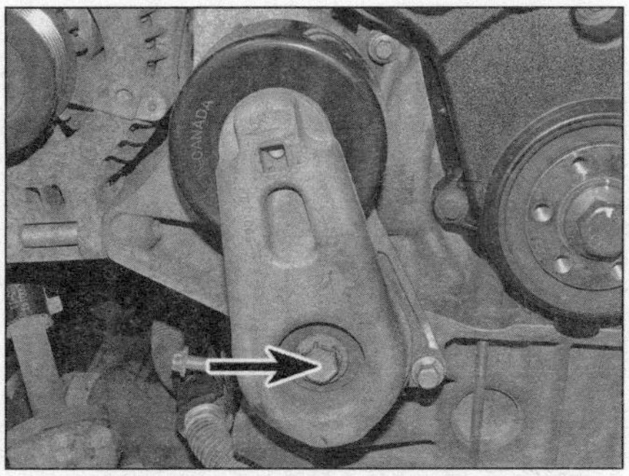

11.2 Auxiliary drivebelt tensioner bolt (arrowed)

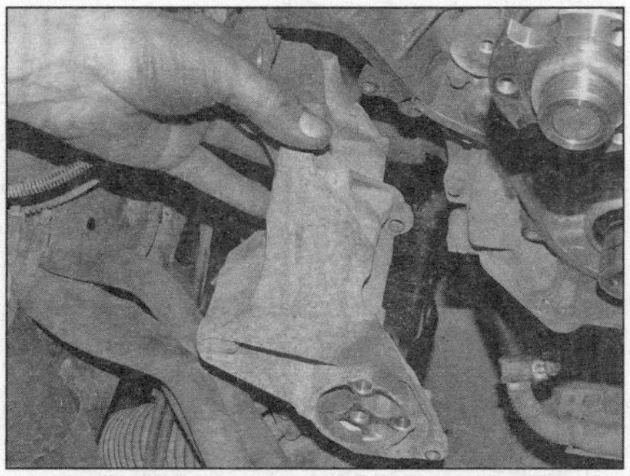

11.5 Remove the alternator mounting bracket

11.7 Undo the bolts and remove the oil pump

2 Undo the bolt and remove the auxiliary drivebelt tensioner assembly **(see illustration)**.

3 Remove the sump extension as described in Section 10.

4 Remove the crankshaft front oil seal as described in Section 12.

5 Undo the 4 bolts and remove the alternator mounting bracket **(see illustration)**.

6 Undo the bolt and remove the timing belt idler pulley **(see illustration 7.4)**.

7 Undo the retaining bolts and detach the oil pump from the cylinder block **(see illustration)**. Recover the timing belt cover sealing strips as the pump is withdrawn. Discard the rubber seal.

Inspection

8 With the pump removed from the engine, thoroughly clean the external surfaces.

9 It would appear that, at the time of writing, no components of the oil pump assembly are available separately. Consequently, should the pump be faulty/worn/damaged, the complete assembly must be renewed. Consult your local Land Rover dealer or parts specialist.

Refitting

10 Clean the mating faces of the pump and engine block.

11 Before fitting the pump, it must be primed by filling the orifice with 20 ml of clean engine oil, and rotating the oil pump drive 2 complete revolutions **(see illustration)**.

11.11 Prime the oil pump, and rotate the drive 2 complete revolutions

12 Fit a new seal, and position the oil pump, remembering to refit the timing cover sealing strips **(see illustrations)**.

13 Insert a retaining bolt on each side of the pump finger-tight then, on pumps without locating dowels, make sure the base flange of the pump is flush (± 0.2 mm) with the base of the engine block **(see illustration)**.

14 Refit the remaining retaining bolts and tighten them to the specified torque in the sequence shown **(see illustration)**. Do not allow the pump to move as the bolts are tightened. Check the alignment of the pump/block.

11.12a Refit the sealing strips (arrowed) ...

15 The remainder of refitting is a reversal of removal.

12 Oil seals – renewal

Crankshaft front oil seal

1 Remove the timing belt as described in Section 7.

2 The crankshaft must now be locked so the crankshaft sprocket bolt can be unscrewed. The tool (303-1117 or 303-1116 – see Section 3) or equivalent used to lock the flywheel is insufficient to counterhold the crankshaft

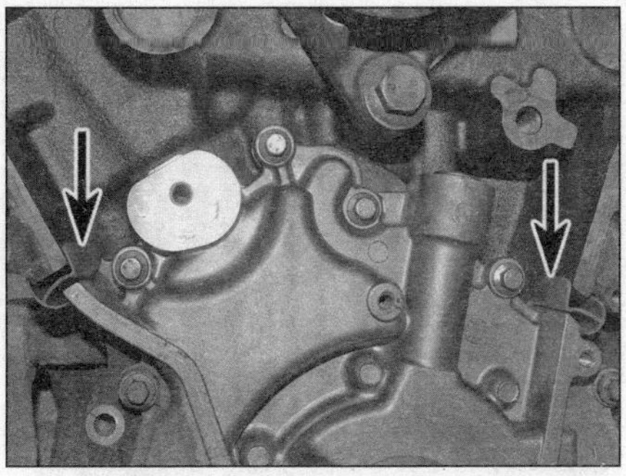

11.12b ... each side (arrowed)

11.13 The base of the pump should be flush (± 0.2 mm) with the base of the cylinder block

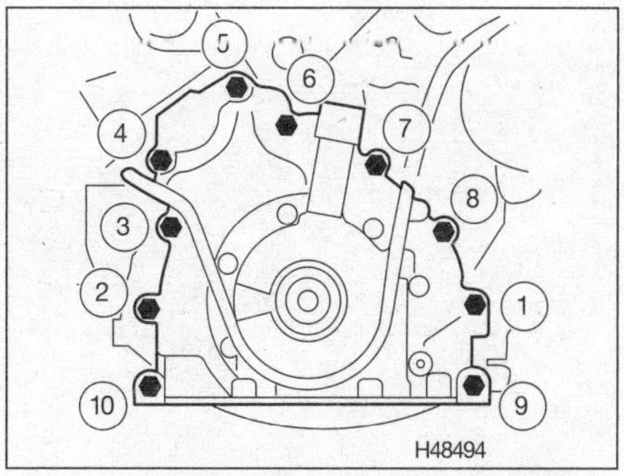

11.14 Oil pump bolts tightening sequence

12.2a The special tool fits into the starter motor aperture ...

12.2b ... and engages with the teeth on the ring gear

12.3a Slacken ...

12.3b ... and remove the bolt ...

12.3c ... followed by the sprocket. Note there is no keyway

12.4 Pierce the seal and lever it from the housing

whilst the bolt is released. So, remove the locking tool, and fit tool No. 303-1123. This tool engages with the ring gear on the edge of the flywheel/driveplate **(see illustrations)**.

3 With the flywheel/driveplate locked, slacken and remove the crankshaft sprocket bolt. Withdraw the sprocket from the crankshaft **(see illustrations)**. Discard the bolt – a new one must be fitted.

Caution: The bolt is extremely tight.

4 Use a sharp, pointed tool to pierce the seal and lever from the oil pump housing. Take great care not to mark the crankshaft **(see illustration)**.

5 Ensure the seal bore in the oil pump housing is clean. The new seal must be installed dry – do not lubricate any part of the new seal. It **must** be fitted to the correct depth, otherwise the seal drain holes will be blocked. It's correct depth is 1.0 mm underflush with the machined front face of the oil pump housing. Land Rover tool No. 303-1122 is available to safely slide the seal into place. If using this tool, fit the seal over the tapered section of the tool and onto the cylindrical section. Remove the tapered part, position the tool/seal at the end of the crankshaft, and slide the seal into place. Land Rover tool No. 303-1121 is available to press the seal into the correct position. Position the tool at the end of the crankshaft and use the

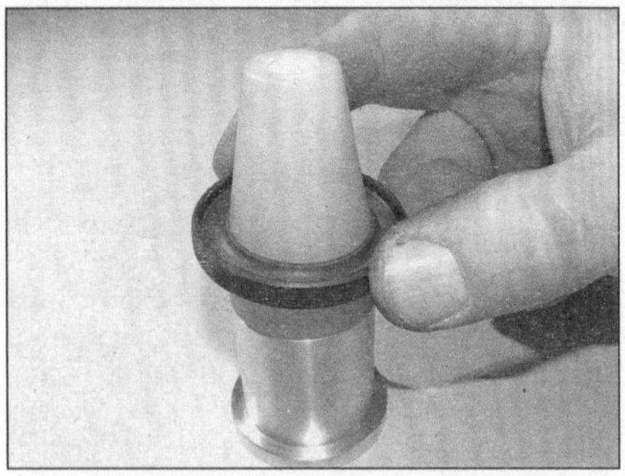

12.5a Slide the new seal onto the cylindrical section of the tool

12.5b Fit the tool onto the end of the crankshaft ...

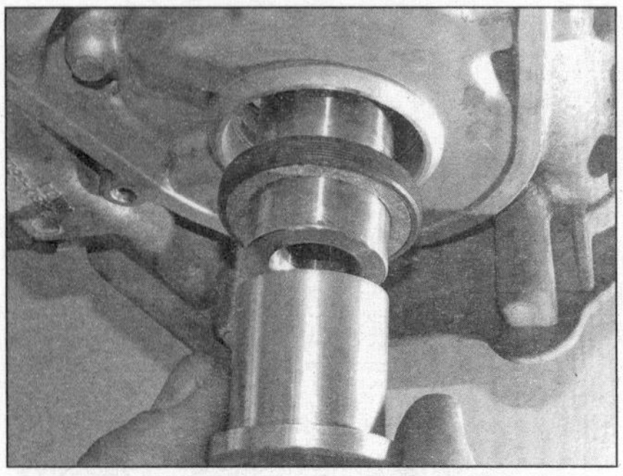

12.5c ... and slide the seal onto the crankshaft

12.5d Using the Land Rover tool to draw the seal into place

12.5e The seal should be 1.0 mm below the machined face of the oil pump housing

12.9 Use a long Allen key to undo the sensor retaining bolt

12.10 Prise the sensor ring from the end of the crankshaft

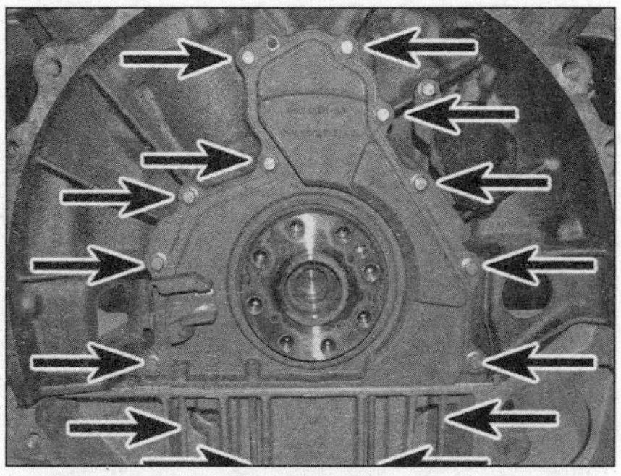

12.11 Oil seal housing retaining bolts (arrowed)

12.12a Apply sealant to the areas indicated (arrowed) ...

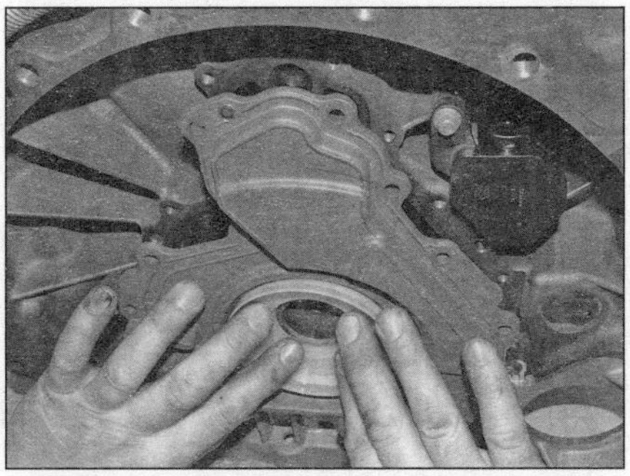

12.12b ... then locate the seal guide over the end of the crankshaft and push the housing into place over the locating dowels

12.14a Align the hole in the sensor ring with the pin on the tool (arrowed) ...

old sprocket retaining bolt to draw the tool/ seal into place. With care, the same result can be achieved using a socket or tubular spacer. Use a vernier caliper depth gauge to check the seal fitted depth **(see illustrations)**.

6 With the seal correctly fitted, position the crankshaft sprocket and tighten the new retaining bolt to the specified torque.

7 Fit the new timing belt as described in Section 7.

Crankshaft rear oil seal

8 Remove the flywheel/driveplate as described in Section 13.

9 Undo the bolt and move the crankshaft position sensor to one side **(see illustration)**. Note that the bolt is captive within the sensor.

10 Carefully prise the sensor ring from the end of the crankshaft **(see illustration)**. Discard the sensor ring – a new one must be fitted. Take great care not to damage the crankshaft surface.

11 Undo the 14 bolts (4 on the underside) and withdraw the oil seal and housing from place **(see illustration)**. Note that the seal is not available separately from the housing.

12 Ensure the seal housing mating face on the engine block is clean, and apply a little RTV sealant to the joint between the sump extension and the cylinder block each side. The new seal/housing is supplied with a guide sleeve already fitted to the centre of the seal. Locate the assembly over the end of the crankshaft and push it into place. Note that the seal must be fitted dry. Push the seal housing over the dowels, and finger-tighten 2 bolts each side **(see illustrations)**.

13 Remove the seal fitting guide, then loosely fit the remaining retaining bolts. Beginning with the seal housing-to-cylinder block bolts, tighten them to the specified torque.

14 A new crankshaft position sensor ring must now be fitted to the end of the crankshaft. This can only be achieved satisfactorily using Land Rover tool No. 303-1130. Without this tool it is impossible to accurately position the ring, and the engine would subsequently run very poorly if at all. Position the new sensor ring on the tool, locating the hole in the ring over the pin on the tool **(see illustrations)**.

15 Align the dowel of the tool with the hole in the crankshaft and secure it with the Allen bolts **(see illustrations)**.

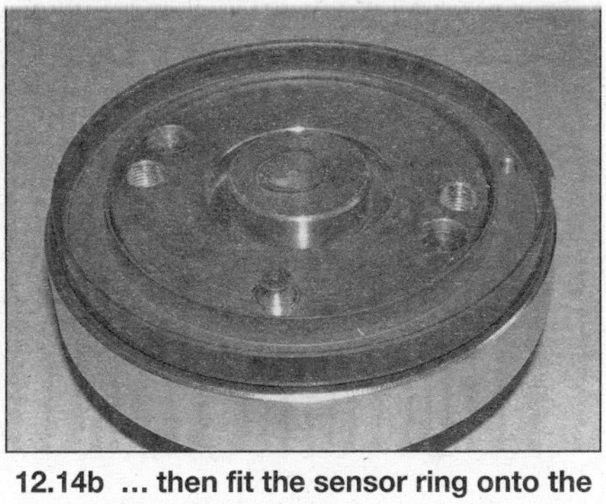

12.14b ... then fit the sensor ring onto the tool

12.15a Align the dowel with the hole in the crankshaft (arrowed)

12.15b Fit the tool, insert and tighten the Allen bolts supplied

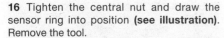

12.16 Tighten the nut and draw the sensor ring into place

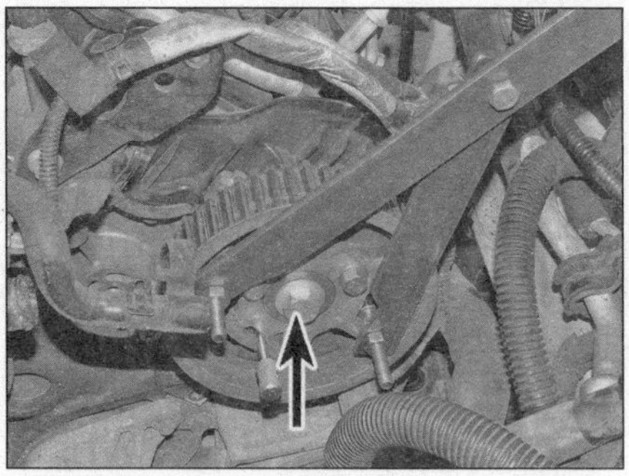

12.20 Slacken the camshaft hub bolt (arrowed)

12.22 Pierce the oil seal and lever it from place

16 Tighten the central nut and draw the sensor ring into position **(see illustration)**. Remove the tool.

17 Refit the crankshaft position sensor and tighten the Allen screw to the specified torque.

18 The remainder of refitting is a reversal of removal.

Camshaft front oil seal

19 Remove the timing belt as described in Section 7.

20 Using a tool similar to the one used to counterhold the sprocket, prevent the camshaft from rotating and slacken the hub retaining bolt **(see illustration)**.

21 Completely unscrew the bolt and remove the camshaft hub, complete with sprocket. Discard the bolt – a new one must be fitted.

22 Note its fitted depth, then using a large, sharp screwdriver (or similar), pierce the centre of the rear camshaft oil seal and lever it from position **(see illustration)**. Take great care not to damage the surfaces of the camshaft or housing.

23 Ensure the bore in the camshaft bearing cap/cylinder head is clean, then drive the new seal into position using a suitable tubular spacer or socket **(see illustration)**. Do not lubricate the seal – it must be fitted dry. If required, Land Rover tool No. 303-1119 is available to draw the seal into place.

24 Refit the hub over the end of the camshaft, counterhold it using the tool used during disassembly, and tighten the new retaining bolt to the specified torque **(see illustration)**.

25 If removed, refit the camshaft sprocket, and finger-tighten the retaining bolts.

26 Renew the timing belt as described in Section 7.

Camshaft rear oil seal

27 Remove the fuel injection pump drivebelt as described in Chapter 4A, Section 11.

28 Bearing in mind that access to the rear of the cylinder head is extremely limited, the use of Land Rover's special tools is essential. Begin by installing Land Rover tool No. 303-1145/1 over the camshaft rear sprocket to prevent rotation. The tool is retained by a bolt to the engine lifting bracket **(see illustrations)**.

29 Fit tool No. 303-1145/3 to the camshaft rear sprocket retaining bolt then, using tool No. 303-1145/2, slacken and remove the retaining bolt **(see illustrations)**. Discard the bolt – a new one must be fitted.

30 Remove the special tools and withdraw the sprocket from the rear of the camshaft.

31 Remove the oil seal using Land Rover

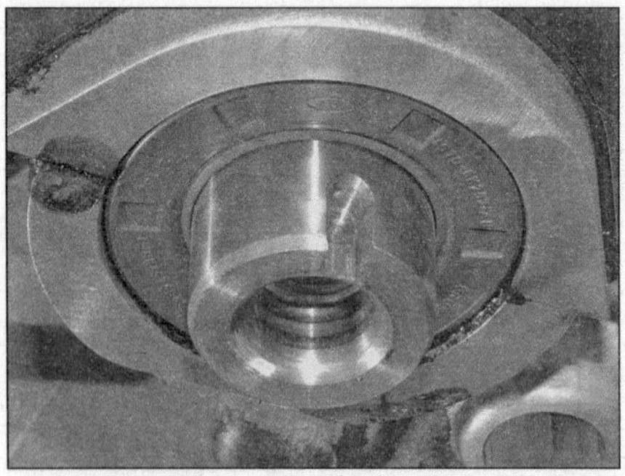

12.23 Fit the new seal just underflush with the cylinder head/carrier surface

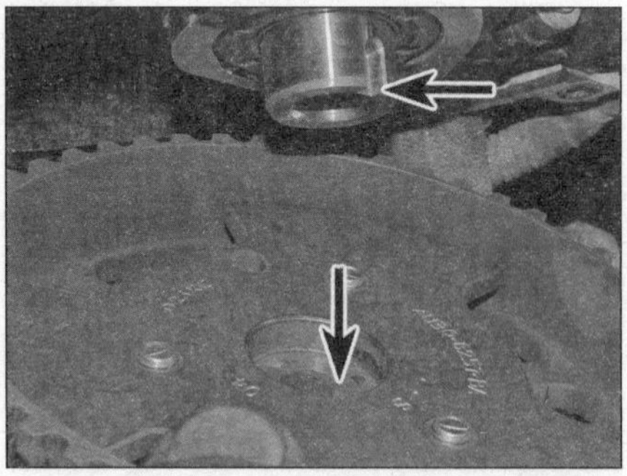

12.24 Note the key in the hub must align with the keyway in the camshaft (arrowed)

12.28a The Land Rover special tool engages with the pump drive sprocket ...

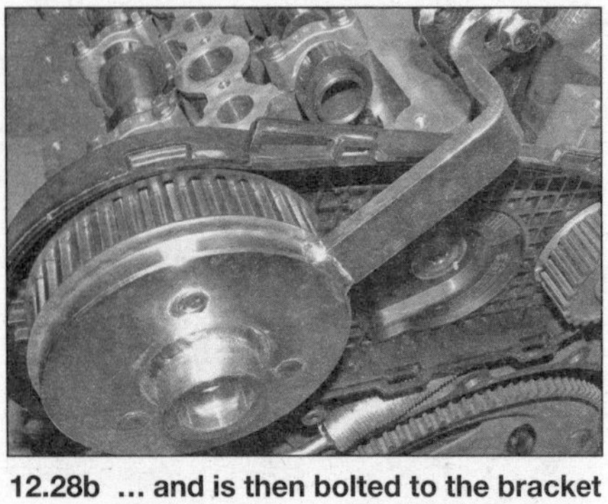

12.28b ... and is then bolted to the bracket to prevent rotation – shown with the engine removed for clarity

12.29a Fit the adapter tool to the sprocket retaining bolt ...

12.29b ... then use the special tool to slacken the bolt

12.31a Screw the threaded sleeve into the end of the camshaft ...

12.31b ... hook one leg of the special tool behind the seal lip ...

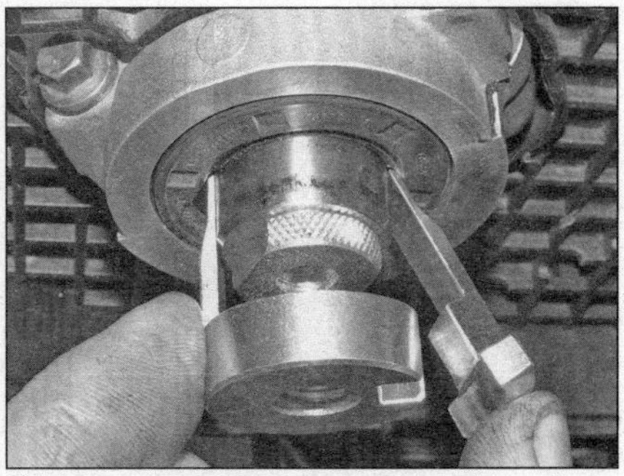

12.31c ... then hook the other leg behind the seal lip, and clip it to the tool

12.31d Screw in the central bolt ...

12.31e ... and draw out the oil seal

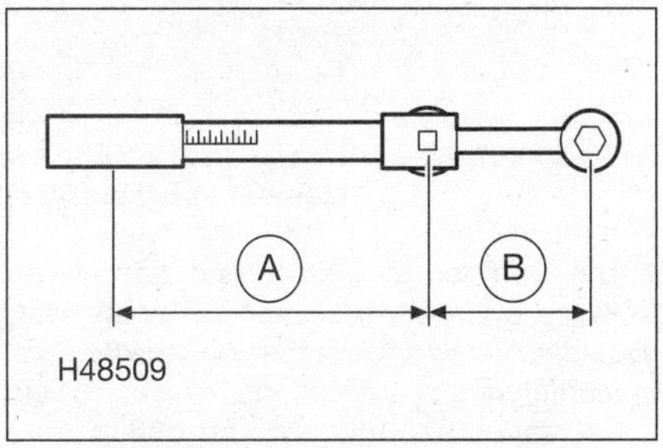

12.35 Length of torque wrench (A)
B Length of special tool

tool No. 303-1118 **(see illustrations)**. Take great care not to damage the surfaces of the camshaft or housing.

32 Ensure the bore in the camshaft bearing cap/cylinder head is clean, then draw the new seal into place using Land Rover tool No. 303-1119.

33 With the seal correctly fitted, refit the camshaft sprocket, and the new retaining bolt. Do not tighten the bolt at this stage.

34 Fit the special tools No. 303-1145/1 and 303-1145/3 to the sprocket/bolt, as described in paragraphs 28 and 29.

35 The sprocket retaining bolt must now be tightened to the specified torque. As it's necessary to use Land Rover tool No. 303-1145, the actual torque value used must be calculated, bearing in mind the length of the special tool:

*a) Multiply the required torque by the length of the torque wrench **(see illustration)**.*

b) Add the length of the torque wrench to the length of the special tool No. 303-1145/2.

c) Divide the total of Step a) by the total of Step b), and set the torque wrench to the figure arrived at.

36 After tightening the sprocket retaining bolt to the specified torque, angle-tighten it to the Stage 2 setting (see Specifications).

37 Remove the special tools, and fit the fuel pump drivebelt as described in Chapter 4A, Section 11.

13 Flywheel/driveplate – removal, inspection and refitting

Removal

1 On manual transmission models, remove the clutch as described in Chapter 6, Section 2. On models with automatic transmissions, remove the gearbox as described in Chapter 7B, Section 3.

2 Undo the 8 bolts and remove the flywheel/driveplate from the end of the crankshaft. Discard the bolts – new ones must be fitted. Note the flywheel/driveplate locates on a dowel.

Warning: The flywheel is heavy – take care not to drop it.

Inspection

3 If the flywheel-to-clutch mating surface is deeply scored, cracked or otherwise damaged, then the flywheel must be renewed, unless it is possible to have it surface ground. Seek the advice of a Land Rover dealer or engine reconditioning specialist.

4 If the ring gear is badly worn or has missing teeth, then the flywheel/driveplate must be renewed. It's not possible to renew the ring gear.

5 Vehicles with manual transmissions are fitted with dual mass flywheels. Whilst Land Rover do not publish any checking procedures, some olutoh and flywhool manufaoturoro do publioh some information concerning rotational and lateral movement.

6 In order to check the rotational movement, lock the flywheel in place. Rotate the flywheel secondary element (drive surface) by hand anti-clockwise, mark its position in relation to the primary flywheel element (bolted to the crankshaft), then rotate it by hand clockwise and mark its position. Bear in mind, that the *free* rotational movement is being measured here – do not use excessive force to rotate the secondary element. Mark the limits of the rotational movement is relation to the number of flywheel starter ring gear teeth **(see illustrations)**.

13.6a Turn the flywheel secondary element anti-clockwise and mark the limit of its travel on the starter ring gear ...

13.6b ... then turn the secondary element clockwise, and mark its travel limit again

13.8a Attach a length of steel strip to the flywheel secondary element (drive surface) ...

13.8b ... and mount a DTI gauge in line with the edge of the secondary element

7 The number of starter ring gear teeth travelled by the flywheel secondary element, should be noted and compared to the flywheel manufacturers specification. The permissible travel varies enormously, and differs from one flywheel part number to the next. If in any doubt, consult a Land Rover dealer or transmission specialist as to whether a new unit is needed.

8 In order to check the lateral movement of the flywheel, attach a length of steel strip to the flywheel secondary element (drive surface), and mount a DTI gauge so that it measures in-line with the edge of the secondary flywheel element **(see illustrations)**. Pull the steel strip away from the flywheel, zero the DTI gauge, then push the strip towards the flywheel and read off the measurement. Again, the permissible amount of lateral movement varies from one flywheel part number to the next. If in any doubt, consult a Land Rover dealer or transmission specialist as to whether a new unit is needed.

Refitting

9 Commence refitting by thoroughly cleaning the mating faces of the flywheel/driveplate and the crankshaft.

10 Align the dowel hole in the flywheel/driveplate with the crankshaft dowel, then lift the flywheel/driveplate onto the end of the crankshaft.

11 Fit the new flywheel/driveplate bolts, and tighten them to the specified torque settings.

12 Refit the clutch as described in Chapter 6, Section 2, or the automatic transmission as described in Chapter 7B, Section 3 (as applicable).

14 Crankcase vent oil separator – removal and refitting

Removal

1 Disconnect the battery negative lead as described in Chapter 5, Section 4.

2 Pull up the engine cover, then depress the release buttons, and disconnect the low pressure fuel hoses from the fuel pump. Plug/cover the openings to prevent contamination.

3 Use clamps on the coolant hoses to minimise fluid loss, then disconnect both EGR coolant crossover pipe hoses **(see illustration)**.

4 Undo the 2 retaining bolts, and remove the EGR coolant crossover pipe **(see illustration)**.

5 Disconnect the wiring plug from the oil pressure sensor at the top, front of the engine.

6 Slacken the oil filter cover 4 complete turns, allow the oil within to drain, then remove the filter cover and element – refer to Chapter 1, Section 3. Clean-up any spilled oil immediately.

7 Unclip and remove the breather hose on each cylinder head cover **(see illustration 4.4)**.

8 Unclip and disconnect the glow plug harness wiring plugs **(see illustration 4.3)**.

9 Depress the release buttons and disconnect the low pressure fuel hoses from the fuel cooler in front of the oil filter housing. Plug/cover all openings to prevent contamination.

10 On vehicles up to 2007 model year, slacken the unions and remove the high-pressure fuel pipe from the pump to the diverter rail **(see illustration)**. **Note:** *It's absolutely essential that the highest standards of cleanliness are observed to prevent contamination of the fuel system. Keep the pipe in contact with the pump and the diverter rail until both unions are undone and the area around the pipes/unions cleaned. Plug/cover the openings to prevent contamination.* Discard the pipe – a new one must be fitted.

11 Undo the nut, depress the release buttons,

14.3 Disconnect the EGR crossover pipe hose each side (right-hand hose arrowed)

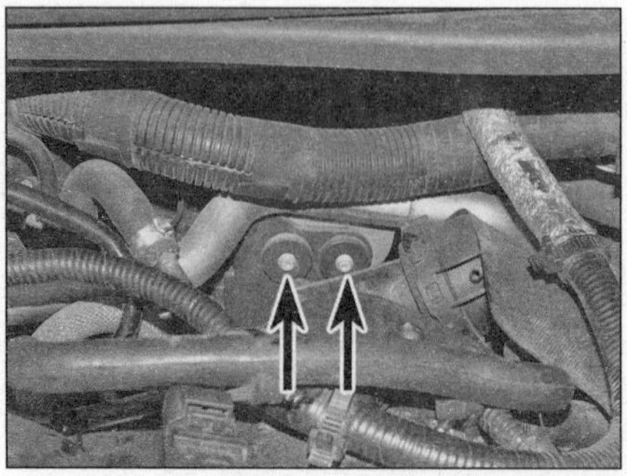

14.4 Undo the 2 bolts (arrowed) and remove the crossover pipe. The bolts are inserted from the rear

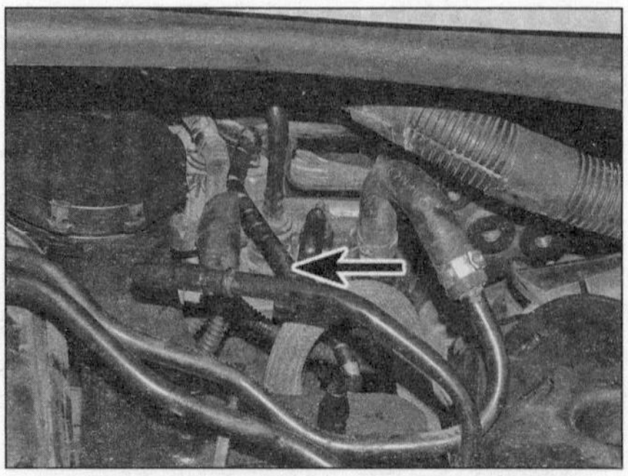

14.10 Disconnect the pipe from the fuel pump to the diverter rail (arrowed)

14.12 Pull up the glow plug wiring connector/harness each side of the oil separator

disconnect the low pressure fuel hose and move the plastic support bracket to one side.

12 Pull up the glow plug harnesses each side of the oil separator **(see illustration)**.

13 Pull the oil separator slightly upwards, then disconnect the wiring plugs from the fuel injection pump, and the fuel rail pressure sensor, then move the wiring harness to one side **(see illustration)**.

14 Pull up the separator, and manoeuvre it from place. Recover the seals **(see illustrations)**. Note that the separator O-ring seals can be re-used providing it is undamaged.

Refitting

15 Refitting is a reversal of removal, noting the following points:

a) Renew the high-pressure fuel pipe.
b) Top-up the cooling system as described in Weekly checks.
c) Renew the oil filter element as described in Chapter 1, Section 3.
d) Reconnect the battery negative lead as described in Chapter 5, Section 4.

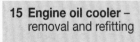

15 Engine oil cooler – removal and refitting

Removal

1 Drain the cooling system as described in Chapter 1, Section 31.

15.5 Remove the left-hand side knock sensor (arrowed)

14.13 Pull up the separator slightly and disconnect the wiring plugs from the pressure sensor (arrowed)

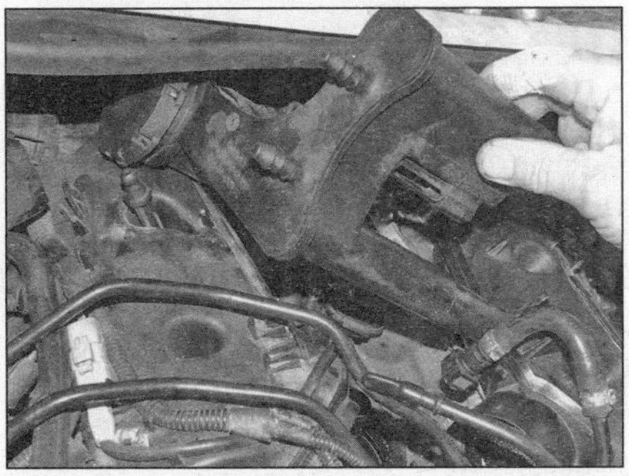

14.14b ... and manoeuvre it from place

2 Remove the crankcase vent oil separator as described in Section 14.

3 Unclip the coolant bleed hose from the left-hand side EGR coolant inlet hose at the front of the engine.

4 Release the clips, disconnect the coolant hoses, then undo the bolts and remove the cylinder head coolant elbow **(see illustrations 9.8a and 9.8b)**. Discard the O-ring seals – new ones must be fitted.

5 Disconnect the wiring plug, then undo the bolt and remove the left-hand side knock sensor **(see illustration)**.

6 Undo the retaining bolts and remove the oil cooler **(see illustration)**. Be prepared for fluid spillage. Discard the gasket and O-ring seal.

Refitting

7 Ensure the mating faces of the cooler and engine block are clean. Position a new gasket

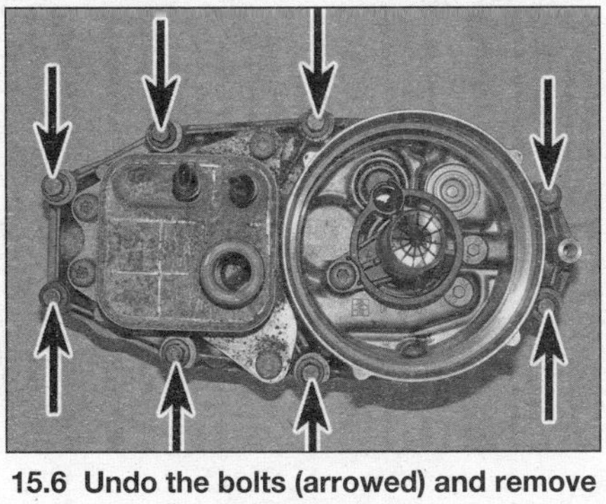

15.6 Undo the bolts (arrowed) and remove the cooler assembly

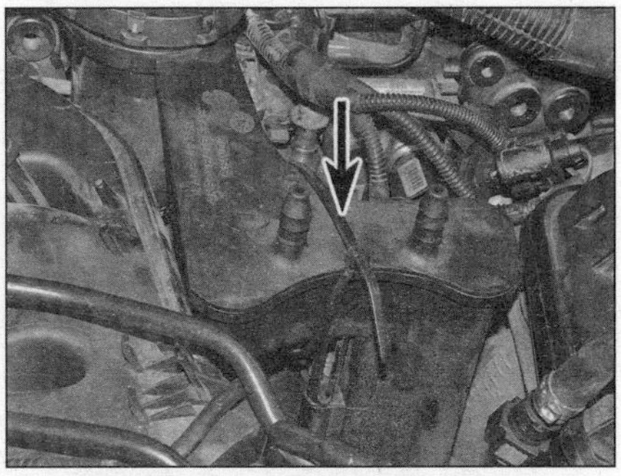

14.14a Pull up the oil separator (arrowed) ...

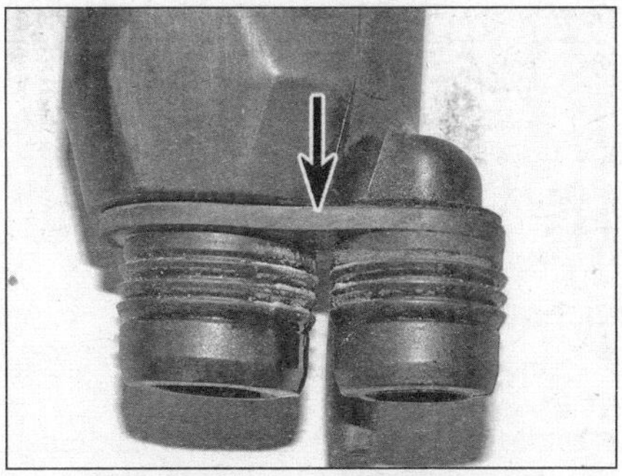

14.14c Check the condition of the separator seals (arrowed)

and O-ring seal, then refit the oil cooler. Tighten the retaining bolts to the specified torque.

8 The remainder of refitting is a reversal of removal, noting the following:

a) Refill the cooling system as described in Chapter 1, Section 31.
b) Tighten all fasteners to the specified torque where given.

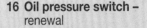

16 Oil pressure switch – renewal

1 Remove the oil filler cap, then pull up the engine top cover **(see illustration 8.2)**.

2 Disconnect the wiring plug, then unscrew the switch **(see illustration)**.

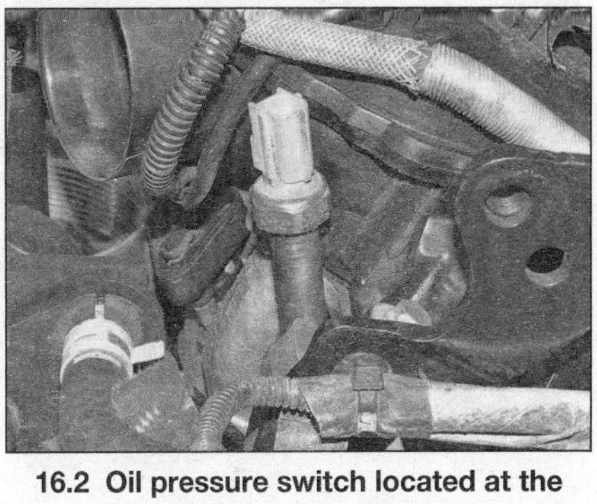

16.2 Oil pressure switch located at the front/top of the engine

3 Ensure the switch threads are clean then refit it, and tighten it to the specified torque.
4 The remainder of refitting is a reversal of removal, remembering to top-up the engine oil as described in *Weekly checks*.

17 Engine mountings – removal and refitting

Removal

Left-hand mounting

1 Remove the turbocharger as described in Chapter 4A, Section 13.
2 Suspend the engine using a hoist and lifting chains/straps, or place a workshop jack under the engine sump with a piece of wood on the jack head to protect the sump casing. Take the weight of the engine.
3 Undo the nuts/bolts and remove the mounting. Discard the bolts – new ones must be fitted.

Right-hand mounting

4 Remove the alternator as described in Chapter 5, Section 6.
5 Undo the bolt and disconnect the earth strap from the mounting bracket **(see illustration)**.
6 Undo the nut securing the mounting to the engine bracket.
7 Suspend the engine using a hoist and lifting chains/straps, or place a workshop jack under the engine sump with a piece of wood on the jack head to protect the sump casing. Take the weight of the engine.
8 Undo the retaining bolts and detach the engine mounting bracket from the side of the engine. Manoeuvre the bracket from place.
9 Undo the bolts and remove the mounting **(see illustration)**. Discard the bolts – new ones must be fitted.

Refitting

10 Refitting is a reversal of removal, but tighten all fixings to the specified torque.

18 Engine removal

In order to remove the complete engine, the vehicle body must be lifted from the chassis. This can **only** be accomplished using a 2-post powered ramp – not normally available to a DIY repairer. Consequently, although the procedure itself is not technically demanding, we have had to conclude that engine removal and refitting is beyond the scope of this manual.

However, for information, and for those fortunate enough to have access to the necessary equipment, the following is provided as a brief summary of the procedure.

1 Have the air conditioning refrigerant circuit evacuated by a suitably-equipped specialist.
2 Remove the front and rear propeller shafts.

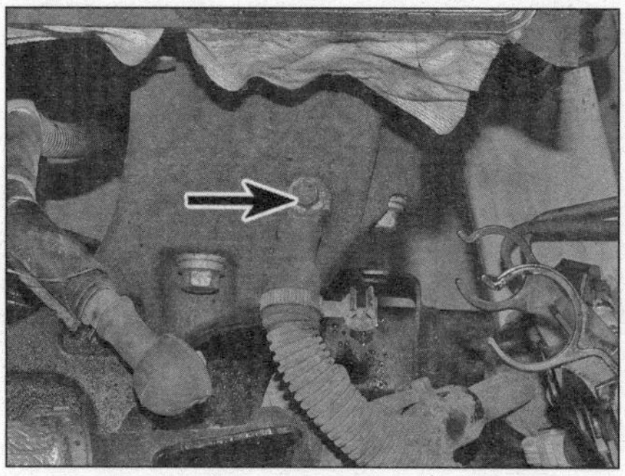

17.5 Earth strap (arrowed) on the right-hand engine mounting bracket

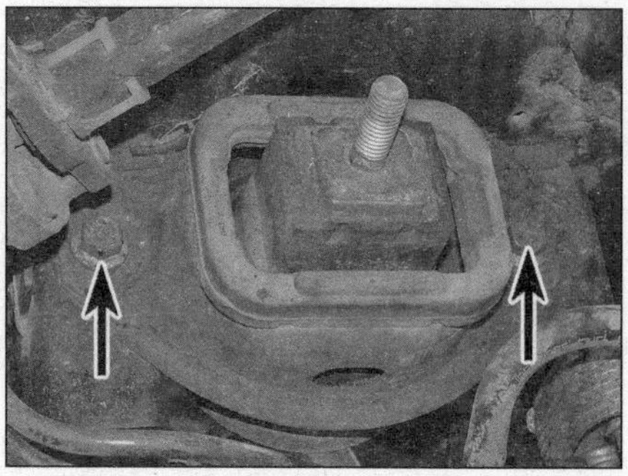

17.9 Right-hand engine mounting retaining bolts (arrowed) – shown with the engine removed for clarity

3 Remove the bonnet.
4 Remove the battery and battery tray.
5 Remove the coolant expansion tank.
6 Remove the air cleaner.
7 Remove the Transmission Control Module (TCM).
8 Detach the lower shaft from the steering column
9 Disconnect the engine and transmission wiring harnesses in the engine compartment.
10 Disconnect the servo vacuum hose.
11 Disconnect the refrigerant pipes and heater hoses.
12 Remove the radiator.
13 Remove the fuel filler flap and detach the filler neck from the body.
14 Remove the front wheel arch liners.
15 Remove the front and rear bumpers.
16 Disconnect the wiring from the following: low pressure AC switch, cooling fan, washer reservoir/pump, ambient air temperature sensor, ABS wheel speed sensors, earth strap (RH and LH front), body harness (RH front, LH front and LH rear), brake pad wear sensors
17 Disconnect the brake pipes/hoses at each corner.
18 Unclip the air suspension pipes at each wheel arch.
19 Disconnect the air suspension compressor intake pipe.
20 Disconnect the handbrake cable from the lever/body.
21 Remove the transmission undershield and heat shield.
22 Disconnect the selector lever cable or gearchange rod from the transmission.
23 Undo the mounting bolts, and lift the body from the chassis ***(see illustration)***. Recover the spacing washers.
24 Remove the idle air shut-off valve.
25 Disconnect any remaining coolant hoses/wiring which would prevent engine and transmission removal.
26 Detach the power steering pump and move it to one side.
27 Disconnect the compressor refrigerant pipes.
28 Disconnect the exhaust system from the turbocharger.
29 Disconnect the intercooler hoses.
30 Disconnect any necessary fuel/breather hoses.
31 Remove the LH upper suspension arm and brake pipe heat shields.
32 Remove the exhaust crossover pipe bracket.
33 Remove the turbocharger support bracket.
34 Undo the engine mounting-to-bracket nuts.
35 Remove the transmission mounting bolt.
36 Attach an engine hoist/crane and lift the engine/transmission assembly from place.

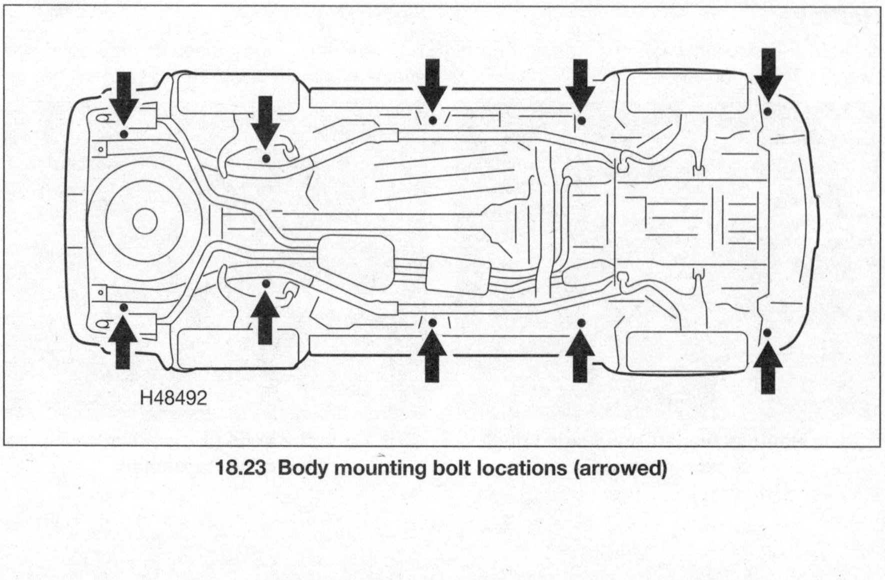

18.23 Body mounting bolt locations (arrowed)

Chapter 3
Cooling, heating and ventilation systems

Contents

Degrees of difficulty

Easy, suitable for novice with little experience	**Fairly easy,** suitable for beginner with some experience	**Fairly difficult,** suitable for competent DIY mechanic	**Difficult,** suitable for experienced DIY mechanic	**Very difficult,** suitable for expert DIY or professional

Specifications

General

Expansion tank cap opening pressure	1.1 bar

Thermostat

Starts to open at	88°C
Fully open at	95°C

Refrigerant

Capacity:	
Front air conditioning only fitted	550 g
Front and rear air conditioning fitted	810 g

Torque wrench setting	**Nm**	**lbf ft**
Compressor mounting bolts	23	17
Coolant pump bolts	10	7
Coolant pump pulley bolts	25	18
Coolant temperature sensor	15	11
Cooling fan to viscous coupling	10	7
Facia crossmember fasteners	25	18
Viscous coupling*	65	48

* *Left-hand thread*

1 General information and precautions

The cooling system is of pressurised type, comprising of a belt-driven coolant pump, an aluminium crossflow radiator, the cooling fan, and a thermostat. The coolant pump is driven by the auxiliary drivebelt. The system functions as follows. Cold coolant from the radiator passes through the hose to the coolant pump, where it is pumped around the cylinder block and head passages. After cooling the cylinder bores, combustion surfaces and valve seats, the coolant reaches the underside of the thermostat, which is initially closed. The coolant passes through the heater, and is returned via the cylinder block to the coolant pump.

When the engine is cold, the coolant circulates only through the cylinder block, cylinder head, expansion tank and heater. When the coolant reaches a predetermined temperature, the thermostat opens and the coolant passes through to the radiator. As the coolant circulates through the radiator, it is cooled by the inrush of air when the car is in forward motion; the coolant is now cooled, and the cycle is repeated.

The electro-viscous cooling fan is driven by the auxiliary drivebelt. The viscous coupling varies the fan speed according to engine temperature. At low temperatures, the coupling provides very little resistance between the fan and pump pulley, so only a slight amount of drive is transmitted to the cooling fan. As the temperature of the coupling increases, so does its internal resistance, therefore increasing drive to the cooling fan. The flow of the fluid within the viscous fan is controlled by an electronic solenoid, itself controlled by the engine management ECM using data received from the engine coolant temperature sensor.

Refer to Section 10 for information on the air conditioning system.

Warning: Do not attempt to remove the expansion tank filler cap, nor disturb any part of the cooling system, while the engine is hot, as there is a high risk of scalding. If the expansion tank filler cap must be removed before the engine and radiator have fully cooled (even though this is not recommended) the pressure in the cooling system must first be relieved. Cover the cap with a thick layer of cloth, to avoid scalding, and slowly unscrew the filler cap until a hissing sound can be heard. When the hissing has stopped, indicating that the pressure has reduced, slowly unscrew the filler cap until it can be removed; if more hissing sounds are heard, wait until they have stopped before unscrewing the cap completely. At all times keep well away from the filler cap opening.

Warning: Do not allow antifreeze to come into contact with skin, or with the painted surfaces of the vehicle. Rinse off spills immediately with plenty of water. Never leave antifreeze lying around in an open container, or in a puddle in the driveway or on the garage floor. Children and pets are attracted by its sweet smell, but antifreeze can be fatal if ingested.

Warning: Refer to Section 10 for precautions to be observed when working on models with air conditioning.

2 Cooling system hoses – disconnection and renewal

Note: *Refer to the warnings given in Section 1 of this Chapter before proceeding.*

1 If the checks described in Chapter 1, Section 5, reveal a faulty hose, it must be renewed as follows.

2 First drain the cooling system (see Chapter 1, Section 31). If the coolant is not due for renewal, it may be re-used if it is collected in a clean container.

3 To disconnect a hose, use a screwdriver to slacken the clips, then move them along the hose, clear of the relevant inlet/outlet union. On some applications, the clips are released by squeezing together the tangs at the ends of the clips. This can be achieved using pliers/pipe grips, or using a tool specifically for this purpose **(see illustration)**. Carefully work the hose free. The hoses can be removed with relative ease when new – on an older vehicle, they may have stuck.

4 If a hose proves stubborn, try to release it by rotating it on its unions before attempting to work it off. Gently prise the end of the hose with a blunt instrument (such as a flat-bladed screwdriver), but do not apply too much force, and take care not to damage the pipe stubs or hoses. Note in particular that the radiator hose unions are fragile; do not use excessive force when attempting to remove the hoses.

HAYNES HiNT ***If all else fails, cut the hose with a sharp knife, then slit it so that it can be peeled off in two pieces. While expensive, this is preferable to buying a new radiator. Check first, however, that a new hose is readily available.***

5 When fitting a hose, first slide the clips onto the hose, then work the hose into position. If clamp-type clips were originally fitted, it is a good idea to update them with screw-type clips when refitting the hose. If the hose is stiff, use a little soapy water as a lubricant, or soften the hose by soaking it in hot water.

6 Work the hose into position, checking that it is correctly routed, then slide each clip along the hose until it passes over the flared end of the relevant inlet/outlet union, before tightening the clips securely.

7 Refill the cooling system with reference to Chapter 1, Section 31.

8 Check thoroughly for leaks as soon as possible after disturbing any part of the cooling system.

3 Radiator – removal, flushing and refitting

HAYNES HiNT ***If leakage is the reason for wanting to remove the radiator, bear in mind that minor leaks can be often be cured using a radiator sealant, with the radiator in situ.***

Removal

1 Drain the cooling system as described in Chapter 1, Section 31.

2 Remove the cooling fan as described in Section 5.

3 Working underneath, undo the bolts and remove the radiator access panel **(see illustration)**.

4 Unclip the coolant pipes and hoses from the lower cooling fan shroud.

5 Release the clip each side, undo the screw and remove the cooling fan lower shroud **(see illustrations)**.

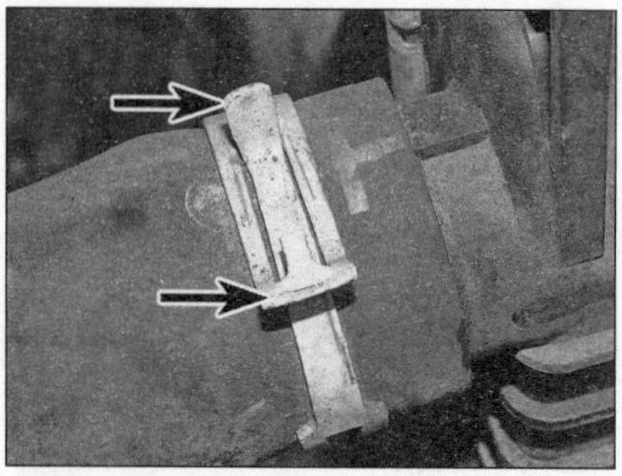

2.3 Squeeze together the tangs (arrowed)

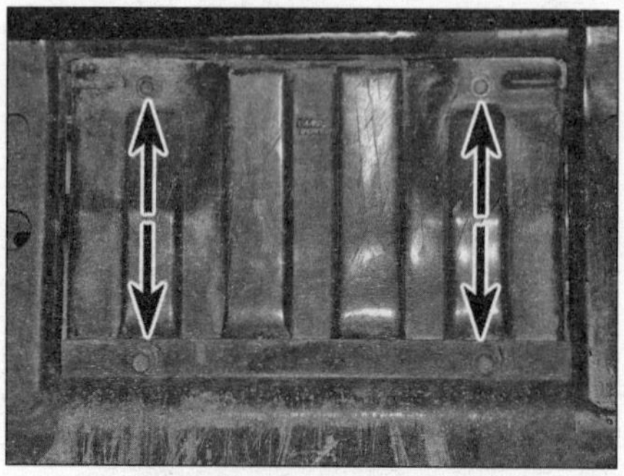

3.3 Radiator panel retaining bolts (arrowed)

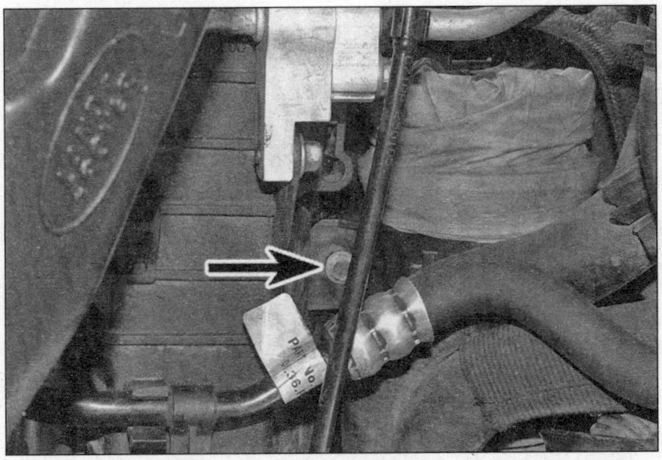

3.5a Undo the screw securing the intake duct at the left-hand side of the radiator

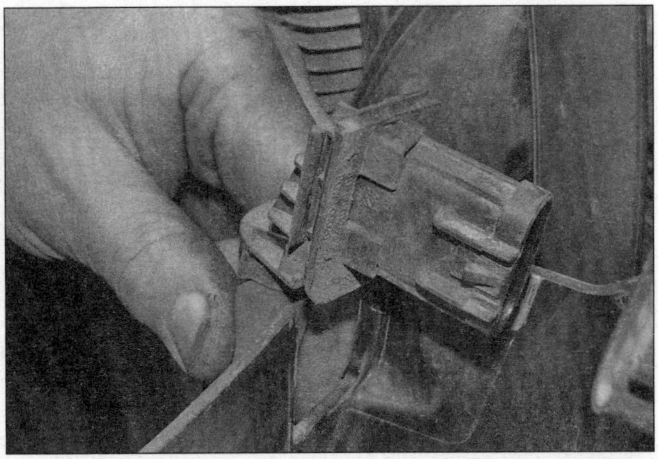

3.5b Slide the wiring plug from the lower cooling fan shroud

3.5c Press the clip (arrowed) rearwards and slide the cooling fan shroud up from place

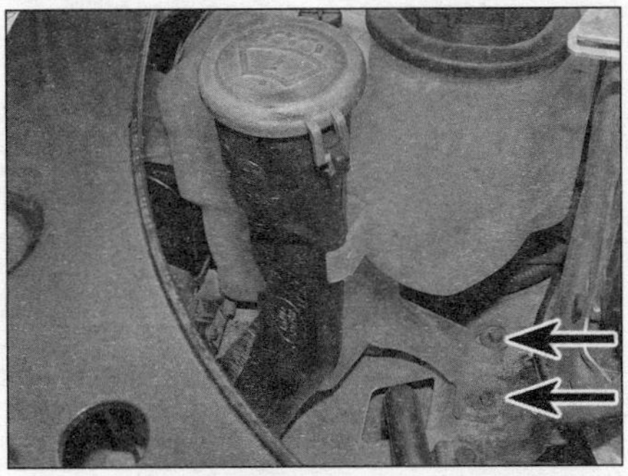

3.8 Unclip the screenwash reservoir filler neck, and undo the coolant expansion tank retaining bolts (arrowed)

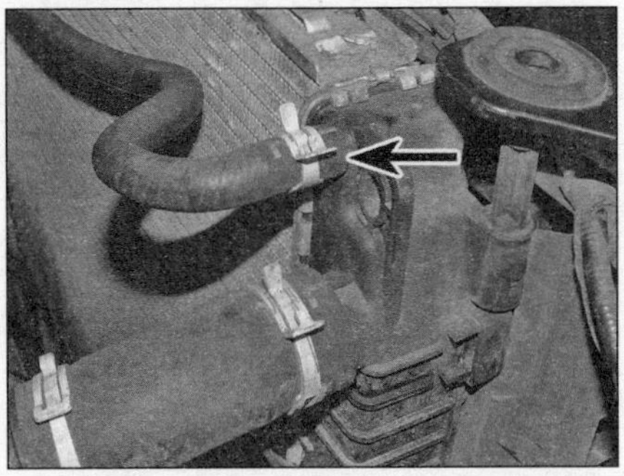

3.9 Disconnect the bleed hose (arrowed) from the radiator

6 Remove the radiator grille as described in Chapter 12, Section 29.

7 Remove the left-hand headlight as described in Chapter 13, Section 7.

8 Undo the 2 retaining bolts and move the coolant expansion tank to one side **(see illustration)**.

9 Release the clip and disconnect the bleed hose and top hose from the radiator **(see illustration)**.

10 Unclip and remove the front splash shield each side **(see illustration)**.

11 Release the clamps and disconnect the intercooler inlet and outlet hoses **(see illustration)**. Plug/cover the openings to prevent contamination.

12 Release the clips and disconnect the coolant hoses from the radiator **(see illustrations)**.

13 Tie the engine air intake duct towards the front of the engine.

14 On models with automatic transmission, release the clamps, disconnect the fluid hoses from the left-hand side of the radiator, and drain the fluid into a container. Be prepared for fluid spillage.

3.10 Remove splash shield (arrowed) each side

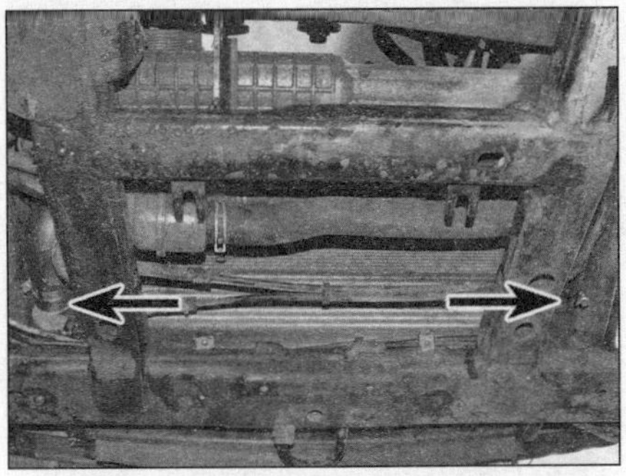

3.11 Release the clamps and disconnect the intercooler hoses each side (arrowed)

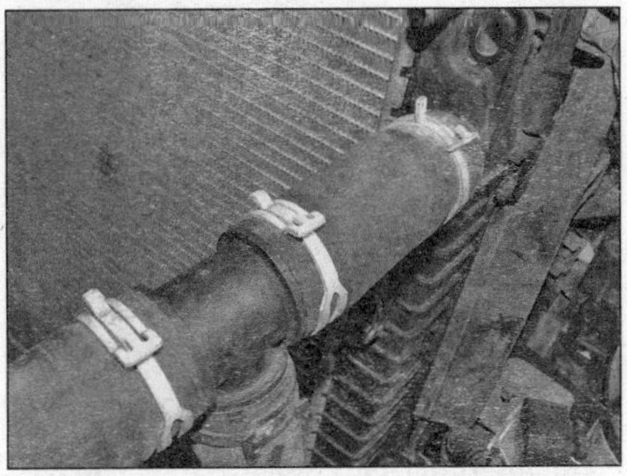

3.12a Disconnect the radiator upper hose ...

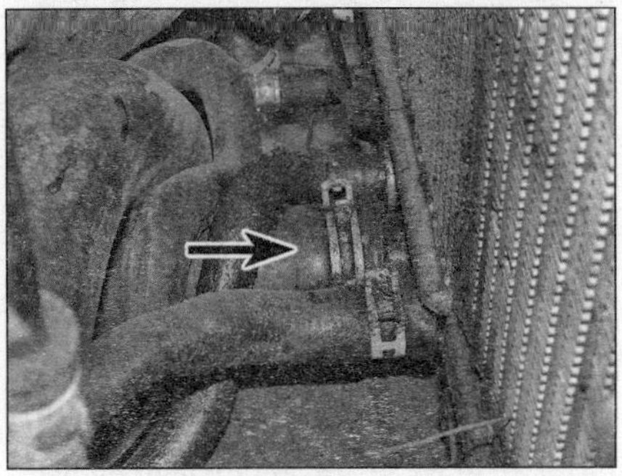

3.12b ... and lower radiator hose (arrowed)

3.15a Depress the clip (arrowed) ...

3.15b ... and slide up the radiator securing peg each side

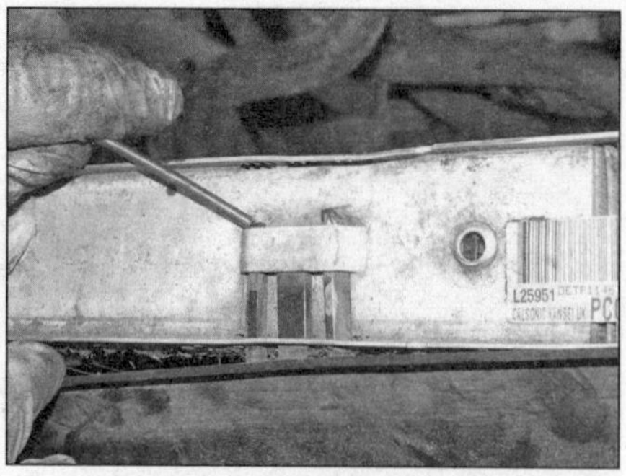

3.16 Release the clips and remove the upper deflector panel from the radiator

15 Depress the clip and withdraw the radiator securing pegs from position **(see illustrations)**.

16 Release the clips and remove the upper radiator deflector **(see illustration)**.

17 Unclip the power steering fluid cooler, and the front differential breather hose **(see illustration)**.

18 Undo the 3 retaining bolts, and lift the condenser a little to release it from the radiator **(see illustrations 11.31a and 11.31b)**.

19 Undo the bolt each side securing the front shroud to the radiator **(see illustration)**.

20 Undo the radiator mounting bolts each side and lift the radiator upwards a little, clear of the mountings **(see illustration)**.

21 Tie the condenser forwards to clear the radiator.

22 Prise out the pins securing the intercooler to the radiator each side **(see illustration)**.

23 Carefully lift the radiator from place.

24 Lift the left-hand side of radiator upwards first, and manoeuvre it from the engine compartment. Recover the rubber mountings at the base of the radiator.

Radiator flushing

25 Disconnect the top and bottom hoses and any other relevant hoses from the radiator.

26 Insert a garden hose into the radiator top inlet. Direct a flow of clean water through the radiator, and continue flushing until clean water emerges from the radiator bottom outlet.

27 If after a reasonable period, the water still does not run clear, the radiator can be flushed with a good proprietary cleaning agent. It is important that their manufacturer's instructions are followed carefully. If the contamination is particularly bad, insert the hose in the radiator bottom outlet, and reverse-flush the radiator.

Refitting

28 Refitting is the reverse of the removal procedure, noting the following points:

a) Ensure that the radiator is correctly engaged with its lower mounting rubbers.
b) Securely tighten all hose retaining clips.
c) On completion, refill the cooling system as described in Chapter 1, Section 31.
d) Check the transmission fluid level – automatic transmissions only (Chapter 7B, Section 7).

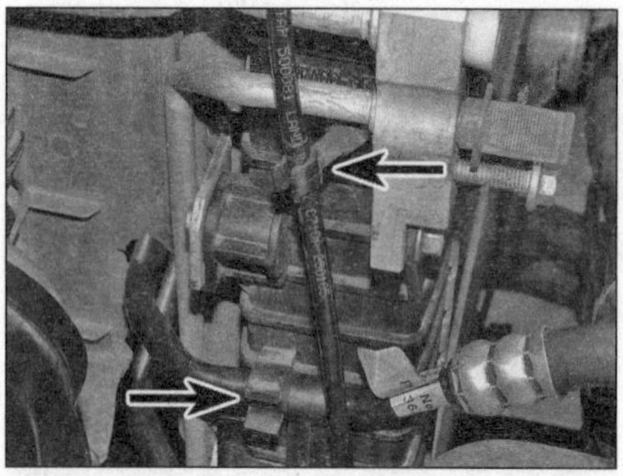

3.17 Unclip the power steering fluid cooler pipe and the differential breather hose (arrowed)

3.19 Undo the bolt (arrowed) each side securing the front shroud

4 Thermostat – removal and refitting

Removal

1 Drain the cooling system as described in Chapter 1, Section 31.

2 Release the clamps and disconnect the coolant hoses from the thermostat **(see illustration)**.

3 Manoeuvre the thermostat from position.

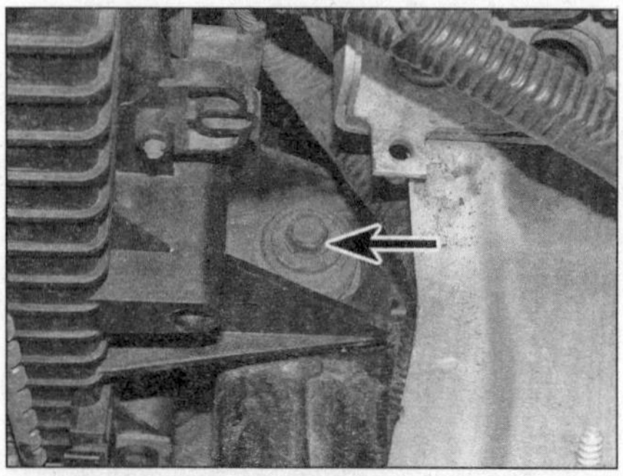

3.20 Remove the radiator mounting bolt (arrowed) each side

3.22 Intercooler-to-radiator retaining pin (arrowed)

4.2 The thermostat housing is located under the left-hand end of the radiator (arrowed)

5.3a Unclip the coolant bleed hose ...

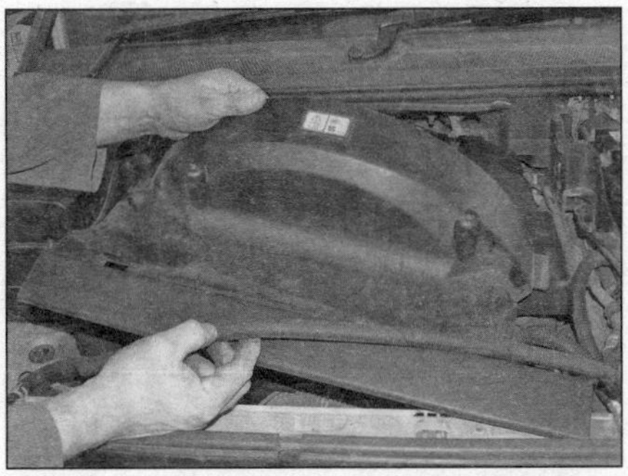

5.3b ... and unclip the upper shroud

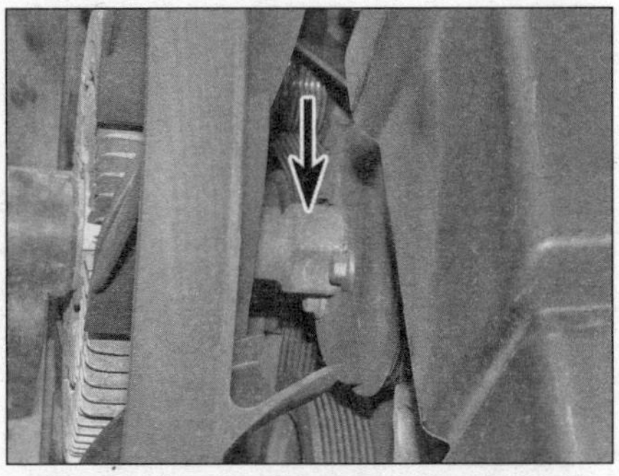

5.5a The viscous coupling nut (arrowed) has a left-hand thread. Undo the nut ...

Refitting

4 Refitting is the reverse of the relevant removal procedure. On completion, refill the cooling system as described in Chapter 1, Section 31.

5 Cooling fan – removal and refitting

Note: *A special narrow open-ended spanner will be required to unscrew the coupling assembly.*

Removal

1 Disconnect the battery negative lead, as described in Chapter 5, Section 4.

2 Remove the air cleaner assembly as described in Chapter 4A, Section 2, then undo the oil filler cap and pull the engine cover upwards from its mountings.

3 Release the coolant hose, then unclip and pull the cooling fan upper shroud upwards **(see illustrations)**.

4 Disconnect the cooling fan wiring plug.

5 Using the special 36 mm open-ended spanner (Land Rover tool No. 303-1142 and 303-1143 or equivalent), unscrew the viscous coupling. If necessary, use home-made tool to prevent the pulley from rotating **(see illustrations)**. **Note:** *The viscous coupling has a* ***left-hand thread*** *– ie, it unscrews* ***clockwise****.*

6 If required, undo the bolts securing the cooling fan to the viscous coupling.

Refitting

7 Refitting is the reverse of removal, making sure that the cooling fan is fitted the correct way around.

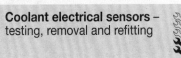

6 Coolant electrical sensors – testing, removal and refitting

Testing

1 Should either sensor fail, a fault code should be stored in the ECM memory by the self-diagnosis system, which can be interrogated

5.5b ... and lift out the cooling fan assembly

5.5c Using a home-made tool to prevent the cooling fan pulley from rotating (fan removed for clarity)

using a suitable fault code reader – see Chapter 4A, Section 1.

Removal

Engine coolant temperature sensor

2 Disconnect the battery negative lead as described in Chapter 5, Section 4.

3 Either partially drain the cooling system to just below the level of the sensor (as described in Chapter 1, Section 31), or have ready a suitable plug which can be used to plug the sender aperture whilst it is removed. If a plug is used, take great care not to damage the sender unit threads, and do not use anything which will allow foreign matter to enter the cooling system.

4 Remove the engine oil filler cap, then pull the plastic cover from the top of the engine.

5 Disconnect the wiring from the sensor, then lift the tang, rotate the sensor anti-clockwise and remove it. Discard the O-ring seal **(see illustrations)**.

Engine coolant level sensor

6 Release the power steering fluid reservoir upwards from its bracket.

7 Unclip the windscreen washer fluid reservoir from its bracket.

8 Undo the 2 retaining bolts and lift the coolant expansion tank from place **(see illustration 3.8)**.

9 Disconnect the wiring plug, then remove from the level sensor on the base of the

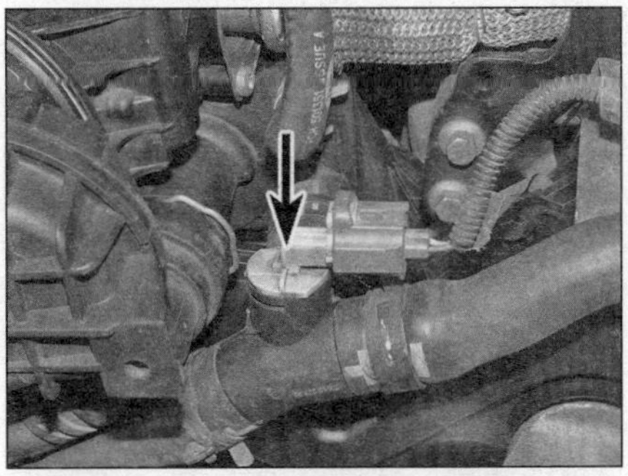

6.5a The engine coolant temperature sensor (arrowed) is located at the front of the engine on vehicles up to 2007 model year ...

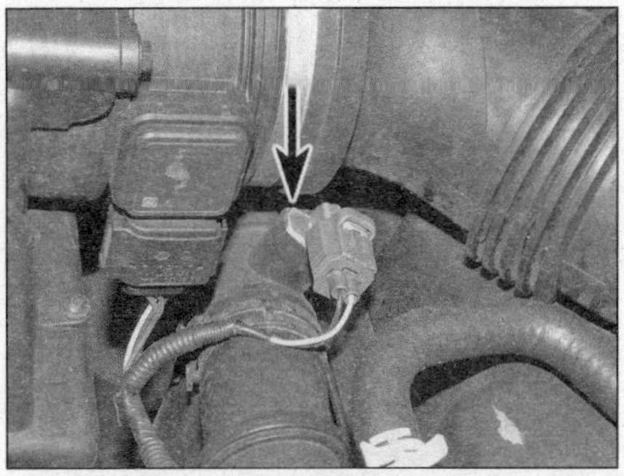

6.5b ... and to the right-hand side of the radiator (arrowed) on vehicles 2007 model year on

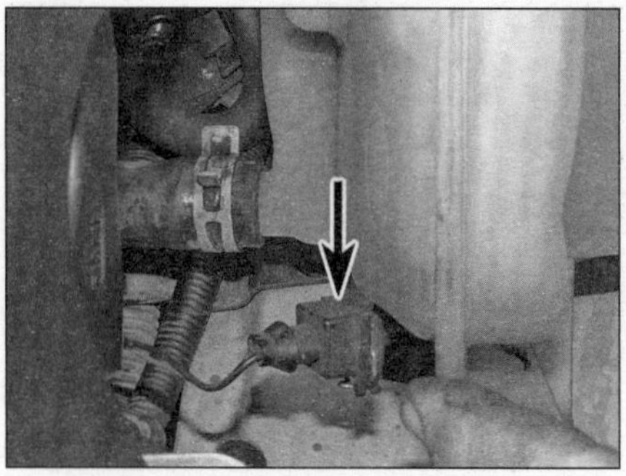

6.9 Disconnect the coolant level warning sensor wiring plug (arrowed)

7.3 Undo the coolant pump pulley bolt (arrowed)

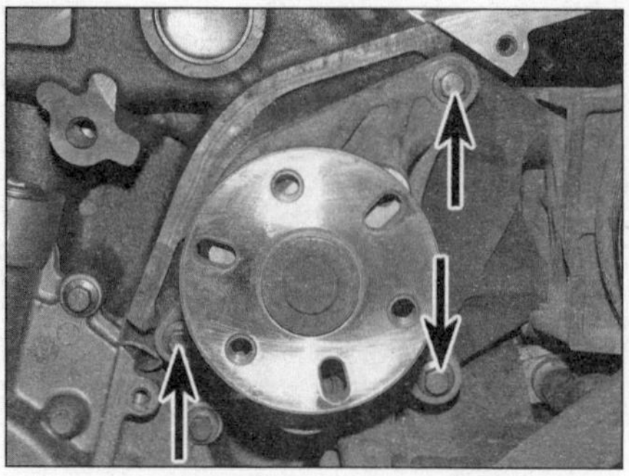

7.4a Coolant pump retaining bolts (arrowed)

expansion tank **(see illustration)**. Be prepared for fluid spillage.

Refitting

10 Refitting is a reversal of removal.

11 Top-up the coolant as described in Chapter 1, Section 31, or *Weekly checks*.

7 Coolant pump – removal and refitting

Removal

1 Drain the cooling system as described in Chapter 1, Section 31.

2 Slacken the coolant pump pulley bolts, then remove the auxiliary drivebelt as described in Chapter 1, Section 9.

3 Completely unscrew the retaining bolts and remove the coolant pump pulley **(see illustration)**.

4 Undo the retaining bolts and remove the coolant pump **(see illustrations)**. Discard the O-ring – a new one must be fitted.

Refitting

5 Ensure that the pump and housing mating surfaces are clean and dry, then refit the pump and cover using new O-ring seals. Tighten the retaining bolts to the specified torque.

6 Reconnect the hose to the pump, and secure it in place with the clip.

7 The remainder of refitting is a reversal of removal, remembering to refill the cooling system as described in Chapter 1, Section 31.

8 Heating and ventilation system – general information

1 The heating/ventilation system consists of a multi-speed blower motor, face-level vents in the centre and at each end of the facia, and air ducts to the front and rear footwells.

2 On some models, a rear heater/climate control unit was available. This consisted of a heater matrix, blower motor, evaporator and the necessary controls/air distribution elements.

3 The front control unit is located in the facia, and the controls operate flap valves to deflect and mix the air flowing through the various parts of the heating/ventilation system. The flap valves are contained in the air distribution housing, which acts as a central distribution unit, passing air to the various ducts and vents.

4 Cold air enters the system through the grille at the side of the engine compartment.

5 The airflow, which can be boosted by the blower, then flows through the various ducts, according to the settings of the controls. Stale air is expelled through ducts at the rear of the vehicle. If warm air is required, the cold air is passed through the heater matrix, which is heated by the engine coolant.

6 A recirculation lever enables the outside air supply to be closed off, while the air inside the vehicle is recirculated. This can be useful to prevent unpleasant odours entering from outside the vehicle, but should only be used briefly, as the recirculated air inside the vehicle will soon deteriorate.

Fuel-burning heater (FBH)

7 On some models, a fuel-fired booster heater is fitted to supplement the heating system, and compensate for the slow warm-up characteristics of the diesel engine. This unit is fully automatic, and consists of a pump and a fuel-burning unit with integral ECU. The system is controlled by the climate control module.

9 Heater/ventilation components – removal and refitting

Heater unit assembly

1 Have the air conditioning system refrigerant discharged by a Land Rover dealer of specialist.

2 Drain the cooling system as described in Chapter 1, Section 31.

Front unit

3 Remove the complete facia as described in Chapter 12, Section 28.

4 Undo the nuts and disconnect the earth cables on the driver's and passenger's side lower A-pillars **(see illustration)**.

5 Disconnect the wiring plugs from the driver's side lower A-pillar, and the plugs from the passenger's side lower A-pillar, so the loom can be removed along with the crossmember **(see illustration)**.

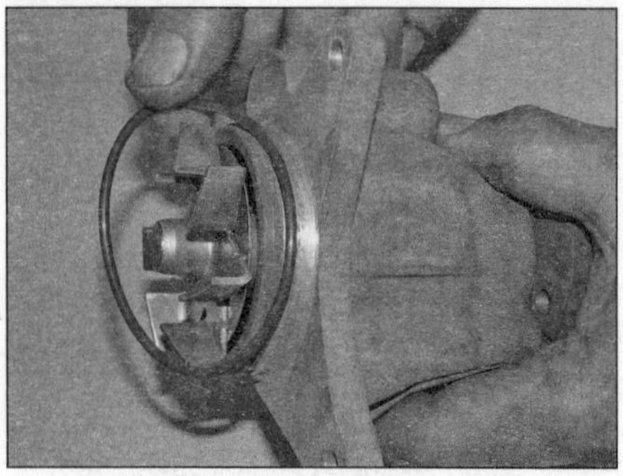

7.4b Renew the O-ring

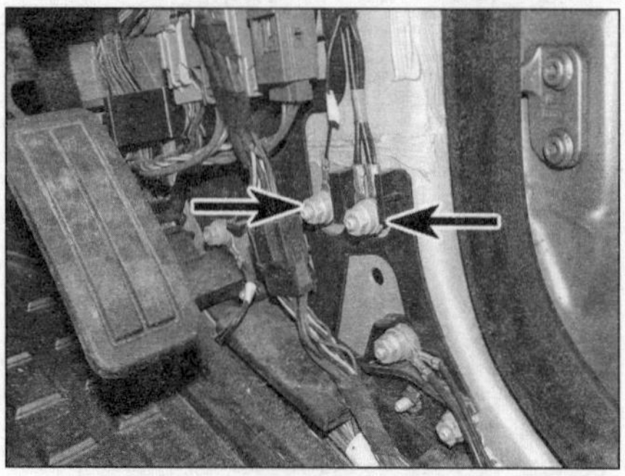

9.4 Earth connections (arrowed) at the base of each A-pillar

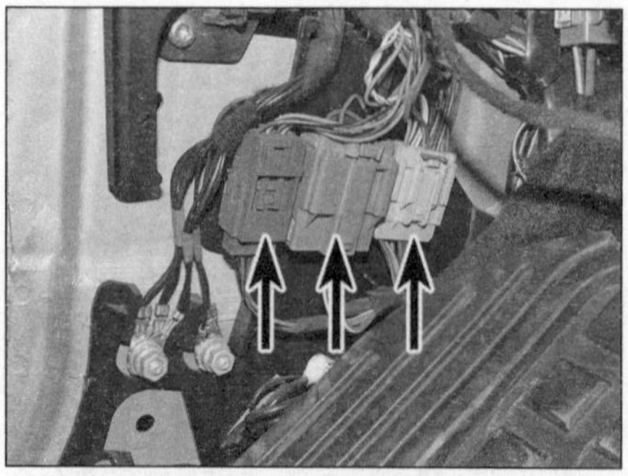

9.5 Disconnect the wiring plugs (arrowed) at the base of each A-pillar

9.6 Disconnect the wiring plugs (arrowed) from the central junction box

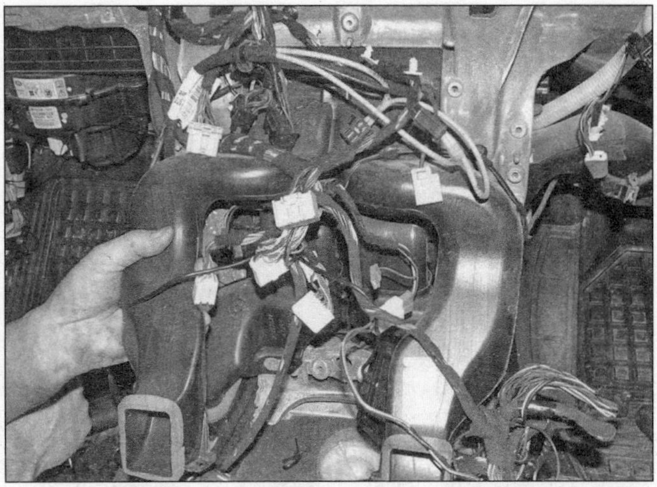

9.8 Remove the central air duct assembly

6 Disconnect the 2 wiring plugs from the central junction box **(see illustration)**.

7 Disconnect the wiring plugs from each side of the centre console location. **Note:** *Cover the fibre optic connectors to minimise dust ingress. Do not bend the fibre optic cable in a radius of less than 30 mm.*

8 Unclip the heater housing centre air ducts, and driver's side air ducts **(see illustration)**.

9 Undo the bolt/nut, and disconnect the intermediate shaft from the steering column **(see illustration)**. Discard the nut – a new one must be fitted.

10 The heater unit assembly is secured to the facia crossmember by 7 Torx screws **(see illustrations)**. Undo the screws.

11 Open the bonnet and remove the exterior A-pillar trim panels each side **(see illustration)**. Note that new clips must be used upon refitting.

12 Remove the wiper arms as described in Chapter 13, Section 12.

13 Pull up the rubber weather strip, and release the 8 clips and pull the plenum chamber trim panel upwards from place **(see illustrations)**.

14 Undo the bolt in the plenum chamber aperture securing the facia crossmember **(see illustration)**.

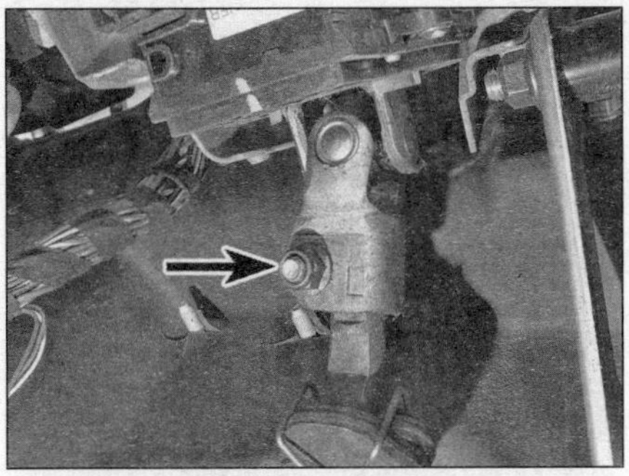

9.9 Intermediate shaft-to-steering column bolt/nut (arrowed)

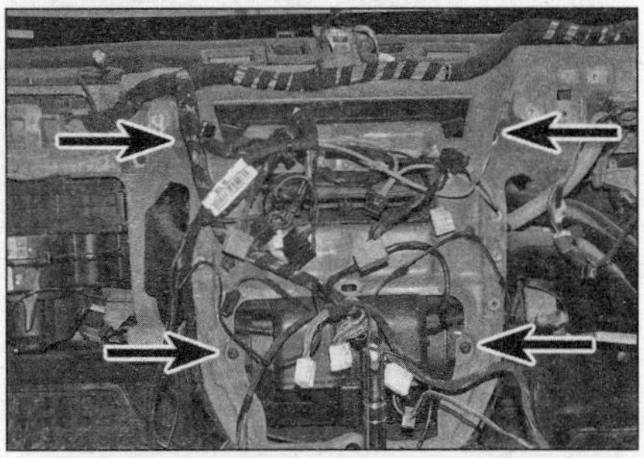

9.10a The heater unit is secured to the facia crossmember by 4 screws in the central area (arrowed) ...

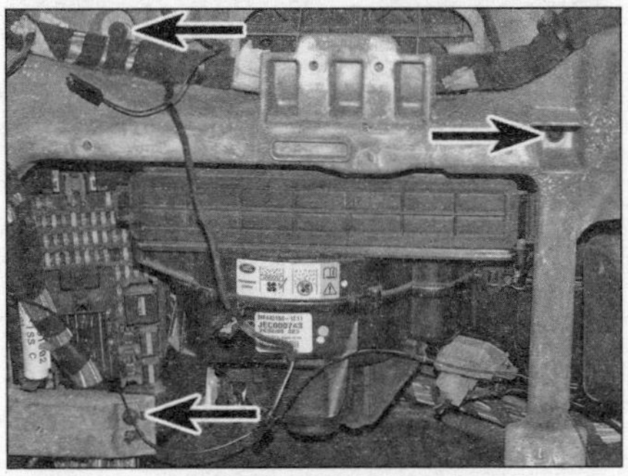

9.10b ... and 3 screws in the passenger's area (arrowed)

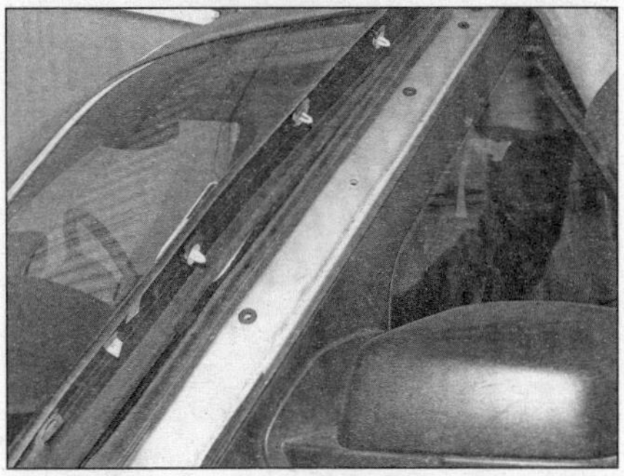

9.11 Pull the trim panel from the A-pillar each side

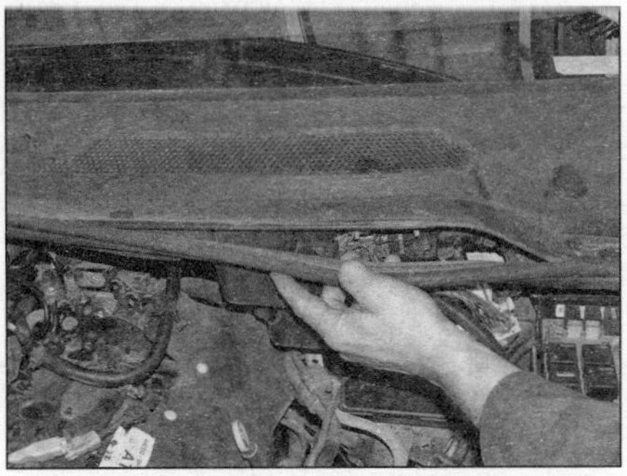

9.13a Pull up the rubber weatherstrip ...

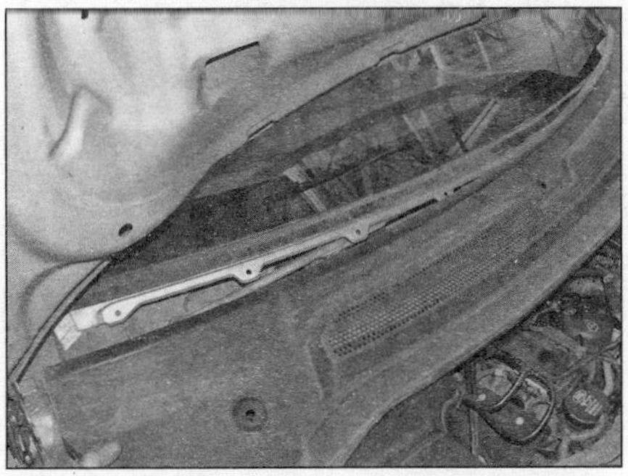

9.13b ... then pull up the plenum chamber trim panel to release the clips

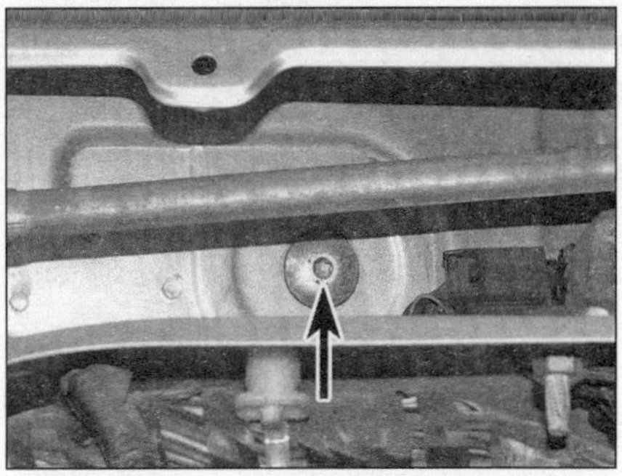

9.14 Remove the bolt in the plenum chamber (arrowed)

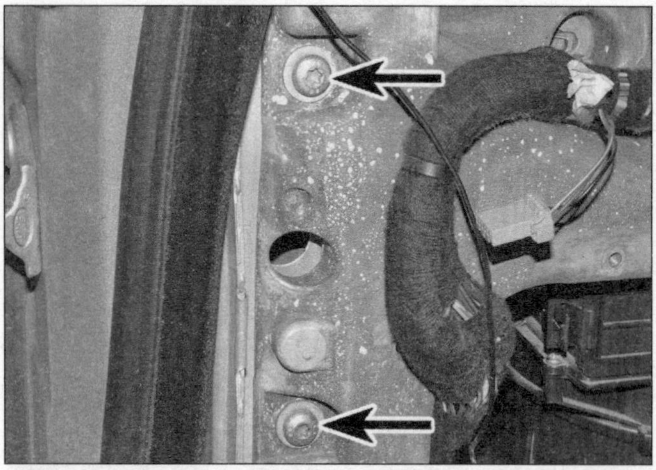

9.15a The facia crossmember is secured by 2 bolts (arrowed) at each end ...

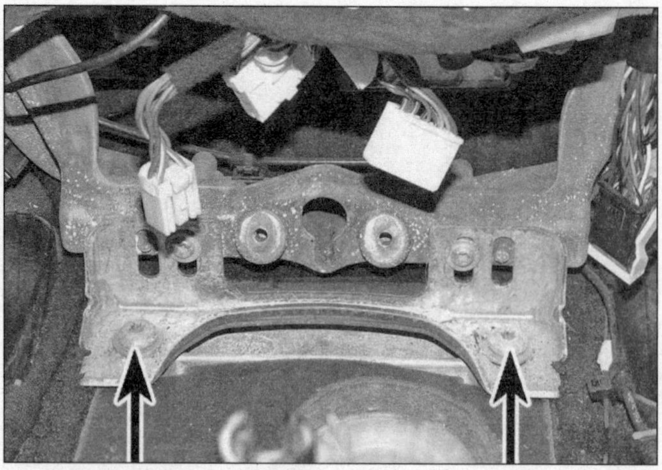

9.15b ... 2 bolts (arrowed) in the centre ...

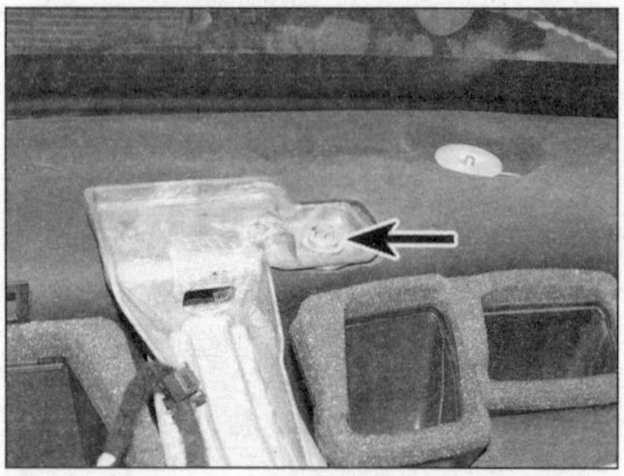

9.15c ... and 1 on the driver's upper side (arrowed)

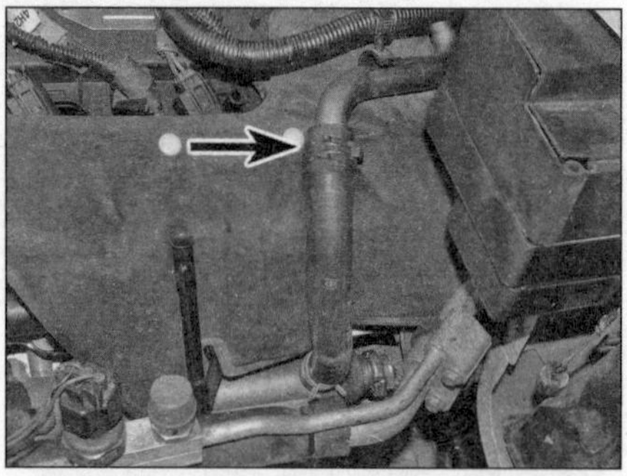

9.16 Release the clips and disconnect the EGR crossover pipe each side

15 Undo the remaining bolts and, with the help of an assistant, manoeuvre the facia crossmember from the passenger cabin **(see illustrations)**. Ensure all relevant wiring plugs/harnesses are disconnected.

16 Working in the engine compartment, release the clips and disconnect both EGR coolant rail crossover hoses **(see illustration)**.

17 Undo the 2 bolts, release the 2 clips and remove the EGR coolant crossover pipe **(see illustration)**.

18 Depress the release buttons, and disconnect the heater hoses at the engine compartment bulkhead **(see illustration)**. Plug/cover the openings to prevent contamination.

19 Undo the nut securing the pipe support bracket, then undo the bolt and disconnect the refrigerant pipes from the connection at the engine compartment bulkhead **(see illustration)**. Plug/cover the openings to prevent contamination. Note that the pipe's O-ring seals must be renewed. If the refrigerant circuit is open to the atmosphere for more than 24 hours, the receiver/drier must be renewed.

20 Undo the nuts and remove the pipe connections adapter panels from the bulkhead **(see illustration)**.

21 Disconnect the 2 drain tubes from the base of the heater assembly unit **(see illustration)**.

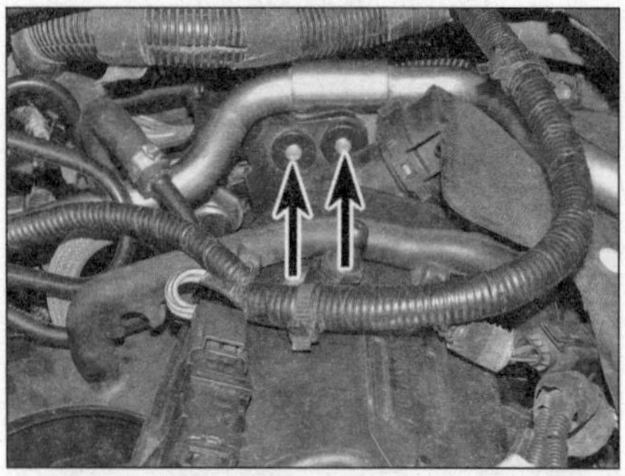

9.17 EGR crossover pipe retaining bolts (arrowed). Note that the bolts are inserted from the rear

9.18 Depress the release buttons (arrowed) and disconnect the heater hoses

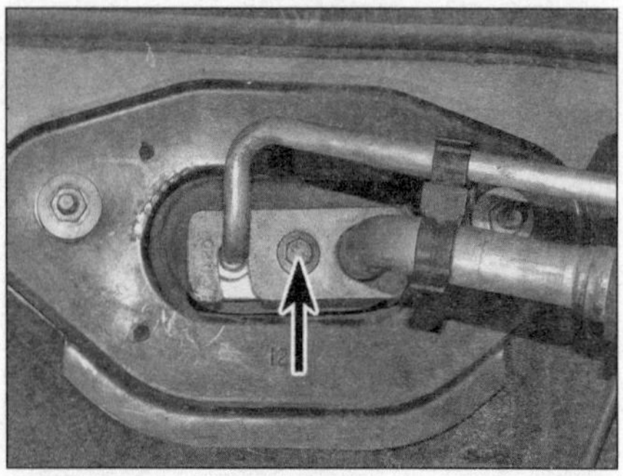

9.19 Refrigerant pipe connection retaining bolt (arrowed)

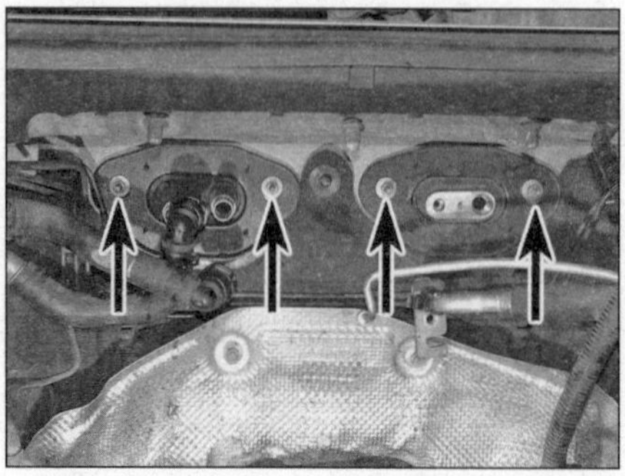

9.20 Undo the pipe connection panels nuts (arrowed)

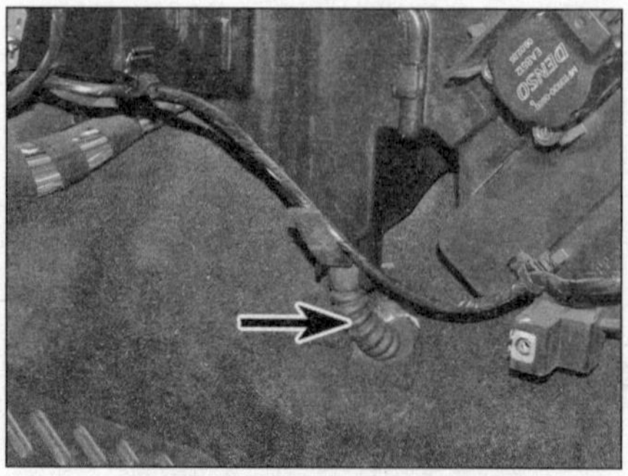

9.21 Disconnect the drain tube (arrowed) each side of the heater unit

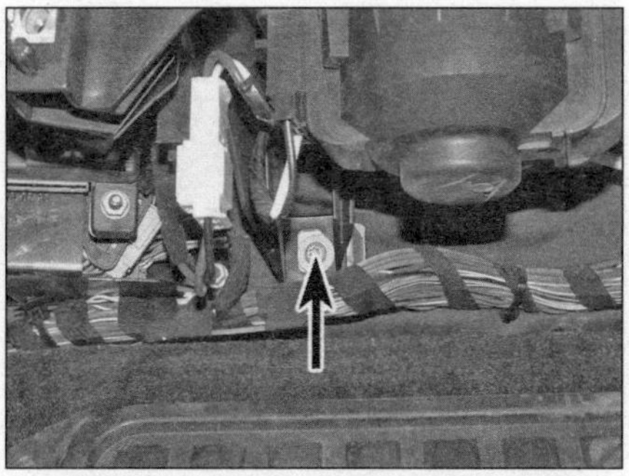

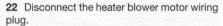

9.23a The heater unit is secured to the bulkhead by a bolt (arrowed) on the left-hand side ...

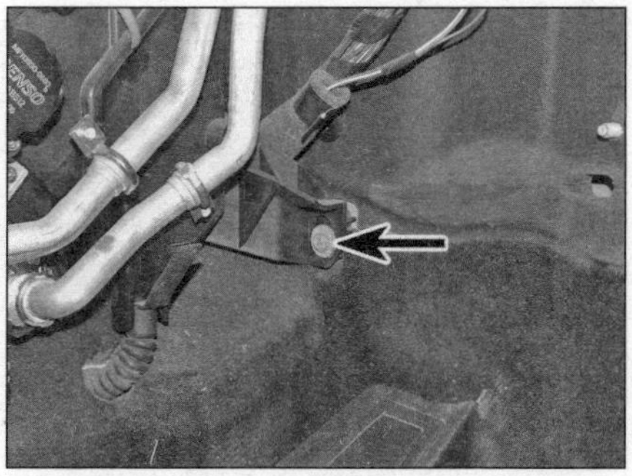

9.23b ... and a bolt (arrowed) on the right-hand side

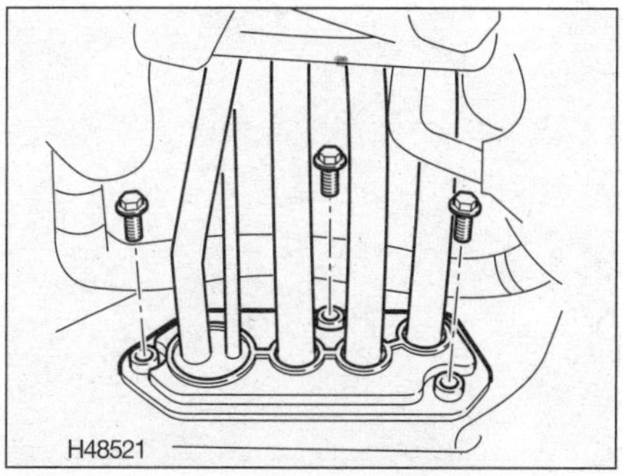

9.33 Undo the 3 bolts securing the pipes sealing plate

22 Disconnect the heater blower motor wiring plug.

23 Remove the Torx bolt each side securing the heater assembly to the bulkhead **(see illustrations)**.

24 With the help of an assistant, manoeuvre the heater assembly from the cabin.

> **HAYNES HiNT** *Be prepared for some coolant spillage as the heater is removed; wash off any spilled coolant immediately with cold water.*

25 Refitting is the reverse of removal, ensuring that an airtight seal is made between the heater unit and bulkhead.

Rear unit

26 Remove the left-hand C-pillar lower trim panel as described in Chapter 12, Section 26.

27 Raise the rear of the vehicle and support it securely on axle stands (see *Jacking and vehicle support*).

28 Support the rear of the exhaust system, then release the centre, left-hand and right-hand rear exhaust system mountings.

29 Undo the nuts and remove the left-hand rear exhaust heat shield.

30 Remove the spare wheel.

31 Undo the bolts and disconnect the refrigerant pipes at the connection on the underside of the floor. Plug the openings to prevent contamination. Note that the O-ring seals must be renewed. If the refrigerant circuit is open to the atmosphere for more than 24 hours, the receiver/drier must be renewed.

32 Release the clamps and disconnect the coolant hoses adjacent to the refrigerant pipes.

33 Working inside the vehicle, undo the 3 bolts securing the sealing plate around the pipes where they enter the cabin **(see illustration)**.

34 Disconnect the wiring plugs, undo the 3 mounting bolts and remove the heater/climate control unit assembly **(see illustration)**.

> **HAYNES HiNT** *Be prepared for some coolant spillage as the heater is removed; wash off any spilled coolant immediately with cold water.*

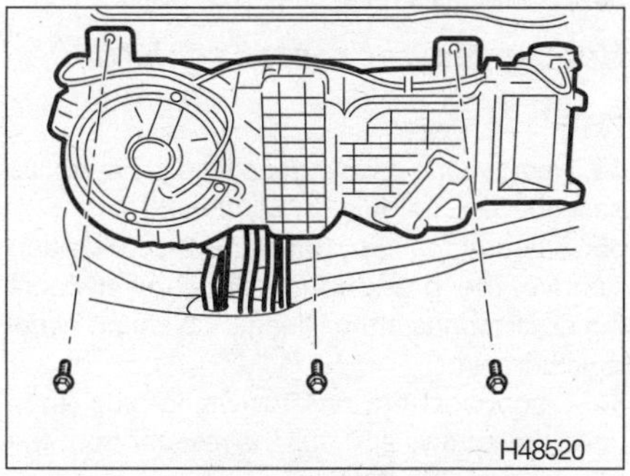

9.34 The rear auxiliary heater unit is secured by 3 bolts

35 Refitting is the reverse of removal, ensuring that an airtight seal is made between the heater unit and bulkhead.

Heater matrix

36 Remove the facia centre reinforcement panel as described in Chapter 12, Section 28.

Front matrix

37 Slacken the retaining screws, release the clamps and disconnect the heater pipes from the matrix **(see illustrations)**. Discard the O-ring seals. Be prepared for coolant spillage.

38 Undo the retaining screw and slide the heater matrix out from the housing **(see illustrations)**.

39 On refitting, slide the matrix into the housing.

40 Ensure that the matrix is correctly seated,

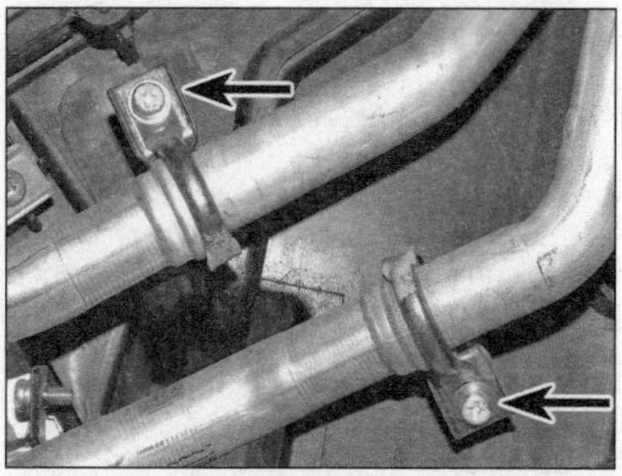

9.37a Disconnect the pipes at the clamps (arrowed) ...

9.37b ... and at the heater matrix (arrowed)

9.38a Undo the screw (arrowed) ...

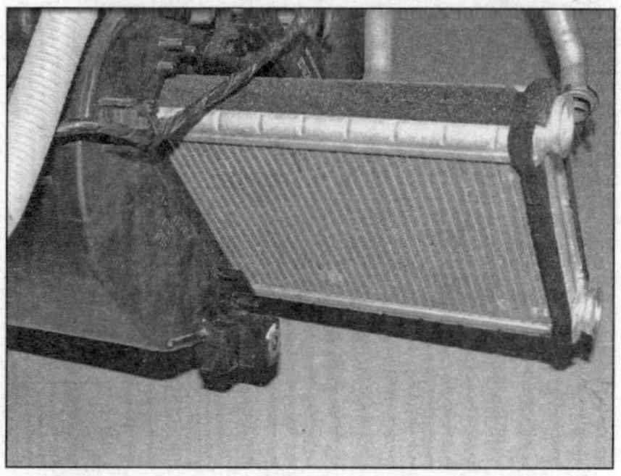

9.38b ... and slide the matrix from the housing

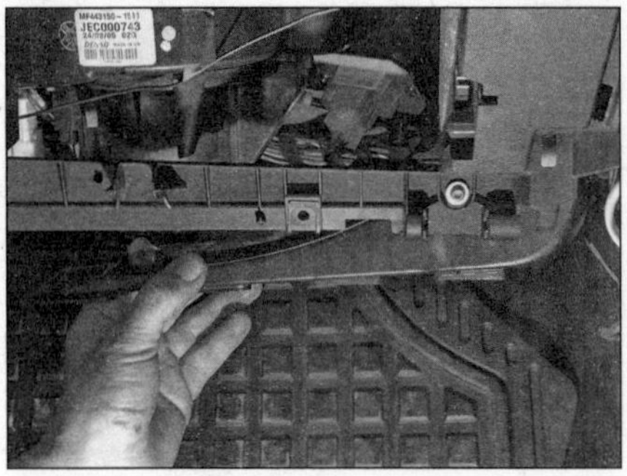

9.48 Move the footwell air duct to one side

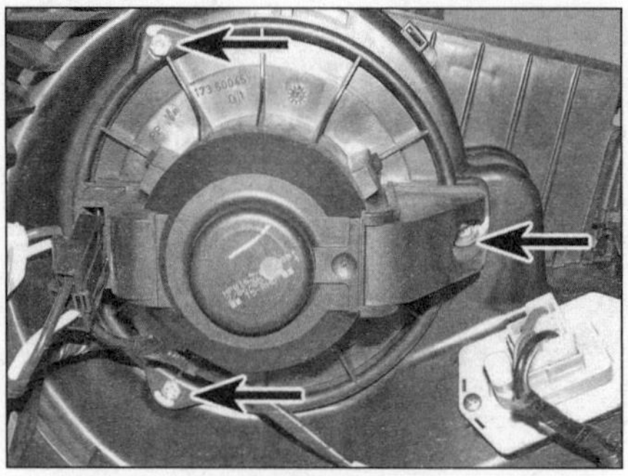

9.49 Blower motor retaining screws (arrowed)

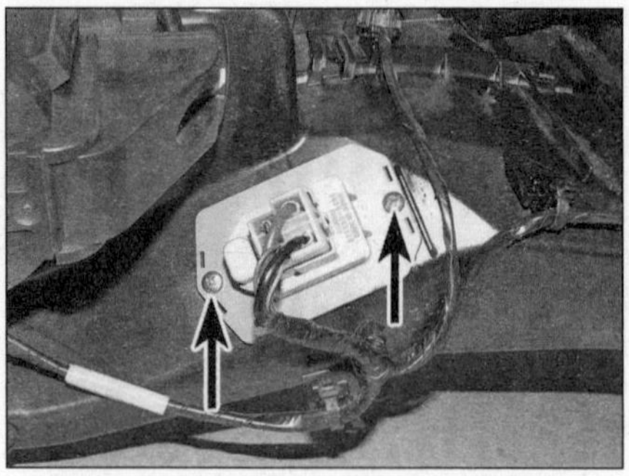

9.56 Blower motor resistor retaining screws (arrowed)

then secure the retaining screw, and refit the pipes using new O-ring seals.

41 The remainder of refitting is a reversal of removal.

Rear matrix

42 Undo the bolts/screws, disconnect the wiring plug, then detach the refrigerant pipes/expansion valve assembly from the heater/climate control unit.

43 Release the pipe clamps, and slide the matrix from the housing.

44 If required, release the clips and detach the coolant pipes from the matrix. Discard the O-ring seals – new ones must be fitted.

45 Refitting is a reversal of removal.

Heater blower motor

Front motor

46 Remove the passenger's side glovebox as described in Chapter 13, Section 26.

47 Release the clip, undo the 2 screws and remove the passenger's side lower facia panel. Disconnect the wiring plug as the panel is withdrawn.

48 Release the clip and move the footwell air duct to one side for access **(see illustration)**.

49 Disconnect the wiring connector, undo the 3 retaining screws, and lower the blower motor from the housing **(see illustration)**.

50 Refitting is the reverse of removal.

Rear motor

51 Remove the left-hand C-pillar lower trim panel as described in Chapter 12, Section 26.

9.64 The FBH (fuel burning heater) is located in the left-hand front corner of the engine compartment (arrowed)

9.61 Pull the instrument panel centre console surround rearwards to release the clips

52 Disconnect the wiring plug, undo the 3 retaining screws and withdraw the blower motor from the heater unit/climate control assembly.

53 Refitting is a reversal of removal.

Heater blower motor resistor

Front

54 Remove the passenger's side glovebox as described in Chapter 13, Section 26.

55 Release the clip, undo the 2 screws and remove the passenger's side lower facia panel. Disconnect the wiring plug as the panel is withdrawn.

56 Disconnect the resistor wiring plug, then undo the screws and pull the resistor from the housing **(see illustration)**.

57 Refitting is a reversal of removal.

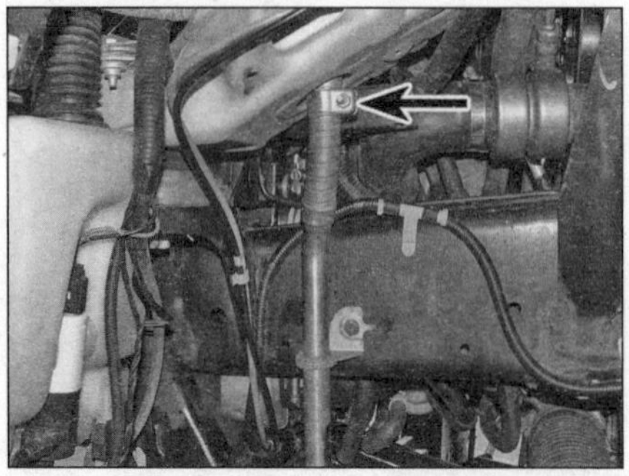

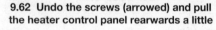

9.67 Undo the FBH exhaust pipe clamp bolt (arrowed)

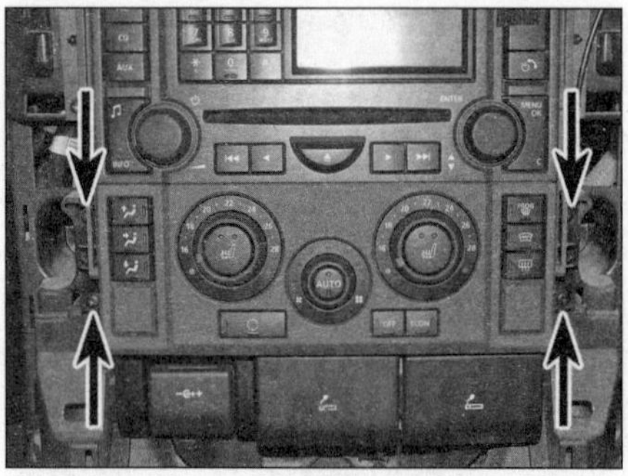

9.62 Undo the screws (arrowed) and pull the heater control panel rearwards a little

Rear

58 Remove the left-hand C-pillar lower trim panel as described in Chapter 12, Section 26.

59 Disconnect the wiring plug, undo the 2 retaining screws and withdraw the resistor from the heater unit/climate control assembly.

60 Refitting is a reversal of removal.

Heater control panel

61 Carefully pull the instrument panel centre console surround rearwards to release the retaining clips **(see illustration)**.

62 Undo the 4 retaining screws and pull the control panel rearwards **(see illustration)**. Disconnect the wiring plugs as the panel is withdrawn.

63 Refitting is a reversal of removal. Note that if a new panel is fitted, it must be configured using Land Rover T4 diagnostic equipment or equivalent. Entrust this task to a Land Rover dealer or suitably-equipped repairer.

Fuel-burning heater (FBH)

64 Disconnect the battery negative lead as described in Chapter 5, Section 4. The FBH is located in the left-hand front corner of the engine compartment **(see illustration)**.

65 Raise the front of the vehicle and support it on axle stands (see *Jacking and vehicle support*). Remove the left-hand front roadwheel.

66 Undo the fasteners and pull back the front section of the left-hand wheel arch liner.

67 Release the FBH exhaust pipe clamp **(see illustration)**.

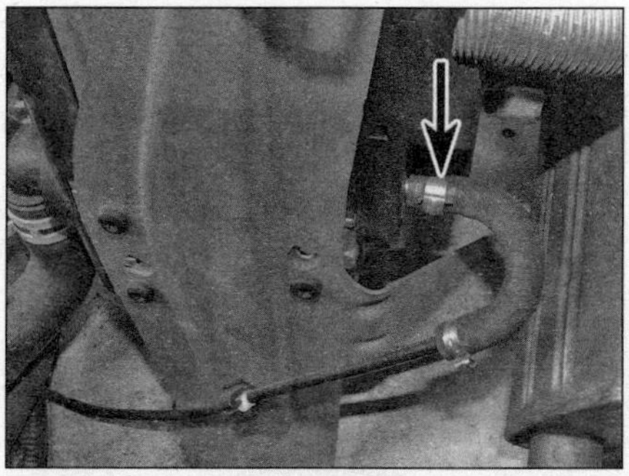

9.68 Disconnect the fuel supply pipe (arrowed)

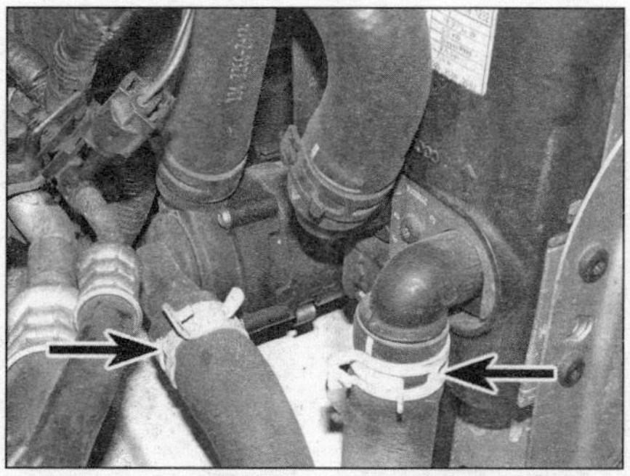

9.70 Disconnect the FBH inlet and outlet coolant hoses (arrowed)

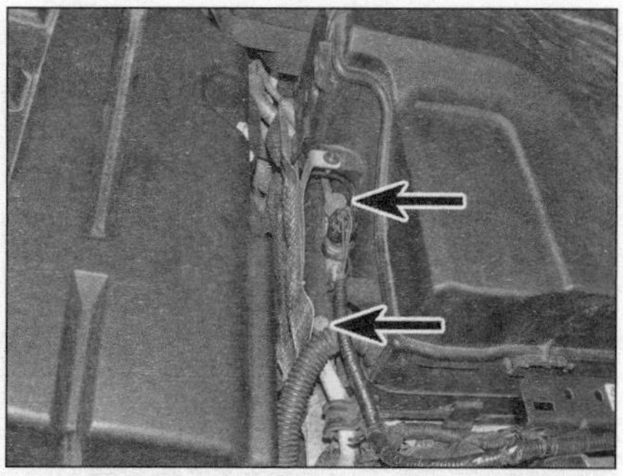

10.5 The high- and low-pressure refrigerant circuit service ports (arrowed) are located on the left-hand side of the engine compartment

68 Disconnect the fuel supply pipe from the FBH. Be prepared for fuel spillage, and plug the ends of the pipe to prevent contamination **(see illustration)**.

69 Slide the power steering fluid reservoir upwards from the mounting bracket.

70 Use suitable clamps to clamp the coolant hoses to and from the heater unit, then release the clips and disconnect the hoses **(see illustration)**.

71 Disconnect the wiring plugs from the FBH.

72 Undo the 3 bolts securing the FBH to the mounting bracket and remove it from the engine compartment. No dismantling of the unit is recommended.

73 Refitting is a reversal of removal, remembering to top-up the coolant as described in Chapter 1, Section 31, or *Weekly checks*.

10 Air conditioning system – general information and precautions

An air conditioning system was standard equipment on all models. It enables the temperature of incoming air to be lowered, and also dehumidifies the air, which makes for rapid demisting and increased comfort.

The cooling side of the system works in the same way as a domestic refrigerator. Refrigerant gas is drawn into a belt-driven compressor, and passes into a condenser mounted in front of the radiator, where it loses heat and becomes liquid. The liquid passes through an expansion valve to an evaporator, where it changes from liquid under high pressure to gas under low pressure. This change is accompanied by a drop in temperature, which cools the evaporator. The refrigerant returns to the compressor, and the cycle begins again.

Air blown through the evaporator passes to the air distribution unit, where it is mixed with hot air blown through the heater matrix, to achieve the desired temperature in the passenger compartment.

The system is controlled electronically by a control unit mounted in the facia centre panel. Any problems with the system should be referred to a Land Rover dealer or specialist.

The high- and low-pressure service ports are located adjacent to the battery in the left-hand corner of the engine compartment **(see illustration)**.

Precautions

When an air conditioning system is fitted, it is necessary to observe special precautions whenever dealing with any part of the system, its associated components and any items which necessitate disconnection of the system. If for any reason the system must be discharged, entrust this task to your Land Rover dealer or a refrigeration engineer.

Do not operate the air conditioning system if it is known to be short of refrigerant, as this may damage the compressor.

Warning: The refrigeration circuit contains a liquid refrigerant (R134a) under pressure, and it is dangerous to disconnect any part of the system without specialised knowledge and equipment. The refrigerant should only be handled by qualified persons. If it is splashed onto the skin, it can cause frostbite. It is not itself poisonous, but in the presence of a naked flame (including a lighted cigarette) it forms a poisonous gas. Uncontrolled discharging of the refrigerant is dangerous and potentially damaging to the environment.

11 Air conditioning system components – removal and refitting

Compressor

1 Have the system refrigerant discharged by a suitably-equipped specialist or Land Rover dealer.

2 Disconnect the battery negative lead as described in Chapter 5, Section 4.

3 Raise the front of the vehicle and support it on axles stands (see *Jacking and vehicle support*). Remove the left-hand front roadwheel.

4 Remove the engine oil filler cap, the pull up and remove the plastic cover from the top of the engine.

5 Remove the auxiliary battery (where fitted) and battery tray as described in Chapter 5, Section 4.

6 Remove the auxiliary drivebelt as described in Chapter 1, Section 9.

7 Release the fasteners and remove the left-hand wheel arch lower splash shield **(see illustration)**.

8 Undo the nuts/bolts and remove the upper suspension arm/brake pipe heat shield **(see illustration)**.

9 Undo the nut/bolts and release the intercooler inlet pipe bracket, then slacken the clamps and remove the inlet pipe.

11.7 Prise up the centre pins (arrowed), lever out the plastic rivets and remove the lower splash shield

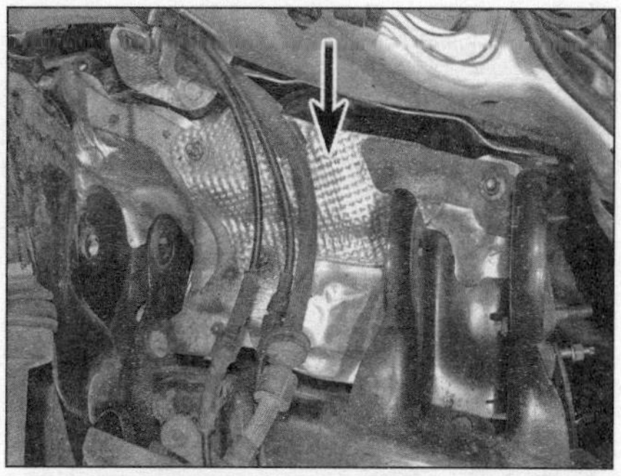

11.8 Remove the heat shield (arrowed – upper arm removed for clarity)

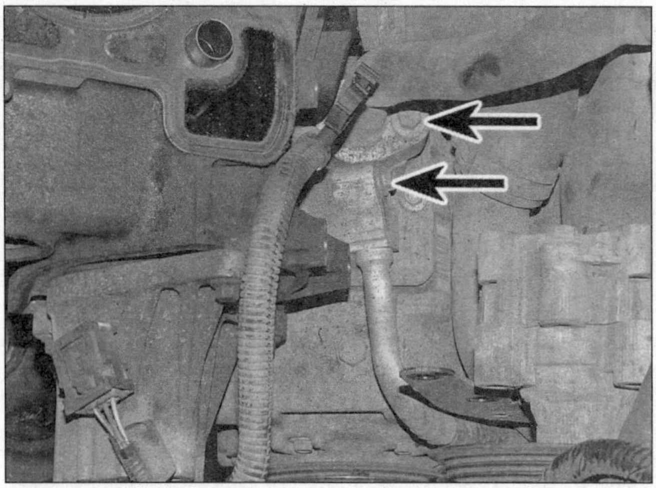

11.10 Compressor refrigerant pipe bolts (arrowed – cylinder head and power steering pump removed for clarity)

11.25 Renew the refrigerant pipe O-ring seals (arrowed)

10 Undo the bolt and detach the low-pressure refrigerant pipe from the compressor **(see illustration)**. Plug the openings to prevent contamination. Note that the pipe's O-ring seal must be renewed. If the refrigerant circuit is open to the atmosphere for more than 24 hours, the receiver/drier must be renewed.

11 Remove the 2 bolts and release the support bracket from the rear of the power steering pump.

12 Undo the bolt and detach the high-pressure refrigerant pipe from the compressor. Plug the openings to prevent contamination. Note that the pipe's O-ring seal must be renewed. If the refrigerant circuit is open to the atmosphere for more than 24 hours, the receiver/drier must be renewed.

13 Undo the bolts securing the front power steering pump bracket, then tie the pump to one side for access to the compressor.

14 Disconnect the compressor wiring plug.

15 Undo the 3 retaining bolts and remove the compressor.

16 Refitting is a reversal of removal, noting the following points:

a) Tighten the compressor mounting bolts to the specified torque.

b) Lubricate the new pipe O-ring seals with refrigerant oil prior to fitting.

c) Top-up the cooling system as described in Weekly checks.

d) Have the refrigerant oil replenished, and the system recharged by a suitably-equipped specialist or Land Rover dealer.

Condenser

17 Have the system refrigerant discharged by a suitably-equipped specialist or Land Rover dealer.

18 Disconnect the battery negative lead as described in Chapter 5, Section 4.

19 Remove the cooling fan as described in Section 5.

20 Working underneath, undo the bolts and remove the radiator access panel **(see illustration 3.3)**.

21 Unclip the coolant pipes and hoses from the lower cooling fan shroud.

22 Release the clip each side, undo the screw and remove the cooling fan lower shroud **(see illustrations 3.5a, 3.5b and 3.5c)**.

23 Remove the radiator grille as described in Chapter 12, Section 29.

24 Undo the 2 bolts and move the coolant expansion tank to one side.

25 Undo the bolts and detach the refrigerant pipes from the condenser **(see illustration)**. Plug the openings to prevent contamination. Note that the pipe's O-ring seals must be renewed. If the refrigerant circuit is open to the atmosphere for more than 24 hours, the receiver/drier must be renewed.

26 Depress the clip and withdraw the radiator securing pegs from position **(see illustrations 3.15a and 3.15b)**.

27 Release the clips and remove the upper radiator deflector **(see illustration 3.16)**.

28 Unclip the power steering fluid cooler, and the front differential breather hose **(see illustration 3.17)**.

29 Tie the engine air intake duct back towards the engine.

30 Undo the radiator mounting bolts each side and lift the radiator upwards a little, clear of the mountings **(see illustration 3.20)**. Tilt the radiator back towards the engine.

31 Undo the retaining bolt, and release the 2 clips securing the condenser **(see illustrations)**. Lift the condenser from place.

32 Refitting is a reversal of removal, noting the following points:

a) Lubricate the new pipe O-ring seals with refrigerant oil prior to fitting.

b) Tighten the refrigerant pipe bolts securely.

c) Top-up the cooling system as described in Weekly checks.

d) Have the refrigerant oil replenished, and the system recharged by a suitably-equipped specialist or Land Rover dealer.

Receiver/drier

33 Remove the condenser as previously described in this Section.

34 Slacken the receiver/drier clamp bolt, then undo the retaining bolt securing the refrigerant

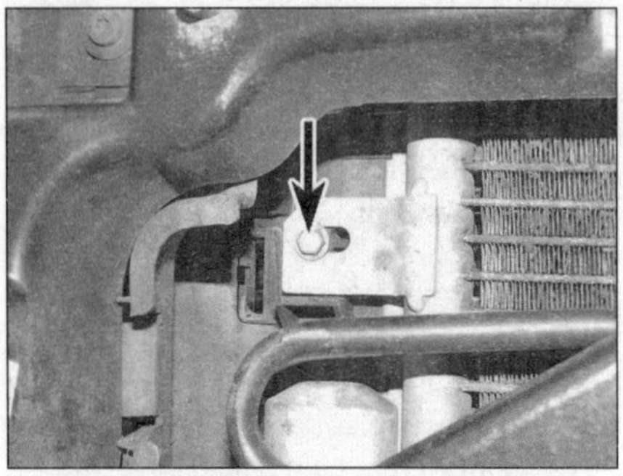

11.31a Undo the bolt at the front right-hand corner (arrowed) ...

11.31b ... then press the clip (arrowed) each side forwards a little

pipes and slide the receiver/drier from the clamp **(see illustration)**. Renew the pipe O-ring seals.

35 Refitting is a reversal of removal, noting the following points:

a) Lubricate the new pipe O-ring seals with refrigerant oil prior to fitting.

b) Tighten the refrigerant pipe bolts securely.

c) Top-up the cooling system as described in Weekly checks.

d) Have the refrigerant oil replenished, and the system recharged by a suitably-equipped specialist or Land Rover dealer.

Evaporator

Front

36 Remove the heater unit assembly as described in Section 9, then undo the clamps

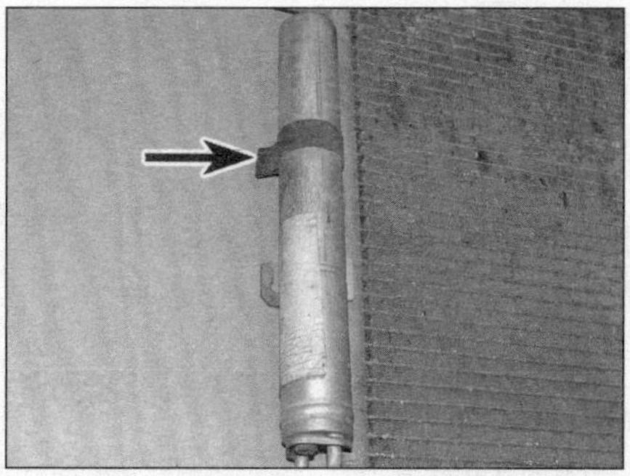

11.34 Receiver/drier clamp bolt (arrowed)

securing the heater matrix pipes on the side of the housing **(see illustration 9.37a)**.

37 Disconnect the wiring plug from the evaporator temperature sensor **(see illustration)**.

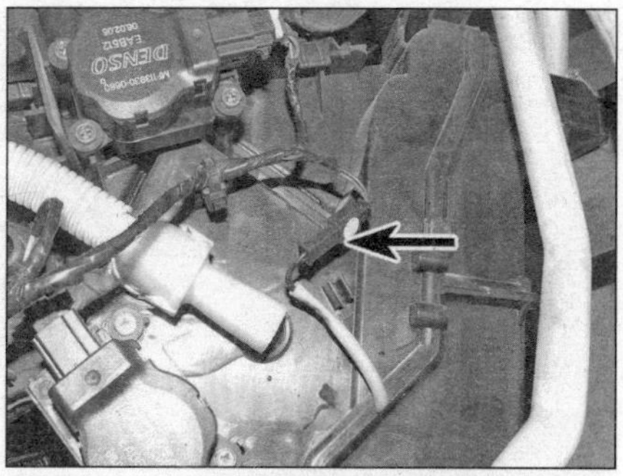

11.37 Disconnect the temperature sensor wiring plug (arrowed)

38 Release the clips and separate the heater matrix housing from the evaporator housing **(see illustrations)**.

39 Remove the temperature sensor (if

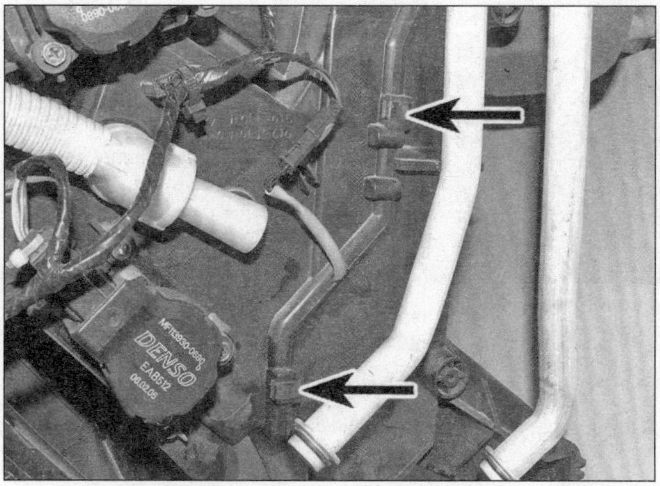

11.38a Release the various clips (arrowed) ...

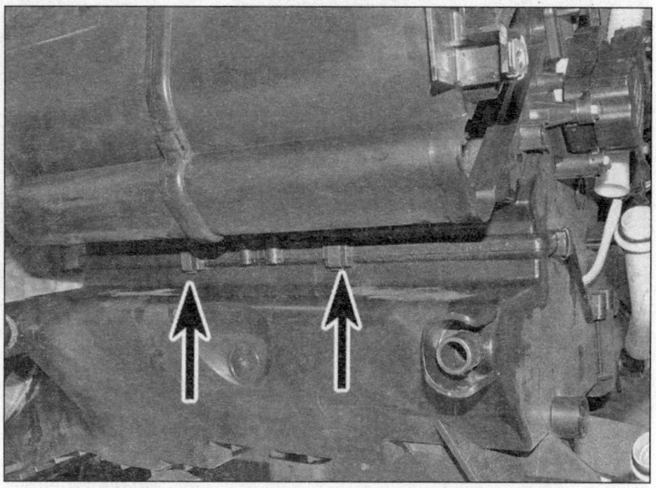

11.38b ... around the circumference (arrowed) ...

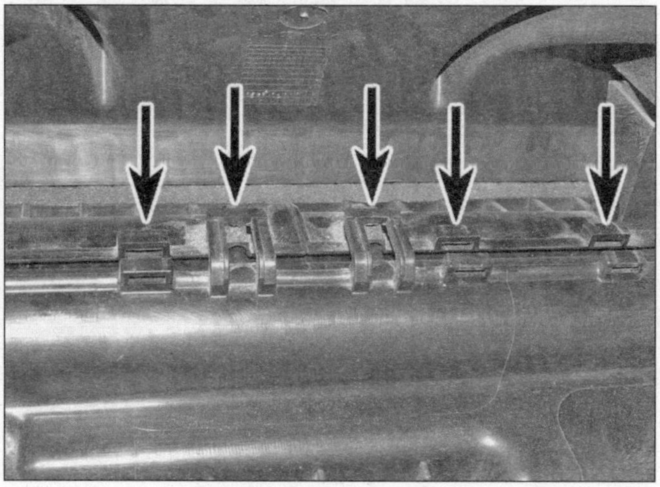

11.38c ... of the casing ...

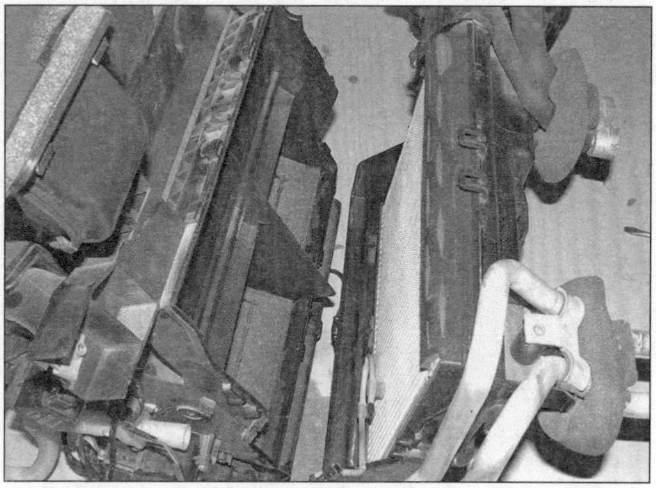

11.38d ... and separate the heater matrix housing from the evaporator housing

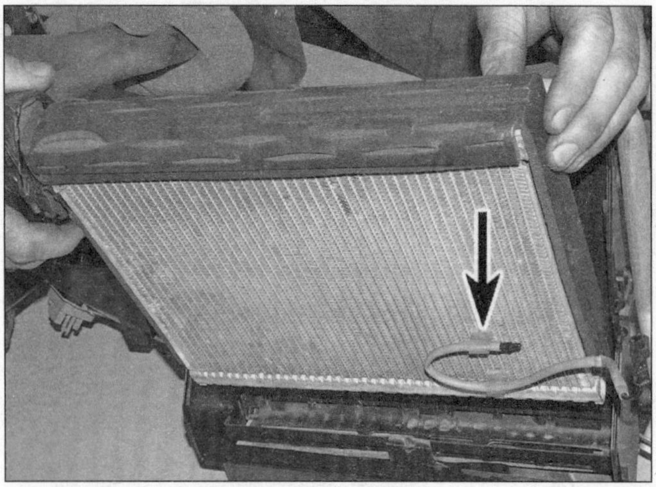

11.39 Lift the evaporator from place. Note the temperature sensor (arrowed)

11.49 The passenger cabin air temperature sensor is located to the left-hand side of the steering column

11.51 Prise up the facia speaker grille

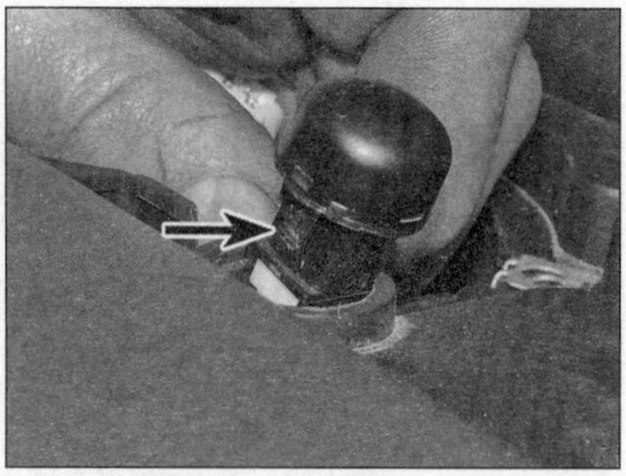

11.52 Carefully prise up the sensor to release the clips (arrowed)

required), and remove the evaporator **(see illustration)**.

40 Refitting is a reversal of removal.

Rear

41 Remove the rear heater matrix as described in Section 9.

42 Undo the screws, release the clips and separate the two halves of the heater unit assembly.

43 Lift the evaporator from place, and recover the end trim.

44 Refitting is a reversal of removal.

Ambient temperature sensor

45 Remove the radiator grille as described in Chapter 12, Section 29.

46 Unclip the sensor from the support bracket, and disconnect the wiring plug.

47 Refitting is a reversal of removal.

Passenger cabin air temperature sensor

48 With reference to Chapter 12, Section 28, remove the steering column shrouds, the steering column side trim panel, and the steering column gaiter panel.

49 Working underneath the facia, release the 2 retaining clips, pull the sensor from place, then disconnect the wiring plug and the hose **(see illustration)**.

50 Refitting is a reversal of removal.

Sunlight sensor

51 Carefully prise the facia upper section speaker grille from place **(see illustration)**.

52 Release the 2 clips and prise the sensor up from the centre of the facia **(see illustration)**. Disconnect the wiring plug as the sensor is removed.

53 Refitting is a reversal of removal.

Chapter 4 Part A:
Fuel and exhaust systems

Contents

Degrees of difficulty

Easy, suitable for novice with little experience	**Fairly easy,** suitable for beginner with some experience	**Fairly difficult,** suitable for competent DIY mechanic	**Difficult,** suitable for experienced DIY mechanic	**Very difficult,** suitable for expert DIY or professional

Specifications

General

System type	Direct injection, with Piezo crystal injectors, belt-driven high-pressure injection pump, tank-mounted lift pump (with integral regulator), fuel coolers. Injector timing controlled by ECM (electronic control module) (not adjustable)

Turbocharger

Type	Variable vane geometry with DC stepper motor control
Maximum boost pressure	ECM controlled

Fuel pump

Tank-mounted pressure	0.5 bar
Injection pump	1650 bar max.

Fuel level sensors

Front sensor:	
Resistance:	
Full tank	872 ohms
1/2 full	281 ohms
Reserve (17 litres) light on at	67 ohms
Empty	51.2 ohms
Rear sensor:	
Resistance:	
Full tank	768 ohms
1/2 full	267 ohms
Reserve (17 litres) light on at	150 ohms
Empty	75 ohms

Torque wrench settings

	Nm	lbf ft
Camshaft position sensor	10	7
Crankshaft position sensor	5	4
EGR valve securing bolts	10	7
Exhaust manifold:		
Nuts*	25	18
Studs*	13	10
Fuel diverter rail studs	23	17
Fuel injector bolts	10	7
High-pressure fuel pipe unions:		
Stage 1	15	11
Stage 2	35	26
Injection pump belt tensioner bolt*	25	18
Injection pump bolts*	23	17
Injection pump sprocket nut/bolt	50	37
Intake air shut-off valve bolt	10	7
Knock sensor	20	15
Oil feed pipe-to-cylinder block	10	7
Oil feed pipe-to-turbocharger banjo bolt	30	22
Oil pressure sensor	15	11
Oil return pipe bolts	10	7
Oil temperature sensor	10	7
Transmission crossmember	90	66
Transmission mounting bolt	175	129
Turbocharger-to-manifold bolts/nuts*	24	18
Turbocharger-to-manifold nuts*	24	18

** Do not re-use*

1 General information and precautions

The fuel system consists of a moulded fuel tank containing a module comprising of a fuel lift pump combined with 2 level sensors, integral pressure regulator, 6 Piezo injectors, belt-driven high-pressure injection pump, two fuel coolers, and a return system. A turbocharger, intercooler and EGR system (exhaust gas recirculation) is fitted to all models.

The engine management ECM (electronic control module) energises a relay which causes the low-pressure side (0.5 bar) of the pump to draw fuel through a coarse filter. A proportion of the low-pressure fuel passes through a restrictor to the jet pump in the swirl pot at the base of the pump, to keep the fuel there circulating. The integral regulator maintains fuel at this pressure. The fuel then passes to the main, external fuel filter, then on to the high-pressure fuel pump on the rear of the engine. This pump is driven by a belt, powered by a sprocket attached to the rear of the left-hand exhaust camshaft. Here, the pressurised fuel (up to 1650 bar) passes through the 'diverter' fuel rail, to a left- and right-hand common fuel rail. Each common fuel rail supplies 3 injectors, mounted centrally in the cylinder heads. The injectors are operated by Piezo crystals controlled by the ECM, based on information supplied by various sensors. The length of the injection period is determined by the ECM based on data concerning engine speed, intake manifold pressure, ambient air pressure, accelerator pedal position/rate of change, coolant temperature, fuel temperature, and airflow volume into the intake manifold. Any fuel not used by the injectors passes through the low-pressure return system, through an engine-mounted cooler, and an external fuel cooler, before passing to the fuel tank.

The EDC (electronic diesel control) system fitted, incorporates a 'drive by wire' system, where the traditional accelerator cable is replaced by an accelerator pedal position sensor. The position and rate-of-change of the accelerator pedal is reported by the position sensor to the ECM, which then adjusts the fuel injectors to deliver the required amount of fuel, and optimum combustion efficiency. The engine ECM also controls the preheating side of the system – refer to Chapter 5, Section 11, for more details.

The exhaust system incorporates a turbocharger, a particulate filter (depending on model) and an EGR system. Further detail of the emission control systems can be found in Chapter 4B, Section 1.

A turbocharger is fitted to the exhaust manifold, which uses the energy from the exhaust gases to spin a turbine on a shaft. The other end of the shaft is attached to another turbine which, when spinning, pressurises the air entering the intake manifold. This results in much improved engine torque and power output, whilst at the same time reducing fuel consumption and noise generation. The intake air leaving the turbocharger passes through an intercooler mounted in front of the coolant radiator. This cools the intake air, increasing its density, which further enhances the efficiency of the combustion process.

Should a fault develop, have the engine management systems self-diagnosis facility interrogated using a fault code reader. Consult a Land Rover dealer or specialist. The diagnostic socket is located in the driver's side lower facia panel **(see illustration)**.

Warning: It is necessary to take certain precautions when working on the fuel system components, particularly the fuel injectors. Before carrying out any operations on the fuel system, refer to the precautions given in 'Safety first!' at the beginning of this manual, and to any additional warning notes at the start of the relevant Sections. Absolute cleanliness is essential when working on the fuel system – do not allow dirt to enter when any part of the system is disconnected.

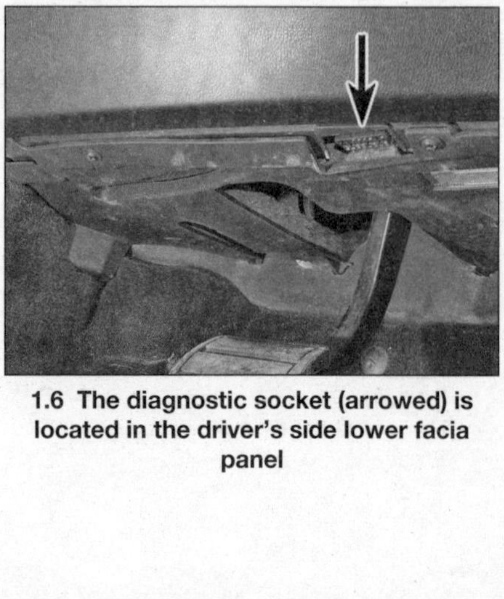

1.6 The diagnostic socket (arrowed) is located in the driver's side lower facia panel

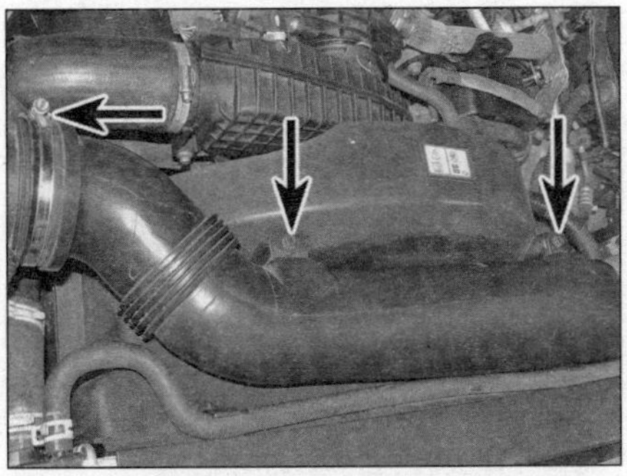

2.1 Intake duct screws and clamp (arrowed)

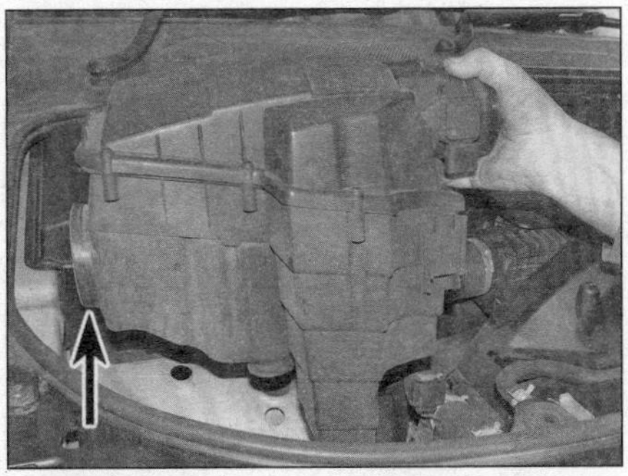

2.3 Pull the air cleaner housing upwards, noting how the intake locates in the inner wing (arrowed)

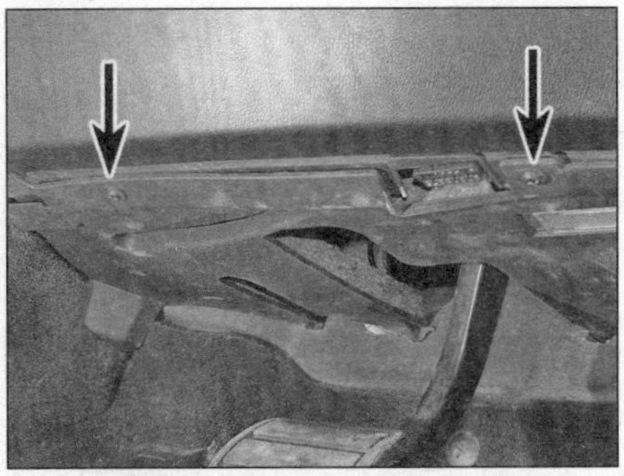

3.1 Undo the screws (arrowed) and remove the lower facia panel

2 Air cleaner assembly – removal and refitting

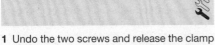

1 Undo the two screws and release the clamp securing the air intake duct **(see illustration)**.
2 Disconnect the wiring plug from the mass airflow sensor.
3 Pull the air cleaner assembly upwards, releasing it from the 2 mounting grommets **(see illustration)**.
4 Refitting is a reversal of removal.

3 Accelerator pedal – removal and refitting

Removal

1 Working in the driver's footwell, undo the fasteners and remove the trim panel for access to the pedals. Disconnect the wiring plug as the panel is withdrawn **(see illustration)**.
2 Slide back the locking catch, depress the clip and disconnect the wiring plug **(see illustration)**.
3 Undo the 3 nuts and manoeuvre the accelerator pedal assembly from position **(see illustration)**.
4 If required, undo the 3 nuts/bolts and detach the pedal/sensor from the bracket. Note that the position sensor is integral with the pedal assembly and no attempt should be made to disassemble it.

Refitting

5 Refitting is a reversal of removal.

4 Fuel coolers – removal and refitting

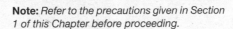

Note: *Refer to the precautions given in Section 1 of this Chapter before proceeding.*

Removal

Engine-mounted cooler

1 The engine-mounted cooler is integral with the oil cooler, located between the cylinder heads, in the V of the engine. Engine coolant circulates around the cooler to regulate the temperature of the fuel in the return circuit.
2 Removal of the cooler is described within the oil cooler removal procedure – see Chapter 2, Section 15.

External cooler

3 The external fuel cooler is located under the vehicle, to the right-hand side of the engine. Raise the front of the vehicle and support it securely on axle stands. Remove the engine undershield.
4 Note their fitted locations, then depress the release buttons, and disconnect the fuel hoses from the cooler **(see illustration)**. Be prepared for fuel spillage. Plug all fuel cooler/hose openings, it is essential that the fuel system is not contaminated by dirt, etc.
5 Undo the bolt and lift the cooler upwards to disengage the mounting lugs.

Refitting

6 Refitting is a reversal of removal.

5 Fuel system – priming and bleeding

Note: *Refer to the precautions given in Section 1 before proceeding.*

1 It is necessary to purge the air from the system if the vehicle runs out of fuel, or if any of the following components are removed, disconnected or renewed:
a) Fuel tank.
b) Low-pressure fuel hoses/pipes.
c) Fuel filter element.
d) Fuel coolers.
e) Injection pump.
f) Fuel rail pressure sensor.
g) Fuel injector.
2 Switch off the ignition and wait for 30 seconds for any residual fuel pressure to dissipate.

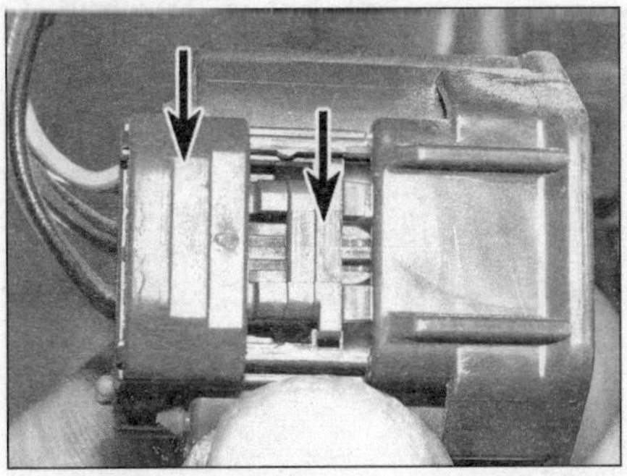

3.2 Slide back the locking catch (arrowed) and depress the clip (arrowed)

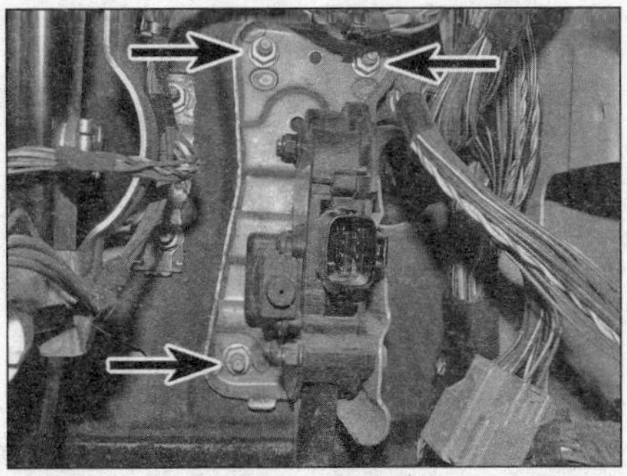

3.3 Accelerator pedal assembly retaining nuts (arrowed)

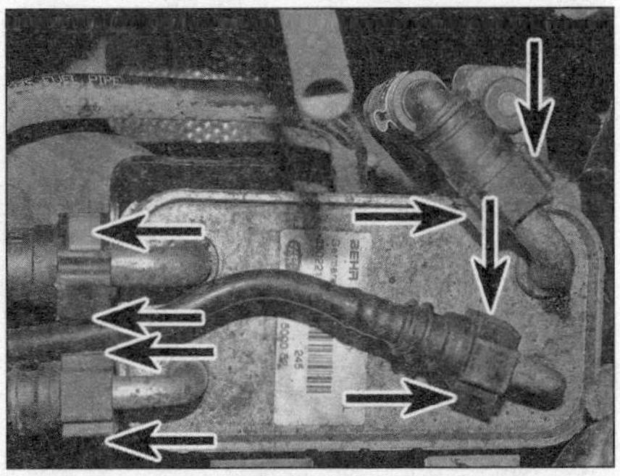

4.4 The release buttons are located each side of the connectors (arrowed)

5.3 Pull the engine top cover upwards to release it

3 Remove the engine oil filler cap, then pull the engine cover upwards and remove it **(see illustration)**.

4 The system is bled via a Schrader valve on the fuel rail. Remove the plastic cap from the valve **(see illustration)**.

5 Land Rover tool No. 310-116 screws onto the valve, and has an integral tap to open, and close the valve. In the absence of this tool, depress the valve core with a screwdriver to open it. Be prepared for fuel spillage.

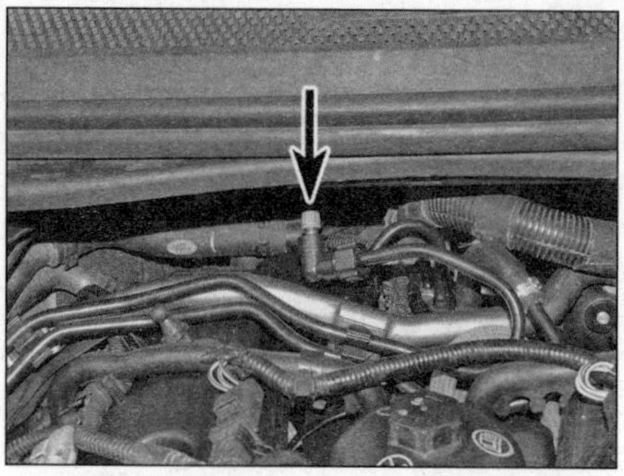

5.4 The bleed valve (arrowed) is located at the rear of the engine compartment

6 Open the valve, and turn the ignition switch to the 'on' position for 25 seconds. The fuel mounted pump will be heard to operate.

7 Repeat this procedure until clean, bubble-free fuel is seen to emerge through the pipe. Whilst the fuel is still pumping, close the Schrader valve. Remove the tool, and refit the cap. **Note:** *If a new fuel injection pump has been fitted, repeat the procedure in paragraph 6 at least 5 times to ensure the pump is fully primed.*

8 Start the engine and allow it to idle for at least 2 minutes to allow any trapped air to be purged.

Warning: Do not crank the engine for more than 20 seconds at a time. Allow the starter motor/ battery to rest for a few minutes.

9 Mop-up any spilled fuel and refit the engine top cover.

6 Fuel level sensors and pump – removal and refitting

Note: *Refer to the precautions given in Section 1 before proceeding.*

Removal

1 Remove the fuel tank as described in Section 7.

2 Note their fitted positions then, using 3 small screwdrivers, spread apart the 3 clips and disconnect the fuel supply and return hoses from the access cover. Where applicable, disconnect the hose for the fuel-burning heater **(see illustrations)**.

3 Slacken the screw and remove the cover clamp **(see illustrations)**.

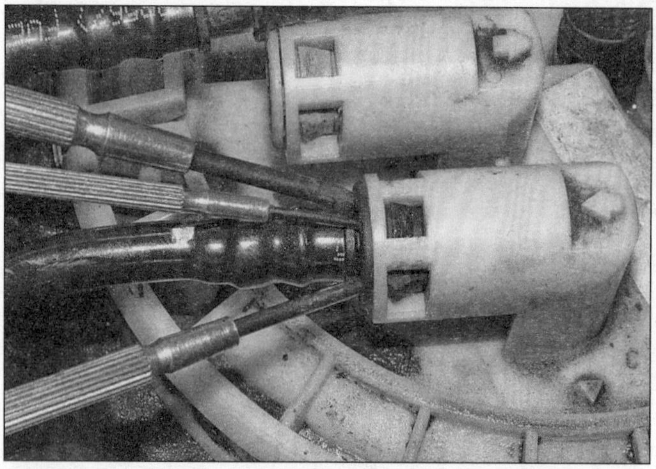

6.2a Spread apart the clips and disconnect the hoses from the access cover

6.2b Disconnect the fuel burning heater hose (arrowed)

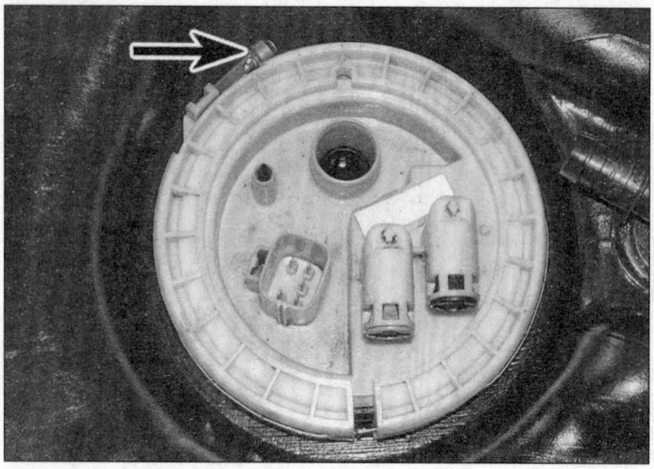

6.3a Slacken the screw (arrowed) ...

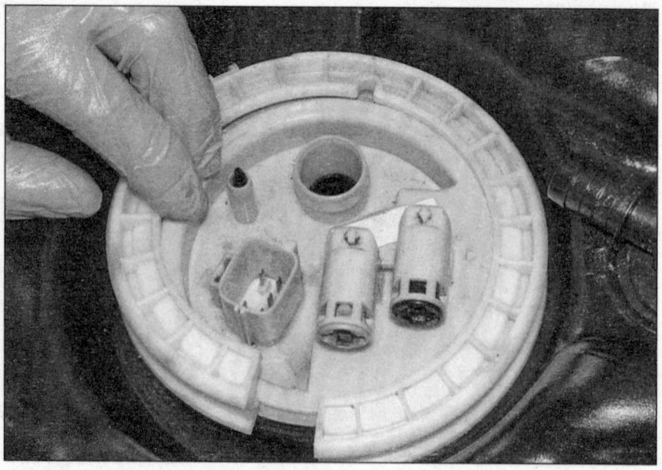

6.3b ... and remove the cover clamp

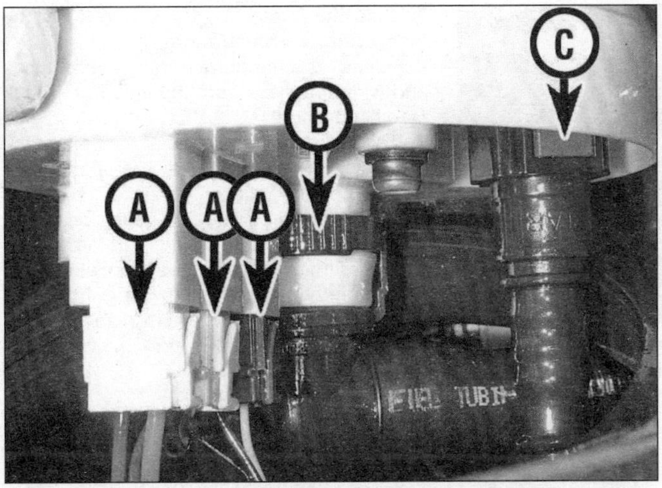

6.4a Disconnect the wiring plugs (A), squeeze together the sides of the collar (B), disconnect the vent hose, then depress the release button (C) and disconnect the fuel hose

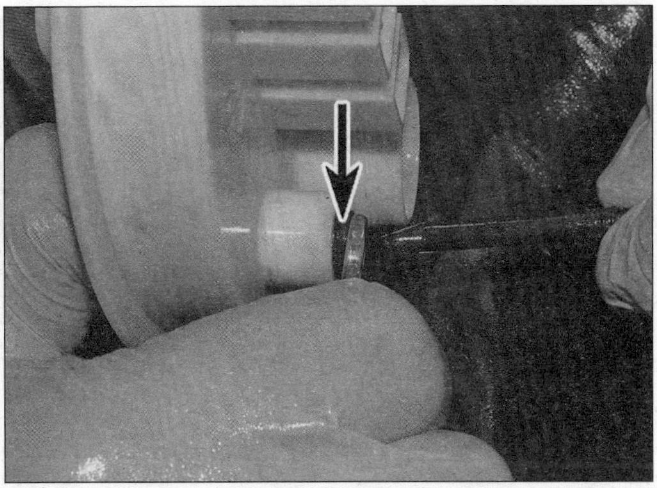

6.4b Push up the collar (arrowed) and disconnect the fuel-burning heater hose

4 Lift the access cover, and disconnect the fuel hose, vent hose and the 3 wiring plugs from the underside of the cover. On models with a fuel-burning heater, press up the collar and pull the hose from the cover **(see illustrations)**. Remove the cover and discard the seal – a new one must be fitted.

5 Release the strap securing the pump module, unclip the regulator and disconnect the 2 fuel hoses **(see illustrations)**.

6 Manoeuvre the regulator through the access hole, followed by the pump module **(see illustrations)**. Take care not to damage the float arm.

7 The rear level sensor is attached to the pump module. To remove the sensor, carefully prise the base of the sensor from the pump module housing, and slide the sensor downwards **(see illustrations)**.

8 The front level sensor is attached to the internal framework within the tank. Reach through the module aperture, and pull the retaining clip outwards then rearwards to release the sensor. Disconnect the sensor wiring plug as it becomes accessible. **Note:** *Access to the sensor is extremely limited – it's located on the left-hand side of the tank and is only just reachable by someone with long, thin arms.*

Refitting

9 Refitting is a reversal of removal, but fit the new sealing ring before reconnecting the

6.5a Release the strap and unclip the hose (arrowed) ...

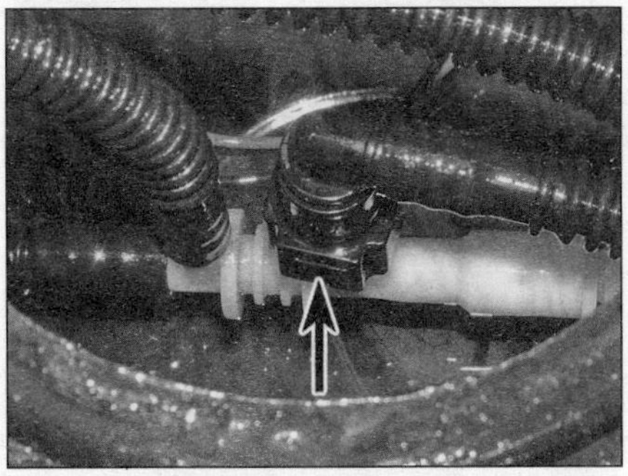

6.5b ... depress the button (arrowed) and disconnect the hose

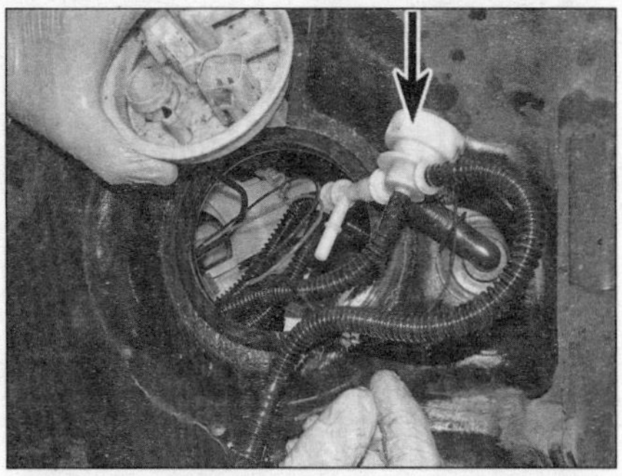

6.6a Unclip the regulator (arrowed) and manoeuvre it through the access hole ...

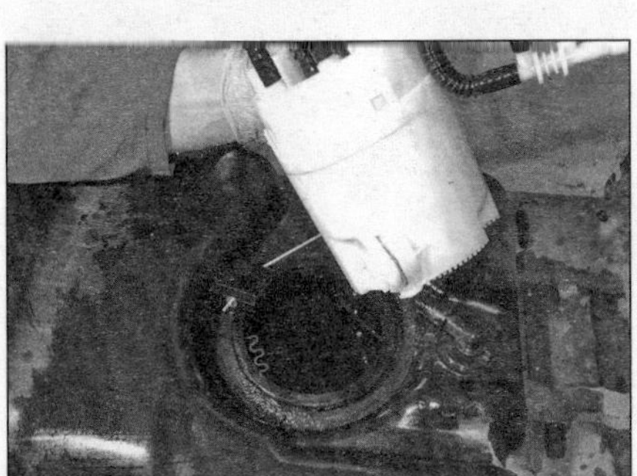

6.6b ... followed by the pump module

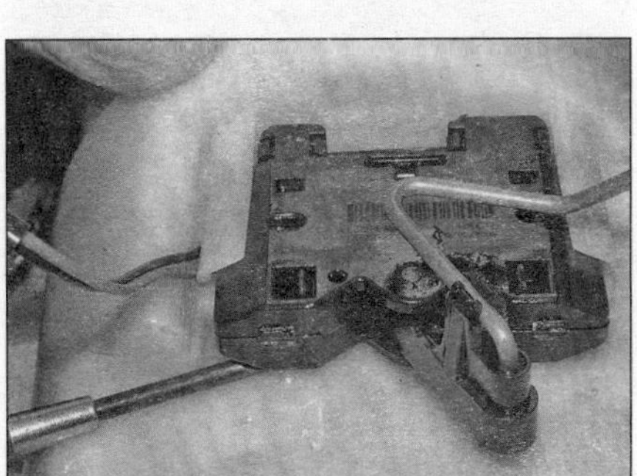

6.7a Carefully prise the base of the sensor from the housing ...

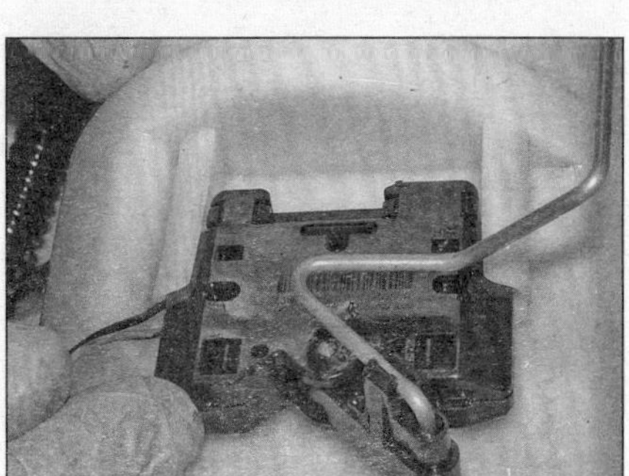

6.7b ... and slide it downwards

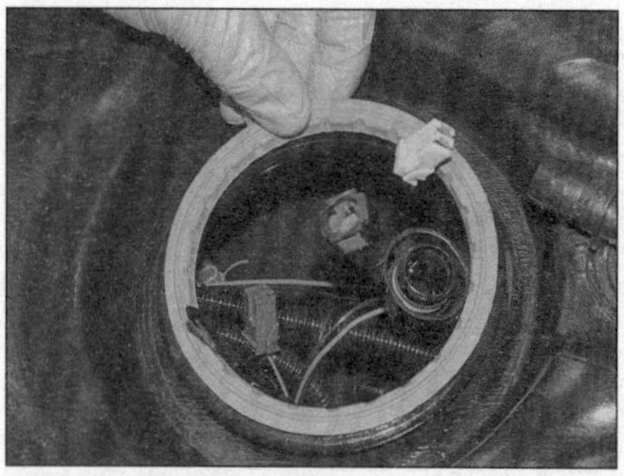

6.9a Renew the sealing ring

hoses and wiring plugs to the underside of the access cover **(see illustrations)**. Ensure that the marks on the access cover align with those on the tank.

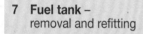

7 Fuel tank – removal and refitting

Note: *Refer to the precautions given in Section 1 before proceeding.*

Removal

1 As no drain plug is fitted to the base of the moulded tank, this procedure is best performed when the tank is almost empty. If this is not possible, use a siphoning device

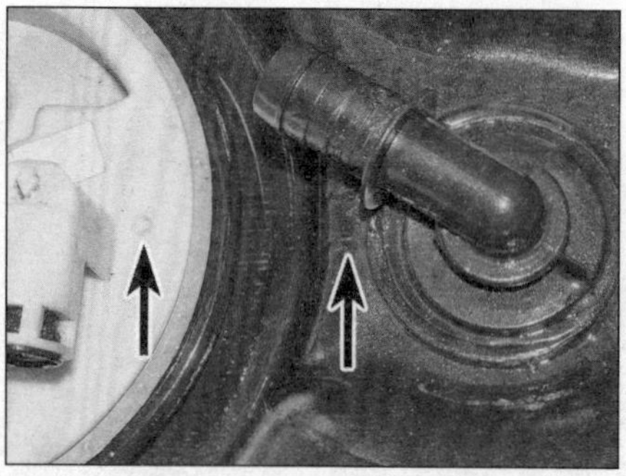

6.9b Align the mark on the cover with the mark on the tank (arrowed)

to remove as much fuel from the tank as possible.

2 Raise the rear of the vehicle and support it securely on axle stands (see *Jacking and vehicle support*).

3 Disconnect the battery negative lead as described in Chapter 5, Section 4.

4 Undo the nuts/bolts and remove the heat shield alongside the fuel tank **(see illustration)**.

5 Prise off the tamperproof cap (where fitted), then slacken the fuel filler neck hose clip. Disconnect the hose from the tank **(see illustration)**.

6 Position a workshop jack under the fuel tank, with a length of wood on the jack head to prevent any damage to the tank. Take the weight of the tank.

7 Undo the 6 retaining bolts, and lower the tank a little **(see illustration)**.

8 Release the handbrake cable, vent hoses and wiring harness from the side of the tank **(see illustration)**.

9 Disconnect the fuel hoses at the front of the tank **(see illustration)**. Plug the openings to prevent contamination.

10 Clean the area around the vent hoses at the pump module access cover, then disconnect the hoses from the cover **(see illustration)**.

11 Disconnect the wiring plug from the access cover, and with the help of an assistant, manoeuvre the tank from under the vehicle.

Refitting

12 Refitting is a reversal of removal.

8 Fuel injectors – testing, removal and refitting

Warning: Exercise extreme caution when working on the fuel injectors. Never expose the hands, or any part of the body, to injector spray, as the high working pressure can cause the fuel to penetrate the skin, with possibly fatal results. You are strongly advised to have any work which involves testing the injectors under pressure carried out by a Land Rover dealer or diesel injection specialist. Refer to the precautions given in Section 1 of this Chapter before proceeding.

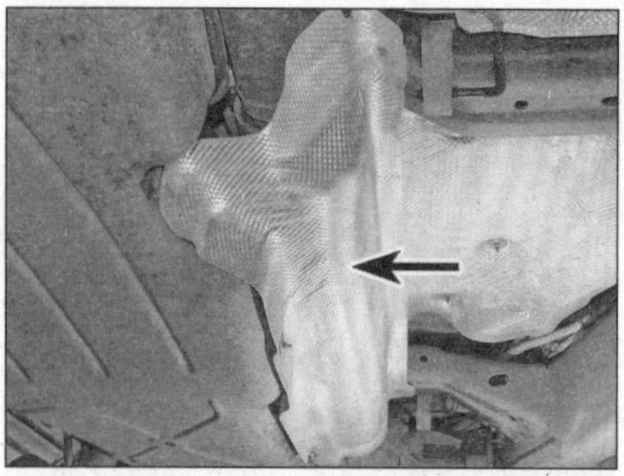

7.4 Remove the heat shield (arrowed)

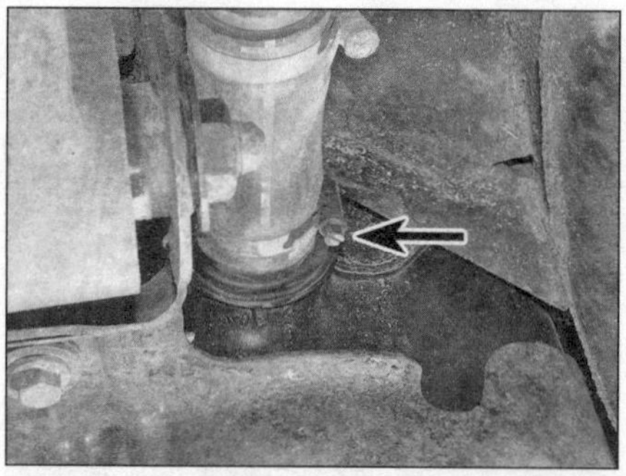

7.5 Slacken the filler hose clamp (arrowed)

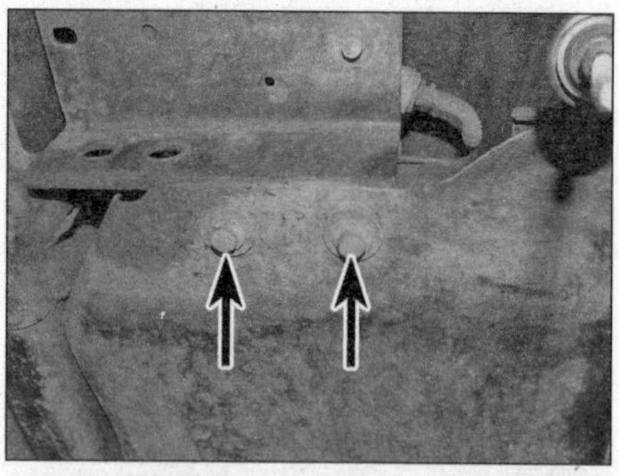

7.7 Undo the tank retaining bolts (front bolts arrowed)

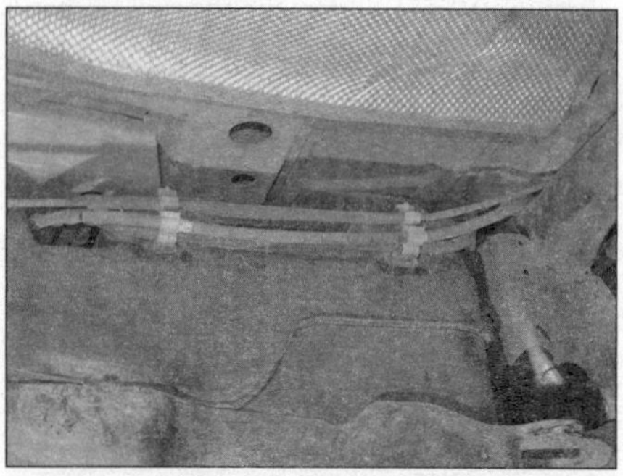

7.8 Release the handbrake cable, hoses and wiring harness from the side of the tank

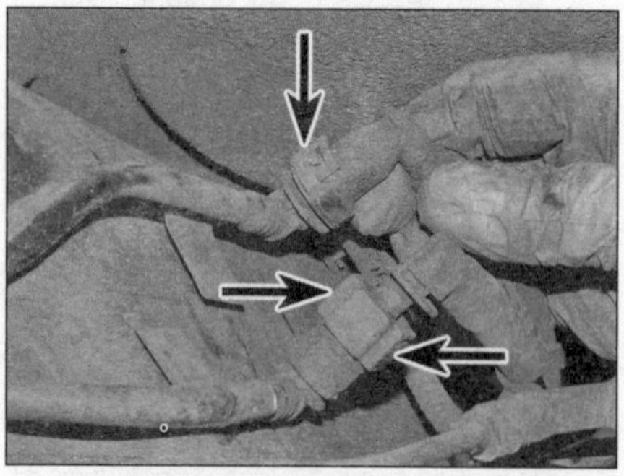

7.9 Prise out the clip (arrowed), depress the release buttons (arrowed) and disconnect the fuel pipes at the front of the tank

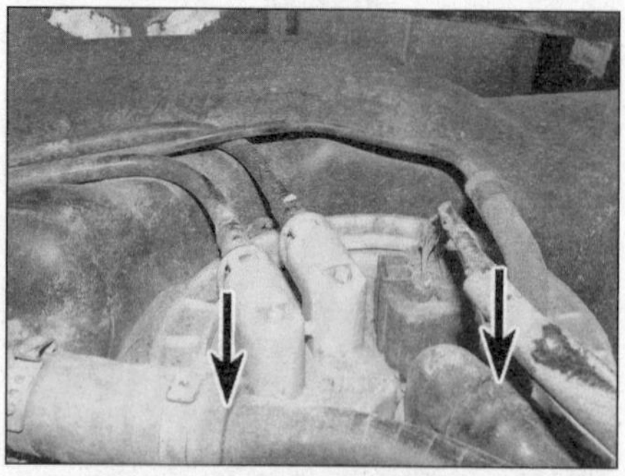

7.10 Disconnect the vent hoses (arrowed) from the access cover

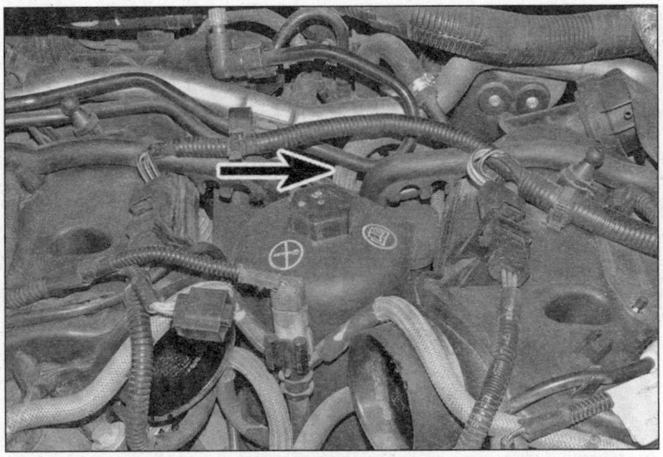
8.4 Disconnect the low-pressure fuel hoses (arrowed) at the fuel pump/rail

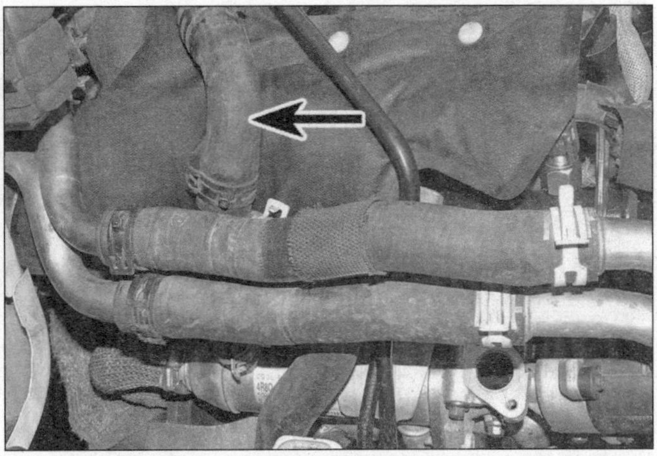
8.5 Disconnect the EGR coolant crossover hose each side (arrowed)

Testing

1 Injectors deteriorate with prolonged use, and it is reasonable to expect them to need reconditioning or renewal after 100 000 miles or so. Accurate testing, overhaul and calibration of the injectors must be left to a specialist.

Removal

Note: *Whenever working on any part of the fuel system, High standards of cleanliness must be observed. The smallest amount of foreign material could cause extensive damage to fuel system/engine components. Clean around the area before opening any part of the system. Plug all openings to prevent contamination.*

2 Remove the battery as described in Chapter 5, Section 4.

3 Remove the engine oil filler cap, then pull up and remove the engine top cover **(see illustration 5.3)**.

4 Depress the release buttons, and disconnect the low-pressure fuel hoses from the fuel injection pump at the rear of the engine **(see illustration)**.

5 Clamp the EGR coolant hoses to minimise loss, then disconnect both EGR coolant crossover hoses **(see illustration)**.

6 Lever over the locking catches, and disconnect the 4 engine harness wiring plugs at the rear of the main battery tray location **(see illustrations)**. Unclip the harness from the bulkhead.

7 Undo the retaining bolts and remove the EGR coolant crossover pipe **(see illustration)**.

8 Remove the acoustic pads from each cylinder bank **(see illustration)**.

9 Release the clips and disconnect the wiring plug from each injector **(see illustration)**.

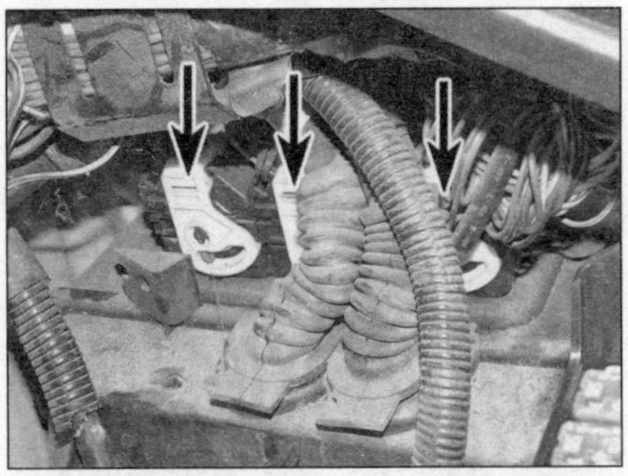
8.6a Lever over the catches (arrowed) and disconnect the 3 wiring plugs at the left-hand rear of the engine compartment ...

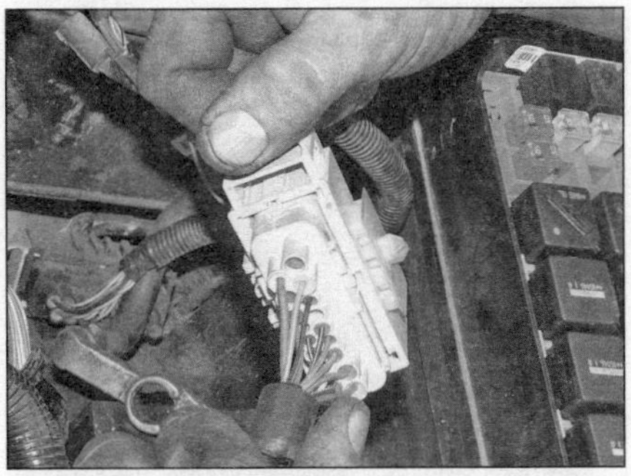
8.6b ... and the connector at the rear of the battery tray

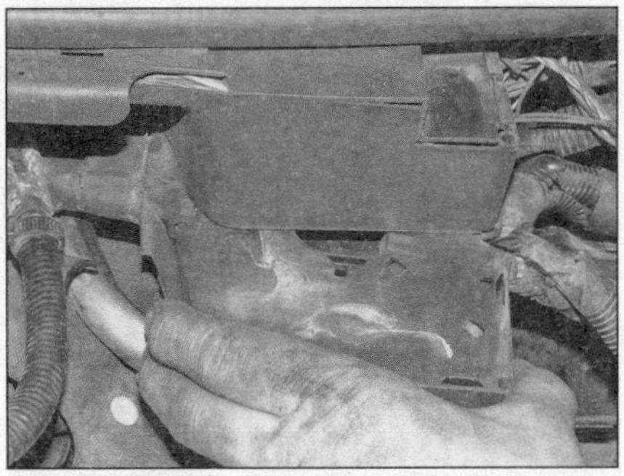
8.6c Unclip the harness block from the bulkhead

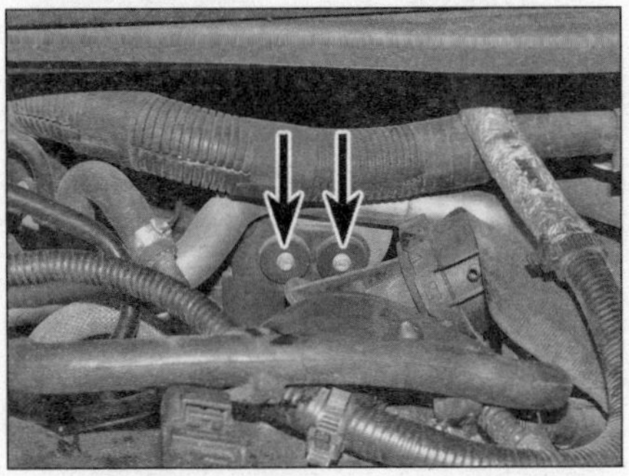
8.7 Undo the bolts (arrowed) and remove the EGR coolant crossover pipe. The bolts are inserted from the rear

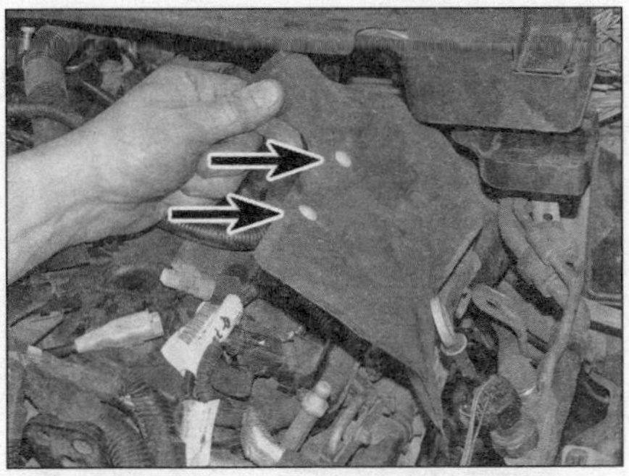
8.8 Release the clips (arrowed) and remove the acoustic pad each side

8.9 Prise up the clip and disconnect the injector wiring plugs

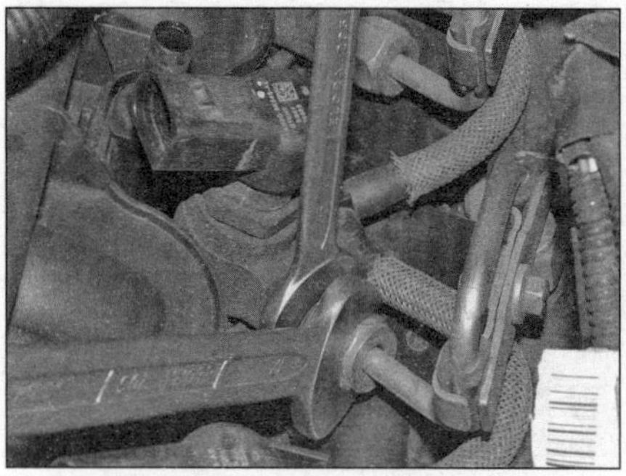

8.11a Slacken the union nuts – counterholding with a second spanner ...

8.11b ... and remove the high-pressure pipes (arrowed)

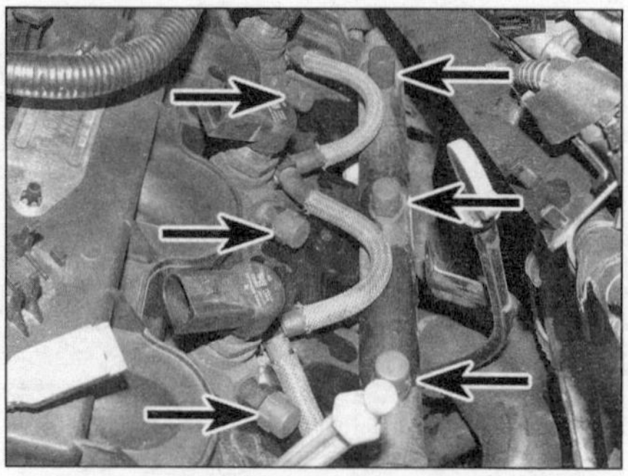

8.11c Plug the openings (arrowed) to prevent contamination

10 Unclip the injector wiring harnesses guide trays and move them to one side.

11 Using a second open-ended spanner to counterhold, slacken the unions and remove the high-pressure fuel pipes between the common fuel rails and the injectors **(see illustrations)**. Keep the pipe in contact with the injector and fuel rail until both unions are undone and the area around the pipes/unions cleaned. Plug/cover the openings to prevent contamination. Discard the pipes – new ones must be fitted.

12 Prise out the clips and disconnect the fuel return hoses from the injectors **(see illustrations)**. Discard the clips – new ones must be fitted. Inspect the hose O-ring seals, and renew if they show any signs of damage or deterioration.

13 Undo the retaining bolts, and remove each injector's clamp spacer **(see illustrations)**.

14 In order to remove the injectors, they must be pulled straight upwards sharply. Twist and pull the injectors from position. The injectors will normally pull up with hand-force alone. However, if necessary, Land Rover special tools 303-1127 are intended for this task, and may be available from Land Rover dealers. Screw the tool's studs into the clamp retaining bolt holes, then fit the tool's extractors over the studs, and locate the crossbar of the tool under the extractors. Ensure the crossbar is correctly located in the injector body. Evenly tighten the bolts on the extractors, and pull each injector from the cylinder heads **(see illustrations)**. Discard the clamps and sealing washers – new ones must be fitted. **Note:** *If the injectors are to be re-used, store them in their fitted order, so they can be refitted to their original positions.* No further dismantling of the injectors is recommended. If the injectors are not to be refitted for some time, cover the holes in the cylinder head to prevent dirt ingress. Land Rover insist that not attempt be made to clean the injector nozzles.

Refitting

15 Prior to refitting the injectors, the sealing washer, clamp and return hose clip on each

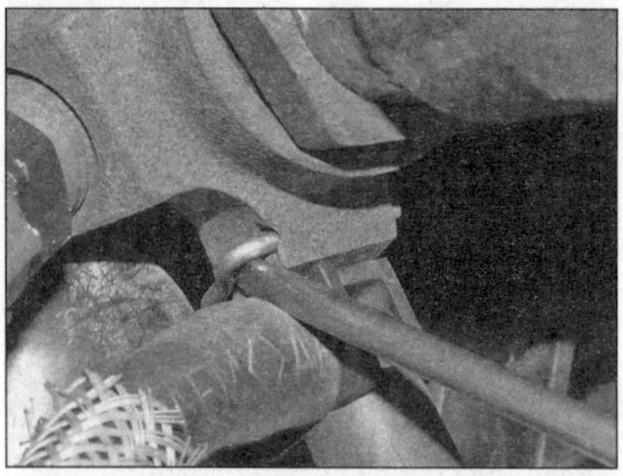

8.12a Prise out the clip and pull the return hoses from the injectors

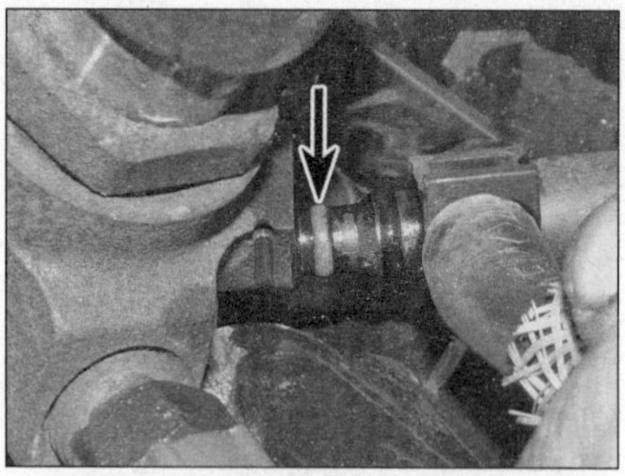

8.12b Check the condition of the O-ring seals (arrowed)

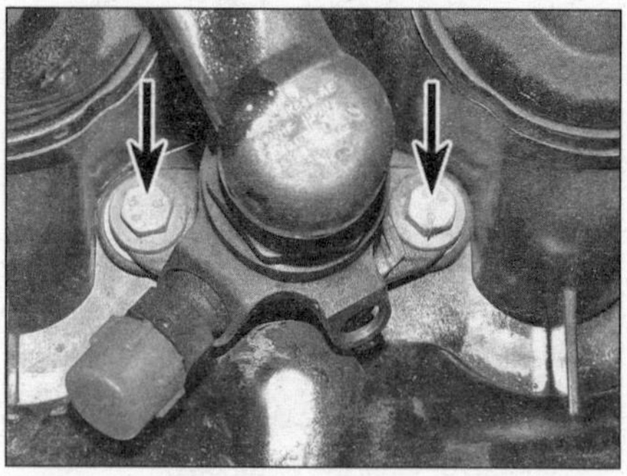

8.13a Remove the injector retaining bolts (arrowed) ...

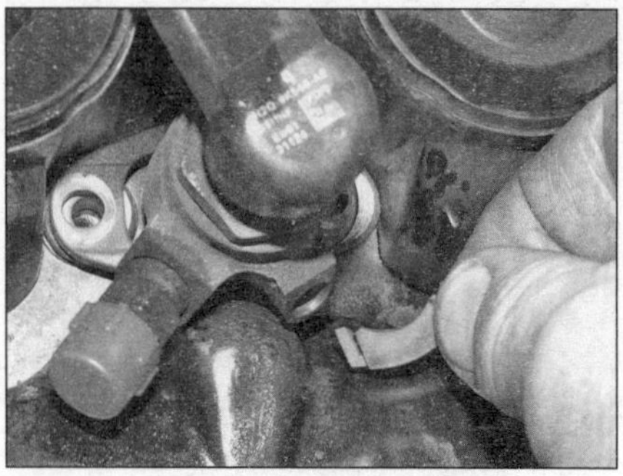

8.13b ... and the plastic spacer above the clamp

8.14a The injectors will normally pull up by hand

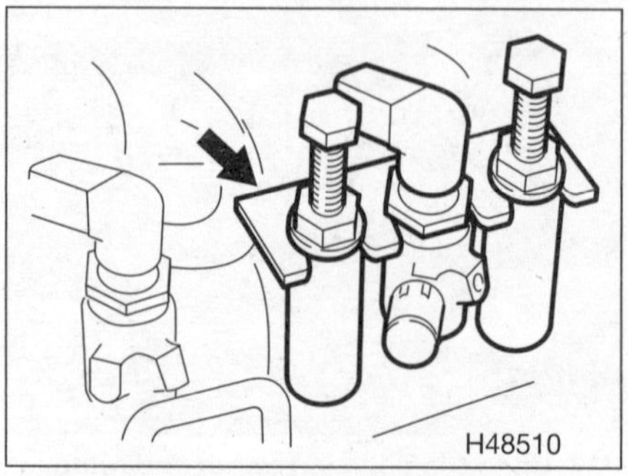

8.14b Injector removal using Land Rover special tools (arrowed)

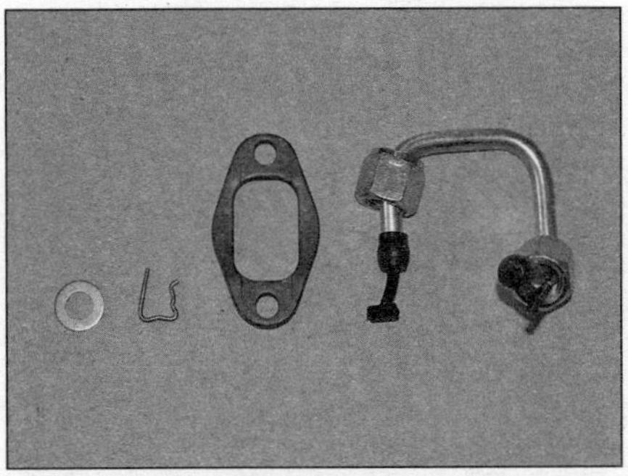
8.15a New sealing washers, clamps, pipes and return hose clips are supplied in a kit from Land Rover

8.15b Fit the new clamp ...

8.15c ... refit the spacer ...

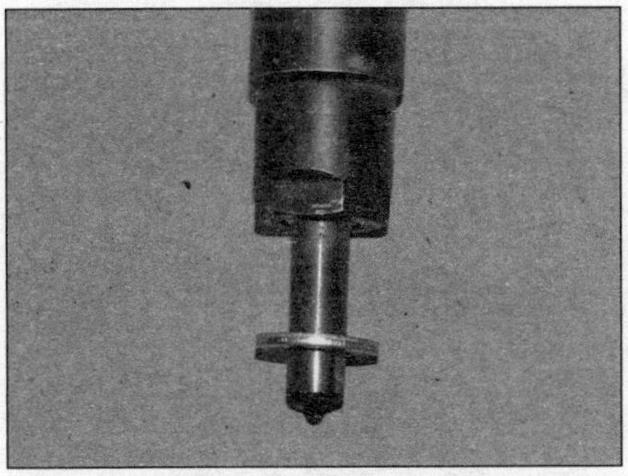
8.15d ... the new sealing washer ...

8.15e ... return hose clip ...

8.15f ... then fit the injector

injector must be renewed. Renew these components, then fit the injectors into the cylinder head **(see illustrations)**. If the original injectors are being refitted, ensure they are returned to their original locations.

16 With the injectors correctly fitted, tighten the retaining bolts to the specified torque.

17 Apply a little petroleum jelly to the fuel return hose O-ring seals, then reconnect the hose to each injector.

18 Transfer the brace from each old high-pressure pipe to the new ones **(see illustration)**.

19 Position the new high-pressure fuel pipes against the ports on the common rail and injector. Maintain pressure, holding the pipes olives against the ports, then finger-tighten the unions.

20 Using a second open-ended spanner to counterhold, tighten the pipe unions in the following sequence:

a) Pipe-to-injector union – Stage 1 torque.
b) Pipe-to-common rail union – Stage 1 torque.
c) Pipe-to-injector union – Stage 2 torque.
d) Pipe-to-common rail union – Stage 2 torque.

21 The remainder of refitting is a reversal of removal, noting the following points:

a) Top-up the cooling system as described in Weekly checks.
b) Bleed the fuel system as described in Section 5.

9 Air shut-off valve – removal and refitting

Note: *Refer to the precautions given in Section 1 of this Chapter before proceeding.*

Removal

1 Remove the oil filler cap, then pull up and remove the plastic cover from the top of the engine **(see illustration 5.3)**.

2 Disconnect the wiring plugs from the shut-off valve, and release the fuel temperature sensor **(see illustrations)**.

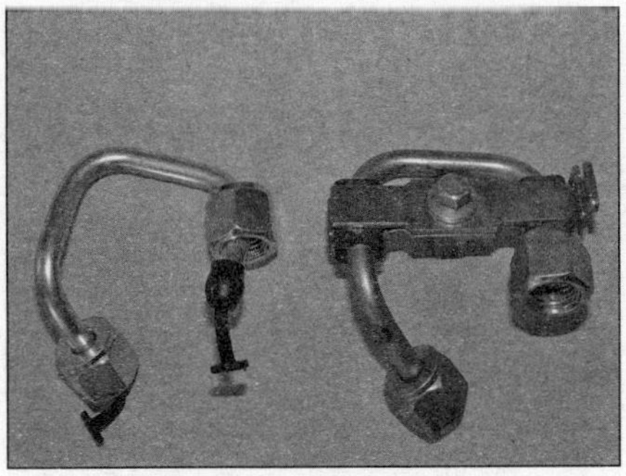
8.18 Transfer the brace from the old pipe to the new

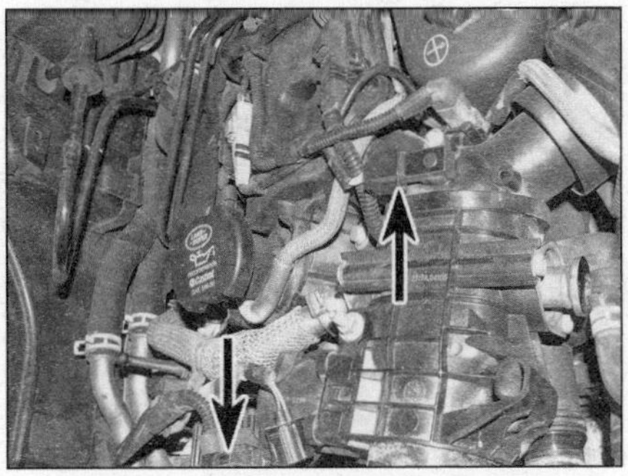
9.2a Disconnect the wiring plugs (arrowed) ...

9.2b ... and slide up the fuel temperature sensor

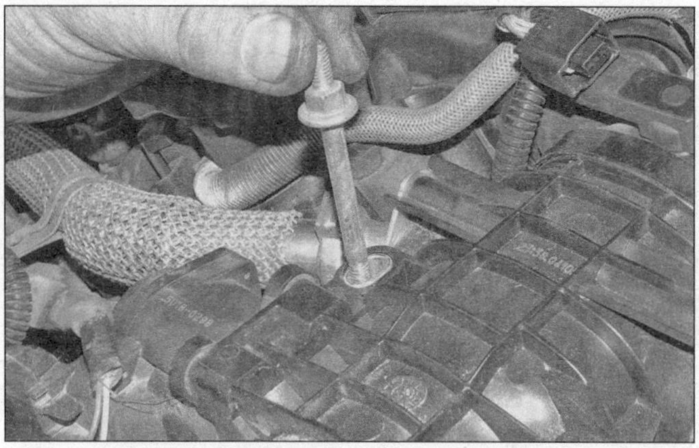

9.3 Undo the shut-off valve retaining bolt

9.4 Release the clamps securing the EGR pipes to the valve

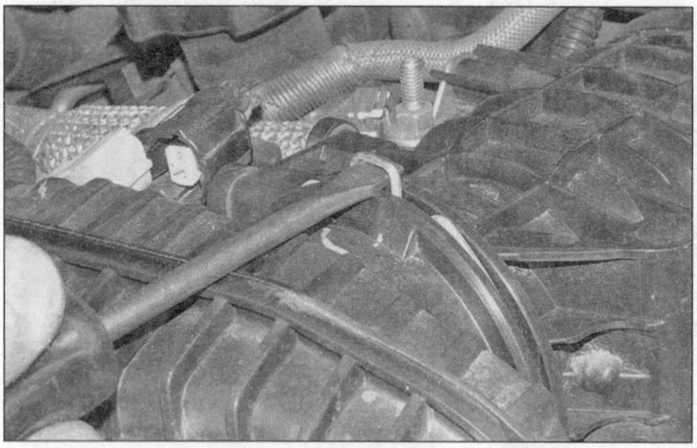

9.5 Air intake elbow-to-valve retaining clip

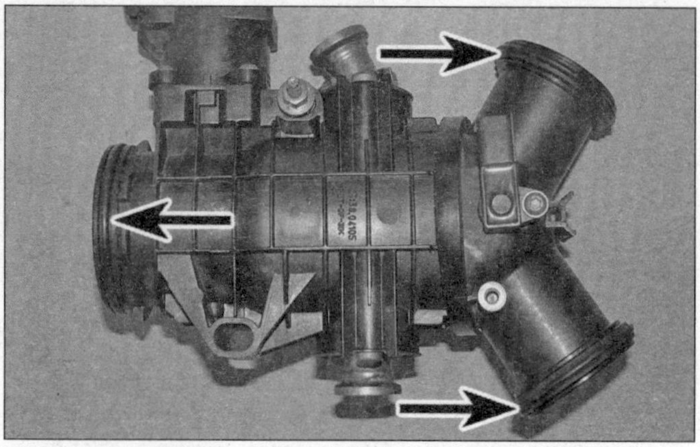

9.6 Check the condition of the O-ring seals (arrowed)

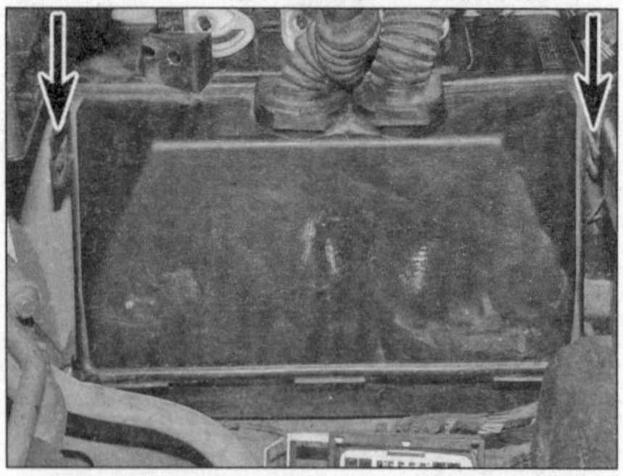

10.2a Release the clip (arrowed) each side ...

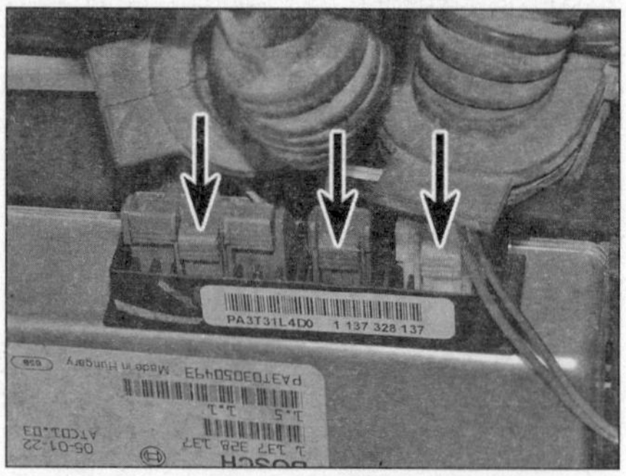

10.2b ... depress the clips (arrowed), disconnect the wiring plugs ...

10.2c ... then release the clips (arrowed) and remove the 4x4 ECM

10.3 Lever over the catches (arrowed) and disconnect the ECM wiring plugs

3 Remove the shut-off valve retaining bolt **(see illustration)**.

4 Release the clamps and disconnect the left- and right-hand EGR tubes from the valve **(see illustration)**.

5 Prise up the clip, undo the retaining bolt and detach the air intake elbow from the valve **(see illustration)**.

6 Manoeuvre the shut-off valve from place. Examine the valve O-ring seals, and renew if they show signs of damage or deterioration **(see illustration)**.

Refitting

7 Refitting is a reversal of removal.

10 Engine management electronic components – removal and refitting

ECM (electronic control module)

1 Remove the battery as described in Chapter 5, Section 4, then wait at least 10 minutes for any residual electrical energy to dissipate.

2 Release the clip each side, pull the top edge forwards, and lift the 4x4 ECM cover from place. Disconnect the wiring plugs, depress the 2 clips and remove the 4x4 ECM **(see illustrations)**.

3 Starting with the plug nearest the left-hand

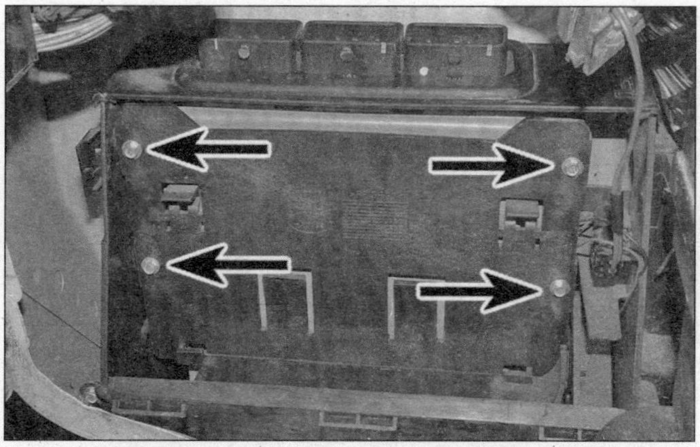

10.4 ECM securing plate retaining bolts (arrowed)

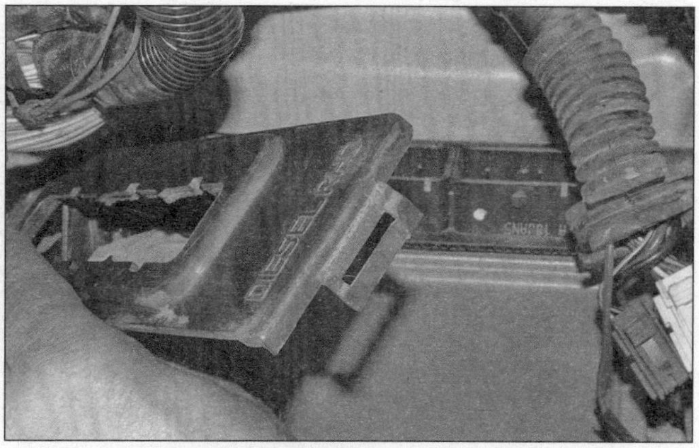

10.5a Unclip the cover ...

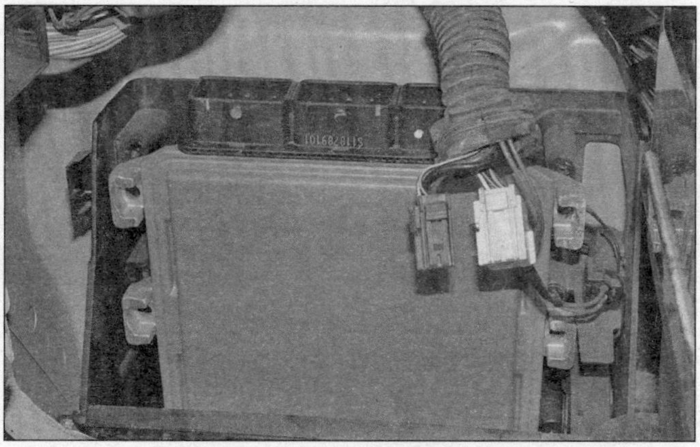

10.5b ... and remove the ECM

10.5c Note the cooling fan (arrowed)

side, lever over the locking catches, and disconnect the wiring plugs from the ECM **(see illustration)**.

4 Undo the 4 retaining bolts and remove the ECM securing plate **(see illustration)**.

5 Lift up the cover and remove the ECM **(see illustrations)**. Note the cooling fan in the left-hand lower corner of the ECM box.

6 Refitting is a reversal of removal. Note that if a new ECM is fitted, it must to be calibrated using Land Rover test equipment (T4) – refer to a Land Rover dealer or specialist.

Fuel temperature sensor

7 Remove the engine oil filler cap, then pull up and remove the plastic cover from the top of the engine.

8 Disconnect the battery negative lead as described in Chapter 5, Section 4.

9 The sensor is fitted to the air shut-off valve located at the front, top of the engine. Disconnect the sensor wiring plug **(see illustration)**.

10 Thoroughly clean the area around the sensor, release the clip each side, and pull the sensor upwards from place. Discard the O-ring seal – a new one must be fitted. Be prepared for fuel spillage, and plug the open fuel port to prevent dirt ingress.

11 Refitting is a reversal of removal, remembering to fit a new O-ring seal.

Mass airflow sensor (MAF)

12 Remove the air cleaner as described in Section 2.

13 Undo the screw and detach the sensor from the air cleaner **(see illustration)**. Examine the O-ring seal, and renew if it shows signs of damage or deterioration.

14 Refitting is a reversal of removal.

Manifold absolute pressure sensor (MAP)

15 Remove the engine oil filler cap, then pull up and remove the cover from the top of the engine **(see illustration 5.3)**.

16 Disconnect the sensor wiring plug **(see illustration)**.

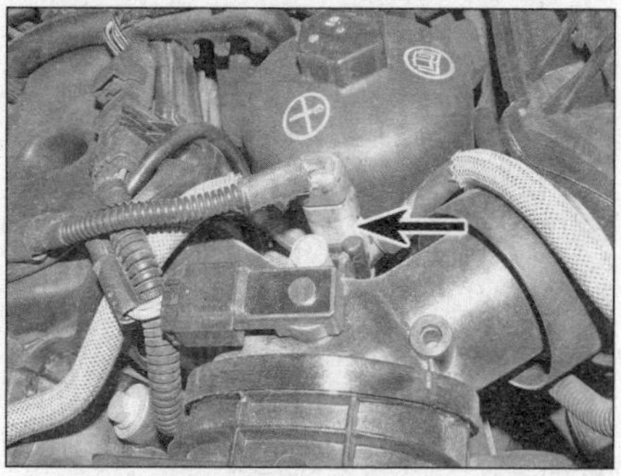

10.9 Fuel temperature sensor (arrowed)

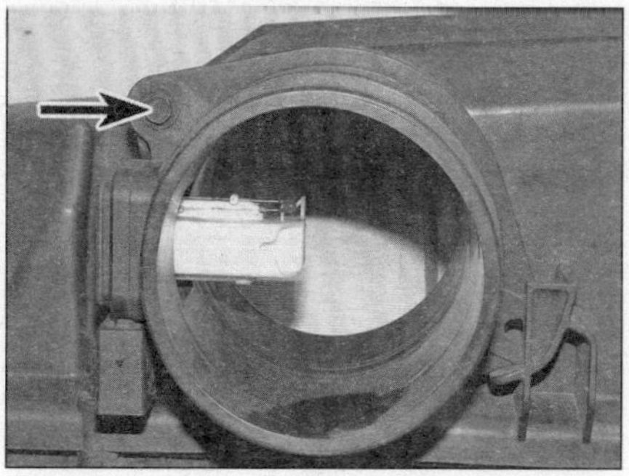

10.13 Mass airflow sensor retaining screw (arrowed)

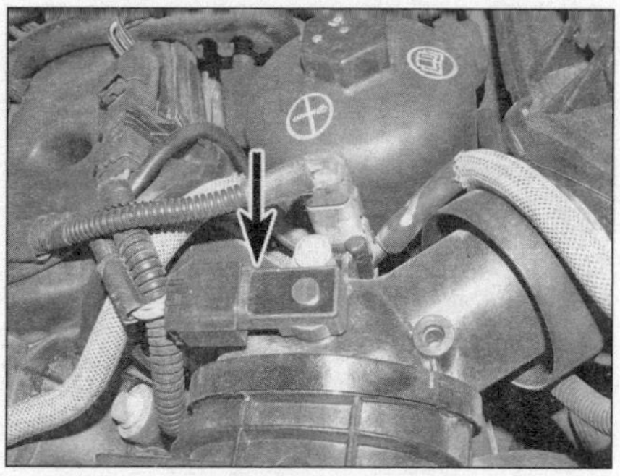

10.16 Manifold absolute pressure sensor (arrowed)

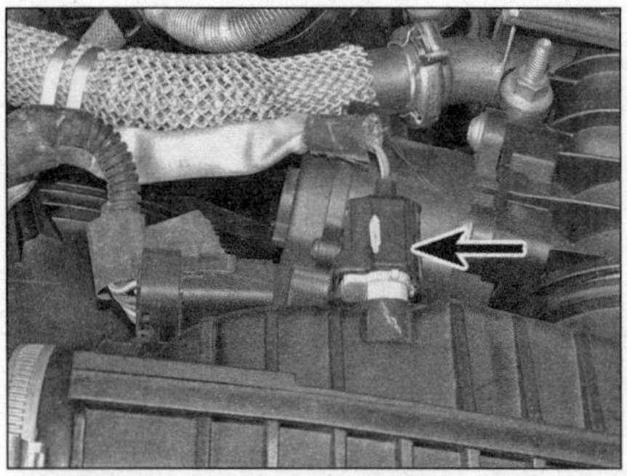

10.20 Intake air temperature sensor wiring plug (arrowed)

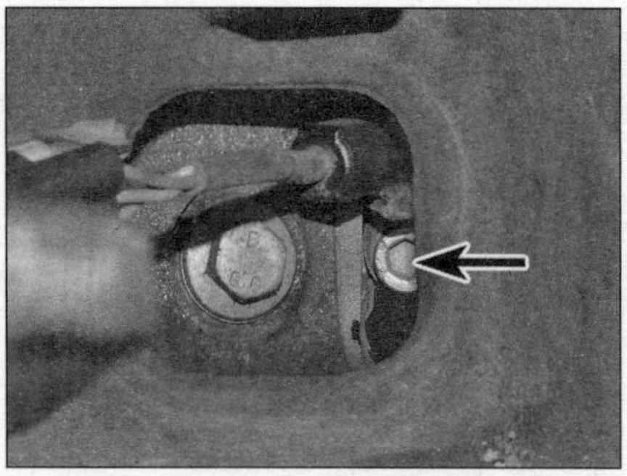

10.33a Crankshaft position sensor retaining bolt (arrowed)

10.33b Use an long Allen bit to unscrew the bolt – shown with the flywheel/driveplate removed for clarity

17 Undo the Torx screw and pull the sensor from place. Examine the O-ring seal, and renew if it shows signs of damage or deterioration.

18 Refitting is a reversal of removal.

Intake air temperature sensor (IAT)

19 Remove the engine oil filler cap, then pull up and remove the cover from the top of the engine.

20 Disconnect the sensor wiring plug **(see illustration)**.

21 Rotate the sensor anti-clockwise and remove it from the air intake elbow.

22 Refitting is a reversal of removal. Tighten the retaining bolts securely.

Accelerator pedal position sensor

23 The accelerator pedal position sensor is integral with the accelerator pedal. Refer to Section 3.

Fuel rail pressure sensor (FRP)

24 The fuel rail pressure sensor must not be removed from the rail. If defective, the complete rail assembly must be renewed. See Section 11.

Camshaft position sensor (CMP)

25 Remove the left-hand EGR valve as described in Chapter 4B, Section 2.

26 Disconnect the wiring plug from the camshaft position sensor. The sensor is located on the left-hand cylinder head, behind the exhaust camshaft sprocket position. Access is very limited.

27 Undo the retaining bolt and remove the sensor.

28 Use a mirror to observe the back of the camshaft sprocket through the position sensor aperture, then using a socket on the crankshaft sprocket bolt, rotate the crankshaft clockwise until one of the sprocket webs is visible.

29 Insert the camshaft position sensor, so the sensor tip rests against the sprocket web. Tighten the retaining bolt to the specified torque.

30 The remainder of refitting is a reversal of removal.

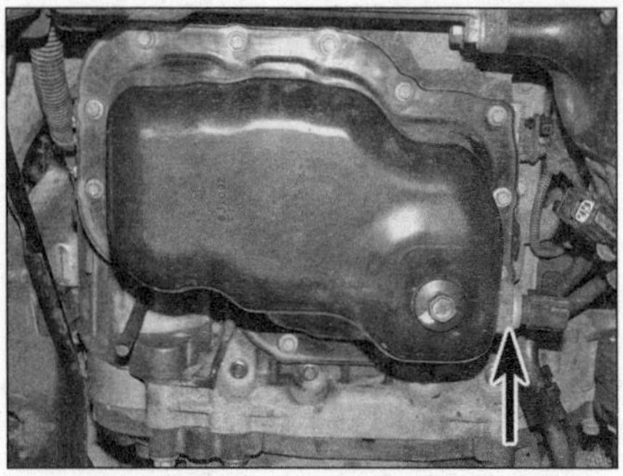

10.37 The engine oil temperature sensor (arrowed) is fitted to the sump

Crankshaft position sensor (CKP)

31 The crankshaft speed and position sensor is located on the rear crankshaft oil seal housing, and is accessible through a blanking cover in the cylinder block. Begin by removing the turbocharger as described in Section 13.

32 Trace the sensor wiring back to the plug and disconnect it.

33 Prise out the blanking cover (where fitted) from the casing, then undo the retaining bolt and pull the sensor from place **(see illustrations)**. Note that the retaining bolt is captive and should not be removed from the sensor.

34 Refitting is a reversal of removal.

Coolant temperature sensor

35 Refer to Chapter 3, Section 6.

10.42 Knock sensor retaining bolts (arrowed)

Engine oil temperature sensor

36 Drain the engine oil as described in Chapter 1, Section 3.

37 Disconnect the wiring plug, then unscrew the sensor from the sump **(see illustration)**. Discard the O-ring seal – a new one must be fitted. Be prepared for fluid spillage.

38 Install a new O-ring seal, then screw the sensor into the sump. Tighten the sensor to the specified torque.

39 The remainder of refitting is a reversal of removal.

Knock sensors (KS)

40 Remove the engine oil filler cap, then pull up and remove the engine top cover.

41 Disconnect the knock sensor wiring plugs.

42 The knock sensors are located each side of the engine oil/fuel cooler in the central V of the engine. Undo the bolts and remove the sensors **(see illustration)**.

43 Fit the sensors to their original positions, then tighten the retaining bolts to their specified torque.

44 Refit the engine top cover and oil filler cap.

11 Fuel injection pump and drivebelt – removal and refitting

Note: *Refer to the precautions given in Section 1 of this Chapter before proceeding.*

Drivebelt

1 Disconnect the battery negative lead as described in Chapter 5, Section 4.

2 Remove the engine oil filler cap, then pull up and remove the engine top cover **(see illustration 5.3)**.

3 Depress the release buttons, and disconnect the low-pressure fuel hoses from the fuel pump at the rear of the engine **(see illustration 8.4)**.

4 Clamp the EGR coolant hoses to minimise loss, then disconnect the both EGR coolant crossover hoses **(see illustration 8.5)**.

5 Undo the retaining bolts and remove

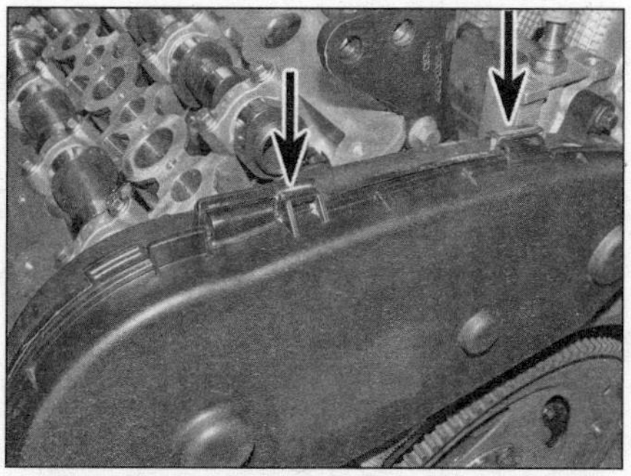

11.7 The pump drivebelt cover is secured by 2 clips (arrowed) – shown with the engine removed for clarity

11.8 Undo the bolt (arrowed) and remove the drivebelt tensioner

11.10 The tang (arrowed) engages with the belt inner cover

the EGR coolant crossover pipe **(see illustration 8.7)**.

6 Unclip the wiring harness at the back of the left-hand cylinder head, and move it to one side for access to the fuel pump drivebelt cover.

7 Remove the pump drivebelt cover **(see illustration)**.

8 Undo the retaining bolt and remove the belt tensioner assembly **(see illustration)**. Discard the tensioner – a new one must be fitted.

9 Remove the pump drivebelt. Note that Land Rover insist the belt must be renewed if it is removed.

Models up to VIN SALLA000304 (end of 2006 model year)

10 Position the new tensioner, but only screw in the retaining bolt 2 to 3 threads at this stage. Ensure the tang on the tensioner engages correctly with the belt inner cover. Note that the tensioner is supplied with a locking pin already fitted – don't remove this pin yet **(see illustration)**.

11 Ensure the sprockets are clean, then fit the new drivebelt around the camshaft and fuel pump sprockets, noting the direction of rotation arrows on the belt **(see illustration)**.

12 Tighten the tensioner retaining bolt to the specified torque, then withdraw the locking pin to tension the belt **(see illustration)**.

Models from VIN SALLA000304 (2007 model year on)

13 Position the new tensioner assembly on the belt inner cover, ensuring the tensioner tang engages correctly with the belt inner cover **(see illustration 11.10)**. Tighten the new retaining bolt to the specified torque. Note that the tensioner is supplied with a locking pin already fitted – don't remove this pin yet.

14 Ensure the sprockets are clean, then fit the new drivebelt around the sprockets.

15 Withdraw the tensioner locking pin to tension the belt.

All models

16 The remainder of refitting is a reversal of removal.

Fuel injection pump

17 Remove the drivebelt as described in this Section.

18 Remove the crankcase vent oil separator as described in Chapter 2, Section 14, then unscrew the separator locating stud **(see illustration)**.

Models up to VIN SALLA000304 (end of 2006 model year)

19 Using a second open-ended spanner to counterhold, slacken the unions and remove the high-pressure fuel pipes between the pump and the diverter rail, and the diverter rail to the common rail each side. Keep the pipes in contact with the pump and fuel rails until both unions are undone and the area around the pipes/unions cleaned. Plug/cover the openings to prevent contamination. Discard the pipes – new ones must be fitted.

20 Disconnect the wiring plugs/harness from the fuel injection pump/diverter rail **(see illustration)**.

21 Undo the 2 mounting studs and remove the fuel diverter rail **(see illustration)**.

11.11 Observe the direction-of-rotation arrows on the drivebelt

11.12 Withdraw the tensioner locking pin (arrowed)

11.18 Unscrew the oil separator locating stud (arrowed)

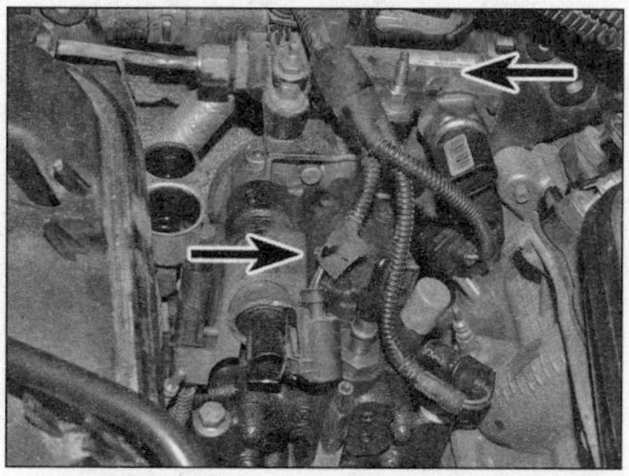

11.20 The fuel pump and diverter rail are located at the centre, rear of the engine (arrowed)

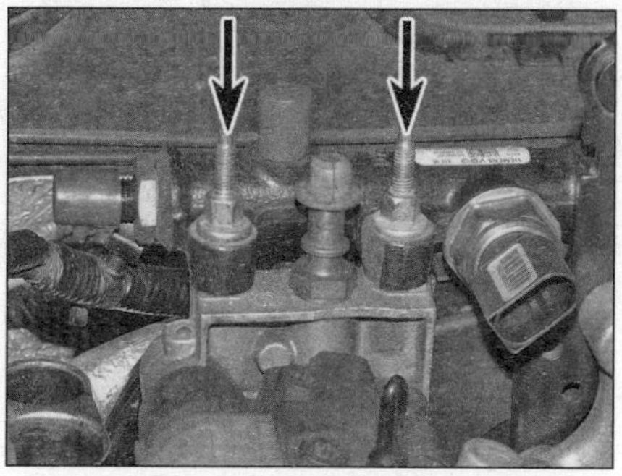

11.21 Fuel diverter rail mounting studs (arrowed)

11.22 Drivebelt inner cover bolts (arrowed) – shown with the engine removed for clarity

11.24 Fuel pump retaining bolts (arrowed)

11.26 Remove the high-pressure pipes (left-hand pipe arrowed) between the pump and common rail each side

22 Undo the 2 bolts securing the drivebelt inner cover **(see illustration)**.

23 Undo the bolt securing the engine breather tube to the rear of the right-hand cylinder head.

24 Remove the 4 retaining bolts and manoeuvre the pump from place **(see illustration)**.

Models from VIN SALLA000304 (2007 model year on)

25 Unclip the fuel injector soundproofing panel each side **(see illustration 8.8)**.

26 Using a second open-ended spanner to counterhold, slacken the unions and remove the high-pressure fuel pipes between the pump and the common rail each side **(see illustration)**. Keep the pipes in contact with the pump and fuel rails until both unions are undone and the area around the pipes/unions cleaned. Plug/cover the openings to prevent contamination. Discard the pipes – new ones must be fitted.

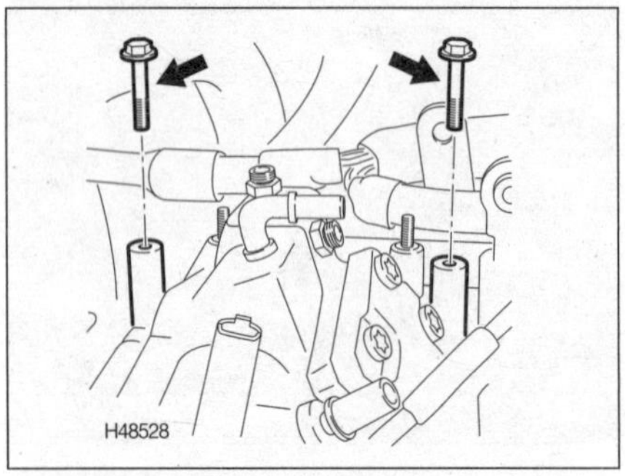

11.27 Undo the belt rear cover access panel bolts (arrowed)

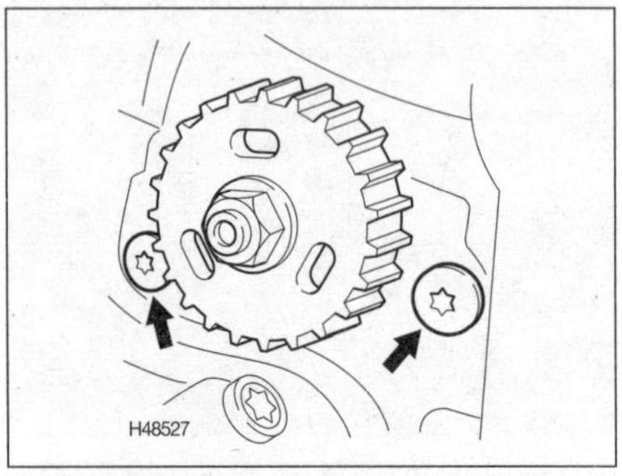

11.28a Undo the bolts at the rear of the pump (arrowed) ...

27 Undo the 2 bolts securing the belt rear cover access panel **(see illustration)**.

28 Disconnect the wiring plugs, undo the retaining bolts and manoeuvre the pump from place **(see illustrations)**. Discard the bolts – new ones must be fitted.

All models

29 If required, undo the retaining bolt/nut and remove the pump sprocket. Note that a puller maybe required to remove the sprocket.

30 If removed, refit the drive sprocket to the pump and tighten the bolt/nut to the specified torque.

Models up to VIN SALLA000304 (end of 2006 model year)

31 Position the pump, and tighten the retaining bolts to the specified torque.

32 Refit the engine breather tube retaining bolt and tighten it securely.

33 Refit the diverter rail, but only finger-tighten the mounting studs at this stage.

34 Reconnect the wiring plugs/harness to the pump and diverter rail.

35 Position the new high-pressure fuel pipes against the ports on the common rails, diverter rail and injection pump. Maintain pressure, holding the pipes olives against the ports, then finger-tighten the unions.

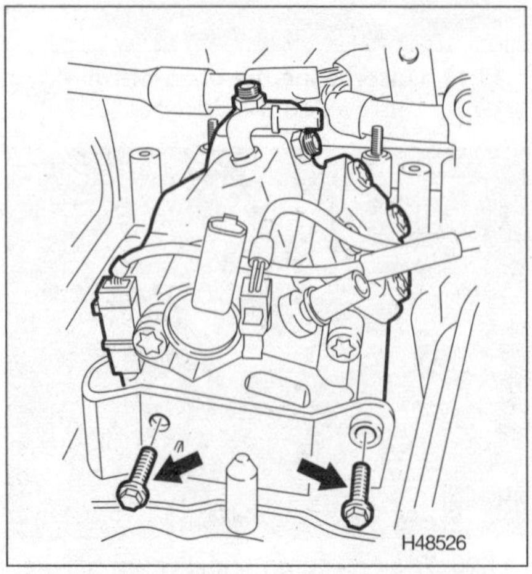

11.28b ... and at the front (arrowed)

36 Tighten the fuel diverter rail mounting studs to the specified torque.

37 Using a second open-ended spanner to counterhold, tighten the pipe unions in the following sequence **(see illustration)**:

a) Pipe-to-common rail union – Stage 1 torque.
b) Pipe-to-diverter rail union – Stage 1 torque.
c) Pipe-to-injection pump – Stage 1 torque.
d) Pipe-to-common rail union – Stage 2 torque.
e) Pipe-to-diverter rail union – Stage 2 torque.
f) Pipe-to-injection pump – Stage 2 torque.

38 Repeat this procedure for the remaining common rail high-pressure pipes.

39 Refit the bolts securing the high-pressure pipe clamp brackets.

40 Refit the crankcase vent oil separator locating stud, and tighten it securely.

41 Refit the injection pump drivebelt rear cover retaining bolts and tighten them securely.

Models from VIN SALLA000304 (2007 model year on)

42 Position the fuel pump, install the new retaining bolts and tighten them to the specified torque. Tighten the Torx bolts first, followed by the M8 bolts.

43 Reconnect the pump wiring plugs.

44 Refit the belt rear cover access panel, and tighten the retaining bolts securely.

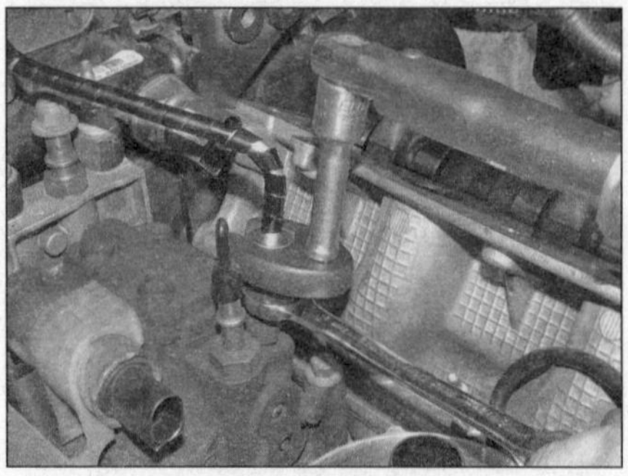

11.37 Use a 'crows foot' adapter to tighten the fuel pipe unions

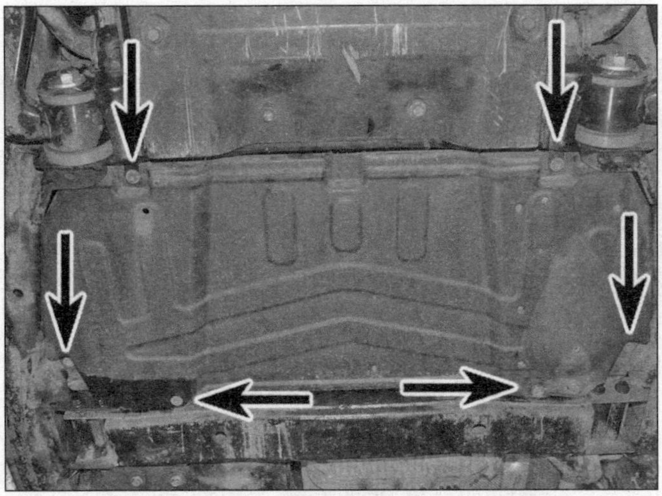

13.4a Transmission undershield bolts (arrowed)

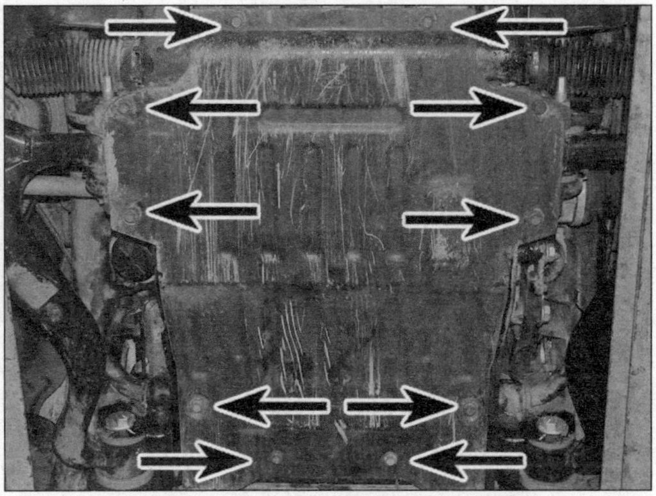

13.4b Engine undershield bolts (arrowed)

45 Position the new high-pressure fuel pipes against the ports on the common rails and injection pump. Maintain pressure, holding the pipes olives against the ports, then finger-tighten the unions.

46 Using a second open-ended spanner to counterhold, tighten the pipe unions in the following sequence:

a) Pipe-to-common rail union – Stage 1 torque.
b) Pipe-to-injection pump union – Stage 1 torque.
c) Pipe-to-common rail union – Stage 2 torque.
d) Pipe-to-injection pump union – Stage 2 torque.

47 Refit the bolts securing the high-pressure pipe clamp brackets.

48 Refit the injector sound proofing panels, and secure them with the clips.

All models

49 The remainder of refitting is a reversal of removal, remembering to bleed the fuel system as described in Section 5.

12 Turbocharger – description and precautions

1 The turbocharger increases engine efficiency by raising the pressure in the intake manifold above atmospheric pressure. Instead of the air simply being sucked into the cylinders, it is forced in. Additional fuel is supplied by the injectors, in proportion to the increased amount of air.

2 Energy for the operation of the turbocharger comes from the exhaust gas. The gas flows through a specially-shaped housing (the turbine housing) and in so doing, spins the turbine wheel. The turbine wheel is attached to a shaft, at the end of which is another vaned wheel, known as the compressor wheel. The compressor wheel spins in its own housing, and compresses the inducted air on the way to the intake manifold.

3 The compressed air passes through an intercooler, between the turbocharger and the intake manifold. The intercooler is an air-to-air heat exchanger, mounted at the front of the vehicle, under to the radiator, and supplied with air through the front grille. The purpose of the intercooler is to remove from the inducted air some of the heat gained in being compressed. Because cooler air is denser, removal of this heat further increases engine efficiency.

4 Boost pressure (the pressure in the intake manifold) is limited by the position of the guide vanes within the turbocharger – no wastegate is fitted. The position of the guide vanes is controlled by an electrical stepper motor, which in turn is controlled by the engine management ECM. A vane position sensor and temperature sensor is fitted to the turbocharger assembly.

5 The turbo shaft is pressure-lubricated by an oil feed pipe from the main oil gallery. The shaft 'floats' on a cushion of oil. A drain pipe returns the oil to the sump.

Warning: The turbocharger operates at extremely high speeds and temperatures. Certain precautions must be observed to avoid premature failure of the turbo, or injury to the operator.

Warning: Do not operate the turbo with any parts exposed. Foreign objects falling onto the rotating vanes could cause excessive damage and (if ejected) personal injury.

Warning: Do not race the engine immediately after start-up, especially if it is cold. Give the oil approximately 15 seconds to circulate.

Warning: Always allow the engine to return to idle speed before switching it off – do not blip the throttle and switch off, as this will leave the turbo spinning without lubrication. Allow the engine to idle for several minutes before switching off after a high-speed run.

Warning: Observe the recommended intervals for oil and filter changing, and use a reputable oil of the specified quality. Neglect of oil changing, or use of inferior oil, can cause carbon formation on the turbo shaft, and subsequent failure.

13 Turbocharger – removal and refitting

Removal

1 Disconnect the battery negative lead, as described in Chapter 5, Section 4.

2 Pull the cover upwards from the top of the engine.

3 Slacken the left-hand front roadwheel nuts then raise the front of the vehicle and support it securely on axle stands (see *Jacking and vehicle support*). Remove the roadwheel.

4 Undo the fasteners, remove the transmission undershield, and the engine undershield **(see illustrations)**.

5 Release the front exhaust pipe bracket from the rubber mounting.

6 Position a trolley/transmission jack to support the transmission, then undo the bolt securing the transmission mounting to the crossmember **(see illustration)**.

7 Undo the bolts/nuts and remove the

13.6 Remove the transmission mounting-to-crossmember bolt (arrowed)

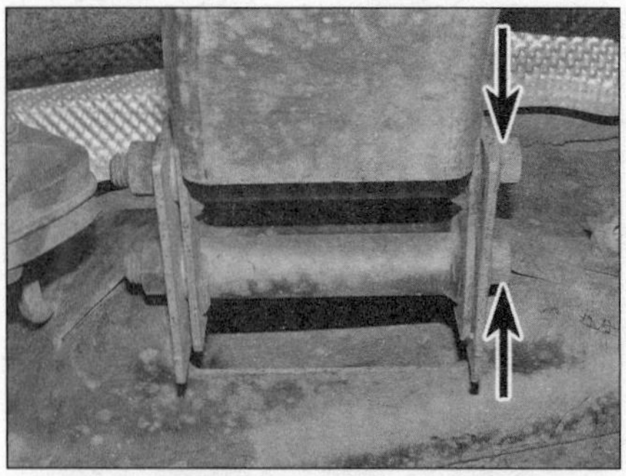
13.7 Undo the crossmember bolts (arrowed) each side

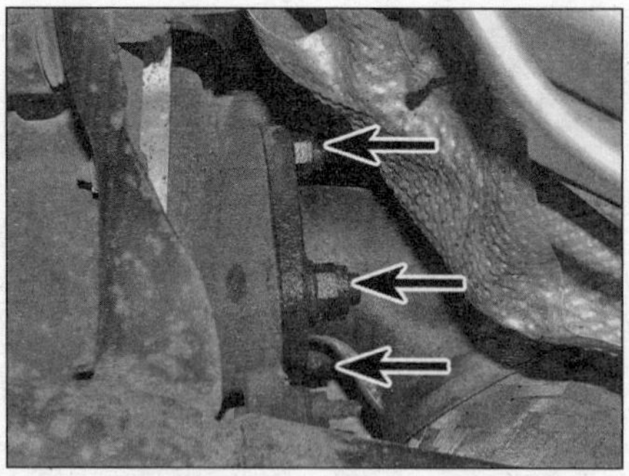
13.8 Catalytic converter-to-turbocharger nuts (arrowed)

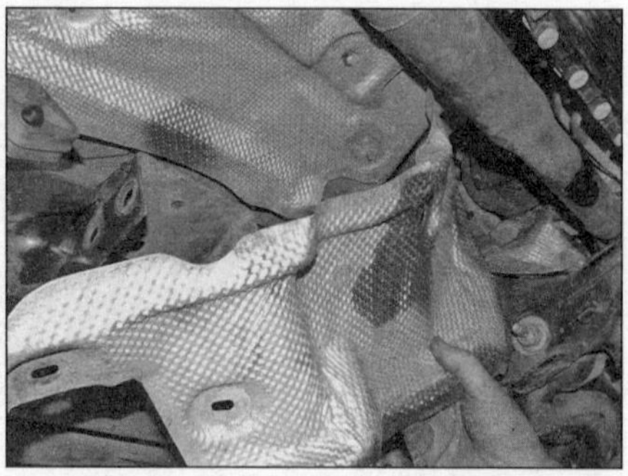
13.9 Remove the exhaust pipe front heat shield

transmission crossmember **(see illustration)**. **Note:** *Enlist the help of an assistant – the crossmember is heavy.*

8 Undo the nuts securing the catalytic converter to the turbocharger, and slacken the clamp securing it to the exhaust system **(see illustration)**. Remove the catalytic converter. Discard the nuts and the gasket – new ones must be fitted. Force a clean rag into the turbocharger opening to prevent contamination.

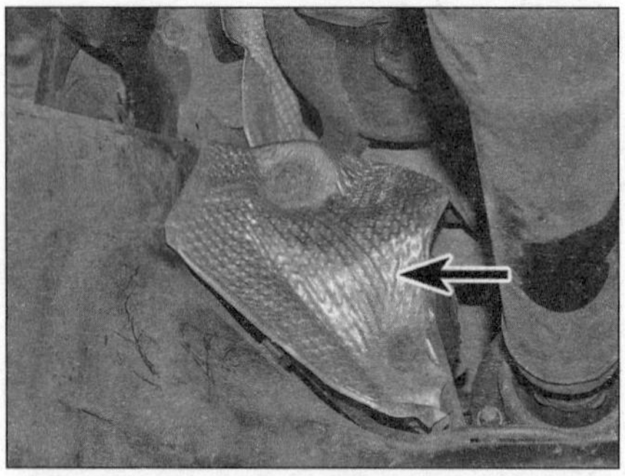
13.12 Differential mounting bracket heat shield (arrowed)

9 Undo the nuts/bolt and remove the exhaust front heat shield **(see illustration)**.

10 Temporarily refit the transmission crossmember, then refit the bolt securing the transmission mounting – do not fully-tighten the bolts at this stage. Remove the jack.

11 Remove the front final drive assembly as described in Chapter 9, Section 4.

12 Undo the 2 bolts and remove the differential mounting bracket heat shield **(see illustration)**.

13 Undo the bolts/nut and remove the turbocharger rear support bracket, then undo the 2 bolts securing the front support bracket to the cylinder block **(see illustration)**.

14 Slacken the turbocharger-to-manifold lower retaining nut **(see illustration)**. Note that a new nut must be fitted.

15 Remove the left-hand upper suspension arm as described in Chapter 11, Section 6.

16 Unclip the left-hand wheel arch lower splash shield.

17 Undo the bolts and remove the heat shields from the upper arm mounting bracket **(see illustration)**.

18 Undo the 2 bolts and securing the turbocharger heat shield **(see illustrations)**. Note that it's not possible to remove the heat shield until the oil feed pipe has been released as described in the next paragraph.

19 Undo the Torx banjo bolt securing the oil feed pipe to the turbocharger **(see illustration)**. Discard the sealing washers – new one must be fitted. Plug/cover the openings to prevent contamination, and remove the heat shield (paragraph 18).

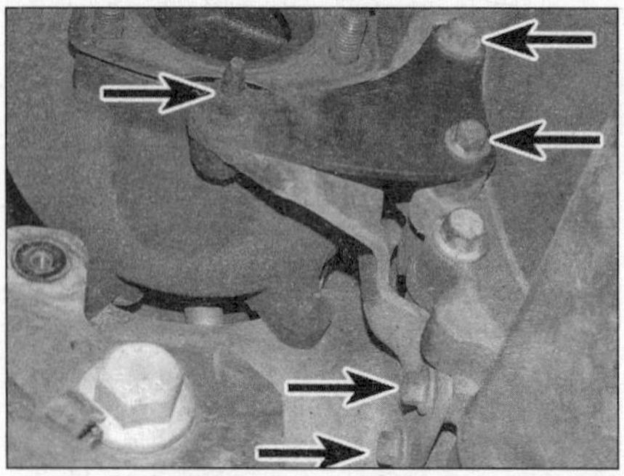
13.13 Turbocharger support brackets bolts/nut (arrowed)

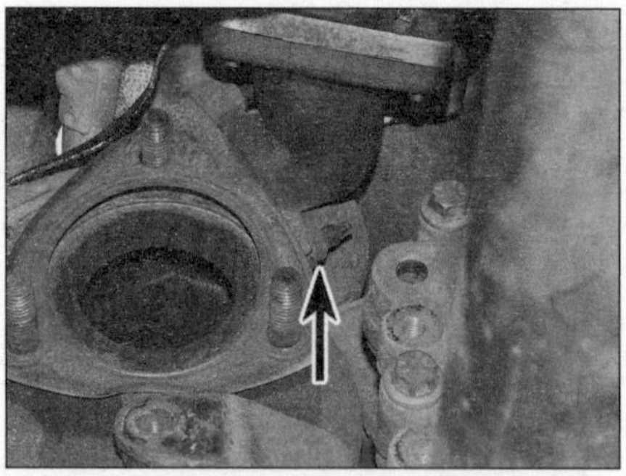
13.14 Slacken the lower turbocharger retaining nut (arrowed)

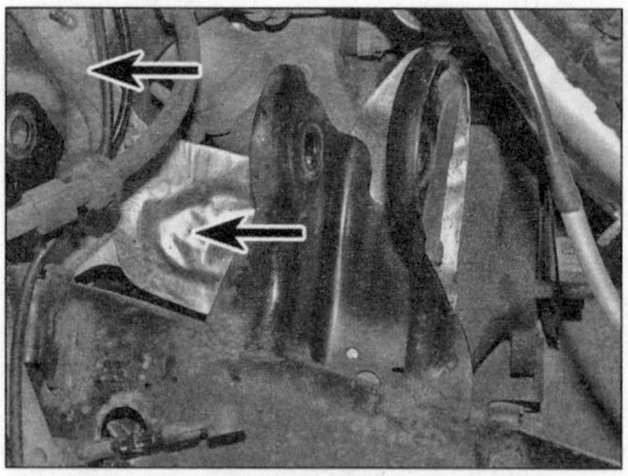
13.17 Remove the upper arm heat shields (arrowed)

13.18a Turbocharger heat shield front bolt (arrowed) ...

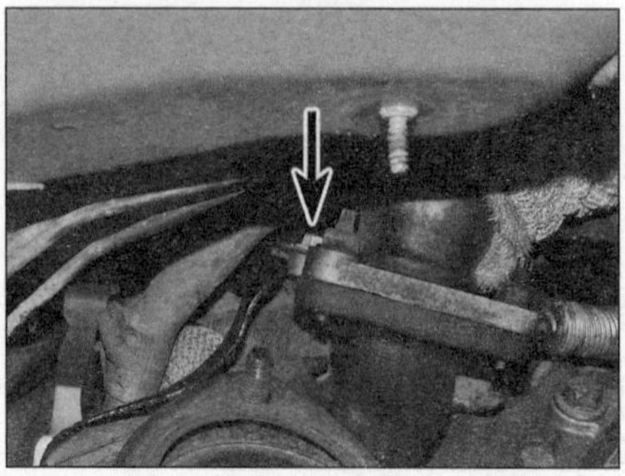
13.18b ... and rear bolt (arrowed)

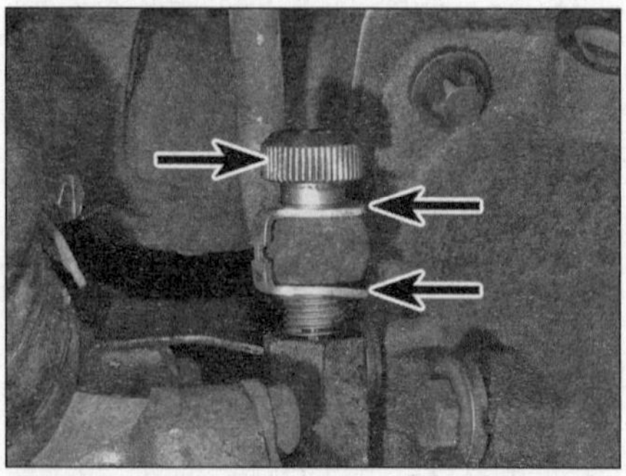
13.19 The sealing washer fits around the oil feed pipe banjo bolt (arrowed)

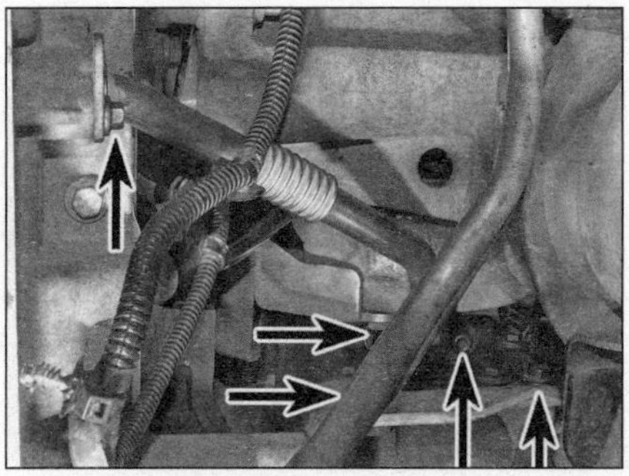

13.20a Oil return pipe bolts (arrowed), and support bracket bolts (arrowed)

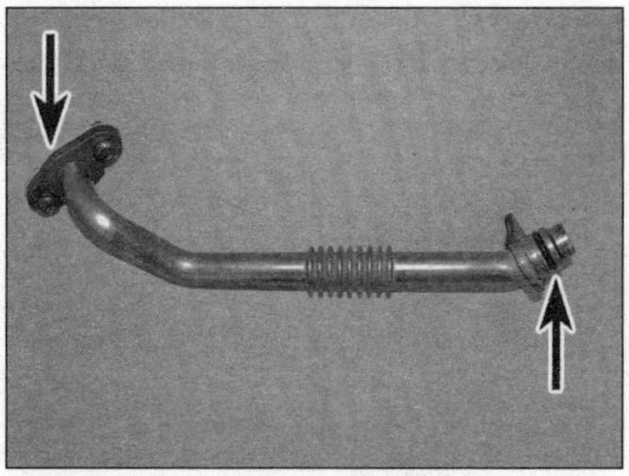

13.20b Renew the gasket and O-ring seal (arrowed)

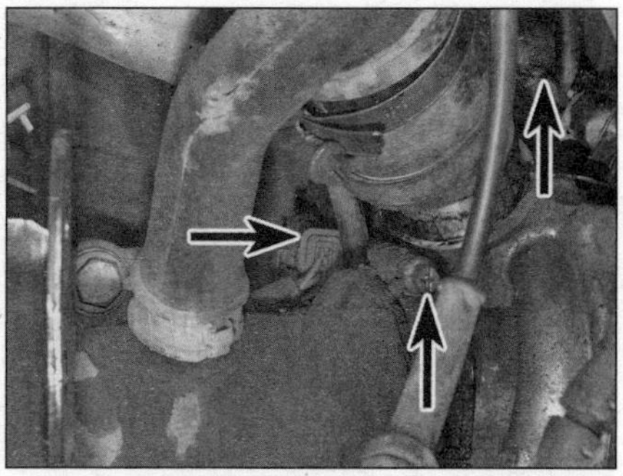

13.22 Slacken the turbocharger intake/outlet pipe clamps (arrowed), and disconnect the control motor wiring plug (arrowed)

20 Unclip the wiring harness, then undo the bolts and detach the oil return pipe from the cylinder block and turbocharger **(see illustrations)**. Discard the gasket/O-ring seal – new ones must be fitted. Manoeuvre the pipe from place.

21 Undo the 2 bolts and remove the support bracket from the base of the turbocharger.

22 Slacken the clamps and disconnect the turbocharger intake and outlet pipes **(see illustration)**.

23 Disconnect the wiring plug from the turbocharger control motor.

24 Drill pilot holes, then carefully drill an 8.0 mm hole in the centre of each of the turbocharger upper mounting studs to remove them **(see illustrations)**. Use a centre punch and pilot drill. Ensure the holes are in the exact centre of the studs. When refitting, the studs are renewed with nuts and bolts.

Caution: Do not exceed a depth of 14 mm.

25 With the help of an assistant, manoeuvre the turbocharger rearwards from place **(see illustration)**.

Refitting

26 Drill out any remains of the upper mounting studs from the turbocharger, leaving two 8 mm diameter holes **(see illustration)**.

27 Fit a new mounting stud in the turbocharger lower mounting hole.

28 Manoeuvre the turbocharger into place, engine engage it with the intake and outlet hoses.

29 Fit the new turbocharger upper mounting bolts/nuts, but only tighten them once the lower support bracket has been fitted.

30 Tighten the turbocharger lower retaining nut, but again, only tighten it once the lower support bracket has been fitted.

31 The remainder of refitting is a reversal of removal, bearing in mind the following points:

a) Tighten all fasteners to the specified torque where given.

b) Renew the oil feed pipe banjo bolt sealing washers.

c) Check, and if necessary, top-up the engine oil level as described in Weekly checks.

d) Reconnect the battery negative lead as described in Chapter 5, Section 4.

14 Turbocharger – examination and overhaul

1 With the turbocharger removed, inspect the housing for cracks or other visible damage.

2 Spin the turbine or the compressor wheel, to verify that the shaft is intact, and to feel for excessive shake or roughness. Some play is normal, since in use the shaft is 'floating' on a film of oil. Check that the wheel vanes are undamaged.

3 The wastegate actuator would appear not to be available as a separate unit. If faulty, the complete turbocharger must be renewed.

4 If the exhaust or intake passages are oil-contaminated, the turbo shaft oil seals have probably failed. (On the intake side, this will also have contaminated the intercooler, which if necessary should be flushed with a suitable solvent.)

5 Check the oil feed and return pipes for contamination or blockage, and clean if necessary.

6 No DIY repair of the turbocharger is possible. A new unit may be available on an exchange basis.

15 Intercooler – removal and refitting

1 Remove the radiator as described in Chapter 3, Section 3.

2 Lift the intercooler from place.

3 Refitting is a reversal of removal.

16 Manifolds – removal and refitting

Intake manifold

1 The intake manifolds are integral with the cylinder head covers – refer to Chapter 2, Section 4.

Exhaust manifold

Left-hand side manifold

2 Remove the turbocharger as described in Section 13.

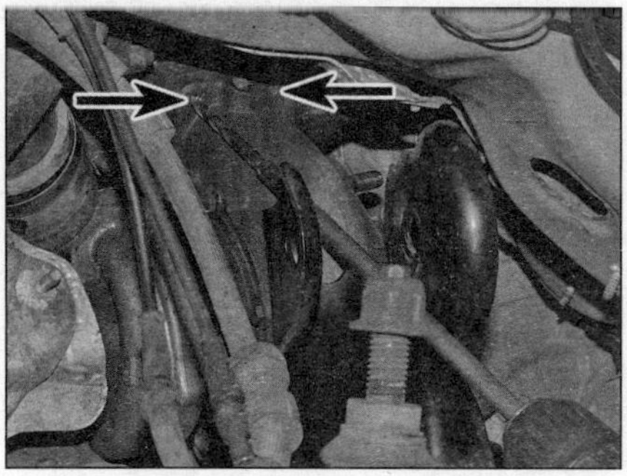

13.24 Drill out the turbocharger upper mounting studs (arrowed) ...

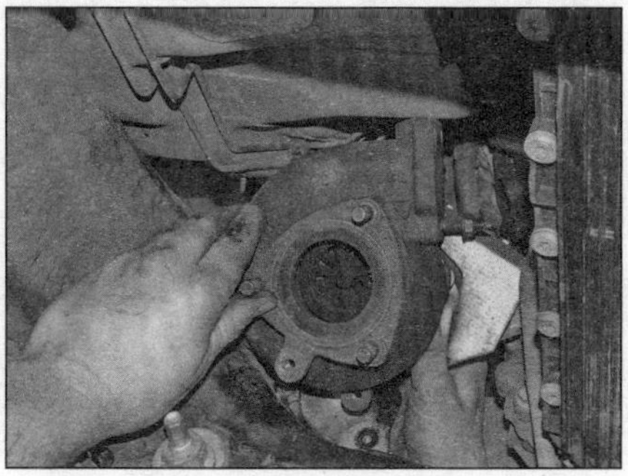

13.25 ... and manoeuvre the turbocharger from place

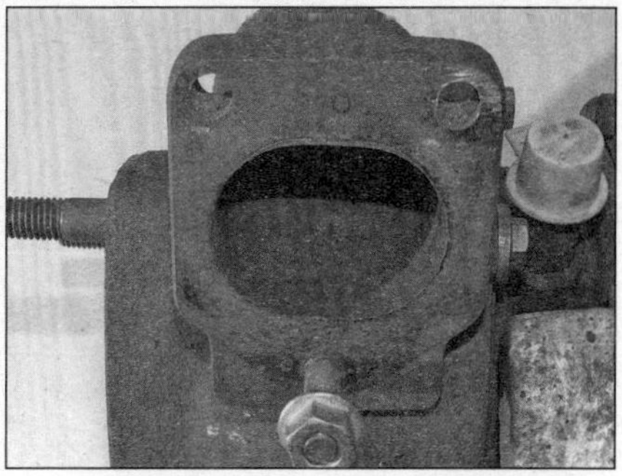

13.26 Drill out any remains of the upper studs, leaving two 8.0 mm holes

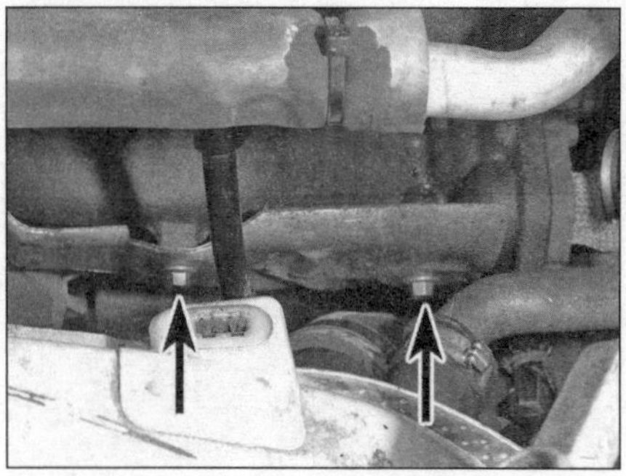

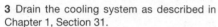

16.6 Manifold heat shield retaining bolts (arrowed)

3 Drain the cooling system as described in Chapter 1, Section 31.
4 Remove the battery and battery tray as described in Chapter 5, Section 4.
5 Remove the left-hand EGR valve/cooler as described in Chapter 4B, Section 2.
6 Undo the 2 retaining bolts and remove the left-hand manifold heat shield **(see illustration)**.
7 Undo the 3 nuts securing the crossover exhaust pipe to the rear of the manifold **(see illustration)**.
8 Undo the 2 bolts and detach the EGR pipe from the manifold. Recover the gasket.
9 Undo the 6 nuts and manoeuvre the exhaust manifold downwards from place **(see illustrations)**. Discard the manifold gasket and the nuts.
10 Remove the manifold mounting studs from the cylinder head and renew them.

Right-hand manifold

11 Disconnect the battery negative lead as described in Chapter 5, Section 4.
12 Slacken the right-hand front roadwheel nuts, raise the front of the vehicle and support it securely on axle stands (see *Jacking and vehicle support*). Remove the roadwheel.

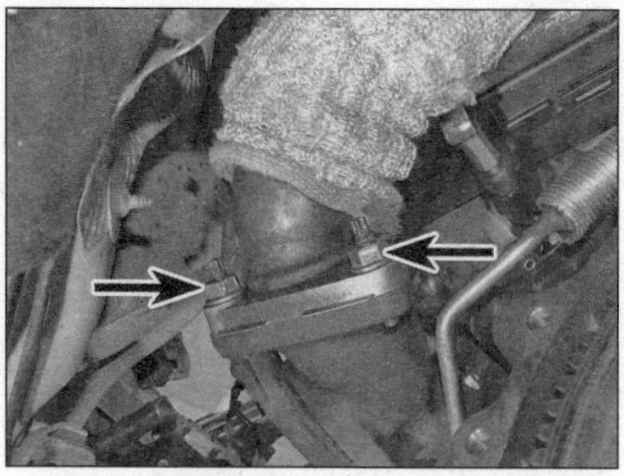

16.7 Crossover pipe-to-manifold nuts (arrowed – one hidden, transmission removed for clarity)

13 Drain the cooling system as described in Chapter 1, Section 31.
14 Remove the auxiliary battery (where fitted) and battery tray as described in Chapter 5, Section 4.
15 Undo the nuts/bolts, then remove the upper suspension arm heat shield and bracket.
16 Remove the right-hand EGR valve and cooler (where applicable) as described in Chapter 4B, Section 2.
17 Undo the bolts and remove the exhaust manifold heat shield.
18 Undo the 3 nuts securing the crossover pipe to the manifold **(see illustration 16.7)**.
19 Undo the 6 nuts and manoeuvre the exhaust manifold from place. Discard the manifold gasket and the nuts.
20 Remove the manifold mounting studs from the cylinder head and renew them.

Both sides

21 Refitting is a reversal of removal, bearing in mind the following points:
- *a) If possible, use a tap to clean the stud threads in the cylinder head, then fit the new manifold mounting studs and tighten them to the specified torque.*
- *b) Thoroughly clean the mating faces of the manifolds and the cylinder heads, and refit the manifolds using new gaskets.*
- *c) Tighten all fasteners to their specified torque (where given).*
- *d) Refill the cooling system as described in Chapter 1, Section 31.*

17 Exhaust system – general information and component renewal

1 The exhaust system consists of 2 separate sections: a front section, incorporating a catalytic converter and a flexible section, and a rear section, incorporating the centre silencer and rear (left- and right-hand) silencers. From 2008 model year, an optional diesel particulate filter (DPF) was available, fitted between the catalytic converter and the centre silencer. Each exhaust section can be renewed individually.
2 To remove the system or part of the system, first jack up the front or rear of the vehicle, as applicable, and support it securely on axle stands (see *Jacking and vehicle support*).

Complete exhaust system

3 Undo the fasteners, then remove the engine and transmission undershields **(see illustrations 13.4a and 13.4b)**.
4 Unclip the fuel hoses from the transmission crossmember.
5 Release the front exhaust mounting rubber.
6 Position a trolley jack beneath the transmission, then remove the bolt securing the transmission mounting to the crossmember **(see illustration 13.6)**.
7 Undo the 4 nuts/bolts and, with the help of an assistant, remove the transmission crossmember.
8 Undo the 3 nuts securing the front of the exhaust pipe to the turbocharger. Discard the gasket and nuts – new ones must be fitted.

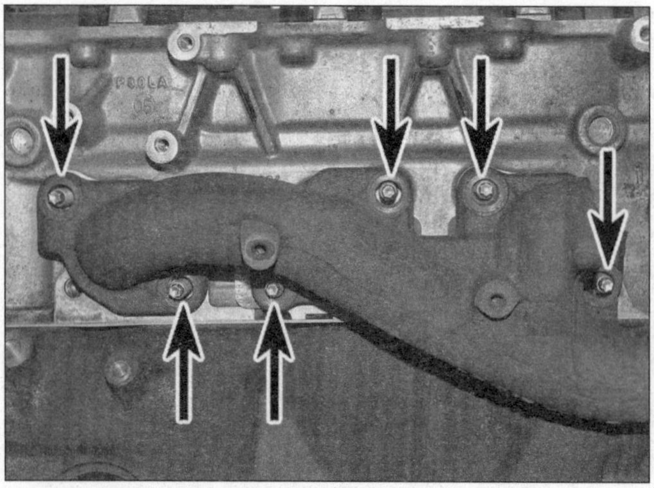

16.9a Manifold retaining nuts locations (arrowed)

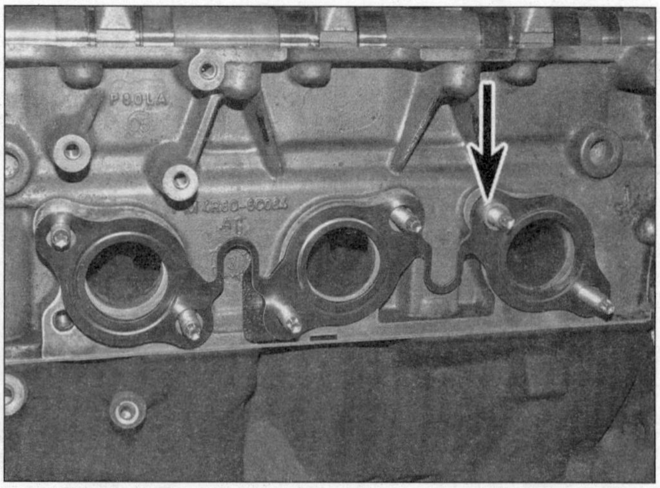

16.9b Renew the gasket. Note the spacer location (arrowed)

Models with DPF

9 Disconnect the wiring plug, then unclip the DPF pressure sensor.
10 Disconnect the DPF exhaust gas temperature sensor wiring plug.
11 Slacken the DPF-to-catalytic converter clamp.
12 Undo the bolt and remove the heat shield over the pre-cat exhaust gas temperature sensor, then disconnect the wiring plug.

All models

13 Release the exhaust system from the various rubber mountings along its length, and, with the help of an assistant, manoeuvre the exhaust system from under the vehicle.

Catalytic converter/ flexible section

14 Remove the complete exhaust system as previously described in this Section.

Models with DPF

15 Undo the bolts and remove the heat shield from the front of the DPF.

All models

16 Release the clamp and detach the catalytic converter from the rest of the system.

Diesel particulate filter (DPF)

17 Remove the complete exhaust system as described in this Section.
18 Undo the bolts and remove the heat shields from the front and rear of the DPF.
19 Undo the 3 nuts, and detach the DPF from the centre silencer.
20 Release the clamp and detach the DPF from the catalytic converter.

DPF pressure sensor

21 Disconnect the wiring plug, then unclip the pressure sensor. Note their fitted positions, and disconnect the hoses from the sensor as it's withdrawn **(see illustration)**.

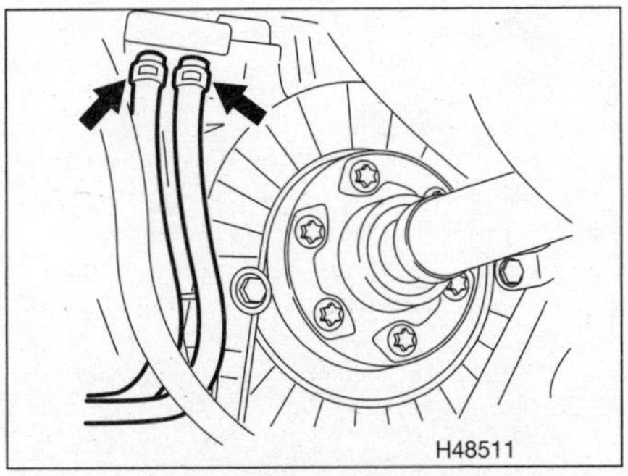

17.21 Disconnect the DPF pressure sensor hoses (arrowed)

Centre silencer

Models without DPF

22 Slacken the clamp securing the catalytic converter to the centre silencer.
23 Release the exhaust system from the various rubber mountings along its length, then with the help of an assistant, detach the silencer from the catalytic converter.

Models with DPF

24 Remove the complete exhaust system as described previously in this Section.

All models

25 The centre silencer can be renewed separately from the rear silencers, and *vice-versa*. There are pre-prepared cutting points in the exhaust pipes between the silencers, indicated by depressions **(see illustration)**. Cut the pipes at these points.
26 New components are supplied with sleeves and clamps to join the sections.

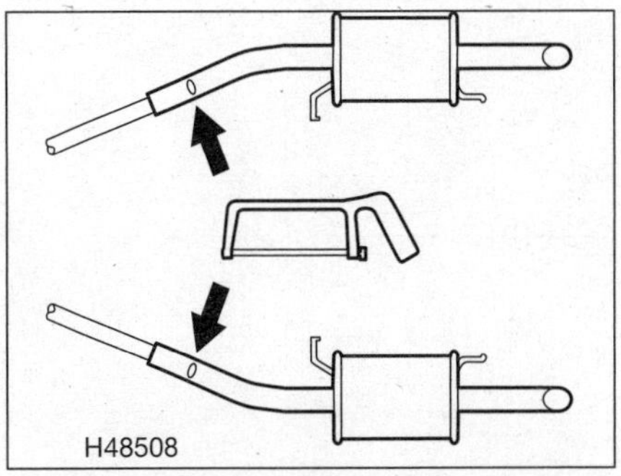

17.25 Pre-prepared cutting points (arrowed)

Tail silencers

27 The tail silencers can be renewed separately from the centre silencer. There are pre-prepared cutting points in the exhaust pipes between the silencers, indicated by depressions **(see illustration 17.25)**. Cut the pipes at these points.
28 New components are supplied with sleeves and clamps to join the sections.

All components

29 Refitting is a reversal of removal, bearing in mind the following points:

a) *Where applicable, check the condition of the exhaust mounting rubbers, and renew if necessary.*
b) *Where applicable, use new exhaust-to-manifold gaskets. On models with a clamped joint, apply a little exhaust jointing compound to the joint before fitting.*
c) *Do not fully-tighten the mountings and clamp nuts and bolts until the completion of refitting.*

Chapter 4 Part B:
Emissions control systems

Contents

Degrees of difficulty

Easy, suitable for novice with little experience	**Fairly easy,** suitable for beginner with some experience	**Fairly difficult,** suitable for competent DIY mechanic	**Difficult,** suitable for experienced DIY mechanic	**Very difficult,** suitable for expert DIY or professional

Specifications

Torque wrench settings	Nm	lbf ft
EGR delivery pipe bolts	10	7
EGR valve securing bolts	10	7
EGR valve-to-cooler bolts	10	7

1 General information and precautions

In order to reduce harmful emissions from the engine, an EGR (exhaust gas recirculation) system, and a crankcase emission control system are fitted. The EGR system allows a controlled amount of the exhaust gases to combine with the fresh air entering the intake system. This reduces the combustion temperature by slowing the fuel-burn rate, which results in lower NO_2 emissions. The flow of exhaust gases into the intake manifolds is controlled by the engine management ECM via solenoid valves which control the flow of vacuum to a diaphragm attached to the EGR valve. The crankcase emission control system allows vapour and gases from the crankcase to pass through a crankcase vent oil separator located between the cylinder heads, then through a breather hose into the intake ducting, to be burnt during the combustion process.

Warning: It is necessary to take certain precautions when working on the fuel system components, particularly the fuel injectors. Before carrying out any operations on the fuel system, refer to the precautions given in 'Safety first!' at the beginning of this manual. Absolute cleanliness is essential when working on the fuel system – do not allow dirt to enter when any part of the system is disconnected.

2 Emissions control systems – general information

1 Certain engines are equipped with systems designed to reduce the emissions of harmful by-products of the combustion process into the atmosphere.

2 The following systems may be fitted according to model.

Crankcase emissions control

3 A crankcase ventilation system is fitted to all models.

4 Oil fumes and piston blow-by gases (combustion gases which have passed by the piston rings) are drawn from the crankcase/ cylinder head cover through an oil separator, into the air intake tract. The gases are then drawn into the engine together with fresh air/ fuel mixture. Condensed oil vapour is returned from the main oil separator to the engine sump.

Exhaust gas recirculation (EGR)

5 The system is designed to recirculate small quantities of exhaust gas into the intake tract, and therefore into the combustion process. This process reduces the level of oxides of nitrogen present in the final exhaust gas which is released into the atmosphere, and also lowers the combustion temperature.

6 The volume of exhaust gas recirculated is controlled by the EGR valve. The solenoid valve is electrically-operated, and is controlled by the engine management ECM.

7 Between idle speed and a pre-determined engine load, the valve is opened to a certain extent. Under full-load conditions, the exhaust gas recirculation is cut off. Operation of the valve is also influenced by engine coolant temperature.

3 Emissions control systems – testing and component renewal

Crankcase emissions control

Testing

1 If the system is thought to be faulty, first check that the hoses are unobstructed. On high-mileage vehicles, particularly those regularly used for short journeys, a jelly-like deposit may be evident inside the system hoses and oil separator. If excessive deposits are present, the relevant component(s) should be removed and cleaned.

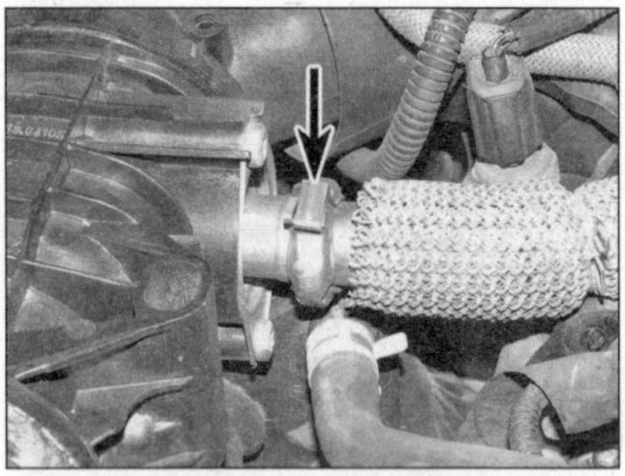

3.9 Release the clamp (arrowed) and disconnect the EGR pipe from the air shut-off valve

2 Periodically inspect the system components for security and damage, and renew them as necessary. Note that damaged or loose hoses can cause various engine running problems (erratic idle speed, stalling, etc) which can be difficult to trace.

Crankcase vent oil separator

3 Renewal of the oil separator is described in Chapter 2, Section 14.

Exhaust emissions control

Testing

4 The system can only be tested accurately using a suitable exhaust gas analyser (suitable for use with diesel engines).

Component renewal

5 The catalytic converter and diesel particulate filter (where fitted) is integral with the exhaust system front section.

6 Removal and refitting are described in Chapter 4A, Section 17.

EGR valve/cooler

7 Remove the battery and battery tray, as described in Chapter 5, Section 4.

8 Pull the plastic cover upwards from the top of the engine.

Models without diesel particulate filter

9 Release the clip securing the EGR outlet pipe to the air shut-off valve **(see illustration)**.

10 Unclip the wiring harness, undo the Torx screw securing the bracket.

11 Undo the 2 bolts and detach the outlet pipe from the EGR valve **(see illustration)**. Discard the gasket – a new one must be fitted.

12 Clamp the hose to minimise fluid loss, the release the clip and disconnect the coolant outlet hose from the EGR cooler **(see illustration)**.

13 Undo the 2 bolts, remove the support bracket, then release the clip and disconnect the EGR inlet pipe from the cooler **(see illustration)**.

14 Disconnect the wiring plug from the EGR valve.

15 Clamp the hose to minimise fluid loss, then release the clip and disconnect the coolant hose from the base of the EGR cooler **(see illustration)**.

16 If removing the left-hand assembly, undo the bolt securing the engine oil level dipstick guide tube to the cylinder head **(see illustration)**.

17 Undo the mounting bolts and manoeuvre the EGR cooler/valve from place **(see illustration)**.

18 If required, undo the 2 bolts and detach the valve from the cooler.

Models with diesel particulate filter

19 Slacken the left-hand front roadwheel bolts/nuts, then raise the front of the vehicle

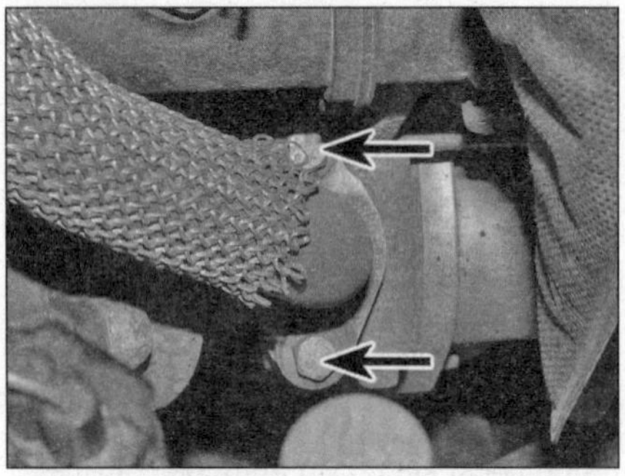

3.11 EGR pipe-to-valve bolts (arrowed)

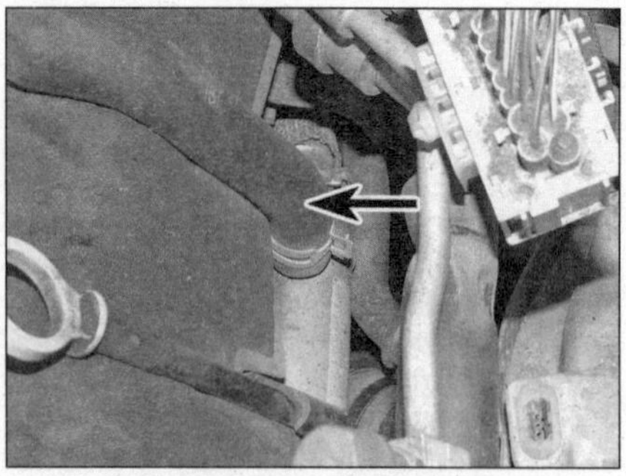

3.12 Disconnect the EGR cooler coolant outlet hose (arrowed)

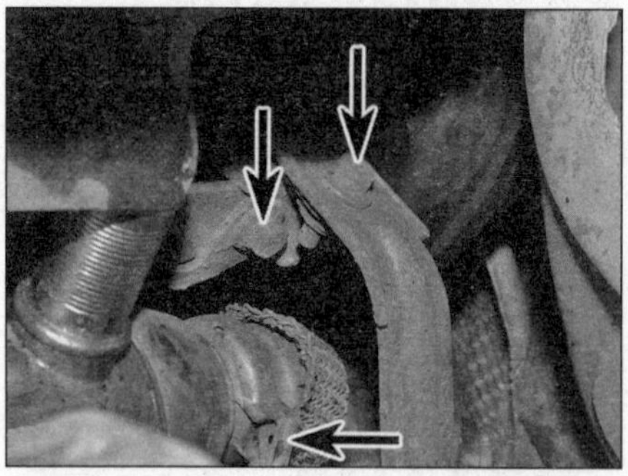

3.13 Undo the bolts (arrowed), remove the bracket to access the pipe clamp (arrowed)

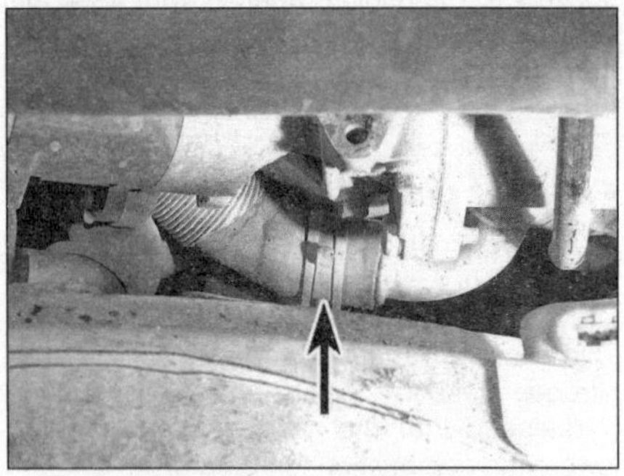

3.15 Disconnect the coolant hose (arrowed) from the base of the EGR cooler

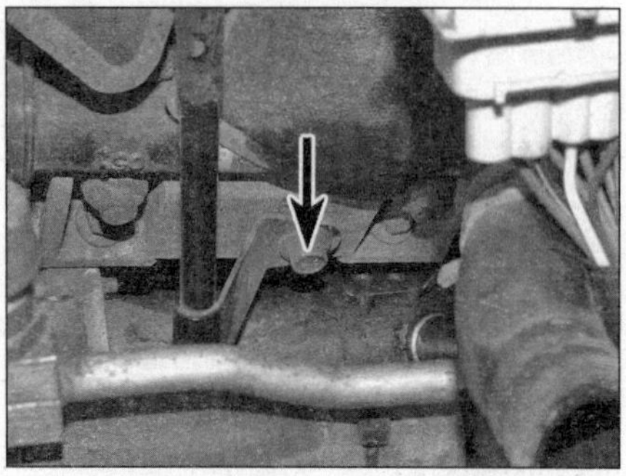

3.16 Dipstick guide tube bolt (arrowed)

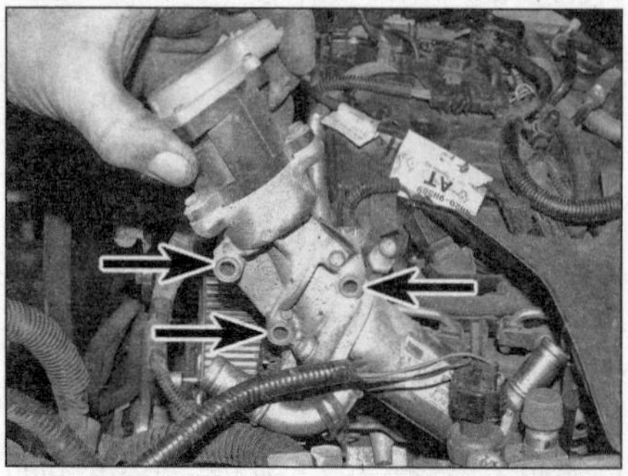

3.17 Undo the 3 bolts (locations arrowed) and remove the EGR valve/cooler

3.34 Disconnect the EGR outlet pipe (arrowed)

3.36 EGR outlet pipe bolts (arrowed)

and support it securely on axle stands (see *Jacking and vehicle support)*. Remove the roadwheel.

20 Working through the wheel arch, undo the 3 nuts and remove the exhaust manifold heat shield.

21 Slacken the clamp securing the outlet hose to the turbocharger.

22 Release the clip securing the EGR outlet pipe to the air-shut off valve.

23 Unclip the wiring harness, undo the Torx screw securing the bracket.

24 Undo the 2 bolts and detach the outlet pipe from the EGR valve. Discard the gasket – a new one must be fitted.

25 Undo the bolts securing the oil level dipstick guide tube brackets, then reposition the tube and tie it against the vehicle body.

26 Disconnect the wiring plug from the EGR valve.

27 Slacken the 2 bolts securing the EGR cooler and release the clip.

28 Clamp the hoses to minimise fluid loss, then release the clip and disconnect the rear coolant hose from the EGR cooler.

29 Undo the 3 bolts securing the EGR valve to the cylinder head, then undo the bolts securing the valve to the cooler. Discard the gasket.

EGR right-hand valve

30 Remove the auxiliary battery (where fitted) and battery tray, as described in Chapter 5, Section 4.

31 Undo the fasteners and remove the plastic cover from the top of the engine.

Models with diesel particulate filter

32 Unclip the low-pressure fuel hoses from the right-hand rear, top of the engine.

33 Undo the bolt and remove the fuel hoses support bracket.

All models

34 Release the clip securing the EGR outlet pipe to the air shut-off valve **(see illustration)**.

35 Unclip the wiring harness, undo the Torx screw securing the bracket.

36 Undo the 2 bolts and detach the outlet pipe from the EGR valve **(see illustration)**. Discard the gasket – a new one must be fitted.

37 Disconnect the wiring plug from the EGR valve.

38 Slacken the bolt securing the EGR cooler and release the clip.

39 Undo the 3 bolts securing the EGR valve to the cylinder head, then undo the bolts securing the valve to the cooler. Discard the gasket.

Notes

Chapter 5
Engine starting and charging

Contents

Degrees of difficulty

Easy, suitable for novice with little experience	**Fairly easy,** suitable for beginner with some experience	**Fairly difficult,** suitable for competent DIY mechanic	**Difficult,** suitable for experienced DIY mechanic	**Very difficult,** suitable for expert DIY or professional

Specifications

General

Electrical system type	12 volt, negative earth

Battery

Type	Lead-calcium maintenance-free 90 amp hr

Alternator

Type	Nippon Denso SC2 150 A
Regulated voltage	13.6 to 14.4 volts at 3000 engine rpm
Minimum brush length	No information available

Starter motor

Make and type	Nippon Denso pre-engaged P76S 2 kW

Glow plugs

Type	Beru GN045
Voltage	11 volts

Torque wrench settings

Torque wrench settings	Nm	lbf ft
Alternator mounting bolt	47	35
Battery terminal nut	11	8
Fuel cooler bolts	10	7
Glow plugs	10	7
Starter motor bolts	48	35
Starter motor support bracket bolts	10	7

1 General information and precautions

The engine electrical system includes all charging, starting and preheating components. Because of their engine-related functions, these components are covered separately from the body electrical devices such as the lights, instruments, etc (which are covered in Chapter 13, Section 2).

The electrical system is of the 12 volt, negative earth type.

The battery is of the low-maintenance or maintenance-free type, and is charged by the alternator, which is belt-driven from a crankshaft-mounted pulley. The alternator pulley incorporates a one-way clutch to reduce belt load during engine overrun.

The starter motor is of the pre-engaged reduction gear type, incorporating an integral solenoid. On starting, the solenoid moves the drive pinion into engagement with the flywheel ring gear before the starter motor is energised. Once the engine has started, a one-way clutch prevents the motor armature being driven by the engine until the pinion disengages from the flywheel. The motor is fitted with a reduction gear mechanism, in order to achieve the high torque necessary to turn the engine against the high compression pressures encountered in a diesel engine.

Further details of the various systems are given in the relevant Sections of this Chapter. While some repair procedures are given, the usual course of action is to renew the component concerned.

Precautions

It is necessary to take extra care when working on the electrical system, to avoid damage to semi-conductor devices (diodes and transistors), and to avoid the risk of personal injury. In addition to the precautions given in *Safety first!* at the beginning of this manual, observe the following when working on the system:

- *Always remove rings, watches, etc, before working on the electrical system.* Even with the battery disconnected, capacitive discharge could occur if a component's live terminal is earthed through a metal object. This could cause a shock or nasty burn.
- *Do not reverse the battery connections.* Components such as the alternator, preheating electronic control unit, or any other components having semi-conductor circuitry could be irreparably damaged.
- If the engine is being started using jump leads and a slave battery, connect the batteries *positive-to-positive* and *negative-to-negative* (see *Jump starting*). This also applies when connecting a battery charger.
- Never disconnect the battery terminals, the alternator, any electrical wiring or any test instruments, when the engine is running.
- Do not allow the engine to turn the alternator when the alternator is not connected.
- Never 'test' for alternator output by 'flashing' the output lead to earth.
- Never use an ohmmeter of the type incorporating a hand-cranked generator for circuit or continuity testing.
- Always ensure that the battery negative lead is disconnected when working on the electrical system.
- Before using electric-arc welding equipment on the car, disconnect the battery, alternator and components such as the preheating electronic control unit, ABS electronic control unit, etc, to protect them from the risk of damage.

The audio unit fitted as standard equipment by Land Rover may have a built-in security code, to deter thieves. If the power source to the unit is cut, the anti-theft system will activate. Even if the power source is immediately reconnected, the unit will not function until the correct security code has been entered. Therefore, if you do not know the correct security code for the audio unit, do not disconnect the battery negative terminal of the battery, nor remove the unit from the vehicle. Refer to the manufacturer's handbook supplied with the vehicle for details of how to enter the security code.

2 Electrical fault finding – general information

Refer to Chapter 13, Section 2.

3 Battery – testing and charging

Note: *Refer to the precautions given in 'Safety first!' and in Section 1 of this Chapter before proceeding.*

Testing

Standard and low maintenance battery

1 If the vehicle covers a small annual mileage, it is worthwhile checking the specific gravity of the electrolyte every three months to determine the state of charge of the battery. Use a hydrometer to make the check and compare the results with the following table. Note that the specific gravity readings assume an electrolyte temperature of 15°C; for every 10°C below 15°C subtract 0.007. For every 10°C above 15°C add 0.007.

	Above 25°C	Below 25°C
Fully-charged	*1.210 to 1.230*	*1.270 to 1.290*
70% charged	*1.170 to 1.190*	*1.230 to 1.250*
Discharged	*1.050 to 1.070*	*1.110 to 1.130*

2 If the battery condition is suspect, first check the specific gravity of electrolyte in each cell. A variation of 0.040 or more between any cells indicates loss of electrolyte or deterioration of the internal plates.

3 If the specific gravity variation is 0.040 or more, the battery should be renewed. If the cell variation is satisfactory but the battery is discharged, it should be charged as described later in this Section.

Maintenance-free battery

4 In cases where a 'sealed for life' maintenance-free battery is fitted, topping-up and testing of the electrolyte in each cell is not possible. The condition of the battery can therefore only be tested using a battery condition indicator or a voltmeter.

5 Certain models may be fitted with a maintenance-free battery, with a built-in charge condition indicator. The indicator is located in the top of the battery casing, and indicates the condition of the battery from its colour. If the indicator shows green, then the battery is in a good state of charge. If the indicator shows black, then the battery requires charging, as described later in this Section. If the indicator shows blue, then the electrolyte level in the battery is too low to allow further use, and the battery should be renewed.

Caution: Do not attempt to charge, load or jump start a battery when the indicator shows clear/yellow.

6 If testing the battery using a voltmeter, connect the voltmeter across the battery. The test is only accurate if the battery has not been subjected to any kind of charge for the previous six hours. If this is not the case, switch on the headlights for 30 seconds, then wait four to five minutes before testing the battery after switching off the headlights. All other electrical circuits must be switched off, so check that the doors and tailgate are fully shut when making the test.

7 If the voltage reading is less than 12.2 volts, then the battery is discharged, whilst a reading of 12.2 to 12.4 volts indicates a partially discharged condition.

8 If the battery is to be charged, remove it from the vehicle (Section 4) and charge it as described later in this Section.

Charging

Note: *The following is intended as a guide only. Always refer to the manufacturer's recommendations (often printed on a label attached to the battery) before charging a battery.*

Standard and low maintenance battery

9 Charge the battery at a rate of 3.5 to 4 amps and continue to charge the battery at this rate until no further rise in specific gravity is noted over a four hour period.

10 Alternatively, a trickle charger charging at the rate of 1.5 amps can safely be used overnight.

11 Specially rapid 'boost' charges which are claimed to restore the power of the battery in 1 to 2 hours are not recommended, as they can cause serious damage to the battery plates through overheating.

12 While charging the battery, note that the temperature of the electrolyte should never exceed 38°C.

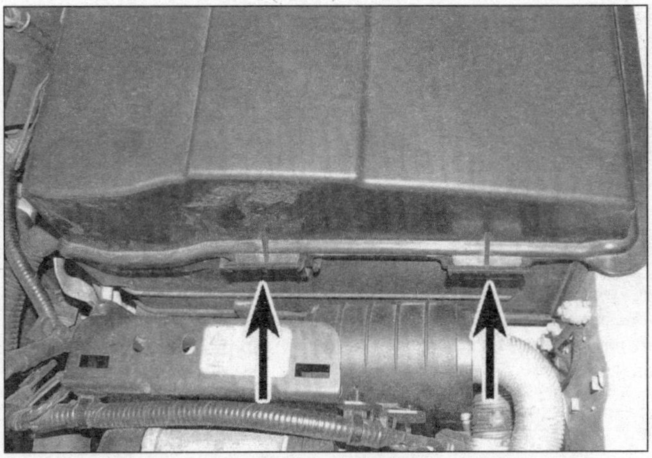

4.3a Release the clips at the front (arrowed) ...

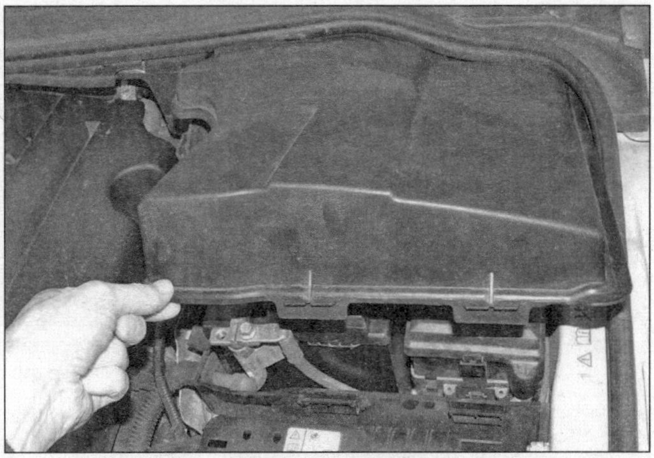

4.3b ... and remove the battery cover

Maintenance-free battery

13 This battery type takes considerably longer to fully recharge than the standard type, the time taken being dependent on the extent of discharge, but it can take anything up to three days.

14 A constant voltage type charger is required to be set, when connected, to 13.9 to 14.8 volts with a charger current below 25 amps. Using this method, the battery should be usable within three hours, giving a voltage reading of 12.5 volts, but this is for a partially-discharged battery and, as mentioned, full charging can take considerably longer.

15 If the battery is to be charged from a fully-discharged state (condition reading less than 12.2 volts), have it recharged by your Land Rover dealer or local automotive electrician, as the charge rate is higher and constant supervision during charging is necessary.

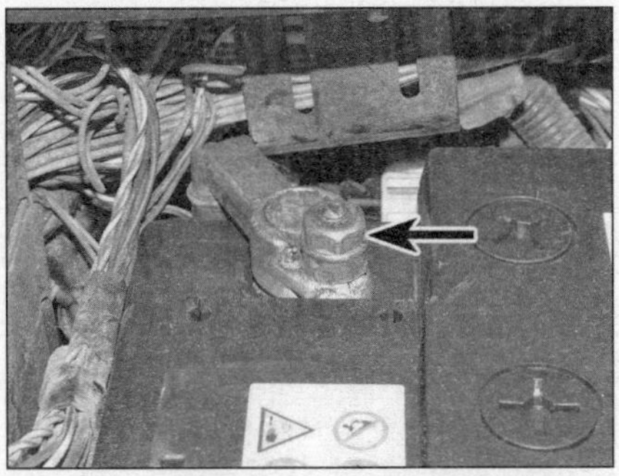

4.4 Slacken the nut (arrowed) and disconnect the negative lead clamp

4 Batteries and trays – disconnection, removal and refitting

Note: *Refer to the precautions given in 'Safety first!' and in Section 1 of this Chapter before proceeding.*

Disconnection

1 The battery is located at the left-hand side of the engine compartment.

2 The battery lead disconnection procedure depends on the vehicle condition. Follow the appropriate procedure:

Engine running

a) Apply the handbrake, switch off the ignition and remove the key.
b) Wait at least 2 minutes for any residual electrical energy to dissipate.

Vehicle powered down, alarmed and locked

a) Unlock the vehicle, and disarm the alarm using the 'plip' button. If the battery is discharged, unlock the vehicle using the key in the passenger's door lock.
b) Turn the ignition switch to position II, apply the handbrake.
c) Turn off the ignition and remove the key.
d) Wait at least 2 minutes for any residual electrical energy to dissipate.

Vehicle unlocked

a) Turn the ignition switch to position II, apply the handbrake.
b) Turn off the ignition and remove the key.
c) Wait at least 2 minutes for any residual electrical energy to dissipate.

All conditions

3 Unclip and remove the battery cover **(see illustrations)**.

4 Slacken the nut and disconnect the battery negative lead clamp **(see illustration)**.

Removal

Main battery and tray

5 Disconnect the battery negative lead as described previously in this Section.

6 Slacken the nut and disconnect the battery positive terminal clamp **(see illustration)**.

7 Undo the bolts and remove the battery clamp **(see illustration)**.

8 Lift the battery from position. Disconnect the vent pipe as the battery is withdrawn **(see illustration)**.

9 If required, undo the screw, and lift the

4.6 Slacken the nut (arrowed) and disconnect the positive lead clamp

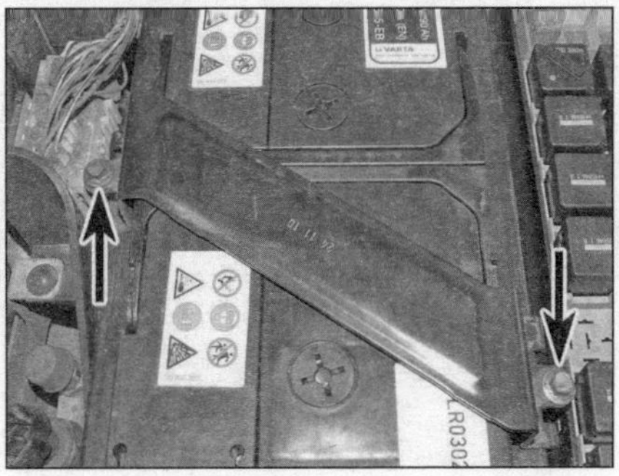

4.7 Undo the bolts (arrowed) and remove the battery clamp

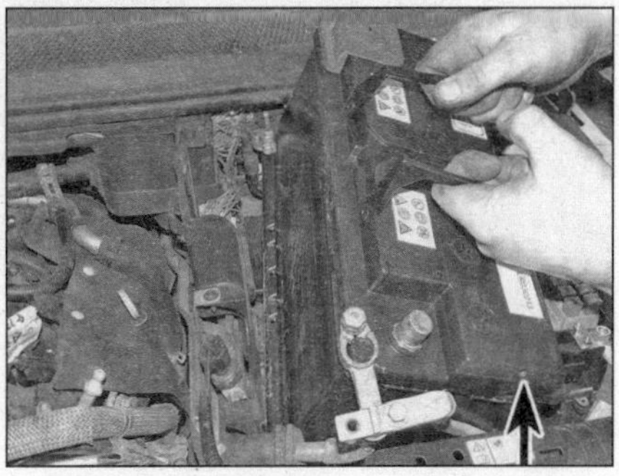

4.8 Lift the battery from place and disconnect the vent hose (arrowed)

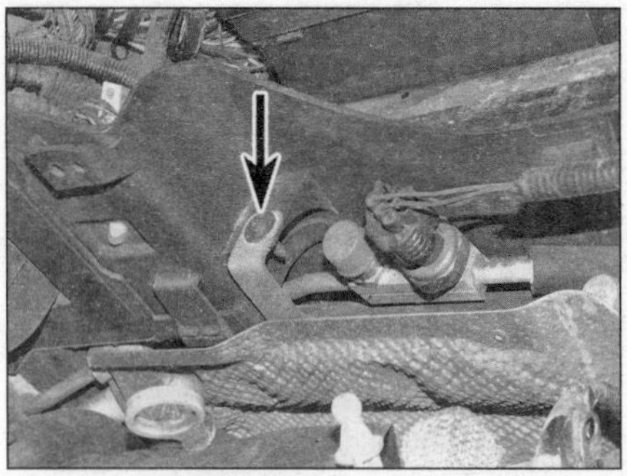
4.9a Undo the screw (arrowed) ...

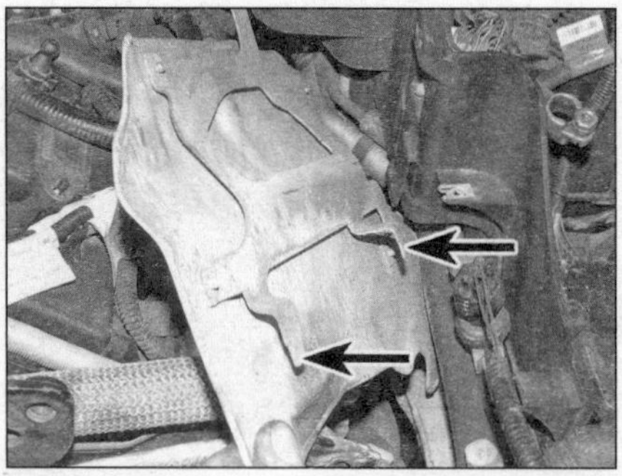
4.9b ... and pull the heat shield upwards to release the clips (arrowed)

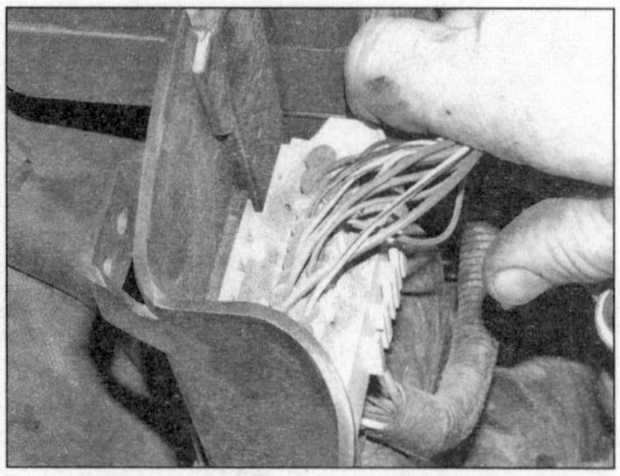
4.10a Unclip the wiring plug ...

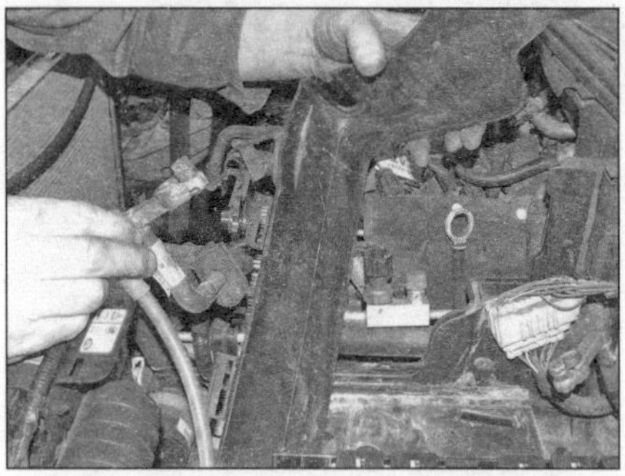
4.10b ... release the cable, and unclip the battery compartment side wall ...

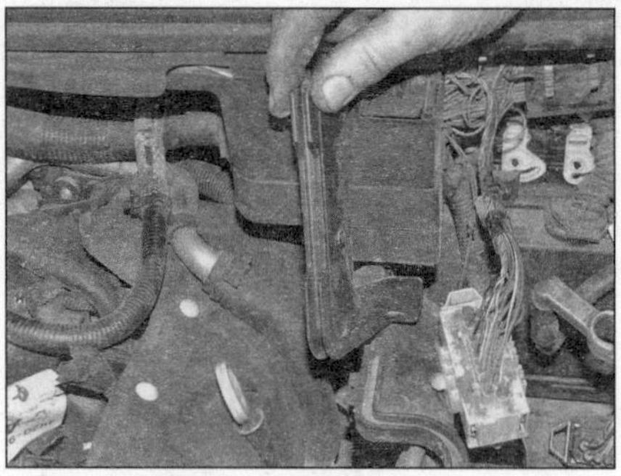
4.10c ... and end piece

4.11 Remove the support bracket screw (arrowed)

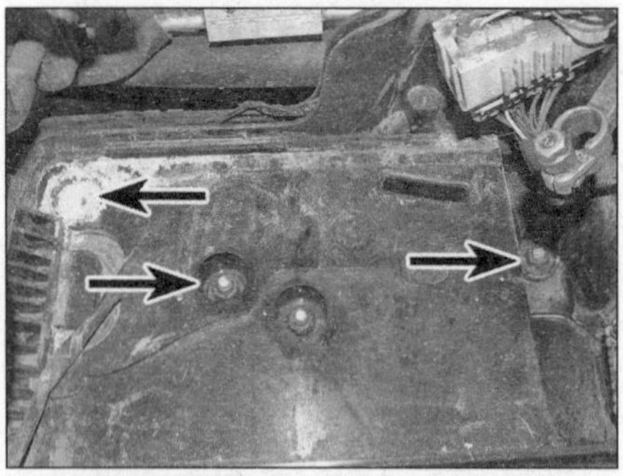
4.12a Undo the nuts (arrowed) ...

engine compartment upper heat shield to release the 2 clips **(see illustrations)**.

10 Release the battery positive lead grommet, unclip the wiring connector block, then unclip the battery compartment side walls **(see illustrations)**.

11 Undo the screw securing the pipe bracket **(see illustration)**.

12 Undo the 3 nuts and remove the battery tray **(see illustration)**.

Auxiliary battery and tray

Note: *Although only some vehicles were fitted with an auxiliary battery, all are fitted with a cover and battery tray.*

13 Unclip the auxiliary battery cover **(see illustration)**. The cover is located on the right-hand side of the engine compartment.

14 Undo the clamp and disconnect the battery negative lead, followed by the positive lead.

15 Release the clamp and remove the battery.

16 Undo the screw, release the clips and remove the battery tray side walls **(see illustrations)**.

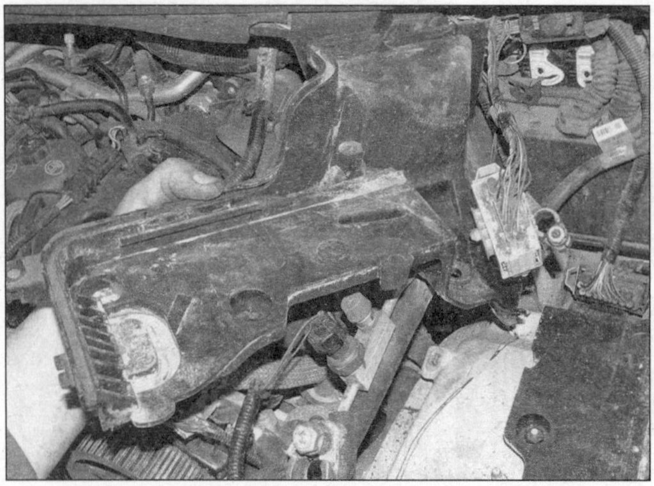
4.12b ... and remove the battery tray

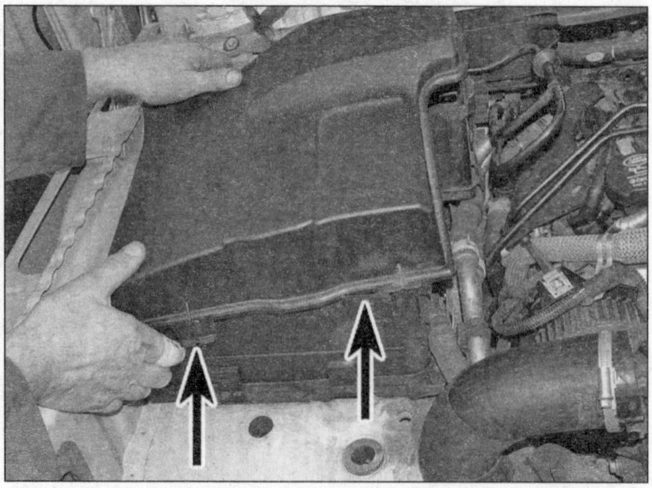
4.13 Release the clips (arrowed) and remove the auxiliary battery cover

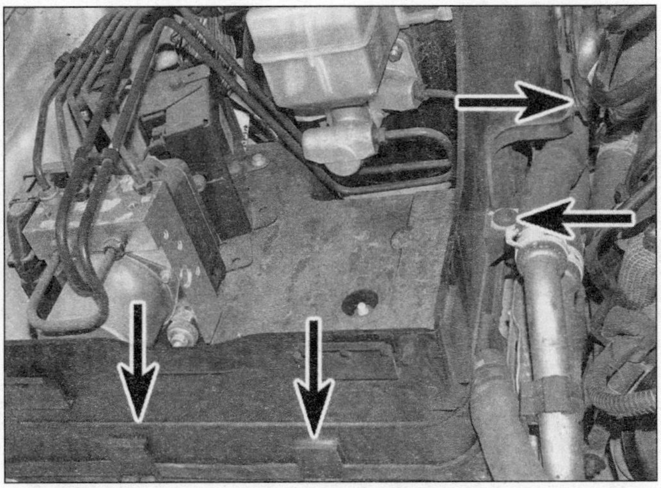

4.16a Undo the screw, release the clips (arrowed) ...

4.16b ... remove the battery tray side wall ...

17 Undo the screw securing the pipe bracket **(see illustration)**.

18 Undo the 3 nuts and remove the battery tray **(see illustration)**.

Refitting

19 Refitting is a reversal of removal, but always connect the positive terminal clamp first and the negative terminal clamp last. After connecting the battery terminals, it's a good idea to apply a layer of petroleum jelly to the terminals to prevent corrosion.

20 After reconnecting the battery leads, switch on the ignition, and apply the handbrake several times until the warning light is extinguished.

21 On models with an electrically-operated sunroof, if the battery has been disconnected, the sunroof will have lost its 'one-touch' and 'anti-trap' functions. To restore these functions the sunroof ECU must be recalibrated by pressing the lower part of the sunroof switch for 20 seconds. The automatic calibration process will commence. This includes fully opening, and closing the sunroof.

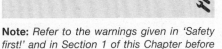

5 Charging system – testing

Note: *Refer to the warnings given in 'Safety first!' and in Section 1 of this Chapter before proceeding.*

1 If the ignition (no-charge) warning light fails to illuminate when the ignition is switched on, first check the security of the alternator wiring connections. If satisfactory, check that the warning light bulb has not blown, and that the bulbholder is secure in its location in the instrument panel. If the light still fails to illuminate, check the continuity of the warning light feed wire from the alternator to the bulbholder. If all is satisfactory, the alternator is at fault, and should be renewed, or taken to an auto-electrician for testing and repair.

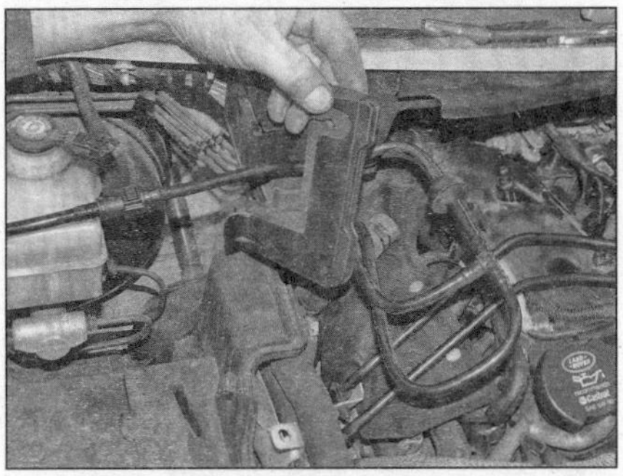

4.16c ... and end piece

2 If the ignition warning light illuminates when the engine is running, stop the engine and check that the drivebelt is correctly tensioned (Chapter 1, Section 9) and that the alternator connections are secure. If the fault persists, the alternator should be renewed, or taken to an auto-electrician for testing and repair.

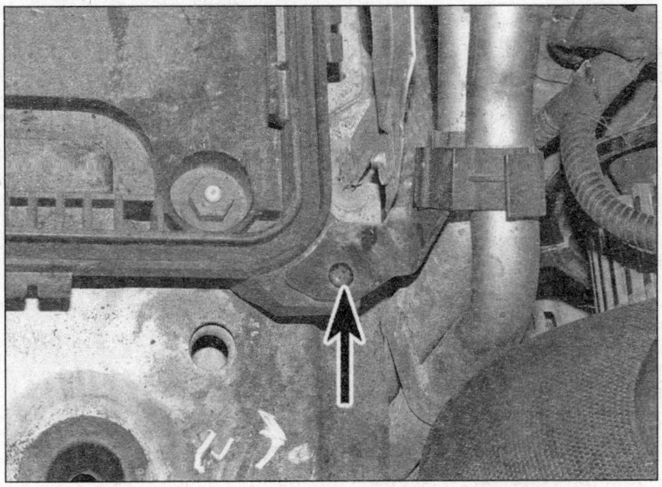

4.17 Undo the pipe support bracket screw (arrowed)

4.18 Undo the nuts (arrowed) and remove the battery tray

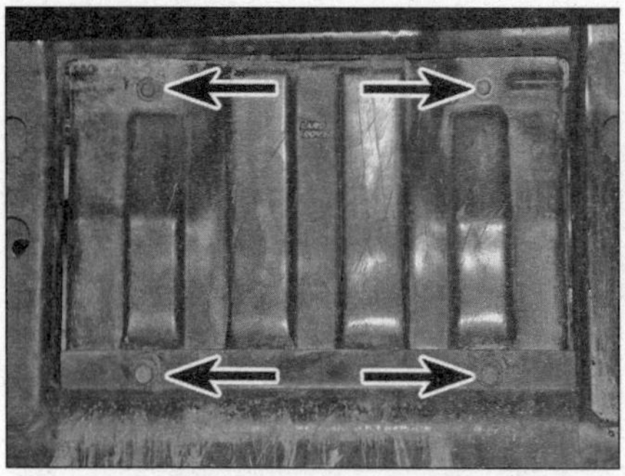

6.4 Undo the bolts (arrowed) and remove the panel beneath the radiator

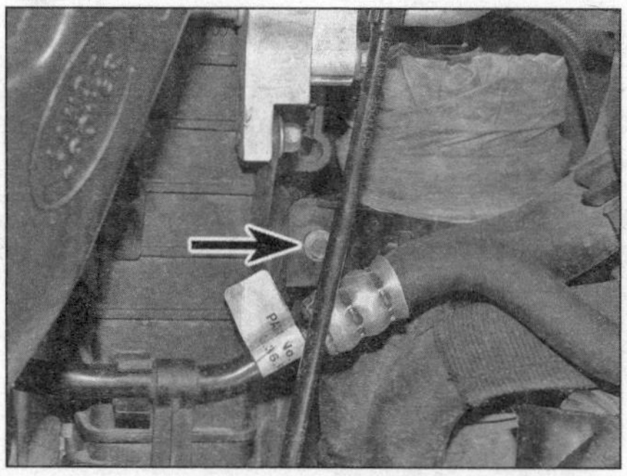

6.6a Undo the air intake pipe bracket screw (arrowed)

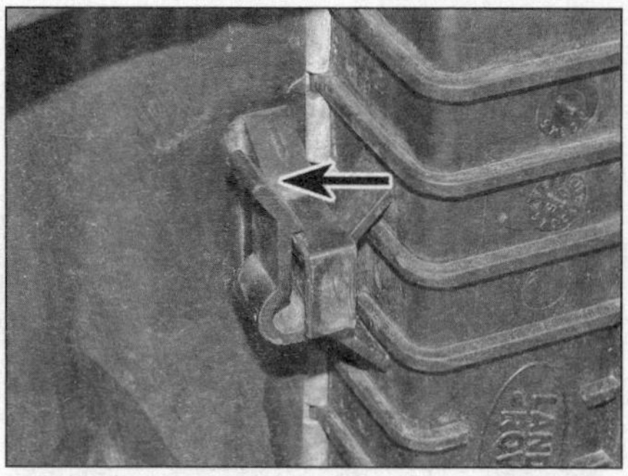

6.6b Release the clip (arrowed) each side and lift out the cooling fan lower shroud

3 If the alternator output is suspect even though the warning light functions correctly, the regulated voltage may be checked as follows.

4 Connect a voltmeter across the battery terminals, and start the engine.

5 Increase the engine speed until the voltmeter reading remains steady; as a rough guide, the reading should be between 13.6 and 14.4 volts.

6 Switch on as many electrical accessories (headlights, heater blower, cigarette lighter, etc) as possible, and check that the alternator maintains the regulated voltage between 13.6 and 14.4 volts. It may be necessary to increase engine speed slightly.

7 If the regulated voltage is not as stated, the fault may be due to worn brushes, weak brush springs, a faulty voltage regulator, a faulty diode, a severed phase winding, or worn or damaged slip-rings. The alternator should be renewed, or taken to an auto-electrician for testing and repair.

6 Alternator – removal and refitting

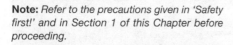

Note: *Refer to the precautions given in 'Safety first!' and in Section 1 of this Chapter before proceeding.*

Removal

1 Disconnect the battery negative lead as described in Section 4.

2 Remove the cooling fan as described in Chapter 3, Section 5.

3 Raise the front of the vehicle and support it securely on axle stands (see *Jacking and vehicle support*).

4 Undo the 4 bolts and remove the access panel beneath the radiator **(see illustration)**.

5 Unclip the pipes and hoses from the cooling fan lower shroud.

6 Undo the screw, release the clip each side, and remove the cooling fan lower shroud **(see illustrations)**.

7 Rotate the tensioner anti-clockwise and remove the auxiliary drivebelt **(see illustration)**.

8 Prise up the rubber boot, undo the nut and disconnect the heavy duty lead from the alternator, then disconnect the wiring plug **(see illustration)**.

9 Undo the 3 alternator mounting bolts **(see illustrations)**.

10 Manoeuvre the alternator from position.

Refitting

11 Refitting is a reversal of removal, but tighten the alternator mounting bolts in the following sequence:

1) *Upper mounting bolt.*
2) *Lower front mounting bolt.*
3) *Lower rear mounting bolt.*

7 Alternator – brush renewal

1 It would appear at the time of writing, that new brushes are not available. However, check with a Land Rover dealer or auto-electrical specialist before dismantling the alternator or renewing it.

8 Starting system – testing

Note: *Refer to the precautions given in 'Safety first!' and in Section 1 of this Chapter before proceeding.*

1 If the starter motor fails to operate when the ignition key is turned to the appropriate position, the possible causes are as follows:

a) *The battery is faulty.*
b) *The electrical connections between the switch, solenoid, battery and starter motor are somewhere failing to pass the necessary current from the battery through the starter to earth.*
c) *The solenoid is faulty.*
d) *The starter motor is mechanically or electrically defective.*
e) *The starter motor solenoid relay is faulty.*

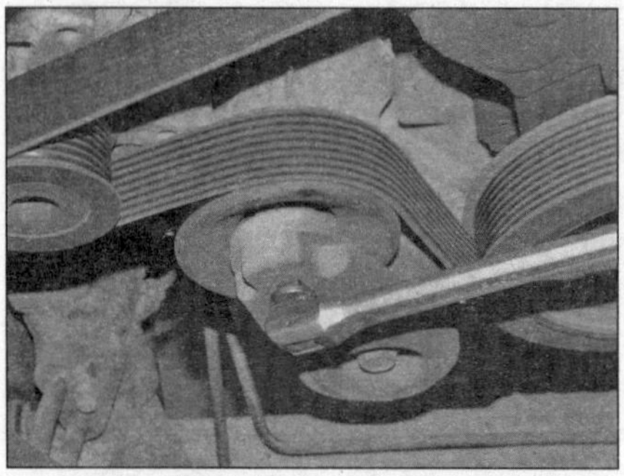

6.7 Rotate the tensioner anti-clockwise and remove the auxiliary drivebelt

6.8 Prise up the rubber boot (arrowed) and disconnect the main lead followed by the plug on the rear of the alternator (arrowed)

6.9 The alternator is secured by 2 bolts on the underside and a bolt on top (arrowed)

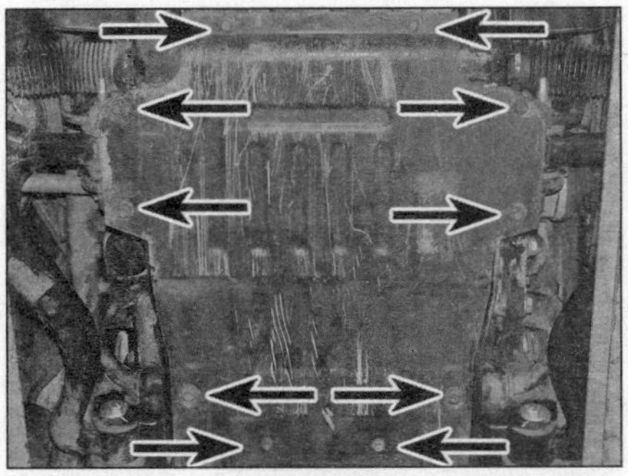

9.3 Engine undershield retaining bolts (arrowed)

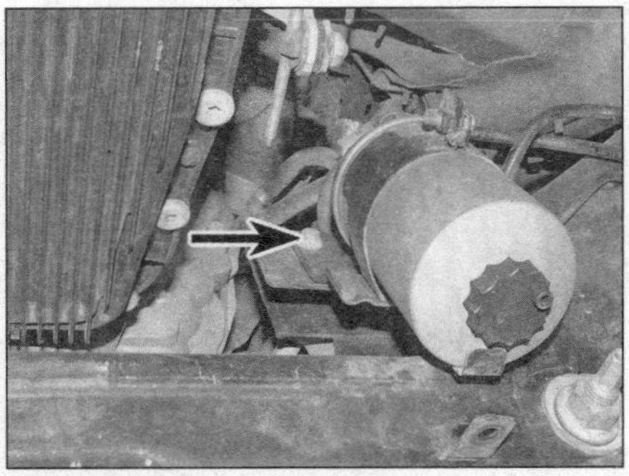

9.4a Fuel filter mounting bolt (arrowed)

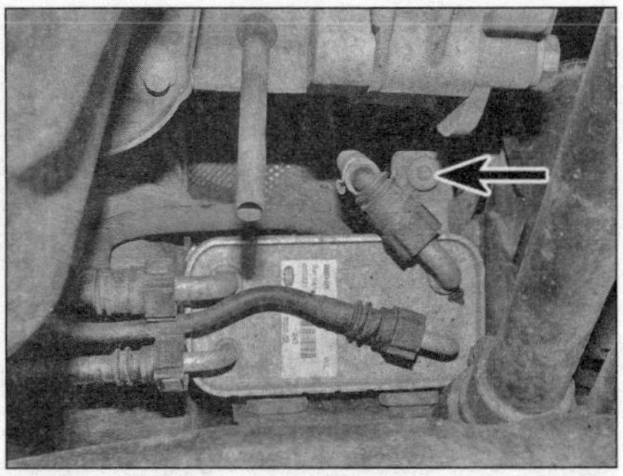

9.4b Fuel cooler mounting bolt (arrowed)

2 To check the battery, switch on the headlights. If they dim after a few seconds, this indicates that the battery is discharged – recharge (see Section 3) or renew the battery. If the headlights glow brightly, operate the starter switch and observe the lights. If they dim, then this indicates that current is reaching the starter motor, therefore the fault must lie in the starter motor. If the lights continue to glow brightly (and no clicking sound can be heard from the starter motor solenoid), this indicates that there is a fault in the circuit or solenoid – see the following paragraphs. If the starter motor turns slowly when operated, but the battery is in good condition, then this indicates either that the starter motor is faulty, or there is considerable resistance somewhere in the circuit.

3 If a fault in the circuit is suspected, disconnect the battery leads, the starter/solenoid wiring and the engine/transmission earth strap(s). Thoroughly clean the connections, and reconnect the leads and wiring. Use a voltmeter or test light to check that full battery voltage is available at the battery positive lead connection to the solenoid. Smear petroleum jelly around the battery terminals to prevent corrosion – corroded connections are among the most frequent causes of electrical system faults.

4 If the battery and all connections are in good condition, check the circuit by disconnecting the wire from the solenoid blade terminal. Connect a voltmeter or test light between the wire end and a good earth (such as the battery negative terminal), and check that the wire is live when the ignition switch is turned to the 'start' position. If it is, then the circuit is sound – if not, there is a fault in the ignition/starter switch or wiring.

5 The solenoid contacts can be checked by connecting a voltmeter or test light between the battery positive feed connection on the starter side of the solenoid, and earth. When the ignition switch is turned to the 'start' position, there should be a reading or lighted bulb, as applicable. If there is no reading or lighted bulb, the solenoid is faulty and should be renewed.

6 If the circuit and solenoid are proved sound, the fault must lie in the starter motor. The starter motor can be checked by a Land Rover dealer or an automotive electrical specialist. A specialist may be able to overhaul the unit at a cost significantly less than that of a new or exchange starter motor.

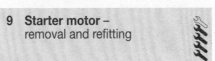

9 Starter motor – removal and refitting

Note: *Refer to the precautions given in 'Safety first!' and in Section 1 of this Chapter before proceeding.*

Removal

1 Disconnect the battery negative lead as described in Section 4.

2 Raise the front of the vehicle and support it securely on axle stands (see *Jacking and vehicle support*).

3 Undo the bolts and remove the engine undershield **(see illustration)**.

4 Undo the fuel filter and cooler bolts, then move the cooler upwards to allow access to the starter motor **(see illustrations)**. There's no need to disconnect any fuel pipes.

5 Undo the bolt (where fitted) securing the wiring harness, then remove the 4 bolts securing the starter motor support bracket **(see illustration)**.

6 Undo the bolts, and detach the starter from the transmission bellhousing **(see illustration)**.

7 Prise up the rubber boot, undo the large upper nut and the smaller nut to the side, then disconnect the electrical connections from the starter motor as it's withdrawn **(see illustration)**. Manoeuvre the starter motor from place.

Refitting

8 Refitting is a reversal of removal. Tighten the fasteners to their specified torque, where given.

10 Starter motor – brush renewal

Starter motor brush renewal is considered to be beyond the scope of the DIY mechanic, and the task should be entrusted to a Land Rover dealer, or an auto-electrical specialist.

9.5 Remove the starter motor support bracket (arrowed)

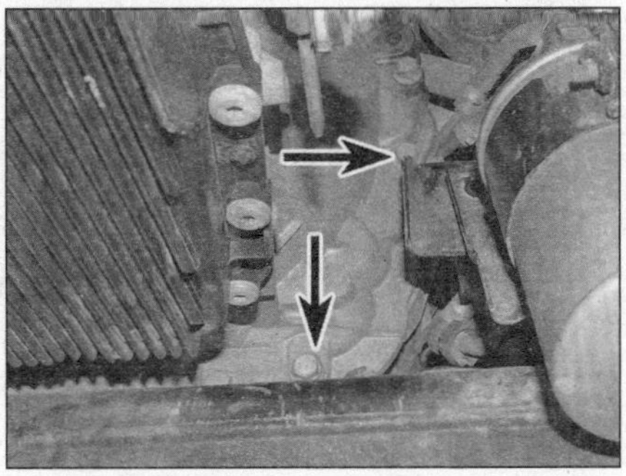

9.6 Starter motor retaining bolts (arrowed)

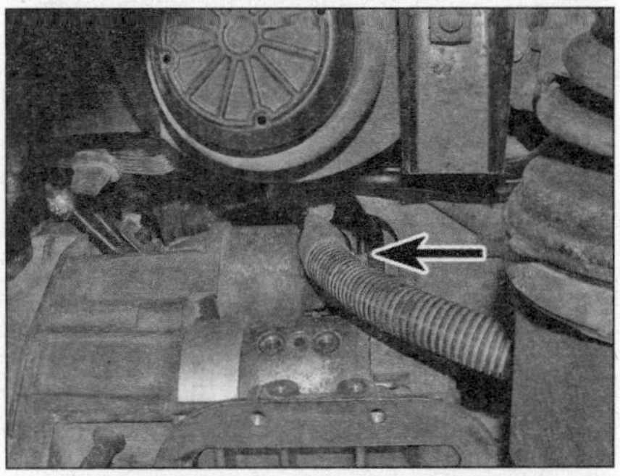

9.7 Disconnect the wiring harness from the top/front of the starter motor (arrowed)

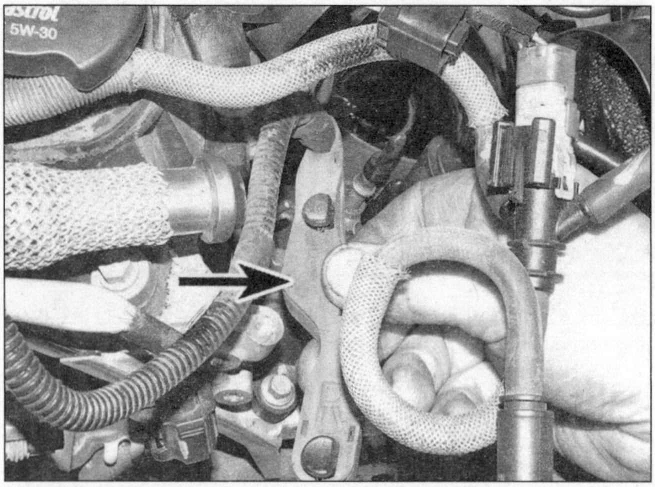

12.3 Pull the connector assembly (arrowed) from the glow plugs

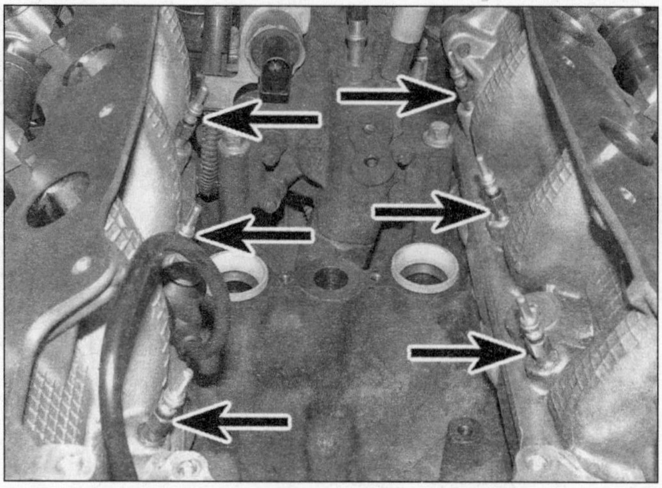

12.4 The glow plugs (arrowed) are located in the V of the engine

11 Preheating system – description and testing

Description

1 Heater (glow) plugs are electrically-operated, and controlled by the engine management ECM. Using information supplied from engine coolant temperature sensors the ECM energises the plugs for a brief period before starting to aid combustion, and for a brief period after starting to reduce the warm up period, reduce combustion noise and improve exhaust emissions. Separate current supply relays are fitted to the engine compartment fuse/relay box for each cylinder bank.

Testing

Note: *Refer to the precautions given in 'Safety first!' and in Section 1 of this Chapter before proceeding.*

2 Remove the glow plugs as described in Section 12.

3 With battery voltage applied, the tip of the plug should start to glow within 5 seconds. If the tip fails to glow first, renew it.

4 If a starting fault is still not evident, have the engine management systems self-diagnosis facility interrogated using a fault code reader. Consult a Land Rover dealer or specialist. The vehicle's diagnostic plug is located in the driver's side lower facia panel.

12 Glow plugs – removal, inspection and refitting

Caution: If the preheating system has just been energised, or if the engine has been running, the glow plugs may be extremely hot.

Removal

1 Disconnect the battery negative lead as described in Section 4.

2 Remove the crankcase vent oil separator as described in Chapter 2, Section 14.

3 Note the wiring routing, and pull the wiring connector assembly from the glow plugs **(see illustration)**.

4 Slacken and remove the glow plugs **(see illustration)**.

Inspection

5 Inspect the glow plugs for physical damage. Burnt or eroded glow plug tips can be caused by a bad injector spray pattern. Have the injectors checked if this sort of damage is found.

6 The glow plugs can be energised by applying 12 volts to them, to verify that they heat up evenly and in the required time. Observe the following precautions:

a) Support the glow plug by clamping it carefully in a vice or self-locking pliers. Remember – it will become ***red-hot****.*

b) Make sure that the power supply or test lead incorporates a fuse or overload trip, to protect against damage from a short-circuit.

c) After testing, allow the glow plug to cool for several minutes before attempting to handle it.

7 A glow plug in good condition will start to glow red at the tip after drawing current for 5 seconds or so. Any plug which takes much longer to start glowing, or which starts glowing in the middle instead of at the tip, is defective – the tip must glow first.

Refitting

8 Refitting is a reversal of removal, bearing in mind the following points:

a) Apply a smear of copper-based anti-seize compound to the plug threads, and tighten the glow plugs to the specified torque. Do not overtighten, as this can damage the glow plug element.

b) Ensure that the glow plug wiring is routed as noted before removal.

Chapter 6
Clutch

Contents

Degrees of difficulty

Easy, suitable for novice with little experience	**Fairly easy,** suitable for beginner with some experience	**Fairly difficult,** suitable for competent DIY mechanic	**Difficult,** suitable for experienced DIY mechanic	**Very difficult,** suitable for expert DIY or professional

Specifications

General

Clutch type	Single dry plate, diaphragm spring, hydraulically-operated, self-adjusting
Adjustment	Automatic
Hydraulic fluid type	DOT 4

Clutch disc

Diameter	258.0 mm
Thickness:	
New	3.2 mm
Minimum above rivet head	0.2 mm

Torque wrench settings

Torque wrench settings	Nm	lbf ft
Clutch cover bolts	25	18
Clutch master cylinder bolts	25	18
Clutch slave cylinder bolts	25	18
Hydraulic fluid pipe and hose unions	15	11

1 General information

All manual transmission models are fitted with a single dry plate clutch, which consists of five main components – friction disc, pressure plate, diaphragm spring, cover, and release bearing.

The friction disc is free to slide along the splines of the gearbox input shaft, and is held in position between the flywheel and the pressure plate by the pressure exerted on the pressure plate by the diaphragm spring. Friction lining material is riveted to both sides of the friction disc. All models are equipped with a dual mass flywheel which incorporates torsional damping to absorb transmission shocks.

The diaphragm spring is mounted on pins, and is held in place in the cover by annular fulcrum rings.

The release bearing is located on a guide sleeve at the front of the gearbox, and is integral with the concentric slave cylinder. The bearing is free to slide on the sleeve, under the action of the slave cylinder.

The release mechanism is operated by the clutch pedal, using hydraulic pressure. The pedal acts on the hydraulic master cylinder pushrod, and a slave cylinder, mounted on the input shaft guide sleeve, which is integral with the release bearing.

When the clutch pedal is depressed, slave cylinder pushes the release bearing forwards, to bear against the centre of the diaphragm spring, thus pushing the centre of the diaphragm spring inwards. The diaphragm spring acts against the fulcrum rings in the cover; as the centre of the spring is pushed in, the outside of the spring is pushed out, so allowing the pressure plate to move backwards away from the friction disc.

When the clutch pedal is released, the diaphragm spring forces the pressure plate into contact with the friction linings on the friction disc, and simultaneously pushes the friction disc forwards on its splines, forcing it against the flywheel. The friction disc is now firmly sandwiched between the pressure plate and the flywheel, and drive is taken up.

All models are fitted with a Self-Adjusting Clutch (SAC), which compensates for friction disc wear by altering the attitude of the diaphragm spring fingers by means of a sprung mechanism within the pressure plate cover. This ensures a consistent clutch pedal 'feel' over the life of the clutch.

2 Clutch assembly – removal, inspection and refitting

Warning: Dust created by clutch wear and deposited on the clutch components may contain asbestos, which is a health hazard. DO NOT blow it out with compressed air, nor inhale any of it. DO NOT use petrol (or petroleum-based solvents) to clean off the dust. Brake system cleaner or methylated spirit should be used to flush the dust into a suitable receptacle. After the clutch components are wiped clean with rags, dispose of the contaminated rags and cleaner in a sealed, marked container.

Removal

1 Remove the gearbox, as described in Chapter 7A, Section 3.

2 If the original clutch is to be refitted, make alignment marks between the clutch cover and the flywheel, so that the clutch can be refitted in its original position.

3 Progressively unscrew the bolts securing the clutch cover to the flywheel **(see illustration)**.

4 Withdraw the clutch cover from the flywheel. Be prepared to catch the clutch friction disc, which may drop out of the cover as it is withdrawn, and note which way round the friction disc is fitted. The greater projecting side of the hub faces the flywheel.

Inspection

5 With the clutch assembly removed, clean off all traces of dust using a dry cloth. Although most friction discs now have asbestos-free linings, some do not, and it is wise to take suitable precautions; *asbestos dust is harmful, and must not be inhaled.*

6 Examine the linings of the clutch disc for wear or loose rivets, and the disc for distortion, cracks and worn splines. The surface of the friction linings may be highly glazed, but, as long as the friction material pattern can be clearly seen, this is satisfactory. If there is any sign of oil contamination, indicated by a continuous, or patchy, shiny black discolouration, the disc must be renewed. The source of the contamination must be traced and rectified before fitting new clutch components; typically, a leaking crankshaft rear oil seal or gearbox input shaft oil seal – or both – will be to blame (renewal procedures are given in Chapter 2, Section 12, and Chapter 7A, Section 5, respectively). The disc must also be renewed if the lining thickness has worn down to, or just above, the level of the rivet heads. Given the amount of labour involved in removing the clutch, if in any doubt, renew the assembly.

7 Check the machined faces of the flywheel and pressure plate. If either is grooved, or heavily scored, renewal is necessary. The pressure plate must also be renewed if any cracks are apparent, or if the diaphragm spring is damaged or its pressure suspect.

8 With the clutch removed, it is advisable to check the condition of the release bearing, as described in Section 3. It is considered good practice to renew the release bearing as a matter of course, whenever new clutch components are fitted, given the amount of work required to gain access to the clutch.

Refitting

9 It is important to ensure that no oil or grease gets onto the friction disc linings, or the pressure plate and flywheel faces. It is advisable to refit the clutch assembly with clean hands, and to wipe down the pressure plate and flywheel faces with a clean rag before assembly begins.

10 Apply a smear of clutch assembly grease to the splines of the friction disc hub, then offer the disc to the flywheel, with the greater projecting side of the hub facing the flywheel (most friction discs will have a 'transmission side' marking, which should face the transmission) **(see illustration)**.

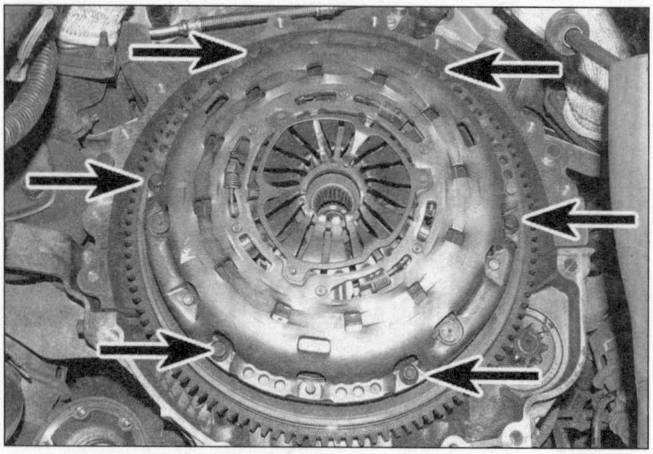

2.3 Undo the clutch cover bolts (arrowed)

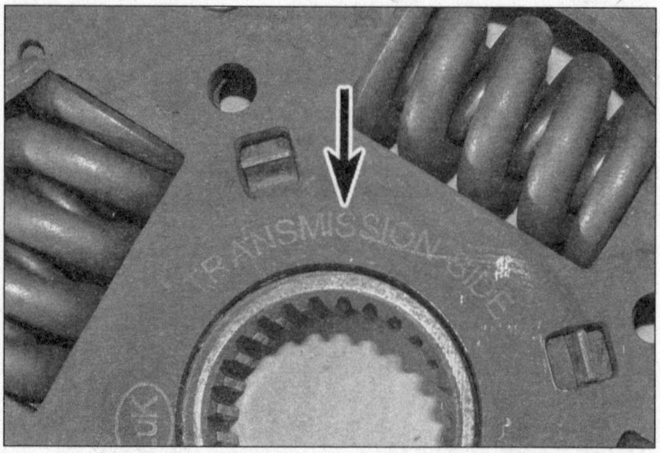

2.10 The disc is marked 'transmission side' (arrowed)

2.11a Compress the diaphragm fingers ...

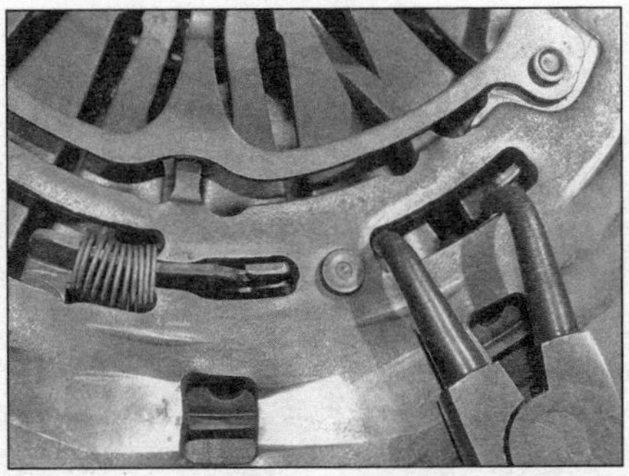

2.11b ... and rotate the adjustment ring fully anti-clockwise

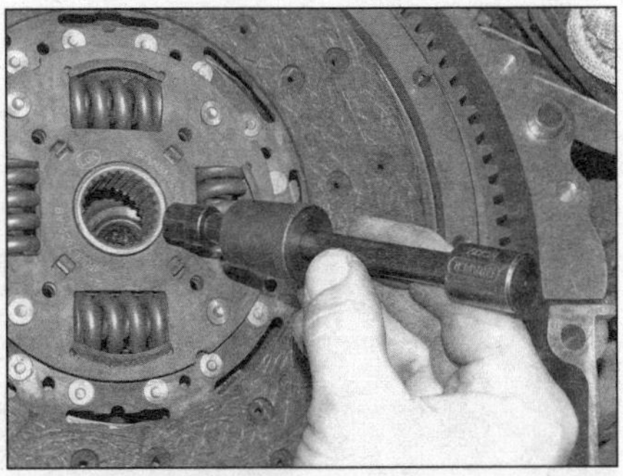

2.14 The centralisation tool must be a good fit in the centre of the friction plate and the flywheel spigot bearing

Hold the friction disc against the flywheel while the cover/pressure plate assembly is offered into position.

11 If the original clutch cover is to be refitted, using a large, circular spacer, compress the diaphragm fingers evenly, until the adjustment ring can be rotated fully anti-clockwise. Holding the adjustment ring in this position, release the fingers. The adjustment ring will be held in this position until the clutch pedal is depressed under normal operation **(see illustrations)**. The pressure plate/clutch cover assembly is now ready for fitting.

12 Fit the clutch cover assembly, where applicable aligning the marks on the flywheel and clutch cover. Refit the securing bolts, and tighten them finger-tight, so that the friction disc is gripped, but can still be moved. Note that the pressure plate assembly locates on dowels.

13 The friction disc must now be centralised, so that when the engine and gearbox are mated, the gearbox input shaft splines will pass through the splines in the friction disc hub.

14 Centralisation can be carried out by inserting a round bar or a long screwdriver through the hole in the centre of the friction disc, so that the end of the bar rests in the spigot bearing in the centre of the crankshaft. Where possible, use a blunt instrument, but if a screwdriver is used, wrap tape around the blade to prevent damage to the bearing surface. Moving the bar sideways or up and down as necessary, move the friction disc in whichever direction is necessary to achieve centralisation. With the bar removed, view the friction disc hub in relation to the hole in the centre of the crankshaft and the circle created by the ends of the diaphragm spring fingers. When the hub appears exactly in the centre, all is correct. Alternatively, use a clutch plate alignment tool **(see illustration)**.

15 Tighten the cover retaining bolts gradually in a diagonal sequence, to the specified torque. Remove the alignment tool.

16 Refit the gearbox as described in Chapter 7A, Section 3.

3 Hydraulic slave cylinder – removal, overhaul and refitting

Warning: Hydraulic fluid is poisonous; wash off immediately and thoroughly in the case of skin contact, and seek immediate medical advice if any fluid is swallowed or gets into the eyes. Certain types of hydraulic fluid are inflammable, and may ignite when allowed into contact with hot components. When servicing any hydraulic system, it is safest to assume that the fluid IS inflammable, and to take precautions against the risk of fire as though it is petrol that is being handled. Finally, it is hygroscopic (it absorbs moisture from the air) – old fluid may be contaminated, and unfit for further use. When topping-up or renewing the fluid, always use the recommended type, and ensure that it comes from a freshly-opened sealed container.

Caution: Hydraulic fluid is an effective paint stripper, and will attack plastics; if any is spilt, it should be washed off immediately, using copious quantities of fresh water

Removal

1 Remove the transmission as described in Chapter 7A, Section 3.

2 Pull out the retaining clip to split the slave cylinder from the connecting pipe in the transmission housing **(see illustration)**.

3 Undo the retaining bolt and pull the connecting pipe from the transmission bellhousing. Discard the O-ring seal, a new one must be fitted **(see illustration)**.

4 Inside the bellhousing, unscrew and remove the 3 mounting bolts, then withdraw the slave cylinder/release bearing over the transmission input shaft **(see illustration)**.

Refitting

5 Refitting is a reversal of removal, noting the following points:

a) Make sure the retaining clip is located securely.

b) Tighten the release bearing/slave cylinder mounting bolts to the specified torque.

c) Refit the transmission as described in Chapter 7A, Section 3.

d) On completion, bleed the clutch as described in Section 4.

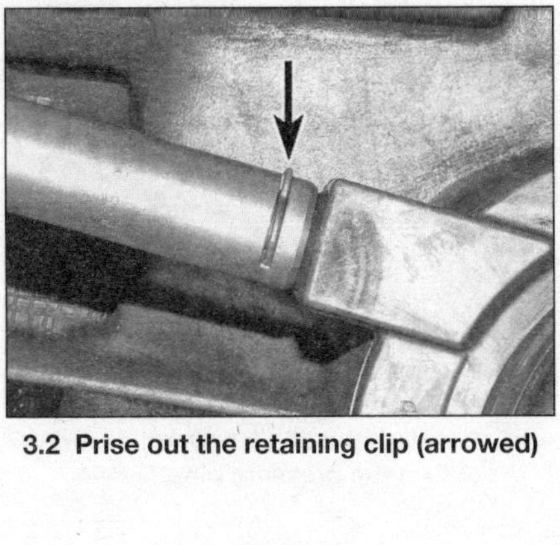

3.2 Prise out the retaining clip (arrowed)

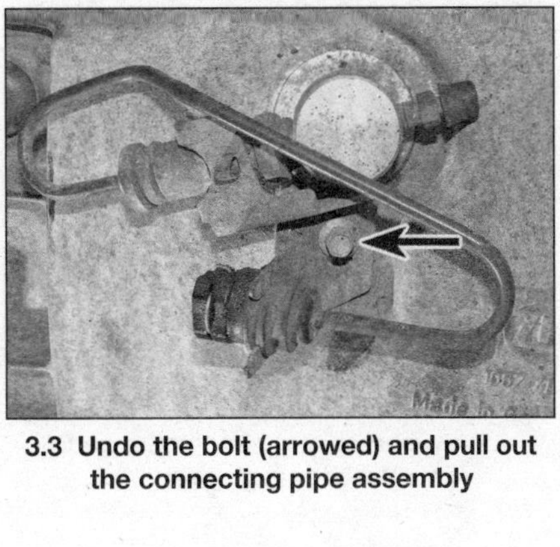

3.3 Undo the bolt (arrowed) and pull out the connecting pipe assembly

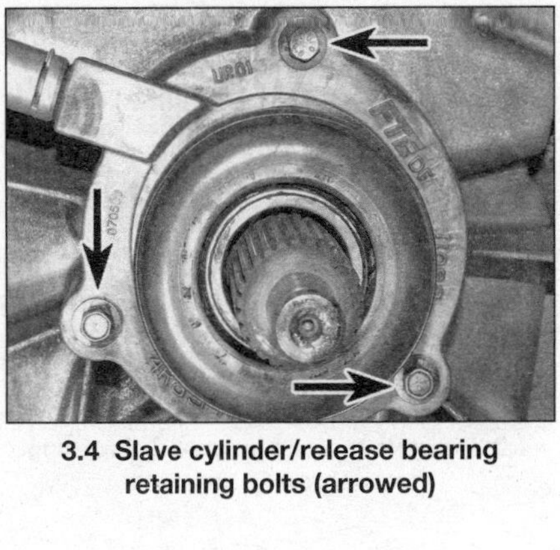

3.4 Slave cylinder/release bearing retaining bolts (arrowed)

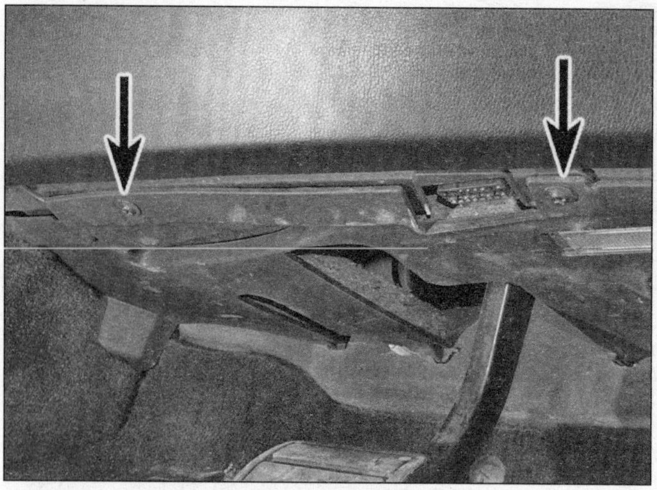
4.1a Undo the 2 screws (arrowed) ...

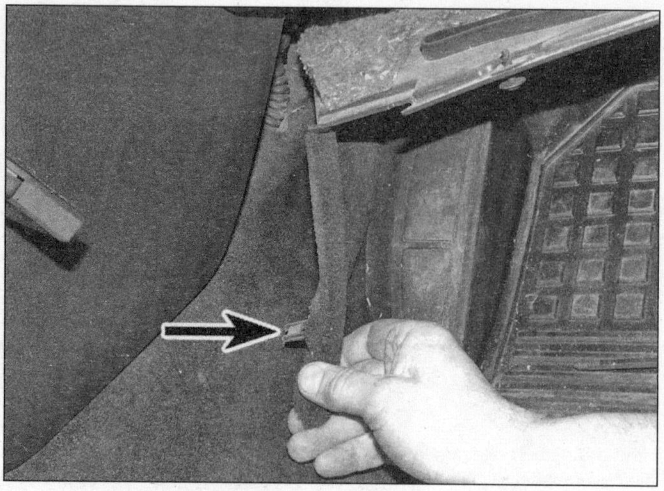
4.1b ... and unclip the panel above the pedals

4 Master cylinder – removal, overhaul and refitting

Warning: Refer to the warning at the beginning of Section 3 before proceeding.

Removal

1 Undo the 2 screws, release the clip, and remove the panel above the driver's pedals **(see illustrations)**. Disconnect the wiring plug as the panel is withdrawn.

2 Release the spring clip securing the master cylinder pushrod to the clutch pedal **(see illustration)**.

3 Remove the pedal spring assister **(see illustration)**.

4 Disconnect the wiring plug from the position sensor on the master cylinder.

5 Position a container beneath the cylinder to collect any fluid, then prise out the clip securing the pressure pipe to the base of the cylinder **(see illustration)**.

6 Undo the 2 retaining bolts and manoeuvre the master cylinder from place, disconnecting the pressure pipe as the cylinder is withdrawn. Plug the open ends of the pipe and master cylinder, to prevent dirt ingress. Be prepared for fluid spillage.

7 Lower the cylinder sufficiently, then use a clamp on the hose, and disconnect the fluid supply hose. Examine the hose O-ring seal, and renew if necessary.

Overhaul

8 At the time of writing, it would appear that no overhaul kits are available for the Discovery. Check with your local dealer, motor factor or specialist.

Refitting

9 Refitting is a reversal of removal. Bleed the hydraulic system as described in Section 6.

5 Hydraulic system – bleeding

Warning: Hydraulic fluid is poisonous; wash off immediately and thoroughly in the case of skin contact, and seek immediate medical advice if any fluid is swallowed or gets into the eyes. Certain types of hydraulic fluid are inflammable, and may ignite when allowed into contact with hot components; when servicing any hydraulic system, it is safest to assume that the fluid is inflammable, and to take precautions against the risk of fire as though it is petrol that is being handled. Hydraulic fluid is also an effective paint stripper, and will attack plastics; if any is spilt, it should be washed off immediately, using copious quantities of fresh water. Finally, it is hygroscopic (it absorbs moisture from the air) – old fluid may be contaminated and unfit for further use. When topping-up or renewing the fluid, always use the recommended type, and ensure that it comes from a freshly-opened sealed container.

General

1 The correct operation of any hydraulic system is only possible after removing all air from the components and circuit; and this is achieved by bleeding the system.

2 During the bleeding procedure, add only clean, unused hydraulic fluid of the recommended type; never re-use fluid that has already been bled from the system. Ensure that sufficient fluid is available before starting work.

3 If there is any possibility of incorrect fluid

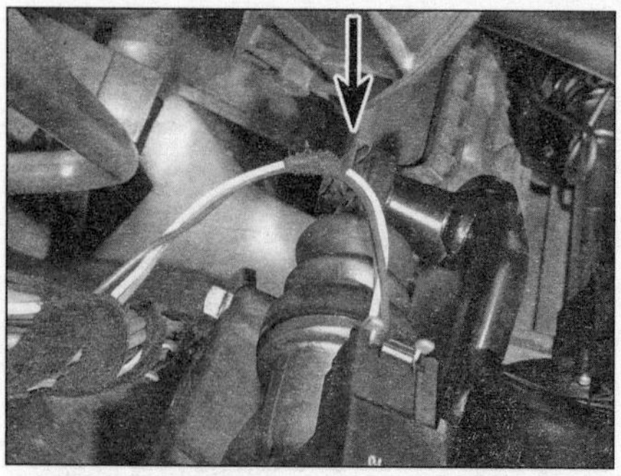
4.2 Remove the clip (arrowed) securing the pushrod to the pedal

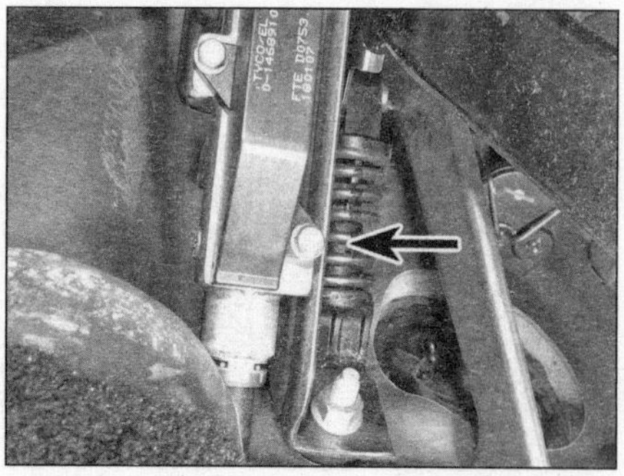
4.3 Compress and remove the pedal assister (arrowed)

4.5 Prise out the clip (arrowed) securing the pressure pipe

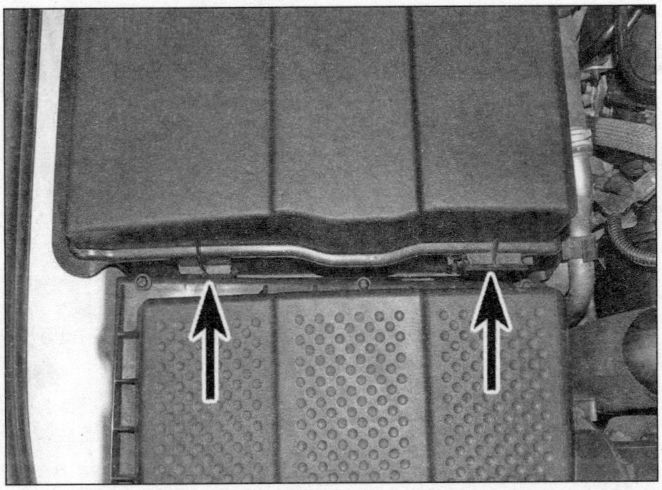

5.7 Release the clips (arrowed) and remove the plastic cover

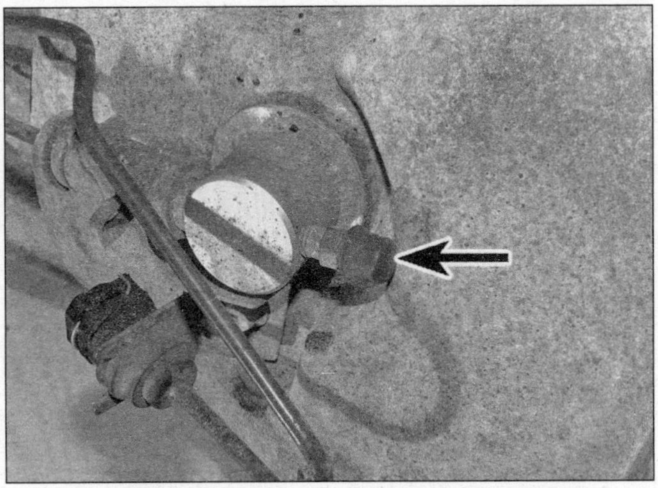

5.11 Slave cylinder bleed screw dust cap (arrowed) – transmission removed for clarity

being already in the system, the hydraulic components and circuit must be flushed completely with uncontaminated, correct fluid, and new seals should be fitted throughout the system.

4 If hydraulic fluid has been lost from the system, or air has entered because of a leak, ensure that the fault is cured before proceeding further.

Bleeding procedure

5 Raise the front of the vehicle and support it securely on axle stands (see *Jacking and vehicle support*).

6 Undo the 6 bolts and remove the transmission undershield.

7 Working in the engine compartment, unclip and remove the plastic cover over the brake master cylinder fluid reservoir **(see illustration)**.

8 Unscrew the master cylinder reservoir cap, and top the master cylinder reservoir up to the MAX level line; refit the cap loosely, and remember to maintain the fluid level at least above the MIN level line throughout the procedure, otherwise there is a risk of further air entering the system.

9 There are a number of one-man, do-it-yourself brake/clutch bleeding kits currently available from motor accessory shops. It is recommended that one of these kits is used whenever possible, as they greatly simplify the bleeding operation, and also reduce the risk of expelled air and fluid being drawn back into the system. If such a kit is not available, the basic (two-man) method must be used, which is described in detail below.

10 If a kit is to be used, prepare the vehicle as described previously, and follow the kit manufacturer's instructions, as the procedure may vary slightly according to the type being used; generally, they are as outlined below in the relevant sub-section.

Basic (two-man) method

11 Clean the area around the bleed screw at the rear of the clutch slave cylinder (located on the gearbox bellhousing). Where applicable, remove the dust cover from the bleed screw **(see illustration)**.

12 Collect a clean glass jar, a suitable length of plastic or rubber tubing which is a tight fit over the bleed screw, and a ring spanner to fit the screw. The help of an assistant will also be required.

13 Fit a suitable spanner and tube to the screw, place the other end of the tube in the jar, and pour in sufficient fluid to cover the end of the tube.

14 Ensure that the master cylinder reservoir fluid level is maintained at least above the MIN level line throughout the procedure.

15 Unscrew the bleed screw (approximately half of one turn).

16 Have the assistant fully depress the clutch pedal, then hold the pedal depressed. When the flow of fluid into the jar stops, tighten the bleed screw again, have the assistant release the pedal slowly, and recheck the reservoir fluid level.

17 Repeat the steps given in paragraphs 15 and 16 until the fluid emerging from the bleed screw is free from air bubbles. If the master cylinder has been drained and refilled, allow approximately five seconds between cycles for the master cylinder passages to refill.

18 When no more air bubbles appear, tighten the bleed screw securely, remove the tube and spanner, and refit the dust cap (where applicable). Do not overtighten the bleed screw.

19 On completion, recheck the fluid level in the reservoir, and top-up if necessary.

20 Discard any hydraulic fluid that has been bled from the system; it will not be fit for re-use.

Using a one-way valve kit

21 As their name implies, these kits consist of a length of tubing with a one-way valve fitted, to prevent expelled air and fluid being drawn back into the system; some kits include a translucent container, which can be positioned so that the air bubbles can be more easily seen flowing from the end of the tube.

22 The kit is connected to the bleed screw, which is then opened. The user returns to the driver's seat, depresses the clutch pedal with a smooth, steady stroke, and slowly releases it; this is repeated until the expelled fluid is clear of air bubbles.

23 Note that these kits simplify work so much that it is easy to forget the master cylinder reservoir fluid level; ensure that this is maintained at least above the MIN level line at all times.

6 Clutch pedal – removal and refitting

Removal

1 Remove the brake servo unit as described in Chapter 10, Section 12.

2 Remove the headlight switch as described in Chapter 13, Section 4.

3 Undo the 2 screws, release the clip, and remove the panel above the driver's pedals **(see illustration 4.1a and 4.1b)**. Disconnect the wiring plug as the panel is withdrawn.

4 Pull the driver's side lower facia panel rearwards to release the 2 clips.

5 Release the wiring harness clip, undo the 4 Torx bolts, and remove the brake pedal bracket.

6 Release the wiring harness clips, disconnect the wiring pug, then rotate the brake light switch anti-clockwise and remove it – refer to Chapter 10, Section 19, if necessary.

7 Release the spring clip securing the master cylinder pushrod to the clutch pedal **(see illustration 4.2)**.

8 Remove the pedal spring assister **(see illustration 4.3)**.

9 Undo the 2 bolts securing the clutch master

cylinder to the bracket and move it to one side.

10 Undo the nuts and remove the pedal assembly.

11 Hold the pedal to counteract the spring pressure, then undo the nut and withdraw the pivot bolt. Carefully release the pedal from the bracket.

12 Remove the bush at each end, and the central pivot bush.

Refitting

13 Lightly grease the pedal pivot bushes.

14 Refit the pedal(s) to the shaft, ensuring all bushes, spacers, etc, are in their original positions.

15 The remainder of refitting is a reversal of removal.

7 Pilot bearing – removal and refitting

Note: *Check availability of the bearing before commencing this procedure.*

Removal

1 A pilot bearing is fitted into the flywheel to provide support for the end of the gearbox input shaft. This ensures accurate and smooth clutch operation. To remove the bearing, begin by removing the flywheel as described in Chapter 2, Section 13.

2 Use a drift to remove the bearing from the flywheel.

Refitting

3 Using a drift which bears only on the outer edge, drive the new bearing into place.

4 Refit the flywheel as described in Chapter 2, Section 13.

Chapter 7 Part A:
Manual transmission

Contents

Degrees of difficulty

Easy, suitable for novice with little experience	**Fairly easy,** suitable for beginner with some experience	**Fairly difficult,** suitable for competent DIY mechanic	**Difficult,** suitable for experienced DIY mechanic	**Very difficult,** suitable for expert DIY or professional

Specifications

General

Transmission type	ZF S6-53 transmission; 6 forward speeds, and reverse
Maximum torque capacity	472 Nm
Fluid capacity	See Chapter 1 Specifications
Ratios:	
1st gear	5.080 : 1
2nd gear	2.804 : 1
3rd gear	1.783 : 1
4th gear	1.260 : 1
5th gear	1.000 : 1
6th gear	0.835 : 1
Reverse	4.725 : 1

Torque wrench settings

Torque wrench settings	Nm	lbf ft
Gear position sensor screws	10	7
Output shaft speed sensor	10	7
Transmission bellhousing-to-engine bolts	40	30
Transmission fluid drain plug*	35	26
Transmission fluid filler plug*	35	26
Transmission undershield bolts	10	7

** Do not re-use*

1 General information

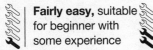

Drive from the clutch is picked up by the input shaft, which runs in parallel with the layshaft and the mainshaft. The input shaft runs on the same axis as the mainshaft, and a bearing between the two shafts allows the shafts to rotate independently. A fixed gear at the rear of the input shaft drives the layshaft. The input shaft and mainshaft gears are in constant mesh, and selection of gears is by sliding synchromesh hubs, which lock the appropriate mainshaft gear to the mainshaft. The direct-drive fifth gear is obtained by locking the input shaft to the mainshaft.

Reverse gear is obtained by sliding an idler gear into mesh with two straight-cut gears on the mainshaft (the 1st/2nd gear synchro sleeve) and the layshaft.

All the forward gear teeth are helically-cut, to reduce noise and to improve wear characteristics.

The mainshaft provides drive to the transfer gearbox, which is described in Chapter 7C, Section 1.

Gear selection is by means of a floor-mounted gearchange lever, with rod linkage to the selector shaft on the transsmission.

2 Sensors – removal and refitting

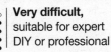

Gear position sensor

Removal

1 Remove the transmission as described in Section 3 of this Chapter.

2 Ensure the area around the sensor is clean to prevent dirt ingress. Plug all open connections to prevent contamination.

3 Undo the 2 Torx screws and remove the sensor from the transmission casing **(see**

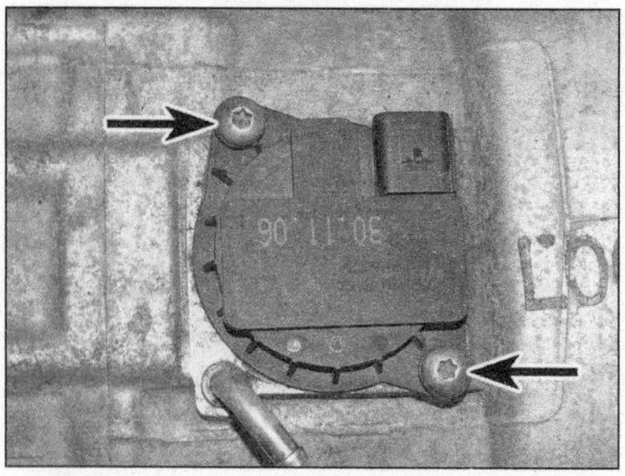

2.3 Gear position sensor retaining screws (arrowed)

illustration). Discard the O-ring seal – a new one must be fitted.

Refitting

4 Ensure the mating faces of the sensor and transmission casing are clean, then fit a new O-ring seal, and install the sensor.

5 Apply a little RTV sealant to the threads, refit the Torx screws and tighten them to the specified torque.

6 The remainder of refitting is a reversal of removal.

Output shaft speed sensor

Removal

7 Raise the front of the vehicle and support it securely on axle stands.

8 Undo the bolts and remove the transmission undershield **(see illustration 4.2)**.

9 Disconnect the wiring plug, undo the retaining bolt and pull the sensor from the transmission casing **(see illustration)**.

2.9 Output shaft speed sensor retaining bolt (arrowed)

Refitting

10 Ensure the mating faces of the sensor and transmission are clean, then fit a new O-ring seal, and fit the sensor to the casing.

11 Apply a little RTV sealant to the threads, refit the Torx screws and tighten them to the specified torque.

12 The remainder of refitting is a reversal of removal.

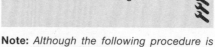

3 Manual transmission – removal and refitting

Note: *Although the following procedure is not difficult, the transmission assembly (the main transmission is removed complete with the transfer gearbox) is heavy, and awkward to handle. Read through the entire procedure before proceeding, to familiarise yourself with the steps. The help of an assistant will prove invaluable during this operation. A suitable engine lifting crane and tackle will be required.*

Removal

1 Disconnect the battery negative lead (see Chapter 5, Section 4).

2 Prise up the gaiter surround, then pull the gearchange knob up sharply to remove it **(see illustrations)**.

3 Starting at the front, carefully prise up and remove the ride/handling optimisation switch assembly from the centre console **(see illustration)**. Disconnect the wiring plugs as the assembly is withdrawn.

4 Undo the 2 retaining bolts, release the gearchange mounting bracket and remove the rubber gaiter **(see illustration)**.

5 Jack up the vehicle, and support securely on axle stands (see *Jacking and vehicle support*). Note that the vehicle must be raised sufficiently to give enough clearance for the transmission assembly to be removed from under the vehicle.

6 Remove the front and rear propeller shafts as described in Chapter 8, Section 2.

7 Undo the fasteners and remove the heat shield above the exhaust pipe **(see illustration)**.

8 Undo the bolts/nut and move the support bracket between the turbocharger and the transmission to one side **(see illustration)**.

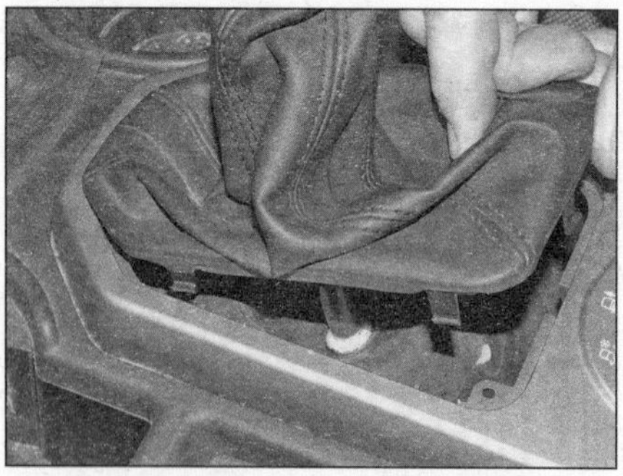

3.2a Prise up the gaiter surround ...

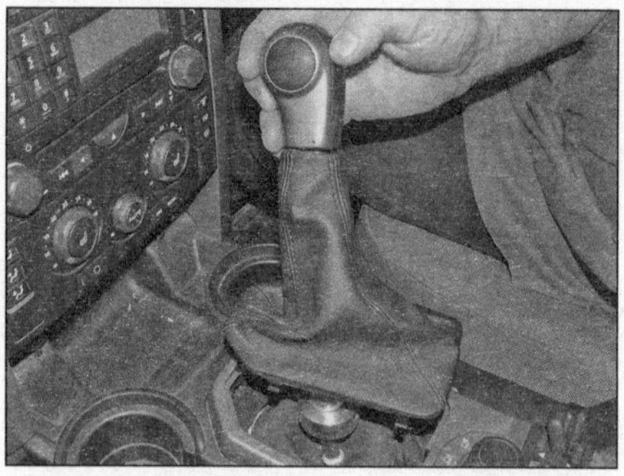

3.2b ... and pull the knob upwards sharply

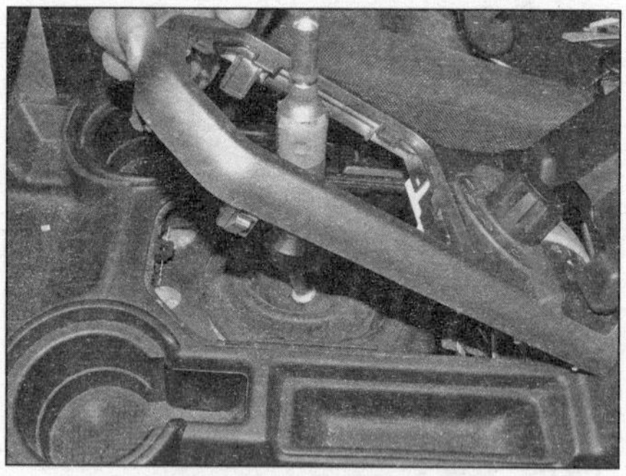

3.3 Starting at the front, prise up the switch panel assembly

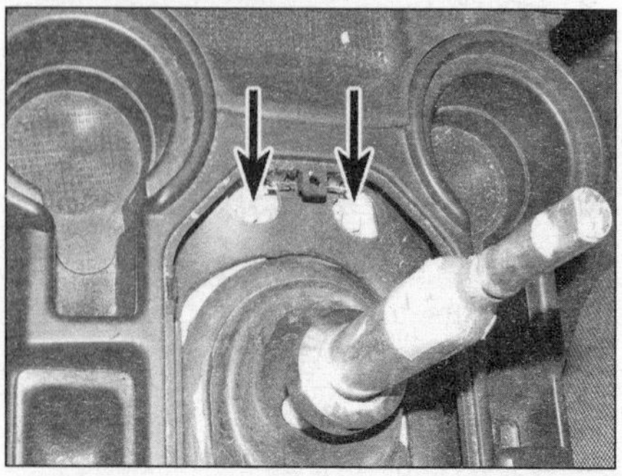

3.4 Remove the gearchange bracket bolts (arrowed)

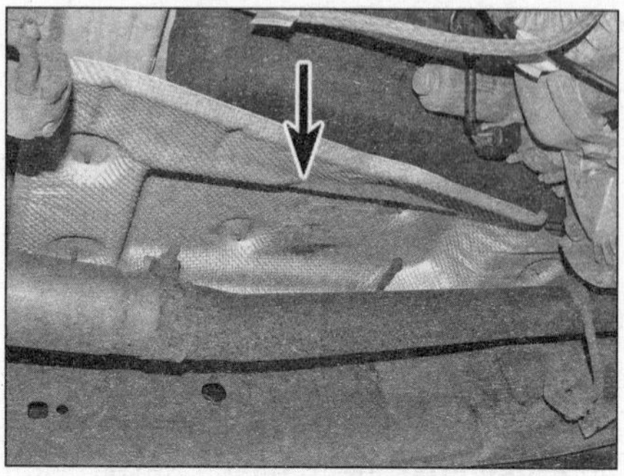

3.7 Remove the exhaust heat shield (arrowed)

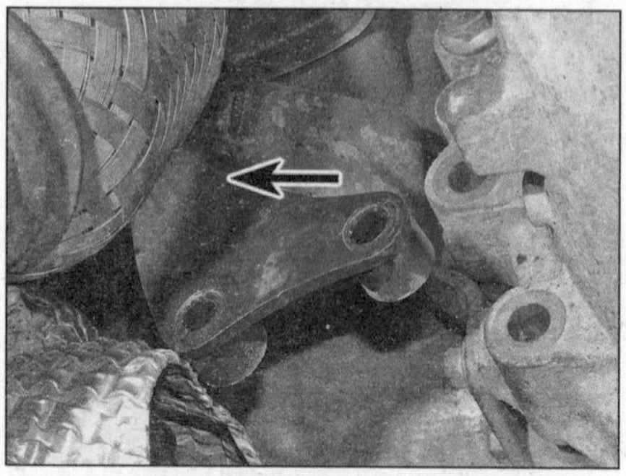

3.8 Allow the turbocharger support bracket (arrowed) to swing down

9 Undo the retaining bolt and move the fuel cooler to one side **(see illustration)**.

10 On vehicles up to 2007 model year, undo the 2 bolts and move the fuel filter assembly to one side.

11 Release the retaining clips, and tape/tie the vacuum hose to the forward edge of the chassis crossmember.

12 Use a clamp to minimise fluid spillage, then prise out the clip and disconnect the fluid hose from the connection at the side of the transmission bellhousing. Plug/cover the openings to prevent contamination.

13 Using a pair of circlip pliers, spread the tabs, slide off the clip, and disconnect the gearchange rod from the base of the gear lever. Discard the O-ring seals – new ones must be fitted **(see illustrations)**.

14 Release the wiring harness from any clips/brackets, then disconnect the wiring plugs from the transfer case.

15 Disconnect the earth lead (where fitted) from the rear of the transfer case **(see illustration)**.

16 Lower the rear of the transmission slightly for access to the upper surfaces.

17 Note their fitted positions, and harness routing, then disconnect the wiring plugs from the transmission, and release the harnesses from the clips/brackets.

18 Undo the support bracket bolt, and disconnect the breather hose from the top of the transmission.

19 Disconnect the breather hose from the top of the transfer case.

20 Undo the bolts securing the support brackets to the transmission casing and exhaust crossover pipe. There are 3 brackets: one each side, and one in the centre **(see illustration)**.

21 Ensure the transmission is securely supported by the workshop jack beneath. Enlist the help of an assistant before proceeding.

22 Undo the 14 bolts securing the transmission to the engine, and ensuring the transmission remains level, slide the assembly 40 mm rearwards, then rotate it slightly to gain access to the gearchange stay bracket.

23 Rotate the clip upwards, and pull out the pin securing the gearchange stay bracket to the transmission **(see illustrations)**.

24 Carefully slide the transmission assembly rearwards and out from under the vehicle, using the trolley jack. Take care when moving the transmission, and do not attempt to lift the assembly without suitable lifting tackle – the assembly is very heavy.

25 If desired, the transfer gearbox can be separated from the main gearbox as described in Chapter 7C, Section 2.

Refitting

26 Where applicable, refit the transfer gearbox to the main transmission, as described in Chapter 7C, Section 2.

27 Ensure the mating faces of the engine and gearbox are clean.

28 Position the transmission assembly under the vehicle using the trolley jack and support block.

29 Lift the transmission assembly into position, then slide the bellhousing into place, leaving a gap of 40 mm between the engine and bellhousing, as during removal. Ensure that the wiring harness and connectors, and the breather pipes, are not trapped as the transmission is moved into position. Note that it will be necessary to tilt the rear of the engine

3.9 Fuel cooler retaining bolt (arrowed)

3.13a Spread and remove the gearchange rod clip ...

3.13b ... remove the outer O-ring seal ...

3.13c ... and the O-ring seal each side of the lever

3.15 Disconnect the earth lead

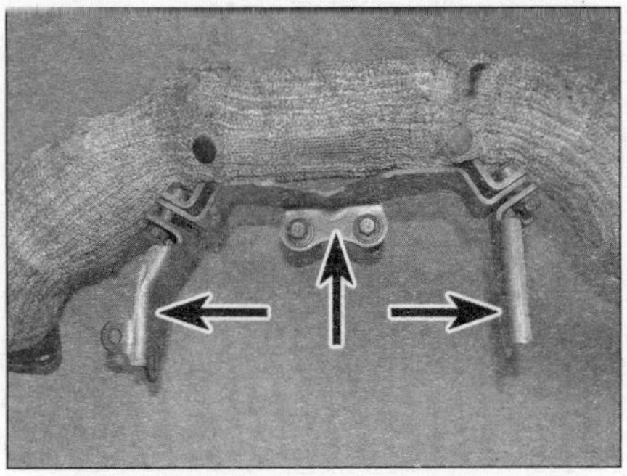

3.20 Undo the bolts and remove the 3 crosspipe support brackets (arrowed)

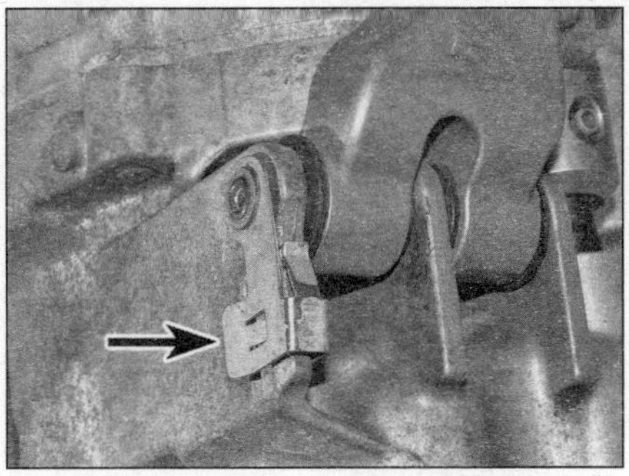

3.23a Rotate the clip (arrowed) upwards ...

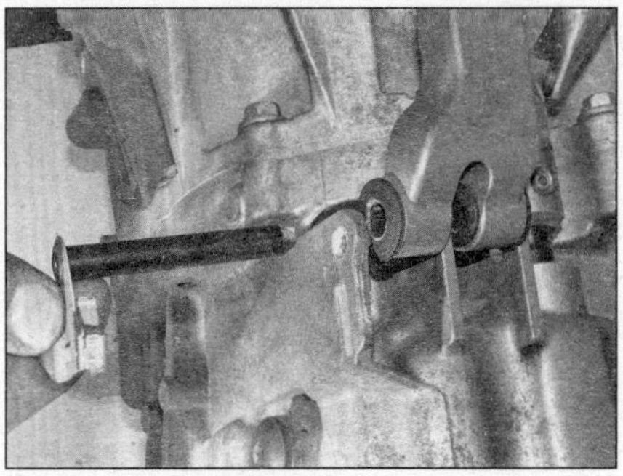

3.23b ... and pull out the pin (transmission removed for clarity)

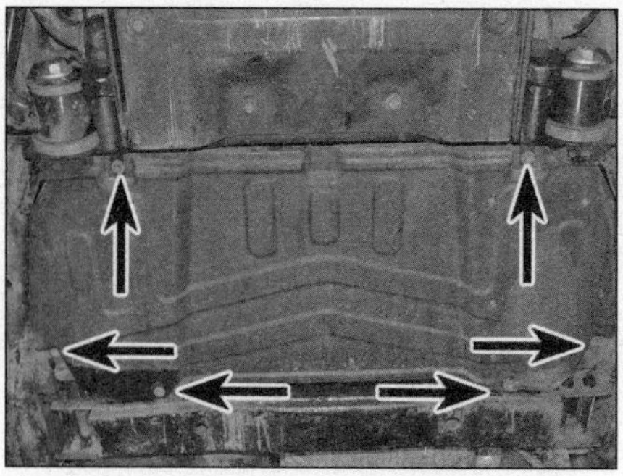

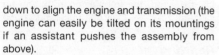

4.2 Transmission undershield bolts (arrowed)

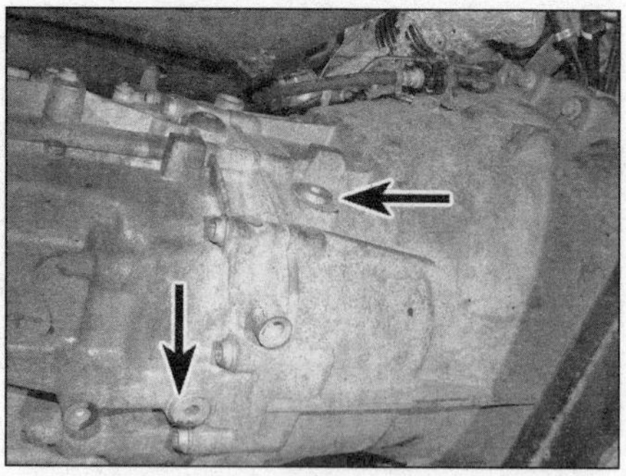

4.3 Transmission fluid drain and filler plugs (arrowed)

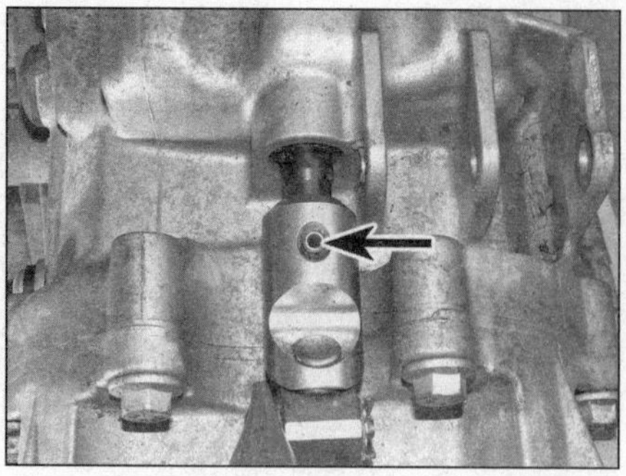

5.7 Drive out the coupling pin (arrowed)

down to align the engine and transmission (the engine can easily be tilted on its mountings if an assistant pushes the assembly from above).

30 Re-attach the gearchange rod to the lever and secure it with the retaining clip.

31 Manipulate the engine and transmission as necessary to align the transmission input shaft splines with the splines in the clutch friction disc hub (it may be necessary to turn the crankshaft using a spanner or socket on the pulley bolt, and push the assembly fully into place.

32 Refit and tighten the engine-to-transmission bolts. Tighten the bolts to the specified torque.

33 The remainder of the refitting procedure is a reversal of removal, bearing in mind the following points:

a) Ensure that all wiring is routed correctly, and that all plugs are reconnected to their correct locations.

b) Refit the propeller shafts with reference to Chapter 8, Section 2.

c) Tighten all fasteners to the specified torque where given.

d) Bleed the hydraulic system as described in Chapter 6, Section 5.

e) Where applicable, on completion, refill the main transmission and transfer gearbox with oil of the correct type.

4 Manual transmission oil renewal

1 Jack up the vehicle, and support securely on axle stands (see *Jacking and vehicle support*).

2 Undo the bolts and remove the transmission undershield **(see illustration)**.

3 Clean the area around the drain and filler plugs **(see illustration)**.

4 Place a container beneath the transmission, then unscrew the filler plug. Discard the filler plug – a new one must be fitted.

5 Unscrew the drain plug, and allow the fluid to drain into the container. Discard the drain plug – a new one must be fitted.

6 Fit the new drain plug, and tighten it to the specified torque.

7 Fill the transmission with 1.6 litres of the correct fluid. Note that the filler plug aperture is not a fluid level aperture.

8 Install a new filler plug and tighten it to the specified torque.

9 Refit the transmission undershield, and lower the vehicle to the ground.

5 Oil seals – renewal

Input shaft seal

1 Remove the clutch slave cylinder/release bearing as described in Chapter 6, Section 3.

2 Note its fitted depth, then drill a small hole in the hard outer surface of the seal, insert a self-tapping screw, and use pliers to extract the seal. Apply a little grease to the drill bit to reduce the risk of swarf entering the transmission.

2 Lubricate the new seal with grease and fit it to the bellhousing, lips pointing to the gearbox side. Use a deep socket or suitable tubing to seat it.

4 Refit the release bearing/slave cylinder using a reversal of removal.

Selector shaft seal

5 Remove the transfer case as described in Chapter 7C, Section 2.

6 Slide off the retaining clip and detach the gearchange rod from the selector shaft. Discard the O-ring seals – new ones must be fitted **(see illustrations 3.13a. 3.13b and 3.13c)**.

7 Release the circlip (where fitted) and drive out the pin securing the coupling to the end of the selector shaft **(see illustration)**.

8 Using a screwdriver or similar, carefully prise the oil seal from the casing. Take great care not to damage the shaft or casing bore.

9 Ensure the shaft and casing bore are clean, then apply a little grease to the seal lips, and use a deep socket to drive seal into place.

10 The remainder of refitting is a reversal of removal.

Output shaft seal

11 Renewal of the output shaft seal requires several Land Rover special tools, skill, dexterity and patience to successfully accomplish. Consequently, we recommend this task is entrusted to a Land Rover dealer or suitably-equipped repairer

6 Manual transmission overhaul – general information

Overhauling a manual transmission is a difficult and involved job for the DIY home mechanic. In addition to dismantling and reassembling many small parts, clearances must be precisely measured and, if necessary, changed by selecting shims and spacers. Transmission internal components are also often difficult to obtain, and in many instances, extremely expensive. Because of this, if the transmission develops a fault or becomes noisy, the best course of action is to have the unit overhauled by a specialist repairer, or to obtain an exchange reconditioned unit.

Nevertheless, it is not impossible for the more experienced mechanic to overhaul a transmission, provided the special tools are available, and the job is done in a deliberate step-by-step manner so that nothing is overlooked.

The tools necessary for an overhaul include internal and external circlip pliers, bearing pullers, a slide-hammer, a set of pin punches, a dial test indicator, and possibly a hydraulic press. In addition, a large, sturdy workbench and a vice will be required.

During dismantling of the transmission, make careful notes of how each component is fitted, to make reassembly easier and more accurate.

Before dismantling the transmission, it will help if you have some idea of which area is malfunctioning. Certain problems can be closely related to specific areas in the transmission, which can make component examination and renewal easier. Refer to the *Fault finding* Section at the end of this manual for more information.

Chapter 7 Part B: Automatic transmission

Contents

Degrees of difficulty

Easy, suitable for novice with little experience	**Fairly easy,** suitable for beginner with some experience	**Fairly difficult,** suitable for competent DIY mechanic	**Difficult,** suitable for experienced DIY mechanic	**Very difficult,** suitable for expert DIY or professional

Specifications

General

Type	ZF 6HP26
Capacity	See Chapter 1 Specifications
Gear ratios:	
1st gear	4.170 : 1
2nd gear	2.340 : 1
3rd gear	1.521 : 1
4th gear	1.143 : 1
5th gear	0.867 : 1
6th gear	0.691 : 1
Reverse	3.403 : 1

Torque wrench settings

Torque wrench settings	Nm	lbf ft
Fluid filler plug	35	26
Sump drain plug	9	7
Sump securing bolts	8	7
Torque converter-to-driveplate bolts	45	33
Transmission bellhousing-to-engine bolts	45	33
Transmission mountings bolt and nut	60	44
Transmission undershield bolts	10	7

1 General information

A 6-speed fully-automatic transmission is available as an option on certain models. The transmission consists of a torque converter, an epicyclic geartrain, and hydraulically-operated clutches and brakes.

The torque converter provides a fluid coupling between the engine and transmission, acts as an automatic clutch, and also provides a degree of torque multiplication when accelerating. The torque converter incorporates a lock-up clutch which improves gearbox throttle response once the converter is fully engaged.

The epicyclic geartrain provides either one of the six forward gear ratios, or reverse gear, according to which of its component parts are held stationary or allowed to turn. The components of the geartrain are held or released by brakes and clutches, which are activated by a hydraulic governor. A fluid pump within the transmission provides the necessary hydraulic pressure to operate the brakes and clutches.

Operation of the transmission is controlled by an transmission control module (TCM) which is networked to the engine management ECM, to enable the TCM to determine the optimum gearchange point, kick-down point, and to improve gearchange quality by reducing engine torque at the change points. The TCM is located within the transmission casing.

Due to the complexity of the automatic transmission, any repair or overhaul work must be entrusted to a Land Rover dealer, or a suitably-qualified transmission specialist, with the necessary specialist equipment and knowledge for fault diagnosis and repair. Refer to the *Fault finding* Section at the end of this manual for further information. Any faults within the transmission should generate a fault code, which should be stored in the TCM. The TCM can be interrogated and the details of any stored faults extracted using dedicated test equipment (fault code reader) via the diagnostic socket located under the facia on the driver's side. Depending on the type of fault, the Sport and Manual warning lamps on the instrument panel may flash or the TCM may enter the limp home mode, where engine performance may be reduced, kick-down disabled, and transmission function reduced (no manual shift, etc).

Note that if necessary, the transmission can be released from the Park position after a complete loss of power (battery failure), by carefully prising up the cover behind the parking brake switch, and pushing up the lever at the rear of the selector mechanism at the same time as pressing the release button on the selector lever, then moving the lever to the required position **(see illustrations)**.

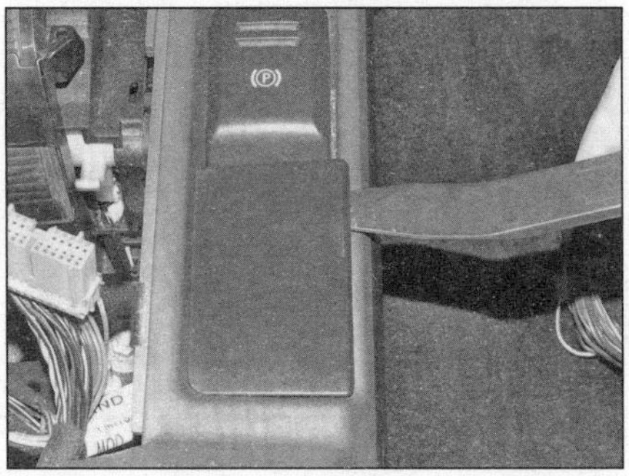

1.6a Prise up the cover behind the parking brake switch ...

1.6b ... and lift up the release button (console top cover removed for clarity)

2 Selector assembly – removal and refitting

Removal

1 Raise the front of the vehicle and support is securely on axle stands (see *Jacking and vehicle support*).

2 Undo the bolts and remove the transmission undershield **(see illustration)**.

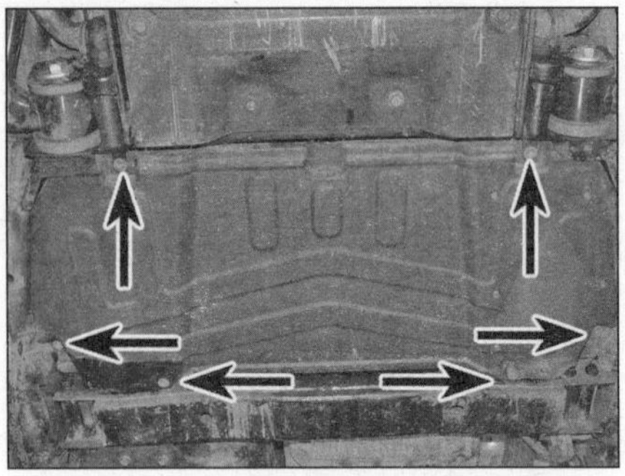

2.2 Transmission undershield retaining bolts (arrowed)

3 Undo the bolts and remove the heat shield (where fitted) from below the transmission.

4 Slacken the selector cable locknut on the transmission lever, then pull back the collar and detach the cable from the bracket **(see illustration)**. Release the cable from the bracket on the side of the transmission.

5 Remove the centre console upper trim panel as described in Chapter 12, Section 27.

6 Undo the retaining nuts, disconnect the wiring plug, and lift the selector lever/cable assembly upwards from the centre console. Release the cable from the floor as it's withdrawn **(see illustration)**.

Refitting

7 Refitting is a reversal of removal, remembering to adjust the cable as described in Section 3.

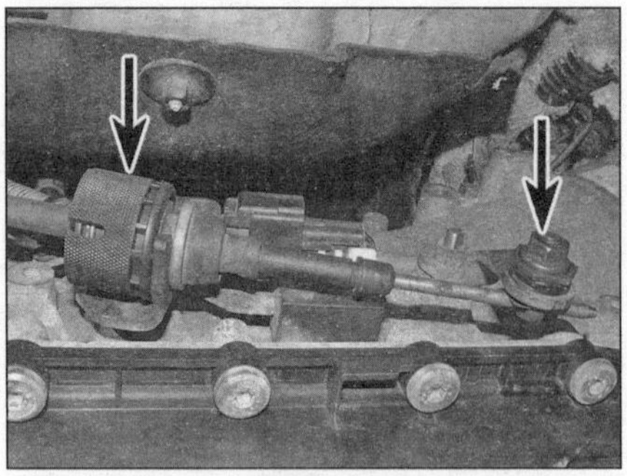

2.4 Undo the locknut and pull back the collar (arrowed)

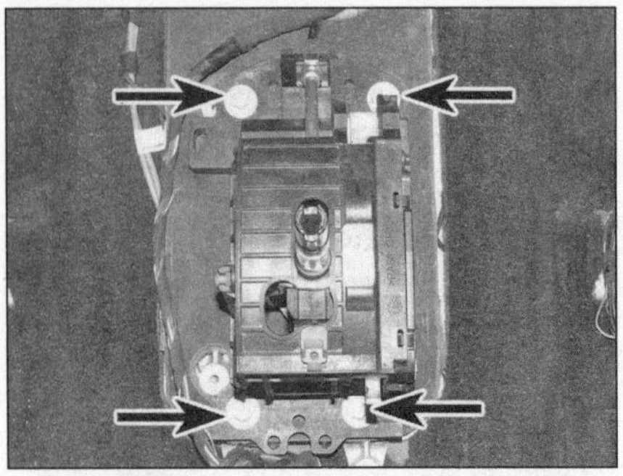

2.6 Selector cable/lever assembly retaining nuts (arrowed)

3 Selector cable – removal, refitting and adjustment

Removal and refitting

1 Remove the selector lever assembly as described in Section 2.

2 Prise up the C-clip securing the outer cable to the selector lever assembly, then prise the inner cable from the balljoint **(see illustrations)**.

3 Refitting is a reversal of removal, but adjust the cable as follows:

Adjustment

4 Raise the front of the vehicle and support is securely on axle stands (see *Jacking and vehicle support*).

5 Undo the bolts and remove the transmission undershield **(see illustration 2.2)**.

6 Undo the bolts and remove the transmission heat shield (where fitted).

7 Working under the vehicle, slacken the selector inner cable clamp nut (located on the right-hand side of the transmission), and push the lever on the side of the transmission fully forward (P position) **(see illustration 2.4)**.

8 Ensure the selector lever in the passenger cabin is in the P position.

9 Tighten the selector inner cable clamp nut securely. Check that the engine can only be started in positions P or N.

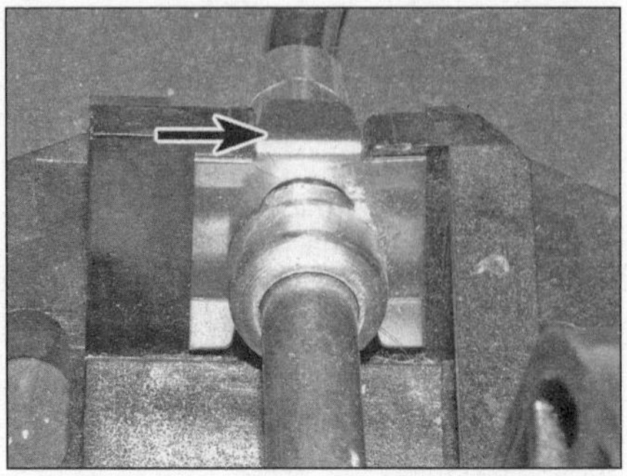

3.2a Slide out the C-clip (arrowed) ...

3.2b ... and prise the inner cable from the balljoint (arrowed)

5.9a Fluid cooler pipes retaining bolt (arrowed)

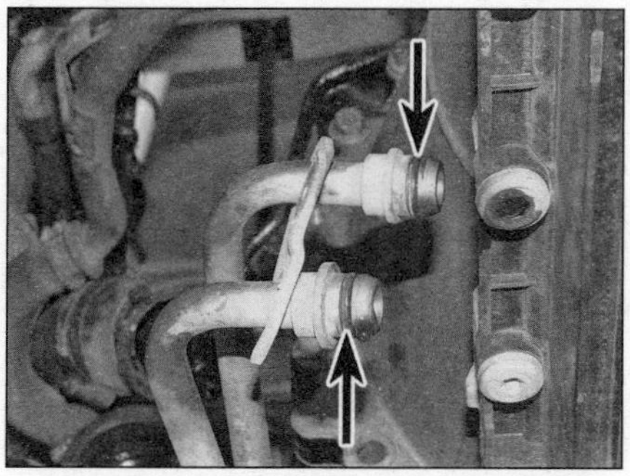

5.9b Renew the O-ring seals (arrowed)

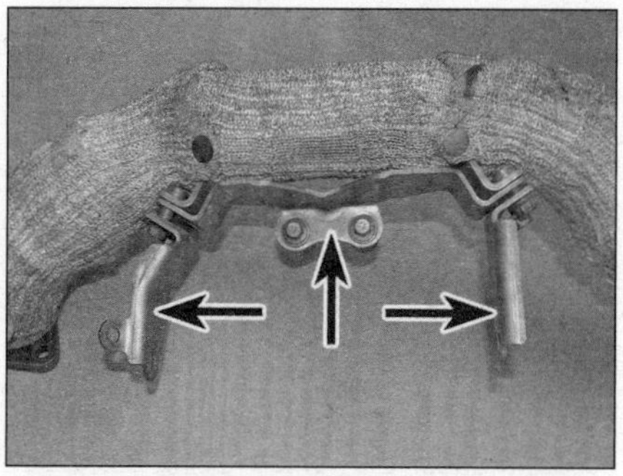

5.12 The exhaust crossover pipe is supported by 3 brackets (arrowed – pipe removed for clarity)

4 Transmission control module (TCM) – general information

1 The TCM is located within the transmission casing. To gain access to the TCM, several special tools, experience and dexterity are required. Consequently, we recommend the renewal of the TCM be entrusted to a Land Rover dealer or suitably-equipped repairer.

2 If a new TCM is fitted, it must be calibrated using Land Rover diagnostic equipment (T4). Entrust this task to a Land Rover dealer or suitably-equipped repairer.

5 Automatic transmission – removal and refitting

Note: *Although the following procedure is not difficult, the transmission assembly (the main transmission is removed complete with the transfer gearbox) is heavy, and awkward to handle. Read through the entire procedure before proceeding, to familiarise yourself with the steps. The help of an assistant will prove invaluable during this operation.*

Removal

1 The automatic transmission is removed with the transfer gearbox as a complete unit.

2 Disconnect the battery negative lead, as described in Chapter 5, Section 4.

3 Jack up the vehicle, and support securely on axle stands (see *Jacking and vehicle support*). Note that the vehicle must be raised sufficiently to give enough clearance for the transmission assembly to be removed from under the vehicle.

4 Remove the front and rear propeller shafts as described in Chapter 8, Section 2.

5 Remove the complete exhaust system as described in Chapter 4A, Section 17.

6 Position a container beneath the transmission, then drain the fluid – see Section 7.

7 Remove the starter motor as described in Chapter 5, Section 9.

8 Disconnect the selector cable from the transmission as described in Section 2.

9 Undo the bolt, release the clips and detach the fluid cooler pipes from the side of the transmission. Discard the O-ring seals – new ones must be fitted **(see illustrations)**. Be prepared for fluid spillage. Plug/cover the openings to prevent contamination.

10 Undo the bolts/nut and remove the support bracket from between the turbocharger and the transmission casing.

11 Undo the nuts and remove the exhaust heat shield alongside the transmission.

12 Undo the bolts securing the support brackets to the transmission casing and exhaust crossover pipe. There are 3 brackets: one each side, and one in the centre **(see illustration)**.

13 The wiring harness is bolted to the left-hand/upper side, and right-hand side of the transmission casing. Release the wiring harness, then rotate the collar anti-clockwise and disconnect the wiring plug from the transmission casing **(see illustration)**. Disconnect any remaining plugs as the harness is released.

14 Release the clips, undo the retaining bracket bolts securing the wiring harness, and disconnect the wiring plugs from the transfer case **(see illustration)**.

15 Disconnect the breather hoses from the top of the casings.

16 Undo the 4 bolts and remove the access panel beneath the radiator.

17 Remove the access plug in the rear of the cylinder block, then using a socket on the crankshaft pulley, rotate the torque converter/ driveplate until one of the retaining bolts is accessible **(see illustration)**. Rotate the crankshaft pulley as necessary to access each of the 4 bolts in turn.

18 Ensure that the transmission assembly is adequately supported on the jack/trolley, then progressively unscrew the transmission-to-engine securing bolts. Note that the transmission assembly may move backwards from the engine once the bolts are removed, and the engine may tip forwards – be prepared for this, and do not allow the assembly to slip from the jack head. Enlist the help of an assistant.

19 Carefully slide the transmission assembly back from the engine.

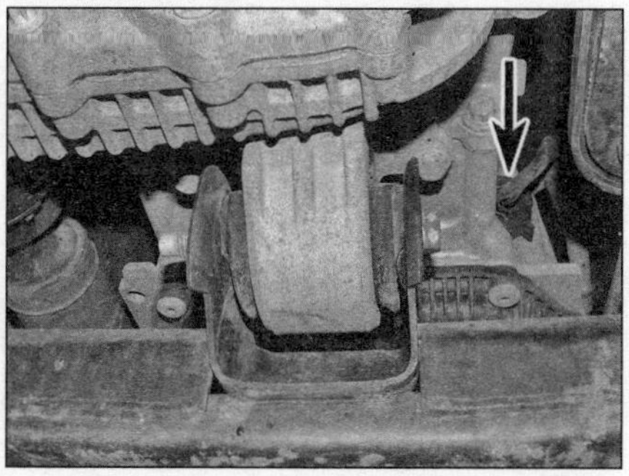

5.13 Rotate the collar (arrowed) anti-clockwise and disconnect the wiring plug

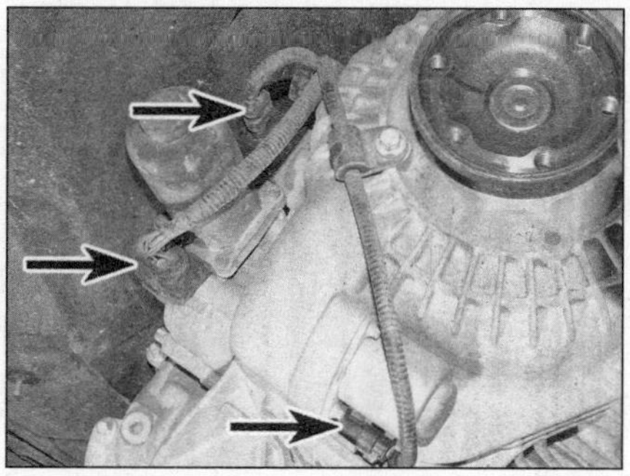

5.14 Disconnect the transfer case wiring plugs (arrowed)

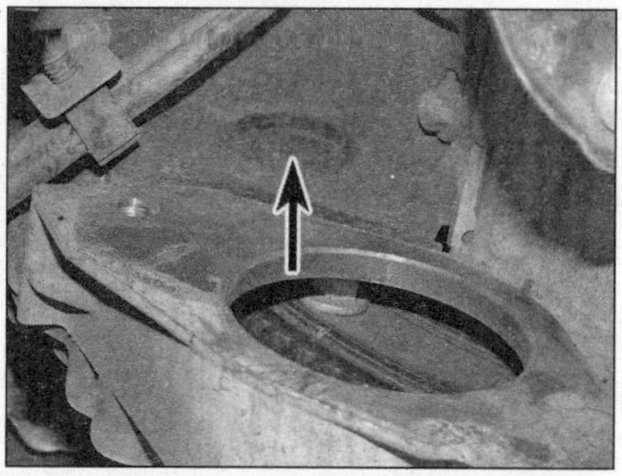

5.17 Prise out the plug (arrowed) to access the torque converter bolts (starter motor removed for clarity)

20 Fit a suitable strip of metal across the bellhousing, to retain the torque converter **(see illustration)**. **Do not** allow the torque converter to fall out of the transmission.
21 Position a trolley jack and a large block of wood under the transmission assembly (the wood should be suitably-shaped to support the transmission when it is lowered), then lower the engine crane to position the transmission assembly on the trolley jack and support block.
22 Carefully slide the transmission assembly out from under the vehicle, using the trolley jack. Take care when moving the transmission, and do not attempt to lift the assembly without suitable lifting tackle – the assembly is very heavy.
23 If desired, the transfer gearbox can be separated from the main gearbox as described in Chapter 7C, Section 2.

Refitting

24 If a new transmission is to be fitted, it will be necessary to transfer the following components from the existing assembly to the new unit. Take great care to prevent dirt from entering the transmission – plug all openings to prevent dirt ingress. Note that if drained fluid is very dirty or contained metallic particles, it's recommended that the fluid cooler and associated pipes/hoses are renewed.
25 Position the transmission assembly under the vehicle using the trolley jack. Remove the torque converter retaining strap from the bellhousing.
26 Apply a little molybdenum disulphide grease to the tip of the torque converter nose.
27 Carefully lift the transmission assembly into position, then slide it into place. Ensure that the wiring harness and connectors, and the breather pipes, are not trapped as the transmission is moved into position. Note that it will be necessary to tilt the rear of the engine down to align the engine and transmission (the engine can easily be tilted on its mountings if an assistant pushes the assembly from above).
28 Progressively tighten the retaining bolts, to draw the transmission bellhousing flush against the engine.
29 The remainder of the refitting procedure is a reversal of removal, bearing in mind the following points:

a) Ensure that all wiring is routed correctly, and that all plugs are reconnected to their correct locations.
b) Refit the propeller shafts with reference to Chapter 8, Section 2.
c) Refit the exhaust system with reference to Chapter 4A, Section 17.

5.20 Attach a metal strip to retain the torque converter

d) Tighten all fasteners to their specified torque where given.
e) Where applicable, on completion, refill the main transmission and transfer gearbox with fluid and oil of the correct type, as described in Section 7.

6 Automatic transmission overhaul – general information

In the event of a fault occurring on the transmission, it is first necessary to determine whether it is of an electrical, mechanical or hydraulic nature, and to achieve this, special test equipment is required. It is therefore essential to have the work carried out by a Land Rover dealer, or a suitably-equipped specialist, if a transmission fault is suspected.

Do not remove the transmission from the vehicle for possible repair before professional fault diagnosis has been carried out, since most tests require the transmission to be in the vehicle.

7 Automatic transmission fluid renewal

Note: *Ensure the transmission fluid temperature is below 30°C before starting out this procedure.*
1 Jack up the vehicle, and support securely on axle stands (see *Jacking and vehicle support*). Ensure the vehicle is level.
2 Remove the transmission undershield, and the heat shield (where fitted) **(see illustration 2.2)**.
3 Clean the area around the transmission drain and filler plugs **(see illustration)**.
4 Place a container below the drain plug, then remove the filler plug, followed by the drain plug. Discard the sealing washers – new ones must be fitted. Allow the fluid to drain. Note that if drained fluid is very dirty or contained metallic particles, it's recommended that the fluid cooler and associated pipes/hoses are renewed.

7.3 Transmission fluid drain and filler plugs (arrowed)

5 Refit the drain plug with a new washer, and tighten it to the specified torque.
6 Add 3.5 to 4.0 litres of the correct specification oil, or until fluid begins to run out of the filler plug aperture. Temporarily refit the filler plug, but don't tighten it at this stage.
7 Ensure the handbrake is fully applied, and if necessary chock the wheels.
8 The temperature of the fluid should be monitored during the checking procedure, using Land Rover diagnostic equipment (or a generic scanner) connected to the diagnostic plug located under the driver's side of the facia. The fluid should be between 30° and 50°C during the check.
9 Start the engine, and move the selector lever from position P through all the other positions, pausing in each position for 2 to 3 seconds, before returning to position P.
10 Allow the engine to idle, and remove the filler plug.
11 If no fluid runs out of the filler plug aperture, add fluid until it a small trickle of fluid begins to emerge.
12 Refit the filler plug and tighten it to the specified torque.
13 Stop the engine.
14 Refit the transmission heat shield and undershield.
15 Lower the vehicle to the ground.

8 Oil cooler – removal and refitting

1 The transmission oil cooler is integral with the engine coolant radiator. Refer to Chapter 3, Section 3.

Chapter 7 Part C: Transfer gearbox

Contents

Degrees of difficulty

Easy, suitable for novice with little experience	**Fairly easy,** suitable for beginner with some experience	**Fairly difficult,** suitable for competent DIY mechanic	**Difficult,** suitable for experienced DIY mechanic	**Very difficult,** suitable for expert DIY or professional

Specifications

General

Type	Magna Steyr DD295
Capacity	See Chapter 1 Specifications

Gear ratios (final drive to axles)

High range	1.10 : 1
Low range	2.93 : 1

Torque wrench settings

	Nm	lbf ft
Fluid drain and level/filler plugs	22	16
Transfer gearbox-to-main gearbox/transmission bolts and nuts	45	33

1 General information

The transfer gearbox is mounted in-line with the main manual gearbox/automatic transmission. The transfer gearbox is a two-speed ratio-reducing gearbox, and provides drive to the front and rear axles via the propeller shafts.

Permanent four-wheel-drive is provided, and the unit incorporates an electronically-controlled differential assembly to allow for any difference in the rotational speed of the front and rear wheels (and a resulting difference in speed between the front and rear propeller shafts). This centre differential (the axles also incorporate differentials, to allow for the difference in rotational speed between left- and right-hand wheels on the same axle) can be locked by mechanical means, to provide increased traction in particularly slippery conditions.

The transfer gearbox is controlled by a module located in the E-box in the engine compartment, behind the battery, adjacent to the engine management ECM.

2 Transfer gearbox – removal and refitting

Removal

1 Disconnect the battery negative lead as described in Chapter 5, Section 4.

2 Raise the vehicle and support it securely on axle stands (see *Jacking and vehicle support*).

3 Remove the front and rear propeller shafts as described in Chapter 8, Section 2.

4 Disconnect the 3 wiring plugs from the transfer case, then note the fitted positions and release the wiring harness brackets **(see illustration)**.

5 Undo the bolt and disconnect the earth

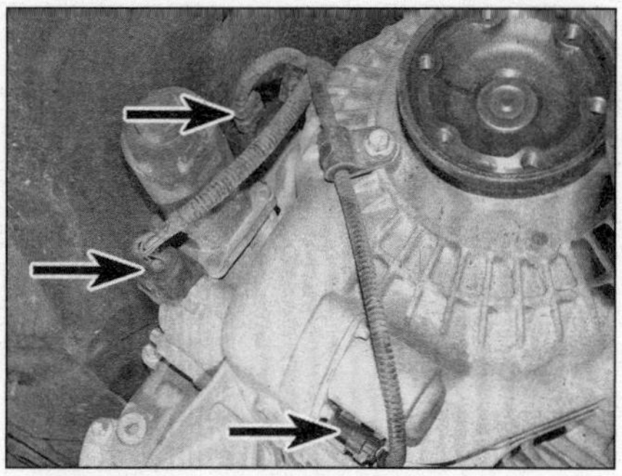

2.4 Disconnect the wiring plugs from the transfer case (arrowed)

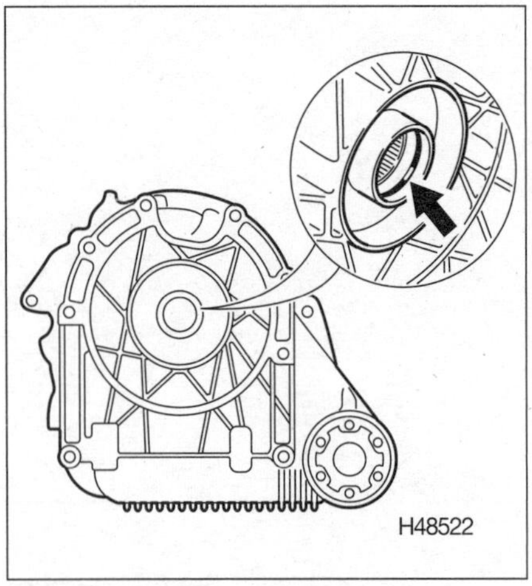

2.9 Renew the coupling O-ring seal (arrowed)

strap (where fitted) from the rear of the transfer case.

6 Depress the lock-ring and disconnect the breather hose from the top of the transfer case.

7 Position a transmission/trolley jack and support the transfer case.

8 Undo the 8 retaining bolts and slide the transfer gearbox rearwards from the main transmission. Enlist the help of an assistant – the gearbox is very heavy.

9 Remove and discard the O-ring seal in the transfer gearbox coupling **(see illustration)**. A new one must be fitted.

Refitting

10 Apply a little Weicon TL7391 (from Land Rover dealers) to the input shaft splines, and fit a new O-ring to the coupling.

11 Install the transfer gearbox to the rear of the main gearbox, and tighten the retaining bolts to the specified torque.

12 The remainder of refitting is a reversal of removal, bearing in mind the following points:

a) Tighten all fasteners to their specified torque where given.

b) Ensure all wiring harnesses are correctly routed and secured.

c) If a new transfer gearbox has been fitted, the ECM must be recalibrated using Land Rover diagnostic equipment. Entrust this task to a Land Rover dealer or suitably-equipped repairer.

3 Transfer gearbox overhaul – general information

Overhauling a transfer gearbox is a difficult and involved job for the DIY home mechanic. In addition to dismantling and reassembling many small parts, clearances must be precisely measured and, if necessary, changed by selecting shims and spacers. Gearbox internal components are also often difficult to obtain, and in many instances, extremely expensive. Because of this, if the gearbox develops a fault or becomes noisy, the best course of action is to have the unit overhauled by a specialist repairer, or to obtain an exchange reconditioned unit.

Nevertheless, it is not impossible for the more experienced mechanic to overhaul a gearbox, provided the special tools are available, and the job is done in a deliberate step-by-step manner so that nothing is overlooked.

The tools necessary for an overhaul include internal and external circlip pliers, bearing pullers, a slide-hammer, a set of pin punches, a dial test indicator, and possibly a hydraulic press. In addition, a large, sturdy workbench and a vice will be required. Certain Land Rover special tools will be required for work on the differential assembly.

During dismantling of the gearbox, make careful notes of how each component is fitted, to make reassembly easier and more accurate.

Before dismantling the gearbox, it will help if you have some idea of which area is malfunctioning. Certain problems can be closely related to specific areas in the gearbox, which can make component examination and renewal easier. Refer to the *Fault finding* Section at the end of this manual for more information.

4 Transfer gearbox fluid renewal

1 Raise the vehicle and support it securely on axle stands (see *Jacking and vehicle support*).

2 Place a container beneath the transfer gearbox, and remove the drain plug **(see illustration)**. Discard the sealing washer – a new one must be fitted. Allow the fluid to drain.

3 Refit the drain plug with a new sealing washer, and tighten it to the specified torque.

4 Undo the filler/level plug. Discard the sealing washer – a new one must be fitted.

5 Fill the transfer gearbox with the recommended fluid, until the fluid is level with the bottom of the filler/level hole.

6 Refit the filler/level plug with a new sealing washer, and tighten it to the specified torque.

5 Four-wheel-drive control module – removal and refitting

1 Remove the battery as described in Chapter 5, Section 4.

2 Release the clips and remove the cover over the control module **(see illustration)**.

3 Release the 2 clips, disconnect the wiring plugs and remove the control module **(see illustrations)**.

4 Refitting is a reversal of removal, noting that if a new unit has been fitted, it must be calibrated using Land Rover diagnostic equipment. Entrust this task to a Land Rover dealer or suitably-equipped repairer.

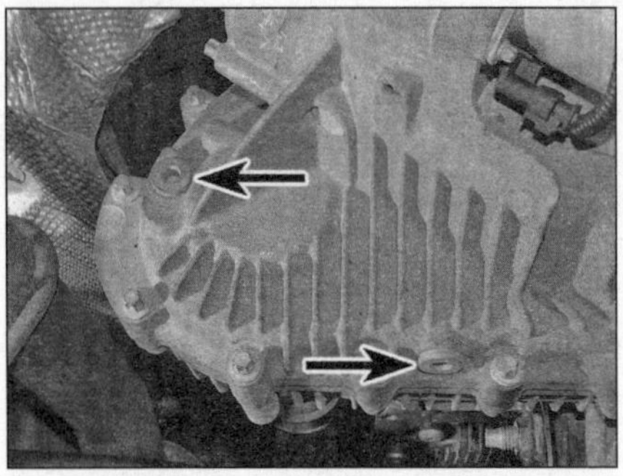

4.2 Transfer gearbox drain and filler/level plugs (arrowed)

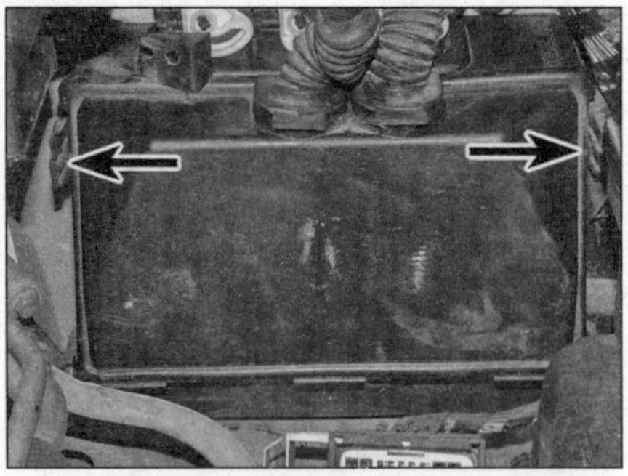

5.2 Release the clips (arrowed) and remove the cover

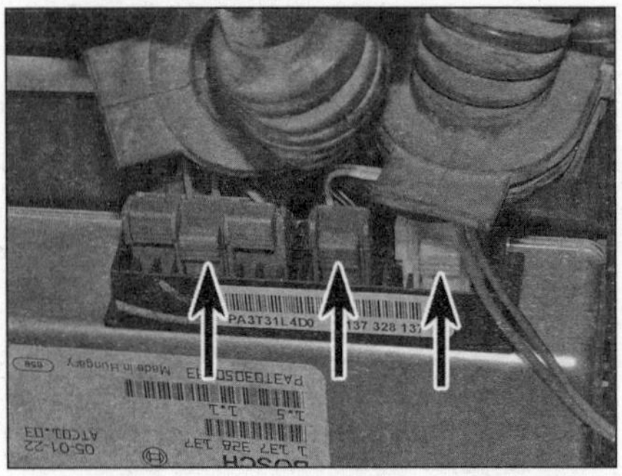

5.3a Depress the clips (arrowed) and disconnect the wiring plugs

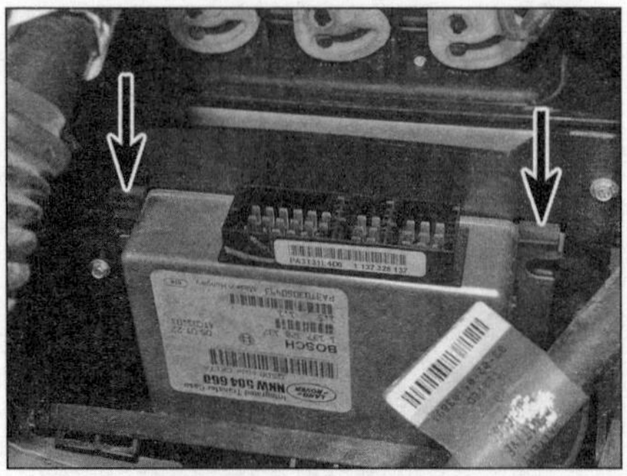

5.3b Lift the clip (arrowed) each side and remove the control module

Chapter 8
Propeller shafts

Contents

Degrees of difficulty

Easy, suitable for novice with little experience	**Fairly easy,** suitable for beginner with some experience	**Fairly difficult,** suitable for competent DIY mechanic	**Difficult,** suitable for experienced DIY mechanic	**Very difficult,** suitable for expert DIY or professional

Specifications

General

Propeller shaft type:	
Front	One-piece steel tube
Rear	Two-piece variable length steel tube
End joints:	
Front shaft	Plunging type constant velocity
Rear shaft	Plunging type constant velocity at the front and centre, with Hookes universal joint at the rear

Torque wrench settings

Torque wrench settings	Nm	lbf ft
Propeller shaft securing bolts:		
Front shaft:*		
Stage 1	45	33
Stage 2	Angle-tighten a further 90°	
Rear shaft to transfer gearbox flange	73	54
Rear shaft to final drive*	150	111
Rear shaft centre bearing bolts	30	22
Transmission crossmember bolts	90	66
Transmission rear mounting through-bolt	175	129

** Do not re-use*

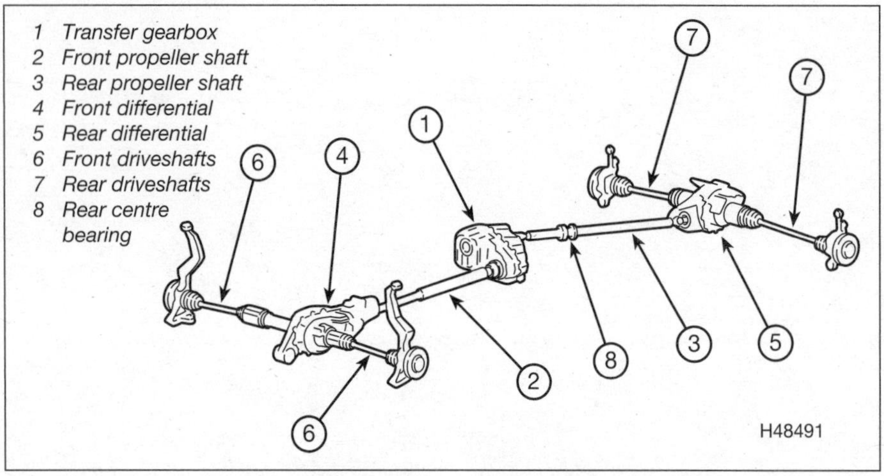

1.2 Four-wheel drivetrain details

1 General information

The drive is transmitted from the transfer gearbox to the front and rear axle differentials/final drives by two tubular propeller shafts.

The front propeller shaft is fitted with constant velocity joints. The joints cater for the varying angle between the final drive and the transmission caused by suspension movement **(see illustration)**.

The rear propeller shaft is fitted with a constant velocity joint at the front end and centre, and a Hookes type universal joint at the rear. Due to the length of the rear shaft, a centre support bearing is fitted.

2 Propeller shaft – removal and refitting

Front propeller shaft

Removal

1 Jack up the vehicle, and support securely on axle stands (see *Jacking and vehicle support*).

2 Undo the bolts and remove the engine and the transmission undershields **(see illustrations)**.

3 Unclip the fuel hoses/pump/wiring plugs from the transmission crossmember. Where applicable, undo the bolts and remove the fuel filter heat shield **(see illustration)**.

4 Detach the exhaust pipe front rubber mounting.

5 Position a trolley jack under the rear of the transfer gearbox, and take the weight.

6 Undo the transmission mounting through-bolt **(see illustration)**.

7 Remove the 4 retaining nuts/bolts and lower the transmission crossmember from place **(see illustration)**.

8 If the original propeller shaft is to be refitted, make alignment marks between the propeller shaft flanges, the differential flange, and the transfer gearbox flange.

9 Undo the flanges retaining bolts, and recover the plates beneath the bolt heads **(see illustrations)**. Discard the bolts – new ones must be fitted.

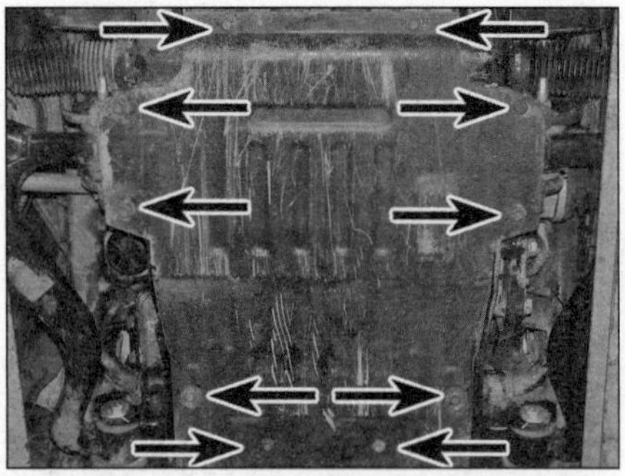

2.2a Engine undershield retaining bolts (arrowed)

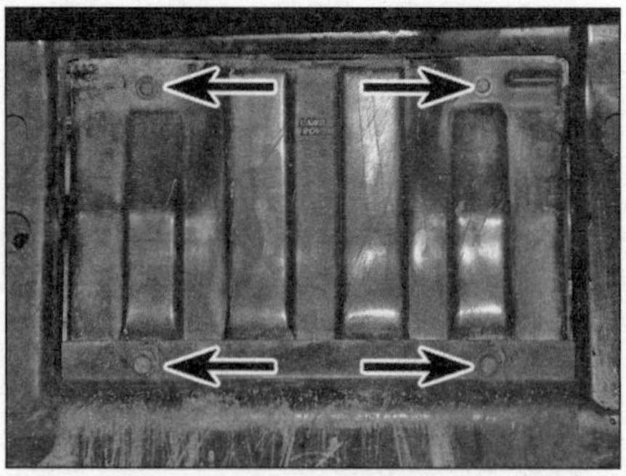

2.2b Transmission undershield retaining bolts (arrowed)

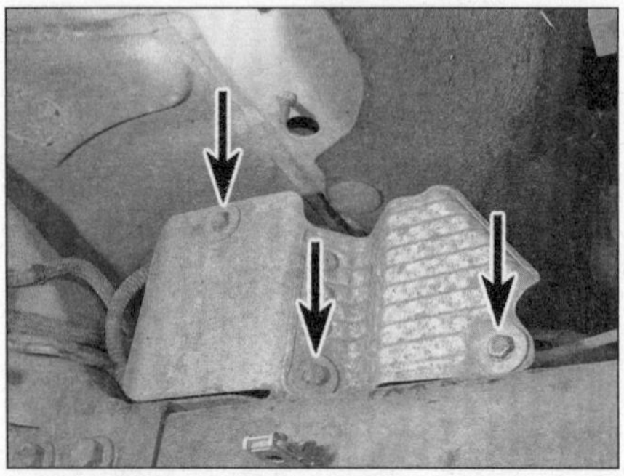

2.3 Fuel filter heat shield retaining bolts (arrowed)

2.6 Remove the transmission mounting through-bolt (arrowed)

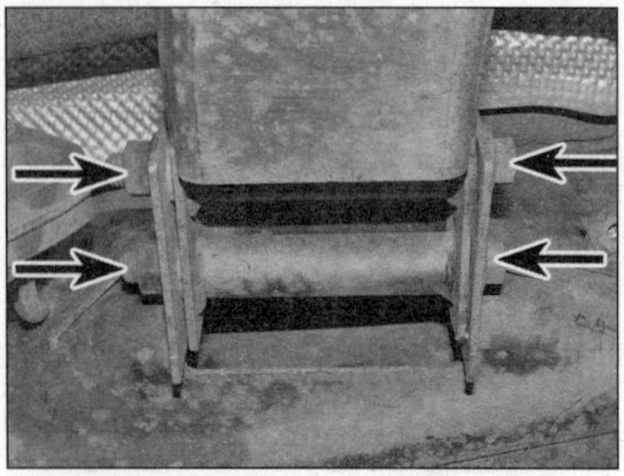

2.7 Remove the bolts/nuts (arrowed) each side securing the transmission crossmember

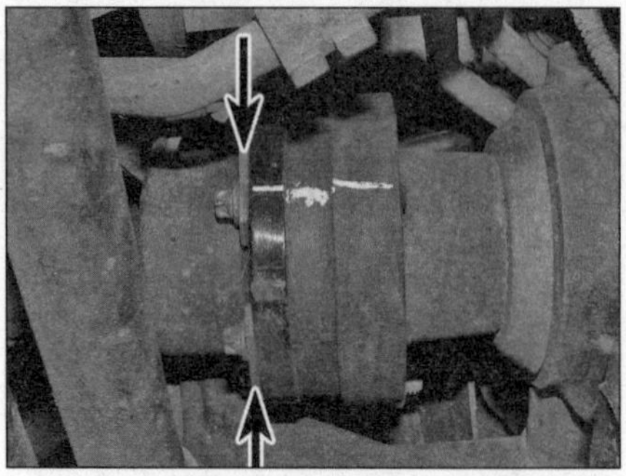

2.9a Make alignment marks between the flanges, and remove the bolts. Recover the plates (arrowed) – front final drive ...

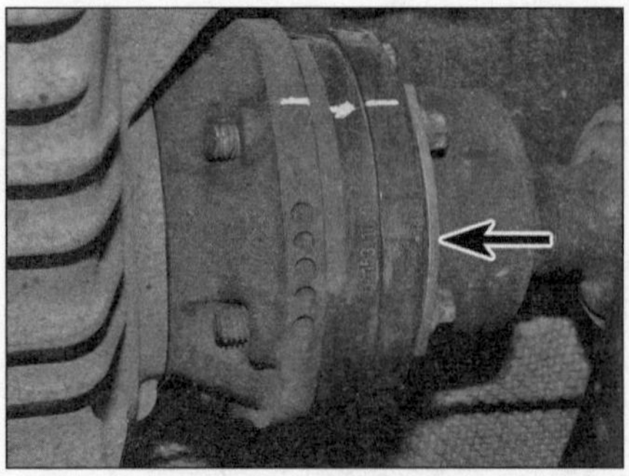

2.9b ... and front propeller shaft to transfer gearbox (plate arrowed)

2.10 Compress the propeller shaft joints slightly, and manoeuvre it from place

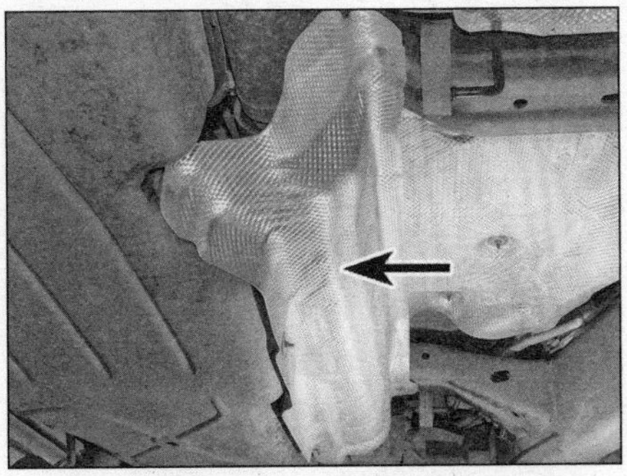
2.13 Remove the heat shield (arrowed) beneath the rear propeller shaft

2.14 Make alignment marks between the propeller shaft flanges and the transfer gearbox output flange ...

10 Raise the gearbox a little, slightly compress the front joint rearwards, and the rear joint forwards, then manoeuvre the shaft from place **(see illustration)**. **Note:** *Do not allow the propeller shaft to hang from one end unsupported – the joint or gaiter may be damaged.*

Refitting

11 Refitting is a reversal of removal, bearing in mind the following points:

a) Don't forget to fit the washer to the transfer gearbox drive flange.
b) If the original propeller shaft is being refitted, align the marks made on the differential flange, transfer gearbox flange, and the propeller shaft flanges before removal.
c) Renew the drive flanges retaining bolts.
d) Tighten all fasteners to their specified torque where given.
e) The shaft is fitted with the smaller diameter at the front.

Rear propeller shaft

Removal

12 Jack up the vehicle, and support securely on axle stands (see *Jacking and vehicle support*).

13 Undo the bolts and remove the heat shield beneath the rear propeller shaft **(see illustration)**.

14 If the original propeller shaft is to be refitted, make alignment marks between the propeller shaft flanges, the rear differential flange and the transfer gearbox flange **(see illustration)**.

15 Undo the propeller shaft front flange's retaining bolts, and recover the plates beneath the bolt heads. Discard the bolts – new ones must be fitted. **Note:** *Do not allow the propeller shaft to hang from one end unsupported – the joint or gaiter may be damaged.*

16 Undo the bolts securing the propeller shaft rear flange **(see illustration)**. Discard the bolts – new ones must be fitted. **Note:** *Do not allow the propeller shaft to hang from one end unsupported – the joint may be damaged.*

17 Have an assistant support the shaft, then undo the centre bearing bracket retaining bolts, and lower the shaft to the ground **(see illustration)**.

Refitting

18 Align the previously-made marks (where applicable), attach the propeller shaft flanges to the transfer gearbox and rear differential flanges, insert the new bolts, and tighten them to the specified torque.

19 Align the centre bearing support bracket with the holes in the vehicle body, insert the bolts and tighten them to the specified torque.

20 Refit the heat shield, and lower the vehicle to the ground.

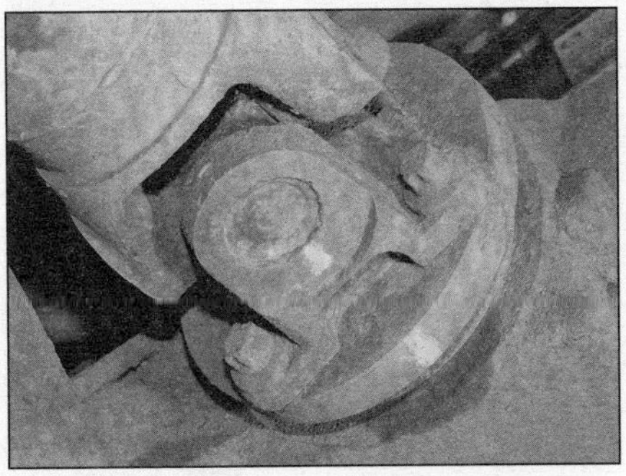
2.16 ... and the rear final drive flange

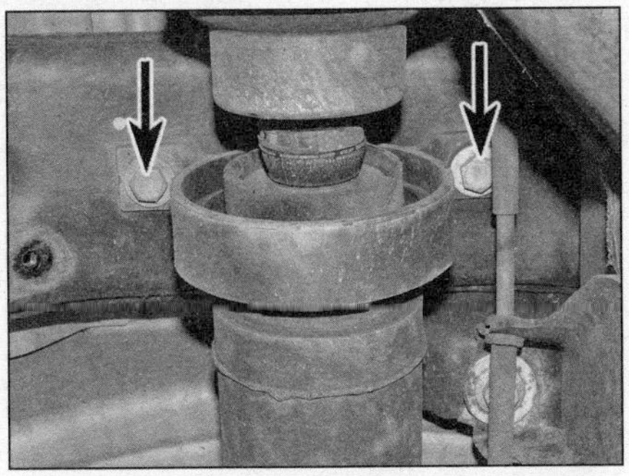
2.17 Centre bearing support bracket bolts (arrowed)

3 Propeller shaft – inspection and overhaul

Inspection

1 Wear in the universal/constant velocity joints is characterised by vibration in the transmission, clonks on taking up the drive, and in extreme cases (lack of lubrication), unpleasant metallic noises as the bearings/surfaces break up.

2 To test the universal/Hookes joints for wear with the propeller shaft in place, apply the handbrake, and chock the wheels.

3 Working under the vehicle, apply leverage between the yokes using a large screwdriver or a flat metal bar. Wear is indicated by movement between the shaft yoke and the coupling flange yoke.

4 Check for play between the constant velocity joint housings and the shaft tubes, any play or stiffness/roughness indicates the joint is defective.

Overhaul

5 If any of the joints are defective, the complete propeller shaft must be renewed. It would appear that no new components are available. Check with a Land Rover dealer or parts specialist.

Notes

Chapter 9
Final drives and driveshafts

Contents

Degrees of difficulty

Easy, suitable for novice with little experience	**Fairly easy,** suitable for beginner with some experience	**Fairly difficult,** suitable for competent DIY mechanic	**Difficult,** suitable for experienced DIY mechanic	**Very difficult,** suitable for expert DIY or professional

Specifications

General information

Differential ratio:	
Manual transmission	3.07 : 1
Automatic transmission	3.54 : 1
Capacity	See Chapter 1 Specifications

Torque wrench settings

	Nm	lbf ft
Front		
Anti-roll bar link nuts*	115	85
Axle carrier-to-final drive bolts:*		
Stage 1	80	59
Stage 2	Angle-tighten a further 60°	
Axle crossmember bolts	115	85
Driveshaft nut*	230	170
Final drive drain plug	54	40
Final drive filler plug	34	25
Final drive mountings:		
Rear bolts:*		
Stage 1	80	59
Stage 2	Angle-tighten a further 60°	
Front bolt (M14)	105	77
Roadwheel nuts	140	103
Steering track rod balljoint nut*	76	56
Upper arm balljoint nut*	70	52
Rear		
Anti-roll bar link nuts*	115	85
Driveshaft nut*	350	258
ETM diff lock motor to casing	12	9
ETM diff lock motor casing to final drive	10	7
Final drive drain plug:		
Hexagonal drive plug	54	40
3/8" square drive plug	28	21
Final drive filler plug	34	25
Final drive mounting bolts:		
Front	275	203
Rear	175	129
Final drive temperature sensor	22	16
Lower arm to hub carrier*	275	203
Roadwheel nuts	140	103
Toe link to hub carrier	175	129

** Do not re-use*

1 General information

The final drive assemblies includes the drive pinion, the ring gear, and the differential. The drive pinion, which drives the ring gear, is also known as the differential input shaft and is connected to the propeller shaft via an input flange. The differential is bolted to the ring gear and drives the wheels through a pair driveshafts with constant velocity (CV) joints at either end. The differential allows the wheels to turn at different speeds when cornering.

The rear final drive may be one of two different types: A traditional 'open' differential – similar to the front unit, or a locking differential, known as an electronic torque managed (ETM) differential. The ETM variant is fitted with a multi-plate clutch mechanism which allows varying degrees of slip (or lock) between the rear wheels. This capacity affords greater traction and enhanced vehicle stability on varying terrain. The multi-plate clutch is controlled electronically by a control module located behind the left-hand C-pillar trim panel. The ECM controls the multi-plate clutch (and therefore the differential lock) based on information received from the wheel speed sensors, transmission sensors, air suspension system, and the ride and handling optimisation controller in the cabin. The ECM is on constant communication with the vehicles other ECM/ECUs, via a CAN bus network.

The driveshafts deliver power from the final drive unit to the wheels. The driveshafts are equipped with constant velocity (CV) joints at both ends. The inner joints are pushed into the differential gears, and secured by circlips, whilst the outer CV joints engage the splines of the wheel hubs, and are secured by a large nut.

Major repair work on the differential assembly components (drive pinion, ring-and-pinion, and differential) requires many special tools and a high degree of expertise, and therefore should not be attempted by the home mechanic. If major repairs become necessary, we recommend that they be performed by a Land Rover service department or other suitably-equipped automotive engineer.

2 Driveshaft – removal and refitting

Front driveshaft

Removal

1 Apply the handbrake, and loosen the nuts on the relevant front roadwheel. Jack up the front of the vehicle and support it securely on axle stands (see *Jacking and vehicle support*). Remove the relevant front roadwheel.

2 Undo the bolts and remove the engine undershield.

3 Place a container beneath the final drive housing, undo the drain plug and allow the fluid to drain **(see illustration)**. Once the fluid has drained, refit the plug and tighten it to the specified torque.

4 Using a chisel or punch, unstake the driveshaft nut, then unscrew it from the driveshaft **(see illustrations)**. Assistance may be required, the nut is very tight. Discard the nut, a new one must be fitted. **Note:** *The driveshaft nut is very tight. It may be prudent to prise out the centre of the roadwheel, refit it, and lower the vehicle to the ground. Then insert the socket through the centre of the wheel and undo the nut.*

5 Using an open-ended spanner to counterhold, undo the nut securing the anti-roll bar link rod to the upper arm **(see illustration)**. Discard the nut – a new one must be fitted.

6 Undo the bolt securing the brake hose bracket to the hub carrier.

7 Slacken the retaining nut, then use a universal balljoint separator tool to detach the steering track rod end balljoint from the hub carrier **(see illustration)**. Discard the nut – a new one must be fitted. Take care not to damage the rubber gaiter on the joint.

8 Place a trolley jack under the hub carrier to support it, then slacken the nut securing the upper balljoint to the hub carrier **(see illustration)**.

9 Using a universal balljoint separator tool, detach the upper balljoint from the hub carrier **(see illustration)**. Discard the nut – a new one must be fitted. Take care not to damage the rubber gaiter on the joint.

10 Carefully, and gently, tap the end of the

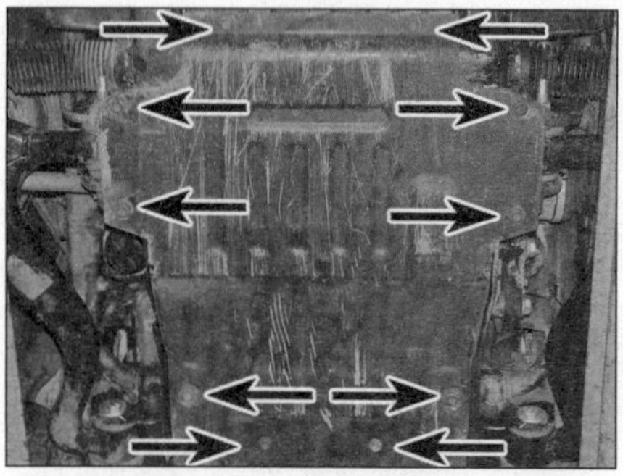

2.2 Engine undershield retaining bolts (arrowed)

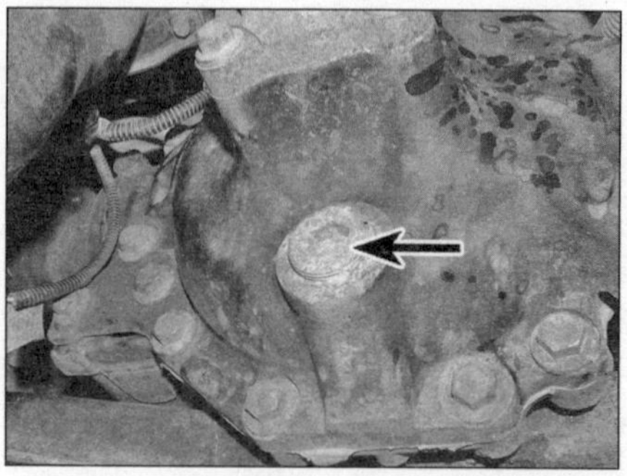

2.3 Front final drive housing drain plug (arrowed)

2.4a Use a chisel to 'un-stake' the driveshaft nut

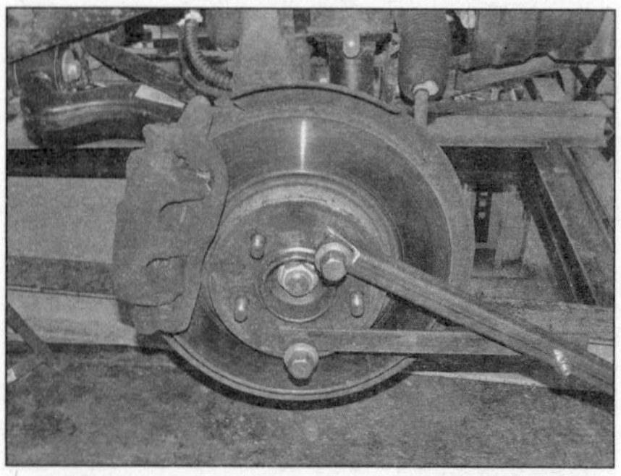

2.4b We used a home-made tool bolted to the hub to prevent rotation whilst slackening the driveshaft nut

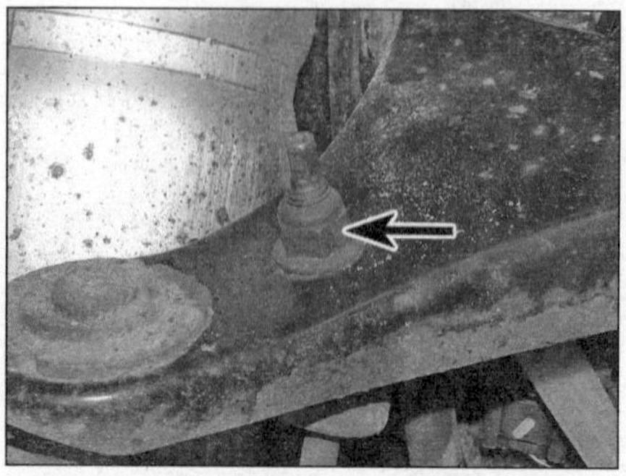

2.5 Undo the nut (arrowed) securing the anti-roll bar link rod to the upper arm

2.7 Detach the steering track rod end from the hub carrier using a separator tool

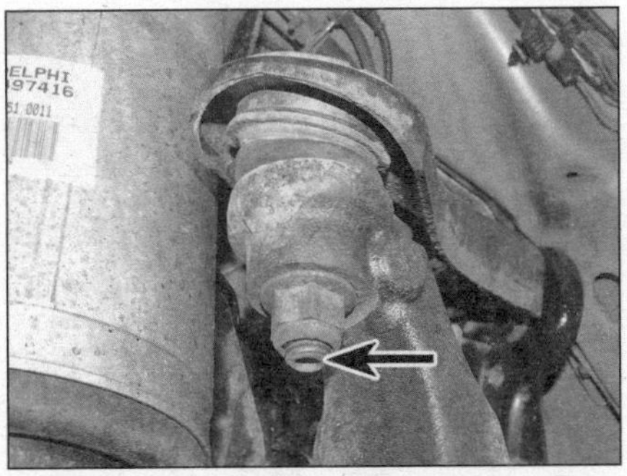

2.8 Insert an Allen key into the end of the balljoint shank (arrowed) to prevent rotation when slackening the retaining nut

driveshaft from the hub with a soft-faced mallet. If the driveshaft is reluctant to move, use a special Land Rover tool (No. 204-506/1, 205-506/3 and 204-506/5) to press the driveshaft from the hub. *Take great care not to damage the end of the shaft.*

11 Allow the hub carrier to tilt outwards, then disengage the driveshaft from it **(see illustration)**. Don't allow the hub carrier to hang on the lower arm, or the lower balljoint may be damaged. Tie it to the suspension strut.

12 Insert a large screwdriver/lever between the differential casing and the inner joint housing, and prise the end of the driveshaft from place **(see illustration)**.

13 Manoeuvre the driveshaft from position.

14 Prise the circlip from the inner end of the shaft **(see illustration)**. Discard the circlip – a new one must be fitted.

15 It is recommended that the driveshaft oil seal in the final drive housing is renewed as described in Section 5.

Refitting

16 Fit a new circlip to the end of the inner joint.

17 Ensure the hub carrier, driveshaft splines, and hub mating faces are clean and free from debris. Apply a little clean oil to the driveshaft seal lips.

18 Push the driveshaft into the final drive casing, then push the inner joint to fully engage it with the differential. Using a lever/ screwdriver, check the circlip is fully engaged, and the joint retained.

19 Remove the oil seal protector. The protector is supplied with genuine Land Rover driveshaft oil seals.

20 Apply a little anti-seize grease to the splines, then refit the end of the driveshaft into the hub assembly. If necessary use Land Rover tool No. 204-506-01, 204-506/1 and 204-506/5 to pull the end of the shaft through the hub.

21 Fit the upper balljoint into the hub carrier, then fit the new nut and tighten it to the specified torque.

22 Refit the steering track rod end balljoint and tighten the new nut to the specified torque.

23 Tighten the driveshaft nut to the specified torque, then 'stake' the nut to the shaft **(see illustration)**. Assistance may be required – the torque for the nut is very high. If necessary refit the roadwheel, then lower the vehicle to the ground and tighten the nut. It will then be necessary to raise the vehicle, remove the roadwheel and stake the nut.

24 The remainder of refitting is a reversal of removal, noting the following points:

a) Tighten al fasteners to their specified torque where given.

b) Refill the final drive with oil as described in Section 10.

Rear driveshaft

Removal

25 Apply the handbrake, and loosen the nuts on the relevant rear roadwheel. Jack up the rear of the vehicle and support it securely on axle stands (see *Jacking and vehicle support*). Remove the relevant roadwheel.

26 Place a container beneath the housing, undo the drain plug and allow the fluid to drain **(see illustration)**. Once the fluid has drained, refit the plug and tighten it to the specified torque.

27 Using a chisel or punch, unstake the driveshaft nut, then unscrew it from the driveshaft **(see illustration 2.4a and 2.4b)**. Assistance may be required, the nut is very tight. Discard the nut, a new one must be fitted. **Note:** *The driveshaft nut is very tight. It may be prudent to prise out the centre of the roadwheel, refit it, and lower the vehicle to the ground. Then insert the socket through the centre of the wheel and undo the nut.*

28 Using an open-ended spanner to

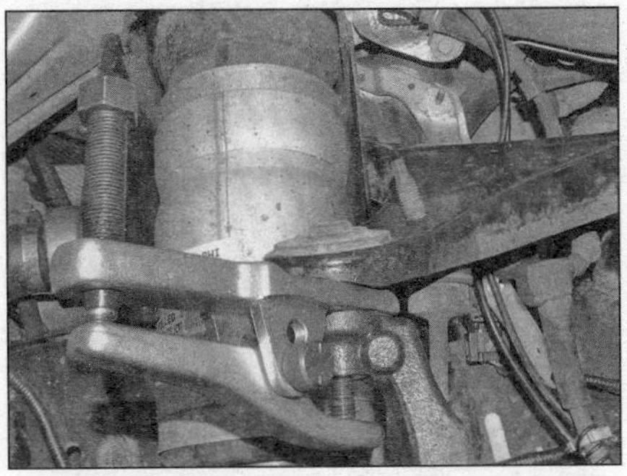

2.9 Detach the upper arm balljoint from the hub carrier using a separator tool

2.11 Disengage the end of the driveshaft from the hub

2.12 Lever between the inner joint housing and the casing/crossmember

2.14 Renew the circlip (arrowed) on the inner end of the driveshaft

2.23 Use a suitable punch to 'stake' the driveshaft nut

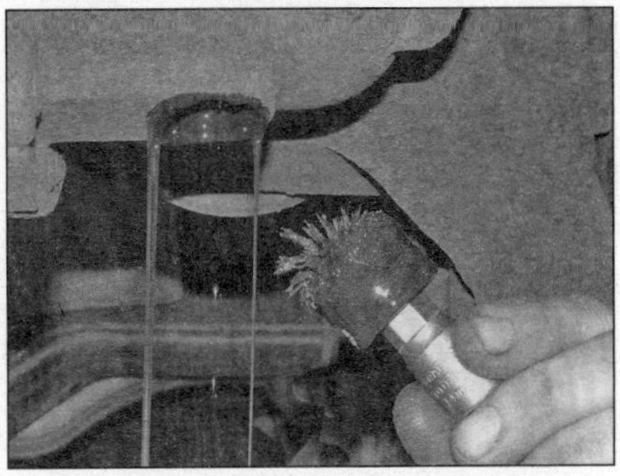

2.26 Note the magnetic drain plug

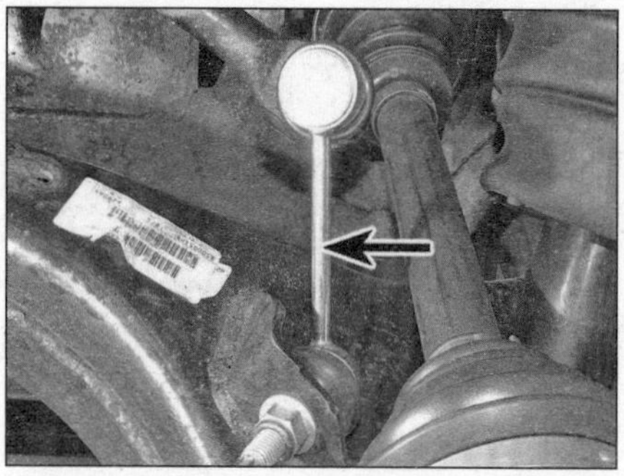
2.28 Remove the rear anti-roll bar link rod (arrowed)

2.30 Toe link retaining bolt (arrowed)

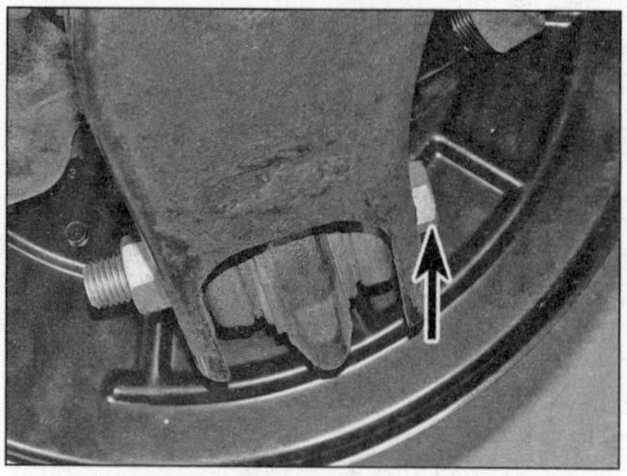
2.31 Undo the bolt (arrowed) securing the lower arm to the hub carrier

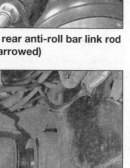

2.34 Carefully drive the inner joint housing from the differential casing

2.36 Renew the circlip on the inner end of the driveshaft

counterhold, undo the nuts and remove the rear anti-roll bar link rod **(see illustration)**. Discard the nuts – new ones must be fitted.

29 Unclip the handbrake cable from the retaining bracket on the lower arm.

30 Undo the bolts securing the toe link to the hub carrier **(see illustration)**.

31 Undo the bolt/nut securing the lower arm to the hub carrier **(see illustration)**. Take care not to damage the rubber seal. Discard the nut – a new one must be fitted.

32 Using a suitable tool, press the end of the driveshaft from the hub. A special Land Rover tool (No. 204-506/1, 205-506/3 and 204-506/5) is available for this task. **Note:** *Use of a hammer to force the shaft from the hub will almost certainly result in damage. Take great care not to damage the end of the shaft.*

33 Pull the hub carrier outwards and disengage the end of the shaft from the hub assembly.

34 Carefully drive the inner joint housing from the differential housing using a block of wood **(see illustration)**.

35 Manoeuvre the driveshaft from position.

36 Prise the circlip from the inner end of the shaft **(see illustration)**. Discard the circlip – a new one must be fitted.

37 It is recommended that the driveshaft oil seal in the final drive housing is renewed as described in Section 5.

Refitting

38 Fit a new circlip to the end of the inner joint.

39 Ensure the hub carrier, driveshaft splines, and hub mating faces are clean and free from debris. Apply a little clean oil to the driveshaft seal lips.

40 Push the driveshaft into the final drive casing, then push the inner joint to fully engage it with the differential. Using a lever/screwdriver, check the circlip is fully engaged, and the joint retained.

41 Remove the oil seal protector. The protector is supplied with genuine Land Rover driveshaft oil seals.

42 Apply a little anti-seize grease to the splines, then refit the end of the driveshaft into the hub assembly. If necessary use Land Rover tool No. 204-506-01, 204-506/1 and 204-506/5 to pull the end of the shaft through the hub.

43 Reconnect the lower arm to the hub carrier, insert the bolt and tighten the new nut to the specified torque.

44 Reconnect the toe link to the hub carrier and tighten the bolt to the specified torque.

45 Refit the anti-roll bar link and tighten the new nuts to the specified torque.

46 Tighten the driveshaft nut to the specified torque, then 'stake' the nut to the shaft **(see illustration 2.23)**. Assistance may be required – the torque for the nut is very high. If necessary refit the roadwheel, then lower the vehicle to the ground and tighten the nut. It will then be necessary to raise the vehicle, remove the roadwheel and stake the nut.

47 The remainder of refitting is a reversal of removal, noting the following points:

a) *Tighten all fasteners to their specified torque where given.*

b) *Refill the final drive with oil as described in Section 10.*

3 Driveshaft overhaul and gaiter renewal

Renewal

1 Remove the driveshaft as described in Section 2.

2 Release the rubber gaiter retaining clips by cutting them off with a pair of side-cutters or hacksaw **(see illustration)**. Remove the clips and slide the gaiter down the driveshaft away from the CV joint.

3 The joint is secured to the driveshaft by an external circlip. Use a soft metal drift to drive the inner spider from the end of the driveshaft **(see illustration)**. Discard the circlip – a new one must be fitted.

3.2 Cut away the old gaiter retaining clips

3.3 Drive the inner spider from the driveshaft

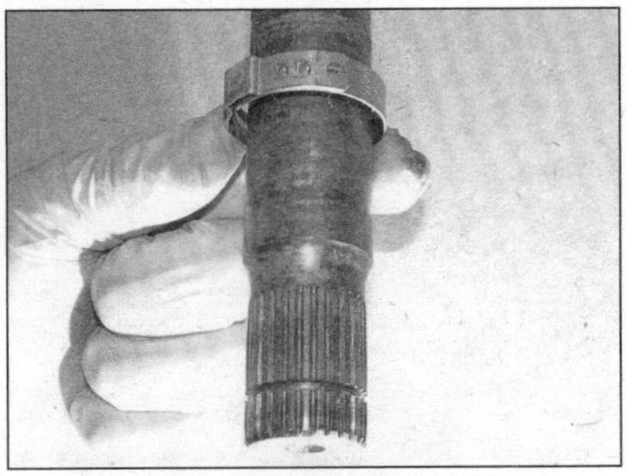
3.9a Slide on the smaller clip ...

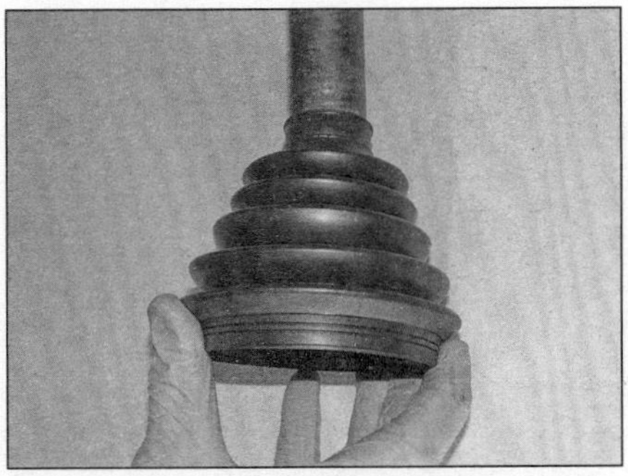
3.9b ... followed by the gaiter and large clip

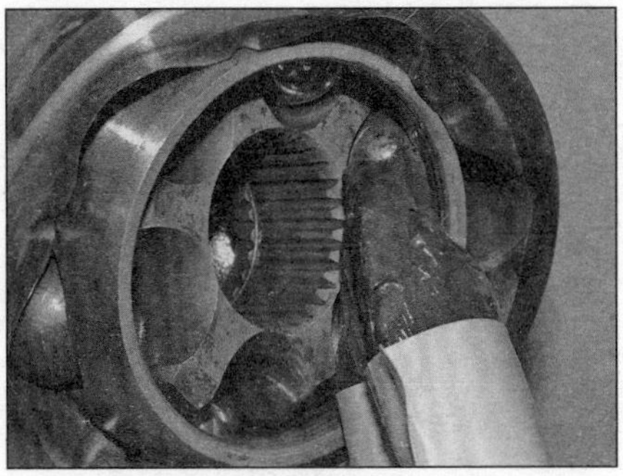
3.11 Pack the joint with grease

3.14a Secure the clips in place ...

3.14b ... using special pliers which squeeze and compress the raised portion

4 Slide the old gaiter off the end of the driveshaft.
5 With the constant velocity joint removed from the driveshaft, thoroughly clean the joint using paraffin, or a suitable solvent, and dry it thoroughly. Carry out a visual inspection of the joint.
6 Move the inner splined driving member from side-to-side, to expose each ball in turn at the top of its track. Examine the balls for cracks, flat spots, or signs of surface pitting.
7 Inspect the ball tracks on the inner and outer members. If the tracks have widened, the balls will no longer be a tight fit. At the same time, check the ball cage windows for wear or cracking between the windows.
8 If any of the constant velocity joint components are found to be worn or damaged, it will be necessary to renew the complete joint assembly as the internal parts are not available separately. If the joint is in satisfactory condition, obtain a new gaiter, retaining clips, circlip, and the correct type of grease. These components are all available as complete kit from Land Rover dealers, and maybe available from other sources.
9 Slide the smaller gaiter securing clip onto the driveshaft, followed by the gaiter and the large securing clip **(see illustrations)**. Note that the closed end of the clips must point in the direction of rotation (when the vehicle moves forwards).
10 Renew the circlip on the end of the shaft.
11 Pack the CV joint with the supplied grease, then twist the joint to ensure that all the recesses are filled **(see illustration)**.
12 Fit the CV joint to the driveshaft, and engage it with the shaft splines. Press the circlip into its groove, then use a mallet to tap the joint onto the shaft until the circlip engages correctly.
13 Slide the large end of the gaiter into position over the joint, ensuring that it is seated squarely over the joint body.
14 Locate the large securing clip over the gaiter and secure the clip in place by squeezing and compressing the raised portion **(see illustrations)**. Note that the 108 mm diameter clip fits on the inner rear joint gaiter.
15 Slide the smaller securing clip over the gaiter, and secure it as described previously.
16 Refit the driveshaft as described in Section 2.

4 Final drives – removal and refitting

Removal

Front

1 Remove both front driveshafts as described in Section 2.
2 Disconnect the front propeller shaft from the final drive flange as described in Chapter 8, Section 2.
3 Undo the bolts/nut and detach the axle tube from the final drive casing. Rotate and remove the tube **(see illustrations)**. Note that early models had an O-ring seal between the tube and the casing – this must be renewed. Later models use sealant (Land Rover No. STC 50550).

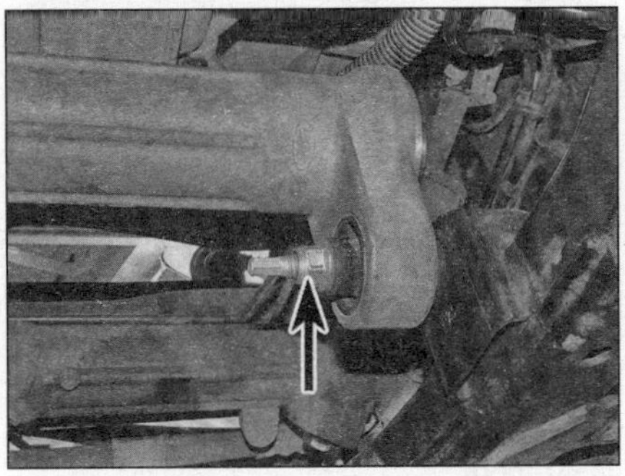
4.3a Undo the mounting nut (arrowed) ...

4.3b ... and the axle tube retaining bolts

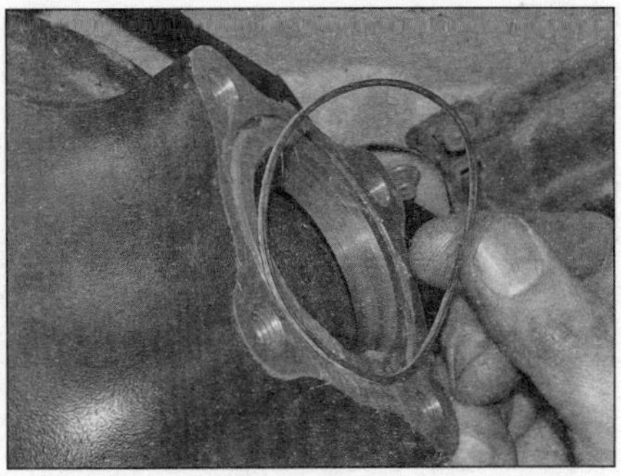
4.3c Renew the O-ring seal on early models

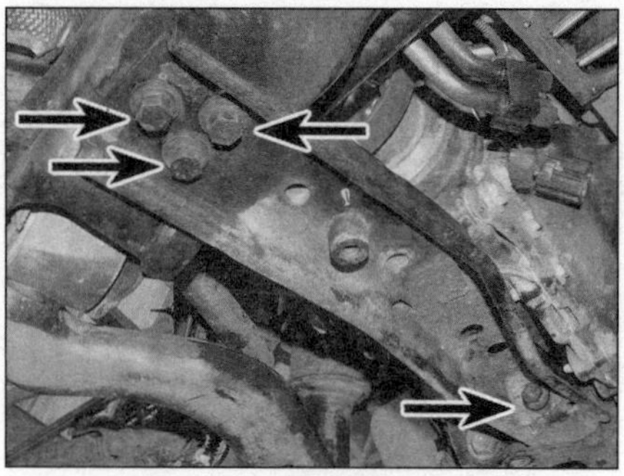
4.4 Undo the bolts (arrowed) and remove the longitudinal crossmember

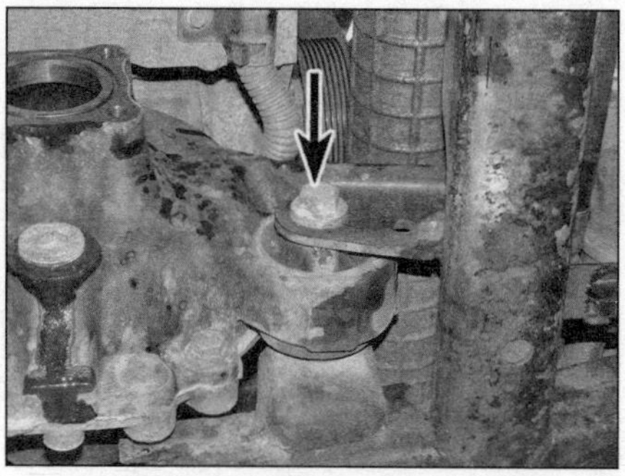
4.6a Undo the mounting bolt (arrowed) on the right-hand side ...

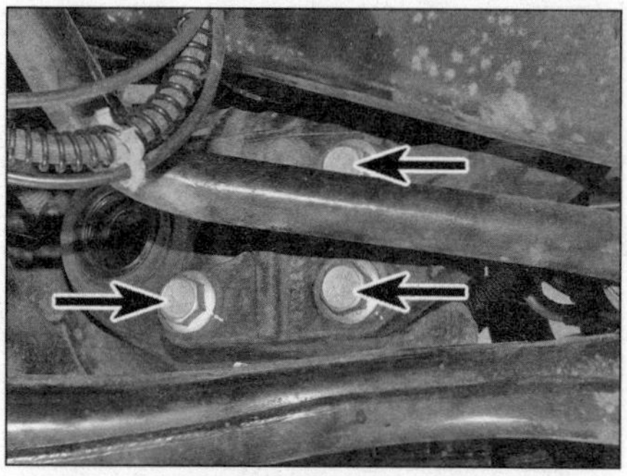
4.6b ... and the bolts (arrowed) on the left-hand side

4.11a Undo the rear final drive front mounting bolt (arrowed) ...

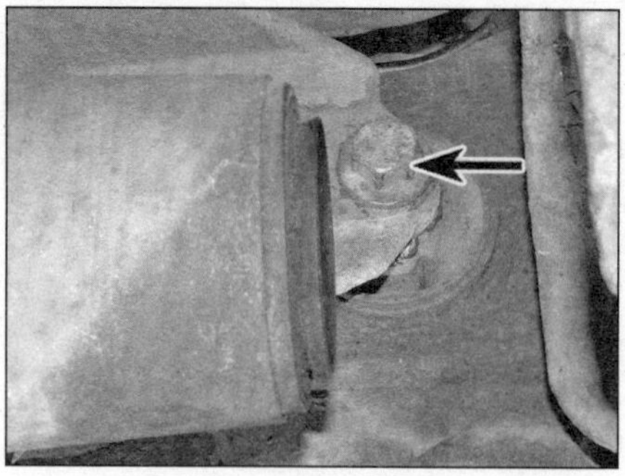
4.11b ...and the one each side (arrowed) at the rear

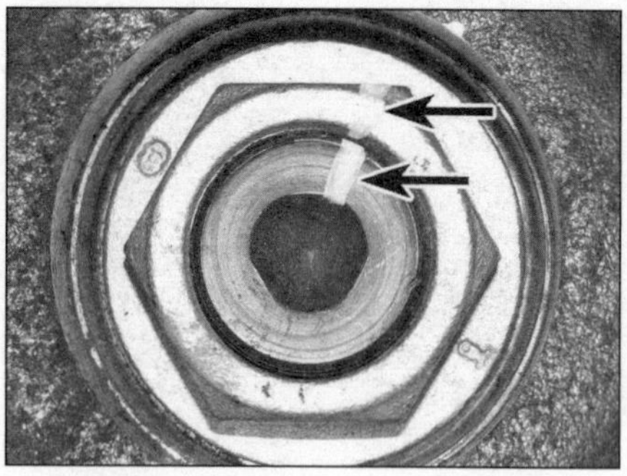
5.2 Make alignment marks (arrowed) between the pinion and the nut

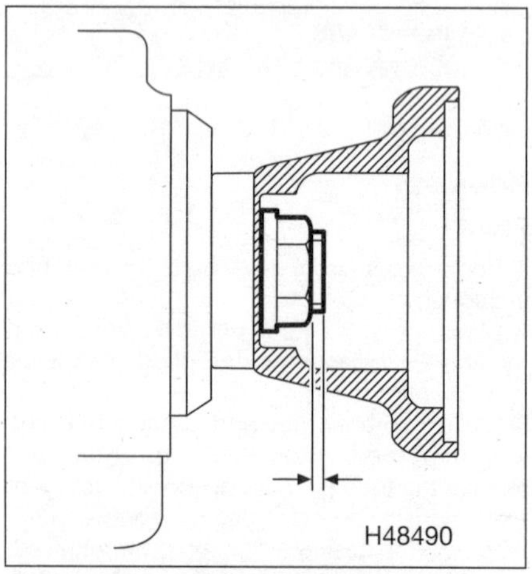

5.3 Note the fitted depth of the pinion retaining nut

4 Undo the 4 bolts and remove the front axle longitudinal crossmember **(see illustration)**.

5 Release the clip and disconnect the breather hose from the final drive casing

6 Position a trolley jack beneath the final drive casing, then remove the mounting bolts, and lower the assembly from place **(see illustrations)**. Enlist the help of an assistant – the final drive assembly is heavy. Renew the 3 rear mounting bolts.

Rear

7 Remove both rear driveshafts as described in Section 2.

8 Remove the rear and centre exhaust silencers as described in Chapter 4A, Section 17.

9 Disconnect the rear propeller shaft from the final drive flange as described in Chapter 8, Section 2.

10 On models with the ETM differential, disconnect the motor wiring plugs, and release the wiring harness from the retaining clips.

11 Position a trolley jack beneath the final drive casing, then the mounting bolts, and lower the assembly from place **(see illustrations)**. Enlist the help of an assistant – the final drive assembly is heavy. Disconnect the breather pipe as the assembly is withdrawn.

Refitting

12 Refitting is a reversal of removal, remembering to tighten the fasteners to their specified torque where given.

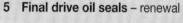

5 Final drive oil seals – renewal

Differential pinion oil seal

1 Detach the propeller shaft from the pinion flange as described in Chapter 8, Section 2. Tie the propeller shaft to one side.

2 Make alignment marks between the flange, retaining nut and the pinion to aid refitting **(see illustration)**.

3 Measure the fitted depth of the pinion nut on the pinion shaft **(see illustration)**. It's essential that the nut is fitted to the original position.

4 Undo the flange retaining nut, noting the exact number of turns to remove it. In order to counterhold the flange, use two strips of steel bolted to the flange as shown **(see illustration)**.

5 Pull the flange from position using a suitable slide hammer **(see illustration)**. If necessary,

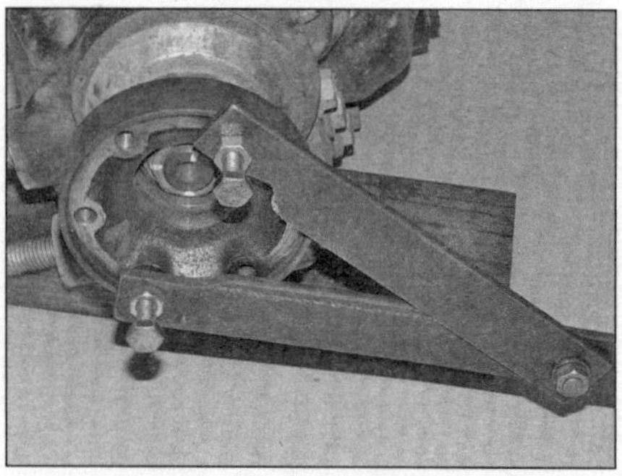
5.4 Use 2 lengths of steel trip to counterhold the pinion flange

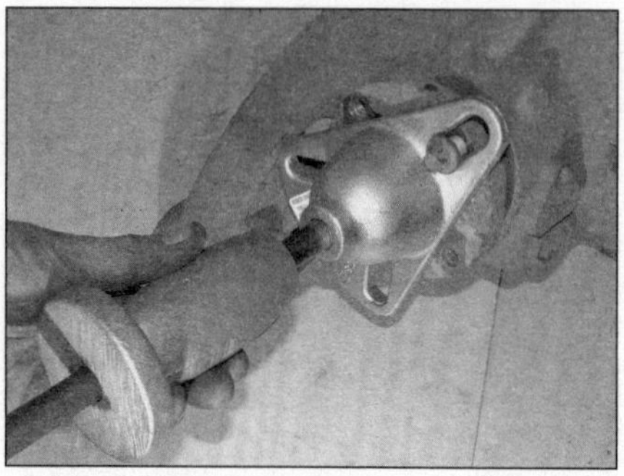
5.5 Use a slide hammer to remove the flange

5.11 Drive the oil seal into position

5.15 Prise the oil seal from the differential casing, or front axle tube as applicable

6.2a Note the fitted depth of the various bushes ...

Land Rover tool attachment No. 205-824 and slide hammer No. 100-012 maybe available for this purpose.

Front pinion seal

6 Note its fitted depth then, using a large screwdriver (or similar), carefully prise the oil seal from position. Take great care not to damage the bore in the differential housing. Be prepared for oil spillage. If necessary, Land Rover tool attachment No. 205-822 and slide hammer No. 100-012 maybe available for this purpose.

7 Clean the pinion flange and the oil seal recess in the casing.

8 Position the new oil seal, then drive it into position using a suitable tubular spacer. If necessary, Land Rover tool No. 205-820 maybe available for this purpose.

Rear pinion seal

9 Note its fitted depth then, using a large screwdriver (or similar), carefully prise the oil seal from position. Take great care not to damage the bore in the differential housing. Be prepared for oil spillage. If necessary, Land Rover tool attachment No. 205-823 and slide hammer No. 100-012 maybe available for this purpose.

10 Clean the pinion flange and the oil seal recess in the casing.

11 Position the new oil seal, then fit special tool No. 205-821-01 onto the face of the seal, and drive it into position using tool No. 205-821 **(see illustration)**.

Front and rear

12 Refit the flange to the pinion, ensuring the previously-made marks align exactly. Refit the nut and tighten it to its exact original position, using the alignment marks made previously, the same number of turns, and to the original fitted depth. Use the steel strip previously described to counterhold the flange. Note the following points:

a) Ensure the mark on the nut is tighten to at least its original position, and not more that 5° past the original marks.

b) Ensure the pinion has no endfloat and is free to rotate.

13 The remainder of refitting is a reversal of removal.

Driveshaft oil seal

14 Remove the relevant driveshaft as described in Section 2.

15 Note its fitted depth, then using a large screwdriver, carefully prise the oil seal from the casing **(see illustration)**. Take great care not to damage the bore in the casing.

16 Clean the oil seal bore in the casing.

17 Position the new seal with the metal part of the seal facing inwards, then drive it into position with a suitably sized-tubular spacer. Note that the seal must be fitted dry.

18 The seals are supplied with a protector sleeve. This must be left in place until the driveshafts are refitted.

19 Refit the driveshaft as described in Section 2.

6 Final drive mountings – renewal

1 The final drive casings are mounting on various metal-rubber bushes. Although various Land Rover special tools may be available to remove and install these bushes, they can be renewed using a combination of tubular spacers, washers, nuts and threaded rod. Begin by removing the relevant final drive assembly as described in Section 4.

2 Make notes of the fitted positions of the bushes. Note the orientation of the rubber webbing inside the bush, and the fitted depth of the metal casing on the outside of the bush **(see illustrations)**.

3 Some of these bushes may be extremely reluctant to move. Generously apply releasing spray/agent to the area where the bush contacts the casing. In extreme cases, it may be necessary to remove the final drive and extract the bushes using a hydraulic press.

4 Select a suitable tubular spacer with an internal diameter larger than the outer diameter of the bush, and a circular spacer with an outer diameter just smaller than the outside diameter of the bush. Pass the threaded rod through the spacers, assemble the washers and nuts, then draw the bush from the casing **(see illustrations)**.

5 Position the new bush, orientated exactly as the original, then use a combination of the

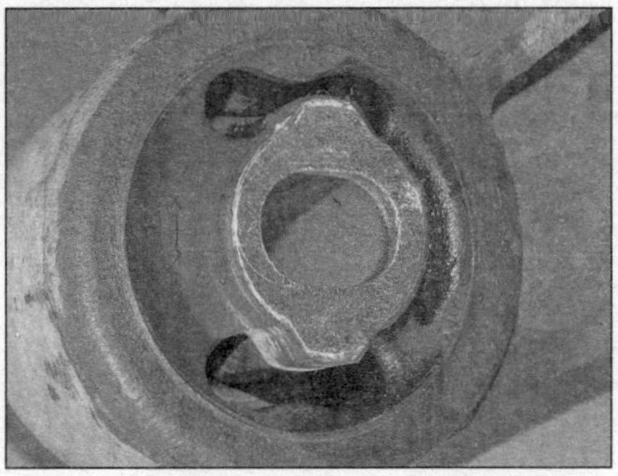

6.2b ... and the orientation of the rubber webbing within the bushes

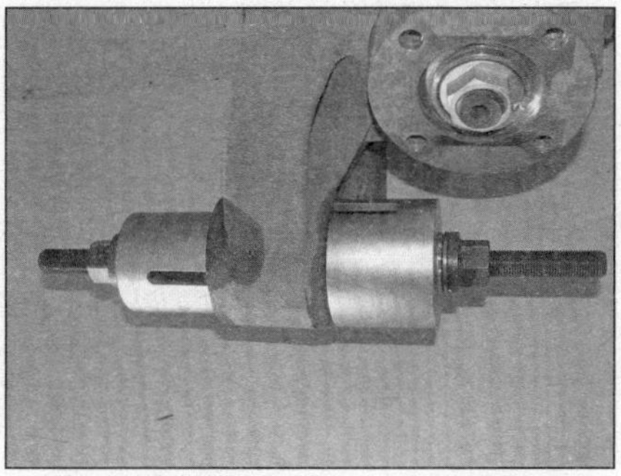

6.4a Use a combination of tubular spacers, washers, nuts and threaded rod ...

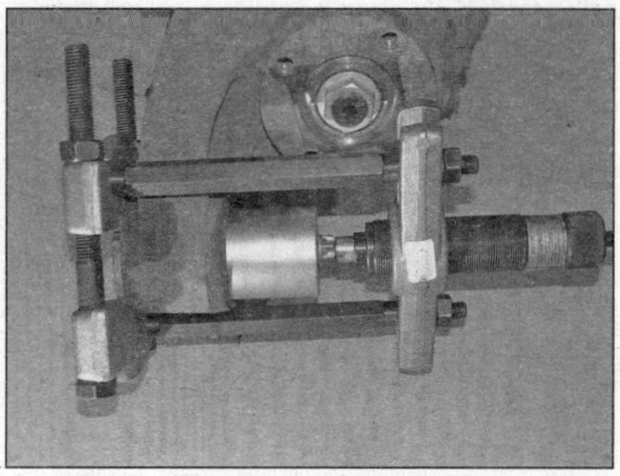

6.4b ... or pull to remove/install the mounting bushes

spacers, washers, nuts and threaded rod to draw the new bush into the original location.

6 With the new bush(es) correctly located, refit the final drive as described in Section 4.

7 Rear final drive ETM motor – removal and refitting

Removal

1 On models with the ETM (electronic torque managed) locking differential, an electric motor is fitted, to control the multi-plate clutch position.

2 Jack up the rear of the vehicle and support it securely on axle stands (see *Jacking and vehicle support*).

3 Disconnect the battery negative lead as described in Chapter 5, Section 4.

4 Undo the 4 retaining bolts and lift the motor, complete with drive casing, from the top face of the final drive. Disconnect the wiring plug as the assembly is withdrawn.

5 With the unit on the bench, undo the retaining bolts and detach the motor from the casing. Discard the O-ring seal – a new one must be fitted.

Refitting

6 Fit a new O-ring seal to the motor.

7 Position the motor in the casing and tighten the retaining bolts to the specified torque.

8 Apply a thin, continuous bead of RTV sealant to the mating face of the casing, then refit the motor assembly to the final drive, remembering to reconnect the wiring plug. Tighten the bolts to the specified torque.

9 The remainder of refitting is a reversal of removal. Note that if a new motor has been fitted, it must be calibrated using Land Rover diagnostic equipment (T4). Entrust this task to a Land Rover dealer or suitably-equipped repairer.

8 ETM control module – removal and refitting

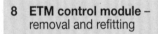

Removal

1 Disconnect the battery negative lead as described in Chapter 5, Section 4.

2 Remove the left-hand C-pillar trim panel as described in Chapter 12, Section 26.

3 Undo the 2 nuts and move the parking aid module to one side.

4 Disconnect the wiring plugs, undo the 3 retaining bolts and remove the ETM module.

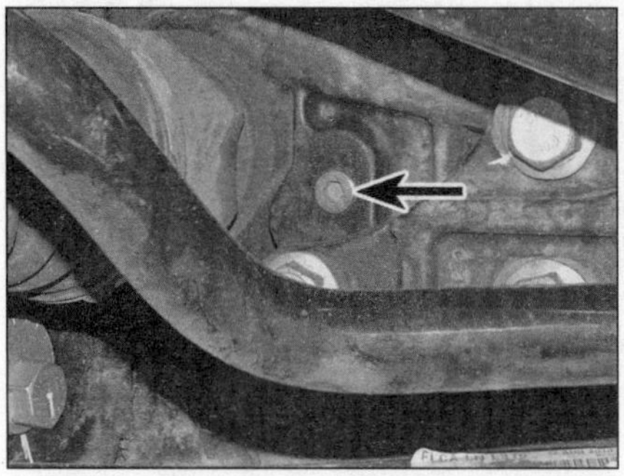

10.4a Front final drive filler plug (arrowed) – viewed through the wheel arch aperture

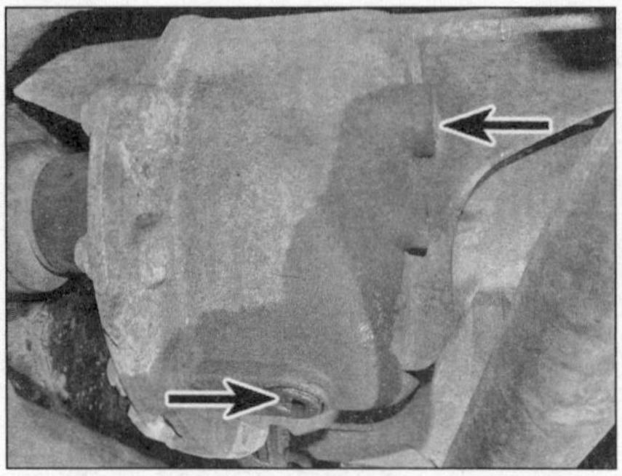

10.4b Rear final drive filler and drain plugs (arrowed)

Refitting

5 Refitting is a reversal of removal, noting that if a new ETM module has been fitted, it must be calibrated using Land Rover diagnostic equipment (T4). Entrust this task to a Land Rover dealer or suitably-equipped repairer.

9 Rear final drive temperature sensor – renewal

Note: *That the sensor is only fitted to models with the ETM locking final drive.*

1 Drain the final drive fluid as described in Section 10.

2 Disconnect the sensor wiring plug, and unclip the wiring harness.

3 Unscrew the sensor from the final drive casing. Discard the O-ring seal – a new one must be fitted.

4 Ensure the mating faces are clean, then fit the sensor, with a new O-ring seal, and tighten it to the specified torque.

5 Top up the final drive fluid oil as described in Section 10.

10 Final drive fluid – renewal

1 Raise the vehicle and support it securely on axle stands (see *Jacking and vehicle support*).

2 If renewing the front final drive fluid, undo the bolts and remove the engine undershield **(see illustration 2.2)**.

3 Clean around the fluid drain and filler plug areas.

4 Unscrew the fluid filler plug **(see illustrations)**.

5 Position a container, then undo the drain plug and allow the oil fluid to flow out **(see illustration 2.3)**.

6 When the flow has stopped, clean around the drain plug area, refit the plug and tighten it to the specified torque.

7 Add the correct specification and quantity of fluid through the filler plug. **Note:** *The filler plug is not a level plug – ensure the only the correct quantity of fluid is added.*

8 Refit the filler plug and tighten it to the specified torque.

9 Lower the vehicle to the ground.

11 Final drive differential overhaul – general information

Overhauling a differential unit is a difficult and involved job for the DIY home mechanic. In addition to dismantling and reassembling many small parts, clearances must be precisely measured and, if necessary, changed by selecting shims and spacers. Components are also often difficult to obtain and in many instances, extremely expensive. Because of this, if the differential develops a fault or becomes noisy, the best course of action is to have the unit overhauled by a specialist repairer, or to obtain an exchange reconditioned unit.

Nevertheless, it is not impossible for the more experienced mechanic to overhaul the differential, if the special tools are available and the job is done in a deliberate step-by-step manner so that nothing is overlooked.

The tools necessary for an overhaul include internal and external circlip pliers, bearing pullers, a slide hammer, a set of pin punches, a dial test indicator, and possibly a hydraulic press. In addition, a large, sturdy workbench and a vice will be required.

During dismantling, make careful notes of how each component is fitted, to make reassembly easier and more accurate.

Before dismantling, it will help if you have some idea what area is malfunctioning. Refer to *Fault finding* at the end of this manual for more information.

Chapter 10
Braking system

Contents

Degrees of difficulty

Easy, suitable for novice with little experience	**Fairly easy,** suitable for beginner with some experience	**Fairly difficult,** suitable for competent DIY mechanic	**Difficult,** suitable for experienced DIY mechanic	**Very difficult,** suitable for expert DIY or professional

Specifications

Front brakes

Type	Ventilated disc, with twin-piston caliper
Disc diameter	320 mm
Disc thickness:	
New	30.0 mm
Service limit	27.0 mm
Maximum disc run-out	0.05 mm
Brake pad friction material minimum thickness	3.0 mm

Rear brakes

Type	Ventilated disc, with single-piston caliper
Disc diameter	325 mm
Disc thickness:	
New	20.0 mm
Service limit	17.0 mm
Maximum disc run-out	0.09 mm
Brake pad friction material minimum thickness	3.0 mm

Control system

Type	Bosch 8.0

Parking brake

Type	Electrically-operated, with shoes fitted within the rear brake discs
Brake shoe friction material minimum thickness	2.0 mm

Torque wrench settings

	Nm	lbf ft
ABS wheel speed sensor bolt	9	7
Brake hose union	28	21
Caliper bracket mounting bolts:		
Front	275	203
Rear	115	85
Caliper guide pin bolts	35	26
Disc retaining screw	35	26
Master cylinder brake pipe union nuts	18	13
Master cylinder mounting nuts	26	19
Parking brake actuator mounting bracket bolts	22	16
Roadwheel nuts	140	103
Vacuum pump:		
Bolts	23	17
Stud/nut	13	10
Vacuum servo unit mounting nuts	23	17
Yaw rate sensor bolts	7	5

1 General information

The braking system is of the servo-assisted, dual-circuit hydraulic type, operating from a tandem master cylinder. On all models, the hydraulic system is split diagonally. Under normal circumstances, both circuits operate in unison. However, in the event of hydraulic failure in one circuit, braking force will still be available at least at two wheels.

Since there is insufficient vacuum in the intake manifold to operate the braking system servo unit, a vacuum pump is fitted to the rear of the right-hand cylinder head, and driven by the exhaust camshaft, to provide the required vacuum.

All models have disc brakes all round and ABS (anti-lock braking system) as standard. The ABS system also incorporates the following features:

- Electronic brake distribution (EBD) which replaces the pressure limiting valve on older models, and controls the distribution of hydraulic pressure between the front and rear brakes.
- Electronic traction control (ETC) to maintain even torque/power distribution to the roadwheels.
- Hill descent control (HDC) to provide a controlled descent ability in off-road conditions.
- Dynamic stability control (DSC), to assist in skid correction, and cornering stability.
- Emergency brake assist (EBA) ensure full brake application in emergency situations.

The front brakes are fitted with ventilated discs, and twin-piston calipers, whilst the rear are also fitted with ventilated discs, but with single-piston calipers.

On all models, an electrically-operated parking brake is fitted. The system is operated from a switch on the centre console, which, when activated, causes the parking brake actuator to tension the left- and right-hand parking brake cables, expanding the brake shoes within the rear brake discs.

When servicing any part of the system, work carefully and methodically; also observe scrupulous cleanliness when overhauling any part of the hydraulic system. Always renew components (in axle sets, where applicable) if in doubt about their condition, and use only genuine Land Rover parts, or at least those of known good quality. Note the warnings given in *Safety first!* and at relevant points in this Chapter concerning the dangers of asbestos dust and hydraulic fluid.

2 Hydraulic system – bleeding

Note: *Hydraulic fluid is poisonous; wash off immediately and thoroughly in the case of skin contact, and seek immediate medical advice if any fluid is swallowed or gets into the eyes. Certain types of hydraulic fluid are inflammable, and may ignite when allowed into contact with hot components. When servicing any hydraulic system, it is safest to assume that the fluid IS inflammable, and to take precautions against the risk of fire as though it is petrol that is being handled. Finally, it is hygroscopic (it absorbs moisture from the air) – old fluid may be contaminated and unfit for further use. When topping-up or renewing the fluid, always use the recommended type, and ensure that it comes from a freshly-opened sealed container.*

Note: *After disconnecting any brake hydraulic components upstream of the HCU (hydraulic control unit) modulator (including the modulator itself), Land Rover insist that the system must be bled using their T4 dedicated test equipment. Have this task carried out be a Land Rover dealer or suitably-equipped specialist.*

General

1 The correct operation of any hydraulic system is only possible after removing all air from the components and circuit; this is achieved by bleeding the system.

2 During the bleeding procedure, add only clean, unused hydraulic fluid of the recommended type; never re-use fluid that has already been bled from the system. Ensure that sufficient fluid is available before starting work.

3 If there is any possibility of incorrect fluid being already in the system, the brake components and circuit must be flushed completely with uncontaminated, correct fluid, and new seals should be fitted to the various components.

4 If hydraulic fluid has been lost from the system (or air has entered) because of a leak, ensure that the fault is cured before proceeding further.

5 Park the vehicle on level ground, switch off the engine and select first or reverse gear, then chock the wheels and release the handbrake.

6 Check that all pipes and hoses are secure, unions tight and bleed screws closed. Clean any dirt from around the bleed screws.

7 Unclip the plastic cover in the right-hand corner of the engine compartment to access the master cylinder fluid reservoir **(see illustration)**.

8 Disconnect the fluid reservoir level sensor wiring plug, then unscrew the master cylinder reservoir cap, and top the master cylinder reservoir up to the MAX level line; refit the cap

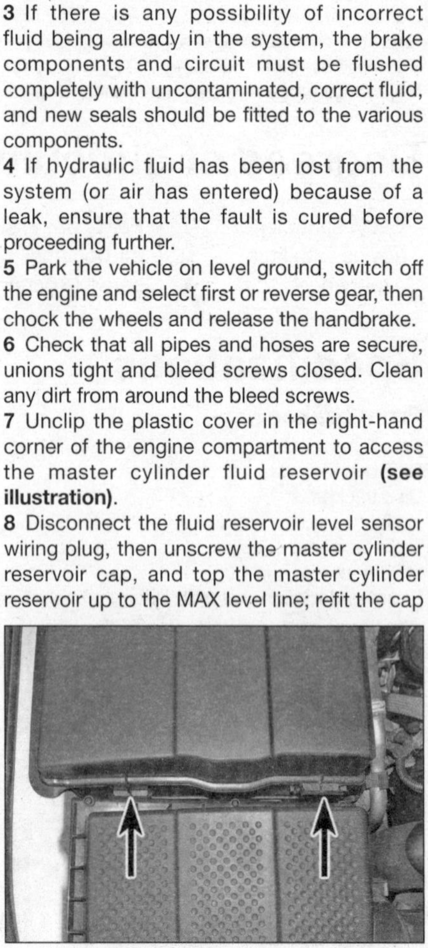

2.7 Release the clips (arrowed) and remove the plastic cover

loosely. Remember to maintain the fluid level at least above the MIN level line throughout the procedure, or there is a risk of further air entering the system.

9 There are a number of one-man, do-it-yourself brake bleeding kits currently available from motor accessory shops. It is recommended that one of these kits is used whenever possible, as they greatly simplify the bleeding operation, and also reduce the risk of expelled air and fluid being drawn back into the system. If such a kit is not available, use the basic (two-man) method which is described in detail below.

10 If a kit is to be used, prepare the vehicle as described previously, and follow the kit manufacturer's instructions as the procedure may vary slightly according to the type being used; generally, they are as outlined below in the relevant sub-section.

11 Whichever method is used, the same sequence must be followed (paragraphs 12 and 13) to ensure the removal of all air from the system.

Bleeding sequence

12 If the system has been only partially disconnected, and suitable precautions were taken to minimise fluid loss, it should be necessary only to bleed that part of the system (ie, the primary or secondary circuit).

13 If the complete system is to be bled, then it should be done starting with the caliper furthest away from the master cylinder, in the following sequence:

a) Passenger's side rear brake.
b) Driver's side rear brake.
c) Passenger's side front brake.
d) Driver's side front brake.

Basic (two-man) method

14 Collect a clean glass jar, a suitable length of plastic or rubber tubing which is a tight fit over the bleed screw, and a ring spanner to fit the screw. The help of an assistant will also be required.

15 Remove the dust cap from the bleed screw on the passenger's side front brake. Fit the spanner and tube to the screw, place the other end of the tube in the jar, and pour in sufficient fluid to cover the end of the tube.

16 Ensure that the master cylinder reservoir fluid level is maintained at least above the MIN level line throughout the procedure.

17 Have the assistant fully depress the brake pedal several times to build up pressure, then maintain it on the final stroke.

18 While pedal pressure is maintained, unscrew the bleed screw (approximately one turn) and allow the compressed fluid and air to flow into the jar. The assistant should maintain pedal pressure, following it down to the floor if necessary, and should not release it until instructed to do so. When the flow stops, tighten the bleed screw again, release the pedal slowly and recheck the reservoir fluid level.

19 Repeat the steps given in paragraphs 17 and 18 until the fluid emerging from the bleed screw is free from air bubbles. If the master cylinder has been drained and refilled, and air is being bled from the first screw in the sequence, allow approximately five seconds between cycles for the master cylinder passages to refill.

20 When no more air bubbles appear, tighten the bleed screw securely, remove the tube and spanner, and refit the dust cap. Do not overtighten the bleed screw.

21 Repeat the procedure on the remaining rear brake.

Using a one-way valve kit

22 As their name implies, these kits consist of a length of tubing with a one-way valve fitted, to prevent expelled air and fluid being drawn back into the system; some kits include a translucent container, which can be positioned so that the air bubbles can be more easily seen flowing from the end of the tube.

23 The kit is connected to the bleed screw, which is then opened **(see illustration)**. The user returns to the driver's seat and depresses the brake pedal with a smooth, steady stroke and slowly releases it; this is repeated until the expelled fluid is clear of air bubbles.

24 Note that these kits simplify work so much that it is easy to forget the master cylinder reservoir fluid level; ensure that this is maintained at least above the MIN level line at all times.

Using a pressure-bleeding kit

Note: *Ensure that the pressure in the reservoir does not exceed 4.5 bars (65 psi approx).*

25 These kits are usually operated by the reservoir of pressurised air contained in the spare tyre, although note that it will probably be necessary to reduce the tyre pressure to a lower level than normal; refer to the instructions supplied with the kit.

26 By connecting a pressurised, fluid-filled container to the master cylinder reservoir, bleeding can be carried out simply by opening each screw in turn (in the specified sequence) and allowing the fluid to flow out until no more air bubbles can be seen in the expelled fluid.

27 This method has the advantage that the large reservoir of fluid provides an additional safeguard against air being drawn into the system during bleeding.

2.23 Attach the tube and spanner to the brake caliper bleed screw

28 Pressure bleeding is particularly effective when bleeding difficult systems, or when bleeding the complete system at the time of routine fluid renewal.

All methods

29 When bleeding is complete and firm pedal feel is restored, wash off any spilt fluid, tighten the bleed screws securely and refit their dust caps.

30 Check the hydraulic fluid level, and top-up if necessary (see *Weekly checks*).

31 Discard any hydraulic fluid that has been bled from the system; it will not be fit for re-use.

32 Check the feel of the brake pedal. If it feels at all spongy, air must still be present in the system, and further bleeding is required. Failure to bleed satisfactorily after a reasonable repetition of the bleeding procedure may be due to worn master cylinder seals.

3 Hydraulic pipes and hoses – renewal

Note: *Before starting work, refer to the note at the beginning of Section 2 concerning the dangers of hydraulic fluid.*

1 If any pipe or hose is to be renewed, minimise fluid loss as follows. Remove the master cylinder reservoir cap, then tighten it down onto a piece of polythene to obtain an airtight seal. Alternatively, flexible hoses can be sealed, if required, using a proprietary brake hose clamp, while metal brake pipe unions can be plugged (if care is taken not to allow dirt into the system) or capped immediately they are disconnected. Place a wad of rag under any union that is to be disconnected, to catch any spilt fluid.

2 If a flexible hose is to be disconnected, unscrew the brake pipe union nut before removing the spring clip which secures the hose to its mounting bracket (where fitted).

3 To unscrew the union nuts, it is preferable to obtain a brake pipe spanner of the correct size; these are available from most large motor accessory shops. Failing this, a close-fitting open-ended spanner will be required, though if the nuts are tight or corroded, their flats may be rounded-off if the spanner slips. In such a case, a self-locking wrench is often the only way to unscrew a stubborn union, but it follows that the pipe and the damaged nuts must be renewed on reassembly. Always clean a union and surrounding area before disconnecting it.

4 If a brake pipe is to be renewed, it can be obtained, cut to length and with the union nuts and end flares in place, from Land Rover dealers. All that is then necessary is to bend it to shape, following the line of the original, before fitting it to the car. Alternatively, most motor accessory shops can make up brake pipes from kits, but this requires very careful measurement of the original to ensure that the new one is of the correct length. The safest answer is usually to take the original to the shop as a pattern.

5 On refitting, do not overtighten the union nuts. It is not necessary to exercise brute force to obtain a sound joint.

6 Ensure that the pipes and hoses are correctly routed with no kinks, and that they are secured in the clips or brackets provided. After fitting, remove the polythene from the reservoir, and bleed the hydraulic system as described in Section 2. Wash off any spilt fluid, and check carefully for fluid leaks.

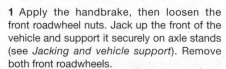

4 Front brake pads – renewal

Warning: Renew BOTH sets of front brake pads at the same time – NEVER renew the pads on only one wheel, as uneven braking may result. Note that the dust created by wear of the pads may contain asbestos, which is a health hazard. Never blow it out with compressed air, and don't inhale any of it. An approved filtering mask should be worn when working on the brakes. DO NOT use petroleum-based solvents to clean brake parts – use brake cleaner or methylated spirit only.

1 Apply the handbrake, then loosen the front roadwheel nuts. Jack up the front of the vehicle and support it securely on axle stands (see *Jacking and vehicle support*). Remove both front roadwheels.

2 Follow the accompanying photos **(see illustrations 4.2a to 4.2u)** for the pad renewal procedure. Be sure to stay in order and read the caption under each illustration. Note that if the pad wear warning light has been activated, the sensor must be renewed. When the sensor has been renewed, the instrument cluster detects the completed sensor circuit, and extinguishes the warning light.

Caution: Pushing back the piston causes a reverse-flow of brake fluid, which has been known to 'flip' the master cylinder rubber

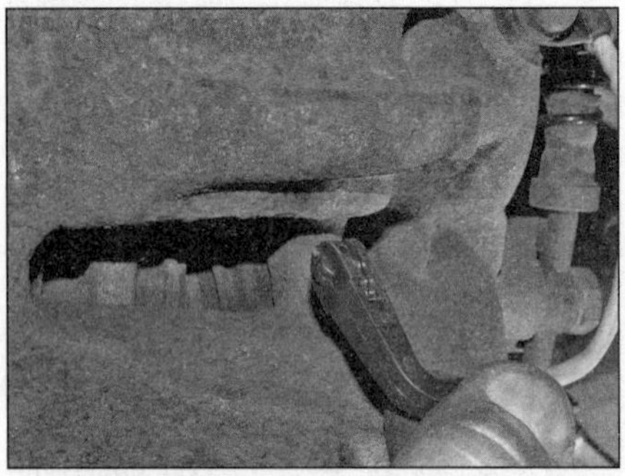

4.2a On the left-hand side caliper, pull the wear sensor from place ...

4.2b ... and unclip the wiring harness

4.2c Using an open-ended spanner to counterhold, remove the lower guide pin bolt ...

4.2d ... pivot the caliper upwards ...

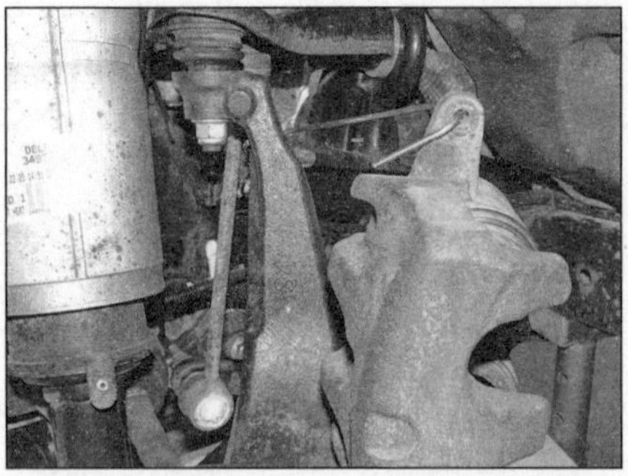

4.2e ... and secure it to the hub carrier with wire/string, etc

4.2f Remove the inner brake pad ...

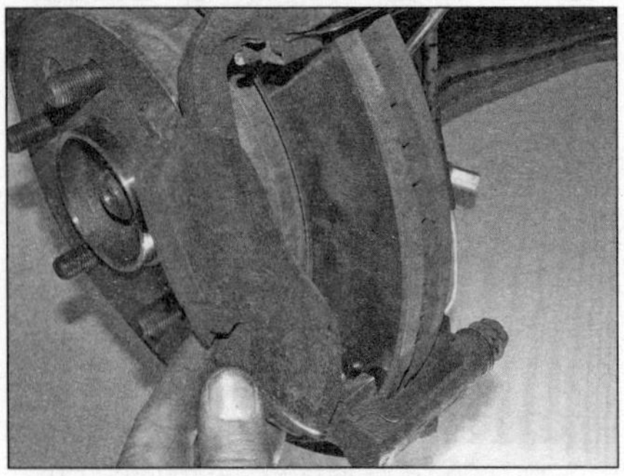

4.2g ... followed by the outer pad

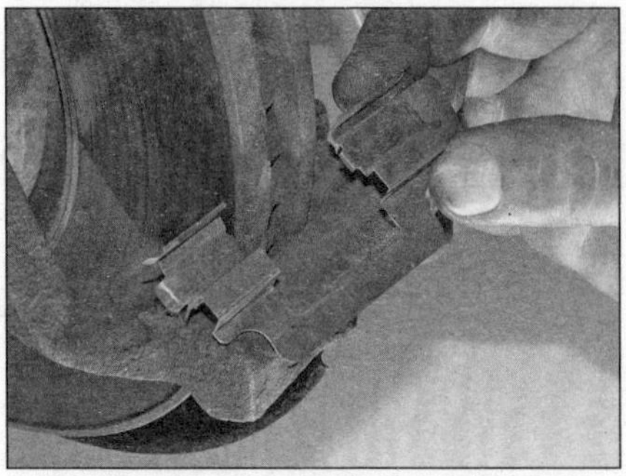

4.2h Remove the lower shim ...

4.2i ... and the upper shim

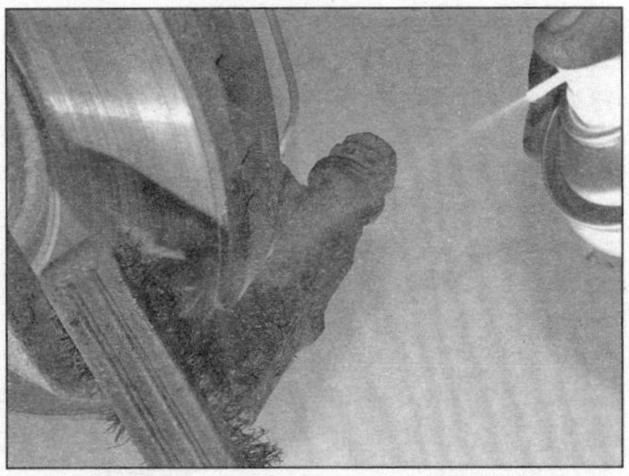

4.2j Clean the pad mounting surfaces with a brush and aerosol brake cleaner

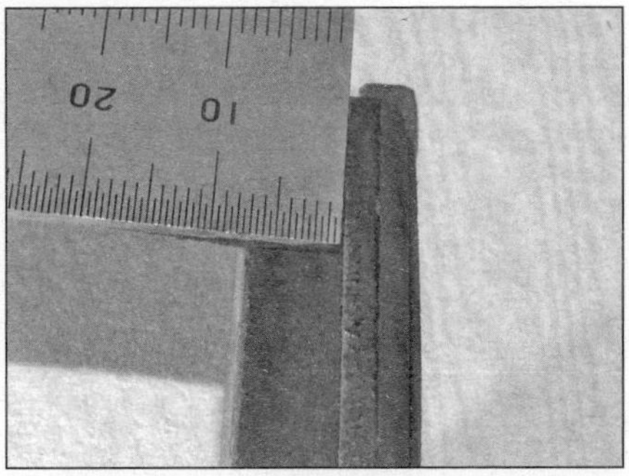

4.2k Measure the thickness of the brake pad friction material. If it's less than 3.0 mm, renew all 4 front brake pads

4.2l If new pads are being fitted, push the pistons back into the caliper body using a piston retraction tool. Keep an eye on the fluid level in the master cylinder reservoir!

4.2m Fit the upper shim ...

4.2n ... and the lower shim

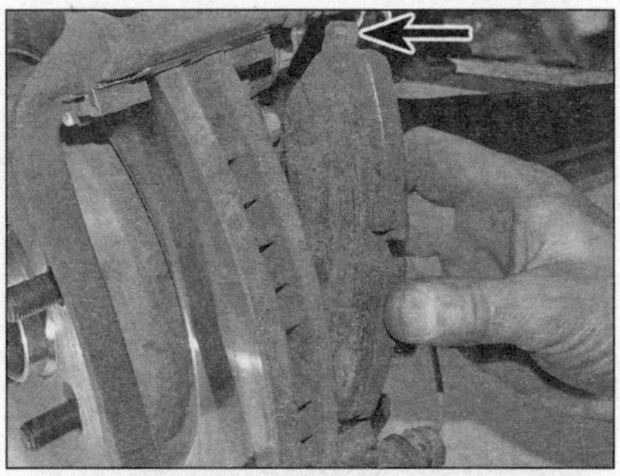

4.2o Apply a little high-temperature anti-seize grease to the pad mounting surfaces (arrowed), then install the inner pad ...

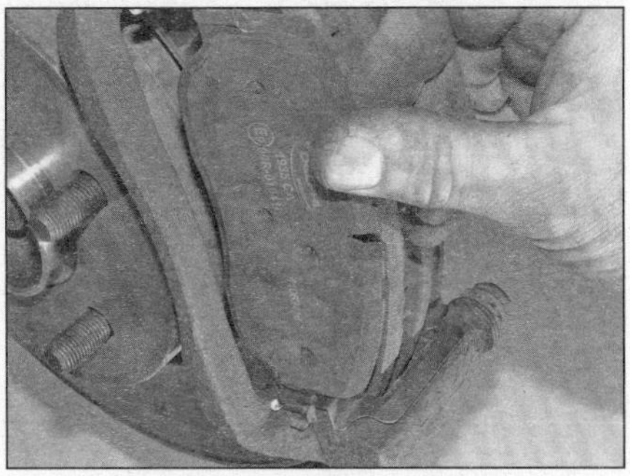

4.2p ... and the outer pad

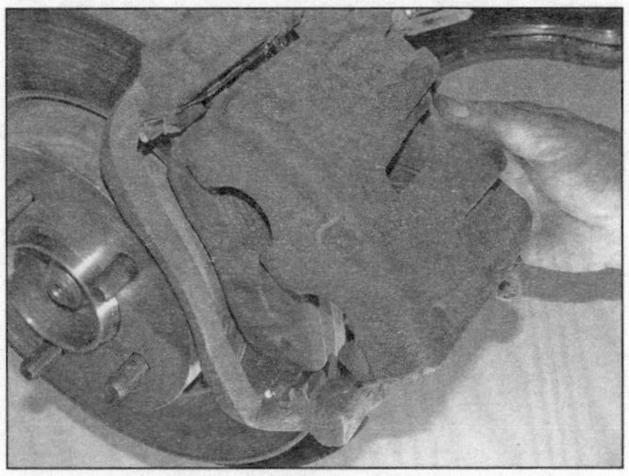

4.2q Pivot the caliper body back down ...

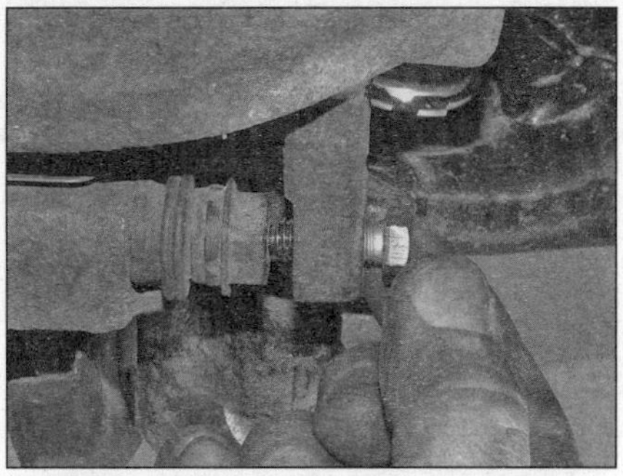

4.2r ... apply a little thread-locking compound, refit the lower guide pin bolt ...

4.2s ... and tighten it to the specified torque

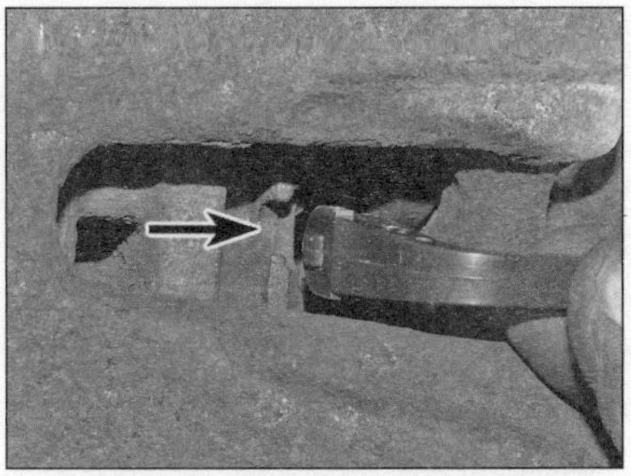

4.2t Slide the wear sensor (where fitted) into the slot (arrowed) in the inner brake pad ...

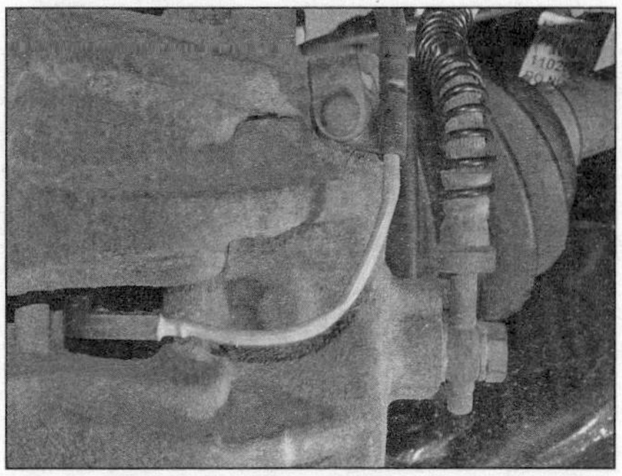

4.2u ... and clip the wiring harness over the bleed nipple

seals, resulting in a total loss of braking. To avoid this, clamp the caliper flexible hose and open the bleed screw – as the piston is pushed back, the fluid can be directed into a suitable container using a hose attached to the bleed screw. Close the screw just before the piston is pushed fully back, to ensure no air enters the system.

3 Depress the brake pedal repeatedly, until the pads are pressed into firm contact with the brake disc, and normal (non-assisted) pedal pressure is restored.

4 Repeat the above procedure on the remaining front brake caliper.

5 Refit the roadwheels, then lower the vehicle to the ground and tighten the roadwheel nuts to the specified torque.

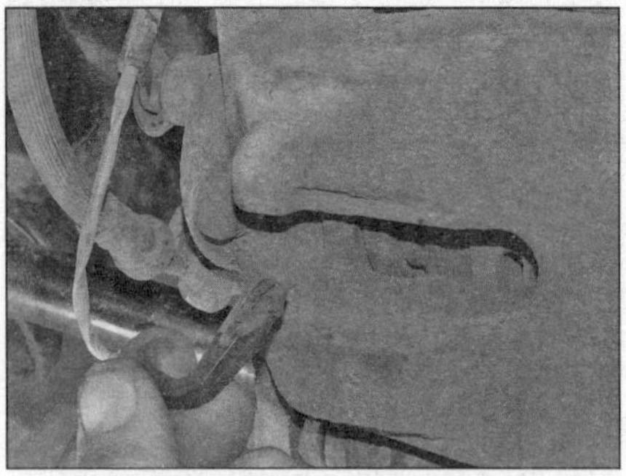

5.2a On the right-hand side caliper, pull the wear sensor from place ...

6 Check the hydraulic fluid level as described in *Weekly checks*.

Caution: New pads will not give full braking efficiency until they have bedded-in. Be prepared for this, and avoid hard braking as far as possible for the first hundred miles or so after pad renewal.

5 Rear brake pads – renewal

Warning: Renew BOTH sets of rear brake pads at the same time – NEVER renew the pads on only one wheel, as uneven braking may result.

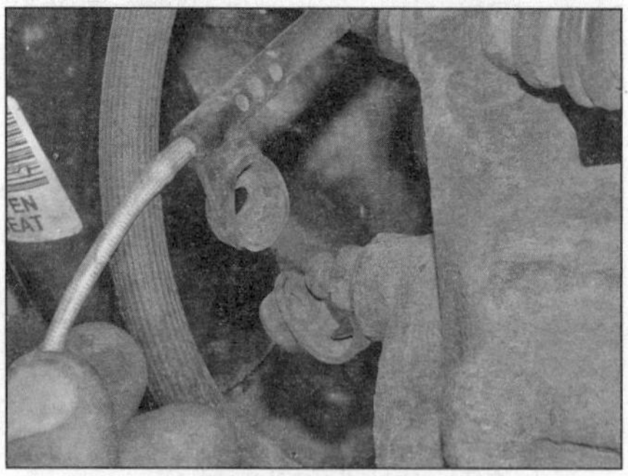

5.2b ... and unclip the wiring harness

Note that the dust created by wear of the pads may contain asbestos, which is a health hazard. Never blow it out with compressed air, and don't inhale any of it. An approved filtering mask should be worn when working on the brakes. DO NOT use petroleum-based solvents to clean brake parts – use brake cleaner or methylated spirit only.

1 Apply the handbrake, then loosen the rear roadwheel nuts. Jack up the rear of the vehicle and support it securely on axle stands (see *Jacking and vehicle support*). Remove both rear roadwheels.

2 Follow the accompanying photos **(see illustrations 5.2a to 5.2t)** for the pad renewal procedure. Be sure to stay in order and read the caption under each illustration. Note that if the pad wear warning light has been activated, the sensor must be renewed. When the sensor has been renewed, the instrument cluster detects the completed sensor circuit, and extinguishes the warning light.

Caution: Pushing back the piston causes a reverse-flow of brake fluid, which has been known to 'flip' the master cylinder rubber seals, resulting in a total loss of braking. To avoid this, clamp the caliper flexible hose and open the bleed screw – as the piston is pushed back, the fluid can be directed into a suitable container using a hose attached to the bleed screw. Close the screw just before the piston is pushed fully back, to ensure no air enters the system.

5.2c Using an open-ended spanner to counterhold, remove the lower guide pin bolt ...

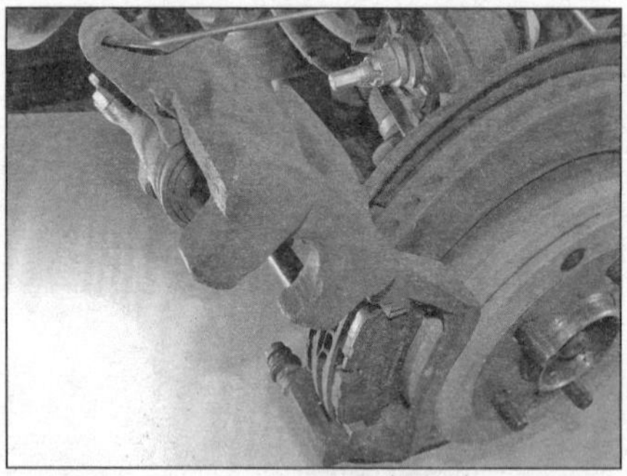

5.2d ... pivot the caliper upwards and secure it to the hub carrier with wire/string, etc

5.2e Remove the inner brake pad ...

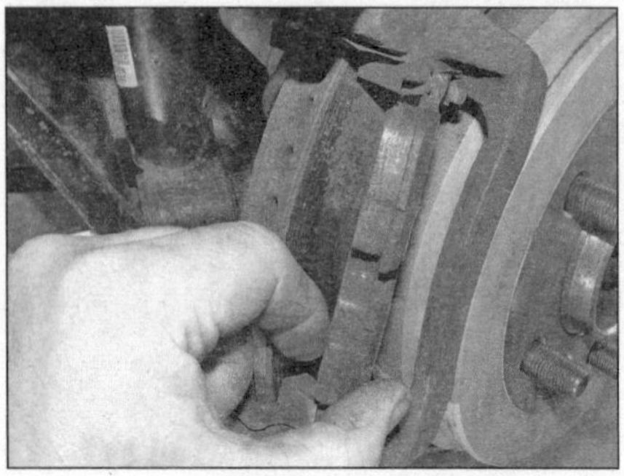

5.2f ... followed by the outer pad

5.2g Remove the lower shim ...

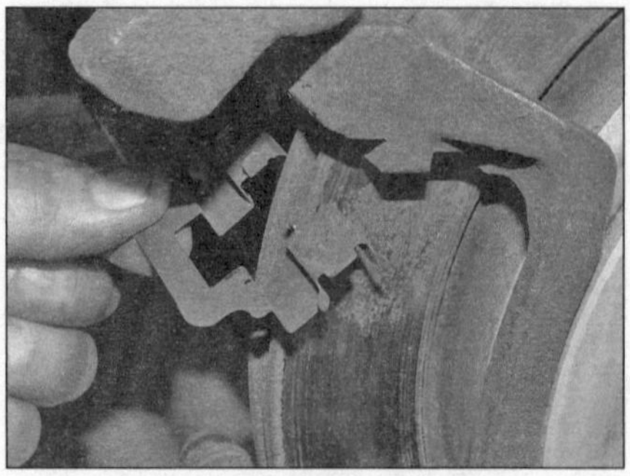

5.2h ... and the upper shim

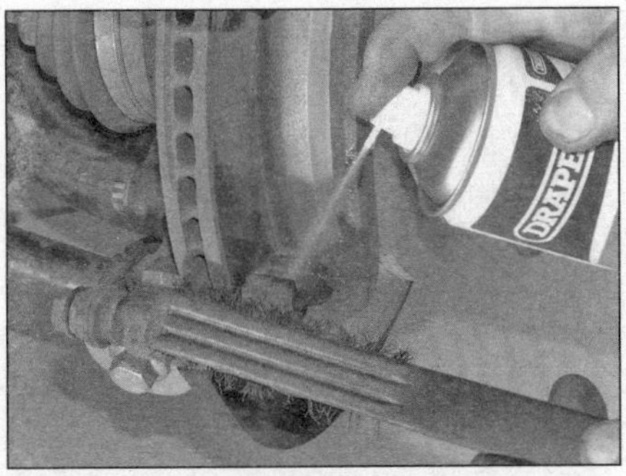

5.2i Clean the pad mounting surfaces with a brush and aerosol brake cleaner

5.2j Measure the thickness of the brake pad friction material. If it's less than 3.0 mm, renew all 4 rear brake pads

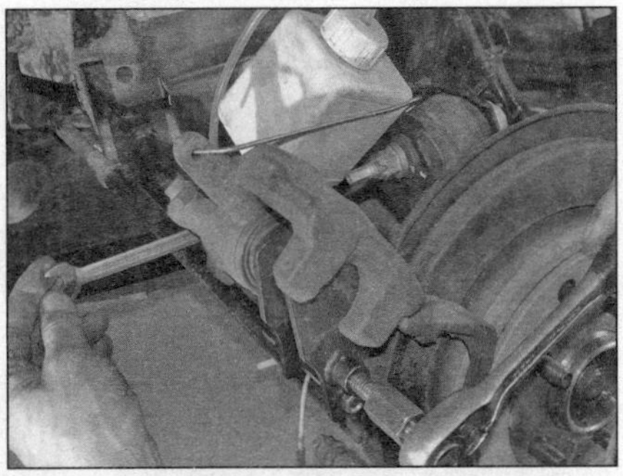

5.2k If new pads are being fitted, use a retraction tool to push the pistons back into the caliper body, whilst opening the bleed nipple to allow the displaced fluid to flow into a suitable container via a tube

5.2l Fit the upper shim ...

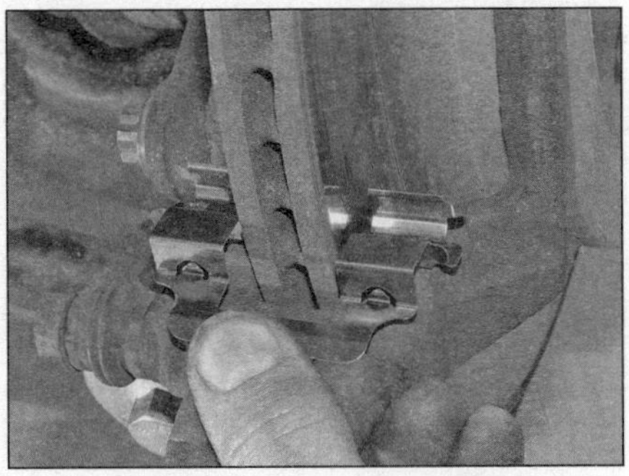

5.2m ... and lower shim

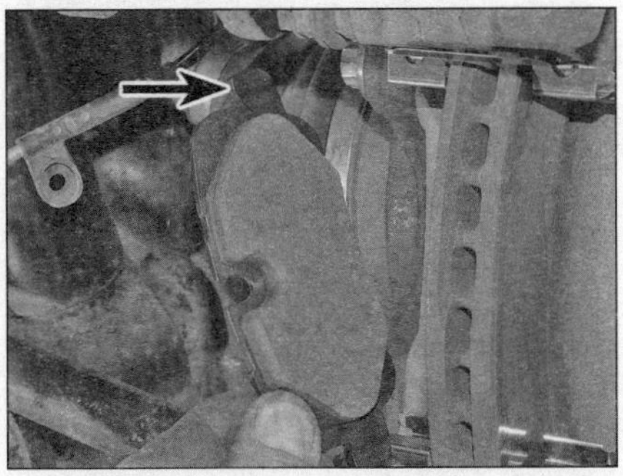

5.2n Apply a little high-temperature anti-seize grease to the pad mounting surfaces (arrowed), then install the inner pad ...

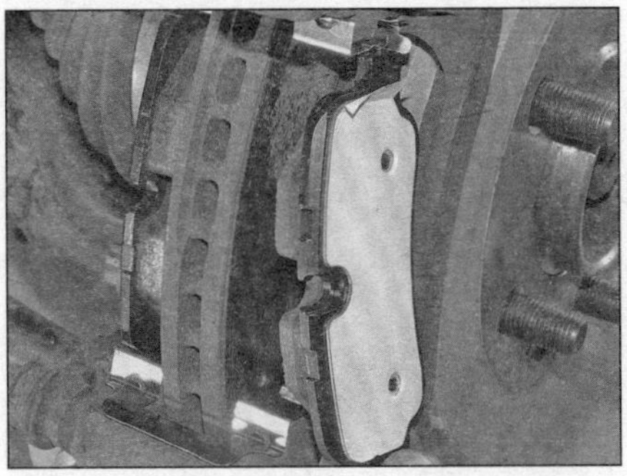

5.2o ... and the outer pad

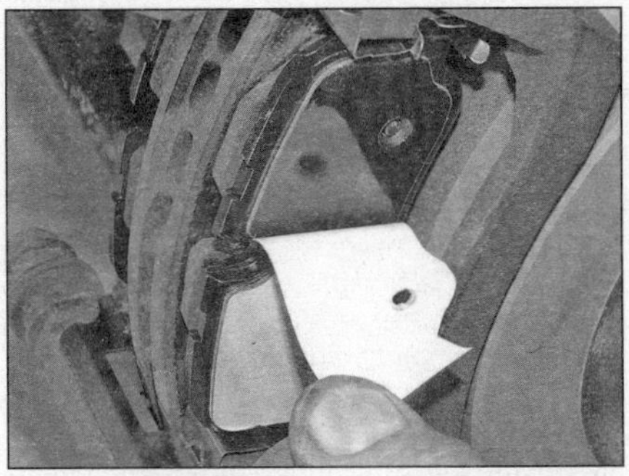

5.2p Where applicable, peel the backing from the adhesive strips

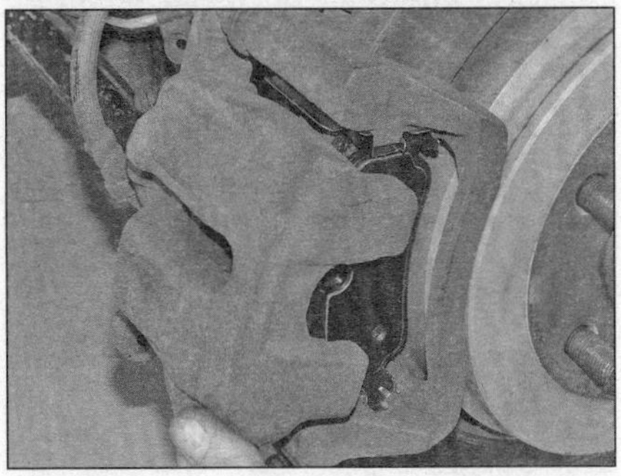

5.2q Pivot the caliper body back down ...

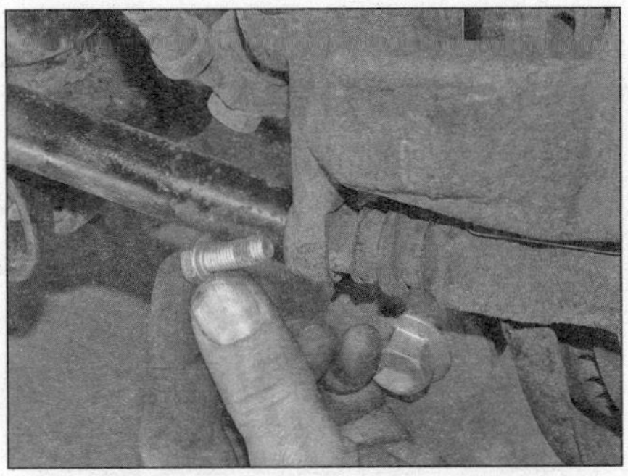

5.2r ... apply a little thread-locking compound, refit the lower guide pin bolt ...

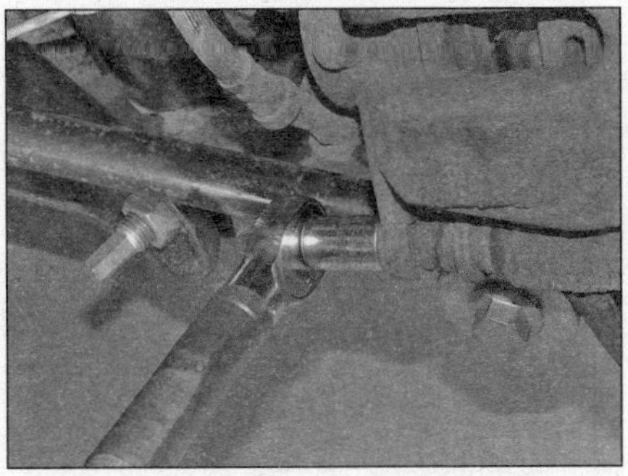

5.2s ... and tighten it to the specified torque

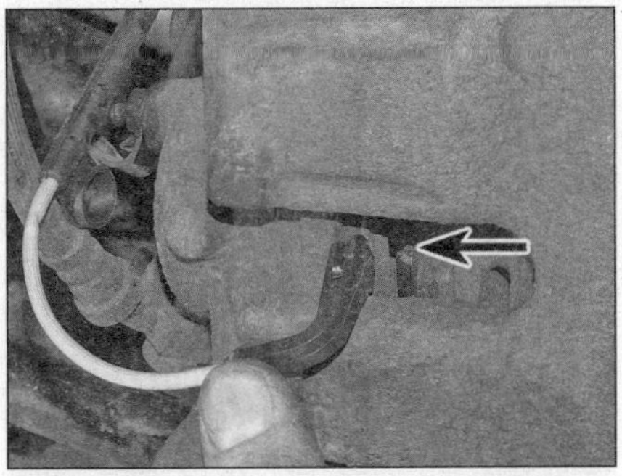

5.2t Slide the wear sensor (where fitted) into the slot (arrowed) in the inner brake pad and clip the wiring harness over the bleed nipple

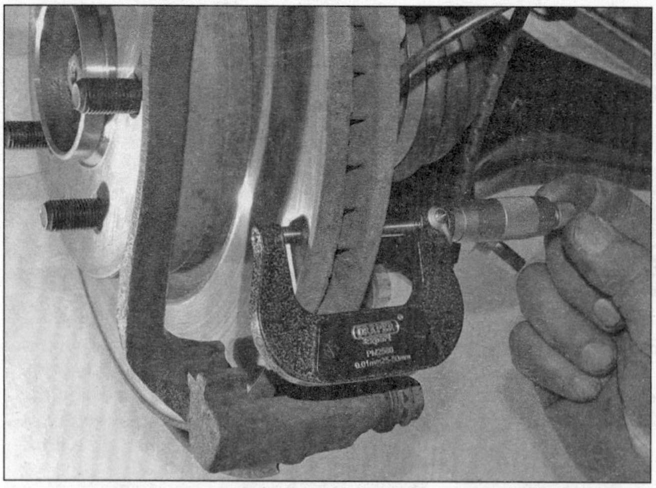

6.3 Measure the thickness of the brake disc using a micrometer

6.8 Undo the caliper mounting bracket bolts (arrowed)

3 Depress the brake pedal repeatedly, until the pads are pressed into firm contact with the brake disc, and normal (non-assisted) pedal pressure is restored.

4 Repeat the above procedure on the remaining rear brake caliper.

5 Refit the roadwheels, then lower the vehicle to the ground and tighten the roadwheel nuts to the specified torque.

6 Check the hydraulic fluid level as described in *Weekly checks*.

Caution: New pads will not give full braking efficiency until they have bedded-in. Be prepared for this, and avoid hard braking as far as possible for the first hundred miles or so after pad renewal.

6 Front brake disc – inspection, removal and refitting

Note: *Before starting work, refer to the warning and note at the beginning of Section 4.*

Inspection

Note: *If either disc requires renewal, BOTH should be renewed at the same time, to ensure even and consistent braking.*

1 Firmly apply the handbrake, then loosen the roadwheel nuts. Jack up the car and support it securely on axle stands (see *Jacking and vehicle support*). Remove the appropriate roadwheel.

6.9 Disc retaining screw (arrowed)

2 Slowly rotate the brake disc, so that the full area of both sides can be checked; remove the brake pads if better access is required to the inner surface. Light scoring is normal in the area swept by the brake pads, but if heavy scoring is found, the disc must be renewed.

3 It is normal to find a lip of rust and brake dust around the disc's perimeter; this can be scraped off if required. If, however, a lip has formed due to excessive wear of the brake pad swept area, then the disc's thickness must be measured using a micrometer **(see illustration)**. Take measurements at several places around the disc, at the inside and outside of the pad swept area. If the measured thickness is below that specified, both front discs must be renewed.

4 If the disc is thought to be warped, it can be checked for run-out as follows. Either use a dial gauge mounted on any convenient fixed point, while the disc is slowly rotated, or use feeler blades to measure (at several points all around the disc) the clearance between the disc and a fixed point such as the brake caliper. If the measurements obtained are at the specified maximum or beyond, the disc is excessively warped and must be renewed; however, it is worth checking first that the axle hub bearing is in good condition.

5 Check the disc for cracks, especially around the wheel studs, and any other wear or damage.

Removal

6 Remove the brake pads as described in Section 4.

7 Undo the caliper upper guide pin bolt, and suspend the caliper from the vehicle body or hub carrier using string or wire. Do not let the caliper hang by the hose.

8 Undo the two bolts securing the brake caliper mounting bracket to the hub carrier, and slide it from the disc **(see illustration)**.

9 Slacken and remove the screw securing the brake disc to the hub assembly, and remove the disc **(see illustration)**.

Refitting

10 Refitting is the reverse of the removal procedure, noting the following points:

a) Ensure that the mating surfaces of the disc and hub are clean and flat.

b) If a new disc has been fitted, use a suitable solvent to wipe any preservative coating from the disc before refitting the caliper.

c) Apply a little locking compound to the threads, then tighten the caliper mounting bracket bolts to the specified torque.

d) Refit the roadwheel, lower the vehicle to the ground, and tighten the roadwheel nuts to the specified torque. On completion, repeatedly depress the brake pedal, until normal (non-assisted) pedal pressure returns.

7 Rear brake disc – inspection, removal and refitting

Removal

1 Chock the front wheels, and set the parking brake into 'Service Mode' using the following procedure:

a) Turn the ignition key to position II.

b) Apply and hold the footbrake.

c) Apply and hold the parking brake switch in the Release position.

d) Turn the ignition key to position 0 and remove the key.

e) Release the footbrake and the parking brake switch.

f) Remove fusible link No. 8 from the engine compartment fusebox to isolate the parking brake circuit.

Caution: Do not turn the ignition on once the 'Service Mode' has been set.

7.5 Rotate the adjuster wheel to move the shoes away from the drum

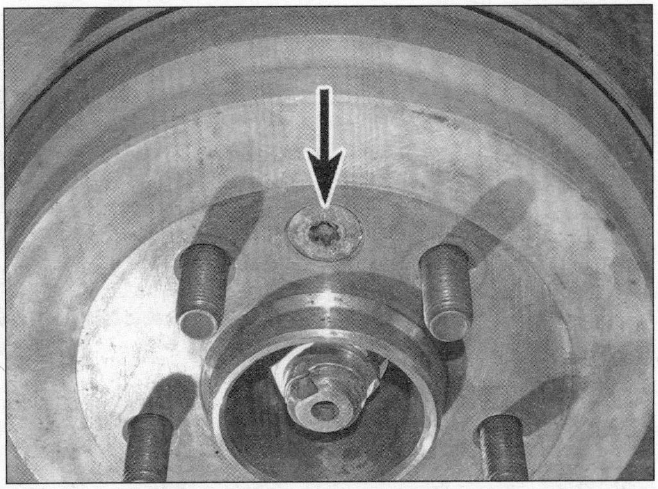

7.6 Rear disc retaining screw (arrowed)

2 Remove the brake pads as described in Section 5.

3 Undo the caliper upper guide pin bolt, and suspend the caliper from the vehicle body using string or wire. Do not let the caliper hang by the hose.

4 Undo the two bolts securing the brake caliper mounting bracket to the hub carrier, and slide it from the disc.

5 Prise out the access plug, then use a screwdriver to rotate the parking brake shoe adjuster wheel, providing clearance between the friction material and the drum **(see illustration)**.

6 Slacken and remove the screw securing the brake disc to the hub assembly, and remove the disc **(see illustration)**.

Inspection

7 Refer to Section 6.

Refitting

8 Ensure the disc and hub mating surfaces are clean and flat.

9 If a new disc has been fitted, use a suitable solvent to wipe any preservative coating from the disc before refitting.

10 Position the disc on the hub and tighten the retaining screw to the specified torque.

11 Refit the caliper mounting bracket and tighten the retaining bolts to the specified torque.

12 Position the caliper, install and tighten the upper guide pin bolt to the specified torque.

13 Fit the brake pads as described in Section 5.

14 Adjust the parking brake as described in Section 18.

15 Refit fuse No. 8 to the fusebox. On completion, repeatedly depress the brake pedal until normal (non-assisted) pedal pressure returns.

8 Front brake caliper – removal, overhaul and refitting

Note: *Before starting work, refer to the note at the beginning of Section 2 concerning the dangers of hydraulic fluid, and to the warning and note at the beginning of Section 4.*

Removal

1 Apply the handbrake, then loosen the relevant front roadwheel nuts. Jack up the front of the vehicle and support it securely on axle stands (see *Jacking and vehicle support*). Remove the appropriate roadwheel.

2 To minimise fluid loss, remove the master cylinder reservoir cap, then tighten it down onto a piece of polythene to obtain an airtight seal. Alternatively, use a brake hose clamp, a G-clamp, or a similar tool to clamp the flexible hose at the nearest convenient point to the caliper.

3 Clean the area around the caliper brake hose union bolt. Undo the union bolt, and disconnect the brake hose from the caliper. Discard the copper sealing washers, new ones must be fitted. Plug the hose end and caliper hole to minimise fluid loss and to prevent the ingress of dirt into the hydraulic system.

4 Carefully pull the wear sensor front the inner pad – left-hand side only.

5 Undo the two caliper guide pin bolts, and slide the caliper from the mounting bracket, leaving the brake pads in position.

Overhaul

Note: *Prior to dismantling the caliper, check the availability of spares from your Land Rover dealer.*

6 With the caliper on the bench, wipe away all traces of dust and dirt, but *avoid inhaling the dust, as it is a health hazard.*

7 Withdraw both the partially-ejected pistons from the caliper body. The pistons can be withdrawn by hand, if loose. If one or both of the pistons are not loose enough to be withdrawn by hand, they can be pushed out by applying compressed air to the brake hose union hole. Only low pressure should be required, such as is generated by a foot pump. Try to ensure both pistons are ejected at the same time.

8 Extract both pistons from the caliper. Make identification marks between the pistons and bore to use on refitting, to ensure each piston is refitted to its original bore.

9 Carefully prise out and remove the rubber dust boots fitted between the top of the pistons and the caliper body.

10 Using a small screwdriver, carefully remove the seals from the caliper, taking great care not to mark the bore.

11 This is the limit of caliper dismantling.

12 Pull the guide pins from the caliper mounting bracket, and examine them for wear or damage. They should be a good sliding fit in the bores, without excessive play or roughness. Discard the guide pin gaiters, new ones should be supplied in the overhaul kit.

13 Thoroughly clean all components, using only methylated spirit, isopropyl alcohol or clean hydraulic fluid as a cleaning medium. Never use mineral-based solvents such as petrol or paraffin, which will attack the hydraulic system's rubber components. Dry the components immediately, using compressed air or a clean, lint free cloth. Use compressed air to blow clear the fluid passages.

14 Check all components, and renew any that are worn or damaged. Check particularly the cylinder bores and pistons; these should be renewed if they are scratched, worn or corroded in any way.

15 If the assembly is fit for further use, obtain the necessary components from your Land Rover dealer.

16 On reassembly, ensure that all components are absolutely clean and dry.

17 Soak the pistons and the new piston (fluid) seals in clean hydraulic fluid. Smear clean fluid on the cylinder bore surface.

18 Fit the new piston seals, using only your fingers to manipulate them into the cylinder bore grooves.

19 Ensure that the piston seals are correctly located, then fit the new dust boots to the base of the piston.

20 Engage the lip of the dust seal with the groove in the caliper body, and fit each piston using a twisting motion, ensuring that they enter the caliper bore squarely. If the original pistons are being re-used, use the marks made on removal to ensure that they are refitted to the correct bores.

21 As the pistons are fitted, ensure the dust boots fit correctly in the piston recesses.

22 Apply a little lithium-based grease to the caliper guide pins, then fit them, with the new gaiters, to the caliper mounting brackets.

Refitting

23 Check that the brake pads are still correctly fitted, then fit the caliper in place on the mounting bracket, ensuring the flats on the guide pins align with the caliper. Insert the guide pin bolts and tighten them to the specified torque.

24 Refit the hose to the caliper using new sealing washers, and tighten the union bolt to the specified torque.

25 Remove the brake hose clamp or polythene, as applicable, and bleed the hydraulic system as described in Section 2. Note that, providing the precautions described were taken to minimise brake fluid loss, it should only be necessary to bleed the relevant front brake.

26 Refit the roadwheel, then lower the vehicle to the ground and tighten the roadwheel nuts to the specified torque.

9 Rear brake caliper – removal, overhaul and refitting

Note: *Before starting work, refer to the note at the beginning of Section 2 concerning the dangers of hydraulic fluid, and to the warning at the beginning of Section 5 concerning the dangers of asbestos dust.*

Removal

1 Remove the rear brake pads as described in Section 5.

9.4 Rear caliper guide pin bolts (arrowed)

2 To minimise fluid loss, remove the master cylinder reservoir cap, then tighten it down onto a piece of polythene to obtain an airtight seal. Alternatively, use a brake hose clamp, a G-clamp, or a similar tool to clamp the flexible hose at the nearest convenient point to the caliper.

3 Clean the area around the caliper brake hose union bolt. Undo the union bolt, and disconnect the brake hose from the caliper. Discard the copper sealing washers, new ones must be fitted. Plug the hose end and caliper hole to minimise fluid loss and to prevent the ingress of dirt into the hydraulic system.

4 Undo the upper caliper guide pin bolts, and slide the caliper from the mounting bracket **(see illustration)**.

Overhaul

Note: *Prior to dismantling the caliper, check the availability of spares from your Land Rover dealer; on some models, it may prove difficult to obtain caliper components.*

5 Overhaul of the rear caliper is identical to the procedure described for the front caliper in Section 8.

Refitting

6 Check that the brake pads are still correctly fitted, then fit the caliper in place on the mounting bracket. Insert the guide pin bolts and tighten them to the specified torque.

7 Refit the hose to the caliper using new sealing washers, and tighten the union bolt to the specified torque.

8 Remove the brake hose clamp or polythene, as applicable, and bleed the hydraulic system as described in Section 2. Note that, providing the precautions described were taken to minimise brake fluid loss, it should only be necessary to bleed the relevant front brake.

9 Refit the roadwheel, then lower the vehicle to the ground and tighten the roadwheel nuts to the specified torque.

10 Master cylinder – removal, overhaul and refitting

Note: *Before starting work, refer to the notes at the beginning of Section 2 concerning the dangers of hydraulic fluid and the need to use the Land Rover equipment for bleeding the hydraulic system.*

Removal

1 Unclip the plastic cover from the right-hand corner of the engine compartment **(see illustration 2.7)**.

2 Disconnect the wiring connector from the brake fluid level sender unit, then remove the master cylinder reservoir cap and siphon the hydraulic fluid from the reservoir. **Note:** *Do not siphon the fluid by mouth, as it is poisonous; use a syringe or an old poultry baster.* Alternatively, open any convenient bleed screw in the system, and gently pump the brake pedal to expel the fluid through a plastic tube connected to the screw (see Section 2).

3 On models with manual transmission, release the clip and disconnect the clutch master cylinder fluid supply pipe from the brake reservoir **(see illustration)**. Plug the pipe openings to prevent dirt ingress and fluid loss.

4 Prise outwards the 2 retaining clips and pull the fluid reservoir upwards from place **(see illustration)**. Discard the 2 rubber seals, new ones must be fitted.

5 Wipe clean the area around the brake pipe unions on the side of the master cylinder, and place absorbent rags beneath the pipe unions to catch any surplus fluid. Make a note of the correct fitted positions of the unions, then unscrew the union nuts and carefully withdraw the pipes. Wash off any spilt fluid immediately with cold water.

6 Slacken and remove the two nuts securing the master cylinder to the vacuum servo unit. Withdraw the master cylinder assembly from the engine compartment **(see illustration)**.

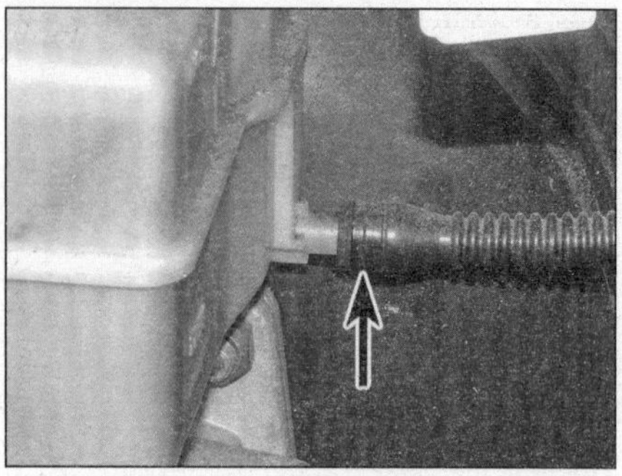

10.3 Disconnect the clutch fluid supply pipe (arrowed)

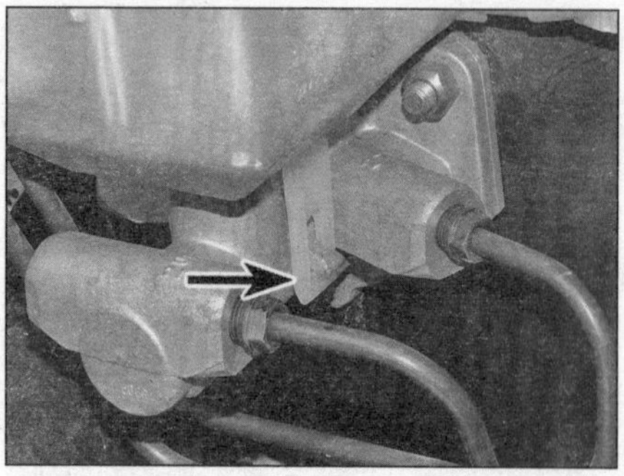

10.4 Prise the clip (arrowed) each side outwards

10.6 Master cylinder retaining nuts (arrowed)

Discard the master cylinder-to-servo O-ring seal – a new one must be fitted.

Overhaul

7 At the time of writing, master cylinder overhaul was not possible, since spares are not available. If the cylinder is thought to be faulty, it must be renewed. Check with your Land Rover dealer or specialist.

Refitting

8 Remove all traces of dirt from the master cylinder and servo unit mating surfaces, then fit the master cylinder, ensuring that the servo unit pushrod enters the master cylinder bore centrally. Refit the master cylinder mounting nuts, and tighten them to the specified torque.

9 Wipe clean the brake pipe unions, then refit them to the master cylinder ports and tighten them to the specified torque setting.

10 Lubricate the new reservoir seals with clean brake fluid, then install them into the master cylinder ports.

11 Press the reservoir into place, ensuring the retaining clips engage correctly.

12 On manual transmission models, reconnect the clutch cylinder fluid supply hose to the reservoir.

13 Refill the master cylinder reservoir with new fluid.

14 Slowly depress the brake pedal to the floor, and then slowly release it – repeat this five times. Wait for 10 seconds, then repeat this process. As this is done, air bubbles will rise into the reservoir, effectively bleeding the master cylinder.

15 Repeat the operations described in paragraph 14 until resistance is felt at the brake pedal, then bleed the complete hydraulic system as described in Section 2.

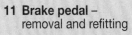

11 Brake pedal – removal and refitting

Manual transmission models

1 On models with manual transmission, the brake pedal removal procedure is described within the clutch pedal removal procedure – refer to Chapter 6, Section 6.

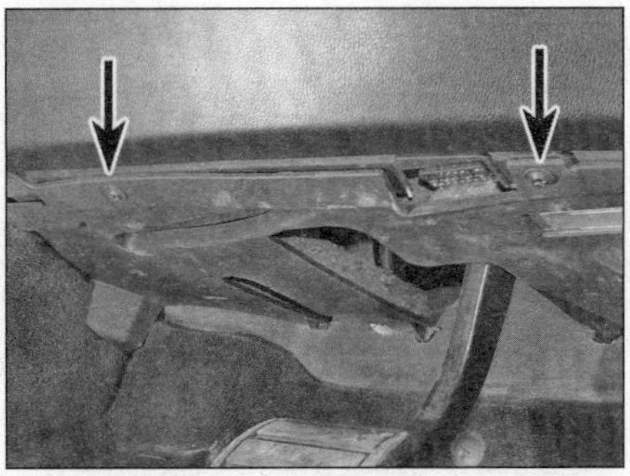

11.3 Undo the screws (arrowed) and remove the panel above the pedals

Automatic transmission models

Removal

2 On automatic transmission models, begin by removing the headlamp switch as described in Chapter 13, Section 4.

3 Undo the 2 screws, release the clip and remove the facia panel above the pedals **(see illustration)**. Disconnect the wiring plug as the panel is withdrawn.

4 Pull the driver's side lower facia panel rearwards to release the retaining clips **(see illustration)**.

5 Disconnect the wiring plug, then rotate the brake light switch clockwise and remove it from the bracket **(see illustration 19.3)**.

6 Release the wiring harness clip, then undo the 4 Torx bolts and remove the bracket to access the brake pedal.

7 Slide off the retaining clip, and remove the pin securing the servo pushrod to the pedal **(see illustration)**.

8 Undo the pivot bolt and nut, then lower the pedal from position **(see illustration)**.

Refitting

9 Lightly grease the pedal pivot bushes.

10 Refit the pedal(s) to the shaft, ensuring all bushes, spacers, etc, are in their original positions.

11 Manoeuvre the pedal into place, insert the pivot bolt and tighten the nut securely.

12 Tighten the pivot shaft bolts securely.

13 Reconnect the pushrod to the brake pedal, and secure it with the clevis pin and clip.

14 The remainder of refitting is a reversal of removal. Check the operation of the brakes before venturing out onto the road.

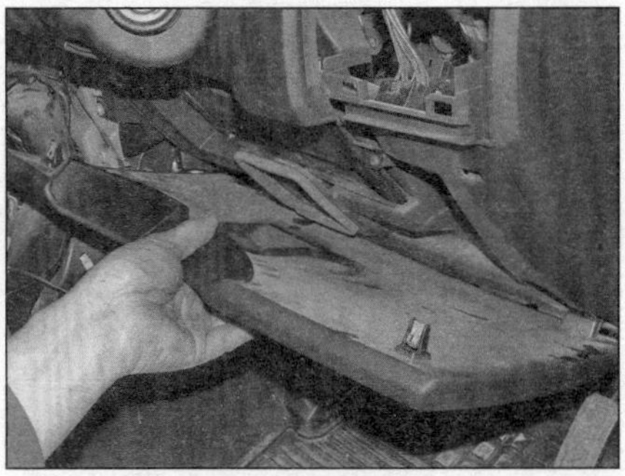

11.4 Pull the lower facia panel rearwards

12 Vacuum servo unit – testing, removal and refitting

Testing

1 To test the operation of the servo unit, with the engine switched off, depress the footbrake several times to exhaust the vacuum. Keeping the pedal depressed, start the engine. As the engine starts, there should be a noticeable give in the brake pedal as the vacuum builds up. Allow the engine to run for at least two minutes, then switch it off. If the brake pedal is now depressed it should feel normal, but further applications should result in the pedal feeling firmer, with the pedal stroke decreasing with each application.

2 If the servo does not operate as described, first inspect the servo unit check valve as described in Section 13.

3 If the servo unit still fails to operate satisfactorily, the fault lies within the unit itself. Repairs to the unit are not possible, and if faulty, the servo unit must be renewed.

Removal

4 Unclip the plastic cover from the right-hand side of the engine compartment **(see illustration 2.7)**.

5 If fitted, remove the auxiliary battery as described in Chapter 5, Section 4.

6 Unclip the battery compartment side wall **(see illustration)**.

11.7 Prise off the clip (arrowed)

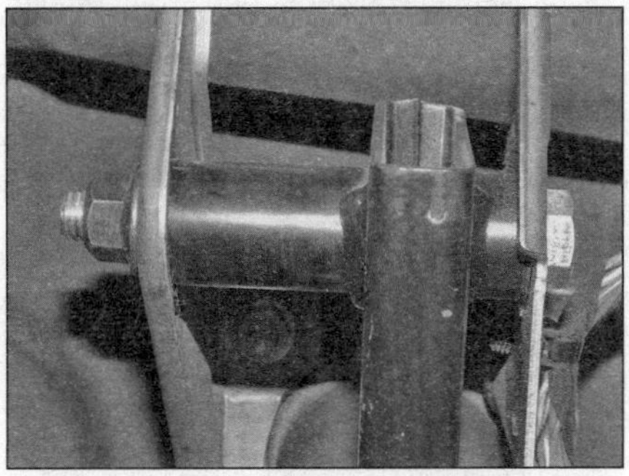

11.8 Brake pedal pivot bolt

12.6 Remove the auxiliary battery compartment side wall (arrowed)

12.7 Heating pipes support bracket screw (arrowed)

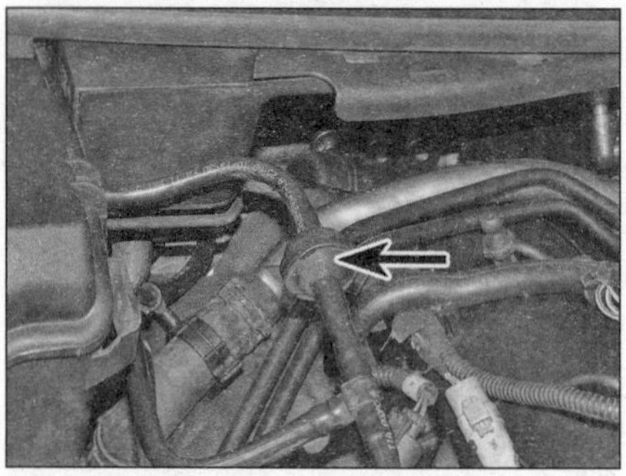
13.1 Vacuum check valve (arrowed)

7 Undo the screw securing the heating pipes support bracket **(see illustration)**.
8 Undo the nuts and remove the auxiliary battery tray **(see illustration)**.
9 Undo the 3 nuts securing the braking HCU (hydraulic control unit) to the vehicle body, and release the brake pipes from the clip.

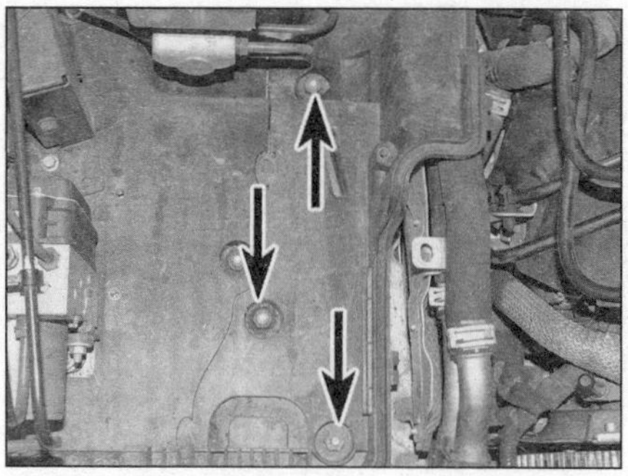
12.8 Undo the nuts (arrowed) and remove the auxiliary battery tray

10 Disconnect the low fluid warning sensor wiring plug **(see illustration)**.
11 On manual transmission models, disconnect the clutch fluid supply pipe from the side of the reservoir. Plug/cover the openings to prevent contamination/fluid loss.
12 Prise out the vacuum hose connection from the servo.
13 Undo the nuts securing the master cylinder to the servo, then carefully lift the master cylinder and HCU, complete with still-connected pipes, upwards to access the servo. Place towels or rags over the wing/ scuttle area to reduce any chance of damage.
14 Undo the 3 retaining nuts and remove the outer plenum chamber base.
15 Undo the 2 screws, release the clip and remove the facia panel above the pedals **(see illustration 11.3)**. Disconnect the wiring plug as the panel is withdrawn.
16 Slide off the retaining clip, and remove the pin securing the servo pushrod to the pedal **(see illustration 11.7)**.

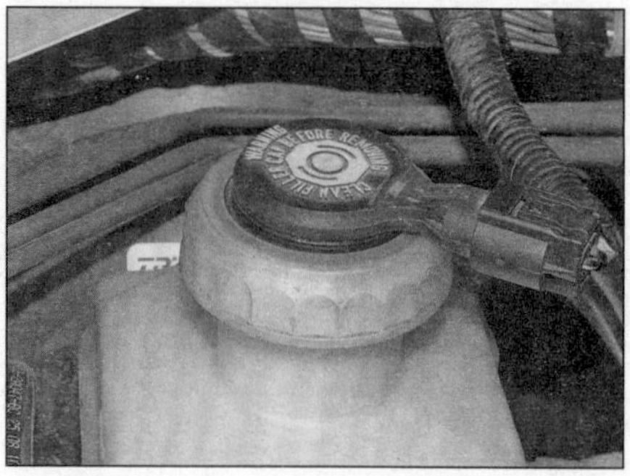
12.10 Disconnect the low fluid warning sensor wiring plug

17 Undo the 4 nuts securing the servo to the bulkhead, and manoeuvre it from position.

Refitting

18 Refitting is a reversal of removal, noting the following points:

a) Tighten all fasteners to their specified torque where given.
b) On manual transmission models, bleed the clutch hydraulic system as described in Chapter 6, Section 5.
c) Check the operation of the brakes before venturing out onto the road.

13 Vacuum servo unit check valve – removal, testing and refitting

Removal

1 Slacken the retaining clip (where fitted), and disconnect the vacuum hoses from the servo unit check valve **(see illustration)**.

Testing

2 Examine the check valve for signs of damage, and renew if necessary. The valve may be tested by blowing through it in both directions, air should flow through the valve in one direction only – when blown through from the servo unit end of the valve. Renew the valve if this is not the case.

Refitting

3 Reconnect the vacuum hoses to the valve, and secure with the retaining clip (where fitted).
4 On completion, start the engine, and check the check valve for signs of air leaks.

14 Parking brake shoes – renewal

1 Remove the rear brake disc as described in Section 7.
2 Note the position of each shoe, and the location of the return springs and self-adjuster mechanism to aid refitting later **(see illustrations)**.
3 Rotate the adjuster star wheel to the

14.2a Nearside upper spring arrangement

14.2b Nearside lower spring arrangement

14.2c Offside upper spring arrangement

14.2d Offside lower spring arrangement

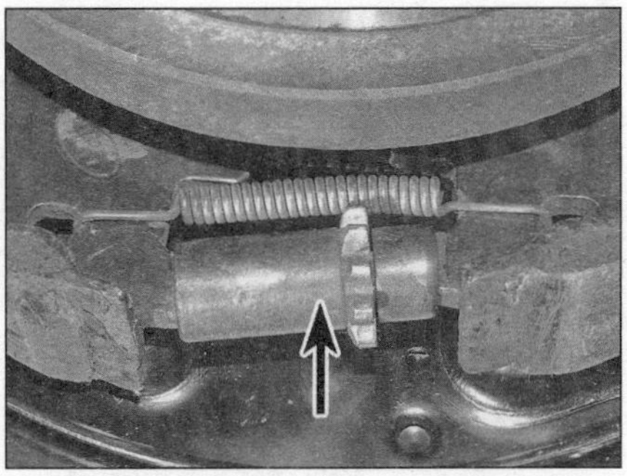
14.3 Remove the star wheel adjuster assembly (arrowed) ...

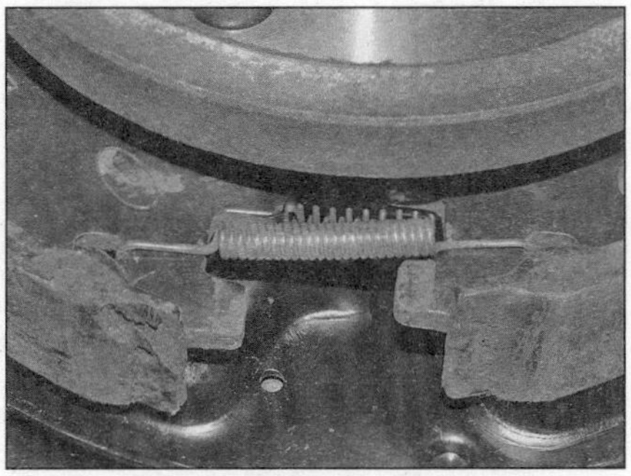
14.4 ... and the return spring

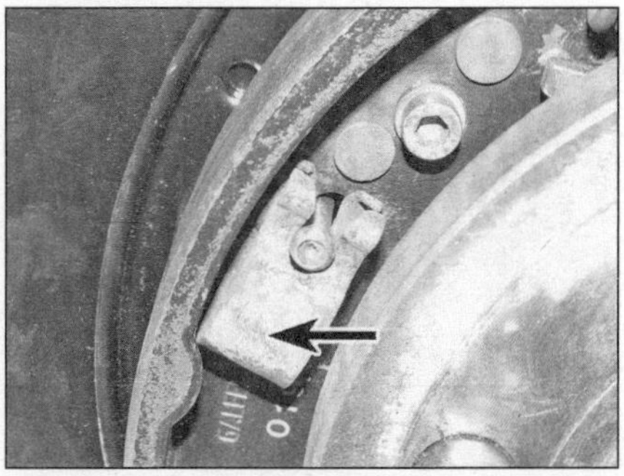
14.5 Depress the clip (arrowed) and slide it out from under the head of the pin

minimum tension position, then manoeuvre it from place **(see illustration)**.

4 Remove the return spring adjacent to the adjuster **(see illustration)**.

5 Depress the leading brake shoe hold-down spring clip and slide the clip out from under the pin head, while holding the pin from the rear **(see illustration)**. Remove the pin from the rear of the backplate.

6 Disconnect the remaining return spring, and remove the shoe, spreader plate and spring **(see illustrations)**.

7 Remove the hold-down spring clip and pin from the trailing brake shoe, then withdraw the shoe from the backplate.

8 Unclip the end of the cable spring and slide the handbrake cable end out of the lever on the trailing shoe **(see illustrations)**. Remove the trailing brake shoe.

9 If refitting the original parking brake shoes, take the opportunity to slacken the retaining screw, and clean the wedge adjuster, removing any built-up debris, rust, etc **(see illustration)**.

10 Apply a smear of high melting-point grease to the contact areas of the shoes and backplate **(see illustration)**. Take care to ensure that the grease does not contaminate the friction material.

11 Engage the shoe with the handbrake cable, secure it with the end of the cable spring, and locate the shoe on the backplate. Install the shoe retainer pin and spring clip. **Note:** *The closed end of the spring clip must point towards the star wheel adjuster position.*

14.6a Remove the return spring ...

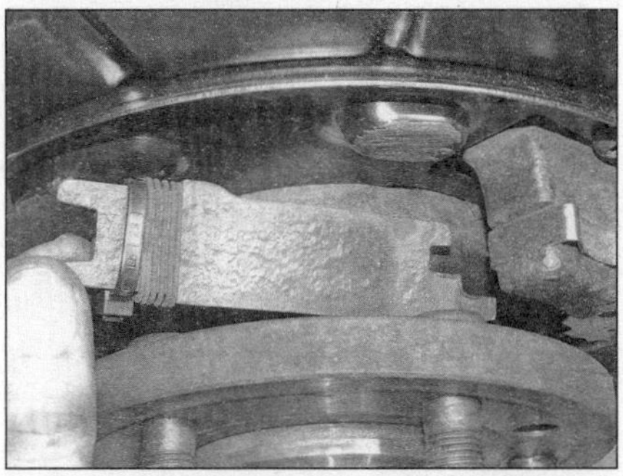
14.6b ... and spreader plate with spring

14.8a Unhook the spring ...

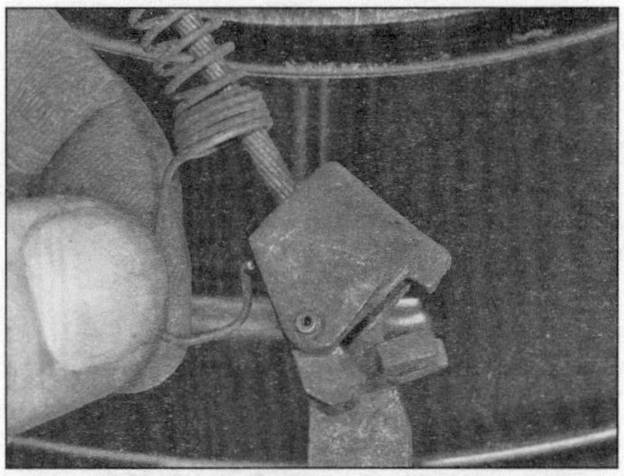
14.8b ... and slide the end of the cable from the lever

12 Refit the spreader plate and spring. Use a cable-tie to hold-back the spring **(see illustration)**.

13 Fit the return spring to the shoes, manoeuvre the leading shoe into position, engaging it with the spreader plate, then

14.9 Slacken the screw (arrowed) remove the wedge adjuster and clean the assembly

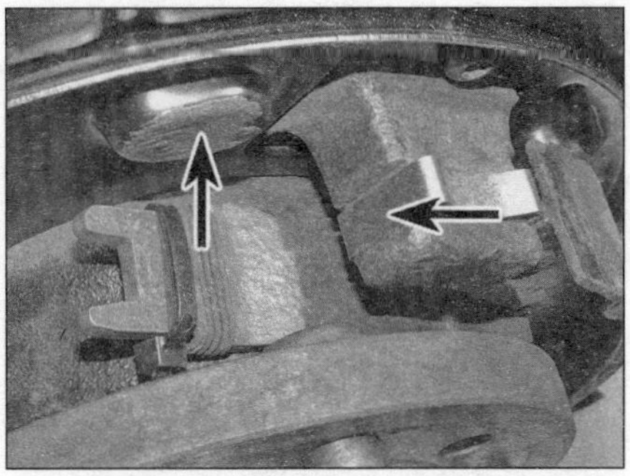
14.10 Apply high-temperature grease to the shoe and backplate contact areas (arrowed)

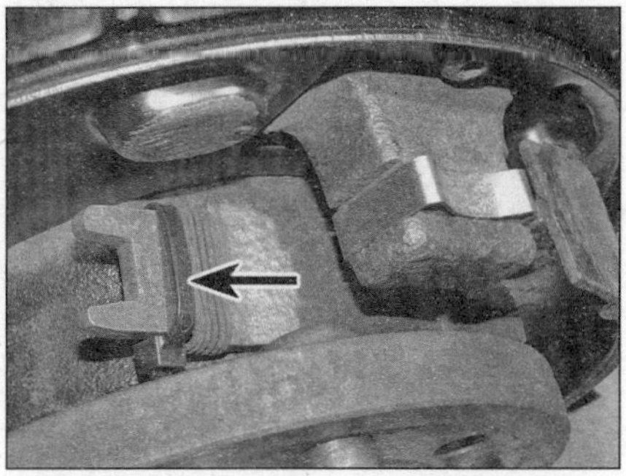
14.12 Use a cable-tie (arrowed) to retain the spring on the spreader plate

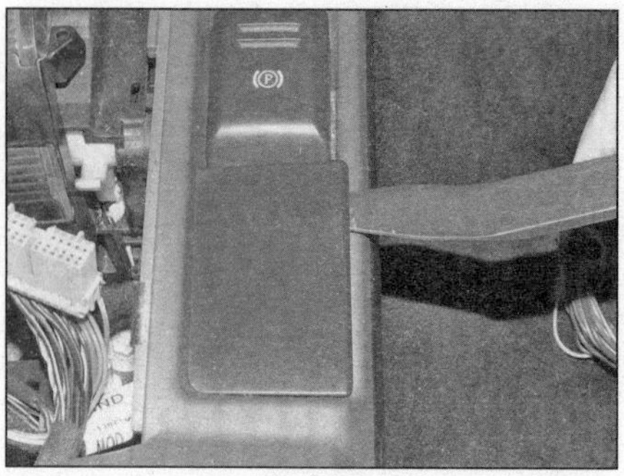

15.1 Prise out the plastic cover behind the switch

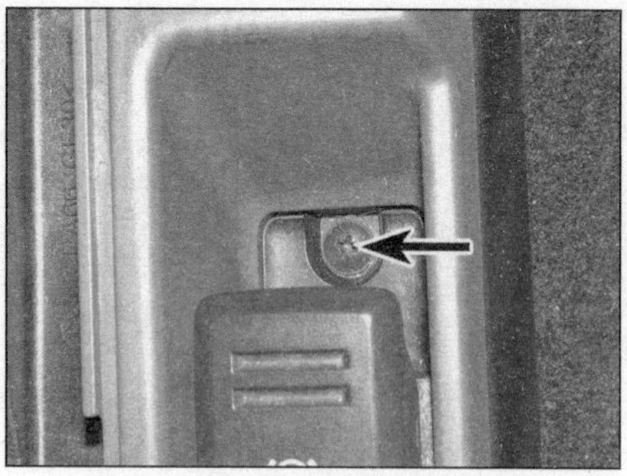

15.2a Undo the screw (arrowed), disconnect the wiring plug ...

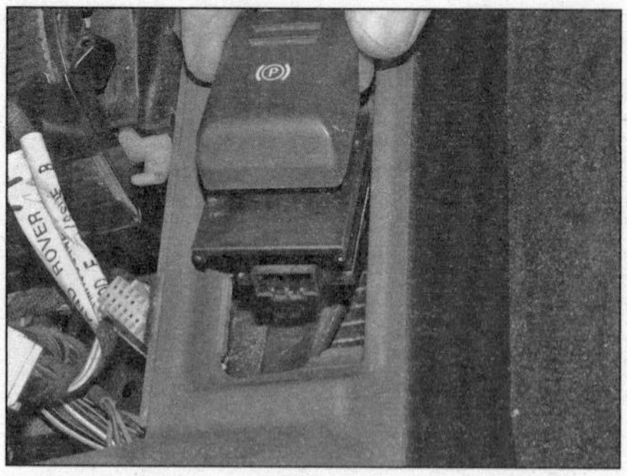

15.2b ... then slide the switch rearwards

install the retainer pin and spring clip. Again, the closed end of the clip must point towards the adjuster.

14 Refit the adjuster and its adjacent return spring. Take care not to over-stretch the spring.

15 Remove the cable-tie, holding back the spreader plate spring

16 Refit the brake disc as described in Section 7.

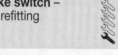

15 Parking brake switch – removal and refitting

1 Prise up the plastic cover behind the switch **(see illustration)**.

2 Undo the retaining screw, disconnect the wiring plug and slide the switch rearwards from place **(see illustrations)**.

3 Refitting is a reversal of removal.

16 Parking brake cables – removal and refitting

Note: *Land Rover insist that the cables can only be refitted if they have performed less than 50 000 applications. The number of applications can only be ascertained using Land Rover diagnostic equipment (T4). If the cables have performed more than 50 000 applications, the complete cables and actuator assembly must be renewed.*

Removal

1 Remove the parking brake shoes as described in Section 14.

2 Rotate the collar anti-clockwise securing the cable to the brake backplate **(see illustration)**.

3 Working along its length, unclip/unbolt the cable from the various retaining clips/brackets.

Left-hand cable

4 Unscrew the cover, pull the outer cable away from the parking brake actuator a little, then rotate the star nut clockwise until the end of the cable detaches from the actuator **(see illustrations)**. If necessary, pull the cable outwards to access the star nut.

Right-hand cable

5 Unscrew the cover, release the clips and detach the end of the cable from the actuator **(see illustrations)**.

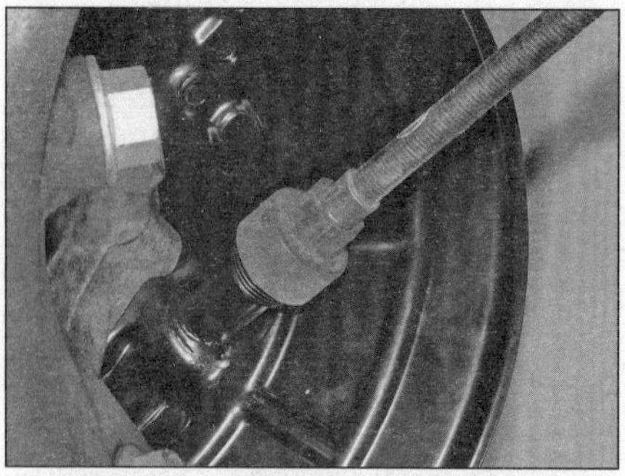

16.2 Unscrew the cable collar from the backplate

16.4a Unscrew the cover (arrowed) ...

16.4b ... rotate the star nut (arrowed) clockwise to unscrew it

16.4c If necessary, pull the cable to withdraw the star nut from the actuator housing

16.5a Unscrew the cover (arrowed) ...

16.5b ... pull out the cable/cap ...

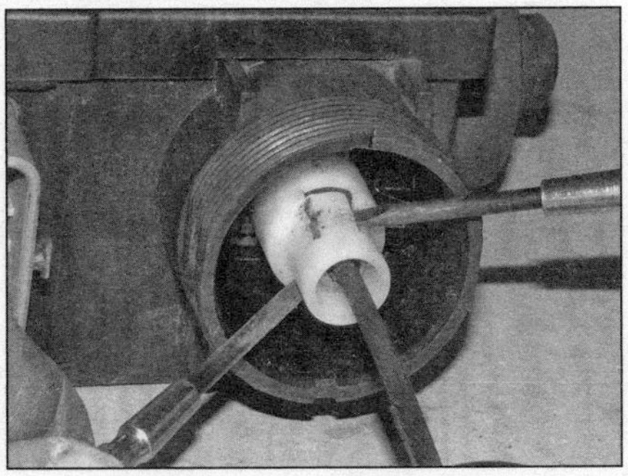
16.5c ... lever out the clips ...

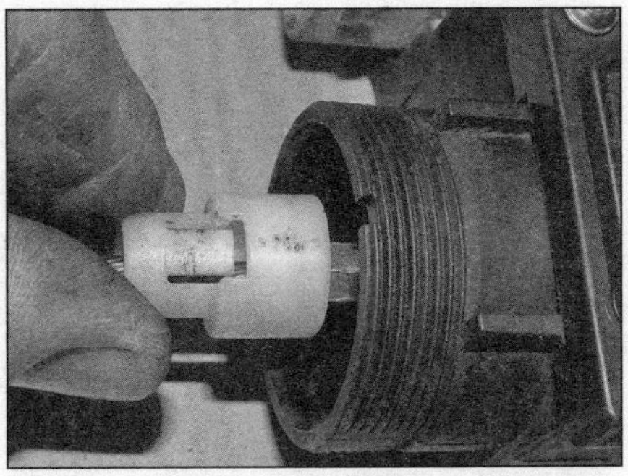
16.5d ... slide back the plastic retainer ...

16.5e ... and detach the end of the cable from the actuator

Refitting

Left-hand cable

6 Insert the end of the cable into the actuator aperture, screw-in the star nut 5 complete revolutions anti-clockwise, the refit the cover **(see illustration)**.

Right-hand cable

7 Attach the cable end fitting to the actuator mechanism, refit the retaining clip, and tighten the cover securely **(see illustrations)**.

Both cables

8 Refit the parking brake shoes as describe in Section 14.

17 Parking brake actuator – removal and refitting

Removal

1 Remove both parking brake cables as described in Section 16.

2 Undo the bolts/nuts and remove the fuel tank heat shield beneath the rear propeller shaft.

3 Note the fitted position of the cable-to-body seal, then unclip the emergency parking brake release cable from the underside of the floor **(see illustration)**. Inspect the cable-to-body seal and renew if necessary.

4 Ensure the immediate area is clean, then undo the union nut, slide out the retaining clip and disconnect the rigid brake pipe on the right-hand side. Plug the openings to prevent contamination and fluid loss.

5 Disconnect the wiring plug, undo the 2 retaining nuts, and manoeuvre the parking brake actuator and release cable assembly from place **(see illustrations)**. Note the routing of the emergency release cable.

Refitting

6 Refitting is a reversal of removal, noting the following points:

a) *Tighten all fasteners to their specified torque where given.*
b) *Bleed the brake hydraulic system as described in Section 2.*
c) *Adjust the handbrake as described in Section 18.*

16.6 The lug on the cap must align with the notch in the actuator housing (arrowed) – left-hand cap ...

16.7 ... and right-hand cap

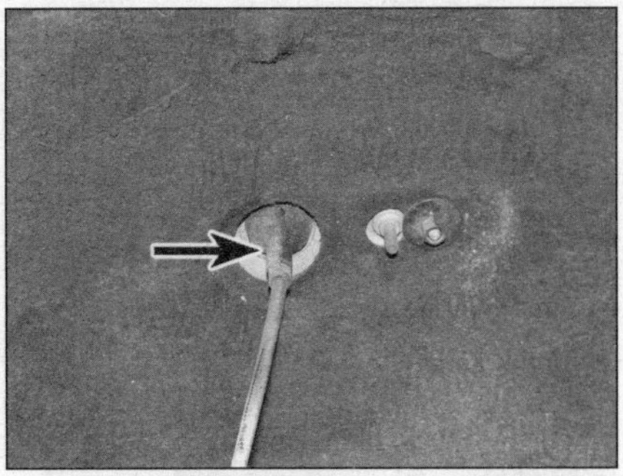
17.3 Note the location of the parking brake emergency release cable grommet (arrowed)

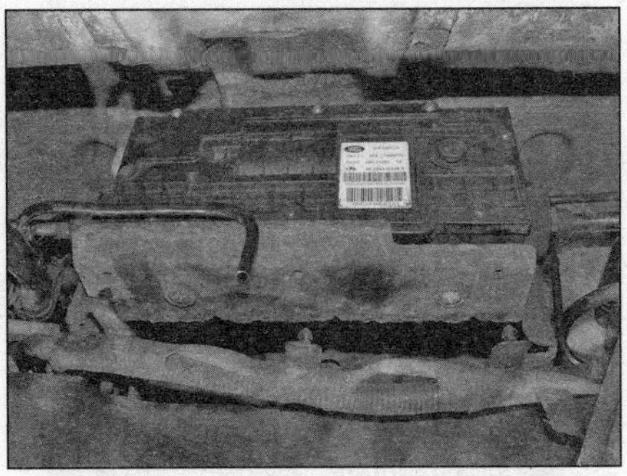
17.5a The parking brake actuator is located above the rear final drive assembly

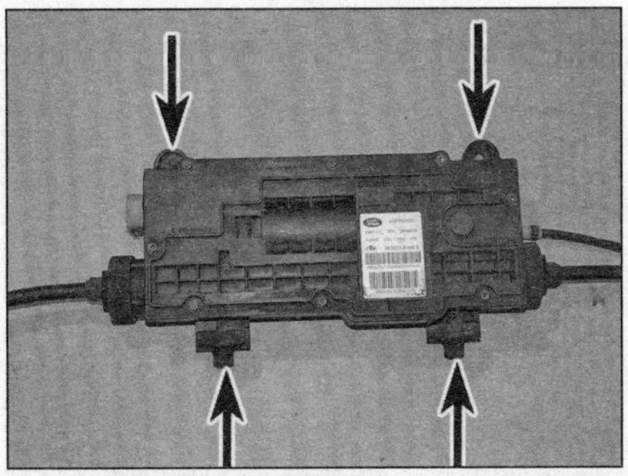
17.5b The actuator locates on rubber mounting below, and is bolted at the top (arrowed – actuator removed for clarity)

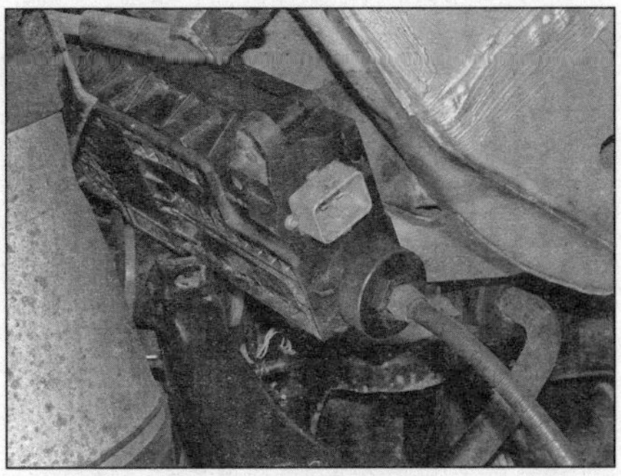
17.5c Manoeuvre the actuator assembly through the right-hand side wheel arch aperture

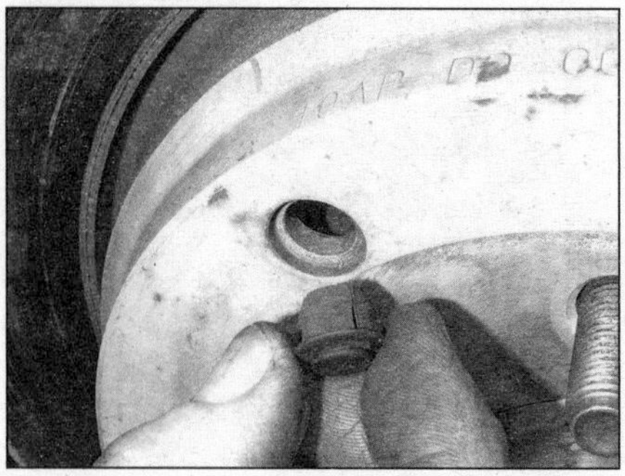

18.3 Prise out the adjuster's access plug

18.4 Lever the ends of the shoes slightly away from the drum surface

18.5 Rotate the star adjuster wheel until the disc/drum can no longer be turned by hand pressure on the studs only

18 Parking brake adjustment and bedding-in

Adjustment

1 Chock the front wheels, and set the parking brake into 'Service Mode' using the following procedure:

a) Turn the ignition key to position II.

b) Apply and hold the footbrake.

c) Apply and hold the parking brake switch in the Release position.

d) Turn the ignition key to position 0 and remove the key.

e) Release the footbrake and the parking brake switch.

f) Remove fuse No. 8 from the fusebox to isolate the parking brake circuit.

Caution: Do not turn the ignition on once the 'Service Mode' has been set.

2 Slacken the rear roadwheel nuts, raise the rear of the vehicle and support it securely on axle stands (see *Jacking and vehicle support*). Remove both rear roadwheels.

3 Prise out the blanking plugs to access the parking shoe adjusters **(see illustration)**.

4 Using a flat-bladed screwdriver through the adjuster aperture, gently lever the ends of the brake shoes away from the surface of the drum **(see illustration)**.

5 Again, using a flat-bladed screwdriver through the aperture, rotate the adjuster star wheel until the disc cannot be turned by hand applying pressure to the wheel studs only **(see illustration)**.

6 Apply a dot of paint on the star wheel to mark its position, then rotate the star wheel exactly one rotation backwards **(see illustrations)**.

7 Rotate the disc so the wedge-adjuster Allen screw is visible **(see illustration)**.

8 Slacken the Allen screw ½ a turn **(seeillustration)**.

9 Using a soft-faced hammer/mallet, tap lightly around the drum part of the disc to ensure the wedge adjuster is properly seated.

10 Tighten the Allen screw to 6 Nm (4 lbft), and refit the blanking plug.

11 Repeat this procedure on the remaining side.

12 Refit the fuse, and discontinue the 'Service mode' by operating the parking brake twice.

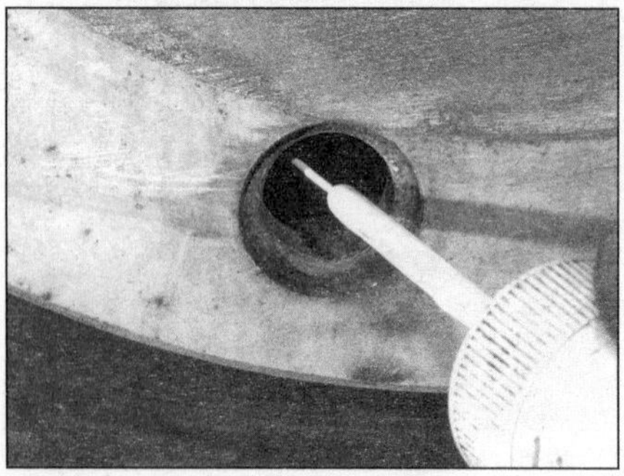

18.6a Use paint ...

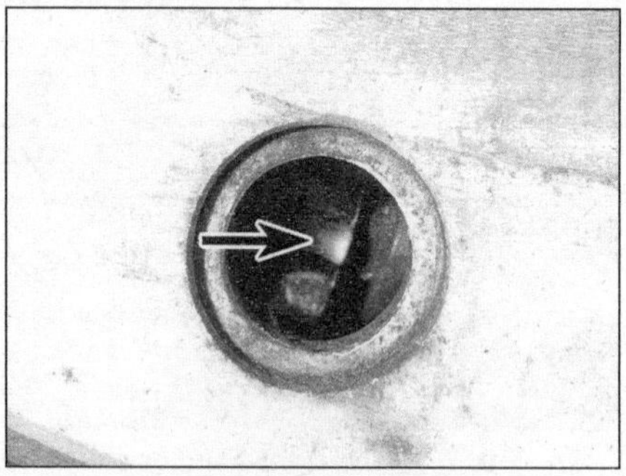

18.6b ... to highlight a single point on the star adjuster wheel (arrowed)

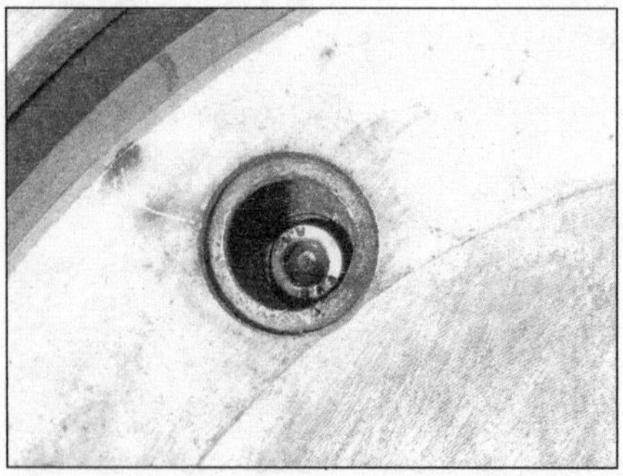

18.7 Rotate the disc/drum until the wedge-adjuster Allen screw is visible ...

18.8 ... then slacken the Allen screw ½ turn

Bedding-in

13 If new shoes or rear discs have been fitted, this 'bedding-in' procedure must be carried out.

14 Enter the 'Service bedding-in procedure mode' using the following procedure:

a) Start the engine, and allow it to idle.

b) Apply the footbrake 3 times within 10 seconds – hold down the 3rd application.

c) Apply the parking brake switch 4 times, followed by 3 release applications, within 10 seconds.

15 Driving along in a straight line, at between 19 to 22 mph, bed the shoes/discs in by conducting 10 repeated stops using the parking brake switch, noting the following:

a) Drive for at least 500 metres between applications, or remain stationary for 1 minute, to allow the brakes to cool.

b) If the switch is in the Neutral or Off positions, the parking brake will be released.

c) The 'Service bedding-in procedure mode' will be exited if the vehicle speed exceeds 31 mph.

d) Take note of other road users – try to perform this procedure without causing inconvenience to others.

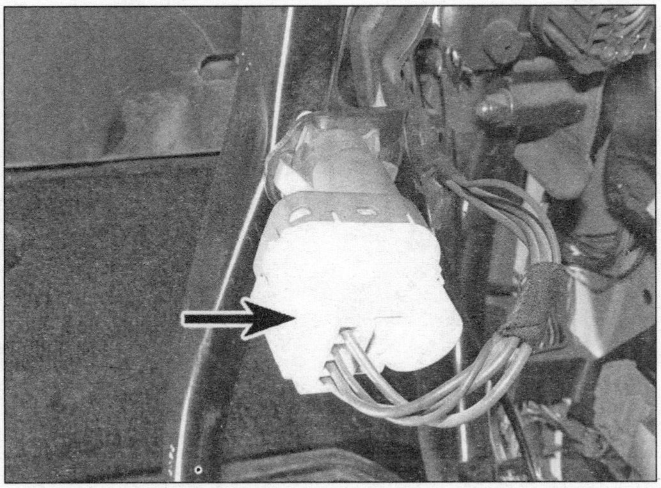

19.2 Disconnect the wiring plug (arrowed) ...

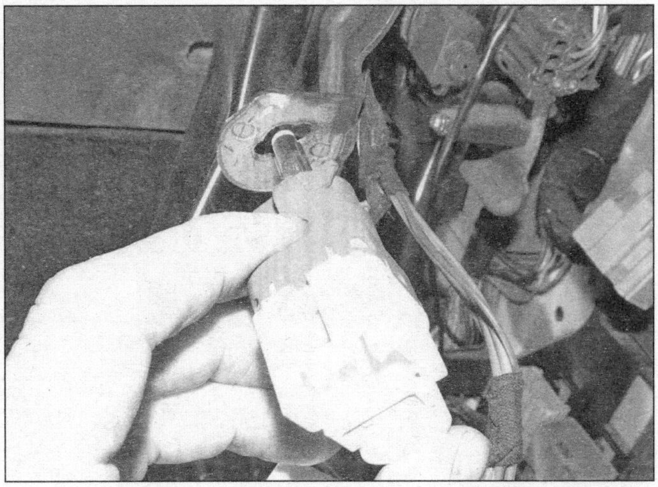

19.3 ... then rotate the switch *clockwise* to remove it

19 Brake light switch – removal, refitting and adjustment

Removal

1 Undo the 2 screws, release the clip and remove the facia panel above the pedals **(see illustration 11.3)**. Disconnect the wiring plug as the panel is withdrawn.

2 Disconnect the wiring connector plug(s) from the brake light switch **(see illustration)**.

3 Twist the switch *clockwise* and pull it from the pedal bracket **(see illustration)**.

Refitting and adjustment

4 Push the switch fully into the mounting bracket and twist it anti-clockwise to lock it in position. Do not depress the brake pedal.

5 Reconnect the switch wiring connector.

6 Check the operation of the switch. It should illuminate after the pedal has been depressed 5.5 to 8.5 mm from the at-rest position. If this is not the case, removing and refitting the switch should reset it.

7 On completion, refit the facia panel.

20 Vacuum pump – removal and refitting

Removal

1 Pull up and remove the plastic cover from the top of the engine **(see illustration)**.

2 Depress the release button and disconnect the vacuum hose from the pump. The pump is located on the rear of the right-hand cylinder head.

3 Remove the complete exhaust system as described in Chapter 4A, Section 17.

4 Undo the bolts securing the support brackets to the transmission casing and exhaust crossover pipe at the rear of the engine. There are 3 brackets: one each side, and one in the centre.

5 Undo the retaining nuts/bolt, remove the turbocharger heat shield, and detach the crossover pipe from the turbocharger.

6 Undo the 3 bolts and remove the right-hand exhaust manifold heat shield.

7 Undo the 3 nuts securing the crossover pipe to the right-hand manifold, and move it rearwards. Recover the gaskets.

8 The high-pressure fuel pipe retaining bracket is secured to the vacuum pump. Undo the bolt securing the bracket to the pump.

9 The vacuum pump is secured by 3 bolts. Undo the bolts and manoeuvre the pump from place **(see illustration)**.

Refitting

10 Ensure the mating faces of the pump and cylinder head are clean and free from any sealant residue.

11 Apply a 2.0 mm square of Loctite 518

20.1 Pull up the plastic cover from the top of the engine

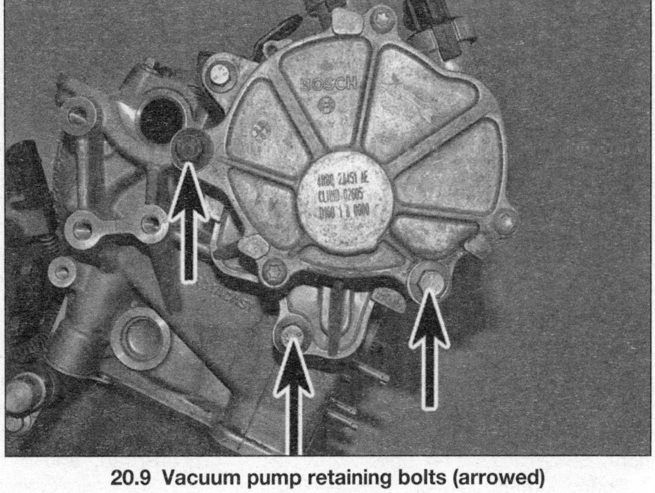

20.9 Vacuum pump retaining bolts (arrowed)

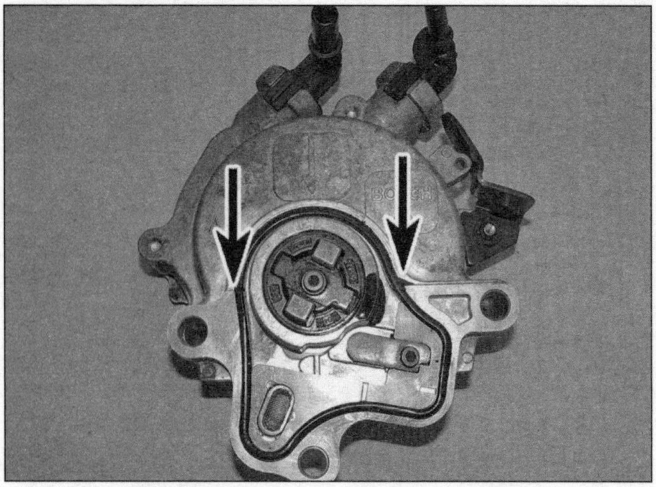

20.11 Apply sealant to the areas arrowed

20.12 Ensure the pump drive dogs engage with the slot in the camshaft

sealant to the pump mating face as shown **(see illustration)**.

12 Immediately after applying the sealant, align the pump drive dogs with the slots in the end of the camshaft and fit the pump to the cylinder head, without smearing the sealant **(see illustration)**. If the sealant is smeared, wipe it off and start again.

13 Refit the bolts, stud and nut, then tighten them to the specified torque.

14 The remainder of refitting is a reversal of removal.

21 Anti-lock braking system (ABS) – general information

ABS is fitted as standard to all models. The system comprises of the hydraulic control unit (HCU), a modulator block (which contains the hydraulic solenoid valves and accumulators, and the electrically-driven pump), and four roadwheel sensors; one fitted to each hub. The brake pedal light switch is used to indicate to the HCU that the brakes are applied. The purpose of the system is to prevent wheel(s) locking during heavy braking. This is achieved by automatic release of the brake on the relevant wheel, followed by reapplication of the brake.

The solenoid valves are controlled by the HCU, which itself receives signals from the four wheel sensors, which monitor the speed of rotation of each wheel. By comparing these speed signals from the four wheels, the HCU can determine the speed at which the vehicle is travelling. It can then use this speed to determine when a wheel is decelerating at an abnormal rate compared to the speed of the vehicle, and therefore predicts when a wheel is about to lock. During normal operation, the system functions in the same way as a non-ABS braking system does.

During normal operation, the solenoid valves in the modulator assembly are closed, and the governor valves are in the at-rest position. The system then functions in the same way as a non-ABS braking system does.

If the HCU senses that a wheel is about to lock, the ABS operates the relevant solenoid valve in the modulator assembly, which then isolates the brake caliper on the wheel which is about to lock from the master cylinder, effectively sealing-in the hydraulic pressure.

If the speed of rotation of the wheel continues to decrease at an abnormal rate, the electrically-driven return pump operates, and pumps the hydraulic fluid back into the master cylinder, releasing pressure on the brake caliper so that the brake is released. Once the speed of rotation of the wheel returns to an acceptable rate, the pump stops and the solenoid valve opens, allowing the hydraulic master cylinder pressure to return to the caliper, which then reapplies the brake. This cycle can be carried out at many times a second.

The action of the solenoid valves and return pump creates pulses in the hydraulic circuit. When the ABS is functioning, these pulses can be felt through the brake pedal.

Other functions are built into the ABS system.

- Using the same sensors and actuators (solenoids), the system is able to regulate the fluid pressure to the rear brakes to compensate for heavy loads, etc – electronic brake force distribution (EBD).
- The system also provides electronic traction control by using the brakes to control the spinning of any wheel that has lost traction, thus diverting the drive to the wheels that still have traction – electronic traction control (ETC).
- In addition the system also provides hill descent control (HDC), where the vehicle's brakes are used by the ECU to maintain vehicle stability during sharp descents off-road, and dynamic stability control (DSC) where cornering stability is enhanced by brake applications at individual wheels.

The operation of the ABS is entirely dependent on electrical signals. To prevent the system responding to any inaccurate signals, a built-in safety circuit monitors all signals received by the HCU. The first time the vehicle exceeds 5 mph after the ignition has been switched on, the HCU tests the readings from each wheel sensor, and the operation of the modulator solenoid valves. If a fault is present, the ABS is automatically shut down by the HCU, and the warning light on the instrument panel is illuminated to inform the driver that the ABS is not operational.

Every time the ignition is switched on, the HCU performs a self-test and checks its memory for faults. This takes approximately 1 to 2 seconds, during which time the ABS warning light in the instrument panel will illuminate. The warning light should then go out, indicating the end of the self-test. If the warning light fails to go out, or illuminates whilst the vehicle is being driven, then a fault is present in the ABS.

If a fault does develop in the ABS, the vehicle must be taken to a Land Rover dealer or specialist for fault diagnosis and repair.

22 Anti-lock braking system (ABS) components – removal and refitting

HCU module assembly

Note: *Before starting work, refer to the note at the beginning of Section 2 concerning the dangers of hydraulic fluid.*

Note: *After refitting the module, Land Rover insist that the system must be bleed using their T4 dedicated test equipment. Have this task carried out be a Land Rover dealer or suitably-equipped specialist.*

Removal

1 Disconnect the battery negative terminal as described in Chapter 5, Section 4.

22.11 Front wheel speed sensor retaining bolt (arrowed)

22.19 Rear wheel speed sensor retaining bolt (arrowed)

2 Unclip the plastic cover from the right-hand corner of the engine compartment **(see illustration 2.7)**.

3 Disconnect the wiring plug from the module.

4 Wipe clean the area around the module brake pipe unions, then make a note of how the pipes are arranged, to use as a reference on refitting. Unscrew the union nuts, and carefully withdraw the pipes. Plug or tape over the pipe ends and modulator orifices, to minimise the loss of brake fluid and to prevent the entry of dirt into the system. Wash off any spilt fluid immediately with cold water.

5 Slacken and remove the mounting nuts, and release the module assembly with its mounting bracket. If necessary, unscrew the module rubber mounting bushes, and remove them. **Note:** *Do not attempt to dismantle the module block hydraulic assembly; overhaul of the unit is not possible.*

Refitting

6 Refitting is the reverse of the removal procedure, noting the following points:

a) Examine the rubber mounting bushes for signs of wear or damage, and renew if necessary.

b) Refit the brake pipes to their respective unions, and tighten the union nuts to the specified torque.

c) Ensure that the wiring is correctly routed, and that the connector is firmly pressed into position.

d) On completion, prior to refitting the battery, bleed the complete braking system using Land Rover dedicated test equipment (T4) – entrust this task to a Land Rover dealer or specialist.

Front wheel sensor

Removal

7 Firmly apply the parking brake, then loosen the relevant front roadwheel nuts. Jack up the front of the vehicle and support it securely on axle stands (see *Jacking and vehicle support*). Remove the appropriate front roadwheel.

8 Undo the fasteners and remove the wheel arch liner from the relevant side.

9 Undo the bolt securing the brake hose bracket to the hub carrier.

10 Undo the 2 bolts securing the brake caliper mounting bracket to the hub carrier, and slide the caliper and bracket from the disc. Suspend the caliper from the vehicle body using string or wire. Do not let the caliper hang by the hose.

11 Clean the area around the sensor, then undo the bolt and pull the sensor from the hub **(see illustration)**.

12 Trace the wiring back to the plug, and disconnect it, Release the wiring harness from the retaining clips.

Refitting

13 Ensure the sensor and hub mating faces are clean and free from debris. Apply a little high-temperature anti-seize grease to the sensor body.

14 Position the sensor in the hub, and tighten the retaining bolt to the specified torque.

15 Ensure that the sensor wiring is correctly routed and retained by all the necessary clips. Reconnect it to its wiring connector, and clip the connector into the retaining clip.

16 The remainder of refitting is a reversal of removal.

Rear wheel sensor

Removal

17 Firmly apply the parking brake, then loosen the relevant rear roadwheel nuts. Jack up the rear of the vehicle and support it securely on axle stands (see *Jacking and vehicle support*). Remove the appropriate rear roadwheel.

18 Trace the sensor wiring back to the plug, and disconnect it. Release the wiring harness from the retaining clips along its length.

19 Undo the bolt and pull the sensor from the hub carrier **(see illustration)**.

Refitting

20 Ensure the sensor and hub mating faces are clean and free from debris. Apply a little high-temperature anti-seize grease to the sensor body.

21 Position the sensor in the hub, and tighten the retaining bolt to the specified torque.

22 Ensure that the sensor wiring is correctly routed and retained by all the necessary clips. Reconnect it to its wiring connector, and clip the connector into the retaining clip.

23 The remainder of refitting is a reversal of removal.

Yaw rate sensor

24 Remove the centre console as described in Chapter 12, Section 27.

25 Undo the 2 retaining bolts, and remove the yaw rate sensor **(see illustration)**. Disconnect the wiring plug as the sensor is withdrawn.

26 Refitting is a reversal of removal. If a new sensor has been fitted, it must be calibrated using Land Rover diagnostic equipment (T4). Entrust this task to a Land Rover dealer or suitably-equipped repairer.

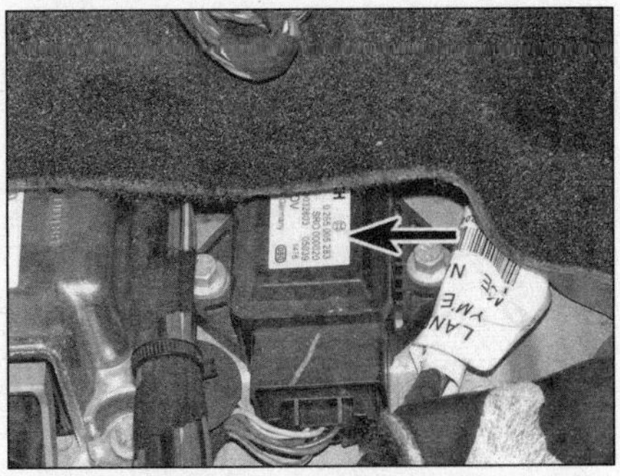

22.25 The yaw rate sensor (arrowed) is located under the rear of the centre console

Chapter 11
Suspension and steering

Contents

Degrees of difficulty

Easy, suitable for novice with little experience	**Fairly easy,** suitable for beginner with some experience	**Fairly difficult,** suitable for competent DIY mechanic	**Difficult,** suitable for experienced DIY mechanic	**Very difficult,** suitable for expert DIY or professional

Specifications

Front suspension

Type	Fully independent, with upper, and lower arms, shock absorber with coil springs or air springs. Anti-roll bar standard on all models

Rear suspension

Type	Fully independent, with upper, and lower arms, shock absorber with coil springs or air springs. Anti-roll bar standard on all models

Steering

Type	Steering rack with speed-proportional hydraulic power assistance
Power steering pump type	Auxiliary belt driven hydraulic

Wheel alignment and steering angles

Note: *All measurements should be taken with the vehicle unladen, with a full tank of fuel, at normal ride height.*

Front

Camber angle	-30' ± 45'
Castor angle	4°1' ± 45'
Toe setting	10' ± 12' (total)

Rear

Camber angle:	
Models with air suspension	-45' ± 45'
Models without air suspension	-30' ± 45'
Toe setting	14' ± 8' (total)

Roadwheels

Type	Pressed-steel or aluminium alloy (depending on model)

Tyres

Pressures	See *Lubricants, fluids and tyre pressures*

Torque wrench settings

	Nm	lbf ft
Front suspension		
Anti-roll bar link nuts*	115	85
Anti-roll bar clamp nuts	115	85
Axle crossmember bolts	115	85
Driveshaft retaining nut*	230	170
Front crossmember bolts	115	85
Hub mounting bolts	115	85
Lower suspension arm bolts	275	203
Lower suspension arm-to-hub carrier nut	115	85
Suspension strut:		
Upper mounting nuts:		
Coil spring strut	70	52
Air spring strut	63	46
Lower mounting bolts	300	221
Piston nut*	98	72
Upper suspension arm-to-hub carrier nut	70	52
Upper suspension arm nuts/bolts	175	129
Voss connector gland nut	4	3
Rear suspension		
Anti-roll bar:		
Connecting link nuts*	115	85
Mounting clamp bolts	62	46
Compressor mounting bolts	23	17
Driveshaft nut*	350	258
Lower arm to hub carrier	175	129
Lower arm pivot bolts	275	203
Suspension strut:		
Lower mounting bolt/nut	300	221
Upper mounting nuts:		
Coil spring strut	70	52
Air spring strut	63	46
Piston nut*	98	72
Toe link bolt (do not use more than 5 times)	175	129
Toe link inner balljoint nut*	133	98
Upper arm to hub carrier	133	98
Upper arm pivot bolts:		
Front	175	129
Rear	275	203
Voss connector gland nut	3.5	2.6
Steering		
Power steering pump:		
Mounting bolts	25	18
Feed pipe union nut	25	18
Pulley retaining bolts	10	7
Steering rack bolts (new captive nuts required)	175	129
Steering column:		
Intermediate shaft-to-upper shaft nut*	22	16
Intermediate shaft-to-lower shaft bolt*	25	18
Universal joint bolt*	25	18
Mounting bolts	25	18
Steering wheel bolt*	63	46
Track rod:		
Locknut	53	39
Balljoint nuts:*		
M12	76	56
M14	150	111
Roadwheels		
Roadwheel nuts	140	103

** Do not re-use*

1 General information

In a change from the beam axle design fitted to previous models, the Discovery 3 is equipped with fully-independent front and rear suspension. Upper and lower suspension arms control the position of the hub carrier, with shock absorbing capacity provided by either steel coil springs, or air springs (depending on model) with integral dampers. A toe link arm is fitted to the rear suspension to control/adjust rear wheel toe position. With the exception of the spring/damper units, the suspension arms/bars are identical regardless of which type of spring is fitted.

Front and rear anti-roll bars are fitted to all models.

Models fitted with air suspension are equipped with vehicle dynamic suspension. This system comprises air springs, height sensors, electronic control module, valve blocks, air supply unit, air reservoir, associated pipes, filter and control switches. The ECM constantly monitors the ride height of the vehicle, maintaining the height under all operating conditions by controlling the air supply to the 4 springs. There are 4 ride states, selectable by the driver via a switch on the centre console.

The steering column is linked to the steering rack by a lower shaft, and intermediate shaft. The lower shaft has an integral universal joint fitted to its lower end, whilst the upper end is bolted to the intermediate shaft. The intermediate shaft is secured to the upper column by a coupling. In the event of a frontal collision, the lower shaft is designed to collapse, whilst the intermediate shaft coupling is designed to shear, minimising steering column intrusion into the cabin.

A conventional power-assisted steering rack is fitted, with speed-proportional assistance provided by an auxiliary belt-driven hydraulic pump.

Note: *Many of the suspension and steering components are secured in position with self-locking nuts. Whenever a self-locking nut is disturbed, it must be discarded and a new nut fitted.*

2 Front strut – removal and refitting

Note: *Shock absorbers must ALWAYS be renewed in pairs, even if only one appears to be defective, in order to preserve safe handling.*

Removal

1 Slacken the roadwheel nuts, raise the front of the vehicle and support it securely on axle stands (see *Jacking and vehicle support*). Remove the front roadwheels.

Coil spring suspension

2 Remove the headlights as described in Chapter 13, Section 7.

3 Undo the screws securing the mud flap at the rear of the front wheel arch.

4 Remove the fasteners/screws and pull the wing/wheel arch moulding out sideways to release the clips **(see illustration)**.

5 Undo the screws, release the clips and remove the wheel arch liner. Disconnect any wiring plugs as the wheel arch liner is withdrawn.

6 Place a trolley jack under the lower suspension arm on the relevant side.

7 Undo the nut and withdrawn the suspension strut lower mounting bolt.

8 In order to access the upper mounting inner nut, undo the bolts/nut and remove the heat shield.

9 Undo the 3 upper mounting nuts and manoeuvre the suspension strut from position.

Air suspension

Note: *Before any part of the pressurised air circuit can be worked on, it's essential to depressurise the system – the pressure in the system can be in excess of 16 bar (230 psi). Land Rover recommend that this must be carried out using their dedicated test equipment (T4). It is possible to depressurise the system without T4 by very slowly undoing the air pipe gland nut on the air spring* **(see illustration 2.13a and 2.13b)** *to allow the pressure within to slowly escape. If in any doubt at all, entrust any work involving the pressurised air circuit to a Land Rover dealer or suitably-equipped specialist.*

Warning: Do not attempt to drive the vehicle with the air suspension system depressurised.

10 Disconnect the battery negative lead as described in Chapter 5, Section 4.

11 Depressurise the air suspension system as described above.

12 Undo the nut and withdrawn the suspension strut lower mounting bolt.

13 Fully undo the gland nut, and detach the air pipe from the top of the strut. Remove the Voss connector (consisting of a split olive and gland nut with integral O-ring seal), and discard it – a new one must be fitted **(see illustrations)**. Plug/cover the openings to prevent contamination.

14 Undo the 3 upper mounting nuts and manoeuvre the suspension strut from position **(see illustrations)**.

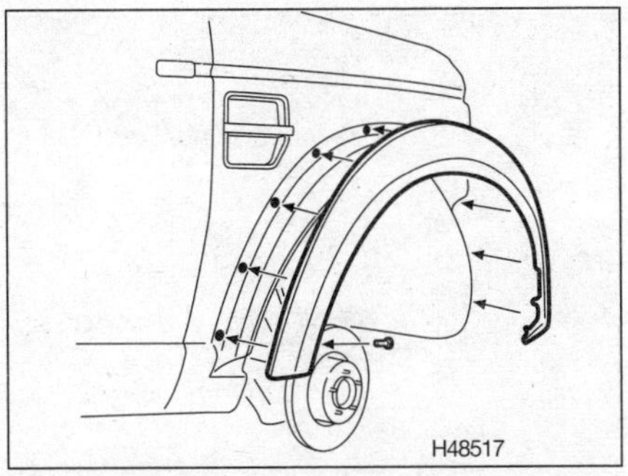

2.4 Undo the screws, release the fasteners, and pull the wheel arch moulding outwards

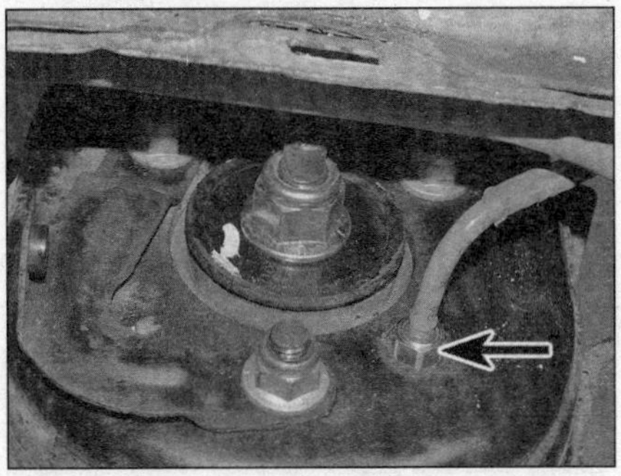

2.13a Undo the gland nut (arrowed) on the top of the strut

2.13b The Voss connector (split olive, gland nut and O-ring) must be renewed

2.14a Undo the 3 nuts (arrowed) ...

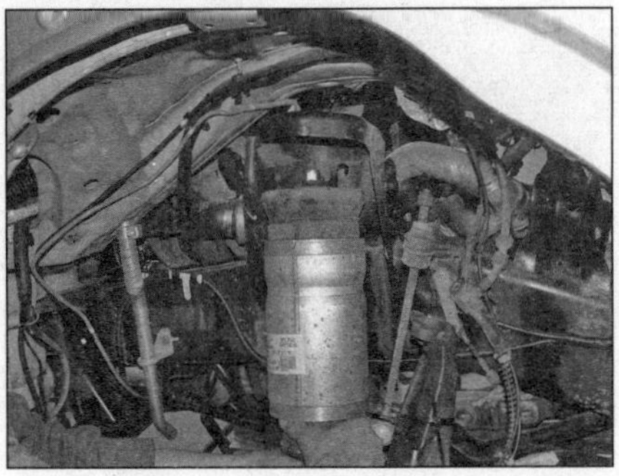

2.14b ... and lower the strut

Refitting

15 Refitting is a reversal of the removal procedure, noting the following points:

a) Tighten all fasteners to their specified torque where given.

b) On air spring models, fit a new Voss connector to the pipe.

c) Start the engine to repressurise the air spring system (where applicable).

3 Front strut – overhaul

Overhaul

1 Remove the front suspension strut as described in Section 2.

Coil spring strut

Note: *Suitable coil spring compressor tools will be required for this operation.*

2 Fit suitable spring compressors to the coil spring, and compress the spring sufficiently to enable the upper mounting to be turned by hand.

Warning: Ensure that the coil spring is compressed sufficiently to remove all the tension from the upper mounting before attempting to remove the piston rod nut.

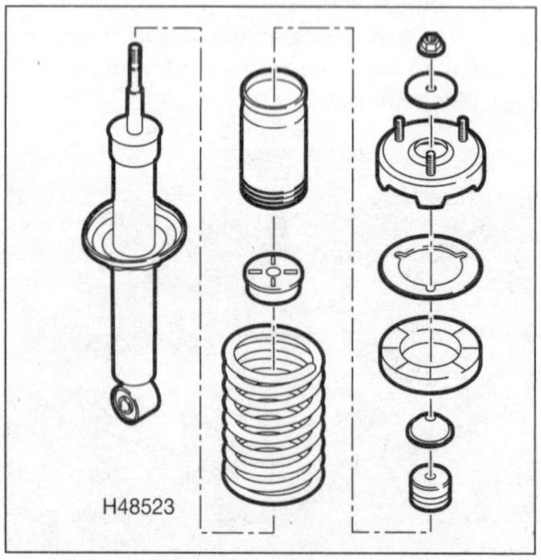

3.4 Coil spring details

3 Unscrew the nut securing the strut piston rod to the upper mounting, while counterholding the piston with a suitable Allen key. Discard the nut – a new one must be fitted.

4 Withdraw the washer, mounting plate, bush, spring seat and spacer, then withdraw the spring, complete with the compressors **(see illustration)**.

5 Withdraw the dust cover and bump rubber.

6 Make alignment marks between the rubber seat and the mounting plate, and remove the seat and spacer from the mounting.

7 With the strut assembly now dismantled, examine all the components for wear, damage or deformation. Renew any components as necessary.

8 Examine the strut body for signs of fluid leakage or damage, and the piston rod for signs of pitting or scoring. If there is any visible sign of wear or damage to the strut, renewal is necessary.

9 If any doubt exists about the condition of the coil spring, carefully remove the spring compressors, and check the spring for distortion and signs of cracking. Renew the spring if it is damaged or distorted, or if there is any doubt about its condition.

Warning: Coil springs are classified by their height when under load – this is indicated by a coloured paint marking on the side of the coil windings. All coil springs fitted to the vehicle must be of the same classification to ensure the correct ride height.

10 Begin reassembly by refitting the dust cover and bump rubber.

11 Ensure that the coil spring is compressed sufficiently to enable the upper mounting components to be fitted, then fit the spring over the piston rod, ensuring that the lower end of the spring is correctly located in the recess on the lower spring seat. Note that the end of the spring with the 'close coils' is fitted at the top.

12 Refit the rubber seat and spacer to the mounting plate, ensuring the previously-made marks are aligned.

13 Locate the upper spring seat over the piston rod, then refit the upper mounting.

14 Fit the new piston rod top nut, then tighten the nut to the specified torque, counterholding the piston rod in a manner similar to that used during dismantling. Note that a suitable crows-foot adapter or flange-drive socket (Vortex) will be required to tighten the piston rod top nut to the specified torque.

15 Remove the spring compressors and refit the strut to the car as described in Section 2.

Air spring

16 Remove the suspension strut as described in Section 2.

17 Prise out the nylon retaining pin on the side of the air spring **(see illustration)**.

18 Unscrew the nut securing the strut piston rod to the upper mounting, while counterholding the piston with a suitable spanner/socket **(see illustration)**. Discard the nut – a new one must be fitted.

19 Clamp the strut lower mounting is a vice, then remove the rebound washer, followed by the 3 spacers and the 2 O-ring seals **(see illustrations)**.

20 Using a soft-faced mallet/hammer, carefully tap the sleeve support to release it **(see illustration)**. Do not unroll the sleeve.

3.17 Prise out the nylon pin

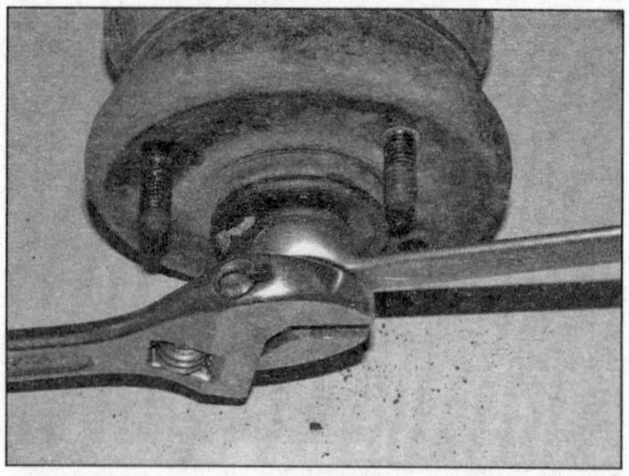

3.18 Hold the piston rod stationary and undo the nut

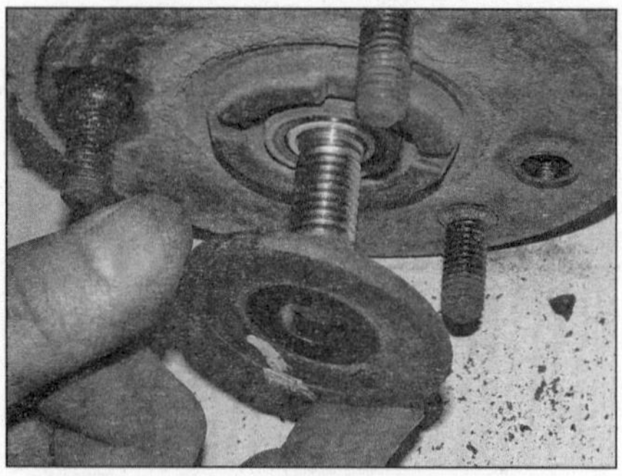

3.19a Remove the rebound washer ...

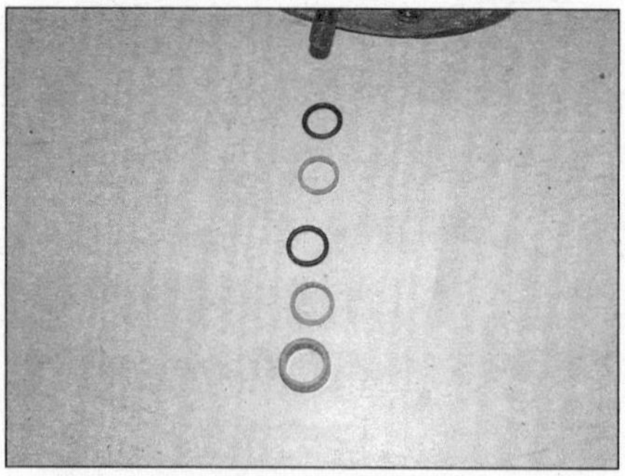

3.19b ... followed by the 3 spacers and 2 O-rings

3.20 Carefully tap the sleeve support to release it

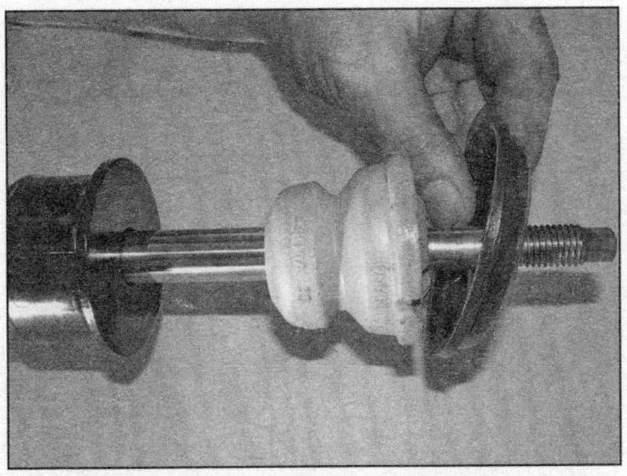

3.21 Remove the bump stop and spring aid

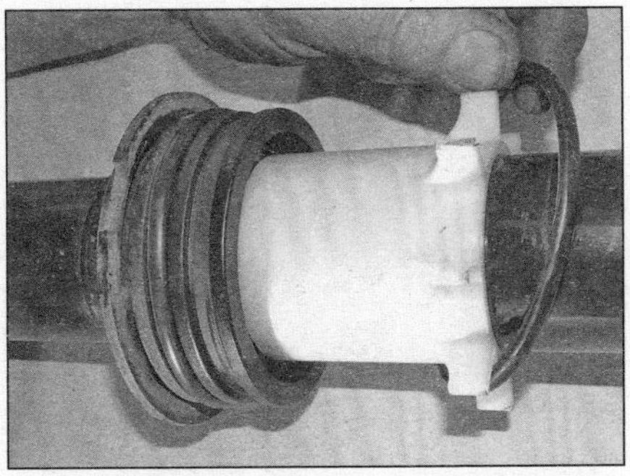

3.22 Renew the O-ring seals on the seal carrier

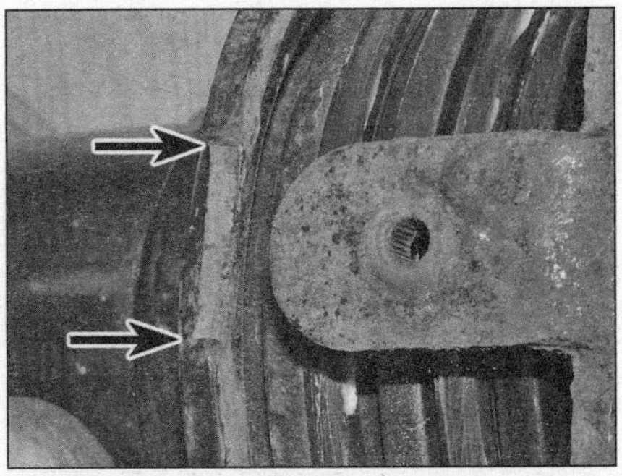

3.26 Align the location tag with the cut-out in the spring seat (arrowed)

3.27 Fit the spacers/O-rings in the order shown

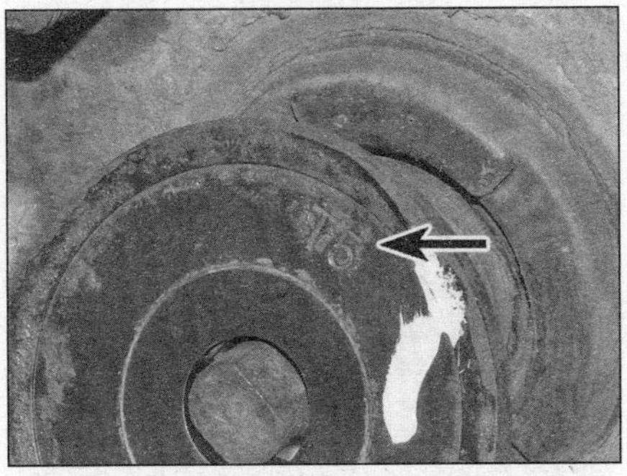

3.28 Fit the rebound washer with the mark T5 uppermost (arrowed)

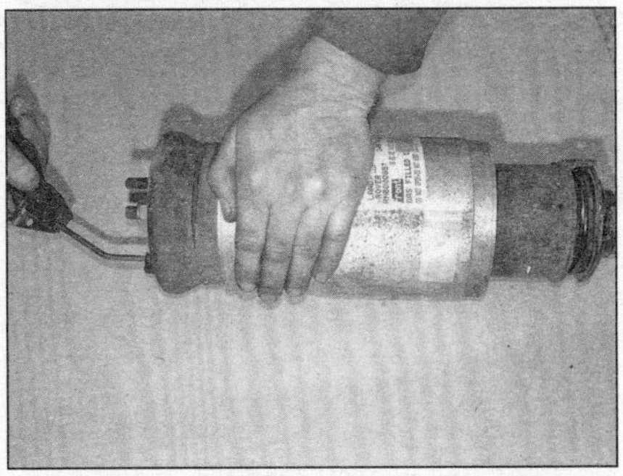

3.30 Apply 2.0 bar of compressed air to seat the sleeve

21 Note its fitted position, then remove the bump stop and spring aid **(see illustration)**.

22 Remove the 2 O-ring seals from the lower seal carrier **(see illustration)**. Discard the O-ring seals – new ones must be fitted.

23 Lift the seal carrier, and check the damper body O-ring seals and spacers are fully seated on the spring seat. Press the seal carrier down into place.

24 Apply a little silicone-based oil (Loctite 8021) to the new O-ring seals, then fit them to the seal carrier.

25 Fit the bump stop and spring aid.

26 Align the sleeve support location tag with the cut-out in the spring seat, then press the sleeve down into position as far as possible **(see illustration)**.

27 Carefully fit the seals/spacers to the piston rod in the following order **(see illustration)**:

a) O-ring seal.
b) Spacer.
c) O-ring seal.
d) Spacer.
e) Large spacer.

28 Refit the rebound washer with the mark T5 uppermost **(see illustration)**.

29 Fit a new piston rod nut and tighten it to the specified torque.

30 The strut must now be connected to a tyre inflation airline/pump and pressurised to 2.0 bar (29 psi) to seat the spring over the O-rings. Land Rover tool No. 204-538 may be available to connect the spring to the hose. In the absence of the tool, use an air gun and a source of compressed air **(see illustration)**.

31 With the spring fully-seated, secure the sleeve in place with the rivet supplied in the seal kit (replacing the nylon retaining pin).

32 Now pressurise the strut to 4.0 bar (58 psi) to check for leaks. If a leak is suspected, immerse the pressurised strut in water and identify the source of the leak. Dismantle the strut and rectify as necessary.

33 Release the air pressure, remove the special tool (or equivalent), and refit the strut as described in Section 2.

4 Front hub carrier – removal and refitting

Removal

1 Slacken the roadwheel nuts, raise the front of the vehicle and support it securely on axle stands (see *Jacking and vehicle support*). Remove the front roadwheels.

3.31 Secure the sleeve with the rivet supplied in the seal kit

2 Using a chisel or punch, un-stake the driveshaft nut, then unscrew it from the driveshaft. Assistance may be required, the nut is very tight. Discard the nut, a new one must be fitted. **Note:** *The driveshaft nut is very tight. It may be prudent to prise out the centre of the roadwheel, refit it, and lower the vehicle to the ground. Then insert the socket through the centre of the wheel and undo the nut.*

3 Remove the brake disc as described in Chapter 10, Section 6.

4 Undo the bolt securing the brake hose bracket to the hub carrier.

5 Undo the retaining bolt and pull the ABS wheel speed sensor from the hub carrier **(see illustration)**.

6 Use a spanner/socket to counterhold the balljoint, then undo the nut securing the

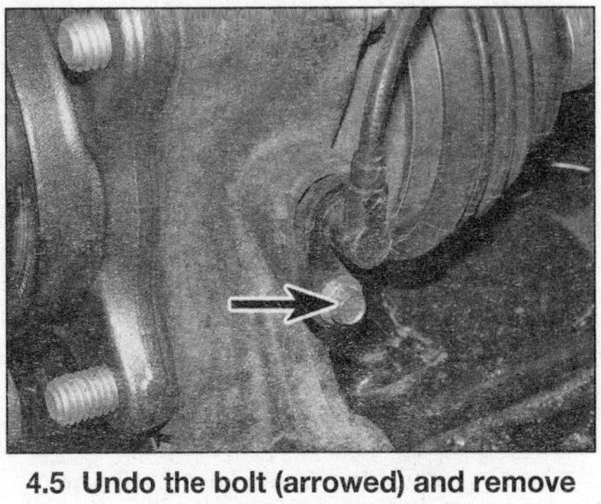

4.5 Undo the bolt (arrowed) and remove the wheel speed sensor

4.6 Counterhold the anti-roll bar link rod balljoint and undo the nut

4.7 Detach the track rod end balljoint with a separator tool

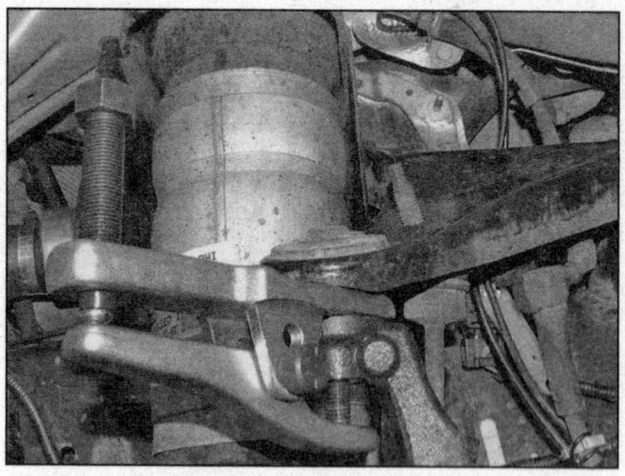

4.9 Use a separator tool to detach the upper arm balljoint ...

anti-roll bar link rod balljoint to the upper arm **(see illustration)**. Discard the nut – a new one must be fitted.

7 Slacken the retaining nut, then use a universal balljoint separator tool to detach the steering track rod end balljoint from the hub carrier **(see illustration)**. Discard the nut – a new one must be fitted. Take care not to damage the rubber gaiter on the joint.

8 Place a trolley jack under the hub carrier to support it, then slacken the nut securing the upper balljoint to the hub carrier.

9 Using a universal balljoint separator tool, detach the upper balljoint from the hub carrier **(see illustration)**. Discard the nut – a new one must be fitted. Take care not to damage the rubber gaiter on the joint.

10 Using a suitable tool, press the end of the driveshaft from the hub. A special Land Rover tool (No. 204-506/1, 205-506/3 and 204-506/5) is available for this task. **Note:** *Use of a hammer to force the shaft from the hub will almost certainly result in damage. Take great care not to damage the end of the shaft.*

11 Allow the hub carrier to tilt outwards, then disengage the driveshaft from it. Don't allow the hub carrier to hang on the lower arm, or the lower balljoint may be damaged.

12 Slacken the lower balljoint nut then, using a universal balljoint separator tool, detach the lower balljoint from the hub carrier **(see illustration)**. Discard the nut – a new one must be fitted. Take care not to damage the rubber gaiter on the joint.

Refitting

13 Refitting is a reversal of removal, noting the following points:

a) *Apply a little anti-seize grease to the splines, then refit the end of the driveshaft into the hub assembly. If necessary use Land Rover tool No. 204-506-01, 204-506/1 and 204-506/5 to pull the end of the shaft through the hub.*

b) *Tighten all fasteners to their specified torque where given.*

c) *After tightening the driveshaft nut, the nut must be 'staked' as described in Chapter 9, Section 2.*

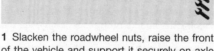

5 Front hub bearing – renewal

1 Slacken the roadwheel nuts, raise the front of the vehicle and support it securely on axle stands (see *Jacking and vehicle support*). Remove the front roadwheels.

2 Using a chisel or punch, un-stake the driveshaft nut, then unscrew it from the driveshaft. Assistance may be required, the nut is very tight. Discard the nut, a new one must be fitted. **Note:** *The driveshaft nut is very tight. It may be prudent to prise out the centre of the roadwheel, refit it, and lower the vehicle to the ground. Then insert the socket through the centre of the wheel and undo the nut.*

3 Remove the brake disc as described in Chapter 10, Section 6.

4 Undo the bolt securing the brake hose bracket to the hub carrier.

5 Undo the retaining bolt and pull the ABS wheel speed sensor from the hub carrier **(see illustration 4.5)**.

6 Using a suitable tool, press the end of the driveshaft inwards and release it from the hub. A special Land Rover tool (No. 204-506/1, 205-506/3 and 204-506/5) is available for this task. **Note:** *Use of a hammer to force the shaft from the hub will almost certainly result in damage. Take great care not to damage the end of the shaft.*

7 Undo the 4 retaining bolts and withdraw the hub and bearing assembly from the hub carrier **(see illustration)**. Note that the hub and bearing is supplied as an assembly – no further dismantling is recommended.

8 Position the new hub/bearing and tighten the retaining bolts to the specified torque.

9 Apply a little anti-seize grease to the splines, then refit the end of the driveshaft into the hub assembly. If necessary use Land Rover tool No. 204-506-01, 204-506/1 and 204-506/5 to pull the end of the shaft through the hub.

10 The remainder of refitting is a reversal of removal, noting the following points:

a) *Tighten all fasteners to their specified torque where given.*

b) *After tightening the driveshaft nut, the nut must be 'staked' as described in Chapter 9, Section 2.*

4.12 ... and the lower arm balljoint

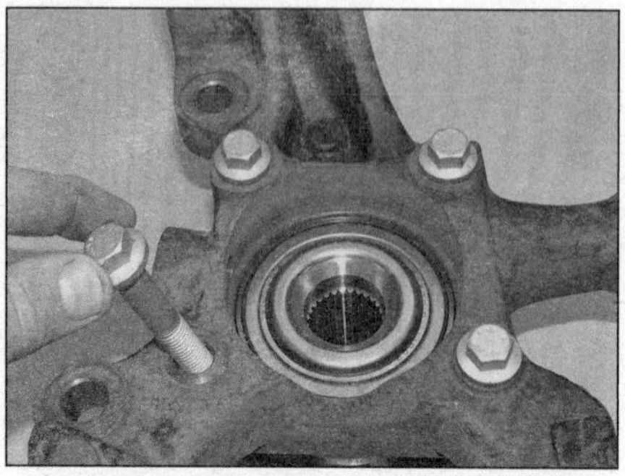

5.7 Undo the bolts and detach the hub/bearing assembly

6 Front suspension arms – removal and refitting

Upper arm

Removal

1 Slacken the roadwheel nuts, raise the front of the vehicle and support it securely on axle stands (see *Jacking and vehicle support*). Remove the front roadwheel.

2 Carefully prise the height sensor link arm

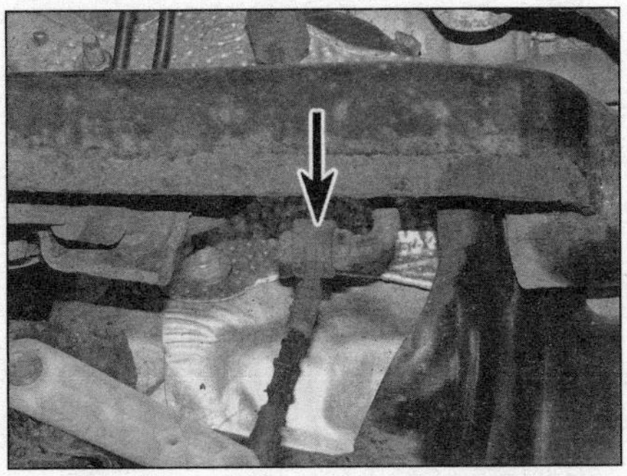

6.2 Prise the sensor arm from the bracket (arrowed)

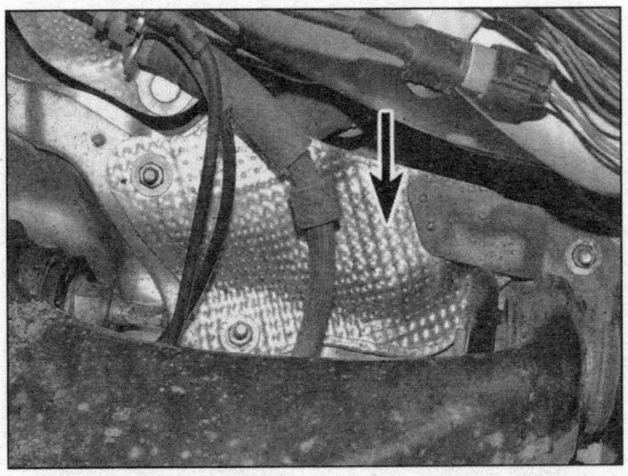

6.3 Remove the heat shield (arrowed)

6.7 Tie the hub carrier to the strut

(where fitted) from the bracket on the upper arm **(see illustration)**.

3 Undo the 3 bolts and 3 nuts, then remove the upper arm/brake pipe heat shield **(see illustration)**.

4 Use a spanner/socket to counterhold the balljoint, then undo the nut securing the anti-roll bar link rod balljoint to the upper arm **(see illustration 4.6)**. Discard the nut – a new one must be fitted.

5 Undo the retaining bolt and release the brake hose and wheel speed sensor wiring harnesses from the upper arm.

6 Place a trolley jack under the lower suspension arm on the relevant side to support the hub carrier.

7 Undo the nut then, using a universal balljoint separator tool, detach the upper balljoint from the hub carrier **(see illustration 4.9)**. If necessary, use an Allen key in the end of the balljoint shank to prevent rotation. Discard the nut – a new one must be fitted. Take care not to damage the rubber gaiter on the joint. Temporarily tie the hub carrier to the suspension strut to prevent the carrier falling outwards **(see illustration)**.

8 Undo the nuts, and withdrawn the upper arm pivot bolts **(see illustration)**. Manoeuvre the arm from position. Discard the nuts – new ones must be fitted.

Refitting

9 Position the upper arm, insert the pivot bolts and fit the new nuts, but only finger-tighten them at this stage.

10 Refit the upper arm balljoint to the hub carrier, fit a new nut and tighten it to the specified torque.

11 Refit the brake hose and wheel speed sensor wiring harnesses.

12 Reconnect the anti-roll bar link rod and tighten the new nut to the specified torque.

13 Refit the heat shield and the height sensor link arm (where fitted).

14 Using a jack under the lower arm/hub carrier, raise the assembly until the distance between the centre of the driveshaft and the highest point of the wheel arch aperture is 466 mm.

15 Tighten the upper arm pivot nuts to the specified torque.

16 The remainder of refitting is a reversal of removal.

Lower arm

Removal

17 Using the height control switch, place the vehicle into 'access mode' (models with air suspension only).

18 Slacken the roadwheel nuts, raise the front of the vehicle and support it securely on axle stands (see *Jacking and vehicle support*). Remove the front roadwheel.

19 Using a chisel or punch, un-stake the driveshaft nut, then unscrew it from the driveshaft. Assistance may be required, the nut is very tight. Discard the nut, a new one must be fitted. **Note:** *The driveshaft nut is very tight. It may be prudent to prise out the centre of the roadwheel, refit it, and lower the vehicle to the ground. Then insert the socket through the centre of the wheel and undo the nut.*

20 Undo the nut and remove the suspension strut lower mounting bolt.

21 Make alignment marks between the lower arm pivot bolt heads/washers and the chassis brackets, then remove the bolts **(see illustration)**.

22 Using a suitable tool, press the end of the driveshaft inwards and release it from the hub. A special Land Rover tool (No. 204-506/1, 205-506/3 and 204-506/5) is available for this task. **Note:** *Use of a hammer to force the shaft from the hub will almost certainly result in damage. Take great care not to damage the end of the shaft.*

23 Disengage the end of the driveshaft from the hub, and position it to one side.

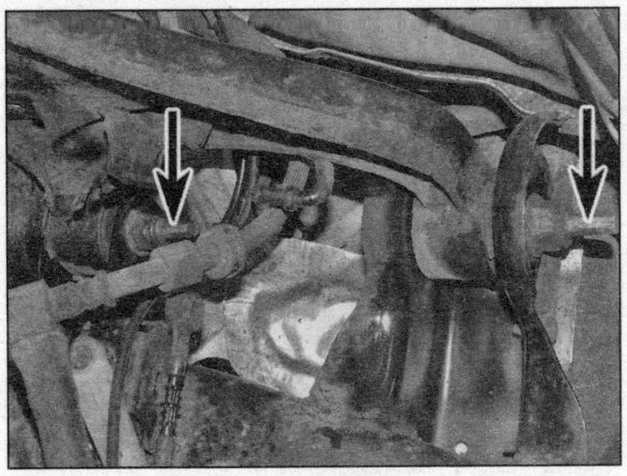

6.8 Undo and remove the upper pivot bolts (arrowed)

24 Slacken the lower balljoint nut then, using a universal balljoint separator tool, detach the lower balljoint from the hub carrier **(see illustration 4.12)**. Discard the nut – a new one must be fitted. Take care not to damage the rubber gaiter on the joint.

25 Manoeuvre the lower arm from position.

Refitting

26 Engage the lower balljoint with the hub carrier, engage the end of the driveshaft with the hub, then position the lower arm. Insert the pivot bolts but only finger-tighten them at this stage.

27 Fit the new lower balljoint nut and tighten it to the specified torque.

28 Using a jack under the lower arm/hub carrier, raise the assembly until the distance between the centre of the driveshaft and the highest point of the wheel arch aperture is 466 mm.

29 Align the previously-made marks, and tighten the lower arm pivot bolts to the specified torque.

30 Refit the suspension strut lower mounting bolts and tighten the nut to the specified torque.

31 The remainder of refitting is a reversal of removal, noting the following points:

a) *Tighten all fasteners to their specified torque where given.*
b) *After tightening the driveshaft nut, the nut must be 'staked' as described in Chapter 9, Section 2.*
c) *Upon completion, have the front wheel alignment checked and, if necessary, adjusted.*

6.21 Make alignment marks between the eccentric bolt head/washer and the chassis

7.2 Remove the balljoint circlip

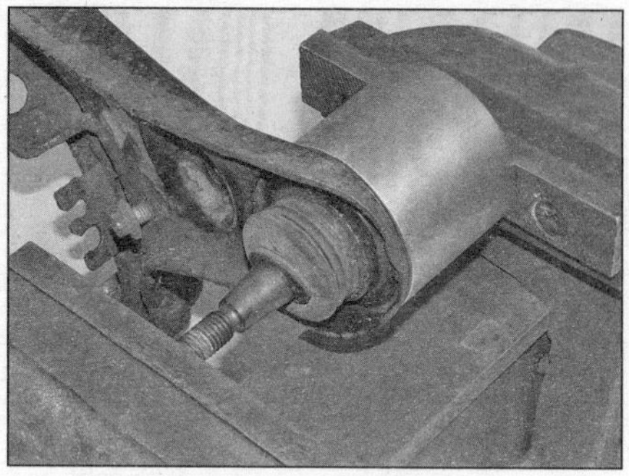

7.3a Use a tubular spacer ...

7.3b ... and force the balljoint from the arm

7 Front suspension arm balljoints and bushes – renewal

Upper arm balljoint

1 Remove the upper arm as described in Section 6.

2 Remove the circlip **(see illustration)**.

3 Note its fitted position then, using a combination of spacers/tubes, press the balljoint from the arm **(see illustrations)**. Note that Land Rover special tools No. 205-503-2 and 204-516-3 may be available instead of using suitable spacers/tubes, etc.

4 Align the cut-out in the balljoint flange with the mark in the upper arm and, again using suitable spacers/tubes, press the new balljoint into position **(see illustrations)**. Land Rover special tools No. 204-530-1 and 204-530-3 may be available instead of using suitable spacers/tubes, etc.

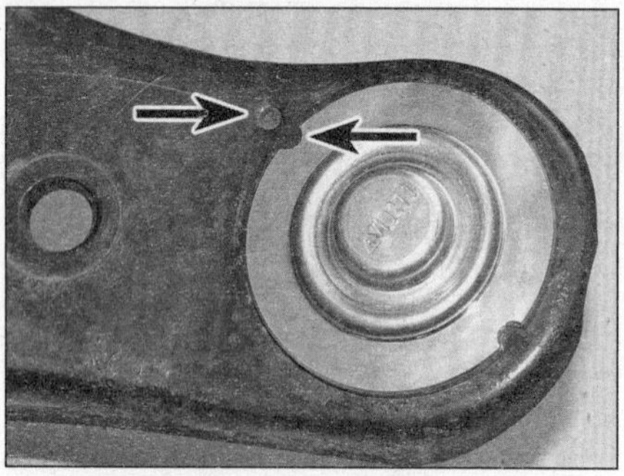

7.4a Align the cut-out in the flange with the mark on the arm (arrowed)

5 Fit the new circlip, ensuring the gap between the eyes at the end of the circlip are positioned 90° to the cut-outs in the balljoint flange **(see illustration)**.

6 Refit the upper suspension arm as described in Section 6.

Upper arm pivot bushes

Note: *Two different procedures are described. One for when Land Rover bushes are used, and one for when Polybush polyurethane bushes are used.*

7 Remove the upper arm as described in Section 6.

Land Rover bushes

8 Note the fitted positions of the bushes in the arm. Make alignment marks between the arrow on the bushes and the upper arm. Make a note of the fitted depth of the bushes. If the original position of the bushes is lost, then Land Rover special tools No. 204-532/1, 205-532/3 and 204-532/4 must be used to fit the new ones.

7.4b Use suitable spacers to press the balljoint into the arm

9 Bend up the bush flanges, and use a hacksaw to remove them **(see illustrations)**.

10 Press the bush(es) from place. Although in theory this can be achieved using suitable spacers and a sturdy bench vice, the bushes are very likely to be corroded into place. Consequently, the use of an hydraulic press is probably essential. Press the old bush out, and install the new bush using a suitable tubular spacer which bears only on the hard outer edge of the bush, not the bush rubber. Align the arrows on the new bushes with the previously-made marks on the upper arms. Fit the bushes to the previously-noted depth.

11 Refit the upper arm as described in Section 6.

Polybush polyurethane bushes

12 Bend up the bush flanges, and use a hacksaw to remove them **(see illustrations 7.9a and 7.9b)**.

13 Press the bush(es) from place. Although in theory this can be achieved using suitable spacers and a sturdy bench vice, the bushes are very likely to be corroded into place. Consequently, the use of an hydraulic press is probably essential.

14 Ensure the bore in the arm is clean and

7.5 Position the ends of the new circlip 90° to the balljoint flange cut-outs

7.9a Use a chisel to bend up the bush flanges ...

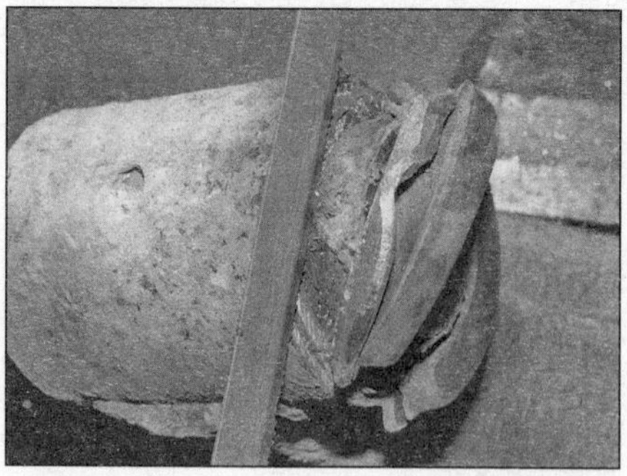

7.9b ... then remove the flanges with a hacksaw

7.15 Fit the bushes to the upper arm with the larger diameter flanges to the outside

7.19 Remove the lower arm balljoint circlip

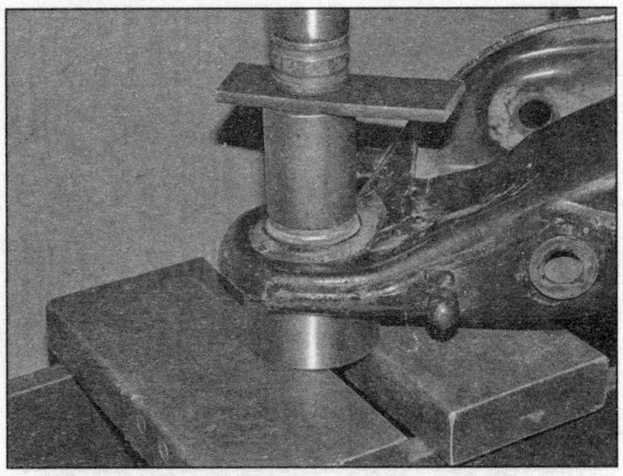
7.20 Press the balljoint from the arm

7.21 Press the new balljoint into the arm ...

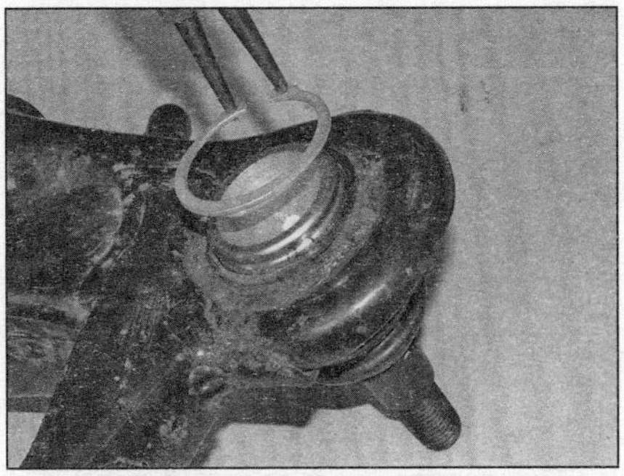
7.22 ... and secure it with the new circlip

free from burrs, etc. Use emery paper to remove all traces of rust, scale, oil and grease, as these will shorten the life of the new bush.

15 Apply a liberal coating of soapy water to the new bush, and using a vice, or G-clamp, press the new bush into place **(see illustration)**. If the bush is reluctant to fit, use a length of threaded rod, 2 large washers and 2 nuts to draw the bush into place.

16 Push the central metal bush into the polyurethane bush, again using a vice, clamp or if necessary the threaded rod, etc **(see illustrations 13.40a, 13.40b, 13.40c and 13.40d)**.

17 Refit the upper arm as described in Section 6.

Lower arm balljoint

18 Remove the lower arm as described in Section 6.

19 Remove the balljoint circlip **(see illustration)**.

20 Note its fitted position then, using a combination of spacers/tubes, press the balljoint from the arm **(see illustration)**. Note that Land Rover special tools may be available instead of using suitable spacers/tubes, etc.

21 Again using suitable spacers/tubes, press the new balljoint into position **(see illustration)**.

22 Secure the balljoint with a new circlip **(see illustration)**.

23 Refit the lower suspension arm as described in Section 6.

Lower arm pivot bushes

Note: *Two different procedures are described. One for when Land Rover bushes are used, and one for when Polybush polyurethane bushes are used.*

Land Rover bushes

24 Before raising the vehicle, use a spirit level type set-square, and make alignment marks through the lower arm rear bush mounting bolt head, and the lowest point on the circumference of the bush boss of the arm **(see illustration)**.

25 Remove the lower arm as described in Section 6.

26 Note the fitted positions of the bushes in the arm. Make a note of the fitted depth of the bushes. If the original position of the bushes is lost, then Land Rover special tools No. 204-535/3, 204-535/5, 205-536/3 and 204-536/1 must be used to fit the new ones.

27 Bend up the front bush flanges, and use a hacksaw to remove them **(see illustrations 7.9a and 7.9b)**.

28 Press the front bush from place. Although in theory this can be achieved using suitable spacers and a sturdy bench vice, the bushes are very likely to be corroded into place. Consequently, the use of an hydraulic press is probably essential.

29 Align the front bush, and using suitable spacers, press the new bush into place.

30 Press the rear bush from place. This is easiest using a hydraulic press, but can be achieved using suitable spacers and a sturdy bench vice. Note that Land Rover tools No. 204-535/1, 2, and 4 may be available for this task.

31 Make alignment guide lines on the installation tool (No. 204-535/3) as follows:

a) *Mark a centre line across the diameter of the tool.*

b) *Mark a line across the top surface, and lower surface of the tool, 3° to the left of the centre line* ***(see illustration)****.*

c) *Mark LH on the top surface, and RH on the lower surface.*

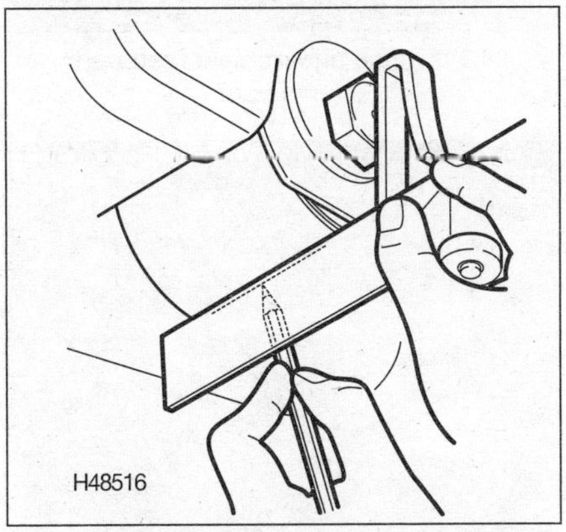

7.24 Mark a line on the lowest point of the bush, in line with the centre of the pivot bolt (arrowed)

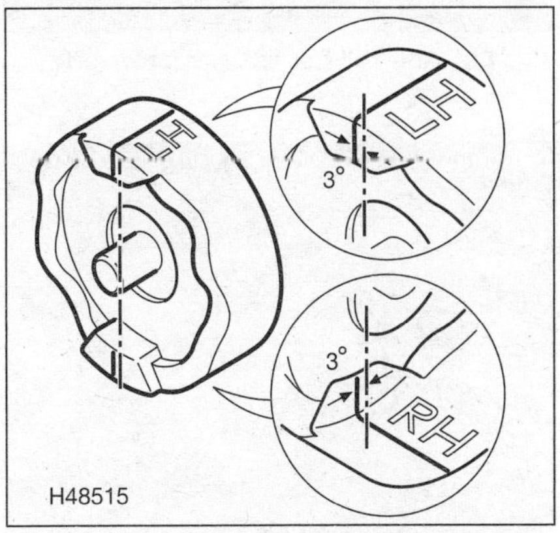

7.31 Mark a line 3° to the left of the centre line

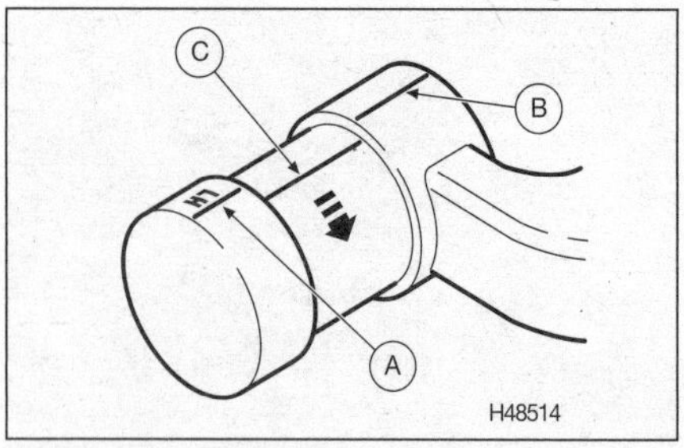

7.32 Align the LH or RH line (A) on the tool with the previously-made line on the arm (B), and mark a line (C) on the bush in line with the 3° line on the tool

32 Position the installation tool against the new rear bush, so the LH or RH line (LH for the left-hand side arm, RH for the right-hand side arm) is aligned with the previously-marked line on the arm's bush boss. Now draw a line across the new bush in line with the others **(see illustration)**.

33 Using a suitable spacer underneath, press the new rear bush into place.

34 Refit the lower arm as described in Section 6.

Polybush polyurethane bushes

35 Remove the lower arm as described in Section 6.

36 If removing the front bush, bend up the bush flanges, and use a hacksaw to remove them **(see illustrations 7.9a and 7.9b)**.

37 Press the bush(es) from place. Although in theory this can be achieved using suitable spacers and a sturdy bench vice, the bushes are very likely to be corroded into place. Consequently, the use of an hydraulic press is probably essential.

7.39 Fit the bushes to the lower arm with the larger diameter flanges to the outside

38 Ensure the bore in the arm is clean and free from burrs, etc. Use emery paper to remove all traces of rust, scale, oil and grease, as these will shorten the life of the new bush.

39 Apply a liberal coating of soapy water to the new bush, and using a vice, or G-clamp, press the new bush into place **(see illustration)**. If the bush is reluctant to fit, use a length of threaded rod, 2 large washers and 2 nuts to draw the bush into place.

40 Push the central metal bush into the polyurethane bush, again using a vice, clamp or if necessary the threaded rod, etc **(see illustrations 13.40a, 13.40b, 13.40c and 13.40d)**.

41 Refit the lower arm as described in Section 6.

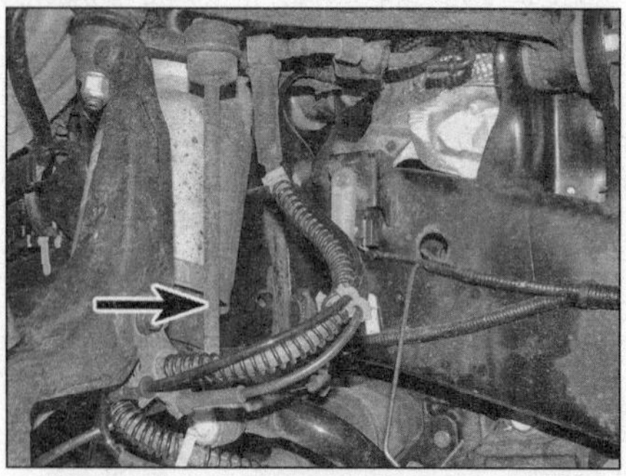

8.2 Anti-roll bar link rod (arrowed)

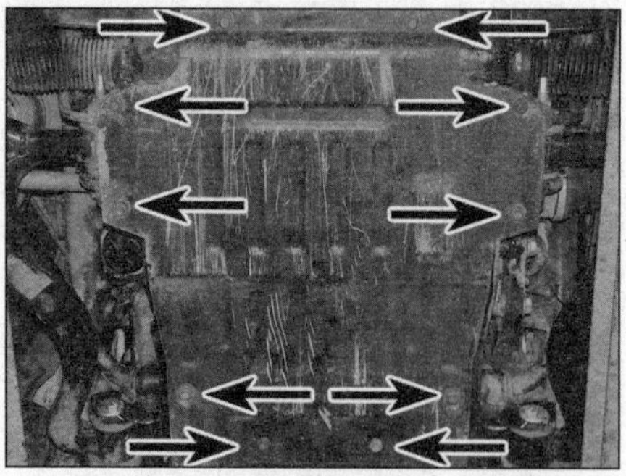

8.3 Engine undershield fasteners (arrowed)

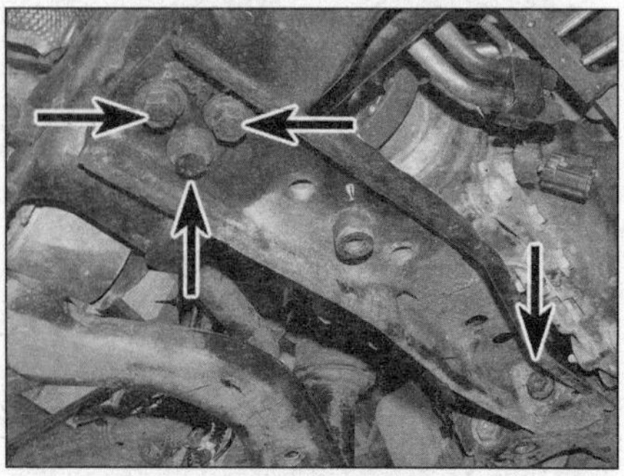

8.4 Undo the bolts (arrowed) and remove the crossmember

8.5 Anti-roll bar clamp nuts (arrowed)

8 Front anti-roll bar – removal and refitting

Removal

1 Slacken the roadwheel nuts, raise the front of the vehicle and support it securely on axle stands (see *Jacking and vehicle support*). Remove the front roadwheel.

2 Undo the nuts securing the ends of the anti-roll bar to the link rods **(see illustration)**. Discard the nuts – new ones must be fitted.

3 Undo the fasteners and remove the engine undershield **(see illustration)**.

4 Undo the 4 bolts/nut and remove the front axle crossmember **(see illustration)**.

5 Unscrew the nuts securing the mounting clamps to the vehicle body, then manoeuvre the bar through the left-hand side wheel arch **(see illustration)**. Discard the nuts – new ones must be fitted.

Refitting

6 Refitting is a reversal of removal. Tighten all fasteners to the specified torque.

9 Front anti-roll bar connecting link – removal and refitting

Removal

1 Slacken the roadwheel nuts, raise the front of the vehicle and support it securely on axle stands (see *Jacking and vehicle support*). Remove the front roadwheel.

2 Undo the nuts securing the ends of the anti-roll bar to the link rods and the upper arms **(see illustration 4.6)**. Discard the nuts – new ones must be fitted.

Refitting

3 Refitting is a reversal of removal. Tighten all fasteners to the specified torque.

10 Rear strut – removal and refitting

Note: *Shock absorbers must ALWAYS be renewed in pairs, even if only one appears to be defective, in order to preserve safe handling.*

Removal

1 Slacken the roadwheel nuts, raise the rear of the vehicle and support it securely on axle stands (see *Jacking and vehicle support*). Remove the rear roadwheels.

Coil spring suspension

2 Slacken the suspension strut upper mounting nuts.

3 Place a trolley jack under the lower suspension arm on the relevant side.

10.9 Rear air spring/strut lower mounting bolt (arrowed)

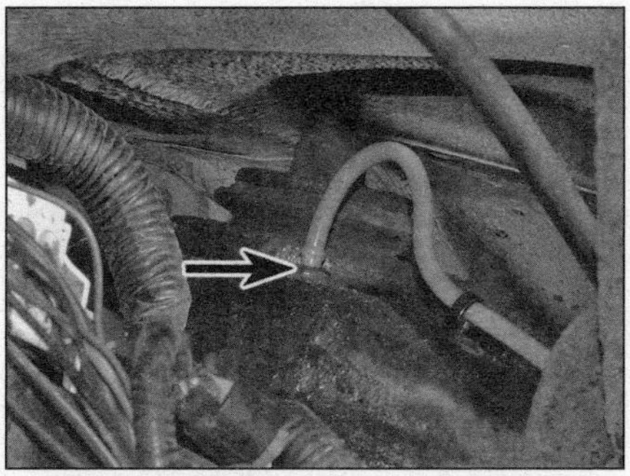

10.10 Undo the air supply pipe gland nut (arrowed) on the top of the strut

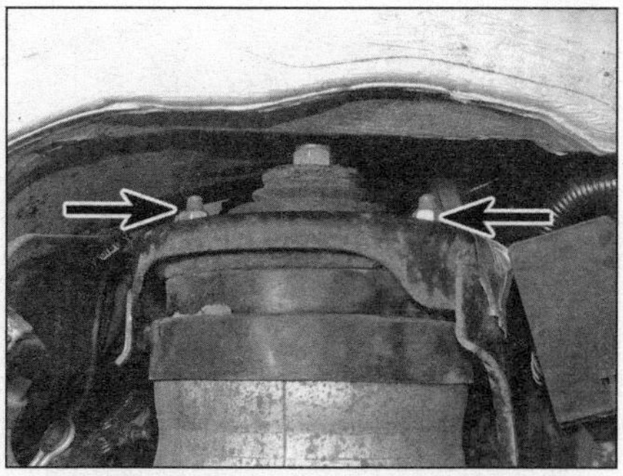

10.12 Strut upper mounting nuts (two arrowed – one hidden)

4 Undo the nut and withdraw the suspension strut lower mounting bolt.

5 Completely unscrew the 3 upper mounting nuts and manoeuvre the suspension strut from position.

Air suspension

Note: *Before any part of the pressurised air circuit can be worked on, it's essential to depressurise the system – the pressure in the system can be in excess of 16 bar (230 psi). Land Rover recommend that this must be carried out using their dedicated test equipment (T4). It is possible to depressurise the system without T4 by very slowly undoing the air pipe gland nut on the air spring* ***(see illustration 10.10)*** *to allow the pressure within to slowly escape. If in any doubt at all, entrust any work involving the pressurised air circuit to a Land Rover dealer or suitably-equipped specialist.*

Warning: Do not attempt to drive the vehicle with the air suspension system depressurised.

6 Disconnect the battery negative lead as described in Chapter 5, Section 4.

7 Remove the spare wheel from under the rear of the vehicle.

8 Depressurise the air suspension system as described above.

9 Undo the nut and withdrawn the suspension strut lower mounting bolt **(see illustration)**.

10 Fully undo the gland nut, and detach the air pipe from the top of the strut **(see illustration)**. Remove the Voss connector (consisting of a split olive and gland nut with integral O-ring seal), and discard it – a new one must be fitted **(see illustration 2.13b)**. Plug/cover the openings to prevent contamination.

11 Disconnect the active damping wiring plug (where fitted) from the top of each strut.

12 Undo the 3 upper mounting nuts and manoeuvre the suspension strut from position **(see illustration)**. Note that it's quite likely the nuts are corroded in place. Soak them with releasing fluid before attempting to undo them.

Refitting

13 Refitting is a reversal of the removal procedure, noting the following points:

a) Ensure the strut and body mating faces are clean.

b) Tighten all fasteners to their specified torque where given.

c) On air spring models, fit a new Voss connector to the pipe.

d) Start the engine to repressurise the air spring system (where applicable).

11 Rear strut – overhaul

Coil spring strut

Note: *Suitable coil spring compressor tools will be required for this operation.*

1 Remove the rear suspension strut as described in Section 10.

2 Fit suitable spring compressors to the coil spring, and compress the spring sufficiently to enable the upper mounting to be turned by hand.

Warning: Ensure that the coil spring is compressed sufficiently to remove all the tension from the upper mounting, before attempting to remove the piston rod nut.

3 Unscrew the nut securing the strut piston rod to the upper mounting, while counterholding the piston with a suitable Allen key. Discard the nut – a new one must be fitted.

4 Withdraw the washer, mounting plate, bush, spring seat, spacer, then withdraw the spring, complete with the compressors **(see illustration)**.

5 Withdraw the dust cover and bump rubber.

6 Make alignment marks between the rubber seat and the mounting plate, and remove the seat and spacer from the mounting.

7 With the strut assembly now dismantled, examine all the components for wear, damage or deformation. Renew any components as necessary.

8 Examine the strut body for signs of fluid leakage or damage, and the piston rod for signs of pitting or scoring. If there is any visible sign of wear or damage to the strut, renewal is necessary.

9 If any doubt exists about the condition of the coil spring, carefully remove the spring compressors, and check the spring for distortion and signs of cracking. Renew the spring if it is damaged or distorted, or if there is any doubt about its condition.

Warning: Coil springs are classified by their height when under load – this is indicated by a coloured paint marking on the side of the coil windings. All coil springs fitted to the vehicle must be of the same classification to ensure the correct ride height.

10 Begin reassembly by refitting the dust cover and bump rubber.

11 Ensure that the coil spring is compressed sufficiently to enable the upper mounting components to be fitted, then fit the spring over the piston rod, ensuring that the lower end of the spring is correctly located in the recess on the lower spring seat. Note that the end of the spring with the 'close coils' is fitted at the top.

12 Refit the rubber seat and spacer to the mounting plate, ensuring the previously-made marks are aligned.

13 Locate the upper spring seat over the piston rod, then refit the upper mounting.

14 Fit the new piston rod top nut, then tighten the nut to the specified torque, counterholding the piston rod in a manner similar to that used during dismantling. Note that a suitable crows-foot adapter or flange-drive socket (Vortex) will be required to tighten the piston rod top nut to the specified torque.

15 Remove the spring compressors and refit the strut to the car as described in Section 10.

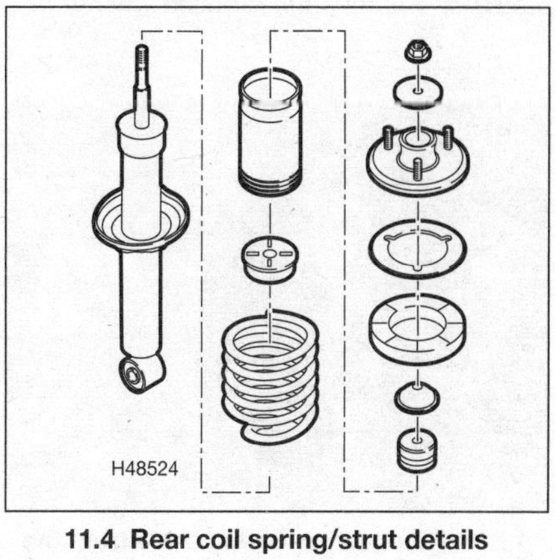

11.4 Rear coil spring/strut details

11.17a Cut through the retaining straps ...

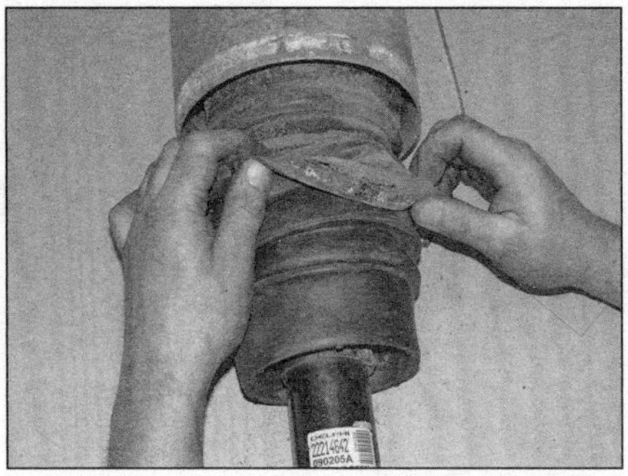
11.17b ... and remove the rubber gaiter

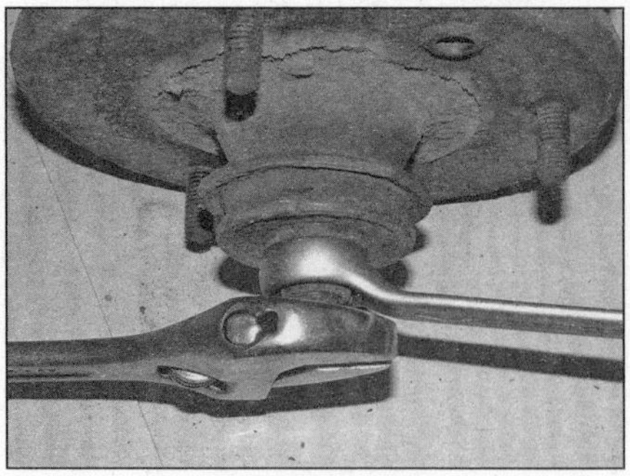
11.18 Counterhold the piston rod and undo the nut

Air spring

16 Remove the suspension strut as described in Section 10.

17 Remove and discard the straps, then remove the gaiter from the spring **(see illustrations)**.

18 Unscrew the nut securing the strut piston rod to the upper mounting, while counterholding the piston with a suitable spanner **(see illustration)**. Discard the nut – a new one must be fitted.

19 Remove the rebound washer, and followed by the O-ring seals and spacers **(see illustrations)**. Discard the O-ring seals – new ones must be fitted.

20 Prise out the nylon retaining pin on the side of the air spring **(see illustration 3.17)**.

21 Using a soft-faced mallet/hammer, carefully tap the sleeve support upwards to release it **(see illustration 3.20)**. Do not unroll the sleeve.

22 Note its fitted position, then remove the bump stop and spring aid **(see illustration)**.

23 Remove the 2 O-ring seals from the lower seal carrier **(see illustration)**. Discard the O-ring seals – new ones must be fitted.

24 Apply a little silicone-based oil (Loctite 8021) to the new O-ring seals, then fit them to the seal carrier.

25 Fit the bump stop and spring aid.

26 Align the sleeve support location tag with the cut-out in the spring seat, then press the sleeve down into position **(see illustration)**.

27 Refit the spacer with the new O-ring seals, then refit the rebound washer **(see illustrations 11.19a and 11.19b)**.

28 Fit a new piston rod nut but only lightly tighten it at this stage.

29 The strut must now be connected to a tyre inflation airline/pump and pressurised to 2.0 bar (29 psi) to seat the spring over the O-ring seals. Land Rover tool No. 204-538 may be available to connect the spring to the hose. In the absence of the tool, use an air gun attached to a compressed air supply **(see illustration)**.

30 Tighten the piston rod nut to the specified torque.

31 Secure the sleeve with the rivet supplied in the overhaul kit (replacing the nylon pin).

32 Now pressurise the strut to 4.0 bar (58 psi) to check for leaks. If a leak is suspected, immerse the pressurised strut in water and identify the source of the leak. Dismantle the strut and rectify as necessary.

11.19a Remove the rebound washer ...

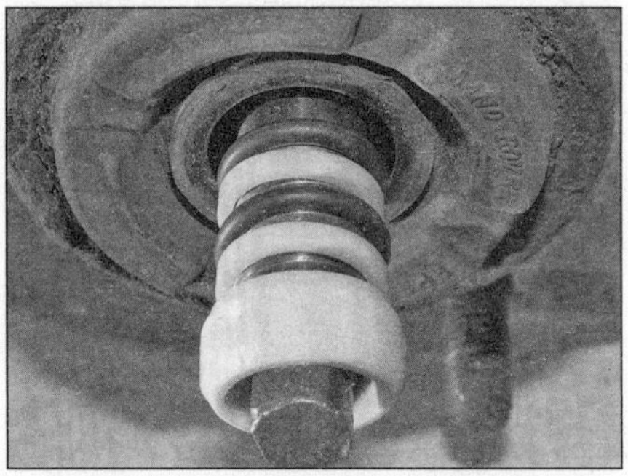
11.19b ... followed by the spacers and O-ring seals

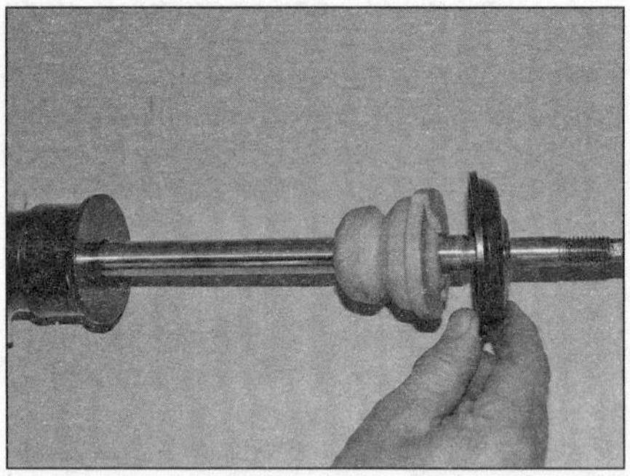
11.22 Remove the bump stop and spring aid

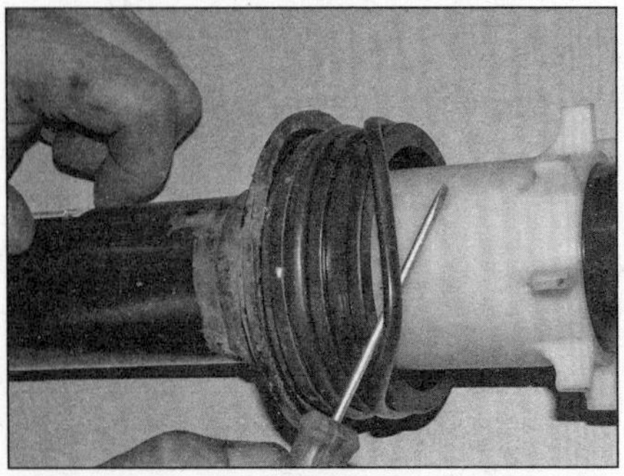
11.23 Remove the O-ring seals from the lower seal carrier

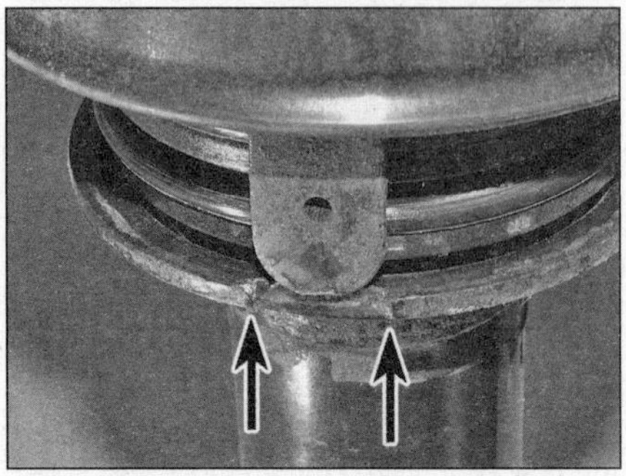
11.26 Align the location tag with the cut-out (arrowed)

11.29 Apply 2.0 bar of compressed air to seat the spring over the O-ring seals

11.34a Slide the new gaiter over the strut ...

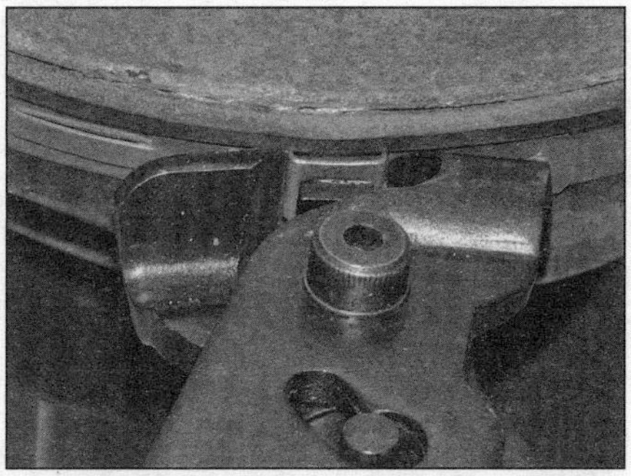

11.34b ... and secure it with the new straps

33 Release the air pressure, remove the special tool (or equivalent).

34 Fit the gaiter and secure it using the new straps **(see illustrations)**.

35 Refit the strut as described in Section 10.

12 Rear suspension arms/links – removal and refitting

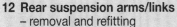

Upper arm

Removal

1 On models with air suspension, disconnect the battery negative lead as described in Chapter 5, Section 4. This is to prevent the system attempting to level the suspension when the vehicle is raised or lowered.

2 Chock the front wheels, then jack up the rear of the vehicle and support it securely on axle stands (see *Jacking and vehicle support*). Remove the relevant rear roadwheel.

3 Unclip the brake pipe/hose and wheel speed sensor wiring harness from the retaining clips on the upper arm.

4 Carefully prise the height sensor link arm (where fitted) from the bracket on the upper arm **(see illustration 16.2)**.

5 Pull the brake pad wear sensor from the brake pads (where applicable), and unclip the wiring harness. Refer to Chapter 10, Section 5, if necessary.

6 Make alignment marks between the upper arm-to-hub carrier bolt eccentric washer and the upper arm **(see illustration)**.

7 Undo and remove the upper arm pivot bolts, and the arm-to-hub carrier bolt, then manoeuvre the arm from place **(see illustration)**.

Refitting

8 Position the upper arm, insert the pivot bolts and fit the new nuts, but only finger-tighten them at this stage.

9 Using a jack under the lower arm/hub carrier, raise the assembly until the distance between the centre of the driveshaft and the highest point of the wheel arch aperture is 485 mm **(see illustration)**.

10 Refit the upper arm-to-hub carrier bolt, align the previously-made marks, and tighten it to the specified torque.

12.6 Make alignment marks between the pivot bolt eccentric head/washer and the upper arm (arrowed)

11 Tighten the upper arm pivot bolts to the specified torques.

12 The remainder of refitting is a reversal of removal. Have the wheel alignment checked at the earliest opportunity.

Lower arm

Removal

13 On models with air suspension, disconnect the battery negative lead as described in Chapter 5, Section 4. This is to prevent the system attempting to level the suspension when the vehicle is raised or lowered.

14 Chock the front wheels, then jack up the rear of the vehicle and support it securely on axle stands (see *Jacking and vehicle support*). Remove the relevant rear roadwheel.

15 Counterhold the balljoint, then undo the retaining nut and detach the anti-roll bar link rod from the lower arm. Discard the nut – a new one must be fitted.

16 Remove the suspension strut lower mounting bolt/nut.

17 Unclip the parking brake cable from the retaining clips on the lower arm.

18 Slacken the lower arm pivot bolts and the bolt securing the arm to the hub carrier **(see illustrations)**. Remove the bolts and manoeuvre the lower arm from position.

Refitting

19 Position the lower arm and insert the pivot bolts, but only lightly tighten them at this stage.

12.7 Rear upper arm pivot bolts (arrowed)

12.9 The distance between the centre of the driveshaft and the highest point of the wheel arch aperture should be 485 mm

12.18a Rear lower arm pivot bolts (arrowed)

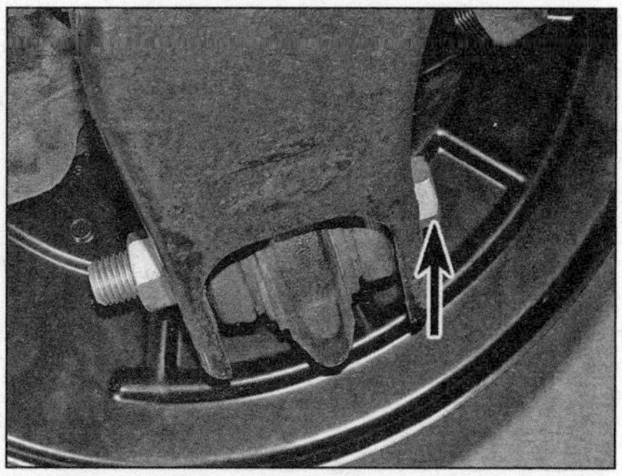

12.18b Rear lower arm-to-hub carrier bolt (arrowed)

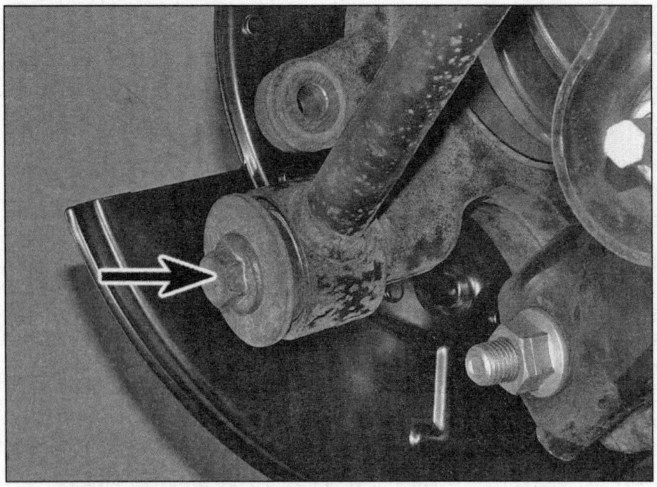

12.26a The toe link is secured by a bolt at the outer end (arrowed) ...

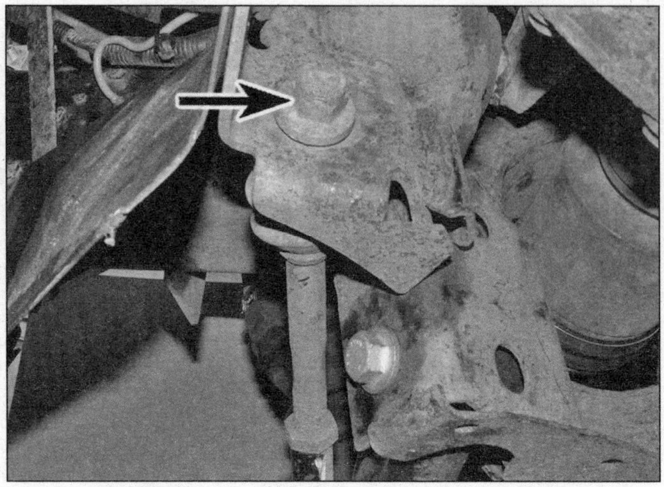

12.26b ... and a nut (arrowed) at the inner end

20 Connect the lower arm to the hub carrier, and tighten the bolt to the specified torque.
21 Reconnect the suspension strut to the lower arm, insert the bolt/nut and tighten them to the specified torque.
22 Using a jack under the lower arm/hub carrier, raise the assembly until the distance between the centre of the driveshaft and the highest point of the wheel arch aperture is 485 mm **(see illustration 12.9)**.
23 Tighten the lower arm pivot bolts to the specified torque.
24 The remainder of refitting is a reversal of removal. Have the wheel alignment checked at the earliest opportunity.

Toe link

Removal

25 Chock the front wheels, then jack up the rear of the vehicle and support it securely on axle stands (see *Jacking and vehicle support*). Remove the relevant rear roadwheel.
26 The toe link is secured by a bolt at its outer end, and a nut at the inner. Undo the bolts and nut, then manoeuvre the toe link from place **(see illustrations)**. Discard the nut – a new one must be fitted. Note that Land Rover state the bolt must not be used more then 5 times.

Refitting

27 Ensure the anti-rotation tang is fully seated in the body bracket, then refit the toe link. Only lightly tighten the new retaining nut at this stage.
28 Land Rover insist that a M14 x 2.0 tap is run though the lower arm mounting hole in the hub carrier. Remove any debris from the hole.
29 Refit the lower arm to the hub carrier, insert the new bolt and tighten it to the specified torque.
30 Set the gap between the toe link rubber gaiter and the body bracket to 10.0 mm **(see illustration)**. Tighten the retaining nut to the specified torque.
31 The remainder of refitting is a reversal of removal. Have the wheel alignment checked at the earliest opportunity.

13 Rear suspension arms bushes and balljoints – renewal

Upper arm balljoint

1 Remove the hub carrier as described in Section 14.
2 Note its fitted position then, using a combination of spacers/tubes, press the balljoint from the hub carrier **(see illustration)**. Note that Land Rover special tools No. 204-525/1/2/3 may be available instead of using suitable spacers/tubes, etc.
3 Position the machined face of the balljoint against the spacer/tube/tool and, again using suitable spacers/tubes, press the new balljoint into position **(see illustration)**. Land Rover special tools No. 204-525/1/2/3 may be available instead of using suitable spacers/ tubes, etc.
4 Refit the hub carrier as described in Section 14.

Upper arm pivot bushes

Note: *Two different procedures are described. One for when Land Rover bushes are used, and one for when Polybush polyurethane bushes are used.*
5 Remove the upper arm as described in Section 12.

Land Rover bushes

6 Note the fitted positions of the bushes in the arm. Make alignment marks between the bushes and the upper arm. Make a note of the fitted depth of the bushes. If the original position of the bushes is lost, then Land Rover

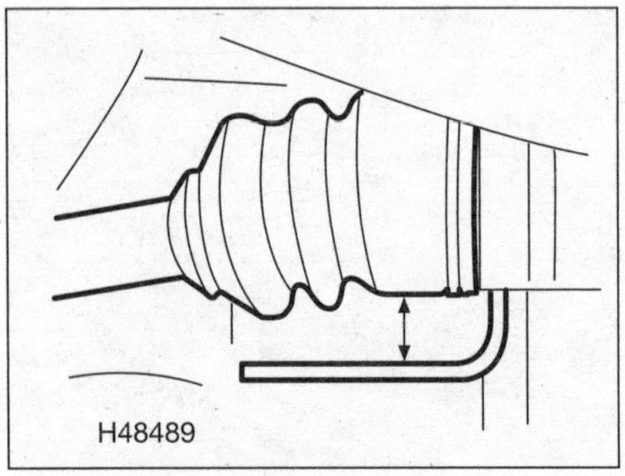

12.30 Set the distance between the toe link gaiter and the upper surface of the bracket to 10.0 mm

13.2 Use spacers and a threaded rod to withdraw the balljoint from the hub carrier

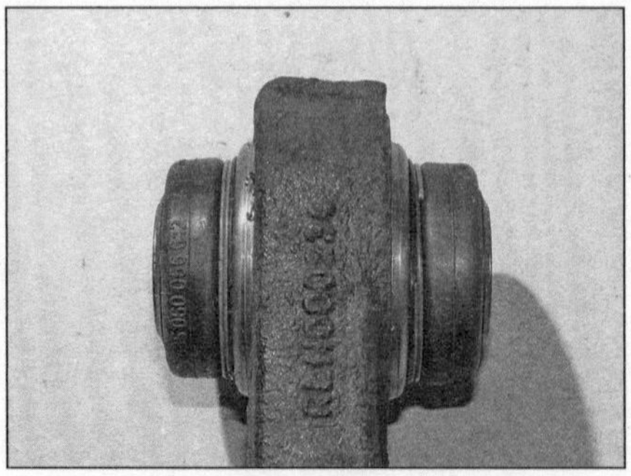

13.3 Press the new balljoint into position in the hub carrier

special tools No. 204-527 and 204-528 *must* be used to fit the new ones.

7 Press the bush(es) from place. Although in theory this can be achieved using suitable spacers and a sturdy bench vice, the bushes are very likely to be corroded into place. Consequently, the use of an hydraulic press is probably essential. Press the old bush out, and install the new bush using a suitable tubular spacer which bears only on the hard outer edge of the bush, not the bush rubber. Align the new bushes with the previously-made marks on the upper arms. Fit the bushes to the previously-noted depth.

8 Refit the upper arm as described in Section 12.

Polybush polyurethane bushes

9 Press the bush(es) from place. Although in theory this can be achieved using suitable spacers and a sturdy bench vice, the bushes are very likely to be corroded into place. Consequently, the use of an hydraulic press is probably essential.

10 Ensure the bore in the arm is clean and free from burrs, etc. Use emery paper to remove all traces of rust, scale, oil and grease, as these will shorten the life of the new bush.

11 Apply a liberal coating of soapy water to the new bush, and using a vice, or G-clamp, press the new bush into place **(see illustration)**. Ensure the larger diameter flanges of the new bushes are fitted to the outside. If the bush is reluctant to fit, use a length of threaded rod, 2 large washers and 2 nuts to draw the bush into place.

12 Push the central metal bush into the polyurethane bush, again using a vice, clamp or if necessary the threaded rod, etc **(see illustrations 13.40a, 13.40b, 13.40c and 13.40d)**.

13 Refit the upper arm as described in Section 12.

Lower arm balljoint

14 Apply the handbrake, and loosen the nuts on the relevant rear roadwheel. Jack up the rear of the vehicle and support it securely on axle stands (see *Jacking and vehicle support*). Remove the relevant roadwheel.

15 Using a chisel or punch, unstake the driveshaft nut, then unscrew it from the driveshaft. Assistance may be required, the nut is very tight. Discard the nut, a new one must be fitted. **Note:** *The driveshaft nut is very tight. It may be prudent to prise out the centre of the roadwheel, refit it, and lower the vehicle to the ground. Then insert the socket through the centre of the wheel and undo the nut.*

16 Undo the bolt securing the toe link to the hub carrier. Note that Land Rover state the bolt must not be used more then 5 times.

17 Unclip the parking brake cable from the hub carrier.

18 Undo the bolt/nut securing the lower arm to the hub carrier **(see illustration 12.18b)**. Take care not to damage the rubber seal. Discard the nut – a new one must be fitted.

19 Using a suitable tool, press the end of the driveshaft from the hub. A special Land Rover tool (No. 204-506/1, 205-506/3 and 204-506/5) is available for this task. **Note:** *Use of a hammer to force the shaft from the hub will almost certainly result in damage. Take great care not to damage the end of the shaft.*

20 Pull the lower part of the hub carrier outwards to access the balljoint, then remove the circlip.

21 Note its fitted position, then using a combination of spacers/tubes/threaded rod/ nuts, draw the balljoint from the hub carrier. Note that Land Rover special tools No. 204-516/1/3/4 may be available instead of using suitable spacers/tubes, etc.

22 Position the balljoint against the chamfered side of the hole in the hub carrier then, again using suitable spacers/tubes, press the new balljoint into position **(see illustration)**. Land Rover special tools No. 204-516/2/3/4 may be available instead of using suitable spacers/ tubes, etc.

23 Secure the balljoint with a new circlip.

24 Apply a little anti-seize grease to the splines, then refit the end of the driveshaft into the hub assembly. If necessary use Land Rover tool No. 204-506-01, 204-506/1 and 204-506/5 to pull the end of the shaft through the hub.

25 Reconnect the lower arm to the hub carrier, insert the bolt and tighten the new nut to the specified torque.

26 Resecure the parking brake cable.

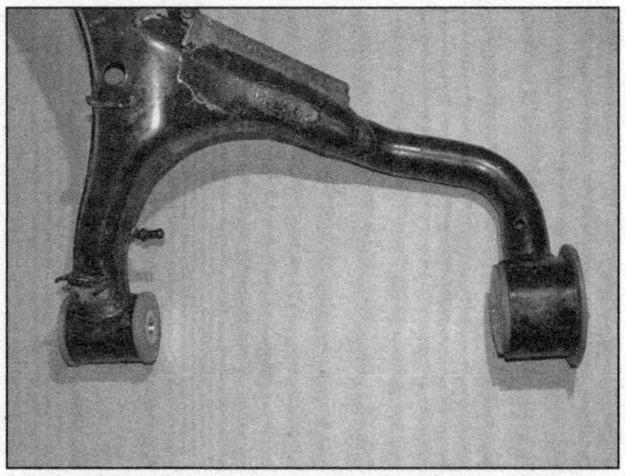

13.11 Fit the new bushes with the larger diameter flanges to the outside

27 Reconnect the toe link to the hub carrier and tighten the bolt to the specified torque. Note that Land Rover state that the bolt must not be used more than 5 times. Each time the bolt is refitted, make a centre punch mark on the bolt head.

28 Tighten the driveshaft nut to the specified torque then 'stake' the nut to the shaft **(see illustration)**. Assistance may be required – the torque for the nut is very high. If necessary refit the roadwheel, then lower the vehicle to the ground and tighten the nut. It will then be necessary to raise the vehicle, remove the roadwheel and stake the nut.

29 The remainder of refitting is a reversal of removal.

Lower arm pivot bushes

Note: *Two different procedures are described. One for when Land Rover bushes are used, and one for when Polybush polyurethane bushes are used.*

Land Rover bushes

30 Remove the lower arm as described in Section 12.

31 Note the fitted positions and fitted depth of the bushes.

32 Bend up the bush flanges, and use a hacksaw to remove them **(see illustrations 7.9a and 7.9b)**.

33 Press the bush(es) from place **(see illustration)**. Although in theory this can be achieved using suitable spacers and a sturdy bench vice, the bushes are very likely to be

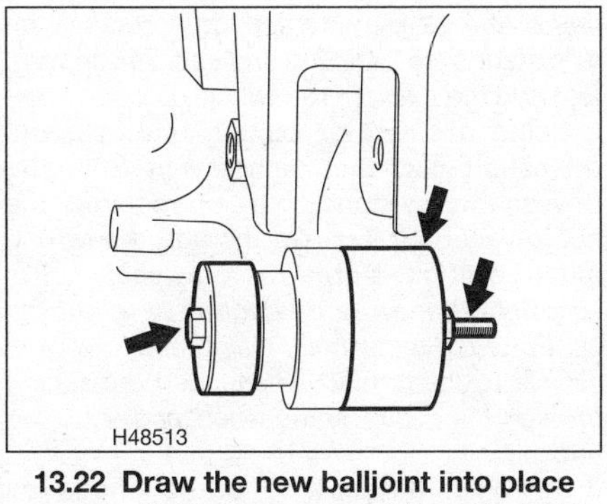

13.22 Draw the new balljoint into place using suitable spacers and threaded rod (arrowed)

13.28 Use a punch to 'stake' the nut to the driveshaft

13.33 Press the old bushes from the arm

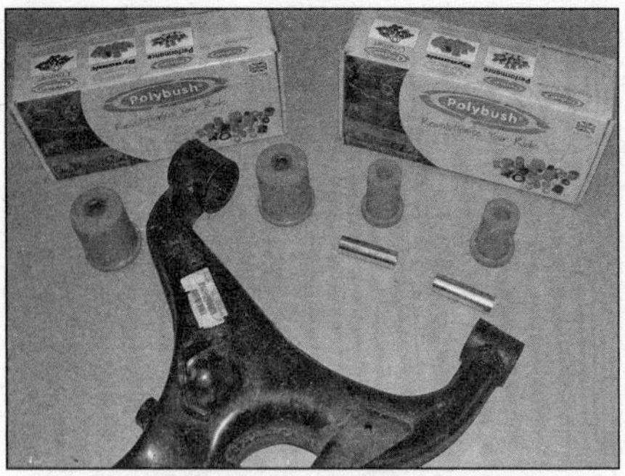

13.39a The Polybush kit comprises of upper and lower arm polyurethane bushes, with central metal bushes

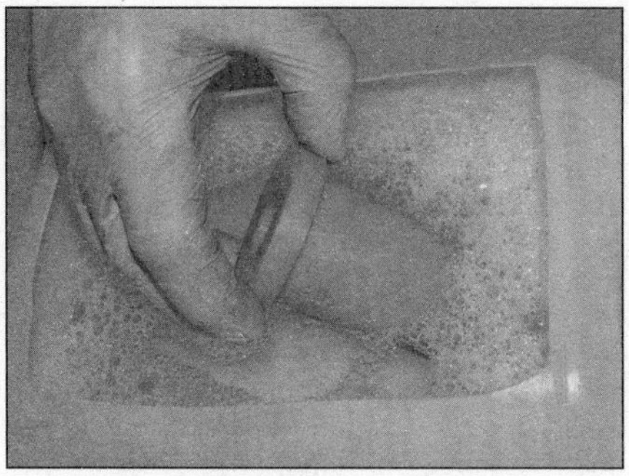

13.39b Apply a liberal coating of soapy water ...

13.39c ... then position the new bushes with the large diameter flanges to the outside ...

13.39d ... and press them into place using a G-clamp (or similar)

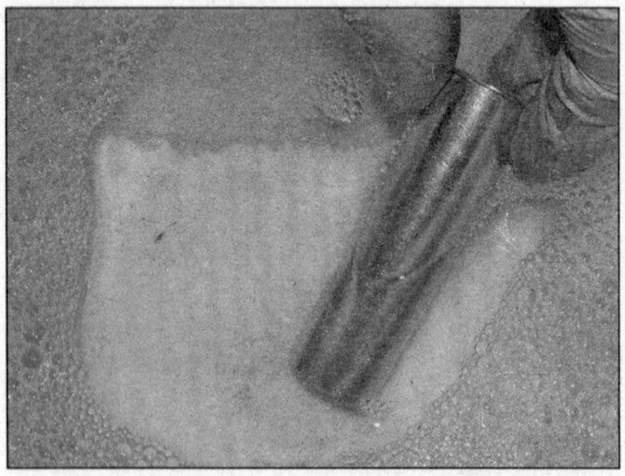

13.40a Apply some soapy water to the central metal bush ...

13.40b ... position it in the bush ...

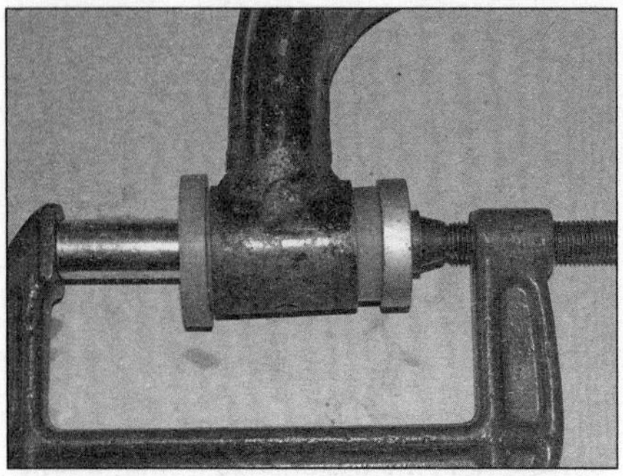

13.40c ... and press it into place

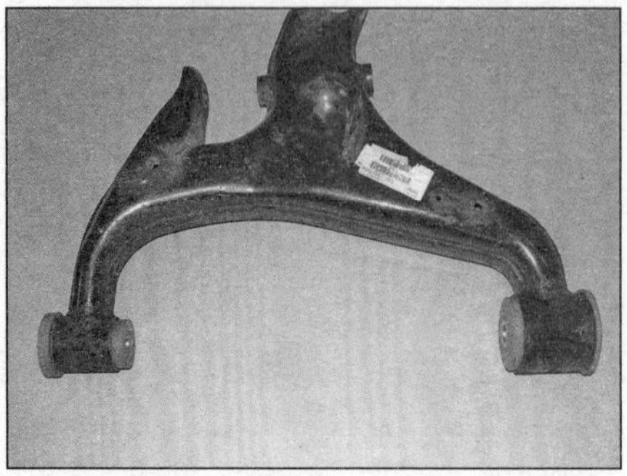

13.40d Final fitted positions of the new bushes

corroded into place. Consequently, the use of an hydraulic press is probably essential. Press the old bush out, and install the new bush using a suitable tubular spacer which bears only on the hard outer edge of the bush, not the bush rubber. Fit the bushes to the previously-noted depth. Land Rover special tools No. 204-540, 204-532 and 204-526 may be available instead of using suitable spacers/tubes, etc.

34 Refit the lower arm as described in Section 12.

Polybush polyurethane bushes

35 Remove the lower arm as described in Section 12.

36 If removing the rear bush, bend up the bush flanges, and use a hacksaw to remove them **(see illustrations 7.9a and 7.9b)**.

37 Press the bush(es) from place **(see illustration 13.33)**. Although in theory this can be achieved using suitable spacers and a sturdy bench vice, the bushes are very likely to be corroded into place. Consequently, the use of an hydraulic press is probably essential.

38 Ensure the bore in the arm is clean and free from burrs, etc. Use emery paper to remove all traces of rust, scale, oil and grease, as these will shorten the life of the new bush.

39 Apply a liberal coating of soapy water to the new bush, and using a vice, or G-clamp, press the new bush into place **(see illustrations)**. If the bush is reluctant to fit, use a length of threaded rod, 2 large washers and 2 nuts to draw the bush into place.

40 Push the central metal bush into the polyurethane bush, again using a vice, clamp or if necessary the threaded rod, etc **(see illustrations)**.

41 Refit the lower arm as described in Section 12.

14 Rear hub carrier – removal and refitting

Removal

1 Apply the handbrake, and loosen the nuts on the relevant rear roadwheel. Jack up the rear of the vehicle and support it securely on axle stands (see *Jacking and vehicle support*). Remove the relevant roadwheel.

2 Using a chisel or punch, un-stake the driveshaft nut, then unscrew it from the driveshaft. Assistance may be required, the nut is very tight. Discard the nut, a new one must be fitted. **Note:** *The driveshaft nut is very tight. It may be prudent to prise out the centre of the roadwheel, refit it, and lower the vehicle to the ground. Then insert the socket through the centre of the wheel and undo the nut.*

3 Remove the parking brake shoes as described in Chapter 10, Section 14.

4 Unclip the parking brake cable from the

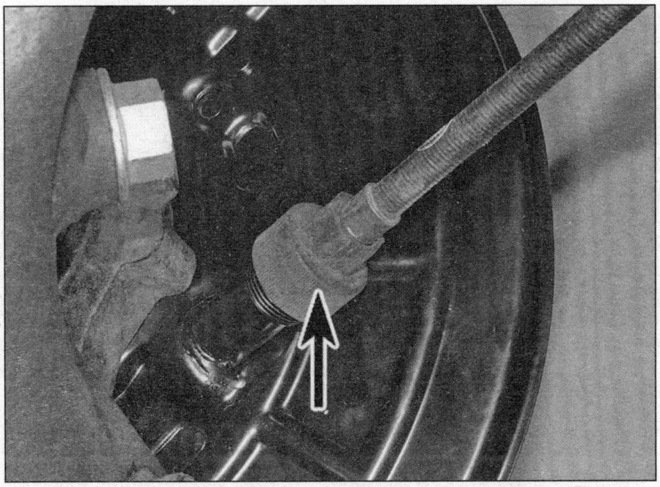
14.4 Unscrew the parking brake collar (arrowed) from the backplate

14.5 Wheel speed sensor retaining bolt (arrowed)

hub carrier, and detach it from the brake disc backplate **(see illustration)**.

5 Undo the retaining bolt, pull the wheel speed sensor from the hub carrier, and unclip the wiring harness from the bracket on the carrier **(see illustration)**.

6 Undo the bolt securing the toe link to the hub carrier. Note that Land Rover state the bolt must not be used more then 5 times.

7 Undo the bolt/nut securing the lower arm to the hub carrier **(see illustration 12.18b)**. Take care not to damage the rubber seal. Discard the nut – a new one must be fitted.

8 Using a suitable tool, press the end of the driveshaft from the hub. A special Land Rover tool (No. 204-506/1, 205-506/3 and 204-506/5) is available for this task. **Note:** *Use of a hammer to force the shaft from the hub will almost certainly result in damage. Take great care not to damage the end of the shaft.*

9 Make alignment marks between the upper arm-to-hub carrier bolt eccentric washer and the upper arm **(see illustration 12.6)**. Remove the bolt/nut. Discard the nut – a new one must be fitted.

10 Manoeuvre the hub carrier from position.

Refitting

11 Apply a little anti-seize grease to the splines, then refit the end of the driveshaft into the hub assembly. If necessary use Land Rover tool No. 204-506-01, 204-506/1 and 204-506/5 to pull the end of the shaft through the hub. Align the hub carrier with the ends of the suspension arms as the driveshaft is refitted.

12 Insert the upper arm-to-hub carrier bolt, aligning the previously-made marks on the eccentric washer and the arm, then tighten the new nut to the specified torque.

13 Insert the lower arm-to-hub carrier bolt and tighten it to the specified torque.

14 Reconnect the toe link to the hub carrier and tighten the bolt to the specified torque. Note that Land Rover state that the bolt must not be used more than 5 times. Each time the bolt is refitted, make a centre punch mark on the bolt head.

15 Tighten the new driveshaft nut to the specified torque, then 'stake' the nut to the shaft **(see illustration 13.28)**. Assistance may be required – the torque for the nut is very high. If necessary refit the roadwheel, then lower the vehicle to the ground and tighten the nut. It will then be necessary to raise the vehicle, remove the roadwheel and stake the nut.

16 The remainder of refitting is a reversal of removal. Have the wheel alignment checked at the earliest opportunity.

15 Rear hub bearing – renewal

Note: *Various special tools, including a hydraulic press will be required for this operation (see text). If the necessary tools are not available, the assembly should be taken to a suitably-equipped engineering works for renewal of the bearing.*

1 Remove the hub carrier as described in Section 14.

2 Press the wheel hub flange from the bearing, together with the bearing inner race. Note that the inner race must be removed from the hub flange **(see illustration)**.

3 Undo the 3 screws and remove the disc backplate from the hub carrier **(see illustration)**.

4 Extract the bearing retaining circlip from the hub carrier **(see illustration)**.

5 Mount the hub carrier on the press bed and press the bearing out of the hub carrier. Note that the bearing must be pressed to the outside of the carrier. The bearing can only be removed in one direction.

6 Before installing the new bearing, thoroughly clean the bearing location in the hub carrier.

7 Fit the new bearing from the outboard

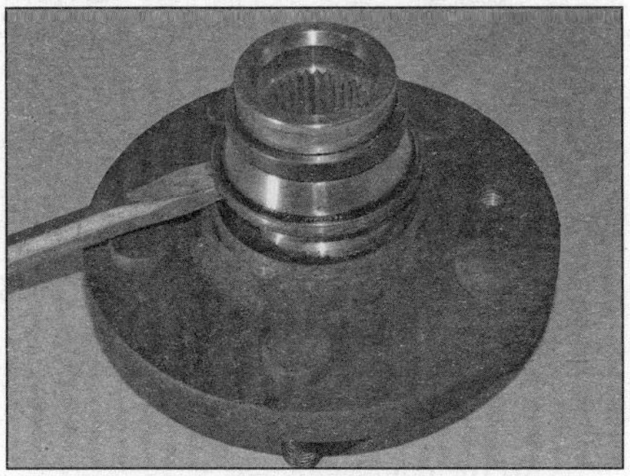
15.2 Carefully remove the inner race from the hub flange

15.3 Undo the screws (arrowed) and remove the backplate

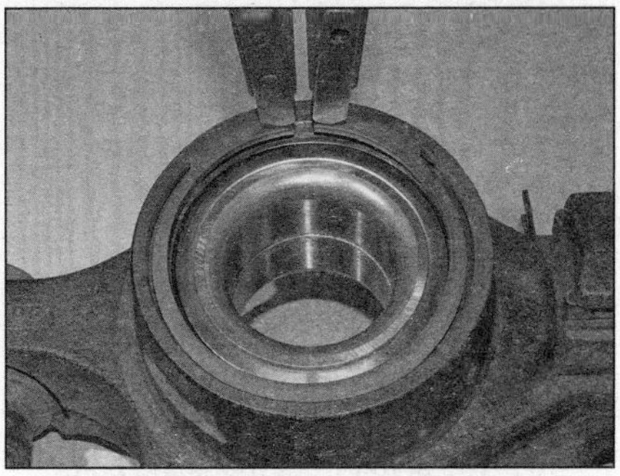
15.4 Extract the bearing circlip

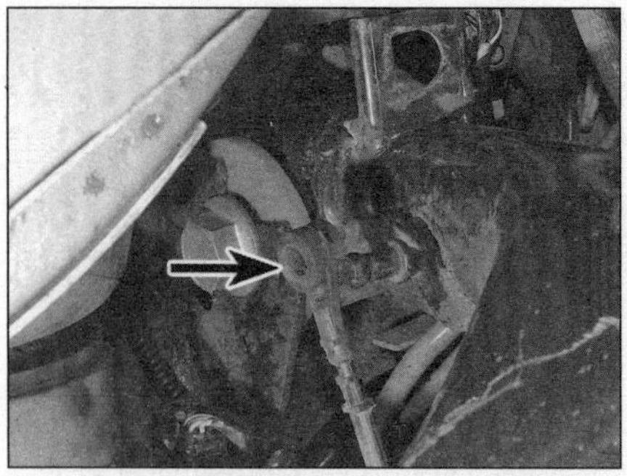
16.2 Pull the sensor link arm (arrowed) from the bracket

16.3 Undo the screws (arrowed) and remove the height sensor

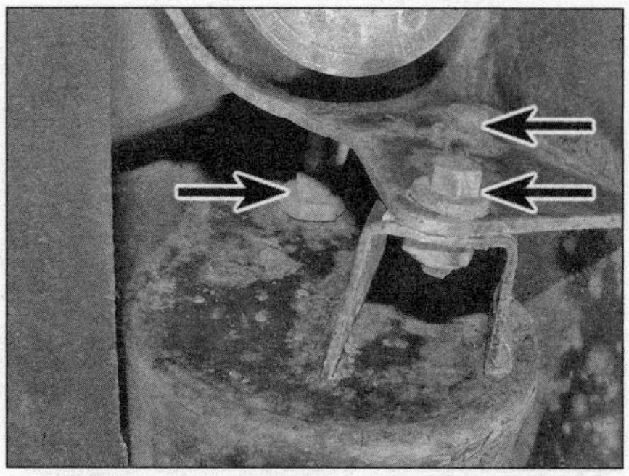
16.8 Reservoir air pipe gland nut and rear mounting bolts (arrowed)

side of the hub carrier and press it fully into position, applying pressure only to the bearing outer race.

8 Fit the bearing retaining circlip to its groove in the hub carrier.

9 Refit the backplate and tighten the retaining screws securely.

10 Refit the parking brake shoes assembly to the backplate as described in Chapter 10, Section 14.

11 Suitably support the bearing inner race on the press bed and press the wheel hub into the bearing.

12 On completion, check that the wheel hub rotates freely in the bearing without resistance or roughness.

13 Refit the hub carrier assembly as described in Section 14.

16 Air suspension system components – removal and refitting

Height sensors

1 Chock the front/rear wheels (as applicable), then raise the front/rear of the vehicle and support it securely on axle stands (see *Jacking and vehicle support*). A sensor is fitted to each corner of the vehicle. Note that the left-hand sensors have a white-coloured lever, whilst the right-hand sensors have a black-coloured lever.

2 Pull the sensor link arm from the bracket **(see illustration)**.

3 Disconnect the wiring plug, then undo the Torx screws and remove the sensor **(see illustration)**.

4 Refitting is a reversal of removal. If a new sensor has been fitted, it must be calibrated using Land Rover diagnostic equipment (T4). Entrust this task to a Land Rover dealer or suitably-equipped repairer.

Air reservoir

Note: *Before any part of the pressurised air circuit can be worked on, it's essential to depressurise the system – the pressure in the system can be in excess of 16 bar (230 psi). Land Rover recommend that this must be carried out using their dedicated test equipment (T4). It is possible to depressurise the system without T4 by very slowly undoing the air pipe union(s) on the air spring* ***(see illustration 10.10)*** *to allow the pressure within to slowly escape. If in any doubt at all, entrust any work involving the pressurised air circuit to a Land Rover dealer or suitably-equipped specialist.*

Warning: Do not attempt to drive the vehicle with the air suspension system depressurised.

5 Raise the vehicle and support it securely on axle stands (see *Jacking and vehicle support*). The reservoir is located under the left-hand side of the vehicle, in line with the front passenger's door.

6 Disconnect the battery negative lead as described in Chapter 5, Section 4.

7 Depressurise the air system as described above.

8 Disconnect the air pipe from the reservoir **(see illustration)**. Remove the Voss connector (consisting of a split olive and gland nut with integral O-ring seal), and discard it – a new one must be fitted **(see illustration 2.13b)**.

9 Undo the mounting bolts and manoeuvre the reservoir from position **(see illustration)**.

10 Refitting is a reversal of removal, using a new Voss connector on the air pipe.

Control module

11 Disconnect the battery negative lead as described in Chapter 5, Section 4.

12 Undo the 2 screws, release the clip and remove the trim panel above the pedals **(see illustration)**. Disconnect any wiring plugs as the panel is withdrawn.

13 Disconnect the wiring plugs, undo the retaining bolt, release the 2 clips and remove the control module **(see illustration)**.

14 Refitting is a reversal of removal. If a new module has been fitted, it must be initiated using Land Rover diagnostic equipment (T4). Entrust this task to a Land Rover dealer or suitably-equipped specialist.

Solenoid blocks

Reservoir block

15 Raise the rear of the vehicle and support it securely on axle stands (see *Jacking and vehicle support*).

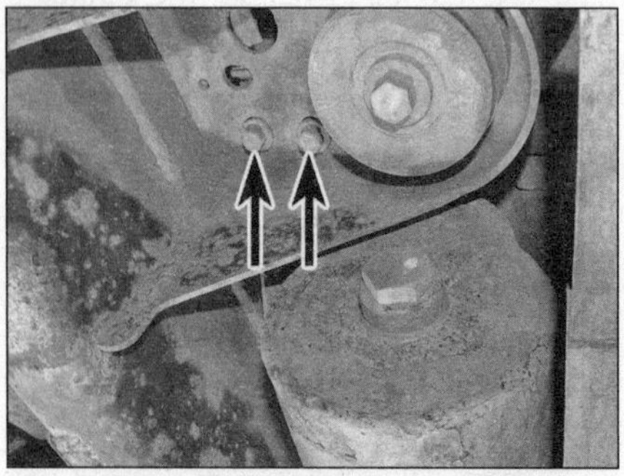
16.9 Reservoir front mounting bolts (arrowed)

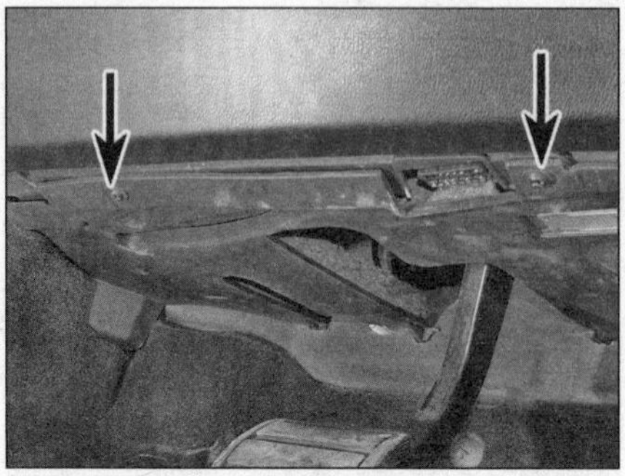
16.12 Trim panel retaining screws (arrowed)

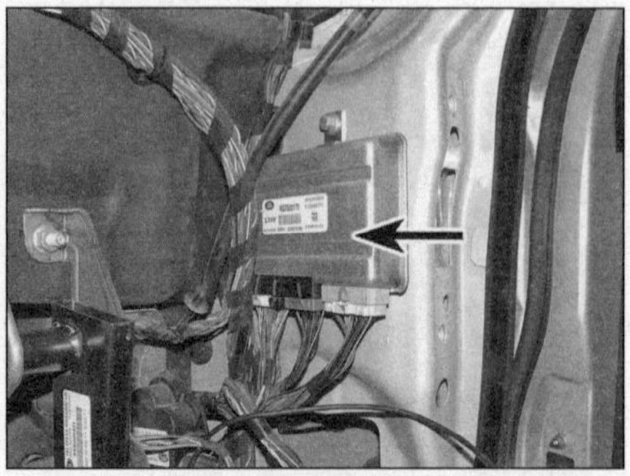
16.13 The control module (arrowed) is attached to the A-pillar (facia removed for clarity)

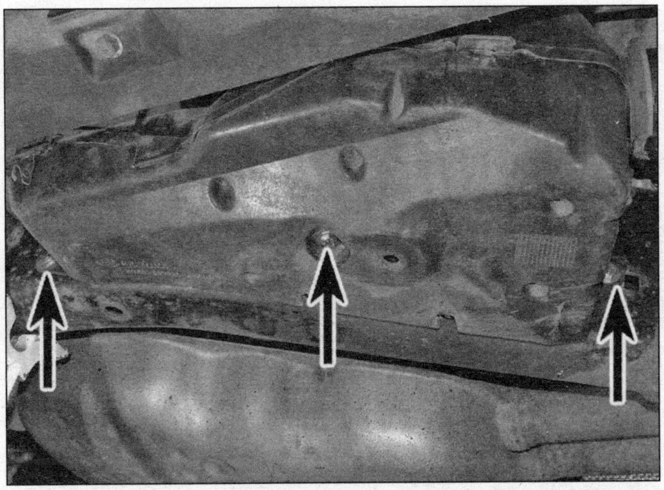

16.17 Undo the bolts (arrowed) and remove the compressor lower cover

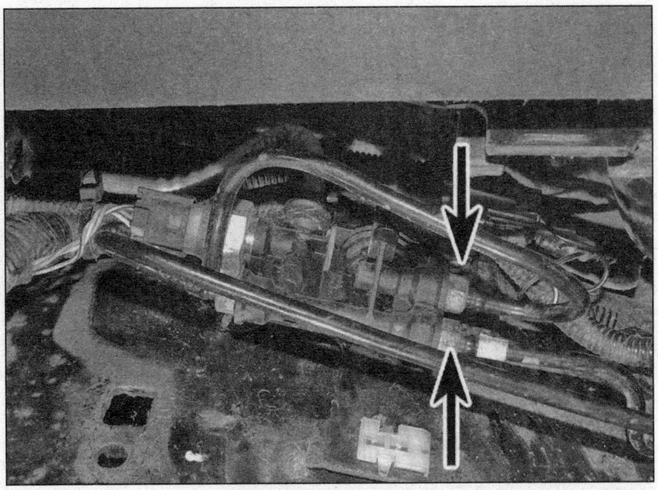

16.19 Undo the unions (arrowed) and disconnect the pipes from the solenoid block

16 Depressurise the air system as described in the Note before paragraph 5.
17 Undo the bolts, release the clips and remove the compressor lower cover **(see illustration)**.
18 Unclip the compressor wiring plug and move it to one side.
19 Note their fitted positions, then undo the unions and disconnect the pipes from the solenoid block. Remove the Voss connector (consisting of a split olive and gland nut with integral O-ring seal), and discard it – a new one must be fitted **(see illustration)**.
20 Disconnect the wiring plugs, and unclip the solenoid block from the rubber mountings.
21 Refitting is a reversal of removal. Note that if a new solenoid block is fitted, new Voss connectors are included with the assembly.

Front block

22 Slacken the right-hand roadwheel nuts, raise the front of the vehicle and support it securely on axle stands (see *Jacking and vehicle support*). Remove the front roadwheel.
23 Depressurise the air system as described in the Note before paragraph 5.
24 Remove the front bumper as described in Chapter 12, Section 6.
25 Note their fitted positions, then undo the unions and disconnect the pipes from the solenoid block. Remove the Voss connector (consisting of a split olive and gland nut with integral O-ring seal), and discard it – a new one must be fitted **(see illustration)**.
26 Disconnect the wiring plug, then slide the solenoid block upwards from the bumper bar **(see illustration)**.
27 Refitting is a reversal of removal. Note that if a new solenoid block is fitted, new Voss connectors are included with the assembly.

Rear block

28 Slacken the left-hand roadwheel nuts, raise the rear of the vehicle and support it securely on axle stands (see *Jacking and vehicle support*). Remove the rear roadwheel.
29 Depressurise the air system as described in the Note before paragraph 5.

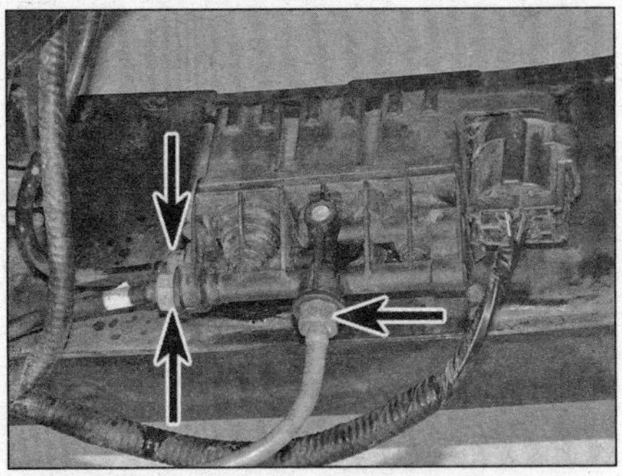

16.25 Front solenoid block air pipe unions (arrowed)

30 Note their fitted positions, then undo the unions and disconnect the pipes from the solenoid block. Remove the Voss connector (consisting of a split olive and gland nut with integral O-ring seal), and discard it – a new one must be fitted **(see illustration)**.
31 Disconnect the wiring plug, and unclip the solenoid block from the rubber mountings.

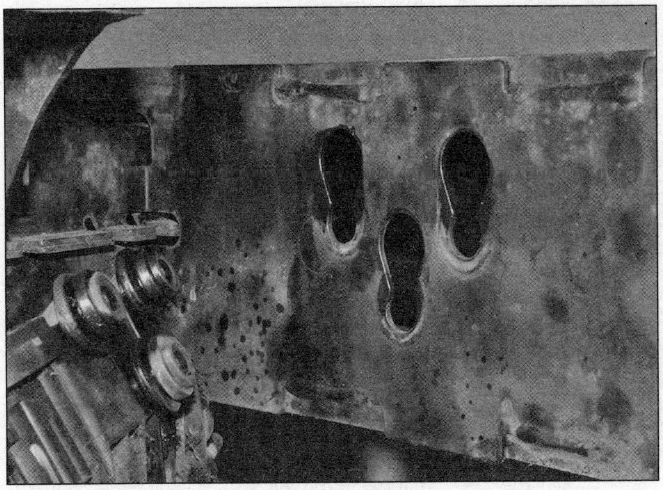

16.26 Slide the solenoid block upwards from the elongated holes in the bumper bar

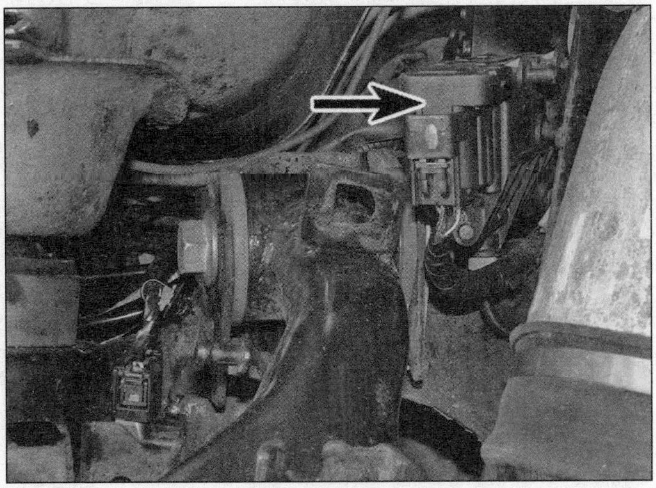

16.30 The rear solenoid block (arrowed) is located in front of the left-hand rear spring/strut

16.36a Depress the collar (arrowed) and disconnect the lower pipe from the front of the compressor ...

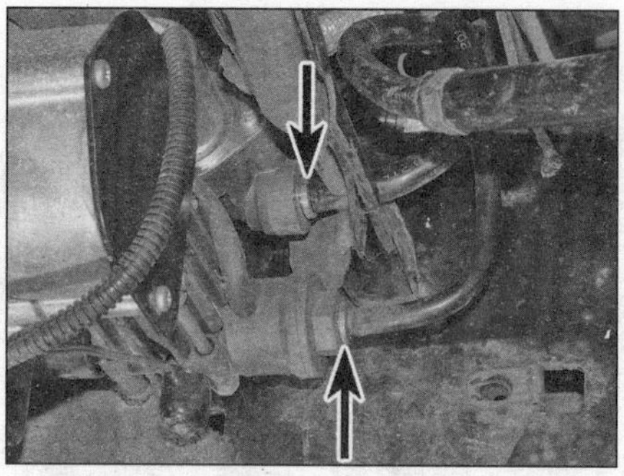

16.36b ... and both pipes from the rear (arrowed)

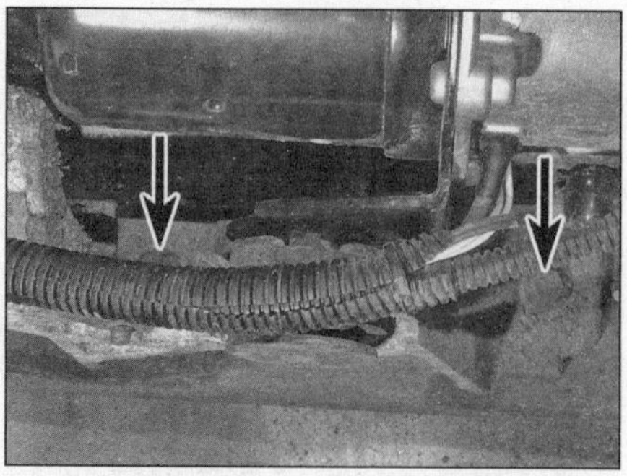

16.37a The compressor is secured by 2 bolts underneath (arrowed) ...

32 Refitting is a reversal of removal. Note that if a new solenoid block is fitted, new Voss connectors are included with the assembly.

Air compressor

33 Disconnect the battery negative lead as described in Chapter 5, Section 4.

34 Raise the rear of the vehicle and support it securely on axle stands (see *Jacking and vehicle support*).

35 Undo the 3 bolts, release the 5 retaining clips and remove the cover from beneath the compressor **(see illustration 16.17)**.

36 Depress the collars and pull the air pipes (1 at the front and 2 at the rear) from the compressor **(see illustrations)**. Plug/cover the openings to prevent contamination.

37 Disconnect the wiring plugs, undo the 3 retaining bolts and manoeuvre the compressor from place **(see illustrations)**. Access to the top mounting bolt is very restricted – use a 3/8" drive socket with a flexible coupling.

38 Refitting is a reversal of removal, noting the following points:

a) *Ensure the compressor upper cover is correctly positioned.*

b) *Ensure the compressor wiring harness and pipes are not trapped behind the mounting bracket.*

c) *Tighten the mounting bolts to the specified torque.*

d) *Due to possible damage to the contacts, the compressor relay (engine compartment relay box – see Chapter 13, Section 3) must be renewed as well.*

16.37b ... and one above (arrowed – compressor removed for clarity)

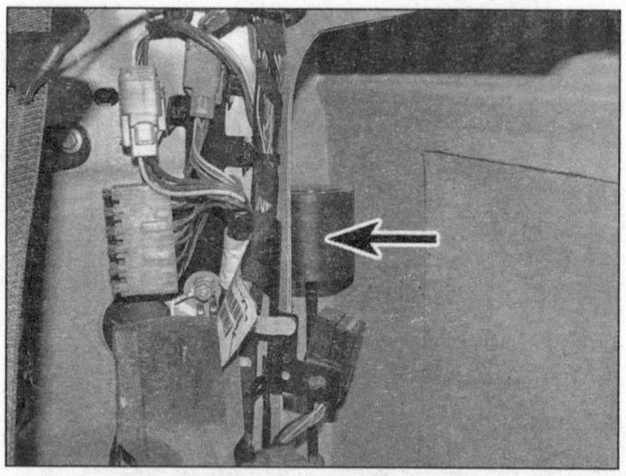

16.43a Air intake filter (arrowed)

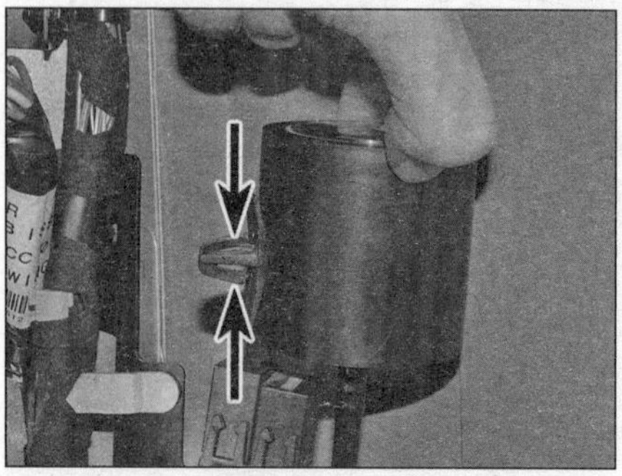

16.43b The retaining clip (arrowed) will probably be damaged during removal

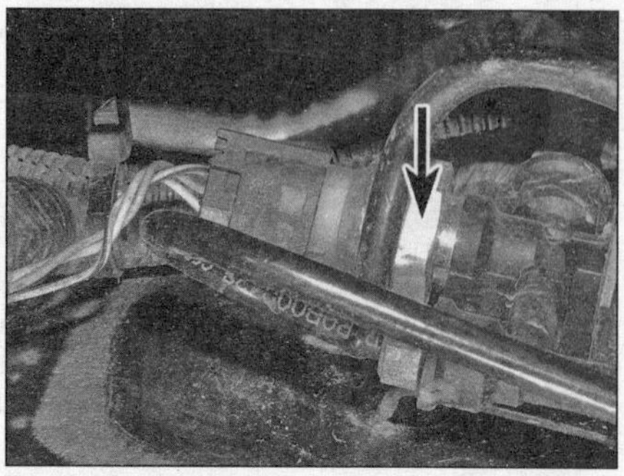

16.48 The air pressure sensor (arrowed) is fitted to the front of the reservoir solenoid block

Air filter

39 Remove the spare wheel.

40 Undo the 4 retaining nuts and remove the left-hand tail silencer heat shield.

41 Disconnect the intake filter pipe, release it from the retaining clip, and prise the rubber grommet from the vehicle floor.

42 Unclip and remove the access panel on the left-hand side of the luggage compartment.

43 Prise the intake filter from the pillar, and manoeuvre it from position **(see illustrations)**. Note that prising the air filter from place will almost certainly result in damage to the integral retaining clip. Only remove the filter if it is to be renewed.

44 Refitting is a reversal of removal.

Air pressure sensor

45 Raise the rear of the vehicle and support it securely on axle stands (see *Jacking and vehicle support*).

46 Depressurise the air system as described in the Note before paragraph 5.

47 Undo the bolts, release the clips and remove the compressor lower cover **(see illustration 16.17)**.

48 Disconnect the wiring plug, then unscrew the sensor **(see illustration)**. Discard the O-ring seal – a new one must be fitted.

49 Refitting is a reversal of removal.

17 Rear anti-roll bar and bushes – removal and refitting

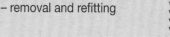

Anti-roll bar

1 Removal of the anti-roll bar requires the complete vehicle body to be lifted. Due to the need for specialist equipment (2-post ramp, etc), this is considered to be beyond the scope of the DIY repairer. We recommend this task is entrusted to a Land Rover dealer or suitably-equipped repairer.

Bushes

2 Slacken the rear wheel nuts on both sides, then raise the rear of the vehicle and support it securely on axle stands (see *Jacking and vehicle support*). Rear both rear wheels.

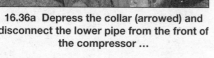

17.3 Rear anti-roll bar clamp bolts (arrowed)

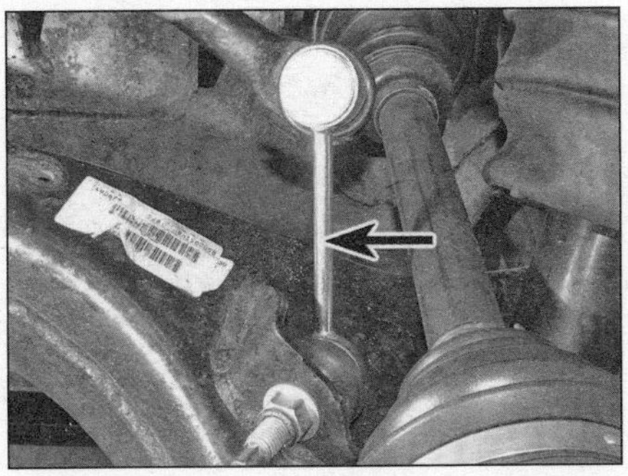

18.2 Rear anti-roll bar link rod (arrowed)

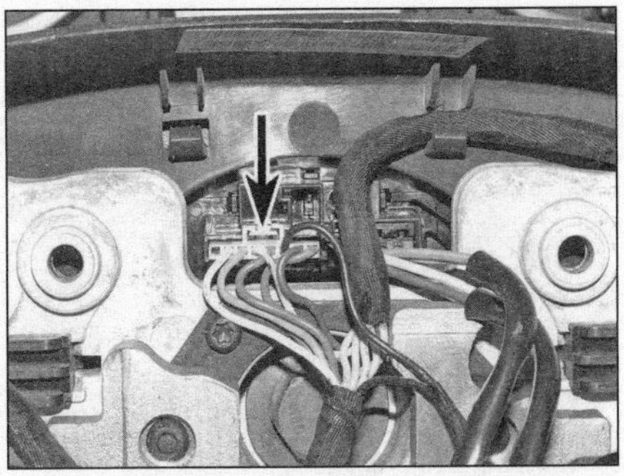

19.3 Depress the clip and disconnect the left-hand wiring plug (arrowed)

3 Undo the bolts securing the anti-roll bar bush clamps to the vehicle chassis **(see illustration)**. Repeat this operation on the remaining side.
4 Prise up the clamps and manoeuvre the bushes from place.
5 Ensure the area where the bushes locate on the bar is free from dirt, rust and grease, then slide the new bushes into place.
6 Refit the clamps and tighten the retaining bolts to the specified torque.
7 Refit the roadwheels and lower the vehicle to the ground. Tighten the wheel nuts to the specified torque.

18 Rear anti-roll bar links – removal and refitting

Removal

1 Slacken the relevant roadwheel nuts, raise the rear of the vehicle and support it securely on axle stands (see *Jacking and vehicle support*). Remove the relevant roadwheel.
2 Undo the nuts securing the ends of the anti-roll bar to the link rods and the upper arms **(see illustration)**. Use a second spanner to counterhold the balljoints. Discard the nuts – new ones must be fitted.

Refitting

3 Refitting is a reversal of removal. Tighten all fasteners to the specified torque.

19 Steering wheel – removal and refitting

Removal

1 Remove the driver's airbag as described in Chapter 13, Section 19.
2 Ensure the front wheels are in the 'straight-ahead' position.
3 Disconnect the wiring plug from the steering wheel **(see illustration)**.
4 Slacken the steering wheel bolt. Do not fully unscrew the bolt at this stage.
5 Pull the wheel from the steering column shaft – it may be tight. Seek assistance if necessary.
6 Remove the steering wheel bolt, and note the alignment marks between the steering wheel and the column shaft. If none are visible, make some **(see illustration)**. Remove the wheel. Discard the wheel retaining bolt, a new one must be fitted. **Note:** *If the steering wheel marks are not aligned, the steering wheel sensor must be calibrated using T4 diagnostic equipment, and a 4-wheel alignment check carried out, after the steering wheel position is reset.*
7 Attach a strip of self-adhesive tape across the airbag rotary contact unit to immobilise it **(see illustration)**.

Refitting

8 Remove the tape from the contact unit, then ensure the wheels are still in the straight-ahead position.
9 Before fitting the steering wheel, check the position of the airbag rotary contact unit. If the position is correct, a yellow or blue marker should be visible through the 'window' on the unit face **(see illustration)**. If it isn't, gently rotate the contact unit until it is. If the force required to rotate the unit increases before the marker is visible, stop and turn it the other way.
10 Locate the steering wheel on the column splines, aligning the marks made on removal.
11 Fit the new retaining bolt, and tighten it to the specified torque setting.
12 Reconnect the wiring plug.
13 Refit the driver's airbag as described in Chapter 13, Section 19.

20 Ignition switch/steering column lock – removal and refitting

Ignition switch

Removal

1 Disconnect the battery negative lead as described in Chapter 5, Section 4.

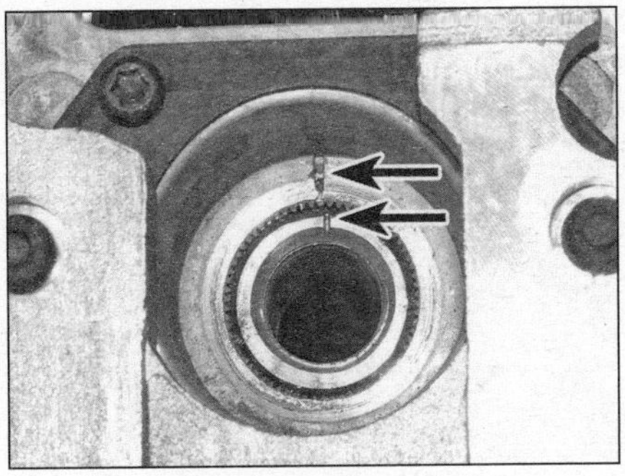

19.6 If there are no alignment marks, make your own (arrowed)

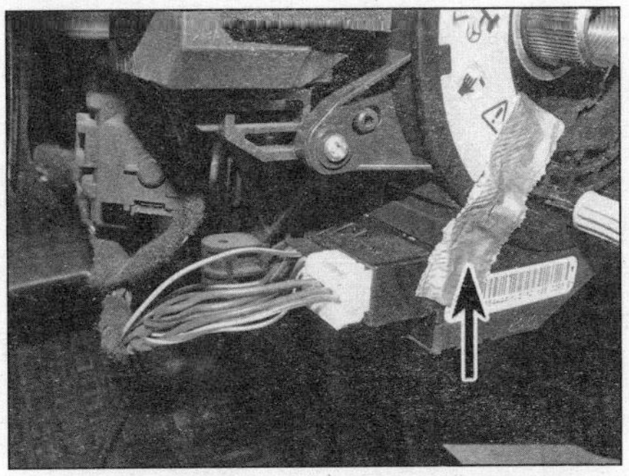

19.7 Immobilise the rotary contact unit with adhesive tape (arrowed)

19.9 The marker should be visible through the window (arrowed)

20.2a Prise the upper shroud upwards to release the clips (arrowed)

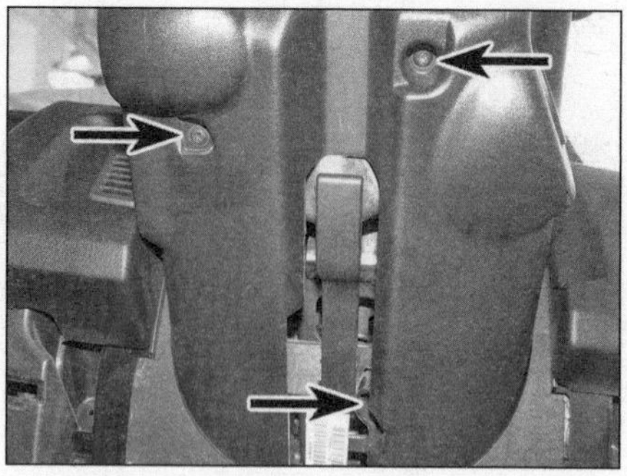

20.2b Lower shroud retaining screws (arrowed)

20.3 Ignition switch retaining clips (arrowed)

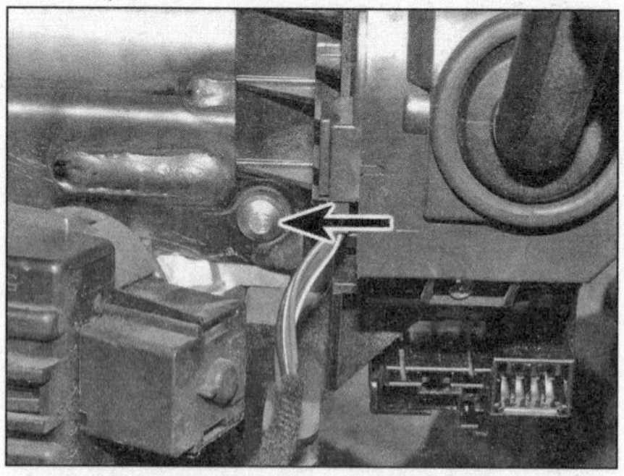

20.7 Steering lock shear-bolt (arrowed)

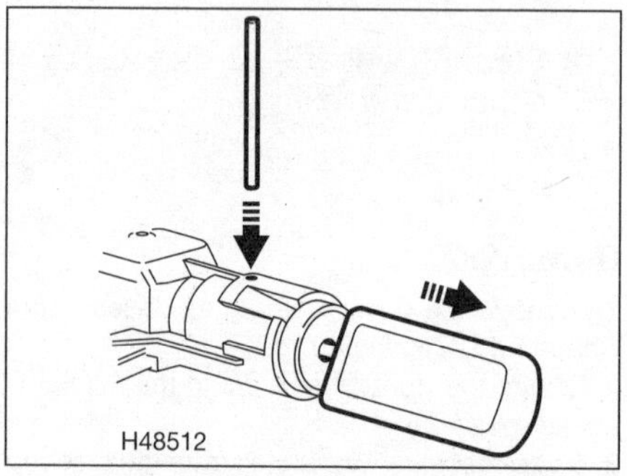

20.10 Insert a 2.0 mm pin and depress the plunger

2 Fully extend the steering column then undo the 3 lower steering column shroud retaining screws, unclip the shroud halves, and remove both the upper and lower shrouds from the steering column **(see illustrations)**.

3 Remove the ignition key, then disconnect the wiring plug, depress the 2 retaining clips and remove the ignition switch **(see illustrations)**.

Refitting

4 Refitting is a reversal of removal.

Lock assembly

Removal

5 Remove the steering column combination switch assembly as described in Chapter 13, Section 4.

6 Disconnect the wiring plug from the transponder ring on the ignition switch.

7 Tap the head of each shear-bolt around anti-clockwise until each bolt is loose enough to be unscrewed by hand **(see illustration)**.

8 Unscrew both shear-bolts, and remove the lock assembly from the steering column.

9 If removal of the barrel is required, insert the ignition key, and turn it to position I.

10 Insert a 2.0 mm rod/drill bit into the access hole, depress the plunger and pull out the lock barrel **(see illustration)**.

Refitting

11 Insert the lock barrel into the housing, turn the key to position 0 and remove the key.

12 Position the lock assembly against the steering column, and fit the new shear-bolts. Tighten the bolts until the heads shear off.

13 The remainder of refitting is a reversal of removal.

21 Steering column – removal, inspection and refitting

Removal

1 Remove the steering wheel as described in Section 19.

2 Remove the steering column combination switch assembly as described in Chapter 13, Section 4.

3 Starting at the lower edge, carefully prise the driver's side trim panel from the end of the facia **(see illustration)**. Disconnect any wiring plug as the panel is withdrawn.

4 Undo the 2 screws, release the clip and remove the trim panel above the pedals **(see illustration 16.12)**. Disconnect any wiring plugs as the panel is withdrawn.

5 Pull the column surround trim panels rearwards to release the clips.

6 Undo the 2 screws, release the clips and remove the steering column gaiter panel from the facia **(see illustration)**.

7 Note their fitted positions, then disconnect the various wiring plugs from the column, and release the wiring harnesses from any clips.

8 Working under the facia, undo the nut and withdraw the bolt securing the upper column to the intermediate shaft **(see illustration)**. Discard the nut – a new one must be fitted.

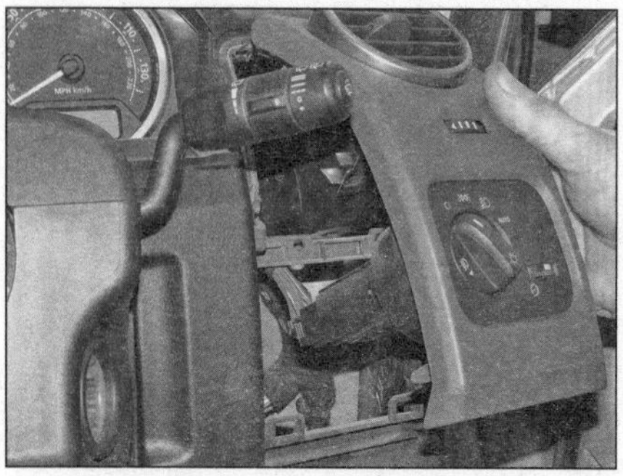

21.3 Starting at the lower edge, pull the panel from the facia

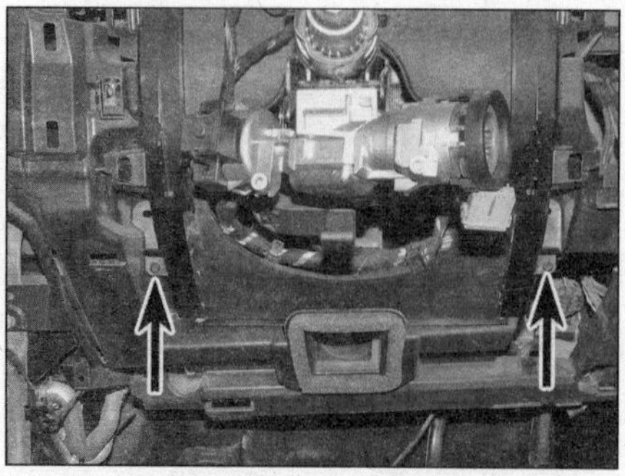

21.6 Undo the screws (arrowed) and pull the panel rearwards

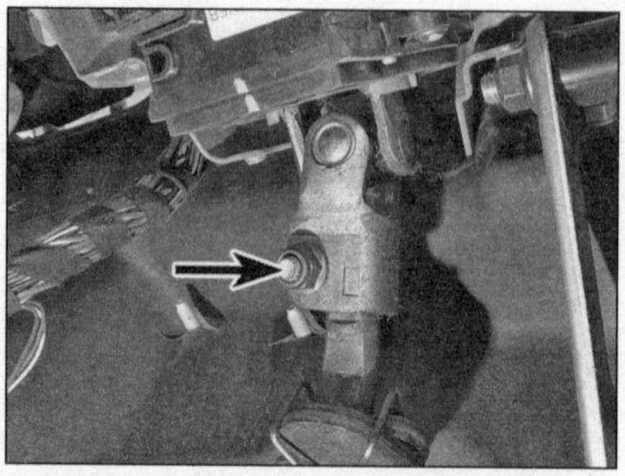

21.8 Upper column shaft-to-intermediate shaft bolt/nut (arrowed)

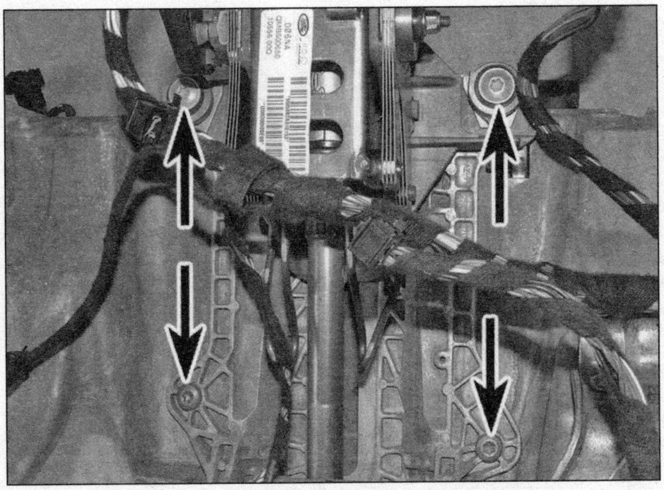

21.9 Steering column mounting bolts (arrowed)

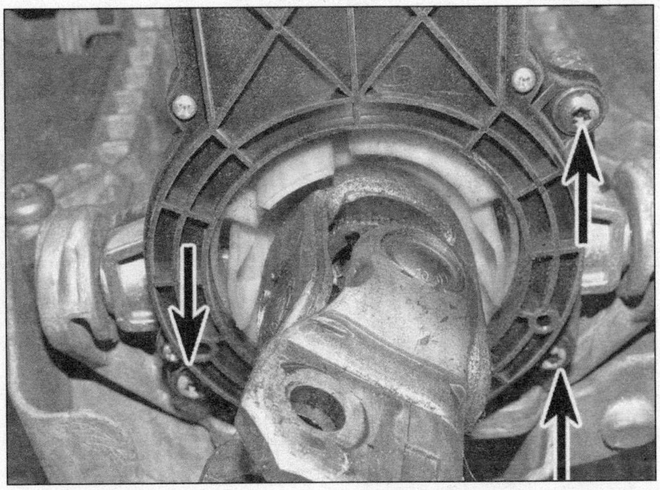

21.10 Steering angle sensor retaining screws (arrowed)

9 Undo the 4 Torx bolts and manoeuvre the column from place **(see illustration)**. Take care not to damage the column components during removal. Enlist the help of an assistant.
10 If required, undo the 3 Torx screws and detach the steering angle sensor from the column **(see illustration)**.

Inspection

11 Examine steering column and mountings for signs of damage and deformation, and check the steering shaft for signs of free play in the column bushes. If there are signs of damage or play, the column must be renewed. Overhaul of the column is not possible.

Refitting

12 On models with an electrically-adjustable steering column, if a new column is being fitted, take a note of the potentiometer hexadecimal code from the sticker on the column. As each column has unique adjustment values, this code will be needed during the calibration procedure.
13 Where applicable, refit the steering angle sensor and tighten the bolts securely.
14 Manoeuvre the steering column into position, and engage it with the intermediate shaft.
15 Install the column retaining bolts and tighten them evenly to the specified torque.
16 Refit the column pinch-bolt, and tighten the new nut to the specified torque.
17 The remainder of refitting is a reversal of removal. Note that if a new column or steering angle sensor has been fitted, they must be calibrated using Land Rover diagnostic equipment (T4). Entrust this task to a Land Rover dealer or suitably-equipped specialist.

22 Steering column intermediate shaft – removal and refitting

Removal

1 Disconnect the battery negative lead as described in Chapter 5, Section 4.
2 Undo the 2 screws, release the clip and remove the trim panel above the pedals **(see illustration 16.12)**. Disconnect any wiring plugs as the panel is withdrawn.
3 Working under the facia, undo the nut and withdraw the bolt securing the upper column to the intermediate shaft **(see illustration 21.8)**. Discard the nut – a new one must be fitted.

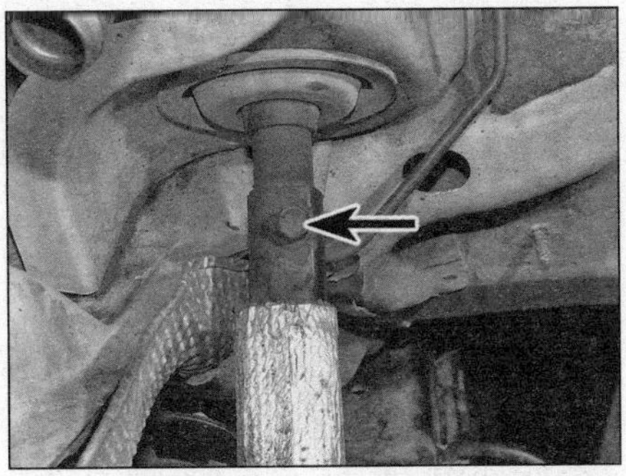

22.4 Intermediate shaft-to-lower shaft bolt (arrowed)

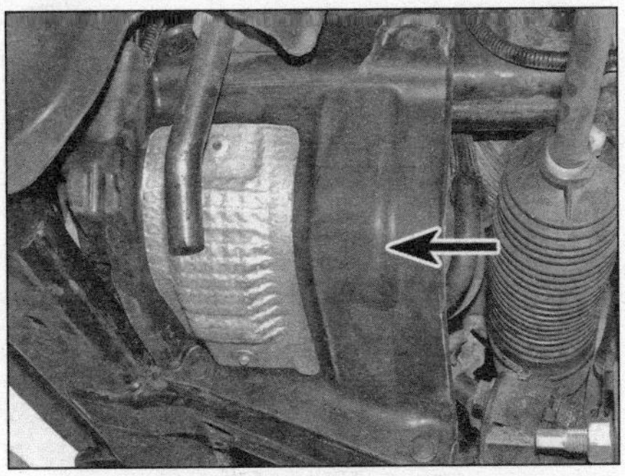

23.5 Remove the lower splash shield (arrowed)

4 Working in the engine compartment, using paint or a marker pen, make alignment marks between the intermediate shaft and the lower shaft, then undo the bolt securing the two shafts together **(see illustration)**. Discard the bolt – a new one must be fitted.
5 Release the 2 rubber grommets from the bulkheads, and manoeuvre the shaft from position.

Refitting

6 Aligning the marks made on removal, engage the shaft with the lower shaft, then engage the upper end of the shaft with the steering column. Install the rubber grommets.
7 The remainder of refitting is a reversal of removal, using a new upper column-to-intermediate shaft pinch-bolt nut, and a new intermediate shaft-to-lower shaft bolt.

23 Steering column lower shaft – removal, inspection and refitting

Removal

1 Ensure the steering wheel is in the 'straight-ahead' position, then disconnect the battery negative lead as described in Chapter 5, Section 4.
2 Working in the engine compartment, using paint or a marker pen, make alignment marks between the intermediate shaft and the lower shaft, then undo the bolt securing the two shafts together **(see illustration 22.4)**. Discard the bolt – a new one must be fitted.
3 Slacken the right-hand side roadwheel nuts, raise the front of the vehicle and support it securely on axle stands (see *Jacking and vehicle support*). Remove the roadwheel.
4 Undo the 3 nuts, and remove the upper suspension arm heat shield.
5 Release the 4 clips and remove the wheel arch lower splash shield **(see illustration)**.
6 Undo the bolt securing the lower shaft

universal joint to the steering rack pinion. If necessary adjust the position of the shaft by moving the roadwheels – do not use the steering wheel. Discard the bolt – a new one must be fitted.
7 Manoeuvre the shaft from position.

Inspection

8 Inspect the universal joint for signs of roughness in its bearings, and check it for ease of movement. If it is damaged in any way, the joint must be renewed.

Refitting

9 Ensure the roadwheels are still in the 'straight-ahead' position.
10 Manoeuvre the lower shaft into place, and engage it with the intermediate shaft and steering rack pinion. Secure the shaft to the pinion and intermediate shaft with new bolts. Tighten them to the specified torque.
11 The remainder of refitting is a reversal of removal.

24 Steering rack – removal, inspection and refitting

Removal

1 Slacken the front roadwheel nuts, raise the front of the vehicle and support it securely on axle stands (see *Jacking and vehicle support*). Remove the roadwheels.
2 Ensure the steering wheel is in the 'straight-ahead' position, then disconnect the battery negative lead as described in Chapter 5, Section 4.
3 Undo the 3 nuts, and remove the upper suspension arm heat shield each side.
4 Release the 4 clips and remove the wheel arch lower splash shield each side **(see illustration 23.5)**.
5 Undo the bolt securing the lower shaft universal joint to the steering rack pinion. If necessary adjust the position of the shaft by moving the roadwheels – do not use the steering wheel. Discard the bolt – a new one must be fitted.
6 Unscrew the nut securing the track rod end to the hub carrier. Release the track rod end tapered shank using a balljoint separator tool **(see illustration 4.7)**.
7 Undo the 4 bolts and remove the access panel beneath the cooling system radiator.
8 Undo the bolt securing the power steering pipe support bracket to the rack housing.
9 Position a container beneath the rack connections, then undo the coupling bolt and detach the fluid pipes from the rack. Be prepared for fluid spillage. Plug/cover the openings to prevent contamination. Discard the pipes O-ring seals – new ones must be fitted.
10 Undo the 2 mounting bolts, and manoeuvre the steering rack from place.

Refitting

11 Refitting is a reversal of removal, noting the following points:
a) *Tighten all fasteners to their specified torque where given.*
b) *Renew the steering rack mounting captive nuts.*
c) *Renew the power steering pipe O-ring seals.*
d) *Bleed the power steering system as described in Section 26.*
e) *Have the front wheel alignment checked at the earliest opportunity.*

25 Power steering pump – removal and refitting

Removal

1 On models from VIN SALLA000305 (from 2007 MY) have the refrigerant circuit discharged by a Land Rover dealer or suitably-equipped repairer.
2 On all models, slacken the left-hand front roadwheel nuts, apply the parking brake, then jack up the front of the vehicle and support it securely on axle stands (see *Jacking and vehicle support*). Remove the roadwheel.
3 Remove the auxiliary drivebelt as described in Chapter 1, Section 9.
4 Remove the auxiliary battery and battery tray as described in Chapter 5, Section 4.
5 Release the clips and remove the lower splash shield form the left-hand wheel arch liner **(see illustration)**.
6 Undo the screws securing the mud flap at the rear of the front wheel arch.
7 Undo the screws and pull the wing/wheel arch moulding out sideways to release the clips **(see illustration 2.4)**.
8 Release the fasteners and remove the wheel arch liner.
9 Undo the 3 nuts, and remove the left-hand upper suspension arm heat shield.
10 Undo the 2 bolts, one nut, and release the intercooler intake pipe.
11 Slacken the clamps and move the intercooler intake pipe to one side, to gain access to the rear power steering pump mounting bolt.

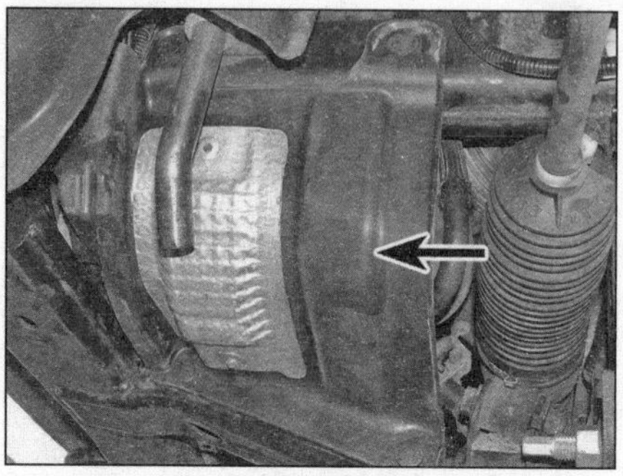

25.5 Left-hand lower splash shield (arrowed)

Models up to VIN SALLA000304 (up to 2007 MY)

12 Remove the rear mounting bolt from the power steering pump.
13 Working in the engine compartment, undo the banjo bolt and disconnect the high-pressure fluid pipe from the pump. Be prepared for fluid spillage. Plug/cover the openings to prevent contamination. Discard the sealing washers – new ones must be fitted.

Models from VIN SALLA000305 (from 2007 MY)

14 Undo the retaining bolt, and detach the refrigerant pipe from the rear of the air conditioning compressor. Move the pipe to one side. Plug the openings to prevent contamination. Discard the pipe seal – a new one must be fitted.
15 Undo the bolt securing the power steering pump rear mounting bracket to the cylinder block.
16 Undo the retaining bolt and detach the high-pressure fluid pipe from the power steering pump. Plug/cover the openings to prevent contamination. Be prepared for fluid spillage. Discard the pipe O-ring seal – a new one must be fitted.

All models

17 Release the clamp and disconnect the fluid supply hose from the pump. Be prepared for fluid spillage. Plug/cover the openings to prevent contamination.
18 Undo the 3 retaining bolts and manoeuvre the pump from place.

Refitting

19 Refitting is a reversal of removal, noting the following points:
a) *Tighten the pump rear mounting bolt before the front ones.*
b) *Renew all disturbed seals.*
c) *All fasteners must be tightened to the specified torque (where given).*
d) *Bleed the steering system as described in Section 26.*

26 Power steering system – bleeding

1 With the engine stopped, top-up the fluid reservoir up to the maximum mark with the specified type of fluid.
2 Start the engine, and allow it to idle for 10 seconds then stop it.
3 Check the fluid level and top-up if necessary. If the fluid is aerated, wait for a few minutes for the bubbles to dissipate.
4 Start the engine and allow it idle. Turn the steering from lock-to-lock, then turn the engine off. Don't hold the steering at full lock for more than 10 seconds. Check, and if necessary, top-up the fluid level.
5 Start the engine, and allow it to idle, turning the steering from lock-to-lock for 2 minutes. Check and if necessary, top-up the fluid level.

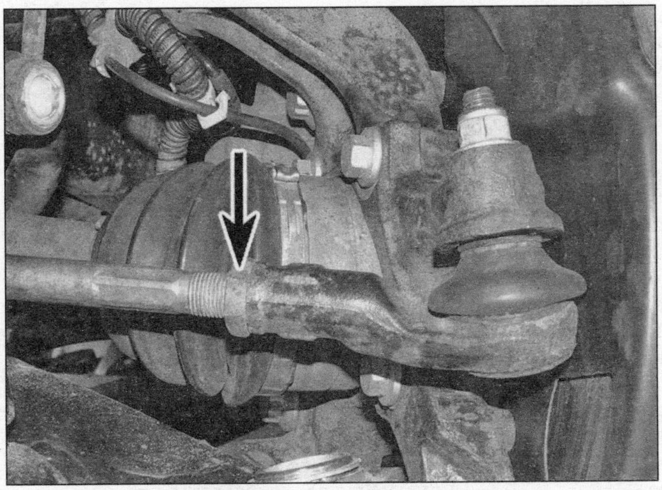

27.2 Slacken the locknut (arrowed)

28.3 Steering rack gaiter securing clamps (arrowed)

27 Track rod end – removal and refitting

Removal

1 Slacken the relevant front roadwheel nuts, then jack up the front of the vehicle, and support it securely on axle stands (see *Jacking and vehicle support*). Remove the front roadwheel.
2 Slacken the track rod end lock nut **(see illustration)**.
3 Unscrew the nut securing the track rod end to the hub carrier. Discard the nut – a new one must be fitted.
4 Using a universal balljoint separator, free the track rod end from the hub carrier **(see illustration 4.7)**.
5 Unscrew the track rod end from the threaded adjuster rod, counting the exact number of threads to aid refitment.

Refitting

6 Screw the track rod end onto the track rod by the same number of turns noted during removal.
7 Engage the balljoint in the hub carrier. Fit a new nut and tighten it to the specified torque.
8 Counterhold the track rod and tighten the locknut.
9 Refit the front wheel, lower the car and tighten the wheel nuts to the specified torque.
10 Have the front wheel toe-in (tracking) checked and adjusted at the earliest opportunity.

28 Steering rack gaiter – renewal

1 Remove the track rod end as described in Section 27.
2 Unscrew the track rod end locknut from the threaded adjuster rod.
3 Release the clamps and slide the rubber gaiter from position **(see illustration)**.
4 Ensure the mating faces are clean and slide the new gaiter into place (complete with clamps). Ensure the clamps are correctly positioned.
5 The remainder of refitting is a reversal of removal.

29 Wheel alignment and steering angles – general information

1 Accurate front wheel alignment is essential for precise steering and handling, and for even tyre wear. Before carrying out any checking or adjusting operations, make sure that the tyres are correctly inflated, that all steering and suspension joints and linkages are in sound condition, and that the wheels are not buckled or distorted, particularly around the rims. It will also be necessary to have the vehicle positioned on flat, level ground, with enough space to push the car backwards and forwards through about half its length.
2 Front wheel alignment consists of four factors **(see illustration)**:

Camber

- Camber is the angle at which the roadwheels are set from the vertical, when viewed from the front or rear of the vehicle. Positive camber is the angle (in degrees) that the wheels are tilted outwards at the top from the vertical.

Castor

- Castor is the angle between the steering axis and a vertical line when viewed from each side of the vehicle. Positive castor is indicated when the steering axis is inclined towards the rear of the vehicle at its upper end.

Steering axis inclination

- Steering axis inclination is the angle, when viewed from the front or rear of the vehicle,

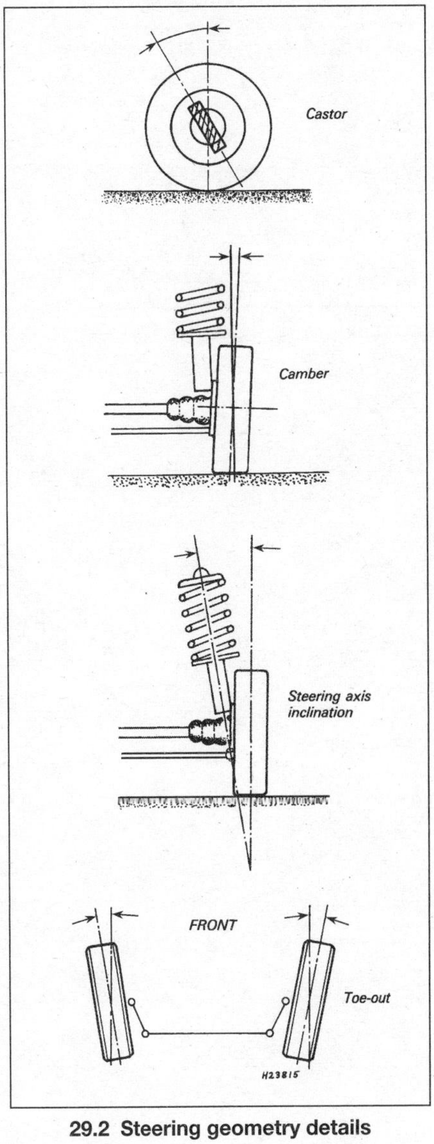

29.2 Steering geometry details

between the vertical and an imaginary line drawn between the upper and lower front suspension strut mountings.

Toe setting

- Toe setting is the amount by which the distance between the front inside edges of the roadwheels differs from that between the rear inside edges, when measured at hub height. If the distance between the front edges is less than at the rear, the wheels are said to toe-in. If it is greater than at the rear, the wheels are said to toe-out. These days, the toe setting dimensions are given as degrees deviation from the central axis of the vehicle.

3 Camber, castor and steering axis inclination are set during manufacture, and are not adjustable. Unless the vehicle has suffered accident damage, or there is gross wear in the suspension mountings or joints, it can be assumed that these settings are correct. If for any reason it is believed that they are not correct, the task of checking them should be left to a Land Rover dealer, who will have the necessary special equipment needed to measure the small angles involved.

4 It is, however, within the scope of the home mechanic to check and adjust the front wheel toe setting. To do this, a tracking gauge must first be obtained, usually from motoring accessory/parts centres. The type of gauge needed is known as a scuff plate, and measures the actual position of the contact surface of the tyre, in relation to the road surface, with the vehicle in motion. This is achieved by pushing or driving the front tyre over a plate, which then moves slightly according to the scuff of the tyre, and shows this movement on a scale.

5 Many tyre specialists will also check toe settings free, or for a nominal charge.

6 Make sure that the steering is in the straight-ahead position when making measurements. The measurement will only be accurate if the vehicle is unladen, but with a full tank of fuel and at normal ride height.

7 If adjustment is necessary, apply the parking brake, then jack up the front of the vehicle and support it securely on axle stands. Slacken the track rod end locknuts, then rotate the adjuster rod to alter the length of the track rod (as necessary); shortening the track rod will reduce toe-in/increase toe-out.

8 When the setting is correct, tighten both the locknuts to the specified torque setting.

9 Recheck the toe setting and, if necessary, repeat the adjustment procedure.

Chapter 12
Bodywork and fittings

Contents

Degrees of difficulty

Easy, suitable for novice with little experience	**Fairly easy,** suitable for beginner with some experience	**Fairly difficult,** suitable for competent DIY mechanic	**Difficult,** suitable for experienced DIY mechanic	**Very difficult,** suitable for expert DIY or professional

Specifications

Torque wrench settings	**Nm**	**lbf ft**
Luggage compartment storage anchors	25	18
Passenger's airbag:		
Module nuts	10	7
Bracket screws	25	18
Seat belt mounting nuts and bolts:		
Inertia reel bolt:		
Front	40	30
Rear*	40	30
Anchorage bolt*	40	30
Front seat belt stalk	40	30
Rear seat belt stalk:		
Centre	25	18
Left-hand	25	18
Right-hand	40	30
Seat mounting bolts	40	30
Tailgate/liftgate hinge bolts	40	30

** Do not re-use*

1 General information

The bodyshell and panels are mainly zinc-coated steel, and posses excellent corrosion resistance properties. The bonnet and tailgate are made from aluminium, whilst the front panel is magnesium. Most components are welded together, but some use is made of structural adhesives.

Extensive use is made of plastic materials, mainly on the interior but also in exterior components. The front and rear bumpers are injection-moulded from a synthetic material, which is very strong and yet light. Plastic components such as wheel arch liners are fitted to the underside of the vehicle, to improve the body's resistance to corrosion.

2 Maintenance – bodywork and chassis

The general condition of a vehicle's bodywork is the one thing that significantly affects its value. Maintenance is easy, but needs to be regular. Neglect, particularly after minor damage, can lead quickly to further deterioration and costly repair bills. It is important also to keep watch on those parts of the vehicle not immediately visible, for instance the underside, inside all the wheel arches, and the lower part of the engine compartment.

The basic maintenance routine for the bodywork is washing – preferably with a lot of water, from a hose. This will remove all the loose solids which may have stuck to the vehicle. It is important to flush these off in such a way as to prevent grit from scratching the finish. The wheel arches and chassis need washing in the same way, to remove any accumulated mud, which will retain moisture and tend to encourage rust. Paradoxically enough, the best time to clean the chassis and wheel arches is in wet weather, when the mud is thoroughly wet and soft. In very wet weather, the chassis is usually cleaned of large accumulations automatically, and this is a good time for inspection.

Periodically, except on vehicles with a wax-based underbody protective coating, it is a good idea to have the whole of the chassis of the vehicle steam-cleaned, engine compartment included, so that a thorough inspection can be carried out to see what minor repairs and renovations are necessary. Steam-cleaning is available at many garages, and is necessary for the removal of the accumulation of oily grime, which sometimes is allowed to become thick in certain areas. If steam-cleaning facilities are not available, there are some excellent grease solvents available which can be brush-applied; the dirt can then be simply hosed off. Note that these methods should not be used on vehicles with wax-based underbody protective coating, or the coating will be removed. Such vehicles should be inspected annually, preferably just prior to Winter, when the underbody should be washed down, and any damage to the wax coating repaired. Ideally, a completely fresh coat should be applied. It would also be worth considering the use of such wax-based protection for injection into door panels, sills, box sections, etc, as an additional safeguard against rust damage, where such protection is not provided by the vehicle manufacturer.

After washing paintwork, wipe off with a chamois leather to give an unspotted clear finish. A coat of clear protective wax polish will give added protection against chemical pollutants in the air. If the paintwork sheen has dulled or oxidised, use a cleaner/polisher combination to restore the brilliance of the shine. This requires a little effort, but such dulling is usually caused because regular washing has been neglected. Care needs to be taken with metallic paintwork, as special non-abrasive cleaner/polisher is required to avoid damage to the finish. Always check that the door and ventilator opening drain holes and pipes are completely clear, so that water can be drained out. Brightwork should be treated in the same way as paintwork. Windscreens and windows can be kept clear of the smeary film which often appears, by the use of proprietary glass cleaner. Never use any form of wax or other body or chromium polish on glass.

3 Maintenance – upholstery and carpets

Mats and carpets should be brushed or vacuum-cleaned regularly, to keep them free of grit. If they are badly stained, remove them from the vehicle for scrubbing or sponging, and make quite sure they are dry before refitting. Seats and interior trim panels can be kept clean by wiping with a damp cloth. If they do become stained (which can be more apparent on light-coloured upholstery), use a little liquid detergent and a soft nail brush to scour the grime out of the grain of the material. Do not forget to keep the headlining clean in the same way as the upholstery. When using liquid cleaners inside the vehicle, do not over-wet the surfaces being cleaned. Excessive damp could get into the seams and padded interior, causing stains, offensive odours or even rot.

4 Minor body damage – repair

Repair of minor scratches

If the scratch is very superficial, and does not penetrate to the metal of the bodywork, repair is very simple. Lightly rub the area of the scratch with a paintwork renovator, or a very fine cutting paste, to remove loose paint from the scratch and to clear the surrounding bodywork of wax polish. Rinse the area with clean water.

In the case of metallic paint, the most commonly-found 'scratches' are not in the paint, but in the lacquer top coat, and appear white. If care is taken, these can sometimes be rendered less obvious by very careful use of paintwork renovator (which would otherwise not be used on metallic paintwork); otherwise, repair of these scratches can be achieved by applying lacquer with a fine brush.

Apply touch-up paint to the scratch using a thin paintbrush; continue to apply thin layers of paint until the surface of the paint in the scratch is level with the surrounding paintwork. Allow the new paint at least two weeks to harden, then blend it into the surrounding paintwork by rubbing the paintwork in the scratch area with a paintwork renovator or a very fine cutting paste. Finally, apply wax polish.

Where the scratch has penetrated right through to the metal of the bodywork, a different repair technique is required. Remove any loose paint, etc from the bottom of the scratch with a penknife. Using a rubber or nylon applicator, fill the scratch with bodystopper paste. If required, this paste can be mixed with cellulose thinners to provide a very thin paste which is ideal for filling narrow scratches. Before the stopper-paste in the scratch hardens, wrap a piece of smooth cotton rag around the top of a finger. Dip the finger in cellulose thinners, and then quickly sweep it across the surface of the stopper-paste in the scratch; this will ensure that the surface of the stopper-paste is lightly hollowed. The scratch can now be painted over as described earlier in this Section.

Repair of dents

The alloy body panels on the Land Rover are easier to work on than steel, and minor dents or creases can be beaten out fairly easily. However, if the damaged area is quite large, prolonged hammering will cause the metal to harden; to avoid the possibility of cracking, it must be softened or 'annealed'. This can be done easily with a gas blowlamp, but great care is required to avoid actually melting the metal. The blowlamp must always be kept moving in a circular pattern, whilst being held a respectable distance from the metal.

One method of checking when the alloy is hot enough is to rub down the surface to be annealed, and then apply a thin film of oil over it. The blowlamp should be played over the rear side of the oiled surface, until the oil evaporates and the surface is dry. Turn off the blowlamp, and allow the metal to cool naturally; the treated areas will now be softened, and it will be possible to work it with a hammer or mallet. After panel-beating, the damaged section should be rubbed down and painted as described later in this Section.

When deep denting of the vehicle's bodywork has taken place, the first task is to pull the dent out until the affected bodywork almost attains its original shape. There is little point in trying to restore the original shape completely, as the metal in the damaged area will have stretched on impact, and cannot be reshaped to its original contour. It is better to bring the level of the dent up to a point which is about 3 mm below the level of the surrounding bodywork. In cases where the dent is very shallow anyway, it is not worth trying to pull it out at all.

If the underside of the dent is accessible, it can be hammered out gently from behind using the method described earlier.

Should the dent be in a section of the bodywork which has a double skin, or some other factor making it inaccessible from behind, a different technique is called for. Drill several small holes through the metal inside the dent area, particularly in the deeper sections. Then screw long self-tapping screws into the holes just sufficiently for them to gain a good purchase in the metal. Now the dent can be pulled out by pulling on the protruding heads of the screws with a pair of pliers.

The next stage of the repair is the removal of the paint from the damaged area, and from an inch or so of the surrounding 'sound' bodywork.

Note: *On no account should coarse abrasives be used on aluminium panels in order to remove paint. The use of a wire brush or abrasive on a power drill for example, will cause deep scoring of the metal and in extreme cases, penetrate the thickness of the relatively soft aluminium alloy.*

Removal of paint is best achieved by applying paint remover to the area, allowing it to act on the paintwork for the specified time, and then removing the softened paint with a wood or nylon scraper. This method may have to be repeated in order to remove all traces of paint. A good method of removing small stubborn traces of paint is to rub the area with a nylon scouring pad soaked in thinners or paint remover. **Note:** *If it is necessary to use this method, always wear rubber gloves to protect the hands from burns from the paint remover. It is also advisable to wear eye protection, as any paint remover that gets into the eyes will cause severe inflammation, or worse.*

Finally, remove all traces of paint and remover by washing the area with plenty of clean fresh water.

To complete the preparations for filling, score the surface of the bare metal with a screwdriver or the tang of a file, or alternatively, drill small holes in the affected area. This will provide a really good 'key' for the filler paste.

To complete the repair, see the Section on filling and respraying.

Repair of holes or gashes

Remove all the paint from the affected area, and from an inch or so of the surrounding 'sound' bodywork, using the method described in the previous Section. With the paint removed, you will be able to gauge the severity of the damage, and therefore decide whether to renew the whole panel (if this is possible) or to repair the affected area. It is often quicker and more satisfactory to fit a new panel than to attempt to repair large areas of damage.

Remove all fittings from the affected area, except those which will act as a guide to the original shape of the damaged bodywork (eg. headlight shells, etc). Then, using tin snips or a hacksaw blade, remove all loose metal and other metal badly affected by damage. Hammer the edges of the hole inwards, in order to create a slight depression for the filler paste.

Before filling can take place, it will be necessary to block the hole in some way. This can be achieved by the use of zinc gauze or aluminium tape.

Zinc gauze is probably the best material to use for a large hole. Cut a piece to the approximate size and shape of the hole to be filled, then position it in the hole so that its edges are below the level of the surrounding bodywork. It can be retained in position by several blobs of filler paste around its periphery.

Aluminium tape should be used for small or very narrow holes. Pull a piece off the roll and trim it to the approximate size and shape required, then pull off the backing paper (if used) and stick the tape over the hole; it can be overlapped if the thickness of one piece is insufficient. Burnish down the edges of the tape with the handle of a screwdriver or similar, to ensure that the tape is securely attached to the metal underneath.

Filling and respraying

Before using this Section, see the Section on dent, deep scratch, hole and gash repairs.

Many types of bodyfiller are available, but generally speaking, those proprietary kits which contain a tin of filler paste and a tube of resin hardener are best for this type of repair. A wide, flexible plastic or nylon applicator will be found invaluable for imparting a smooth and well-contoured finish to the surface of the filler.

Mix up a little filler on a clean piece of card or board. Use the hardener sparingly (follow the maker's instructions on the packet) otherwise the filler will set rapidly.

Using the applicator, apply the filler paste to the prepared area; draw the applicator across the surface of the filler to achieve the correct contour, and to level the filler surfaces. As soon as a contour that approximates the correct one is achieved, stop working the paste; if you carry on too long, the paste will become sticky and begin to 'pick-up' on the applicator. Continue to add thin layers of filler paste at twenty-minute intervals until the level of the filler is just 'proud' of the surrounding bodywork.

Once the filler has hardened, excess can be removed using a metal plane or file. From then on, progressively finer grades of abrasive paper should be used, starting with a 40-grade production paper, and finishing with a 400-grade wet-or-dry paper. Always wrap the abrasive paper around a flat rubber, cork, or wooden block, otherwise the surface of the filler will not be completely flat. During the smoothing of the filler surface, the wet-or-dry paper should be periodically rinsed in water. This will ensure that a very fine smooth finish is imparted to the filler at the final stage.

At this stage, the 'dent' should be surrounded by a ring of bare metal, which in turn should be encircled by the finely 'feathered' edge of the good paintwork. Rinse the repair with clean water, until all the dust produced by the rubbing-down operation is gone.

Spray the whole area with a light coat of grey primer, this will show up any imperfections in the surface of the filler. If at all possible, it is recommended that an etch-primer is used on untreated alloy surfaces, otherwise the primer may not be keyed sufficiently, and may subsequently flake off. Repair imperfections with fresh filler paste or bodystopper and once more, smooth the surface with abrasive paper. Repeat the spray-and-repair procedures until you are satisfied that the surface of the filler, and the feathered edge of the paintwork, is perfect. Clean the repair area with clean water, and allow it to dry fully.

The repair area is now ready for spraying. Paint spraying must be carried out in a warm, dry, windless and dust-free atmosphere. This condition can be created artificially if you have access to a large indoor working area, but if you are forced to work in the open, you will have to pick your day very carefully. If you are working indoors, dousing the floor in the work area with water will 'lay' the dust which would otherwise be in the atmosphere. If the repair is confined to one body panel, mask off the surrounding panels; this will help to minimise the effects of a slight mis-match in paint colours. Bodywork fittings will also need to be masked off. Use genuine masking tape and several thickness of newspaper for the masking operation.

Before commencing to spray, agitate the aerosol can thoroughly, then spray a test area (an old tin, or similar) until the technique is mastered. Cover the repair area with a thick coat of primer; the thickness should be built up using several thin layers of paint, rather than one thick one. Using 400-grade wet-or-dry paper, rub down the surface of the primer until it is really smooth. Whilst doing this, the work area should be thoroughly doused with water, and the wet-or-dry paper periodically rinsed in water. Allow to dry before spraying on more paint.

Spray on the top coat, again building up the thickness by using several thin layers of paint. Start spraying at the top of the repair area and then, using a side-to-side motion, work downwards until the whole repair area and about 50 mm of the surrounding original paintwork is covered. Remove all masking material 10 to 15 minutes after spraying on the final coat of paint.

Allow the new paint at least two weeks to harden, then, using a paintwork renovator or a very fine cutting paste, blend the edges of the paint into the existing paintwork. Finally, apply wax polish.

Plastic components

With the use of more and more plastic body components by the vehicle manufacturers (eg bumpers. spoilers, and in some cases major body panels), rectification of more serious damage to such items has become a matter of either entrusting repair work to a specialist in this field, or renewing complete components. Repair of such damage by the DIY owner is not really feasible, owing to the cost of the equipment and materials required for effecting such repairs. The basic technique involves making a groove along the line of the crack in the plastic, using a rotary burr in a power drill. The damaged part is then welded back together, using a hot-air gun to heat up and fuse a plastic filler rod into the groove. Any excess plastic is then removed, and the area rubbed down to a smooth finish. It is important that a filler rod of the correct plastic is used, as body components can be made of a variety of different types (eg polycarbonate, ABS, polypropylene).

Damage of a less serious nature (abrasions, minor cracks etc) can be repaired by the DIY owner using a two-part epoxy filler repair material. Once mixed in equal proportions, or applied directly from the tube, this is used in similar fashion to the bodywork filler used on metal panels. The filler is usually cured in twenty to thirty minutes, ready for sanding and painting.

If the owner is renewing a complete component himself, or if he has repaired it with epoxy filler, he will be left with the problem of finding a suitable paint for finishing which is compatible with the type of plastic used. At one time, the use of a universal paint was not possible, owing to the complex range of plastics encountered in body component applications. Standard paints, generally speaking, will not bond to plastic or rubber satisfactorily. However, it is now possible to obtain a plastic body parts finishing kit which consists of a pre-primer treatment, a primer and coloured top coat. Full instructions are normally supplied with a kit, but basically, the method of use is to first apply the pre-primer to the component concerned, and allow it to dry for up to 30 minutes. Then the primer is applied, and left to dry for about an hour before finally applying the special-coloured top coat. The result is a correctly-coloured component, where the paint will flex with the plastic or rubber, a property that standard paint does not normally possess.

5 Major body damage – repair

Where serious damage has occurred, or large areas need renewal due to neglect, it means that complete new panels will need welding in, and this is best left to professionals. If the damage is due to impact, it will also be necessary to check completely the alignment of the bodyshell, and this can only be carried out accurately by a Land Rover dealer using special jigs. If the body is left misaligned, it is primarily dangerous, as the car will not handle properly. Secondly, uneven stresses will be imposed on the steering, suspension and possibly transmission, causing abnormal wear, or complete failure, particularly to such items as the tyres.

6 Front bumper – removal and refitting

Removal

1 Raise the front of the vehicle and support it securely on axle stands (see *Jacking and vehicle support*).

2 Remove the headlights as described in Chapter 13, Section 7.

3 Undo the 3 retaining screws and remove the mudflaps.

4 Prise up the centre pins, lever out the 4 plastic expansion rivets, then undo the 2 retaining screws and pull the wheel arch extension outwards to release the retaining clips. Repeat this operation on the remaining side.

5 The bumper is secured by 14 screws. Undo the screws, release the clips, pull out the rear, upper edges and, with the help of an assistant, manoeuvre the bumper forwards a little **(see illustrations)**.

6 Disconnect the wiring plugs and the headlight washer hose from the pump, then remove the bumper completely **(see illustrations)**.

Refitting

7 Refitting is a reversal of removal.

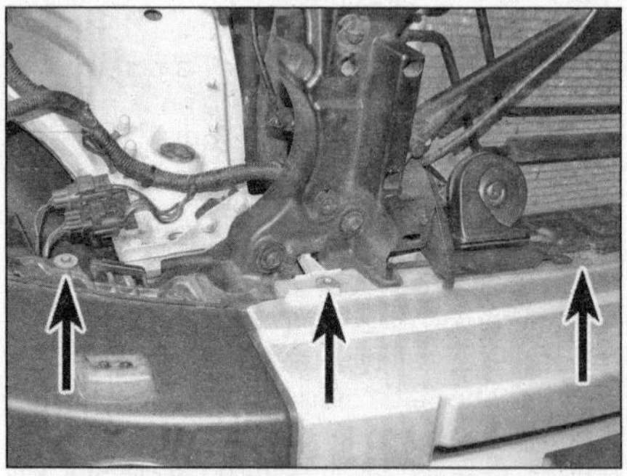

6.5a The front bumper is retained by 3 screws (right-hand screws arrowed) each side on the upper edge ...

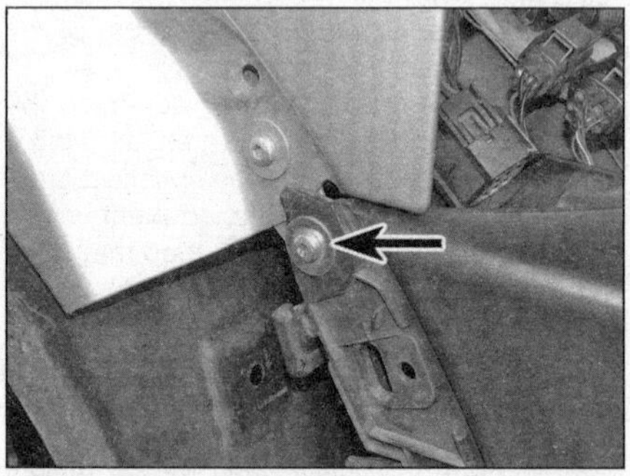

6.5b ... a screw (arrowed) each side on the rear edge ...

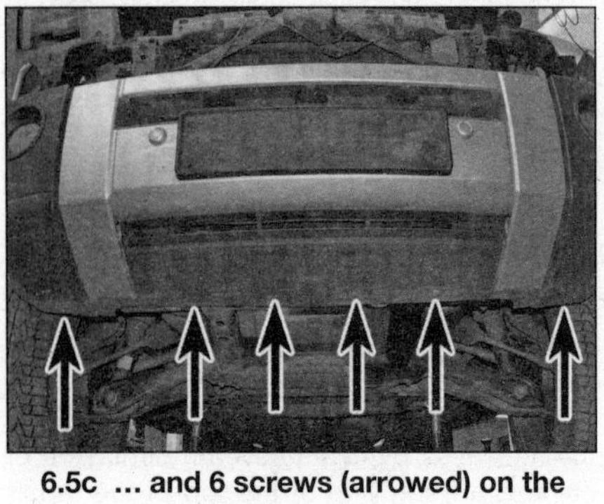

6.5c ... and 6 screws (arrowed) on the lower edge

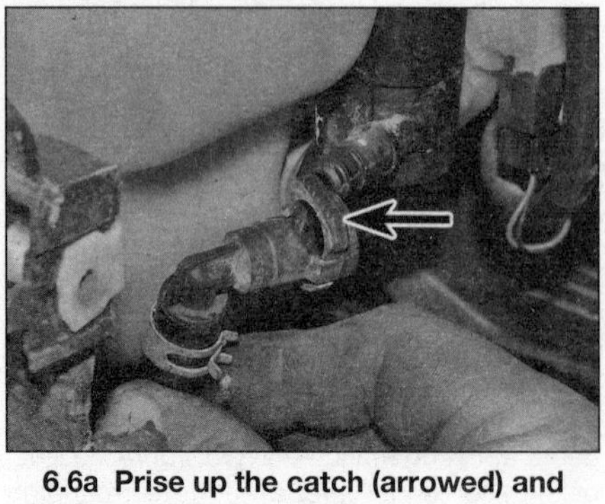

6.6a Prise up the catch (arrowed) and disconnect the headlight washer jet hose

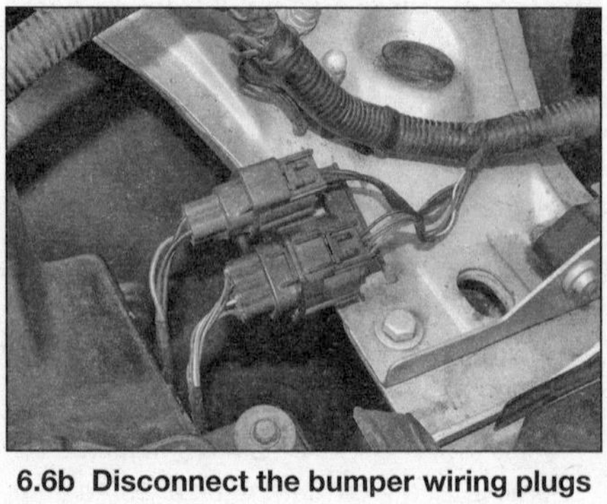

6.6b Disconnect the bumper wiring plugs

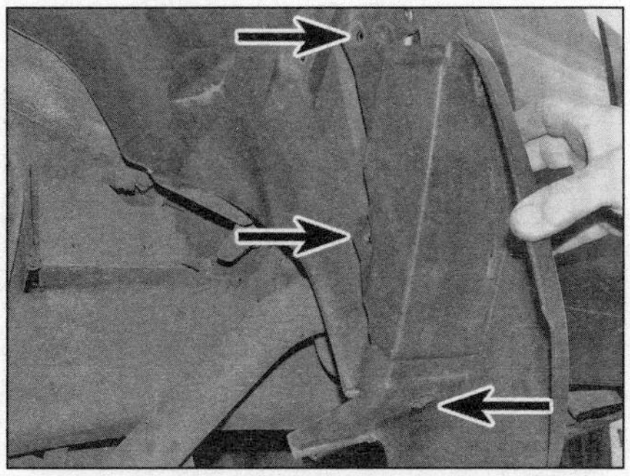

7.3 Undo the screws (arrowed) and remove the rear mudflap each side

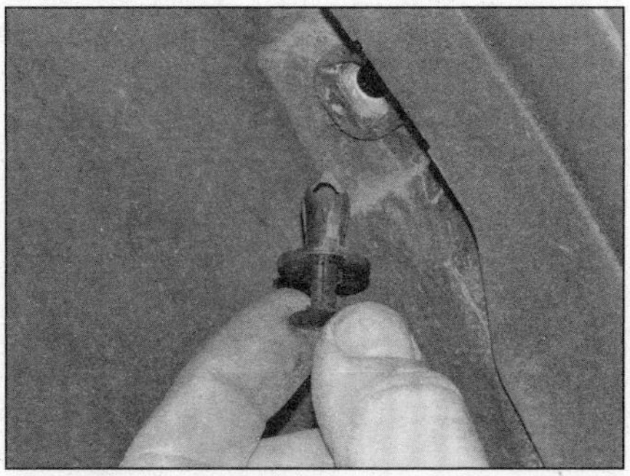

7.4a Prise out the centre pins ...

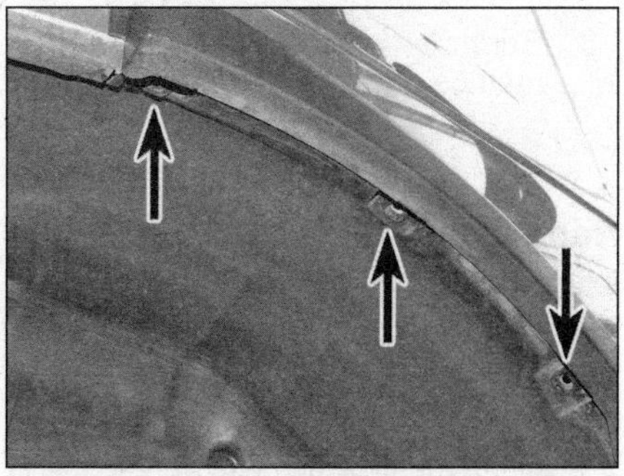

7.4b ... pull out the expansion rivets (arrowed) ...

7.4c ... and pull the wheel arch extension outwards

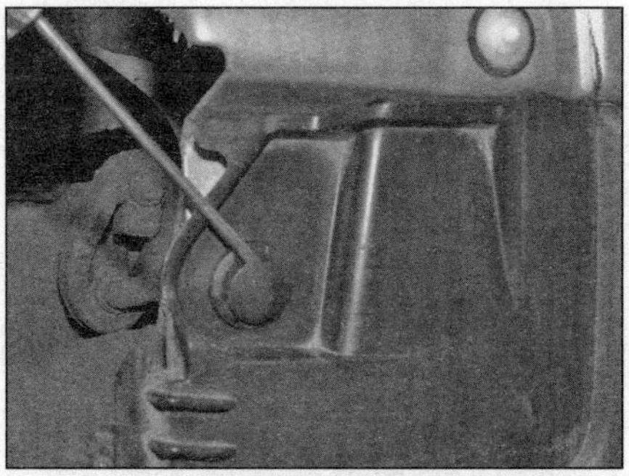

7.5 Remove the expansion rivet at the front edge each side

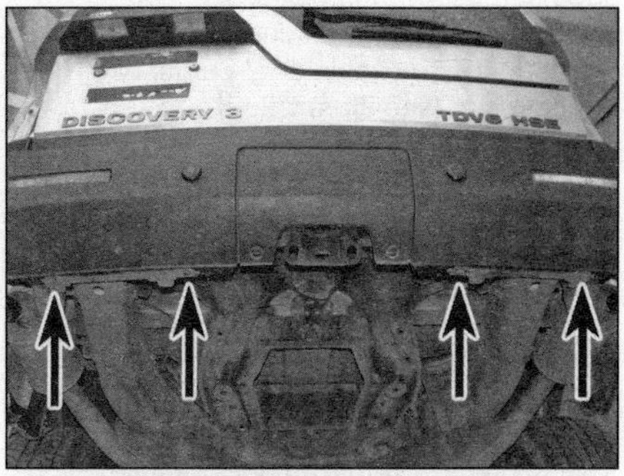

7.6a Undo the screws (arrowed) on the underside of the bumper ...

7 Rear bumper – removal and refitting

Removal

1 Raise the rear of the vehicle and support it securely on axle stands (see *Jacking and vehicle support*).

2 Remove both rear light units as described in Chapter 13, Section 7.

3 Undo the 3 retaining screws and remove the mudflaps **(see illustration)**.

4 Prise up the centre pins, lever out the 3 plastic expansion rivets, then pull the wheel arch extension outwards to release the retaining clips **(see illustrations)**. Repeat this operation on the remaining side.

5 Prise up the centre pin, and lever out the plastic expansion rivet at the front edge of the bumper each side **(see illustration)**.

6 Undo the 4 screws on the underside of the bumper, and the screw each side in the light unit apertures **(see illustrations)**.

7 Fold down the lower tailgate, lift up the hinge cover, then prise up the centre pins and lever out the 4 plastic expansion rivets at the upper edge of the bumper **(see illustrations)**.

8 With the aid of an assistant, support the bumper, then pull the front, outer edges outwards to release the clips, and manoeuvre the bumper rearwards a little. Disconnect any wiring plugs, and withdrawn the bumper **(see illustrations)**.

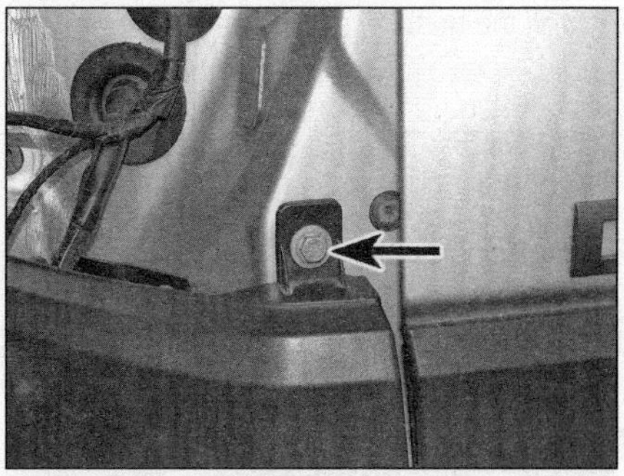

7.6b ... and the screw (arrowed) each side in the light aperture

Refitting

9 Refitting is the reverse of removal.

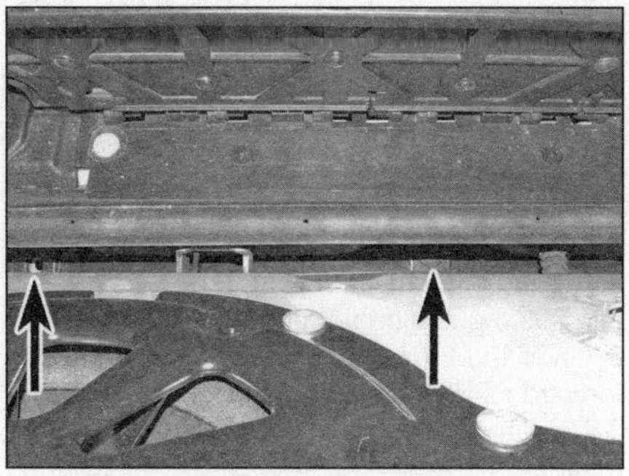

7.7 Prise out the plastic expansion rivets (left-hand rivets arrowed) under the hinge cover

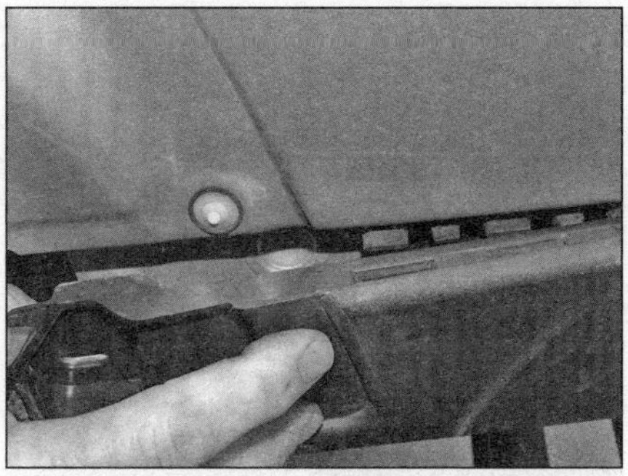

7.8a Pull the front, outer edges outwards

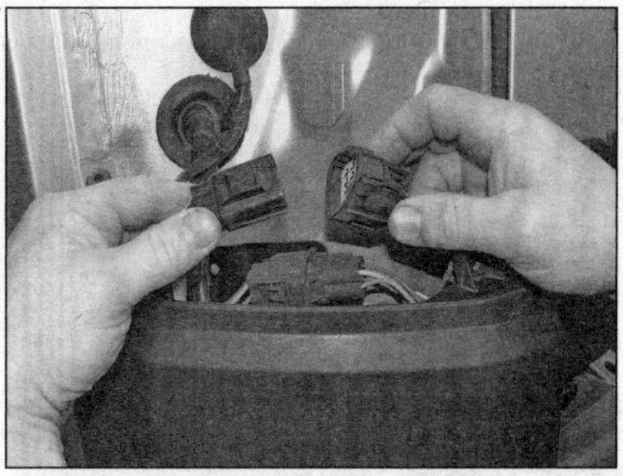

7.8b Disconnect the wiring plugs at the left-hand end of the bumper

8 Bonnet – removal, refitting and adjustment

Removal

1 Open the bonnet, and have an assistant support it. Using a pencil or felt tip pen, mark the outline position of each bonnet hinge relative to the bonnet, to use as a guide on refitting.
2 Prise out the clips and remove the bonnet soundproofing **(see illustration)**.
3 Disconnect the windscreen washer tube and heated jet wiring plugs.
4 Undo the bonnet retaining bolts and, with the help of an assistant, carefully lift the bonnet clear **(see illustration)**.
5 Inspect the bonnet hinges for signs of wear or damage; the hinges are bolted in position, and can easily be renewed.

Refitting and adjustment

6 With the aid of an assistant, offer up the bonnet, and loosely fit the retaining bolts. Align the hinges with the marks made on removal, then tighten the retaining bolts securely.
7 Close the bonnet, and check for alignment with the adjacent panels. If necessary, slacken the bonnet bolts and realign the bonnet to suit. Once the bonnet is correctly aligned, securely tighten the bolts.

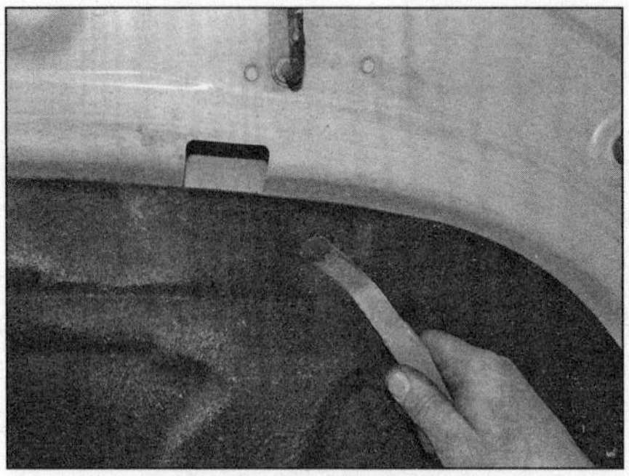

8.2 Prise out the clips securing the bonnet soundproofing panel

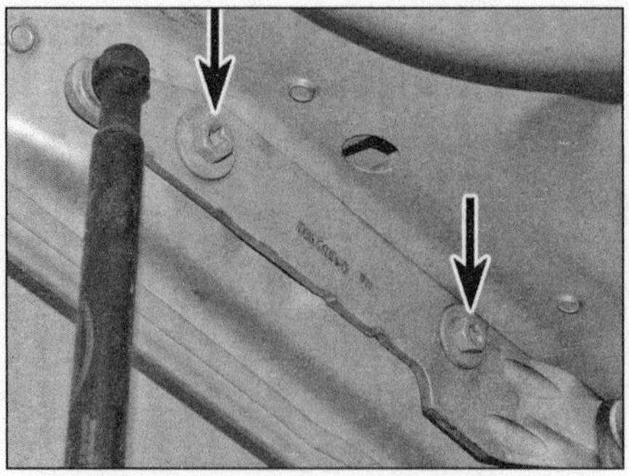

8.4 Hinge-to-bonnet retaining bolts (arrowed)

8 Once the bonnet is correctly aligned, check that the bonnet fastens and releases in a satisfactory manner.

9 Bonnet release cable – removal and refitting

Removal

1 Remove the front grille as described in Section 29.
2 Unclip the junction box from the left-hand inner wing in the engine compartment, then open the junction box on the left-hand inner wing in the engine compartment and disconnect the release cables **(see illustration)**.
3 Release the clips and remove the left-hand side footwell kick panel from the lower A-pillar.
4 Undo the bolt, detach the release handle, then disconnect the cable **(see illustration)**.
5 Pull the sound insulation material from the engine compartment bulkhead, and prise the cable grommet from position.
6 Tie a length of string to the cable in the passenger's compartment, then pull the cable through from the bonnet lock end.
7 Once the cable end appears, untie the string and leave it in position in the vehicle; the string can then be used to draw the new cable back into position. Remove the grommet from the cable.
8 Disconnect the remaining cables from the bonnet locks.

Refitting

9 Fit the grommet to the new cable.
10 Tie the string to the end of the cable, and use the string to draw the bonnet release cable through from engine compartment. Once the cable is through, untie the string.
11 The remainder of refitting is a reversal of removal.

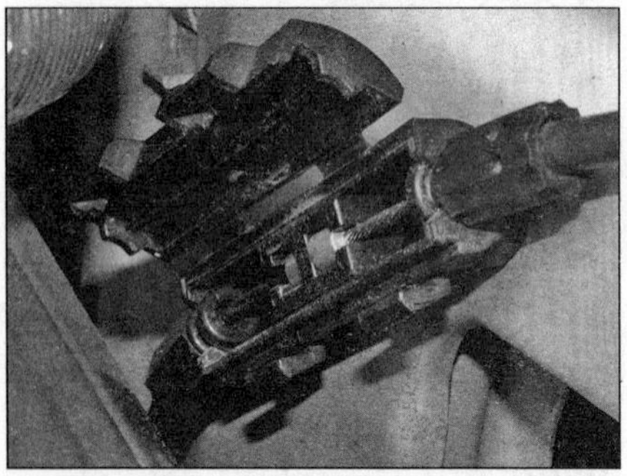

9.2 Open the junction box and disconnect the cables

9.4 Squeeze the clips (arrowed) together and pull the outer cable from the bracket

10 Bonnet locks – removal and refitting

Removal

1 Remove the front radiator grille as described in Section 29.
2 Using a suitable marker pen, draw around the outline of the bonnet lock top plate and adjusting plates. These marks can then be used as a guide on refitting.
3 Undo the 2 retaining bolts and pull the lock forwards a little **(see illustration)**.
4 Disconnect the wiring plug from the rear of the lock.
5 Depress the clip each side and slide the switch from the base of the lock **(see illustration)**.

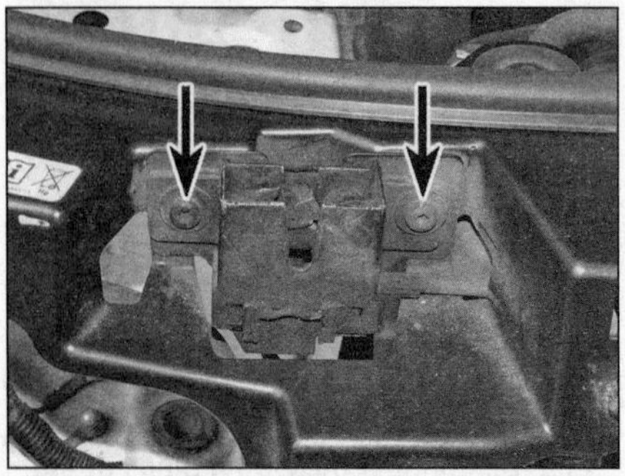

10.3 Bonnet lock retaining bolts (arrowed)

10.5 Depress the clips (arrowed) and slide the switch from the lock

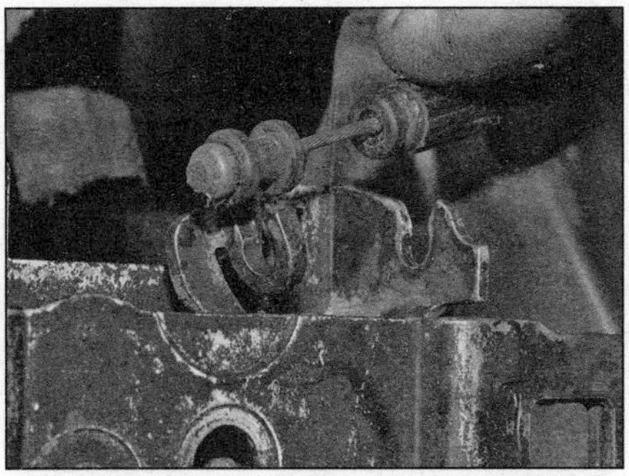

10.6 Detach the cable from the bonnet lock

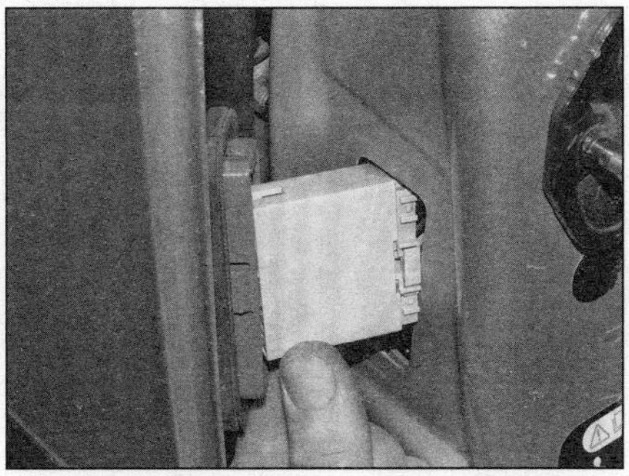

11.1 Prise the rubber sleeve from the pillar, and disconnect the wiring plug

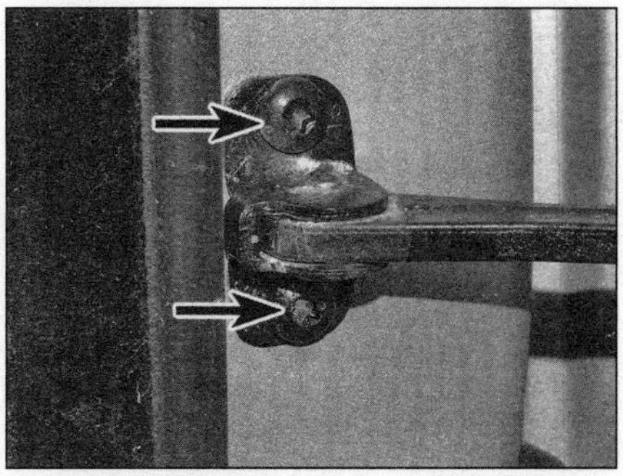

11.2 Door check strap bolts (arrowed)

6 Disconnect the cable from the underside of the lock **(see illustration**.

Refitting

7 Refitting is the reverse of the removal procedure, using the alignment marks made prior to removal. Prior to refitting the radiator grille, check the operation of the release mechanism.

11 Door – removal, refitting and adjustment

Removal

1 Release the wiring harness rubber sleeve from the door pillar, then withdraw and disconnect the wiring plug **(see illustration)**.

2 Undo the bolts securing the check strap to the pillar **(see illustration)**.

3 Undo the hinge pin bolts **(see illustration)** and, with the aid of an assistant, carefully lift the door upwards and away from the vehicle.

4 Examine the hinges for signs of wear or damage. If renewal is necessary, mark the outline of the original hinge on the door/pillar, then slacken and remove the retaining bolts and remove the hinge brackets. Note the correct fitted location of the shim(s) and spacer plates which are positioned behind them. Fit the new brackets, making sure that the shim(s) and spacer plates are correctly arranged, and refit the retaining bolts. Align the brackets with the marks made prior to removal, and securely tighten the retaining bolts.

Refitting

5 Apply a smear of multipurpose grease to the hinge pivots then, with the aid of an assistant, manoeuvre the door back into position. Tighten the hinge pin bolts securely.

6 Align the check strap with the pillar and tighten the bolts securely.

7 Reconnect the wiring connectors, feed the wiring back into the door pillar, and seat the wiring grommet in position.

8 Adjust the door position as described below.

Adjustment

9 Some vertical adjustment of the doors can be achieved by slackening the hinge retaining bolts and repositioning the hinge/door.

10 Some front-to-rear adjustment of the door position can be achieved by adding/removing shims between the door and hinge bracket. To do this, loosen (do not remove) the hinge retaining bolts, then add/remove the relevant number of shims; the shims are slotted to allow the thickness to be adjusted without removing the door. Once the door is correctly positioned, securely tighten the hinge retaining bolts.

11 Door closure may be adjusted by altering the position of the door lock striker on the body. Slacken the striker, reposition it as required, then securely retighten it. The striker can also be adjusted by adding/removing shims from behind it.

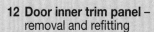

11.3 Door hinge pin bolt (arrowed)

12 Door inner trim panel – removal and refitting

Note: *It is a good idea to obtain a few trim panel retaining clips before starting, as they are often broken in the course of removal, or will be found to have broken during previous removal attempts.*

Removal

1 Release the 2 clips on the underside, then release the 2 upper clips and pull up the cover from the grab handle **(see illustrations)**.

2 Prise out the cover in the release handle recess, and remove the exposed screw **(see illustration)**.

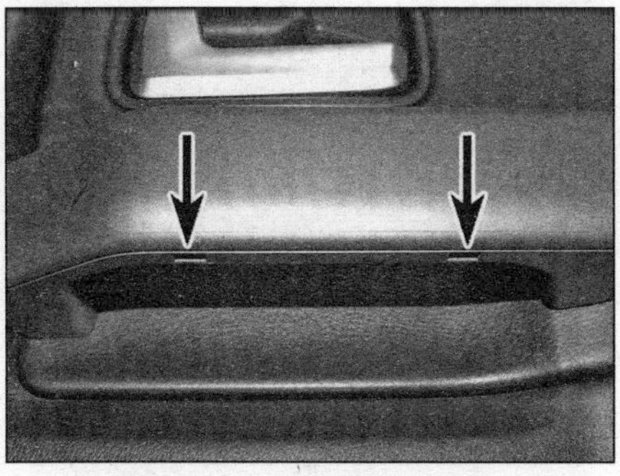

12.1a Release the clips (arrowed) on the underside of the grab handle ...

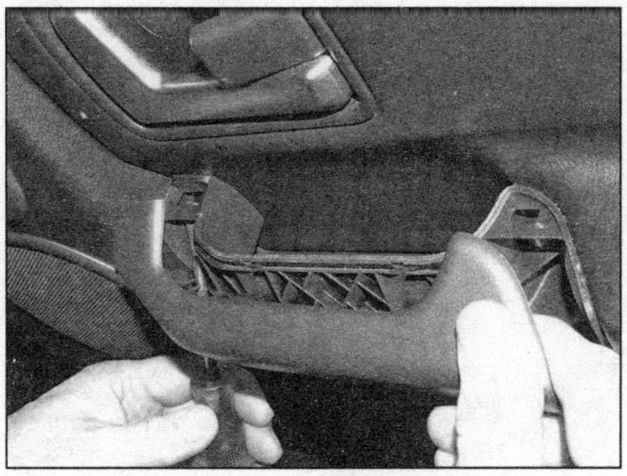

12.1b ... then reach up through and release the clips at the top

12.2 Prise out the cover and under the screw (arrowed)

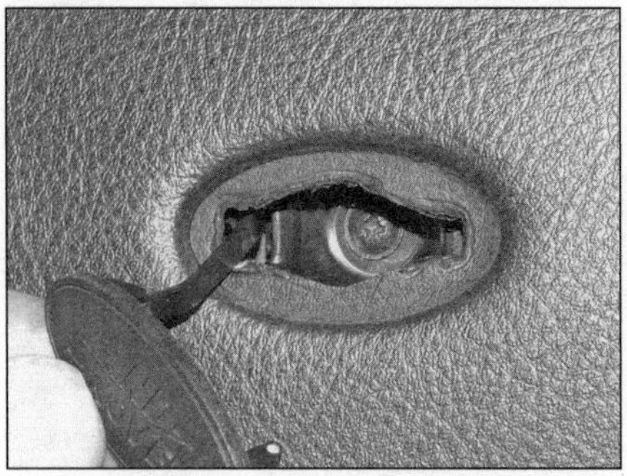
12.3 Undo the screw beneath the cover

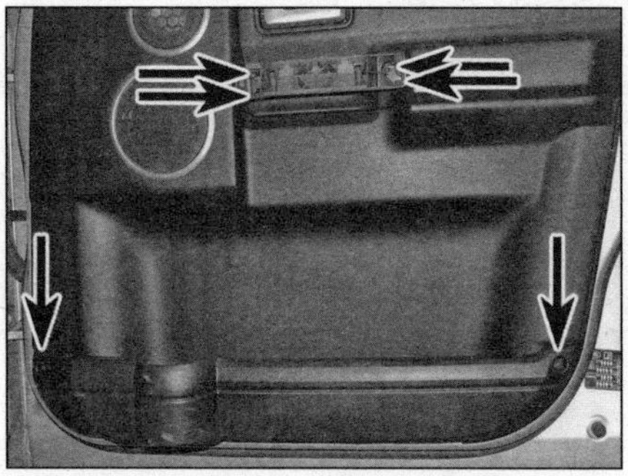
12.4a The front door panel is secured by 6 screws (arrowed)

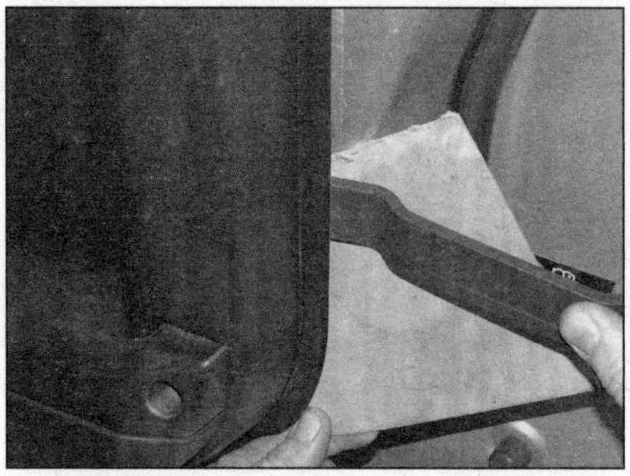
12.4b Prise between the panel and the door to release the clips. Note the cardboard to protect the paintwork

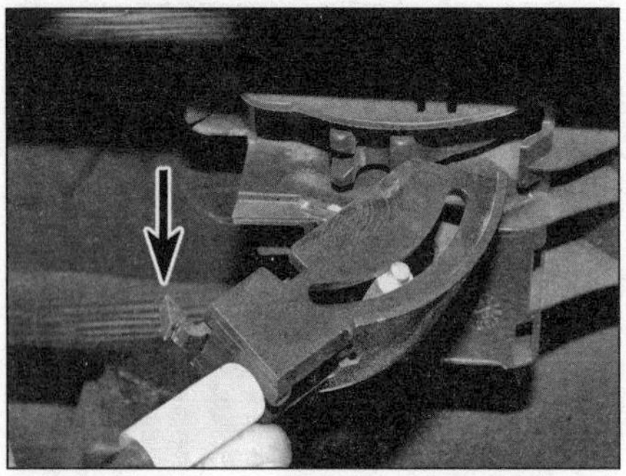
12.5a Release the clip (arrowed) and pull the release cable from the handle

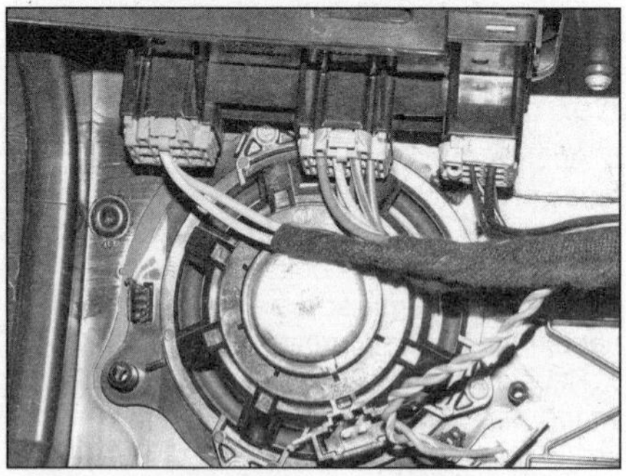
12.5b Disconnect the wiring plugs as they become accessible

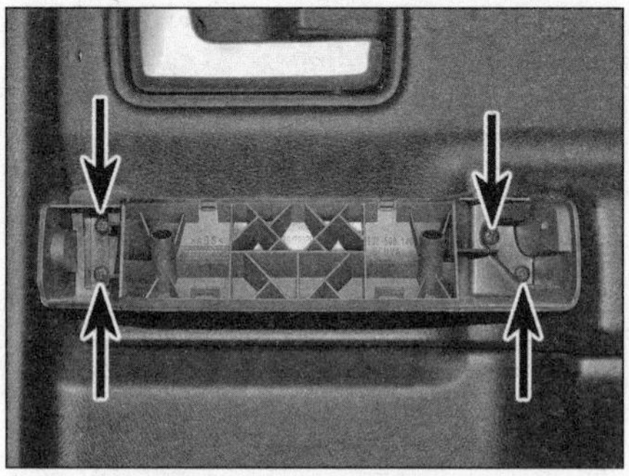
12.6a Undo the screws behind the grab handle (arrowed) ...

Front door

3 Prise out the cover at the rear of the panel and remove the exposed screw **(see illustration)**.

4 The panel is now secured by 6 screws, and 12 clips around its lower, front, and rear edges. Remove the screws, then use a flat-bladed tool to prise between the panel and the door frame to release the clips **(see illustrations)**. Take care not to damage the paintwork – use a piece of card between the tool and the door.

5 Pull the panel away from the door, disconnecting the wiring plugs and release cable as they become accessible **(see illustrations)**.

Rear door

6 The panel is now secured by 6 screws, and 13 clips around its lower, front, and rear edges. Remove the screws, then use a flat-bladed tool to prise between the panel and the door frame to release the clips **(see illustrations)**. Take care not to damage the paintwork – use a piece of card between the tool and the door.

7 Pull the panel inwards and away from the door, disconnecting the wiring plugs and release cable as they become accessible **(see illustration 12.5a)**.

Refitting

8 Refitting is a reverse of the removal procedure. Prior to refitting, examine the panel retaining clips for signs of damage – renew any broken clips.

13 Door handle and lock components – removal and refitting

Interior release handle

1 Remove the door inner trim panel as described in Section 12.

2 Starting at the lower edge, carefully prise the handle assembly from the door trim panel **(see illustration)**.

3 Refitting is a reversal of removal

Exterior handle

4 Remove the window regulator assembly as described in Section 14.

12.6b ... and the screws (arrowed) at the base of the panel

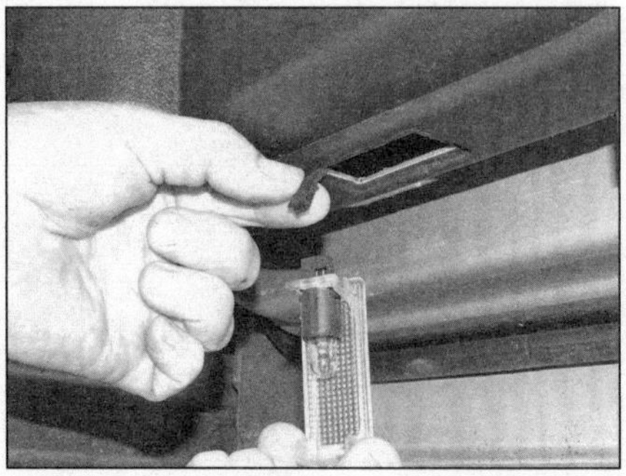
12.6c Disconnect the 'puddle' light wiring plug

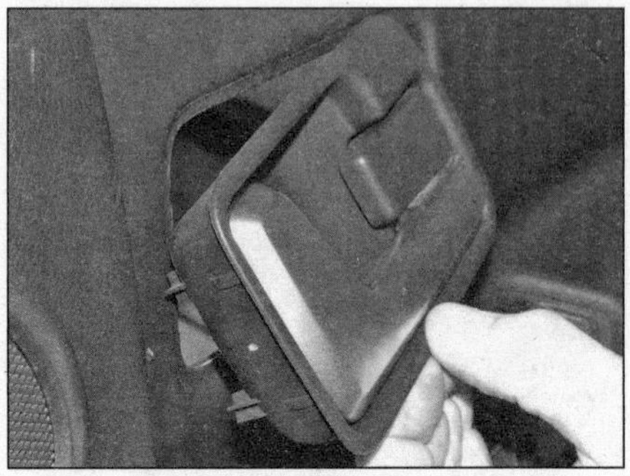
13.2 Prise the lower edge of the handle assembly from the panel

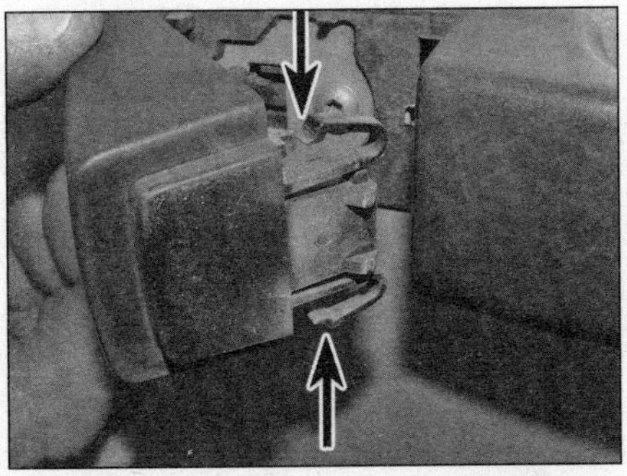

13.7 Carefully pull the cover from place – the clips (arrowed) are easily damaged

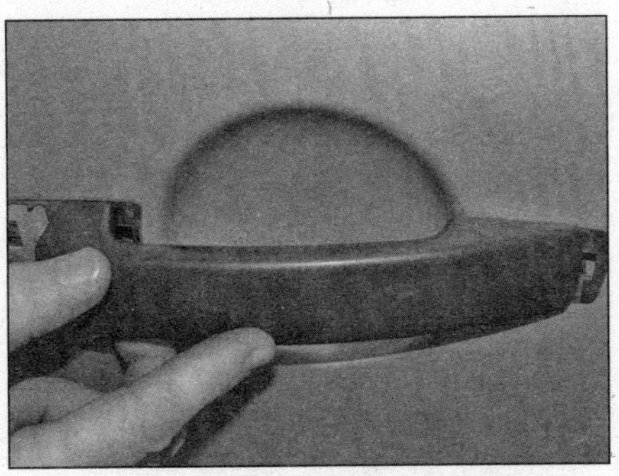

13.9a Slide the exterior handle rearwards ...

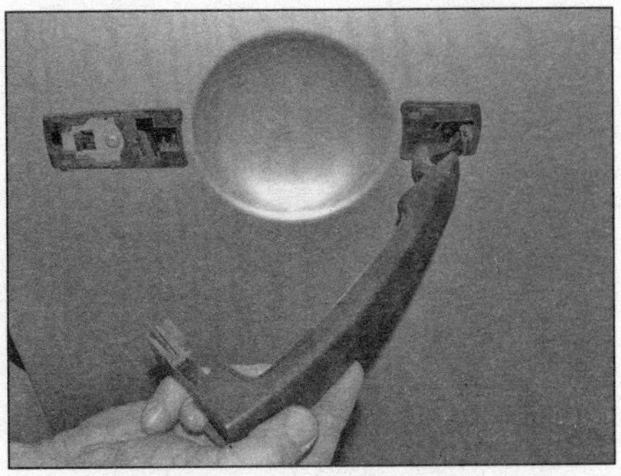

13.9b ... then outwards

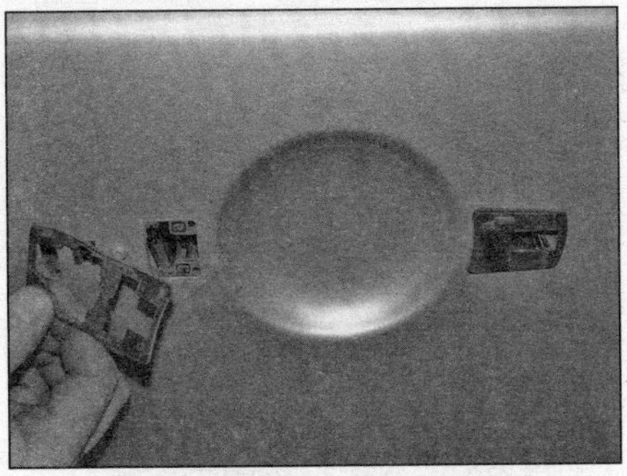

13.9c Recover the gasket

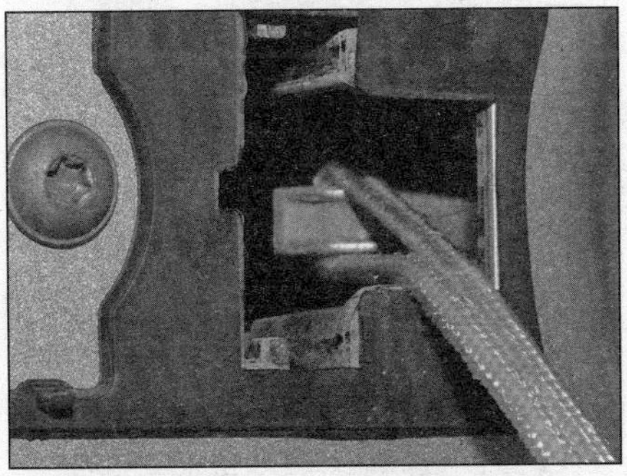

13.10a Use string (or similar) to hold the lock lever against the spring pressure ...

13.10b ... then refit the exterior handle

5 Disconnect the wiring plug from the exterior door handle (models with passive entry system – PES).

6 If working on the driver's door, remove the door lock cylinder (where fitted) as described in this Section.

7 Squeeze together the retaining clips, pull out the handle a little and remove the cover from the rear section of the exterior handle **(see illustration)**. Take care as the clips are easily damaged. These clips are extremely difficult to reach – if necessary, prise the cover from the handle from the outside. Note that this option is quite likely to result in clip/cover breakage.

8 On models with PES, slide the retaining clip forwards, and remove the handle. Recover the gaskets.

9 On models without PES, with the handle closed, slide the exterior handle rearwards then outwards to remove it **(see illustrations)**. Recover the gaskets.

10 Begin refitting by using a length of string (or similar) to hold the lock lever against the spring pressure, then insert the front edge of the handle, followed by the rear edge **(see illustrations)**. As soon as the handle is correctly engaged, release the lock lever.

11 The remainder of refitting is a reversal of removal.

Lock cylinder

Note: *A lock cylinder is not fitted to all models.*

12 Insert the ignition key into the slot on the underside of the lock cylinder cover, and prise the cover from place.

13 Prise out the grommet at the rear edge of the door, and slacken the Torx screw until the cylinder can be withdrawn. Note that the screw remains in the housing.

14 Refitting is a reversal of removal.

Door lock

15 Remove the window regulator assembly as described in Section 14

16 Remove the door exterior handle as described earlier in this Section.

17 Release the rubber grommet where the interior release cable passes through the door panel.

Front door

18 Peel away the adhesive tape, undo the Torx screws, and remove the locking pin securing the exterior handle mechanism to the door **(see illustrations)**.

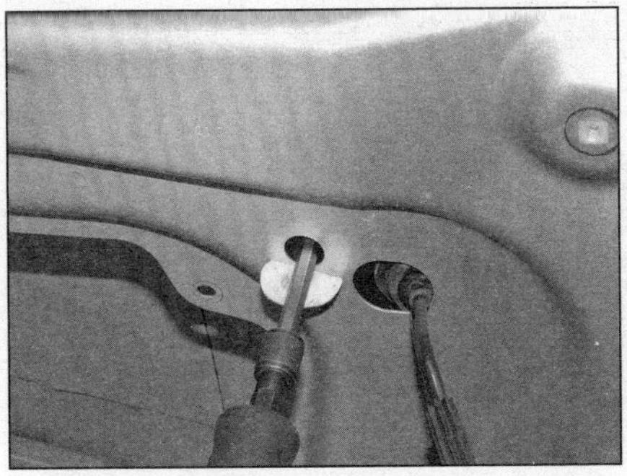

13.18a Undo the screw on the inside of the door ...

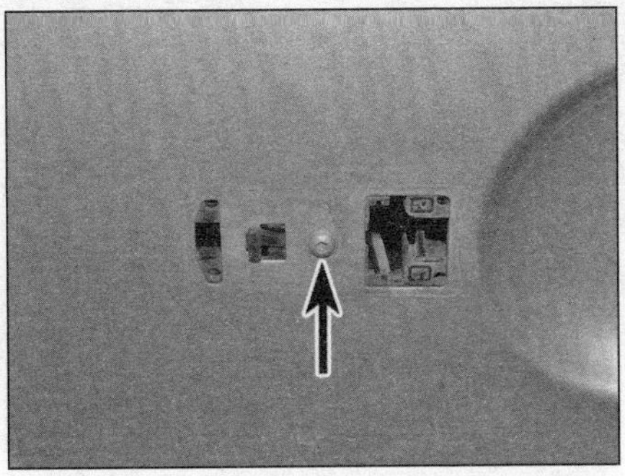

13.18b ... and the screw on the exterior of the door (arrowed)

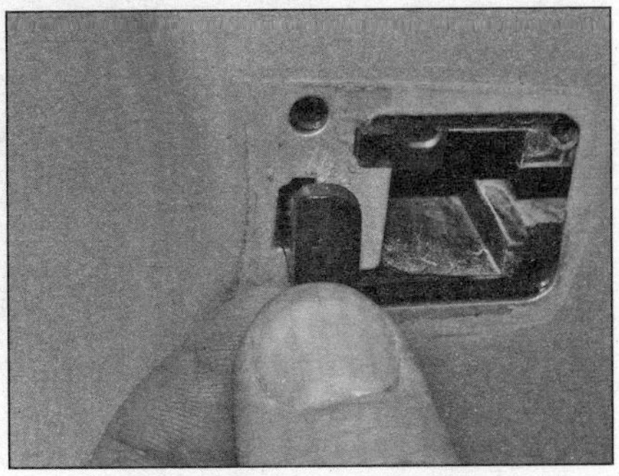

13.18c Pull out the locking pin

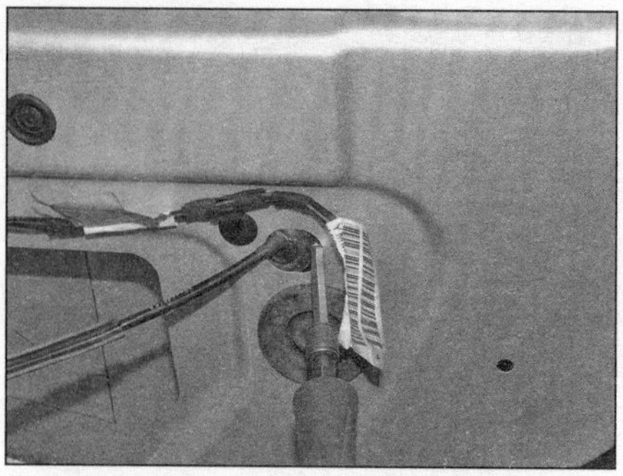

13.19a Release the rubber grommet to access the inner screw ...

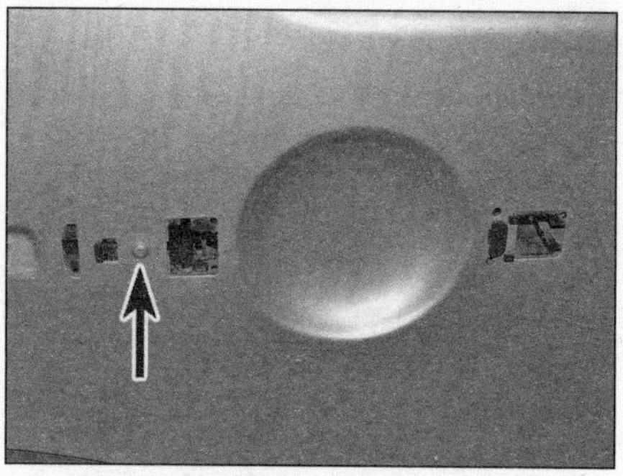

13.19b ... then remove the outer screw (arrowed) ...

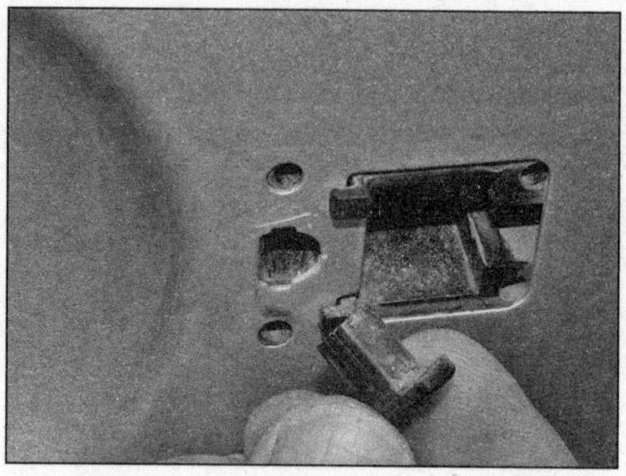

13.19c ... and pull out the locking pin

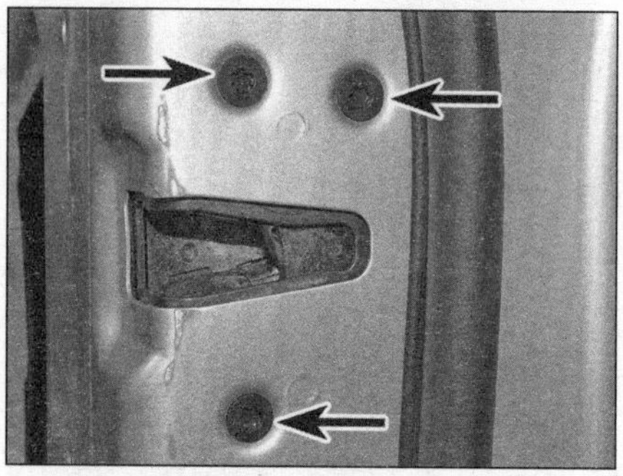

13.20 Undo the lock retaining screws (arrowed)

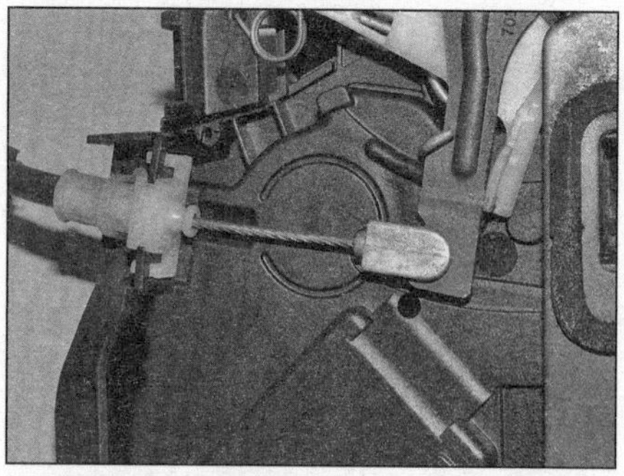

13.21a Disconnect the inner handle release cable ...

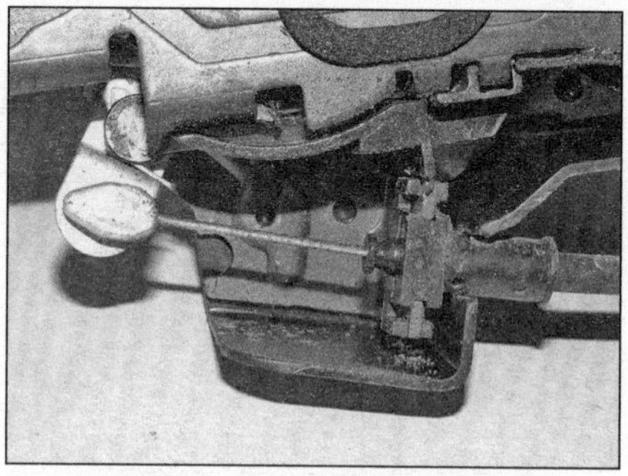

13.21b ... exterior handle cable ...

Rear door

19 Undo the 2 Torx screws, and remove the locking pin securing the exterior handle mechanism to the door **(see illustrations)**.

Both doors

20 Disconnect the wiring plug, undo the 3 Torx screws at the door's rear edge, then manoeuvre the lock, release cable, and the exterior handle mechanism from the door cavity **(see illustration)**.

21 If required, unclip the release cable, exterior handle cable and lock cylinder cable from the lock assembly **(see illustrations)**.

22 Begin refitting by reconnecting the release cable, exterior handle cable, and lock cylinder cable (where applicable).

23 Before refitting the exterior handle mechanism, rotate the lever, and hold it in place with the retaining tang **(see illustration)**.

24 Manoeuvre the lock, exterior handle assembly and release cable into position and secure them with the Torx screws and pin.

25 The remainder of refitting is a reversal of removal. Ensure the lock functions correctly before closing the door.

14 Door window glass and regulator – removal and refitting

Front door drop glass

1 Lower the drop glass approximately 90 mm, then undo the screw at the front and rear

13.21c ... and lock cylinder cable

13.23 Rotate the lever and hold it in place using the spring tang (arrowed)

14.1a Undo the screw at rear of the door (arrowed) ...

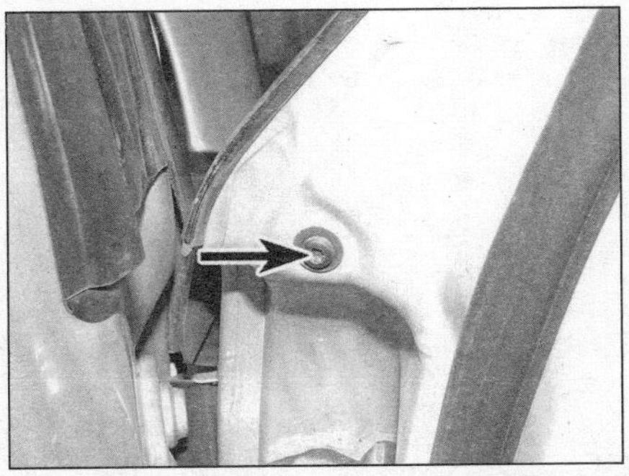

14.1b ... and the front of the door (arrowed) ...

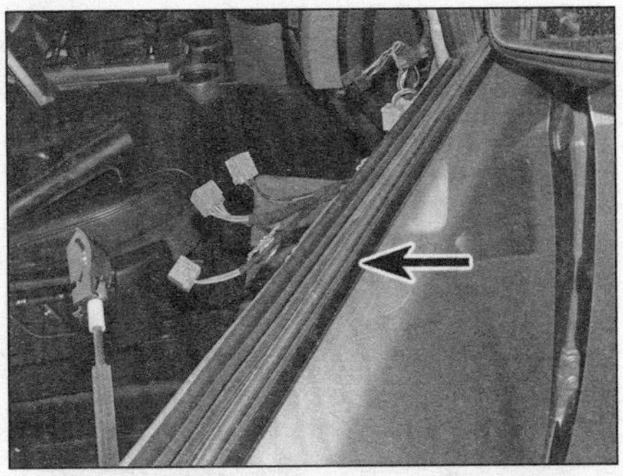

14.1c ... then prise up the outer door weatherstrip

inner edge of the door, and remove the outer weatherstrip from the top edge of the door panel **(see illustrations)**.

2 Undo the screws and remove the door speaker.

3 Reach through the speaker aperture, and press the front and rear retaining clips outwards to release the base of the drop glass from the regulator **(see illustrations)**. Lift the rear edge first, and manoeuvre the glass from the door.

4 When fitting the brackets to the new glass, ensure they are pushed to the edge so there is the minimum gap between them and the glass. Note that the gap must be parallel **(see illustration)**.

5 Refitting is a reversal of removal. Slide the glass down until it can be felt to clip into the regulator assembly.

Rear door drop glass

6 Remove the rear door quarter-light glass as described later in this Section.

7 Lift the glass from the door **(see illustration)**.

8 Refitting is a reversal of removal.

Front door window regulator

9 Remove the front door inner trim panel as described in Section 12.

10 Remove the door drop glass as described earlier in this Section.

11 Release the wiring harnesses from any retaining clips.

12 Undo the retaining bolt and manoeuvre the glass guide channel from the front of the door **(see illustrations)**. Note the locating clip at the top of the guide channel.

13 Disconnect the wiring plugs from the

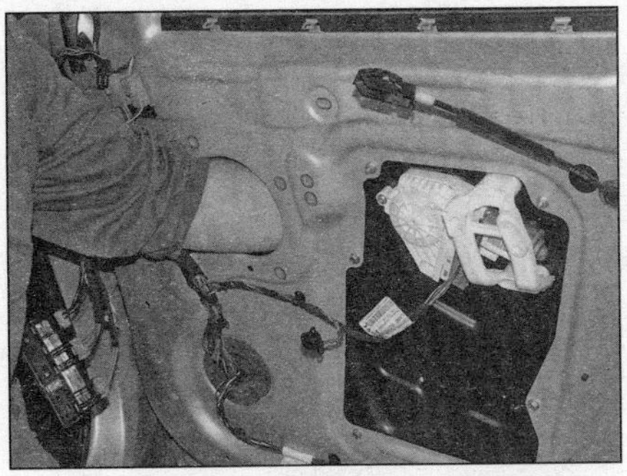

14.3a Reach through the speaker aperture ...

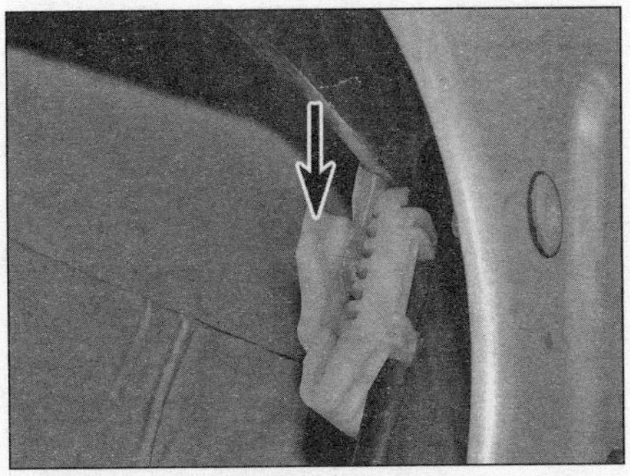

14.3b ... and press the retaining clips (arrowed) outwards to release the glass clamps

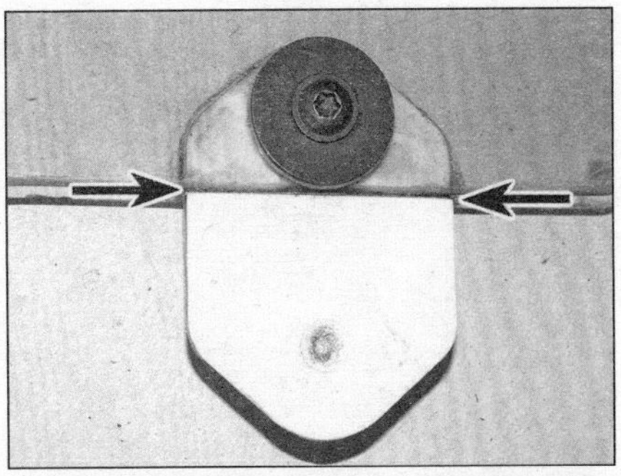

14.4 There must be the minimum clearance between the bracket and the edge of the glass, and it must be parallel

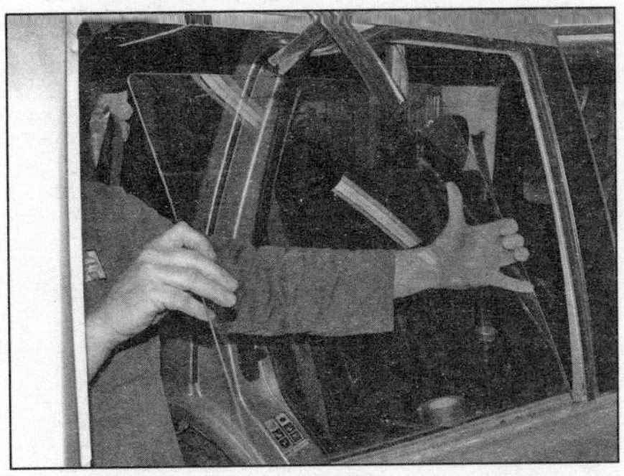

14.7 Lift the drop glass from the rear door

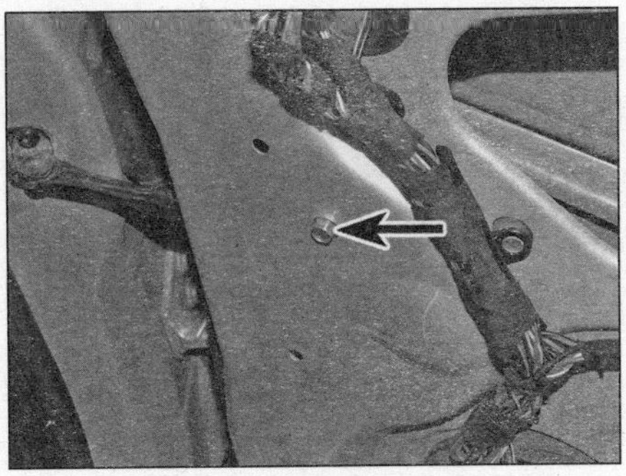

14.12a Undo the retaining bolt (arrowed) ...

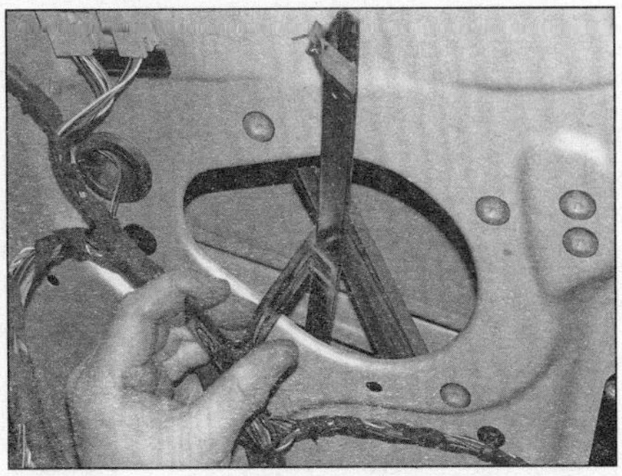

14.12b ... and manoeuvre the glass guide channel from the door

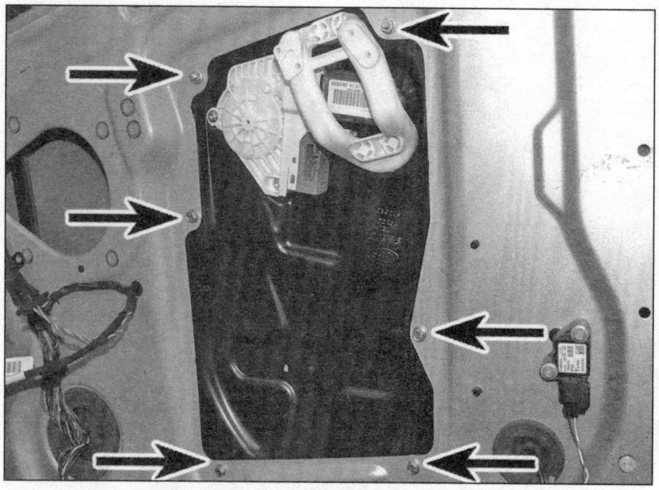
14.14a Remove the retaining bolts/nuts (arrowed) ...

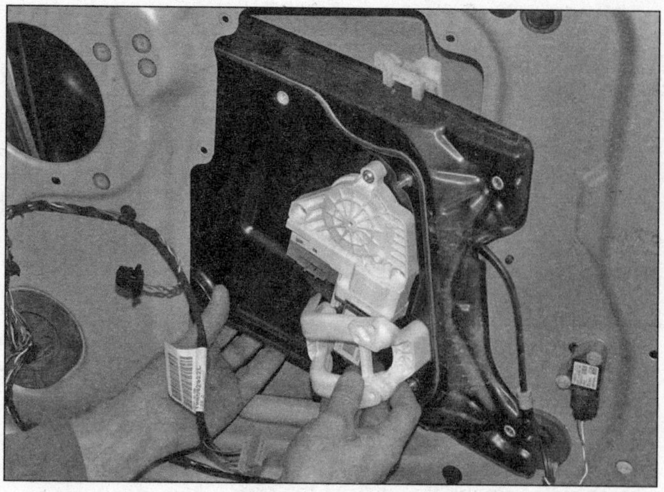
14.14b ... rotate it 90° and manoeuvre the regulator assembly from the door

motor assembly, and move the harness to one side.

14 Undo the 4 bolts and 2 nuts, and manoeuvre the regulator/motor assembly from the door cavity **(see illustrations)**.

15 Refitting is a reversal of removal.

Rear door window regulator

16 Lower the glass approximately a third of the way down, then remove the door inner trim panel as described in Section 12.

17 Disconnect the wiring plug, undo the screws and remove the door speaker.

18 Undo the screw and carefully prise up the outer weatherstrip from the top edge of the door panel **(see illustrations)**.

19 Reach through the speaker aperture, and release the clip securing the glass bracket to the regulator assembly by pressing it outwards a little **(see illustration)**.

20 Slide the glass to the top of the frame and secure it in place with adhesive tape.

21 Disconnect the wiring plug from the regulator motor, then undo the 2 nuts and 4 bolts, and manoeuvre the regulator/motor assembly from the door cavity **(see illustrations)**.

22 To refit, manoeuvre the regulator into place and secure it with the nuts/bolts. Reconnect the wiring plug.

23 Remove the tape and slide the window down until the bracket engages with the regulator assembly.

24 The remainder of refitting is a reversal of removal.

Rear door quarter-light

25 Remove the rear door window regulator as described earlier in this Section.

26 Lower the drop glass to the bottom of the door.

27 Carefully prise the door frame trim inwards to release the clips **(see illustration)**.

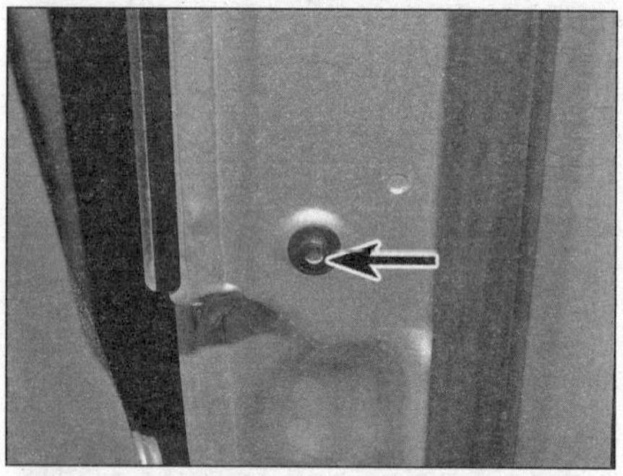
14.18a Undo the screw (arrowed) at the front, inner edge of the door ...

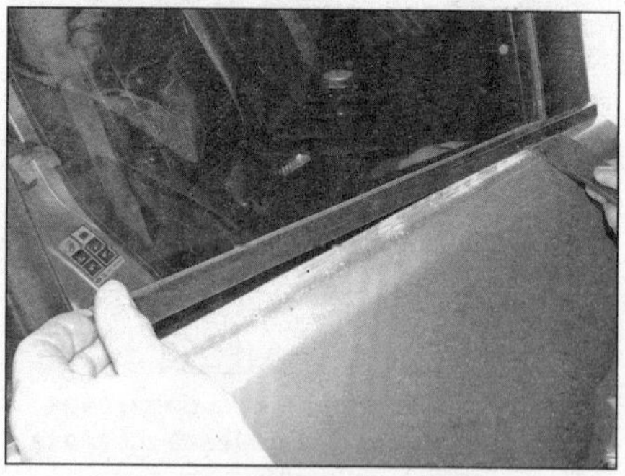
14.18b ... and prise up the outer weatherstrip

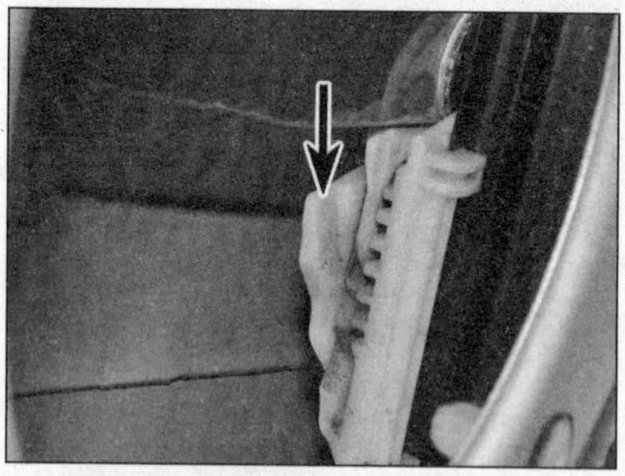
14.19 Press the glass retaining clip (arrowed) outwards a little

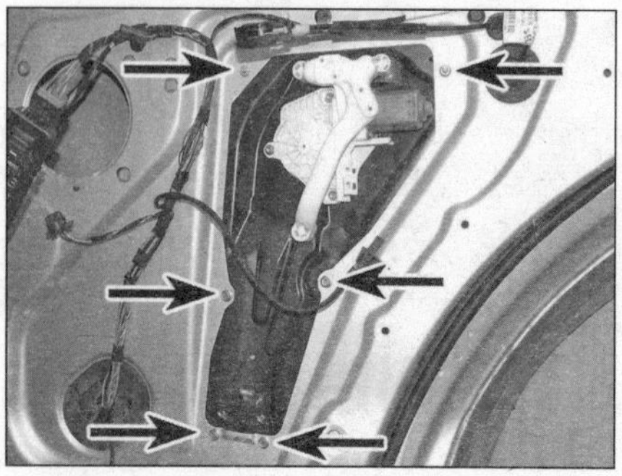
14.21a Undo the bolts/nuts (arrowed) ...

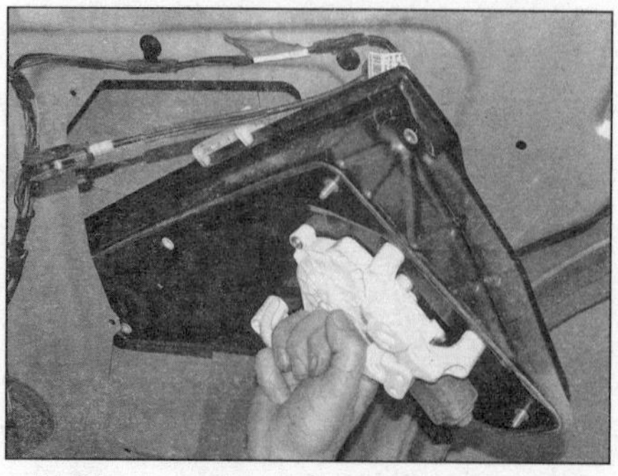
14.21b ... and manoeuvre the regulator from the door

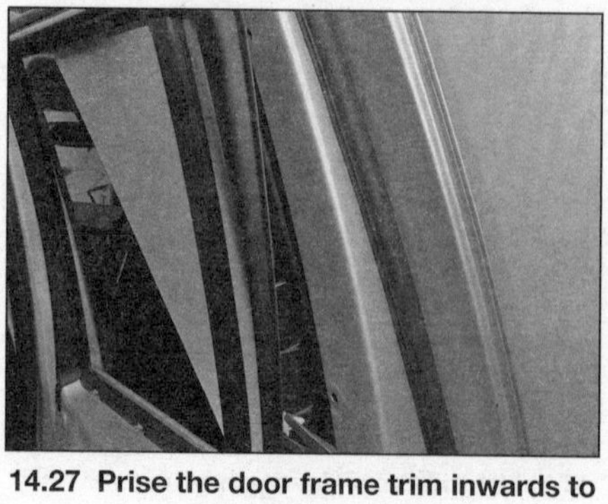
14.27 Prise the door frame trim inwards to release the clips

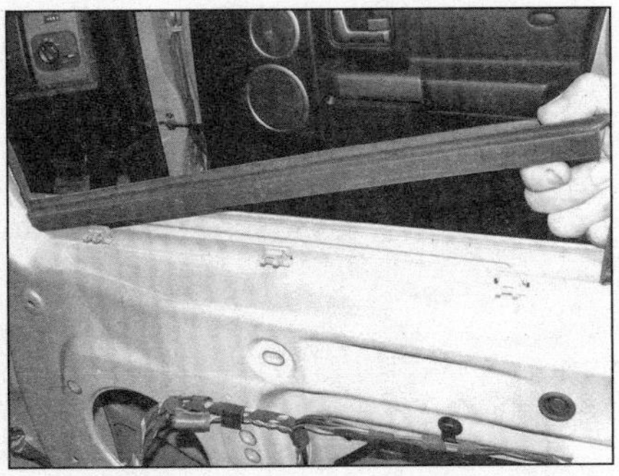

14.28 Prise up the inner weatherstrip

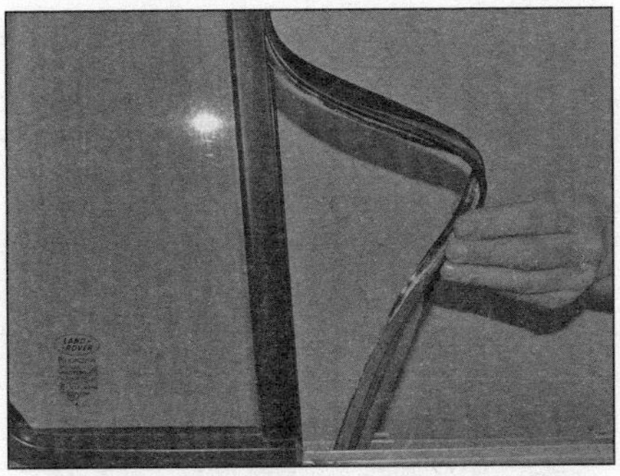

14.29 Pull the rubber guide from the channel

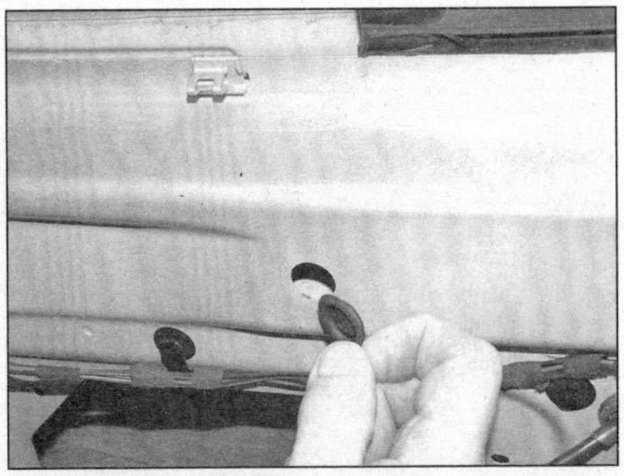

14.30a Prise out the grommet ...

28 Prise up the inner weatherstrip from the top of the door panel **(see illustration)**.

29 Pull the rubber guide from the front edge of the quarter-light glass channel **(see illustration)**. Manoeuvre the drop glass from the lower edge of the channel.

30 Prise out the grommet, slacken the Torx screw, push the screw outwards, and pull the lower edge of the channel/glass assembly forwards **(see illustrations)**. Manoeuvre the assembly from the door.

31 Refitting is a reversal of removal, but ensure the locating peg at the top of the glass/channel engages with the hole in the door frame **(see illustration)**.

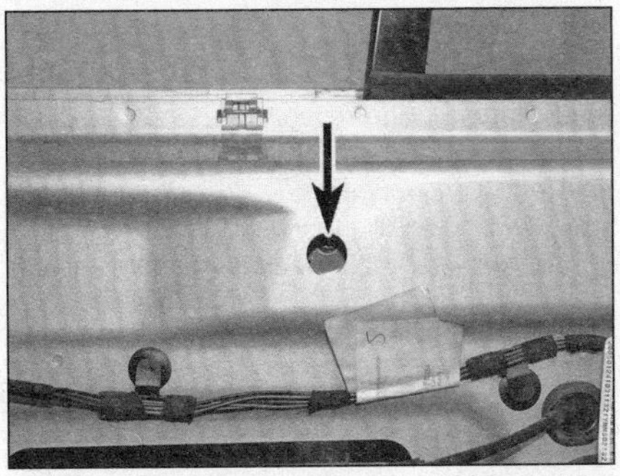

14.30b ... and slacken the screw (arrowed)

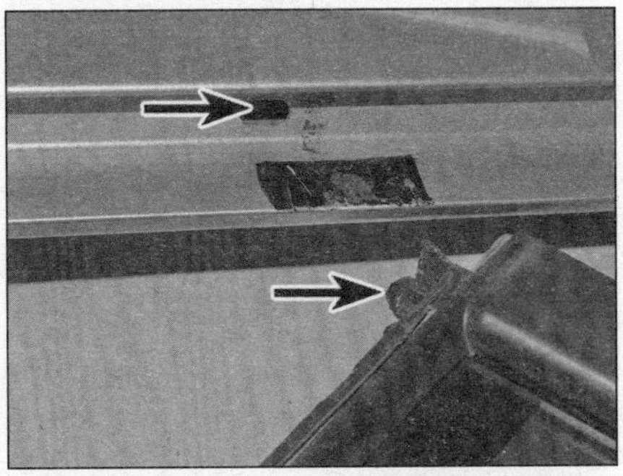

14.31 Ensure the peg (arrowed) aligns with the hole in the door frame (arrowed)

15 Tailgate and liftgate – removal and refitting

Note: *It is a good idea to obtain a few trim panel retaining clips before starting, as they are often broken in the course of removal, or will be found to have broken during previous removal attempts.*

Removal

Liftgate

1 Open the liftgate, then disconnect the battery negative lead as described in Chapter 5, Section 4.

2 Using a blunt, flat-bladed tool, carefully prise the upper panel from the liftgate window aperture to release the clips **(see illustration)**.

3 Prise the liftgate window aperture side trim panels from place **(see illustration)**.

4 Pull down the rear headlining trim panel, then disconnect the liftgate wiring plugs and washer jet hose **(see illustrations)**. Release the rubber grommets.

5 Have an assistant support the liftgate, then prise out the clips a little and disconnect the ends of the lifting strut each side **(see illustration)**.

6 Using a suitable marker pen, make alignment marks between the liftgate hinges and the vehicle body.

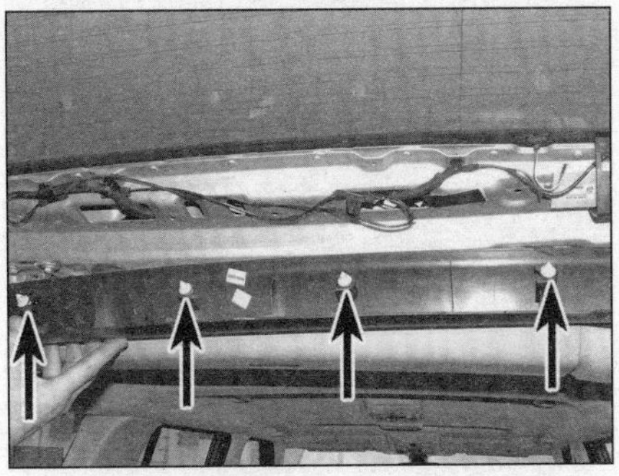

15.2 Prise the upper panel from the liftgate to release the clips (arrowed)

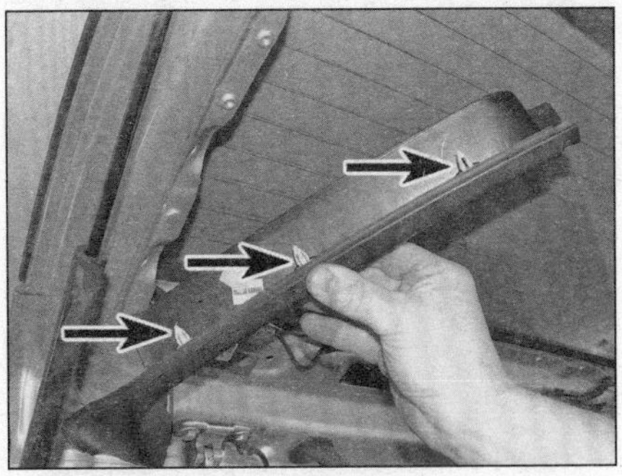

15.3 Side trim panel retaining clips (arrowed)

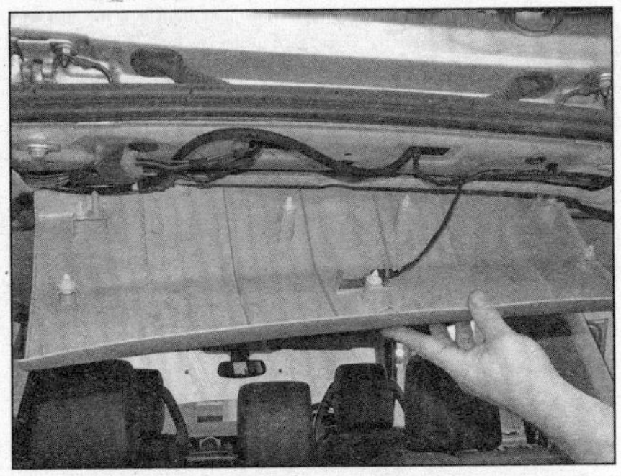

15.4a Pull down the rear headlining trim panel ...

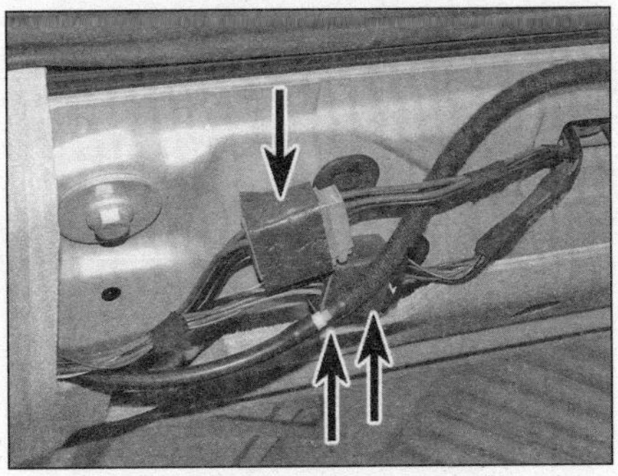

15.4b ... and disconnect the washer hose and wiring plugs (arrowed)

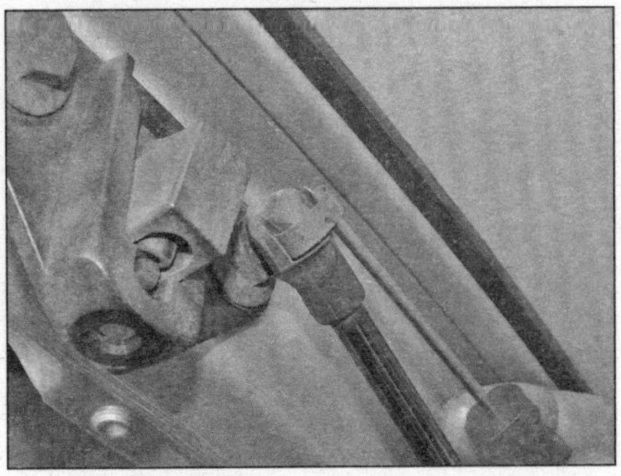

15.5 Prise out the spring clips a little

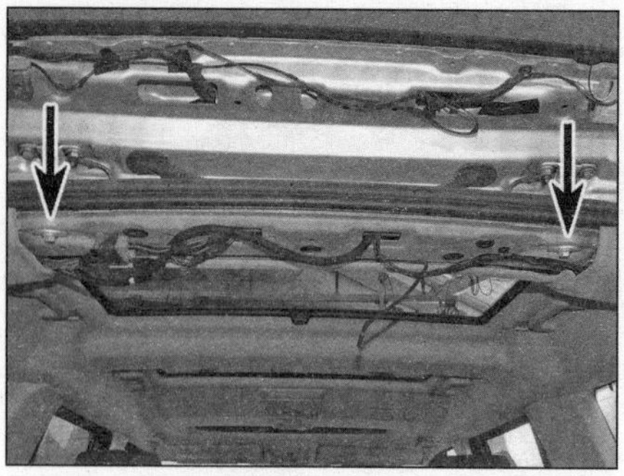
15.7 Liftgate hinge bolts (arrowed)

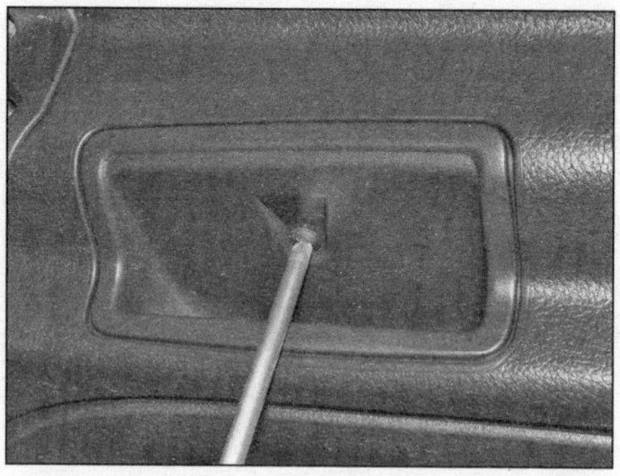
16.1a Undo the screw in the panel handle recess ...

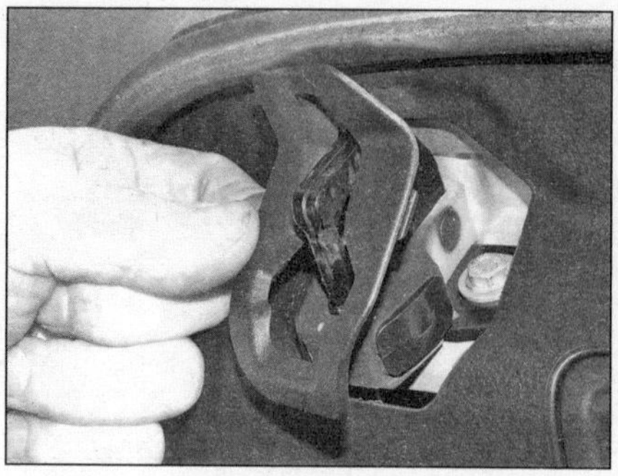
16.1b ... and unclip the striker panel

7 Undo the 2 bolts and washers securing the liftgate hinges, and remove the assembly from the vehicle **(see illustration)**.

Tailgate

8 Remove the tailgate trim panel as described in Section 16.

9 Carefully remove the waterproof membrane from the tailgate. Note that it's quite likely the membrane will be damaged during the process. Renew it if necessary.

10 Undo the screws, lift the tailgate speaker from position and disconnect the wiring plug.

11 Disconnect the wiring plugs from the various tailgate components, and pull the rubber gaiter from the tailgate edge.

12 Undo the hinge-to-tailgate bolts and manoeuvre the tailgate from place.

Refitting

13 Refitting is the reverse of removal, noting the following points:

a) Locate the tailgate/liftgate, and refit the retaining bolts and washers, tightening them by hand only. Align the marks made prior to removal, then tighten the hinge retaining bolts to the specified torque. Reconnect the struts, then close the liftgate and check for alignment with the surrounding body panels. Slight adjustments can be made by loosening the hinge bolts and repositioning the tailgate.

b) Check the trim panel retaining clips for signs of damage – renew any broken ones before installing the panel.

16 Tailgate and liftgate components – removal and refitting

Removal

Liftgate trim panel

1 Undo the screw in the centre of the trim panel and remove the striker panel **(see illustrations)**.

2 Carefully prise between the trim panel and the liftgate to release the 11 clips around its circumference **(see illustration)**. Remove the panel.

Tailgate trim panel

3 Prise out the covers, and remove the 4 upper trim panel retaining screws **(see illustrations)**.

4 Pull the upper trim panel upwards to release the 2 push-in clips.

5 Have an assistant support the tailgate, then prise out the clips a little and disconnect the support cable each side **(see illustration)**. Unscrew the 2 support cable spigots from the tailgate.

6 Lift the hinge cover for access, then prise up the tailgate trim panel to release the 12 retaining clips **(see illustration)**.

Liftgate lock

7 Remove the tailgate trim panel as described previously in this Section.

8 Remove the waterproof membrane from

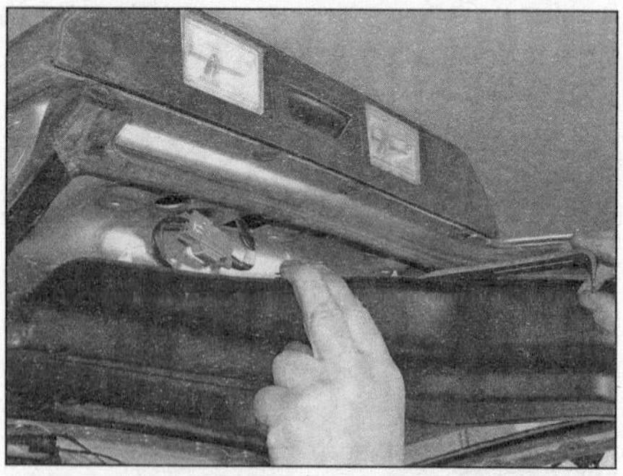
16.2 Prise between the panel and the liftgate to release the clips

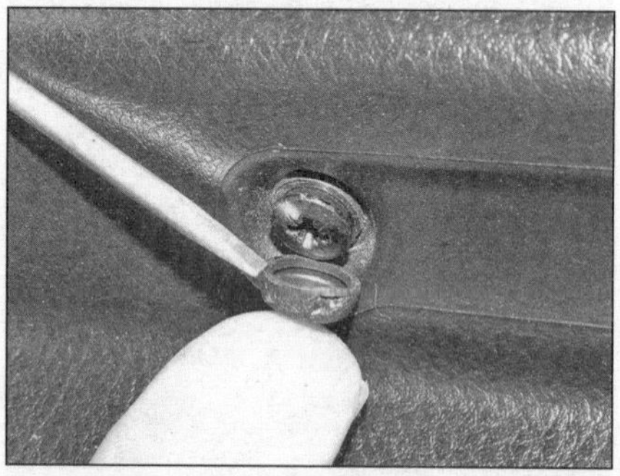
16.3a Prise off the plastic covers ...

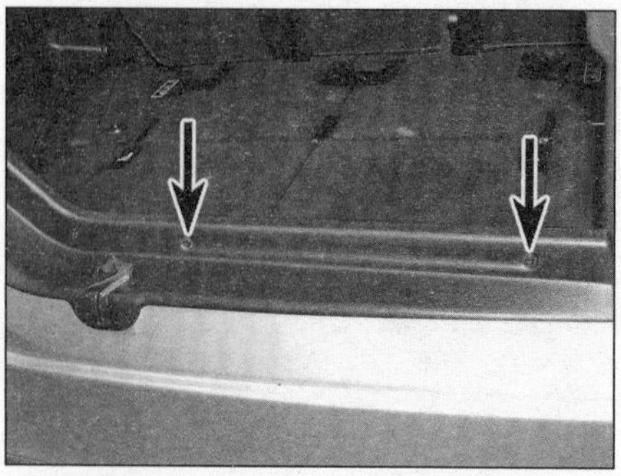
16.3b ... and remove the screws (right-hand screws arrowed)

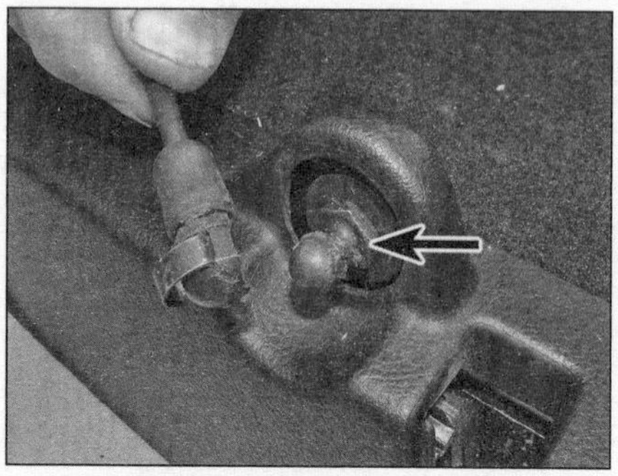
16.5 Disconnect the support cable and unscrew the spigot (arrowed)

16.6 Prise up the tailgate panel

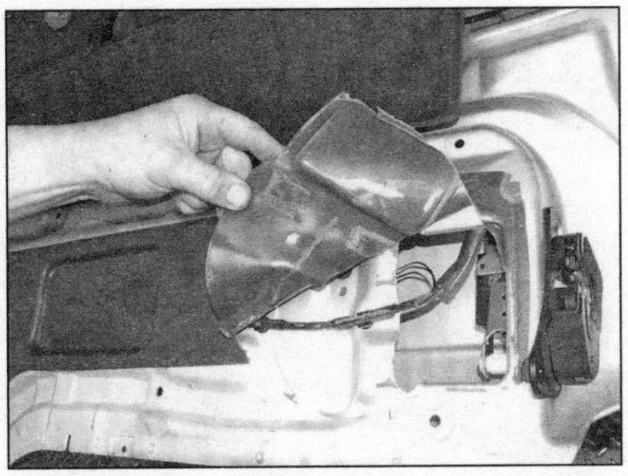

16.8 **Renew the waterproof membrane if it's damaged**

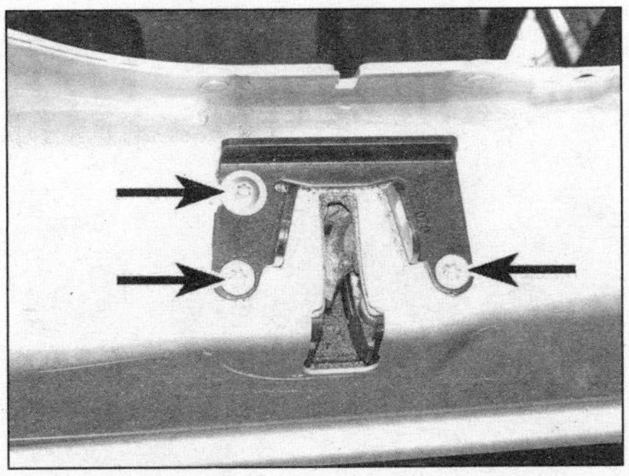

16.9 **Liftgate lock screws (arrowed)**

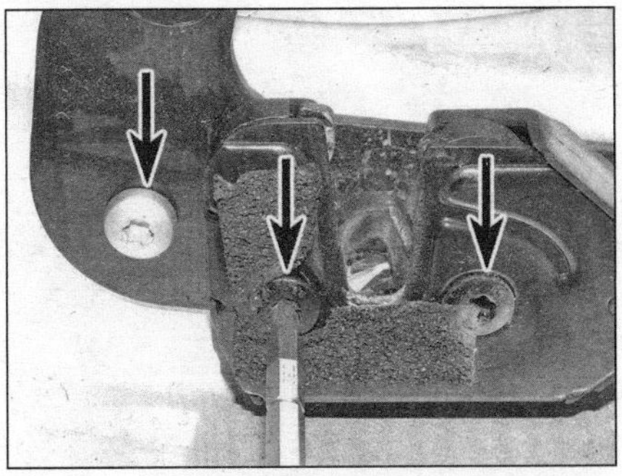

16.13 **Undo the 3 screws (arrowed) and remove the lock/actuator assembly**

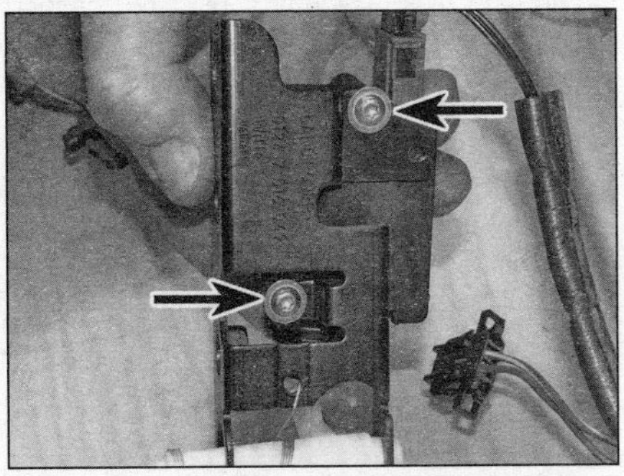

16.14 **The actuator is secured by 2 screws (arrowed)**

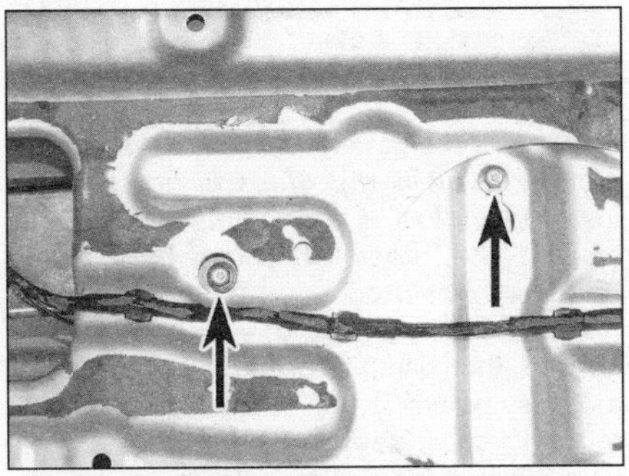

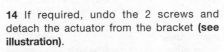

16.16 **Liftgate lock actuator screws (arrowed)**

the tailgate **(see illustration)**. Note that this is almost impossible to do without damaging the membrane – renew if necessary.

9 Undo the 3 Torx screws securing the lock to the tailgate **(see illustration)**.

10 Manoeuvre the lock from position, then disconnect the wiring plug, and the release cable.

Tailgate lock/actuator

11 Remove the tailgate trim panel as described previously in this Section.

12 Undo the 10 Torx screws, lift the tailgate speaker assembly and disconnect the wiring plugs.

13 Undo the 3 lock retaining screws, and remove the lock, plate and actuator assembly **(see illustration)**. Disconnect the wiring plug as the assembly is withdrawn.

14 If required, undo the 2 screws and detach the actuator from the bracket **(see illustration)**.

Liftgate lock actuator

15 Remove the tailgate trim panel as described previously in this Section.

16 Slacken the 2 retaining bolts, disconnect the wiring plug and lift the actuator from position **(see illustration)**.

17 Remove the 2 Torx screws securing the actuator cover **(see illustration)**.

18 Disengage the release cable from the actuator **(see illustration)**.

Liftgate release button

19 Remove the liftgate trim panel as described previously in this Section.

20 Undo the 4 screws and 3 nuts, disconnect the wiring plug, and remove the release button/number plate light assembly from the liftgate **(see illustration)**.

Tailgate release button

21 Remove the tailgate trim panel as described previously in this Section.

22 Undo the 10 Torx screws, lift the tailgate speaker assembly and disconnect the wiring plugs.

23 Disconnect the wiring plug, squeeze together the retaining clips and remove the button.

Refitting

24 Refitting is the reverse of the relevant removal procedure, noting the following:

a) *Ensure that all cables are securely held in position by their retaining clips.*

b) *Apply grease to all locks.*

c) *Before installing the relevant trim panel, thoroughly check the operation of all the lock handles and, where necessary, the central locking system.*

17 Central locking components – removal and refitting

Solenoids and switches

1 The solenoids and switches are integral with the lock assemblies, and if faulty, the complete units must be renewed – see Sections 13 and 16.

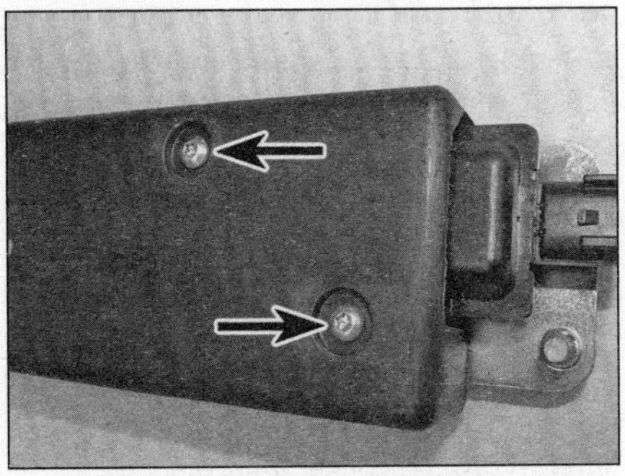

16.17 **Undo the screws (arrowed), remove the cover ...**

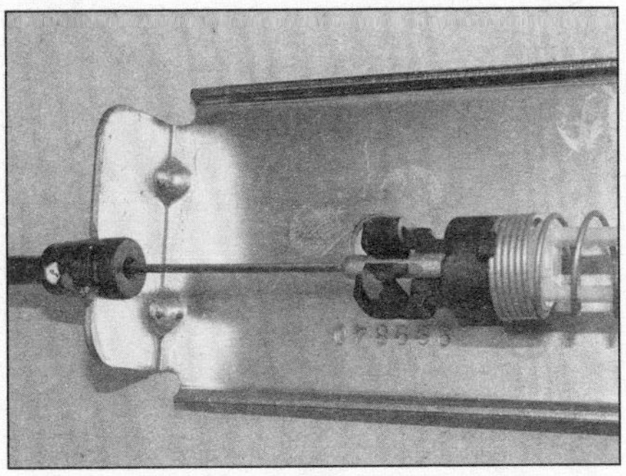

16.18 **... and disconnect the release cable**

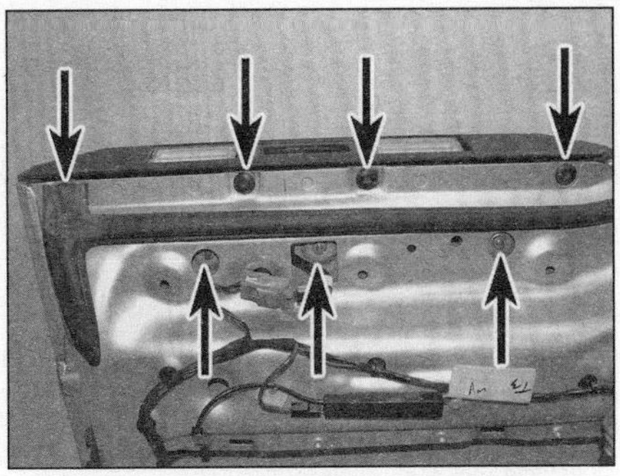

16.20 **Number plate light/release button assembly nuts/bolts (arrowed)**

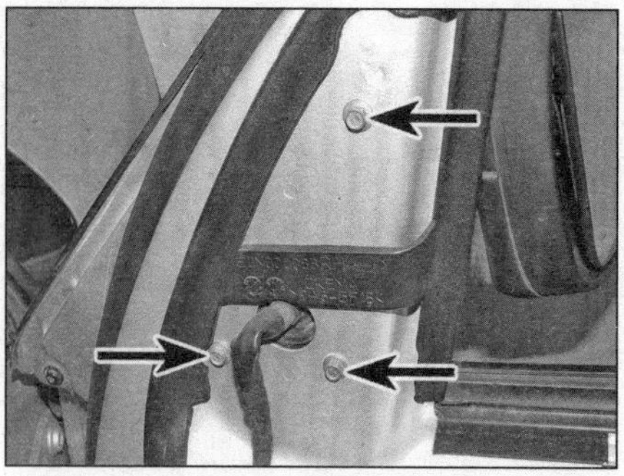
19.3 Mirror retaining screws (arrowed)

19.6 Prise out the lower edge of the mirror glass

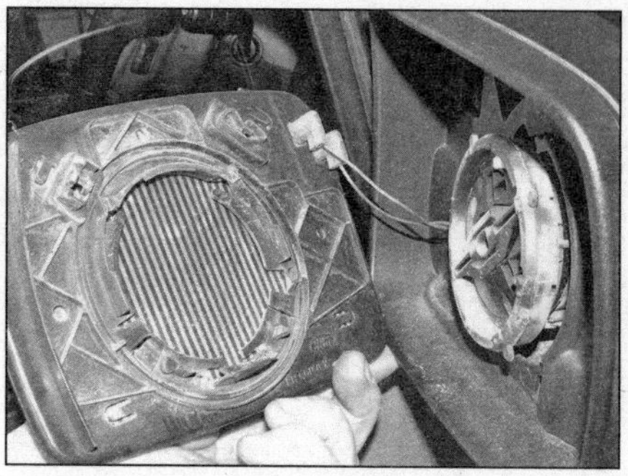
19.7 Disconnect the wiring plugs from the mirror glass

Electronic control unit

2 The function of the central locking system is incorporated into the software installed in the central junction box, located behind the passenger's side of the facia – see Chapter 13, Section 3, for details.

18 Electric window components – removal and refitting

Window switches

1 Refer to Chapter 13, Section 4.

Window lift motor

2 The window lift motors are integral with the window regulator assemblies – see Section 14. Should a fault develop, the complete assembly must be renewed. Consult a Land Rover dealer or parts specialist.

19 Exterior mirrors and associated components – removal and refitting

Door mirror assembly

1 Remove the door inner trim panel as described in Section 12.

2 Disconnect the mirror wiring connector(s).

3 Support the mirror assembly, then undo the 3 retaining screws **(see illustration)**.

4 Remove the mirror assembly from the door.

5 Refitting is the reverse of removal, using a new mirror seal if the original shows signs of damage or deterioration.

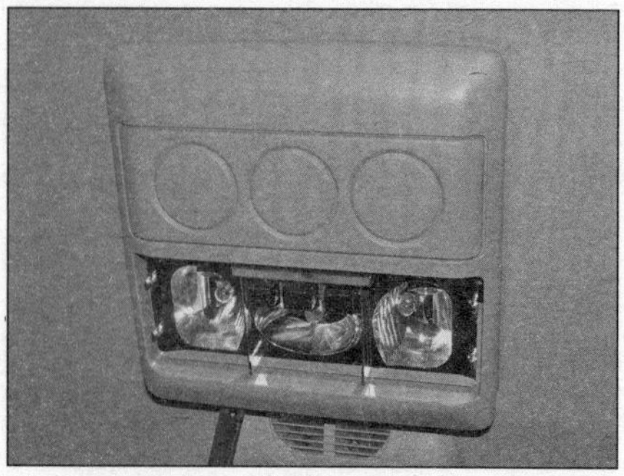
21.3 Starting at the front edge, prise down the overhead console

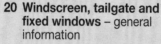

Mirror glass

Caution: If the glass is broken, wear sturdy gloves. Even if the glass is not broken, wearing gloves is a sensible precaution, should the glass break as it is being removed or refitted.

6 Position the glass so its upper edge is fully forward, then carefully prise the lower edge of the glass outwards until it is released from its retaining clips **(see illustration)**. Take great care when removing the glass; do not use excessive force, as the glass is easily broken.

7 Remove the glass from the mirror. On models with electric mirrors, disconnect the wiring connectors from the mirror heating element as they become accessible **(see illustration)**.

8 On refitting, reconnect the wiring connectors (where necessary). Carefully, clip the glass back into position.

Mirror switch

9 Refer to Chapter 13, Section 4.

20 Windscreen, tailgate and fixed windows – general information

These areas of glass are secured by the tight fit of the weatherstrip in the body aperture, and are bonded in position with a special adhesive. The removal and refitting of these areas of fixed glass is difficult, messy and time-consuming task, which is considered beyond the scope of the home mechanic. It is difficult, unless one has plenty of practice, to obtain a secure, waterproof fit. Furthermore, the task carries a high risk of breakage; this applies especially to the laminated glass windscreen. In view of this, owners are strongly advised to have this sort of work carried out by one of the many specialist windscreen fitters.

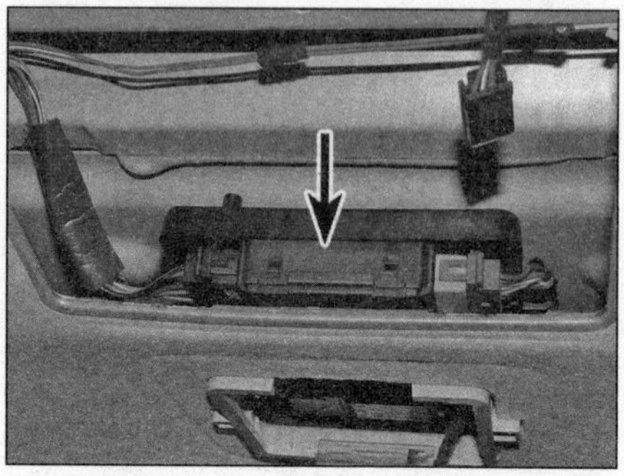
21.4 Slide the sunroof ECU (arrowed) to the left-hand side to release it

21 Sunroof – general information, and component renewal

Twin tilt/sliding sunroofs were fitted as standard to some models, and offered as an optional extra on others. The sunroof(s) is/are either manually or electrically-operated.

Due to the complexity of the tilt/slide sunroof mechanism, considerable expertise is needed to repair, renew or adjust the sunroof components successfully. Removal of the sunroof first requires the headlining to be removed, which is a complex and tedious operation in itself, and not a task to be undertaken lightly (see Section 26). Therefore, any problems with the sunroof should be referred to a Land Rover dealer or specialist.

On models with an electric sunroof, if the sunroof motor fails to operate, first check the relevant fuse. The motor incorporates an automatic cut-out facility, which cuts the motor if the sunroof encounters an obstruction – the motor may therefore cut-out if the mechanism is partially seized.

Sunroof motor

1 Removal of the sunroof motor requires removal of the headlining – see above.

Sunroof ECU

2 Disconnect the battery negative lead as described in Chapter 5, Section 4.

3 Prise down the rear overhead console **(see illustration)**. Disconnect the wiring plugs as the console is withdrawn.

4 Slide the ECU to the left-hand side to release it from the mounting bracket **(see illustration)**. Disconnect the wiring plugs as the ECU is withdrawn.

5 Refitting is a reversal of removal.

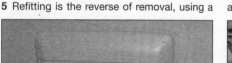

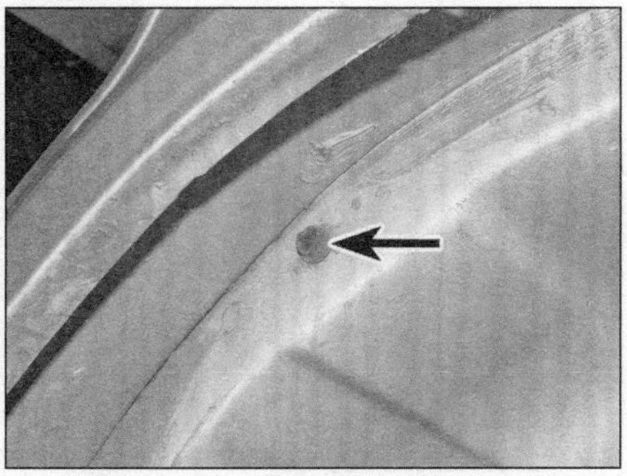

21.9 The sunroof rear drain tubes terminate in the wheel arch areas (arrowed)

Sunroof glass panel

6 Fully tilt (open) the sunroof, then undo the 3 Torx screws each side. Manoeuvre the sunroof panel from place.

7 To refit the panel, position the panel in the frame, but only finger-tighten the screws at this stage.

8 Adjust the position of the panel so that when it's fully closed a gap of 1.0 mm exists between the roof panel and the front edge of the panel. Once this is achieved, tighten the screws securely.

Drain hoses

9 Drain hoses are connected to the front and rear corners of the sunroof frame, and run down the A- and C-pillars of the vehicle **(see illustration)**. One-way valves are fitted to the ends of the hoses to prevent dirt and moisture entering the hoses.

10 The hoses can only be renewed once the headlining has been removed.

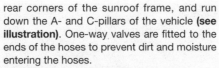

22 Body exterior fittings – removal and refitting

Wheel arch liners and body under-panels

1 The various plastic covers fitted to the underside of the vehicle are secured in position by a mixture of screws, nuts and retaining clips. Removal will be fairly obvious on inspection. Work methodically around the panel, removing its retaining screws and releasing its retaining clips until the panel is free and can be removed from the underside of the vehicle. Most clips used on the vehicle are released by pressing out their centre pins and then removing the outer section of the clip **(see illustration 7.4a)**.

2 On refitting, renew any retaining clips that may have been broken on removal, and ensure that the panel is securely retained by all the relevant clips, nuts and screws.

Body trim strips and badges

3 Most of the various body trim strips and badges are held in position with a special adhesive tape. Removal requires the trim/badge to be heated, to soften the adhesive, and then cut away from the surface. Due to the high risk of damage to the vehicle's paintwork during this operation, it is recommended that this task should be entrusted to a Land Rover dealer.

23 Seats – removal and refitting

Removal

Front seat

1 Slide the seat fully rearwards, prise off the covers, and undo the bolts at the front of the seat rails **(see illustrations)**.

2 Slide the seat to the central position, prise up the covers, and undo the 3 bolts at the rear **(see illustrations)**.

3 Disconnect the battery negative lead as described in Chapter 5, Section 4, then wait at least 10 minutes for any residual electrical energy to dissipate.

4 Pull up the cover from the side of the seat,

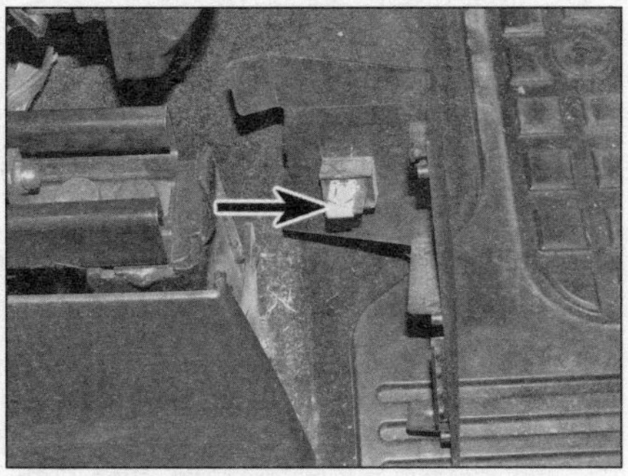

23.1a Prise the front, outer cover inwards to release the clip (arrowed) ...

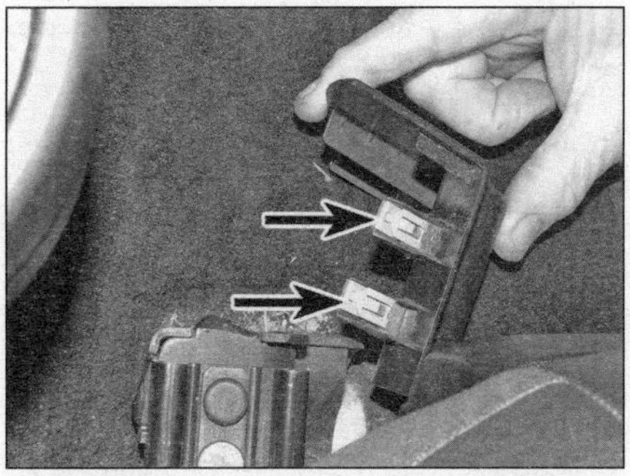

23.1b ... and the front, inner cover outwards to release the clips (arrowed)

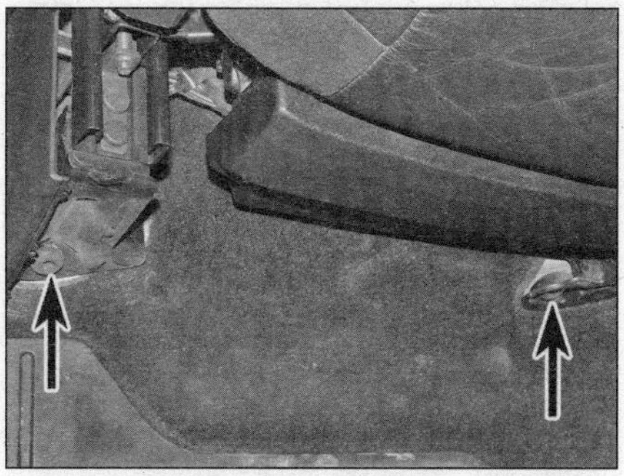

23.1c Front seat, front retaining bolts (arrowed)

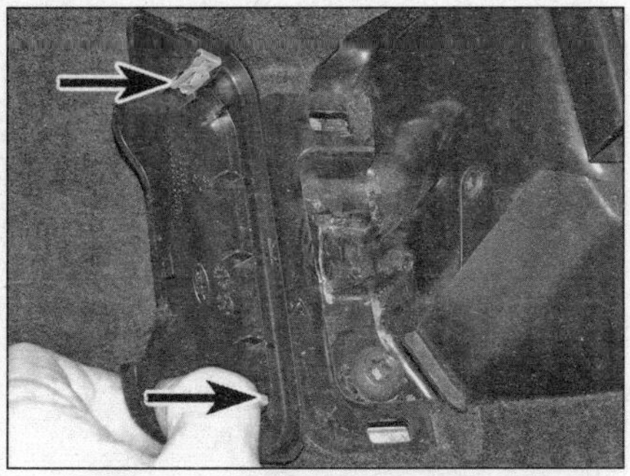

23.2a Prise the front seat, rear outer bolt cover upwards to release the clips (arrowed)

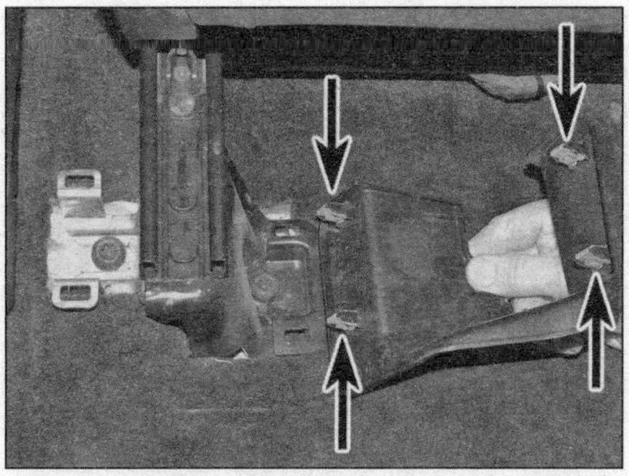

23.2b Prise the front seat, rear inner bolt cover upwards to release the clips (arrowed)

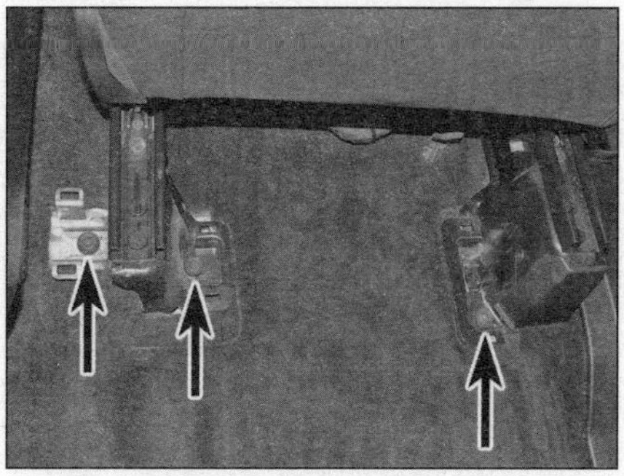

23.2c Front seat, rear retaining bolts (arrowed)

23.4a Slide up the plastic cover ...

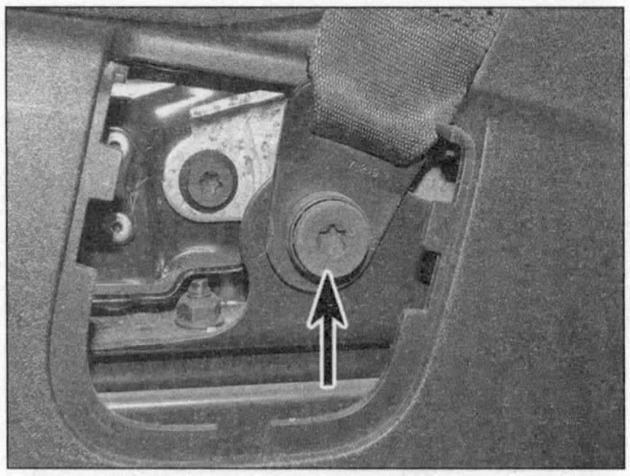
23.4b ... and undo the seat belt anchorage bolt (arrowed)

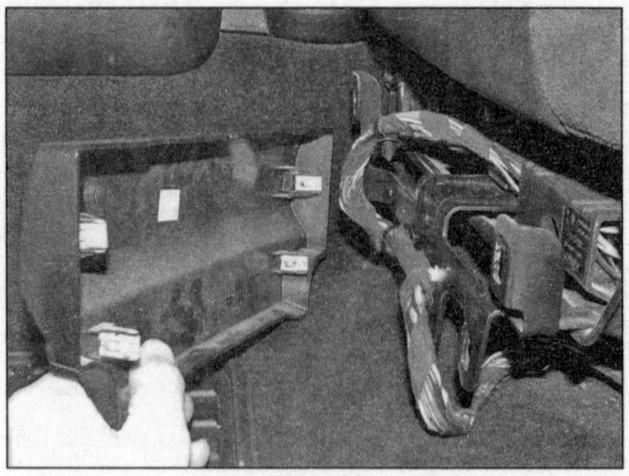
23.5a Pull the plastic cover under the front of the seat forwards

23.5b Undo the bolt (arrowed) and disconnect the wiring plug

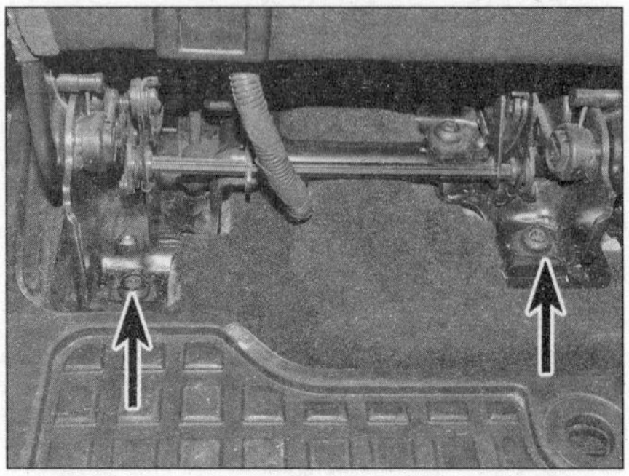
23.9 Undo the rear seat front bolts (arrowed) ...

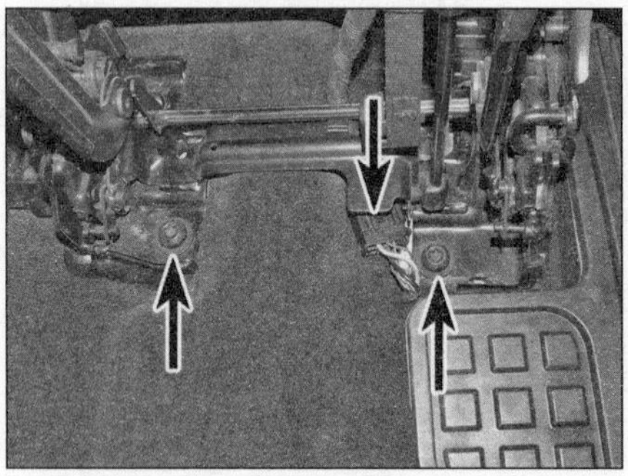
23.10 ... then undo the rear bolts and disconnect the wiring plug (arrowed)

and undo the bolt securing the seat belt lower anchorage **(see illustrations)**.

5 Pull the plastic cover forwards, note their fitted positions, undo the retaining bolt and disconnect the wiring plugs from the seat base **(see illustrations)**.

6 Lift the seat assembly out of the vehicle. Enlist the help of an assistant – the seats are very heavy.

60/40 split rear seat

7 Fold the seat cushion forwards, unto the Torx bolts.

8 Fold the seat backrest forwards, and manoeuvre the rear seat out from the vehicle. Enlist the help of an assistant – the seats are very heavy.

40/20/40 split outer seats

9 Unscrew the front Torx bolts **(see illustration)**.

10 Fold the seat forwards, disconnect the wiring plug and undo the rear Torx bolts **(see illustrations)**. Lift the seat assembly out of the vehicle. Enlist the help of an assistant – the seats are very heavy. Repeat this procedure for the remaining outer seat.

40/20/40 split inner seat

11 Undo the front Torx bolts.

12 Fold the seat forwards, and undo the Torx bolts at the rear. Manoeuvre the seat from the vehicle.

Third row seats (7-seat models only)

13 Undo the load space compartment anchor Torx bolts each side **(see illustration)**.

14 Prise up the load space trim panels each side to release the 4 clips **(see illustrations)**.

15 Fold the trim cover forwards, then undo the 4 Torx bolts at the front **(see illustrations)**

16 Fold the trim covers outwards, then undo the 6 Torx bolts at the rear. With the help of an

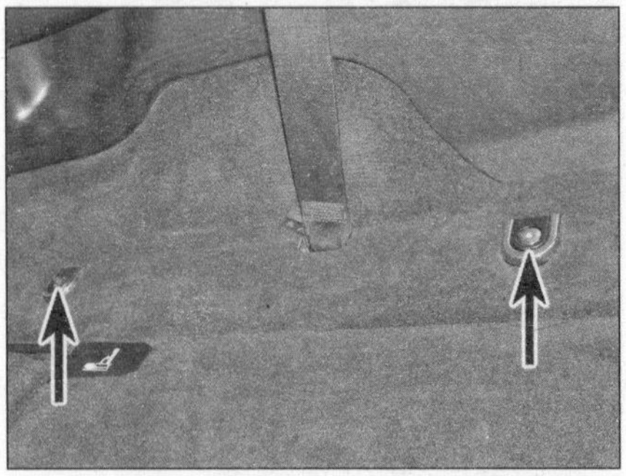
23.13 Undo the load space anchor bolts (arrowed)

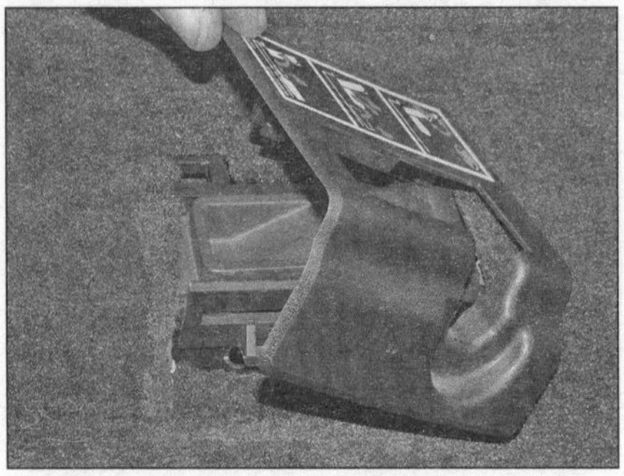
23.14a Carefully prise up the plastic trim around the front catch ...

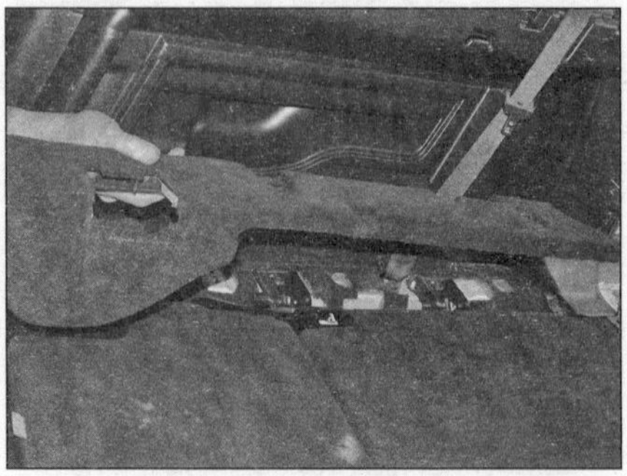
23.14b ... the prise up the load space trim panel each side

23.15a Fold the cover forwards to access the front, inner bolts (arrowed) ...

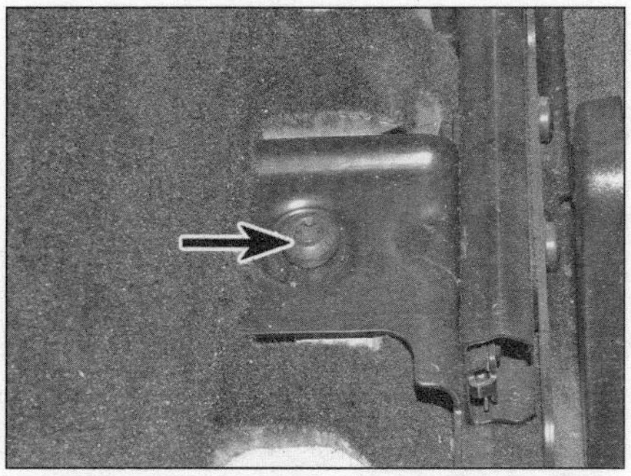

23.15b ... and undo the front outer bolt (arrowed) each side

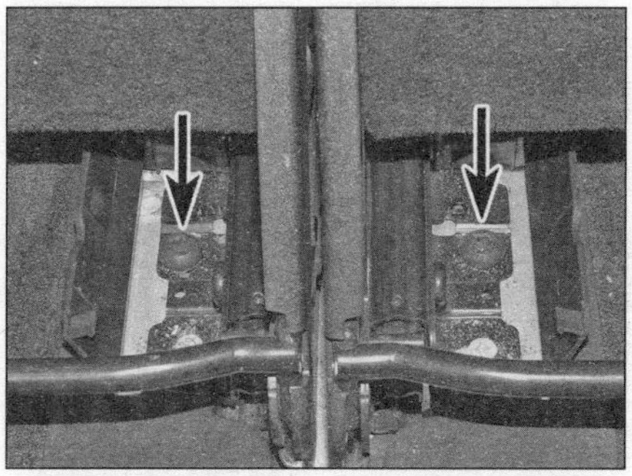

23.16a Fold the covers outwards to access the inner rear bolts (arrowed) ...

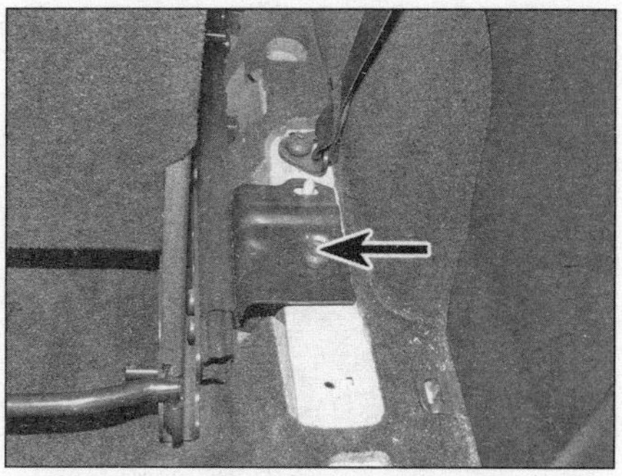

23.16b ... and undo the rear outer bolt each side (arrowed)

assistant, manoeuvre the seat assembly from place **(see illustrations)**.

Refitting

17 Refitting is a reversal of the relevant removal procedure. Make sure that all seat mountings are tightened to the specified torque.

24 Seat positioning motors – removal and refitting

Removal

Fore-and-aft motor

1 Set the front seat to its highest position, then remove it as described in Section 23.

2 Disconnect the motor wiring plug, then remove the drive cable **(see illustration)**.

3 Prise off the 2 retaining clips and manoeuvre the motor from place **(see illustration)**.

Rise-and-fall motor

4 Removal of the height adjustment motor requires the seat cushion cover to be removed. This is a complicated task, requiring patience and experience to successfully complete. For this reason, we recommend the task is entrusted to an upholstery specialist.

Tilt motor

5 Removal of the height adjustment motor requires the seat cushion cover to be removed. This is a complicated task, requiring patience and experience to successfully complete. For this reason, we recommend the task is entrusted to an upholstery specialist.

Seat recline motor

6 Removal of the recline motor requires the seat backrest cover to be removed. This is a complicated task, requiring patience and experience to successfully complete. For this reason, we recommend the task is entrusted to an upholstery specialist.

Refitting

7 Refitting is a reversal of removal.

24.2 Disconnect the wiring plug and pull the drive cable from place (arrowed)

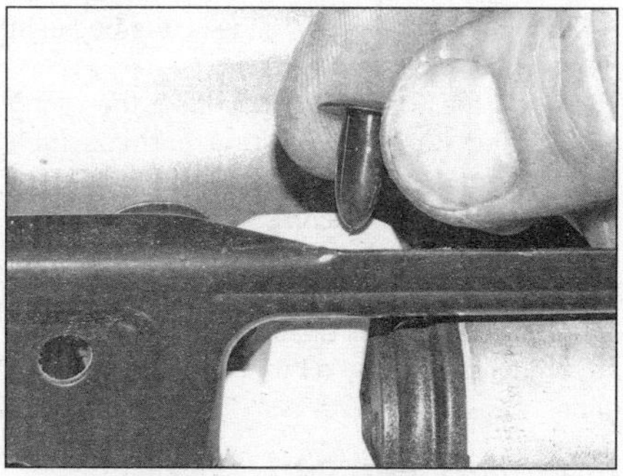

24.3 Prise out the clip each side and remove the seat motor

25 Seat belt components – removal and refitting

1 Disconnect the battery negative lead as described in Chapter 5, Section 4, then wait at least 10 minutes for any residual electrical energy to dissipate.

Front seat belt

2 Remove the B-pillar trim panel as described in Section 26.

3 Slide up the plastic panel and detach the seat belt lower anchorage **(see illustrations 23.4a and 23.4b)**.

4 Pull the top of the sill trim panel inwards a little, then undo the bolt securing the seat belt inertia reel to the B-pillar **(see illustration)**.

5 Remove the seat belt upper anchorage bolt from the B-pillar **(see illustration)**.

6 Refitting is a reversal of the removal procedure, ensuring that all the mounting bolts are tightened to the specified torque (where given) and all disturbed trim panels are securely retained by all the relevant retaining clips.

Front seat belt stalk

7 The front seat belt stalks are equipped with pretensioners. These are pyrotechnic devices designed to quickly retract the stalk, tightening the seat belt in the event of a frontal collision.

8 Remove the front seat as described in Section 23.

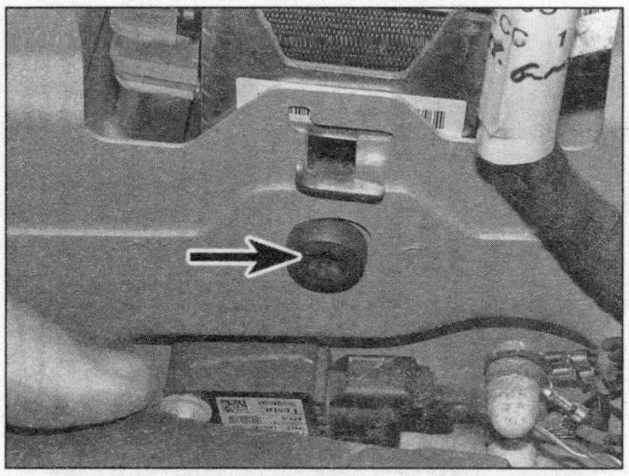

25.4 Pull the sill trim panel inwards slightly to access the front inertia reel retaining bolt (arrowed)

25.5 Front seat belt upper anchorage bolt (arrowed)

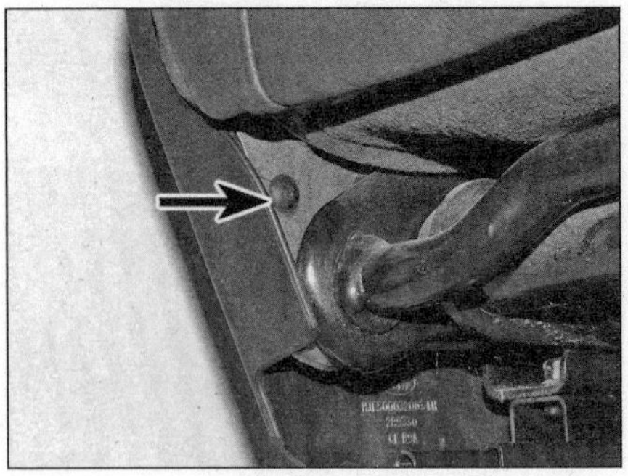
25.9a Undo the screw (arrowed) on the inside ...

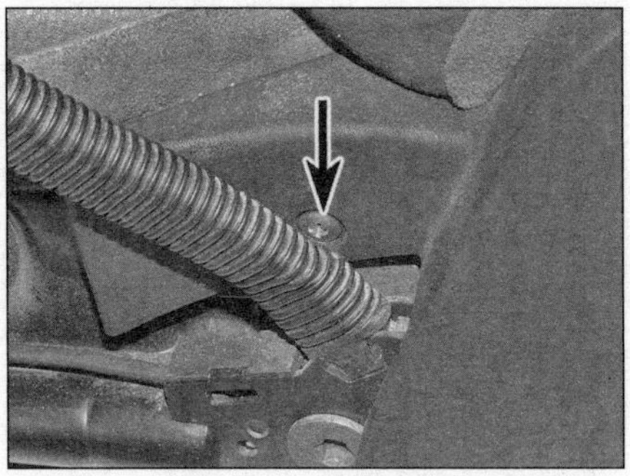
25.9b ... and the screw (arrowed) on the outside of the hinge cover

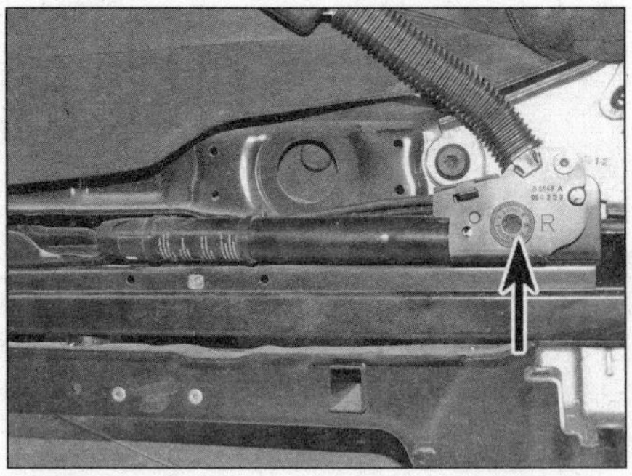
25.10 Front seat belt stalk retaining bolt (arrowed)

9 Undo the 2 screws and slide up the backrest hinge cover **(see illustrations)**.

10 Undo the Torx bolt, disconnect the wiring plugs, and unclip the wiring harness **(see illustration)**. Remove the belt stalk.

11 Refitting is a reversal of the removal procedure, ensuring that all the mounting bolts are tightened to the specified torque (where given) and all disturbed trim panels are securely retained by all the relevant retaining clips.

Rear seat side belt

12 Remove the C-pillar and luggage compartment side trim panels as described in Section 26.

13 Undo the upper seat belt anchorage bolt **(see illustration)**.

14 Undo the seat belt lower anchorage bolt.

15 Undo the bolt securing the inertia seat belt to the vehicle body and remove it from position **(see illustration)**.

16 Refitting is a reversal of the removal procedure, ensuring that all the mounting bolts are tightened to the specified torque (where given) and all disturbed trim panels are securely retained by all the relevant retaining clips.

Rear seat belt centre belt

17 Remove the rear seat as described in Section 23.

18 Undo the 2 screws, and prise up the seat belt guide **(see illustration)**.

19 Prise up the inertia reel cover **(see illustration)**.

20 Remove the lower anchorage bolt **(see illustration)**. Discard the bolt – a new one must be fitted.

21 Undo the retaining bolt and manoeuvre the inertia reel from place **(see illustration)**. Discard the bolt – a new one must be fitted.

22 Refitting is a reversal of the removal procedure, ensuring that all the mounting bolts are tightened to the specified torque (where given) and all disturbed trim panels are securely retained by all the relevant retaining clips.

Rear seat belt stalk

Models with 60/40 seats

23 Remove the rear seat as described in Section 23.

24 Undo the screw and remove the hinge cover panel (right-hand seat only).

25 Undo the bolt, release the retaining strap, and remove the belt stalk. Discard the bolt – a new one must be fitted.

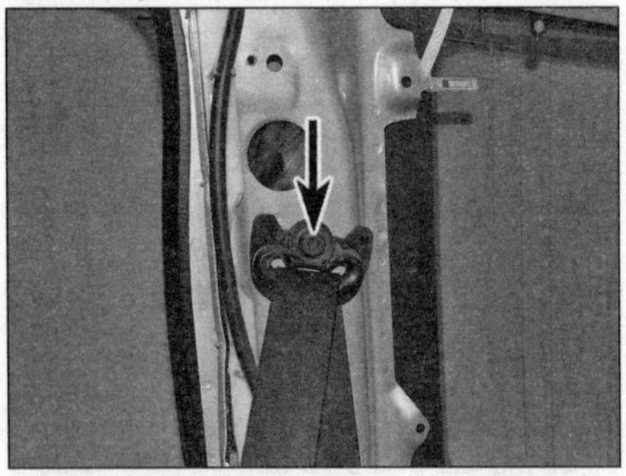
25.13 Rear seat upper anchorage bolt (arrowed)

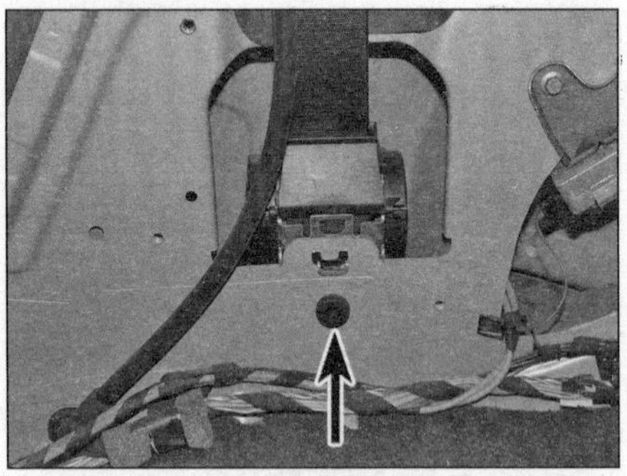
25.15 Rear seat belt inertia reel bolt (arrowed)

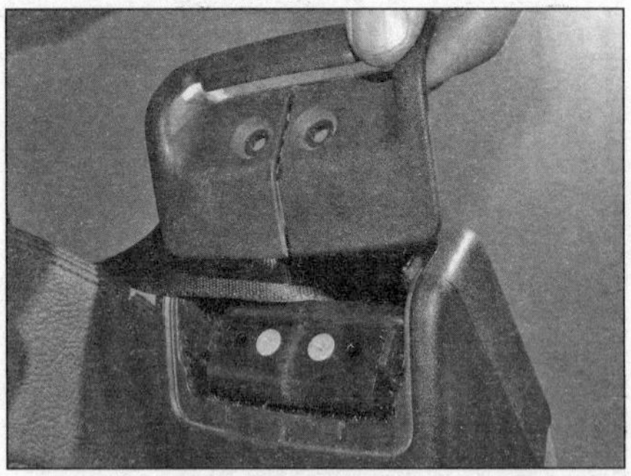
25.18 Undo the screws and remove the seat belt guide

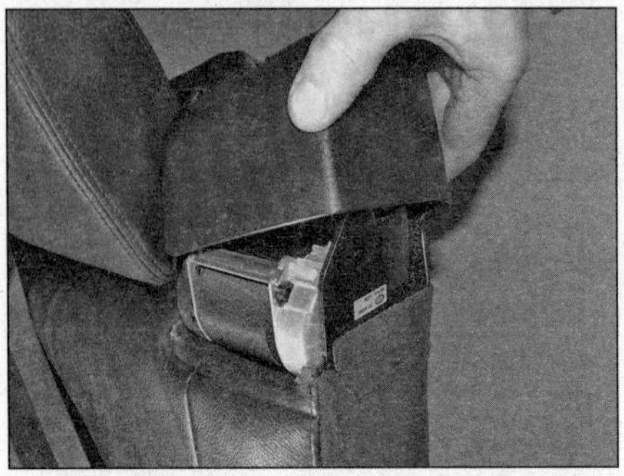
25.19 Prise up the inertia reel cover

25.20 Remove the lower anchorage bolt (arrowed)

25.21 Rear, centre inertia reel retaining bolt (arrowed)

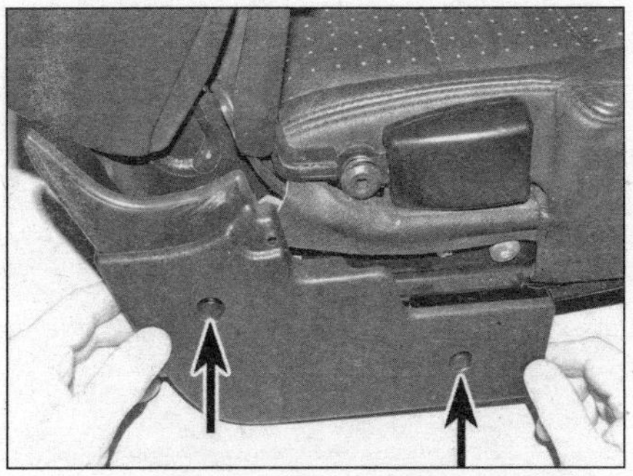

25.27 **Undo the screws (arrowed) and remove the hinge cover panel**

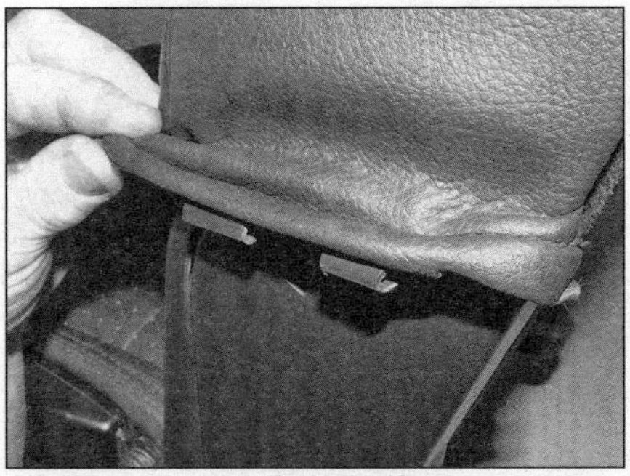

25.28 **Unhook the backrest cover from the panel ...**

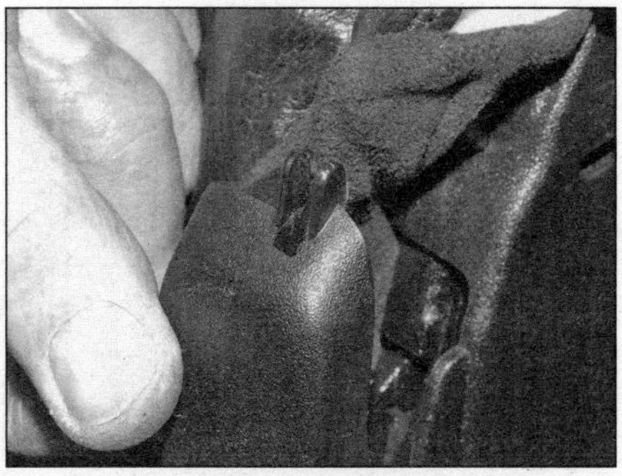

25.29a **... pull the top of the panel forwards ...**

25.29b **... then carefully spread apart the lower edges and remove the panel**

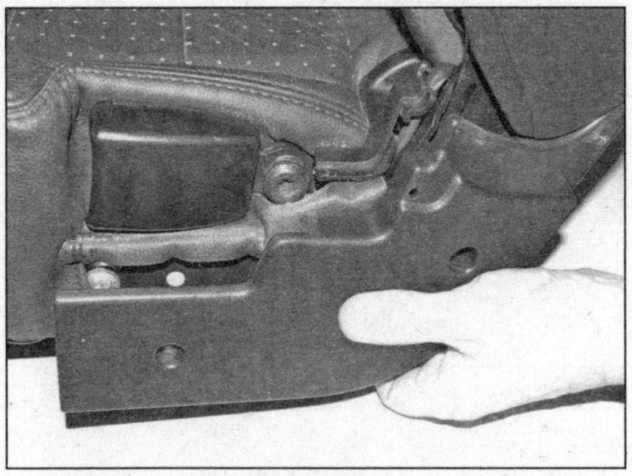

25.30 **Undo the screws and remove the hinge cover panel**

25.34 **Third row seat belt upper anchorage bolt (arrowed)**

Models with 40/20/40 seats

26 Remove the rear seat as described in Section 23.

Centre seat

27 Undo the 2 screws and remove the hinge cover panel **(see illustration)**.

Outer seats

28 Unhook the seat backrest cover from the top of the hinge cover panel **(see illustration)**.
29 Pull the top of the sliding hinge cover forwards, then carefully spread apart the lower edges, disengage the pins and remove it **(see illustrations)**.
30 Undo the 2 screws and remove the hinge cover panel **(see illustration)**.

All seats

31 Undo the Torx bolt, relieve the tension spring and remove the belt stalk.

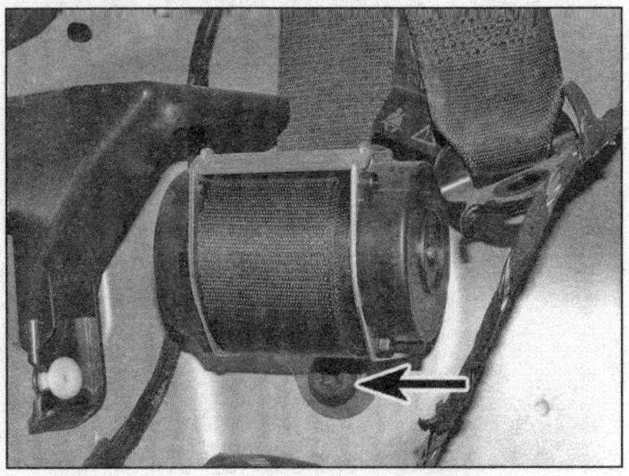

25.35 **Third row seat belt inertia reel bolt (arrowed)**

32 Refitting is a reversal of the removal procedure, ensuring that all the mounting bolts are tightened to the specified torque (where given) and all disturbed trim panels are securely retained by all the relevant retaining clips.

Third row seat belts (7-seat models only)

33 Remove the D-pillar trim panel as described in Section 26.
34 Undo the upper seat belt anchorage bolt **(see illustration)**.
35 Undo the inertia reel retaining bolt, and remove the seat belt from the vehicle **(see illustration)**.
36 Refitting is a reversal of the removal procedure, ensuring that all the mounting bolts are tightened to the specified torque (where given) and all disturbed trim panels are securely retained by all the relevant retaining clips.

26 Interior trim – removal and refitting

Interior trim panels

1 The interior trim panels are secured using either screws or various types of trim fasteners, usually studs or clips.
2 Check that there are no other panels overlapping the one to be removed; usually there is a sequence to be followed that will become obvious on close inspection.
3 Remove all obvious fasteners, such as screws. If the panel will not come free, it is held by hidden clips or fasteners. These are usually situated around the edge of the panel, and can be prised up to release them. Note, however, that they can break quite easily, so replacements should be available. The best way of releasing such clips in the absence of the correct type of tool, is to use a large flat-bladed screwdriver. Note in many cases that an adjacent sealing strip (such as the rubber door seal) must be prised back to release a panel.
4 When removing a panel, **never** use excessive force, or the panel may be damaged. Always check carefully that all fasteners have been removed or released before attempting to withdraw a panel.
5 Refitting is the reverse of the removal procedure; secure the fasteners by pressing them firmly into place, and ensure that all disturbed components are correctly secured, to prevent rattles.

Glovebox

6 Undo the screw, remove the bonnet release lever, pull the weatherstrip from the pillar, then pull the footwell kick panel inwards to release the clips.
7 Undo the 2 screws, release the clip and remove the panel under the facia. Disconnect the footwell light wiring plug as the panel is withdrawn.

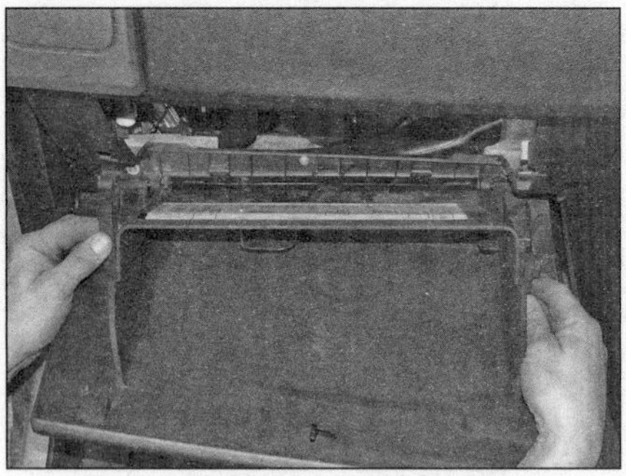

26.8 Press down the upper edges to disengage the latch stop each side

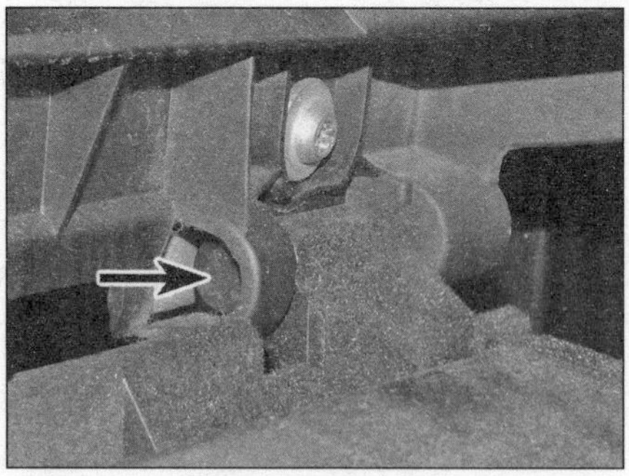

26.9a The glovebox hinge pins are a larger diameter at one end

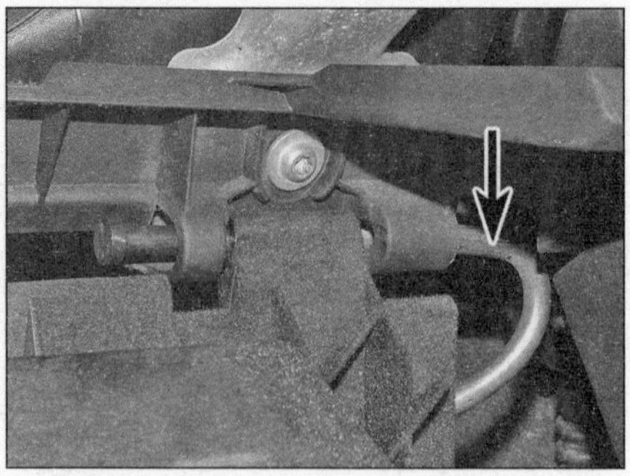

26.9b We used a U-shaped length of rod to drive the inner hinge pin from place

8 Open the glovebox, and release the latch stops each side **(see illustration)**.

9 Carefully drive out the hinge pins and remove the glovebox **(see illustrations)**. Drive the outer pin from outside, and the inner pin from the inside – the pins are a larger diameter at one end. **Note:** *The hinge pins are designed to be only used once. They will be damaged during the removal procedure, and must be renewed.*

10 Refitting is the reverse of removal.

Cool box

11 Disconnect the battery negative lead as described in Chapter 5, Section 4.

12 Remove the centre console upper panel as described in Section 27.

13 Open the cool box lid, undo the Torx screw each side and remove the lid hinge covers.

14 Undo the 2 Torx screws on the front, upper edge, disconnect the wiring plug and lift out the cool box.

15 Refitting is a reversal of removal.

Carpets

16 The passenger compartment floor carpet is secured at its edges by screws or clips, usually the same fasteners used to secure the various adjoining trim panels.

17 Carpet removal and refitting is reasonably straightforward, but very time-consuming, due to the fact that all adjoining trim panels must be removed first, as must components such as the seats, the centre console and seat belt lower anchorages.

Headlining

18 The headlining is clipped to the roof, and can only be withdrawn once all fittings such as the grab handles, sunvisors, windscreen and rear quarter windows, and related trim panels have been removed, and the door, tailgate and sunroof aperture sealing strips have been prised clear.

19 Note that headlining removal requires considerable skill and experience if it is to be carried out without damage, and is therefore best entrusted to an expert.

A-pillar trim

20 Pull away the rubber weatherstrip from the A-pillar.

21 Pull the facia end panel rearwards to release the clip **(see illustration)**.

22 Prise out the plastic cover, undo the Torx screw, then pull the trim away from the pillar to release the retaining clip **(see illustration)**.

23 Refitting is a reversal of removal.

B-pillar trim

24 Pull the rubber weatherstrip seals from the door apertures either side of the B-pillar.

25 Carefully pull the lower pillar trim panel inwards to release the retaining clips **(see illustration)**.

26 Pull up the cover from the side of the seat, disconnect the wiring plug (where applicable), and undo the bolt securing the seat belt lower anchorage **(see illustrations 23.4a and 23.4b)**.

27 Ensure the seat belt height adjuster is at its lowest point, then pull the lower edge of the B-pillar trim inwards, followed by the upper edge. Release the 2 lugs at the top of the trim by pressing them inwards a little **(see illustrations)**. Feed the seat belt through the slot in the trim.

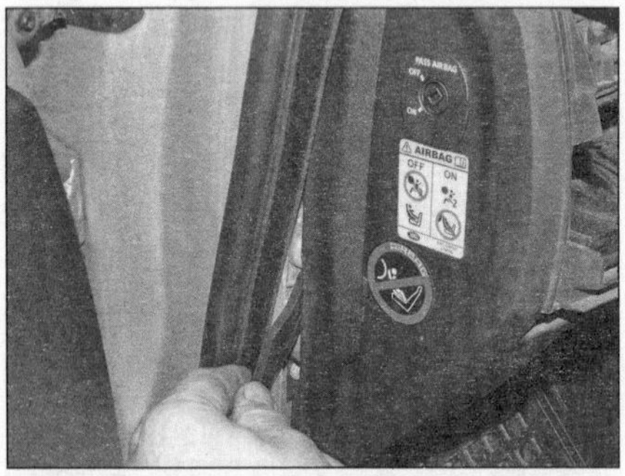

26.21 Pull the trim panel at the end of the facia rearwards to release the clips

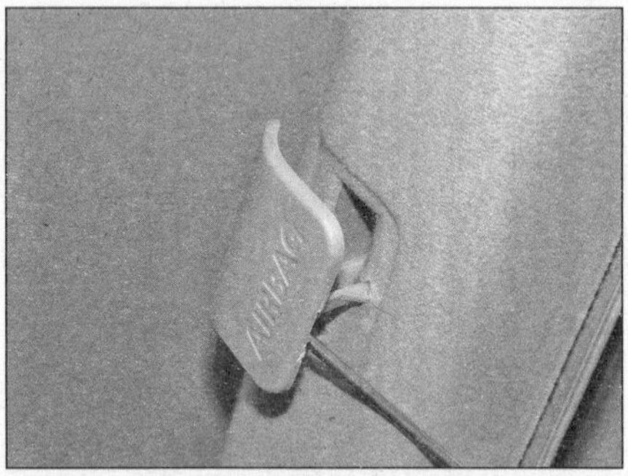

26.22 Prise out the airbag emblem, and undo the screw beneath

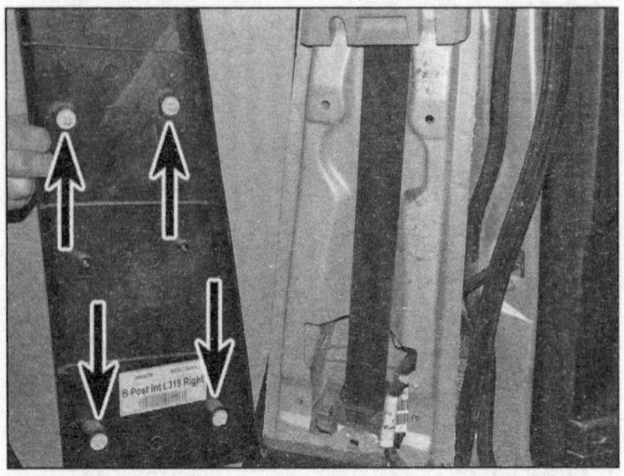

26.25 Pull the B-pillar lower trim panel inwards to release the clips (arrowed)

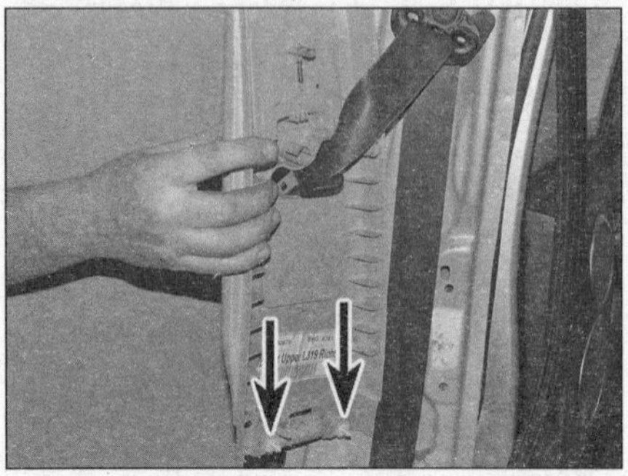

26.27a Pull the lower edge inwards to release the clips (arrowed)

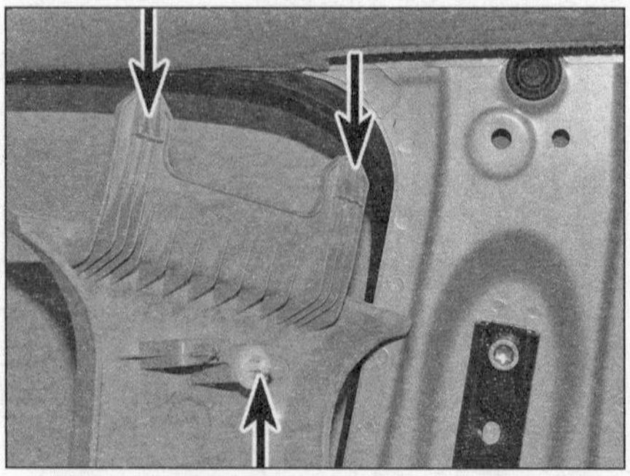

26.27b Release the clip (arrowed), then press the upper lugs (arrowed) inwards to release them

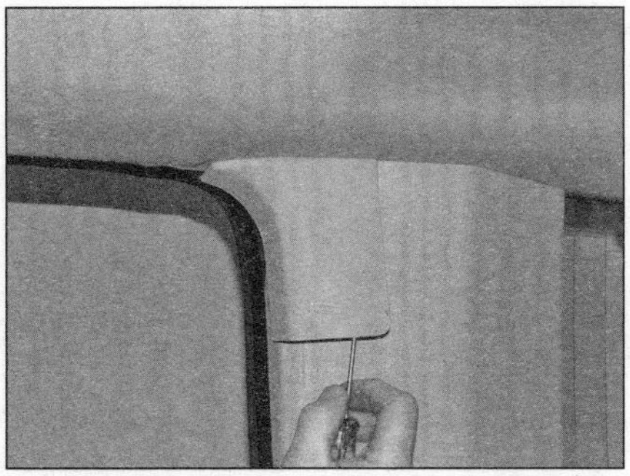
26.32a Prise out the access cover ...

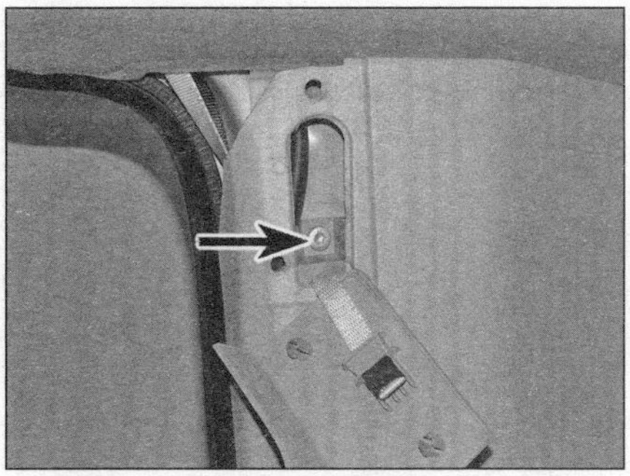
26.32b ... and undo the retaining Torx screw (arrowed)

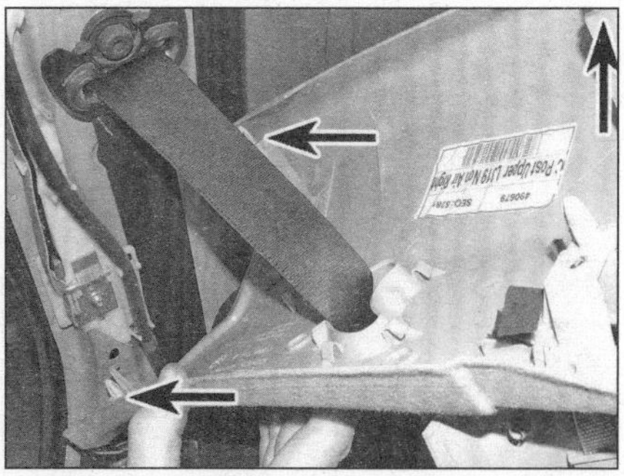
26.33 C-pillar trim panel retaining clips (arrowed)

28 Refitting is a reversal of removal, remembering to tighten the lower seat belt anchorage point bolt to the specified torque.

C-pillar trim

29 Fold down the rear seat backrest, and pull the door weatherstrip from the pillar.
30 Undo the bolt securing the seat belt lower anchorage. Discard the bolt – a new one must be fitted.
31 Prise out the cover, undo the screw, and pull the luggage compartment side trim panel inwards at the top to release it from the base of the C-pillar trim **(see illustrations 26.43a and 26.43b)**.
32 Prise open the C-pillar trim access cover, and undo the Torx screw **(see illustrations)**.
33 Pull the trim inwards from the pillar to release the retaining clips **(see illustration)**. Feed the seat belt through the slot in the trim.
34 Refitting is a reversal of removal.

D-pillar trim

35 Remove the luggage compartment side trim panel as described in this Section.
36 On 7-seater models, undo the third row seat belt lower anchorage bolt **(see illustration)**. Discard the bolt – a new one must be fitted.
37 Pull the pillar trim inwards to release the retaining clips **(see illustration)**. Disconnect the wiring plug and feed the seat belt through the slot (where applicable) as the trim is withdrawn.
38 Refitting is a reversal of removal.

Luggage compartment side trim panel

39 Pull the door weatherstrip from the C-pillar adjacent to the panel.
40 Undo the seat belt lower anchorage bolt. Discard the bolt – a new one must be fitted.
41 Pull the rubber weatherstrip from the tailgate aperture adjacent to the panel.
42 Prise out the spring clip a little, and detach the support from the tailgate **(see illustration 15.5)**.
43 Prise out the cover, undo the screw, and pull the luggage compartment side trim panel inwards to release the 8 retaining clips **(see illustrations)**. Disconnect the wiring plugs as the panel is withdrawn.
44 Refitting is a reversal of removal, remembering to feed the tailgate support through the hole in the trim panel as it's refitted.

Overhead console

45 Carefully prise the front edge of the overhead console from the headlining to release the clips **(see illustrations)**. Disconnect the wiring plug(s) as the console is withdrawn.
46 Refitting is a reversal of removal.

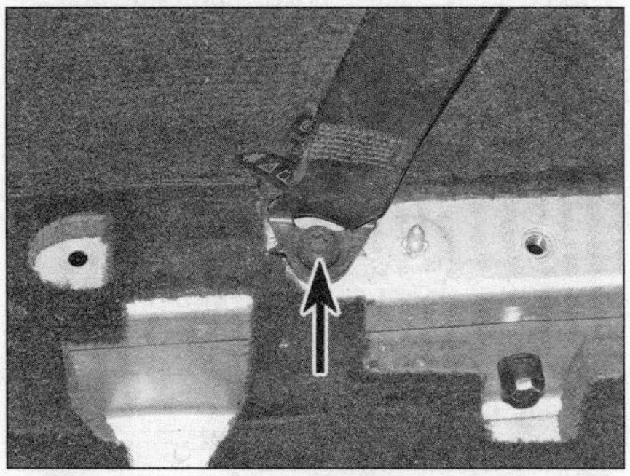
26.36 3rd row seat belt lower anchorage bolt (arrowed)

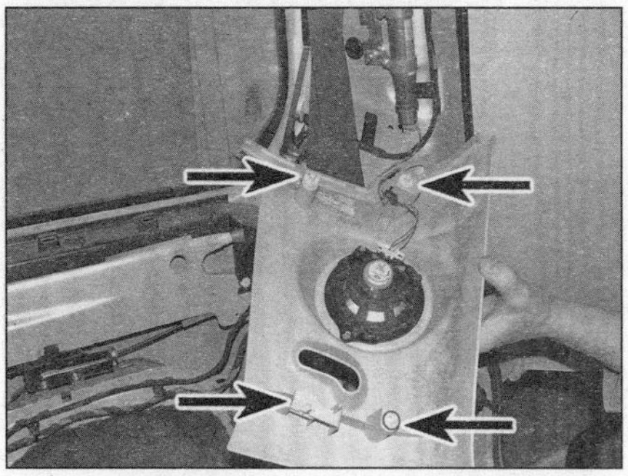
26.37 Pull the D-pillar trim panel inwards to release the clips (arrowed)

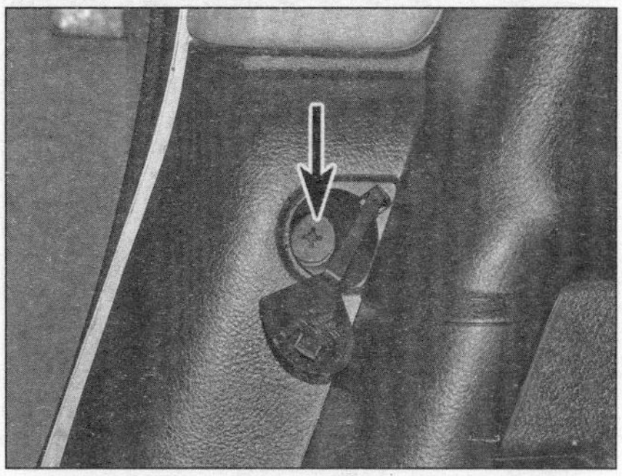
26.43a Prise out the cover and undo the screw (arrowed)

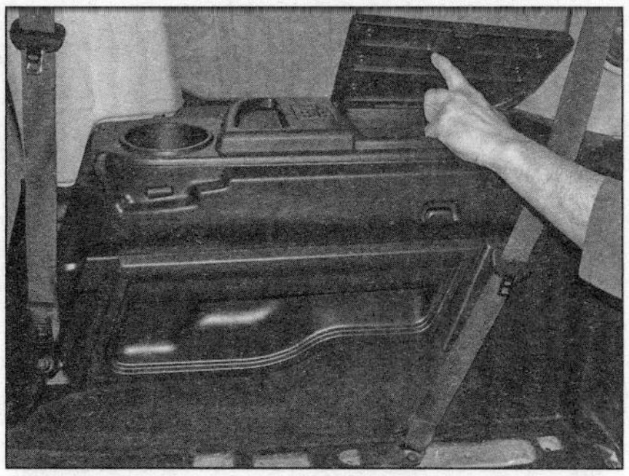
26.43b Open the storage box, and pull the side panel sharply inwards to release the clips

26.45a Prise down the front edge of the overhead console(s)

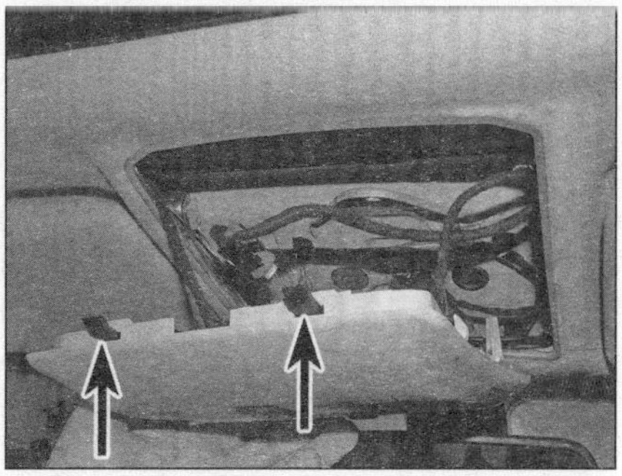
26.45b Note the lugs (arrowed) at the rear of the console

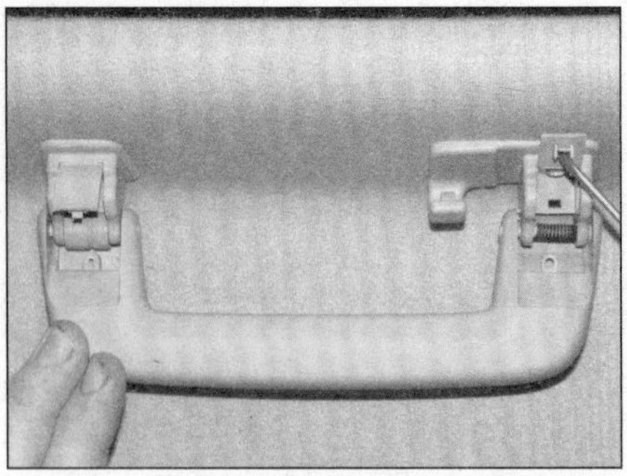

26.47 Lever up the covers and undo the screws beneath

27.5a Prise up the plastic cover ...

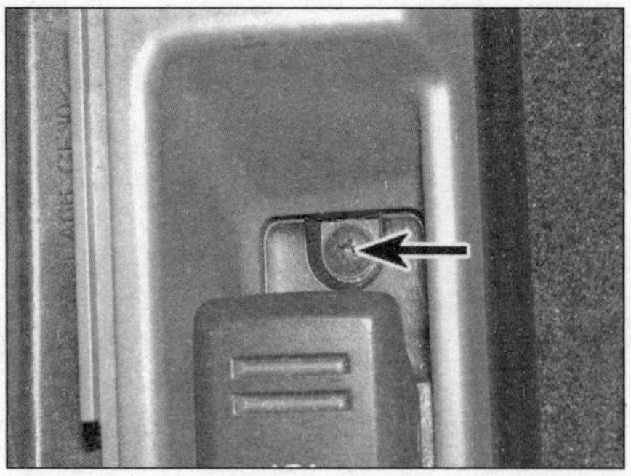

27.5b ... undo the screw (arrowed) ...

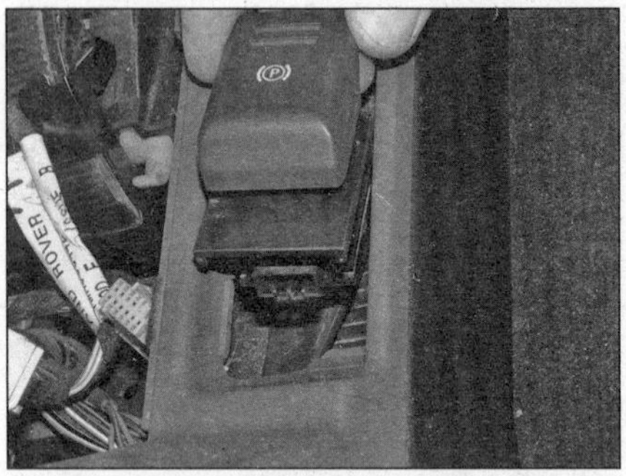

27.5c ... disconnect the wiring plug, and slide the parking brake switch rearwards to remove it

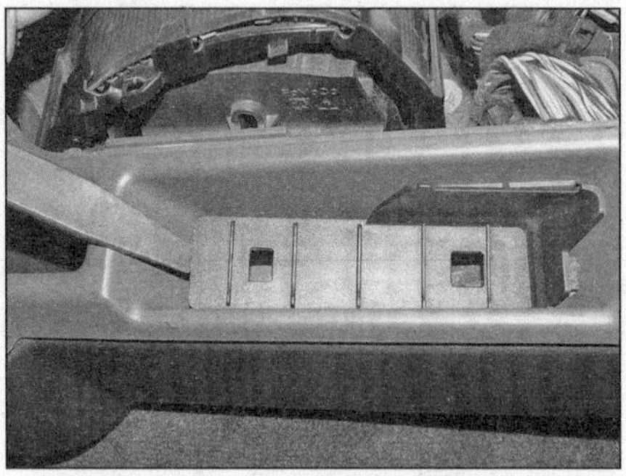

27.6a Prise up the plastic insert ...

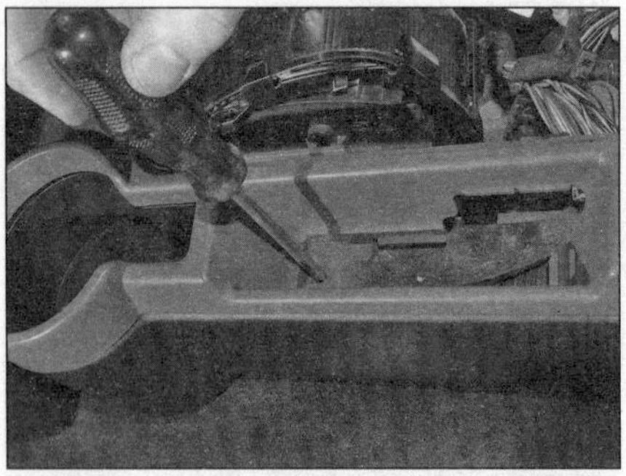

27.6b ... and undo the screw beneath

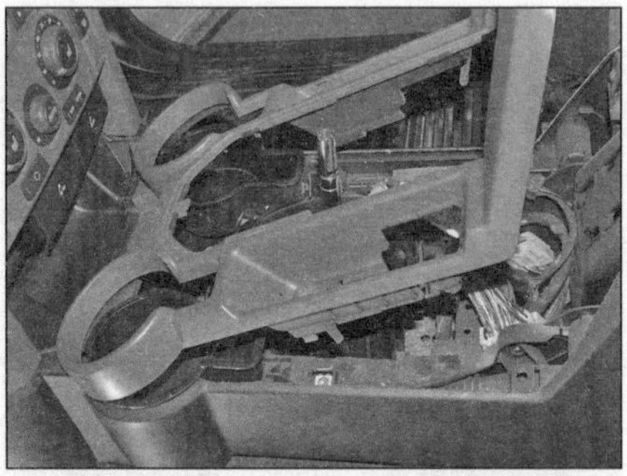

27.6c Pull the console upper panel upwards to release the retaining clips

Grab handles

47 Prise up the covers, undo the screws, and remove the grab handle **(see illustration)**.

48 Refitting is a reversal of removal.

27 Centre console – removal and refitting

Removal

1 Slide the front seats fully forwards, then disconnect the battery negative lead as described in Chapter 5, Section 4.

2 Remove the ride and handling optimisation switch as described in Chapter 13, Section 4.

3 Lift out both front cupholder inserts.

4 Lift out the tray at the front of the console.

5 Prise up the plastic cover, undo the retaining screw, disconnect the wiring plug and slide the parking brake switch rearwards to remove it **(see illustrations)**.

6 Open the storage box lid, remove the rubber and plastic inserts, then undo the retaining screw and pull the console upper panel upwards to release the 8 retaining clips **(see illustrations)**.

7 Release the 4 clips, remove the cigarette lighter closing panel and undo the 2 screws at the front **(see illustrations)**.

8 Note their fitted positions, then disconnect the various console wiring plugs **(see illustration)**.

27.7a Pull out the cigarette lighter closing panel ...

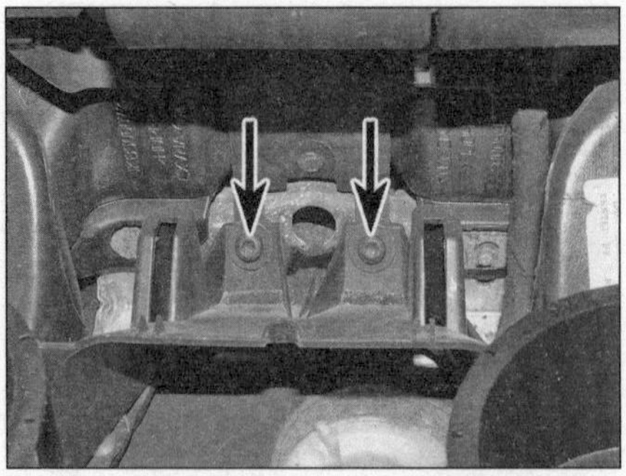

27.7b ... and undo the screws (arrowed) beneath

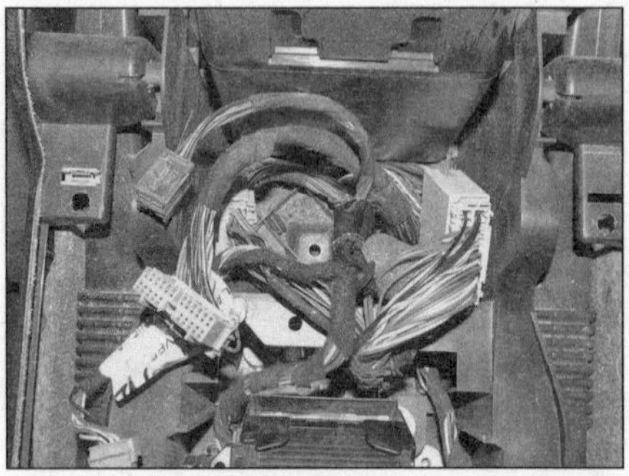

27.8 Note their fitted positions and disconnect the console wiring plugs

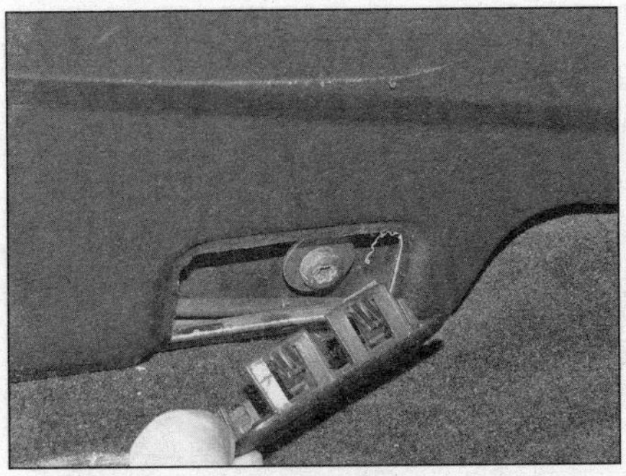

27.9 Prise out the cover and undo the screw each side

9 Prise out the covers, and remove the Torx screw each side at the rear of the console **(see illustration)**.

10 Manoeuvre the console from the cabin **(see illustration)**.

27.10 Lift the rear and manoeuvre the console from place

Refitting

11 Refitting is a reversal of the removal procedure, noting the following:

a) Ensure that all the wiring is correctly routed, and does not become trapped as the console is refitted.

b) Reconnect the battery negative lead as described in Chapter 5, Section 4.

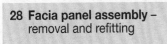

28 Facia panel assembly – removal and refitting

Removal

1 Remove the centre console as described in Section 27.

2 Remove the steering wheel as described in Chapter 11, Section 19.

3 Remove the facia-mounted audio unit as described in Chapter 13, Section 17.

4 Undo the 2 Torx screws, and pull the facia upper switch panel rearwards **(see illustration)**. Disconnect the wiring plug as the panel is withdrawn.

28.4 Upper switch panel retaining screws (arrowed)

5 Undo the 2 Torx screws, release the 3 clips and pull the cigarette lighter panel rearwards **(see illustration)**. Disconnect the wiring plugs as the panel is withdrawn.

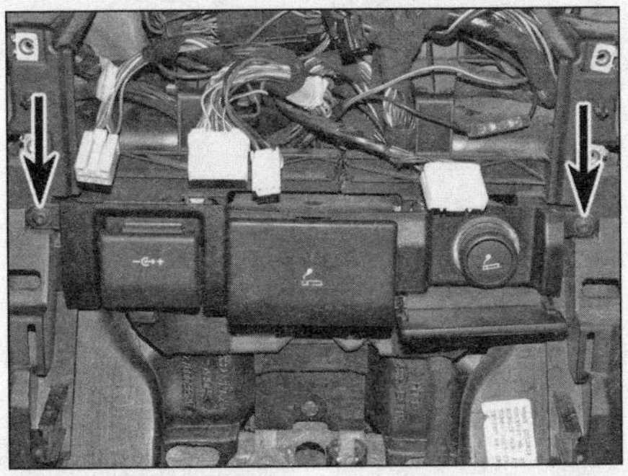

28.5 Undo the screws (arrowed) and pull the cigarette lighter panel rearwards

6 Undo the 2 screws, release the clip and remove the panel above the driver's pedals **(see illustrations)**. Disconnect the wiring plug as the panel is withdrawn.

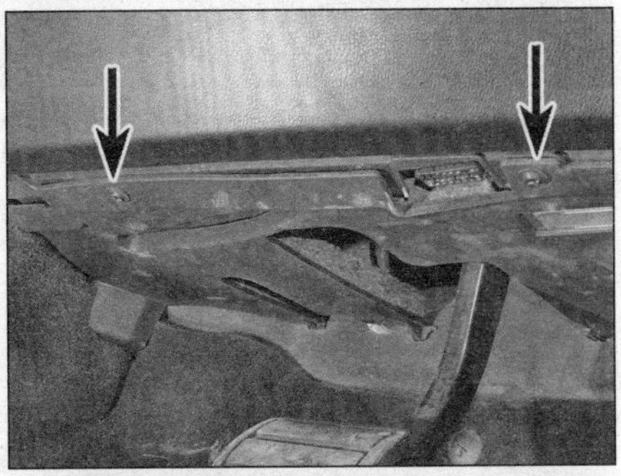

28.6a Undo the screws (arrowed) and remove the panel above the pedals

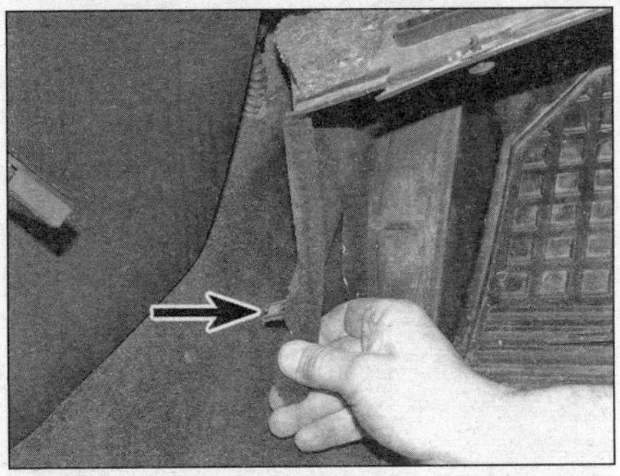

28.6b Note the clip (arrowed) at the inner end of the panel

7 Undo the 2 screws, release the clip and remove the panel above the passenger's footwell. Disconnect the wiring plug as the panel is withdrawn.

8 Undo the screw each side of the facia centre panel **(see illustration)**.

9 On models with the factory-fitted navigation system, undo the 4 screws and remove the display screen **(see illustration)**.

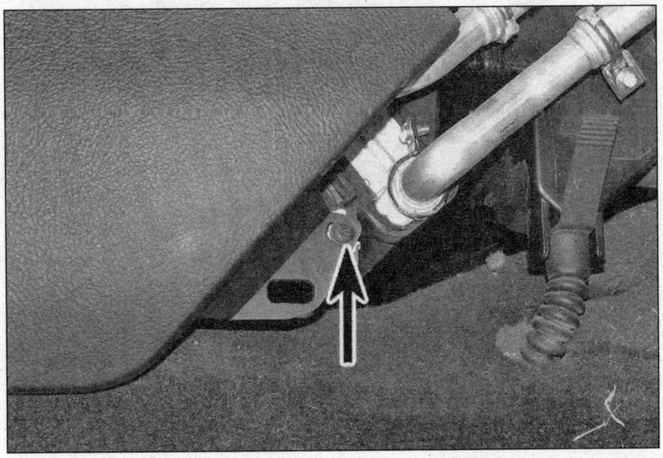

28.8 Remove the screw (arrowed) each side of the centre panel

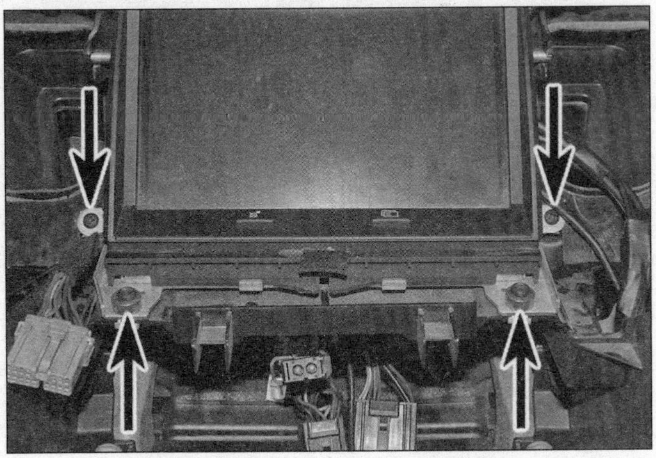

28.9 Display screen retaining screws (arrowed)

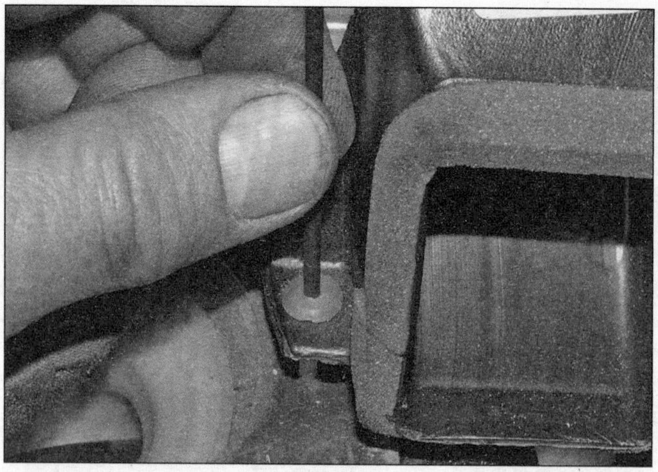

28.10a Press in the centre pins to release the heater duct clips each side ...

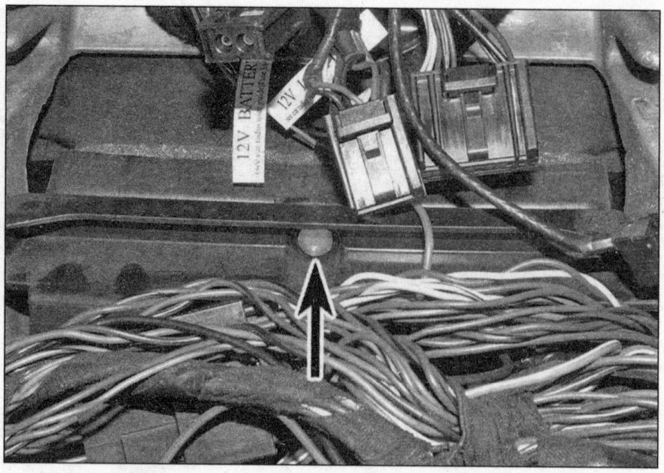

28.10b ... and the one in the centre (arrowed)

Disconnect the wiring plugs as the unit is withdraw. **Note:** *Cover the end of the fibre optic cable to prevent dust/dirt ingress, and don't bend the cable in a radius of less than 30 mm.*

10 On all models, remove the 3 clips securing the central heater duct **(see illustrations)**.

11 Release the wiring harness retaining clips from the base of the left- and right-hand central heater duct.

12 Undo the 8 screws, release the 4 clips and remove the facia centre reinforcement panel **(see illustrations)**. Note the routing of the various wiring harnesses to aid refitment.

13 Starting at the lower edge, pull the driver's

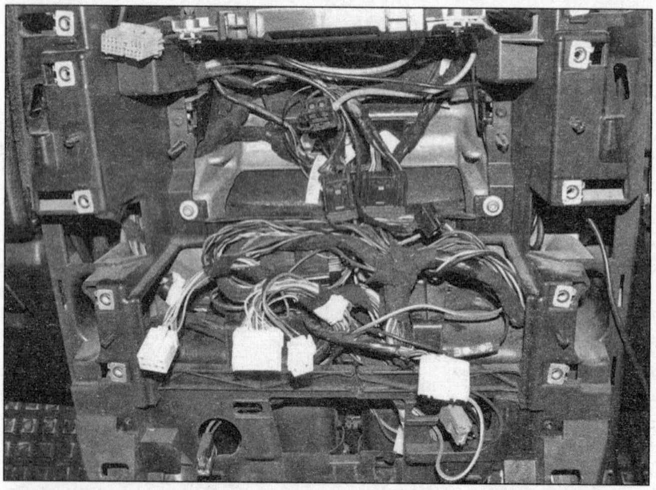

28.12a Note the routing of the various wiring looms to aid refitting

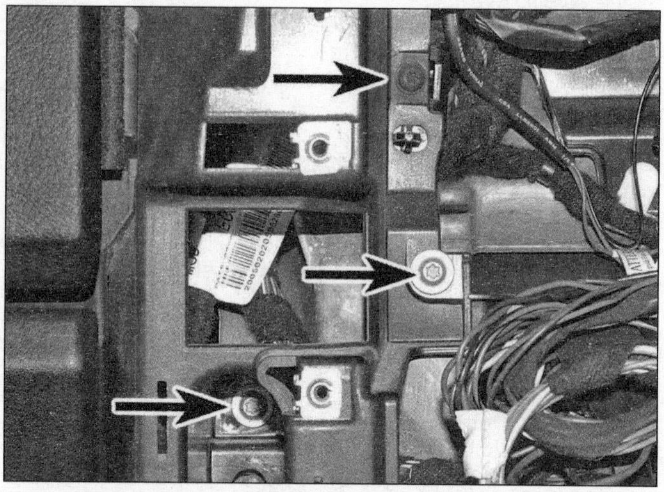

28.12b Undo the 3 screws (arrowed) each side ...

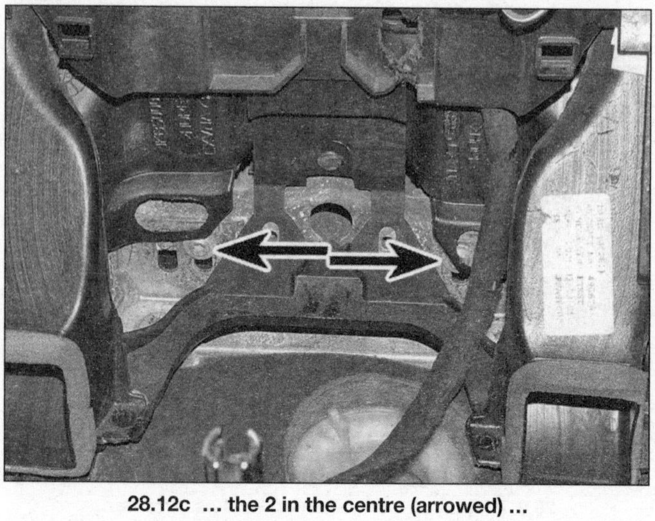

28.12c ... the 2 in the centre (arrowed) ...

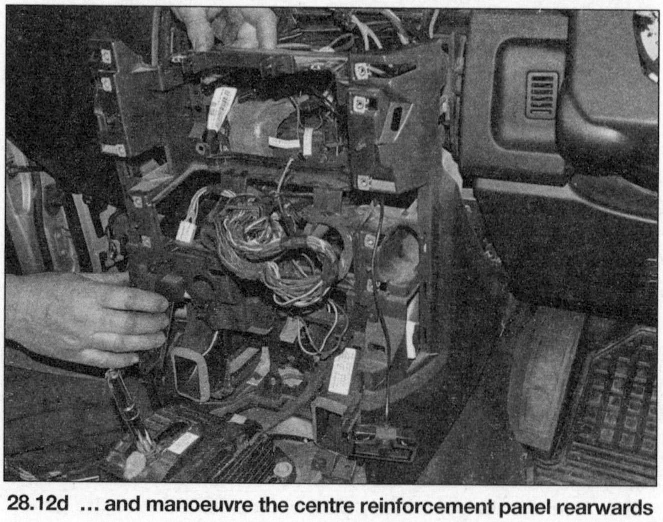

28.12d ... and manoeuvre the centre reinforcement panel rearwards

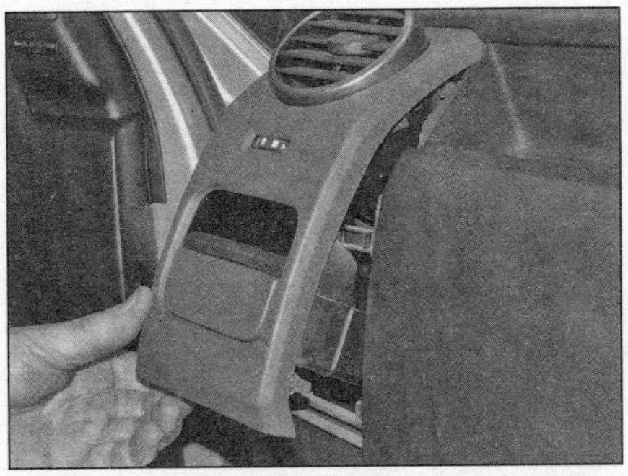

28.13 Pull the lower edge of the side vent panels rearwards

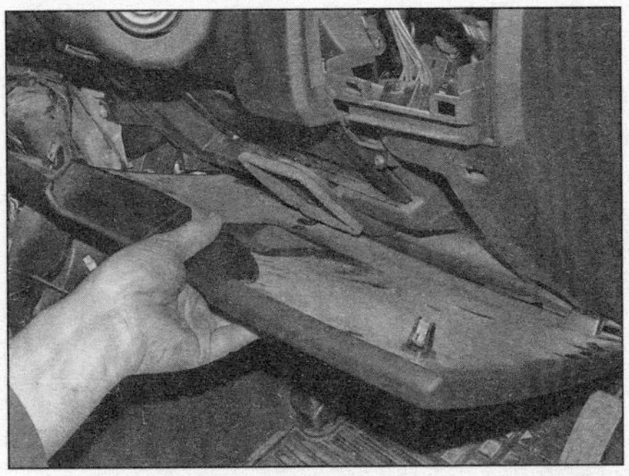

28.14 Pull the upper edge of the driver's side panel rearwards to release the clips

28.15 Upper shroud retaining clips (arrowed)

and passenger's side vent panels from the facia **(see illustration)**. Disconnect the wiring plugs as the panel is withdrawn.

14 Pull the upper edge of the panel beneath the steering column rearwards to release the clips, then remove it **(see illustration)**.

15 Fully extend and lower the column, then carefully prise up the steering column upper shroud to release the clips **(see illustration)**.

16 Undo the 3 retaining screws, release the column adjustment lever (where fitted) and remove the steering column lower shroud **(see illustration)**. Unclip the wiring harness as the shroud is withdrawn.

17 Prise the trim panel each side of the steering column rearwards **(see illustration)**.

18 Disconnect the wiring plugs, undo the 4 screws and remove the steering column combination switch assembly **(see illustrations)**.

19 Undo the 2 screws, release the 2 clips and

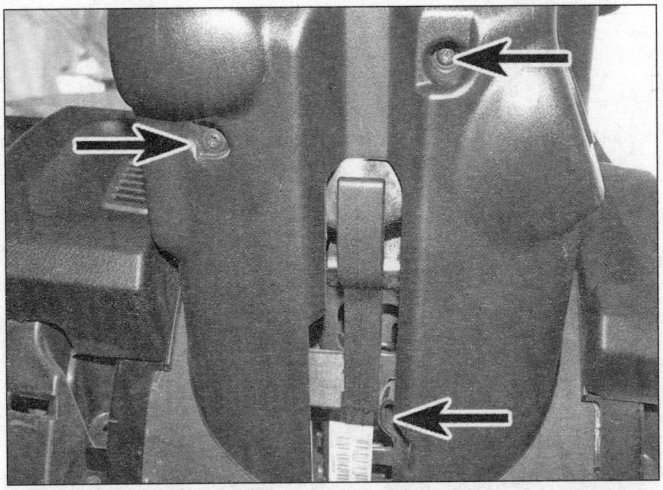

28.16 Lower steering column shroud screws (arrowed)

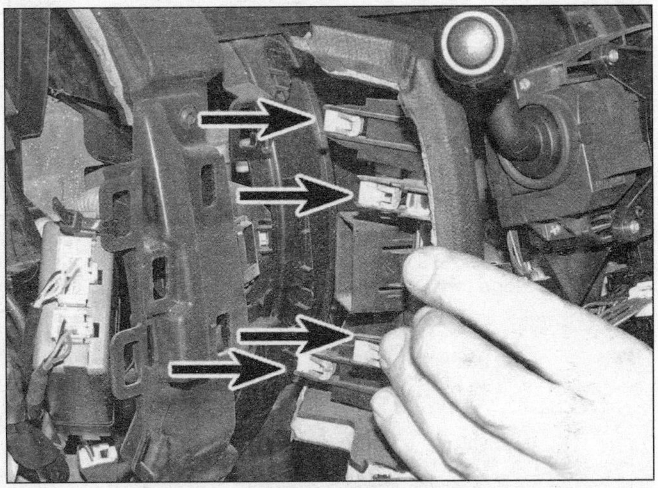

28.17 The panel each side of the steering column is secured by 4 clips (arrowed)

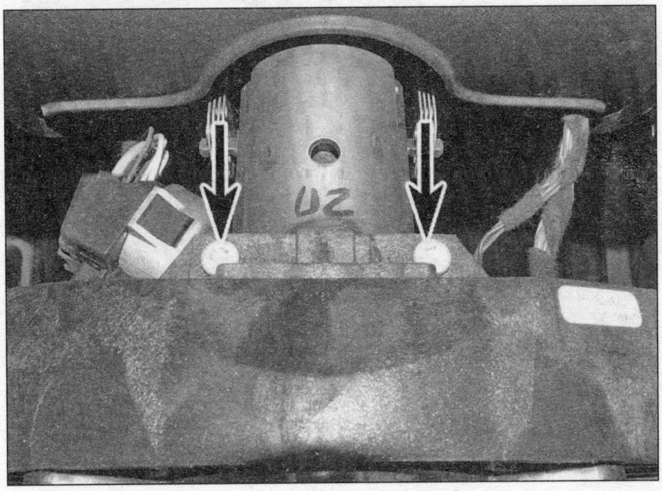

28.18a The steering column combination switch is secured by 2 screws on the top (arrowed) ...

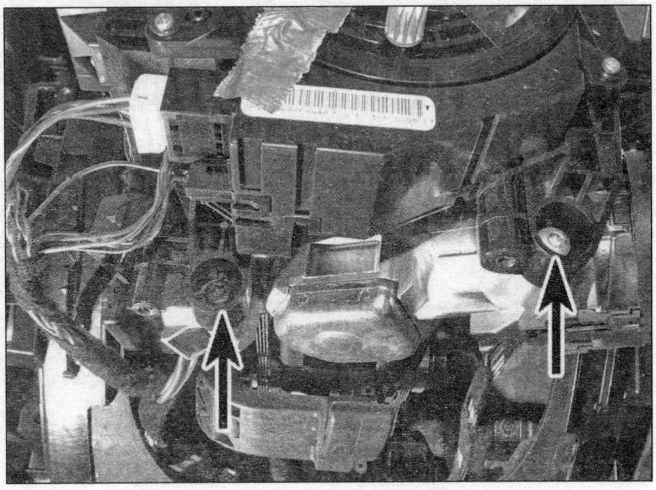

28.18b ... and 2 screws below (arrowed)

28.19 Column gaiter panel screws (arrowed)

28.21 Unclip the temperature sensor from the left-hand side of the column aperture

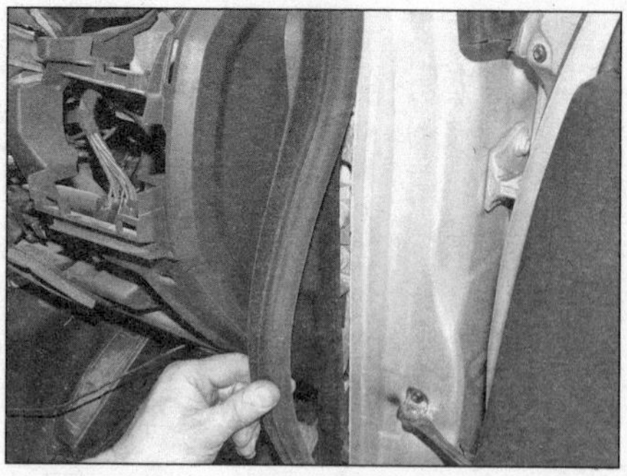

28.23a Pull the weatherstrip from the pillar

remove the steering column gaiter panel **(see illustration)**.

20 Undo the 2 retaining screws at the lower edge and remove the instrument cluster. Disconnect the wiring plug as the unit is withdrawn – refer to Chapter 13, Section 9, if necessary.

21 Unclip the cabin air temperature sensor at the left-hand side of the steering column aperture **(see illustration)**.

22 Undo the 2 screws securing the EOBD plug from the lower edge of the facia panel on the driver's side.

23 Pull away the rubber weatherstrip, prise the trim at the edge rearwards, then undo the 9 screws and remove the driver's side facia reinforcement panel **(see illustrations)**. Unclip the wiring harness as the panel is withdrawn.

24 Disconnect the wiring plug, release the 2 clips and remove the passenger's airbag de-activation switch **(see illustration)**.

25 Remove the passenger's side glovebox as described in Section 26.

26 Remove the clip and withdraw the passenger's side footwell duct **(see illustration)**.

27 Open the lid, then pull the storage compartment rearwards to release the 4 retaining clips **(see illustration)**.

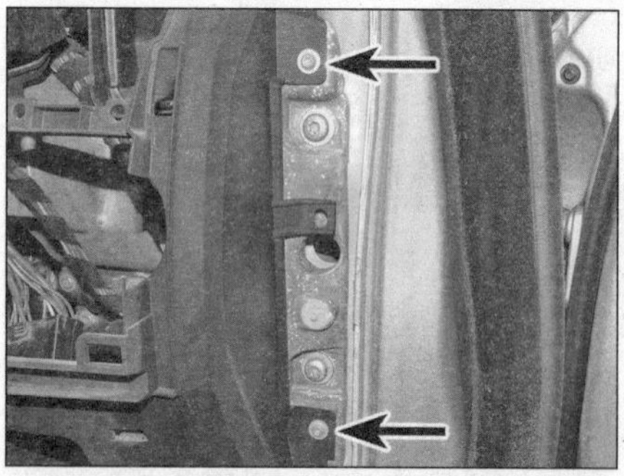

28.23b The driver's side reinforcement panel is secured by 2 screws at the outer edge (arrowed) ...

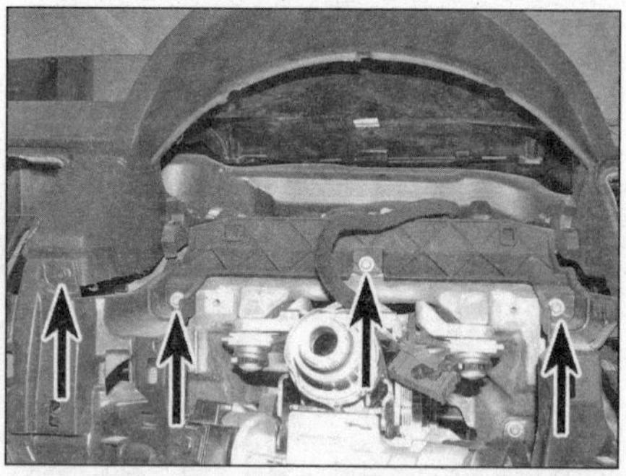

28.23c ... 4 screws in the upper section (arrowed) ...

28.23d ... 2 screws in the lower, left-hand section (arrowed) ...

28.23e ... and a screw in the lower, right-hand section (arrowed)

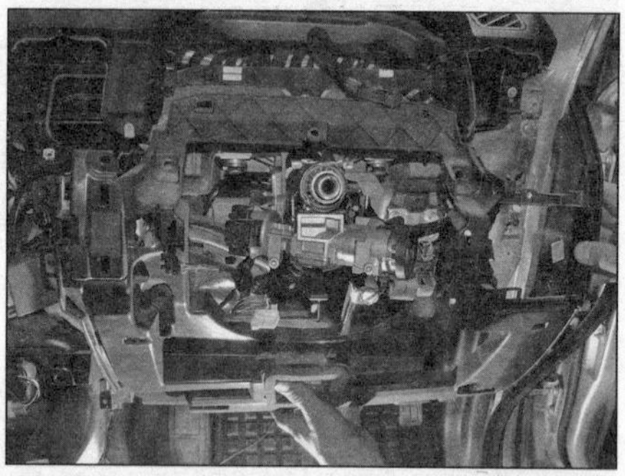

28.23f Manoeuvre the panel from place

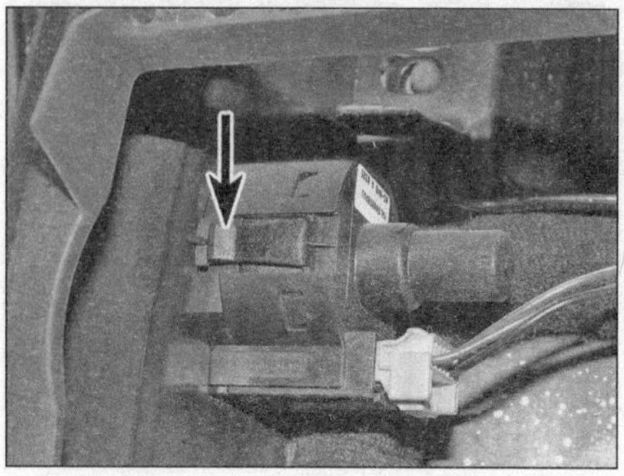

28.24 Squeeze the clip (arrowed) each side and remove the airbag switch

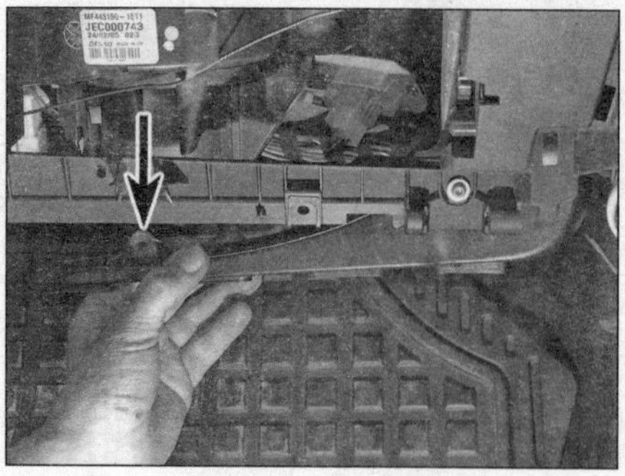

28.26 Release the clip (arrowed) and remove the air duct

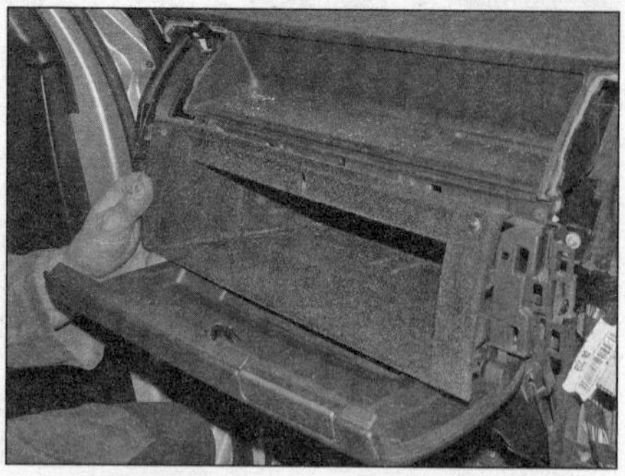

28.27 Pull the storage compartment rearwards to release the clips

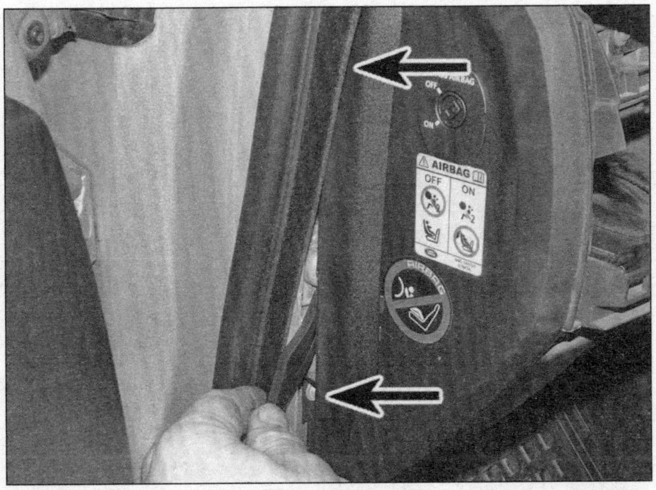

28.28a Prise the trim rearwards and undo the 2 screws (arrowed) at the outer edge

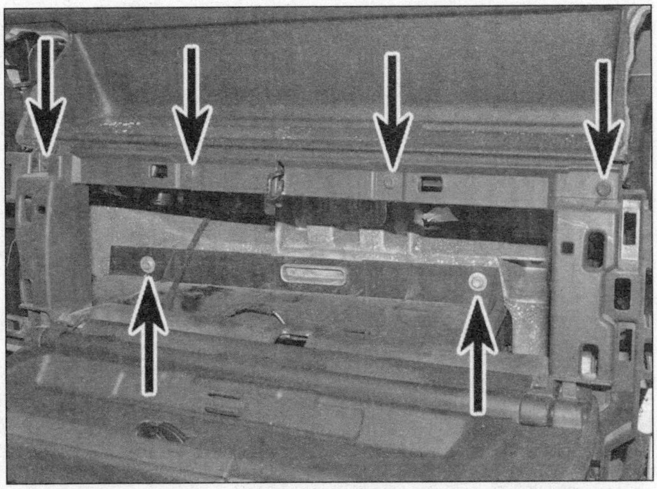

28.28b Undo the screws (arrowed) in/around the storage compartment aperture ...

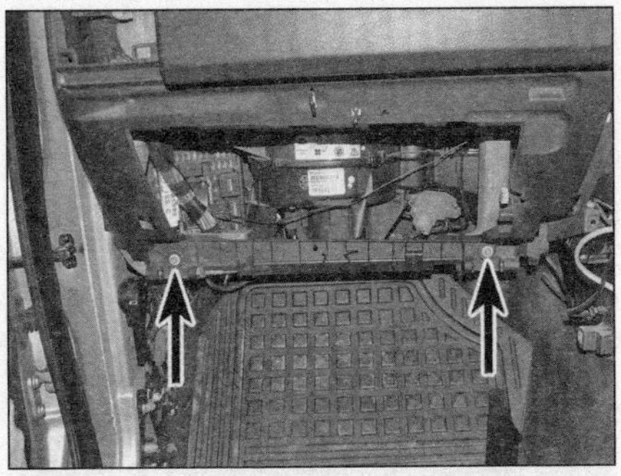

28.28c ... 2 screws (arrowed) at the lower edge ...

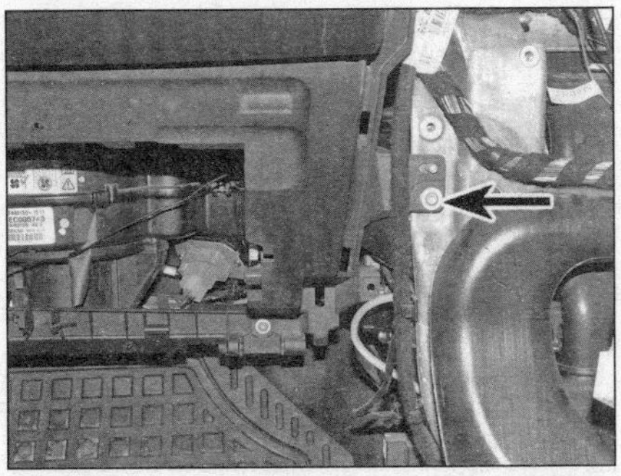

28.28d ... the screw (arrowed) at the inner edge ...

28.28e ... then manoeuvre the reinforcement panel rearwards

28 Pull away the rubber weatherstrip, prise the trim at the edge rearwards, undo the 11 retaining screws and remove the passenger's side facia reinforcement panel **(see illustrations)**. Release any wiring plugs/harnesses as the panel is withdrawn.

29 Remove the facia speaker as described in Chapter 13, Section 17.

30 Remove both A-pillar trims as described in Section 26.

31 Carefully prise up the light sensor from the facia and disconnect the wiring plug.

32 Undo the 2 screws securing the passenger's airbag to the crossmember, and disconnect the 3 wiring plugs from the airbag module **(see illustration)**.

33 Remove the screw in the facia speaker aperture **(see illustration)**. Take care not to drop the screw.

34 Release the wiring harness retaining clips

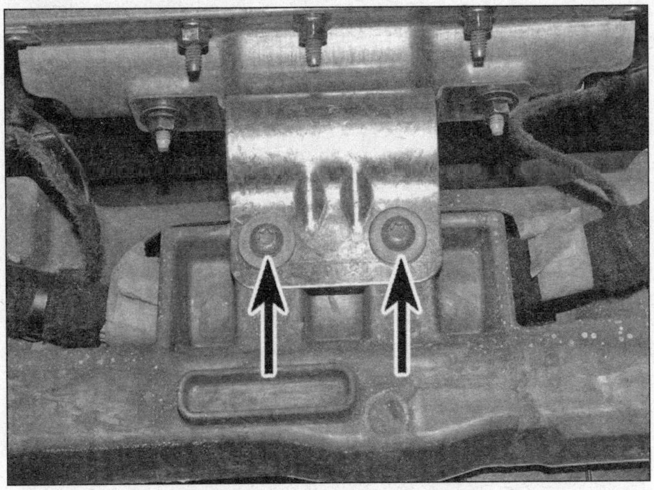

28.32 Undo the airbag bracket screws (arrowed) and disconnect the wiring plugs from the airbag

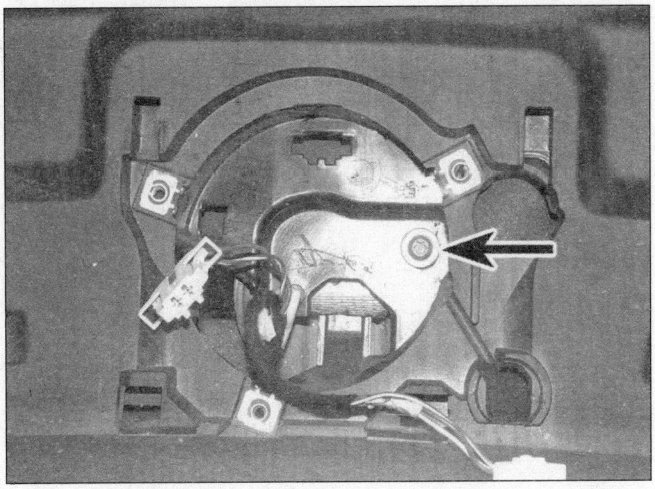

28.33 Undo the screw (arrowed) in the facia speaker aperture

28.35a The facia is secured by 3 screws (arrowed) in the centre ...

28.35b ... and one screw at each end of the facia (right-hand screw arrowed)

in the central facia aperture. Note the wiring loom routing to aid refitting.

35 The facia is now secured by 5 screws **(see illustrations)**. Undo the screws, and with the help of an assistant, manoeuvre the facia from the cabin.

Refitting

36 Refitting is a reversal of the removal procedure, noting the following points:

a) Manoeuvre the facia into position and ensure that the wiring is correctly routed and fed through the relevant facia apertures. Take great care not to trap the wiring as the facia is installed.

b) Clip the facia back into position, then refit all the facia fasteners and tighten them securely.

c) On completion, reconnect the battery (Chapter 5, Section 4) and check that all the electrical components and switches function correctly.

29 Radiator grille – removal and refitting

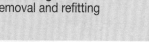

1 Open the bonnet.

2 Release the 4 clips at the top edge of the grille **(see illustration)**.

3 Release the clip each side, and remove the radiator grille **(see illustrations)**.

4 Refitting is the reverse of removal.

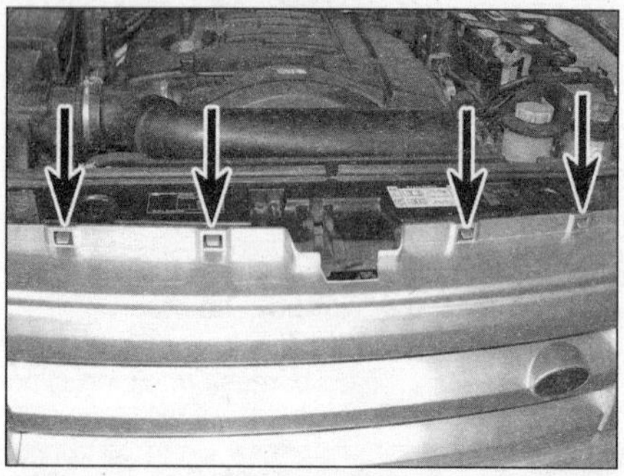
29.2 Depress the clips (arrowed) at the top of the grille ...

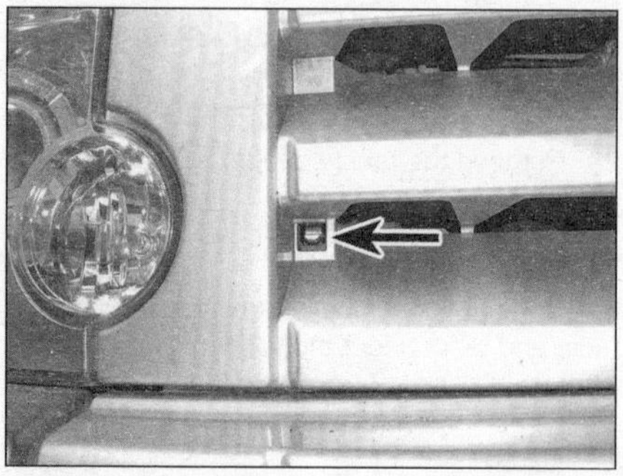
29.3a ... the clip (arrowed) each side ...

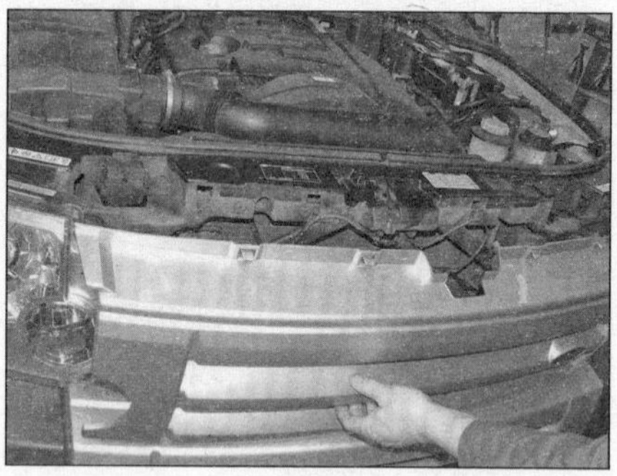
29.3b ... and lift it from place

Chapter 13
Body electrical systems

Contents

Degrees of difficulty

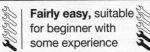

Easy, suitable for novice with little experience	**Fairly easy,** suitable for beginner with some experience	**Fairly difficult,** suitable for competent DIY mechanic	**Difficult,** suitable for experienced DIY mechanic	**Very difficult,** suitable for expert DIY or professional

Specifications

System type	12 volt, negative earth	
Bulbs	**Wattage**	
Brake/tail light	21/5	
Cornering bulb	35 H8	
Direction indicator	21 S8	
Direction indicator side repeater	5 capless	
Foglight:		
Front	55 H11	
Rear	21	
Headlight		
Halogen:		
Dipped beam	55 H7	
Main beam	55 H7	
Xenon:		
Dipped/main beam	35 D2S	
Main beam (halogen)	55 H7	
High-level brake light	LED	
Instrument panel lights	LED	
Interior lights	5 capless	
Number plate light	5 festoon	
Reversing light	21	
Sidelight	5	
Vanity light	1.2 capless	
Torque wrench settings	**Nm**	**lbf ft**
Airbag components:		
Control unit screws	10	7
Passenger's airbag nuts	10	7
Impact sensor	8	6
Side airbag	10	7
Tyre pressure sensor	7	5

1 General information and precautions

Warning: Before carrying out any work on the electrical system, read through the precautions given in Safety first! at the beginning of this manual, and in Chapter 5, Section 1.

The electrical system is of the 12 volt, negative earth type. Power for the lights and all electrical accessories is supplied by a lead-calcium type battery which is charged by the alternator.

This Chapter covers repair and service procedures for the various electrical components not associated with engine. Information on the battery, alternator and starter motor can be found in Chapter 5.

Prior to working on any component in the electrical system, the battery negative terminal should first be disconnected, to prevent the possibility of electrical short-circuits and/or fires. Refer to Chapter 5, Section 4.

2 Electrical fault finding – general information

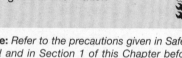

Note: *Refer to the precautions given in Safety first! and in Section 1 of this Chapter before starting work. The following tests relate to testing of the main electrical circuits, and should not be used to test delicate electronic circuits (such as anti-lock braking systems), particularly where an electronic control module is used.*

General

1 A typical electrical circuit consists of an electrical component, any switches, relays, motors, fuses, fusible links or circuit breakers related to that component, and the wiring and connectors which link the component to both the battery and the chassis. To help to pinpoint a problem in an electrical circuit, wiring diagrams are included at the end of this Chapter.

2 Before attempting to diagnose an electrical fault, first study the appropriate wiring diagram to obtain a complete understanding of the components included in the particular circuit concerned. The possible sources of a fault can be narrowed down by noting if other components related to the circuit are operating properly. If several components or circuits fail at one time, the problem is likely to be related to a shared fuse or earth connection.

3 Electrical problems usually stem from simple causes, such as loose or corroded connections, a faulty earth connection, a blown fuse, a melted fusible link, or a faulty relay (refer to Section 3 for details of testing relays). Visually inspect the condition of all fuses, wires and connections in a problem circuit before testing the components. Use the wiring diagrams to determine which terminal connections will need to be checked in order to pinpoint the trouble-spot.

4 The basic tools required for electrical fault finding include a circuit tester or voltmeter (a 12 volt bulb with a set of test leads can also be used for certain tests); a self-powered test light (sometimes known as a continuity tester); an ohmmeter (to measure resistance); a battery and set of test leads; and a jumper wire, preferably with a circuit breaker or fuse incorporated, which can be used to bypass suspect wires or electrical components. Before attempting to locate a problem with test instruments, use the wiring diagram to determine where to make the connections.

Warning: Under no circumstances may live measuring instruments such as ohmmeters, voltmeters or a bulb and test leads be used to test any of the airbag circuitry. Any testing of these components must be left to a Land Rover dealer, as there is a danger of activating the system if the correct procedures are not followed.

Caution: The Land Rover Discovery 3 electrical system is extremely complex. Many of the ECMs are connected via a 'Databus' system, where they are able to share information from the various sensors, and communicate with each other. For instance, as the automatic gearbox approaches a gear ratio shift point, it signals the engine management ECM via the Databus. As the gearchange is made by the transmission ECM, the engine management ECM reduces the injection quantity, momentarily reducing engine output, to ensure a smoother transition from one gear ratio to the next. Due to the design of the Databus system, it is not advisable to backprobe the ECMs with a multimeter in the traditional manner. Instead, the electrical systems are equipped with a sophisticated self-diagnosis system, which can interrogate the various ECMs to reveal stored fault codes, and help pinpoint faults. In order to access the self-diagnosis system, specialist test equipment (fault code reader/scanner) is required.

5 To find the source of an intermittent wiring fault (usually due to a poor or dirty connection, or damaged wiring insulation), a 'wiggle' test can be performed on the wiring. This involves wiggling the wiring by hand to see if the fault occurs as the wiring is moved. It should be possible to narrow down the source of the fault to a particular section of wiring. This method of testing can be used in conjunction with any of the tests described in the following sub-Sections.

6 Apart from problems due to poor connections, two basic types of fault can occur in an electrical circuit – open-circuit, or short-circuit.

7 Open-circuit faults are caused by a break somewhere in the circuit, which prevents current from flowing. An open-circuit fault will prevent a component from working, but will not cause the relevant circuit fuse to blow.

8 Short-circuit faults are caused by a short somewhere in the circuit, which allows the current flowing in the circuit to escape along an alternative route, usually to earth. Short-circuit faults are normally caused by a breakdown in wiring insulation, which allows a feed wire to touch either another wire, or an earthed component such as the bodyshell. A short-circuit fault will normally cause the relevant circuit fuse to blow.

Finding an open-circuit

9 To check for an open-circuit, connect one lead of a circuit tester or voltmeter to either the negative battery terminal or a known good earth.

10 Connect the other lead to a connector in the circuit being tested, preferably nearest to the battery or fuse.

11 Switch on the circuit, bearing in mind that some circuits are live only when the ignition switch is moved to a particular position.

12 If voltage is present (indicated either by the tester bulb lighting or a voltmeter reading, as applicable), this means that the section of the circuit between the relevant connector and the battery is problem-free.

13 Continue to check the remainder of the circuit in the same fashion.

14 When a point is reached at which no voltage is present, the problem must lie between that point and the previous test point with voltage. Most problems can be traced to a broken, corroded or loose connection.

Finding a short-circuit

15 To check for a short-circuit, first disconnect the load(s) from the circuit (loads are the components which draw current from a circuit, such as bulbs, motors, heating elements, etc).

16 Remove the relevant fuse from the circuit, and connect a circuit tester or voltmeter to the fuse connections.

17 Switch on the circuit, bearing in mind that some circuits are live only when the ignition switch is moved to a particular position.

18 If voltage is present (indicated either by the tester bulb lighting or a voltmeter reading, as applicable), this means that there is a short-circuit.

19 If no voltage is present, but the fuse still blows with the load(s) connected, this indicates an internal fault in the load(s).

Finding an earth fault

20 The battery negative terminal is connected to earth – the metal of the engine/transmission and the car body – and most systems are wired so that they only receive a positive feed, the current returning via the metal of the car body.

21 This means that the component mounting and the body form part of that circuit. Loose or corroded mountings can therefore cause a range of electrical faults, ranging from total

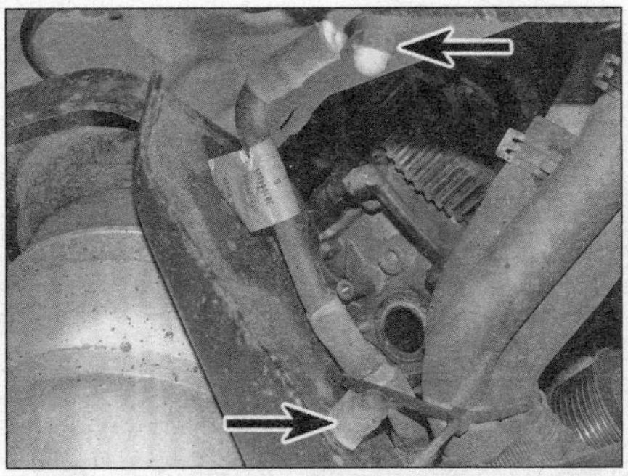
2.22a The main earth strap is bolted to the body, the chassis (arrowed) ...

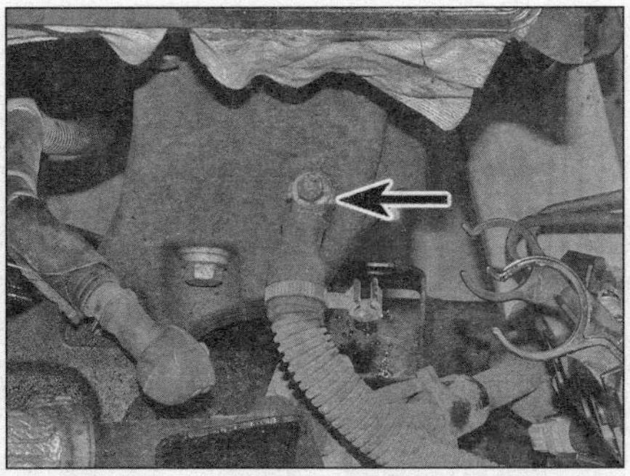
2.22b ... and the right-hand engine mounting bracket (arrowed)

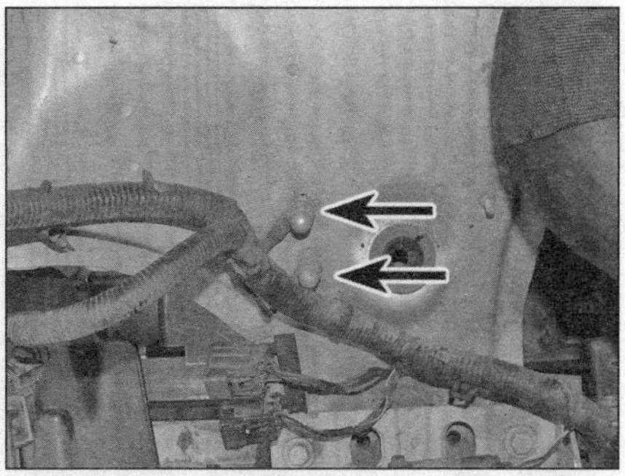
2.22c Other earth connections may be on the inner front wing (arrowed) ...

failure of a circuit, to a puzzling partial fault. In particular, lights may shine dimly (especially when another circuit sharing the same earth point is in operation), motors (eg, wiper motors or the radiator cooling fan motor) may run slowly, and the operation of one circuit may have an apparently-unrelated effect on another.

22 Note that on many vehicles, earth straps are used between certain components, such as the engine/transmission and the body, usually where there is no metal-to-metal contact between components due to flexible rubber mountings, etc **(see illustrations)**.

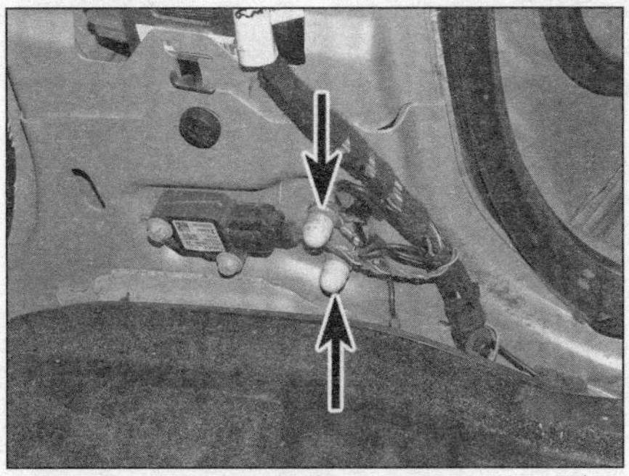
2.22d ... the B-pillar each side (arrowed) ...

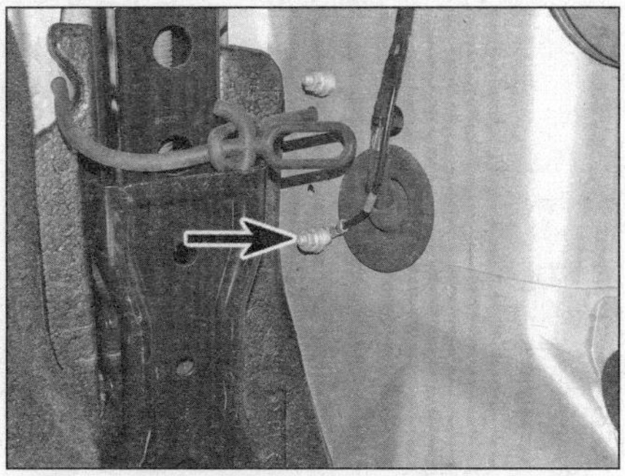
2.22e ... the C-pillar each side (arrowed) ...

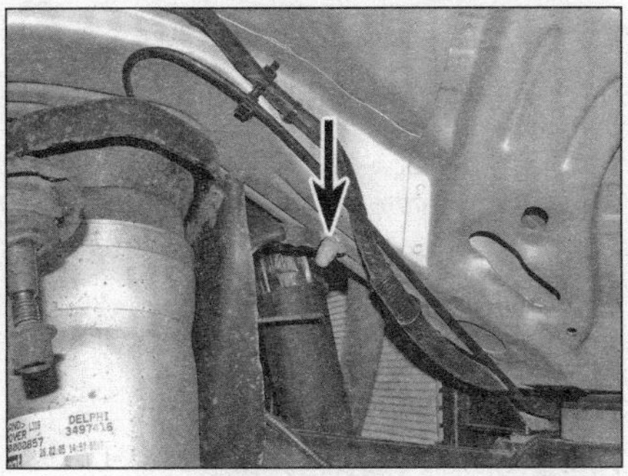
2.22f ... the left-hand wheel arch (arrowed) ...

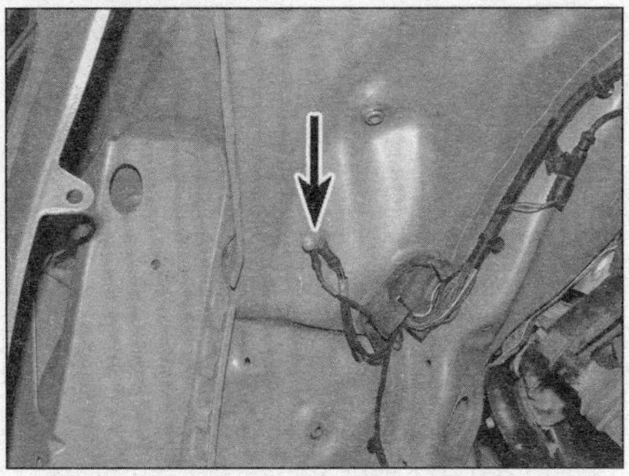
2.22g ... the front wheel arch each side (arrowed) ...

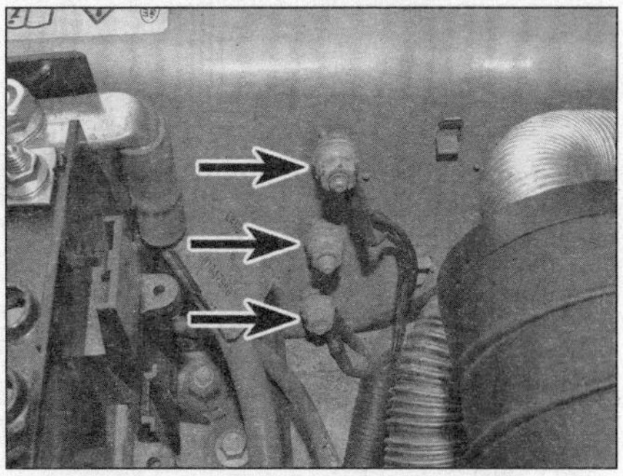
2.22h ... adjacent to the battery (arrowed) ...

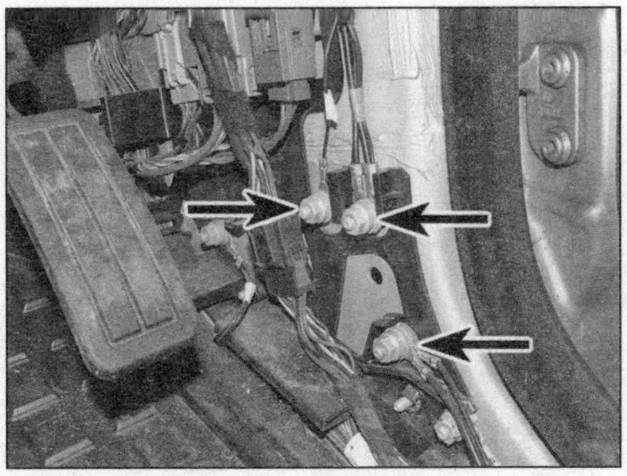
2.22i ... the A-pillar each side (arrowed) ...

2.22j ... adjacent to the liftgate hinge each side ...

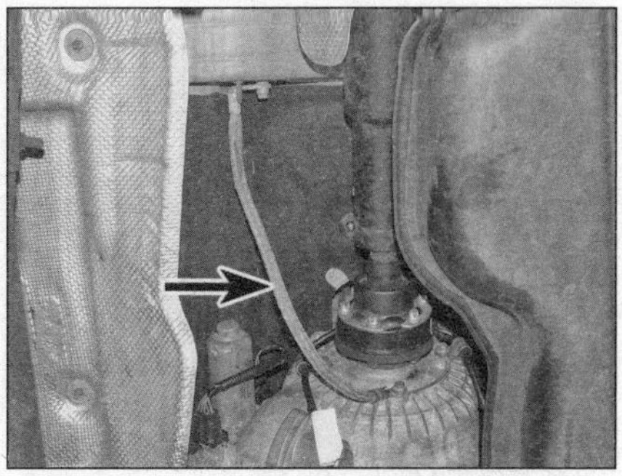
22.2k ... and at the rear of the transfer gearbox (arrowed – not all models)

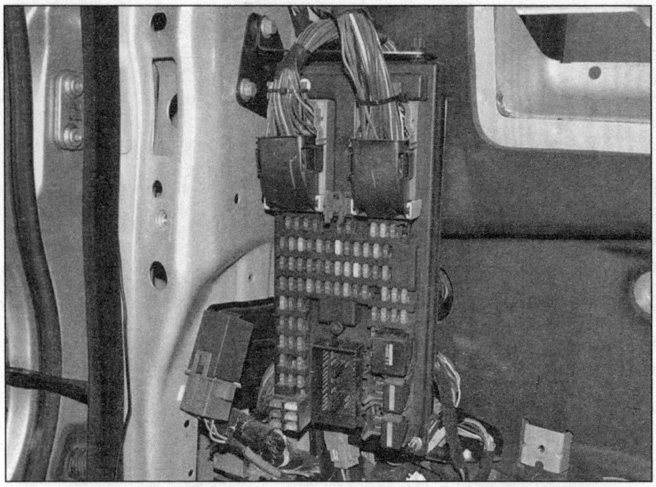

3.1a The central junction box (CJB) is located behind the passenger's side of the facia (facia removed for clarity)

3.1b Release the clips (arrowed) and lift up the engine battery junction box (BJB) cover

23 To check whether a component is properly earthed, disconnect the battery and connect one lead of an ohmmeter to a known good earth point. Connect the other lead to the wire or earth connection being tested. The resistance reading should be zero; if not, check the connection as follows.

24 If an earth connection is thought to be faulty, dismantle the connection and clean back to bare metal both the bodyshell and the wire terminal or the component earth connection mating surface. Be careful to remove all traces of dirt and corrosion, then use a knife to trim away any paint, so that a clean metal-to-metal joint is made.

25 On reassembly, tighten the joint fasteners securely; if a wire terminal is being refitted, use serrated washers between the terminal and the bodyshell to ensure a clean and secure connection. When the connection is remade, prevent the onset of corrosion in the future by applying a coat of petroleum jelly or silicone-based grease. Alternatively, spray on (at regular intervals) a proprietary ignition sealer, or a water-dispersant lubricant.

3 Fuses and relays – general information

Fuses

1 The main fusebox is known as the central junction box (CJB) is located behind the passenger's side of the facia. An auxiliary fuse/relay box, known as the battery junction box (BJB), is located in the left-hand corner of the engine compartment **(see illustrations)**.

2 To gain access to the main fusebox, open the glovebox, pinch together the tops of the support stays, and lower the glovebox.

3 A label identifying each fuse is attached to the rear of the glovebox lid.

4 To remove a fuse, first switch off the circuit concerned (or the ignition), then pull the fuse out of its terminals. The wire within the fuse is clearly visible; if the fuse is blown, it will be broken or melted.

5 Always renew a fuse/fusible link with one of an identical rating; never use one with a different rating from the original, nor substitute anything else. Never renew a fuse/fusible link more than once without tracing the source of the trouble. The rating is stamped on top of the fuse/fusible link; note that are also colour-coded for easy recognition.

6 If a new fuse/fusible link blows immediately, find the cause before renewing it again – a short to earth as a result of faulty insulation is most likely. Where more than one circuit is protected, try to isolate the defect by switching on each circuit in turn (if possible) until it blows again. Always carry a supply of spare fuses/fusible links of each relevant rating on the vehicle; a spare of each fuse rating should be clipped into the base of the fusebox.

7 Note that some circuits are protected by field effect transistors (FETs). These 'fuses' can detect overloads and short circuits, by responding to the heat generated by the increase in current flow. When the heat detected rises above a predetermined level, the FET disconnects the electrical supply to the relevant circuit. When the fault is rectified, or the FET has cooled, it will reset, and operate the circuit normally. Any problems will cause fault codes to be generated and stored by the CJB's self-diagnosis facility. These codes can be retrieved using Land Rover T4 diagnostic equipment, or generic equivalent.

Relays

8 If a circuit or system controlled by a relay develops a fault and the relay is suspect, operate the system; if the relay is functioning, it should be possible to hear it click as it is energised. If it clicks, the fault lies with the components or wiring of the system. If the relay is not being energised, then either the relay is not receiving a main supply or a switching voltage, or the relay itself is faulty. Testing is by the substitution of a known good unit, but be careful; while some relays are identical in appearance and in operation, others look similar but perform different functions.

9 To renew a relay, first ensure that the ignition switch is off. The relays are located in the battery junction box (BJB) in the left-hand corner of the engine compartment. The relay can then simply be pulled out from the socket, and the new relay pressed in.

4 Switches – removal and refitting

Note: *Disconnect the battery negative lead before removing any switch as described in Chapter 5, Section 4. Refer to the precautions in Section 1 before proceeding.*

Ignition switch/ steering column lock

1 Refer to Chapter 11, Section 20.

Steering column switches

Right- or left-hand switch

2 Fully extend the steering column.

3 Carefully prise up the steering column upper shroud to release the clips **(see illustration)**.

4 Undo the 3 retaining screws, release the

4.3 Prise up the steering column upper shroud to release the clips (arrowed)

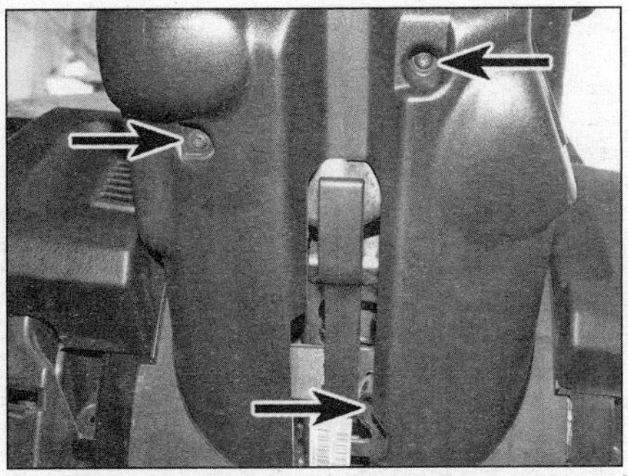

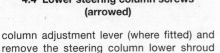

4.4 Lower steering column screws (arrowed)

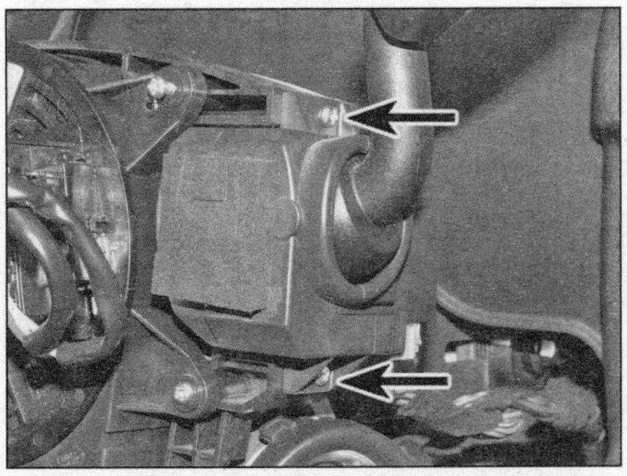

4.5a Undo the screws (arrowed) ...

4.5b ... and remove the switch

column adjustment lever (where fitted) and remove the steering column lower shroud **(see illustration)**.

5 Disconnect the switch wiring plug, then undo the 2 retaining screws, and remove the switch **(see illustrations)**.

6 Refitting is a reversal of the removal procedure.

Complete switch assembly

7 Remove the steering wheel as described in Chapter 11, Section 19.

8 Remove the steering column upper and lower shrouds, as described in paragraphs 3 and 4 of this Section.

9 Disconnect the wiring plugs from the switches, and the airbag rotary contact unit, then undo the 4 screws and slide the switch assembly over the end of the steering column **(see illustrations)**.

Light control switch

10 Starting at the lower edge, pull the driver's side vent panel from the facia **(see illustration)**. Disconnect the wiring plug as the panel is withdrawn.

11 Undo the 4 retaining screws, then detach the lighting switch from the panel **(see illustration)**.

12 Refitting is a reversal of removal.

Instrument panel switches

13 Carefully prise the facia centre panel rearwards to release the 4 retaining clips **(see illustration)**.

14 Undo the 2 retaining screws and pull the switch panel rearwards **(see illustration)**. Disconnect the wiring plug as the switch is withdrawn.

15 Refitting is the reverse of removal, ensuring that the wiring connectors are securely reconnected.

4.9a Undo the screws beneath (arrowed) ...

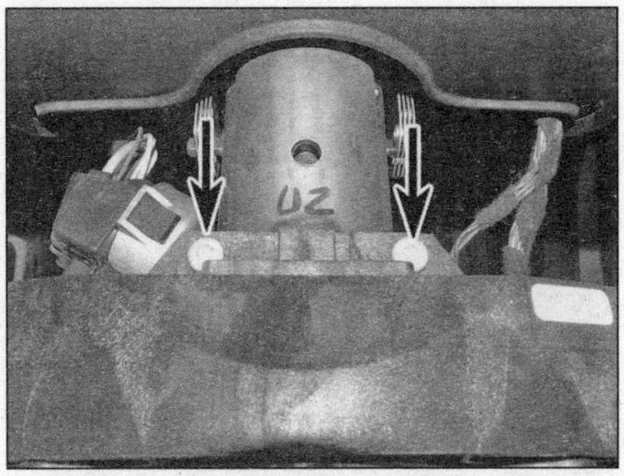

4.9b ... the screws above (arrowed) ...

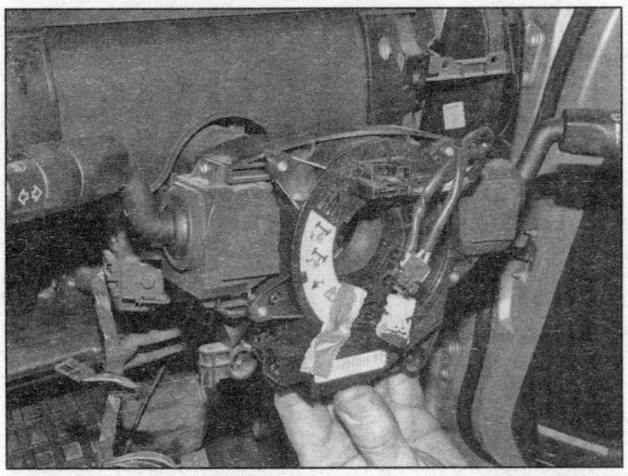

4.9c ... then remove the complete switch

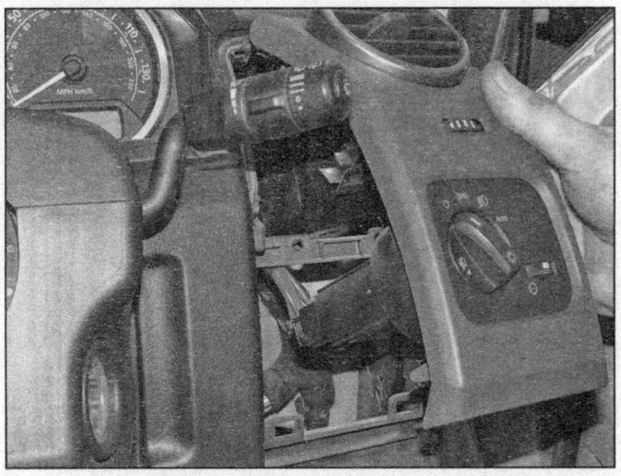

4.10 Pull the lower edge of the facia vent rearwards to remove it

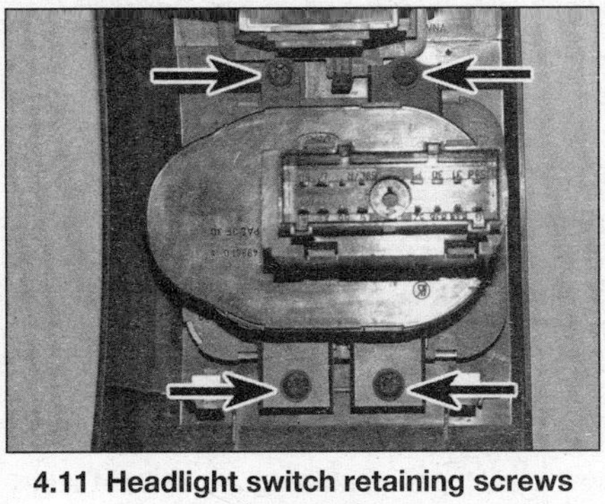

4.11 Headlight switch retaining screws (arrowed)

4.13 Pull the centre facia panel rearwards

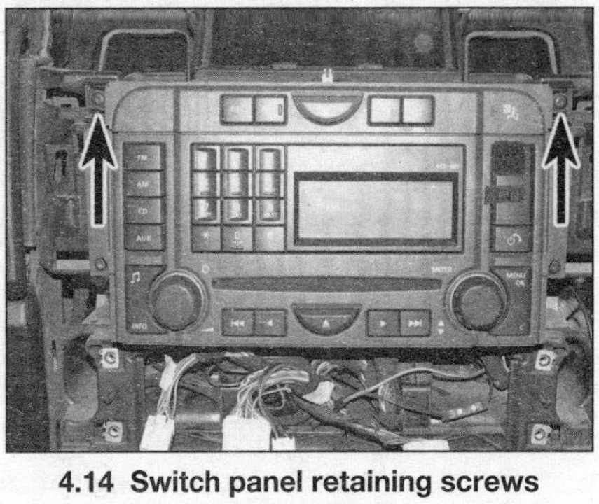

4.14 Switch panel retaining screws (arrowed)

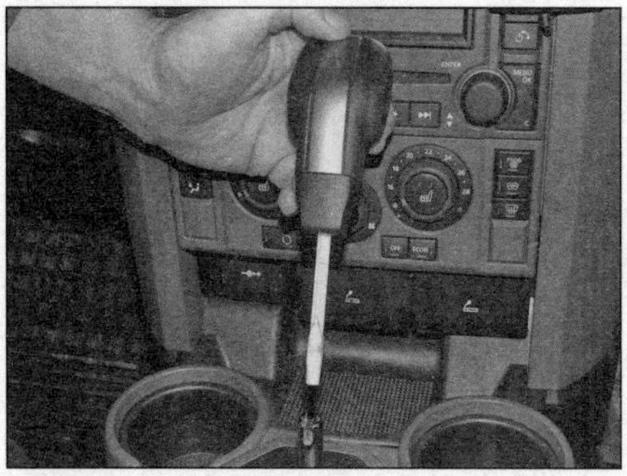

4.16 Pull the selector/change knob sharply upwards

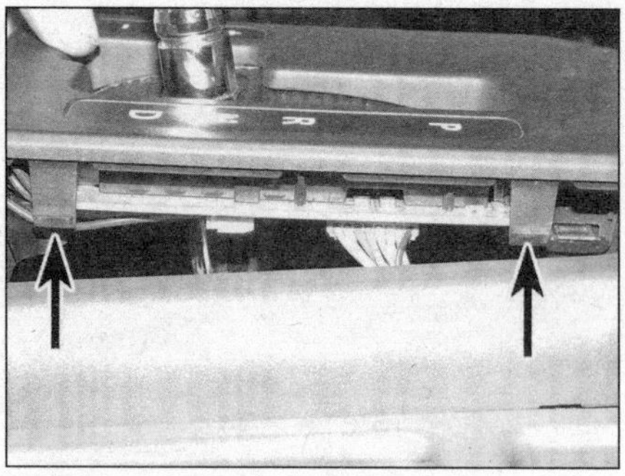

4.17 Release the clip (arrowed) each side and prise up the panel

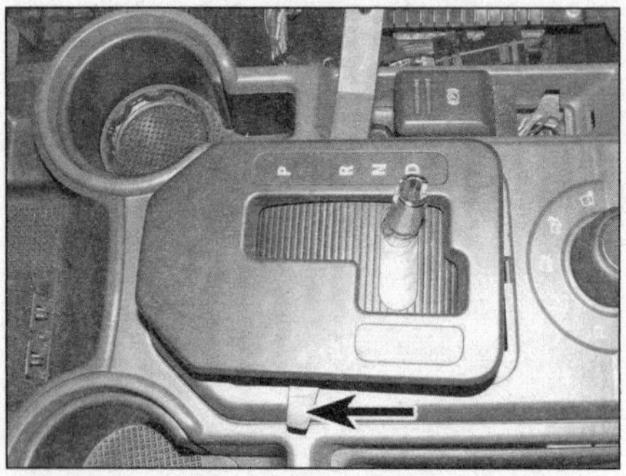

4.18a Slide a thin tool (arrowed) beneath the gate shuttering ...

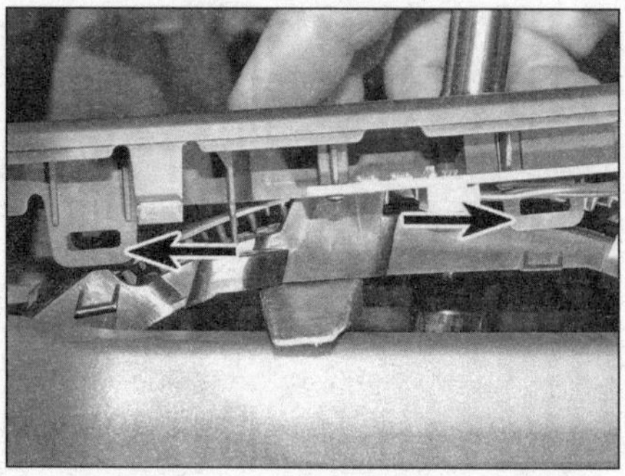

4.18b ... then, using a right-angled tool, pull the clips (arrowed) each side outwards to release the panel from the shuttering

Ride and handling optimisation switch

16 Pull the gear selector/change knob upwards with a sharp tug **(see illustration)**.

17 Prise up the selector/gearchange panel upwards a little to access the lever gate shuttering clips **(see illustration)**.

18 Using a thin, right-angle tool, prise the 4 clips apart, and pull the selector/gearchange panel upwards from place **(see illustrations)**. Do not disconnect the wiring plug at this stage.

19 Prise the switch panel upwards to release the 4 retaining clips, and disconnect the wiring plugs **(see illustration)**. No further dismantling is recommended.

20 Refitting is the reverse of removal.

Brake light switch

21 Refer to Chapter 10, Section 19.

Parking brake switch

22 Refer to Chapter 10, Section 15.

Electric window switches

23 Starting at the front edge, carefully prise the switch from place **(see illustration)**.

24 Disconnect the wiring connectors from the switches.

25 Refitting is the reverse of removal.

Electric mirror switch

26 Remove the door inner trim panel as described in Chapter 12, Section 12.

27 Release the 2 clips and remove the switch from the panel.

28 Refitting is a reversal of removal.

Electric sunroof switch

29 Using a suitable flat-bladed screwdriver, carefully prise the switch panel out from the overhead console, taking care not to mark either.

30 Disconnect the wiring connector from the relevant switch, then depress the retaining clips and push the switch out from the panel.

31 On refitting, clip the switch back into the panel, reconnect the wiring connector, then clip the switch panel back into the overhead console.

Courtesy light switches

32 The function of the courtesy light switch is incorporated into the door lock assemblies. See Chapter 12, Section 13, for details.

Heater control, blower motor and air recirculation switches

33 Remove the heater control panel as described in Chapter 3, Section 9.

34 The switches are integral with the control panel.

35 Refitting is the reverse of removal, ensuring that all wiring connectors are reconnected to their original positions.

Heated seat switches

36 The front seat switches are integral with the heater control panel as described in Chapter 3, Section 9.

37 To remove the rear seat switches, remove the centre console upper panel as described in Chapter 12, Section 27.

4.19 Pull up the ride and handling optimisation switch/panel assembly

4.23 Prise up the window switch panel, starting at the front edge

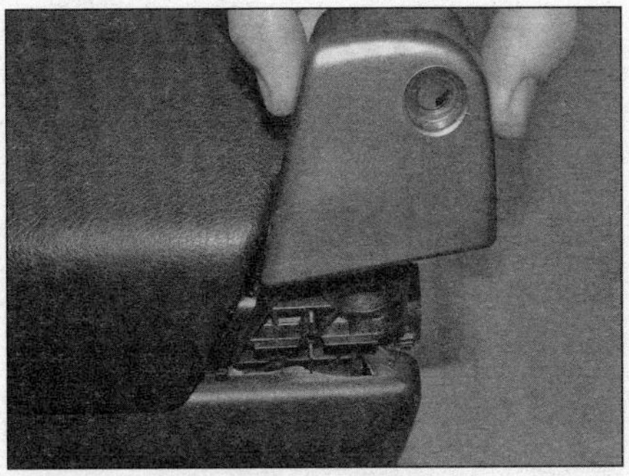

4.38 Undo the screw and pull up the hinge cover each side

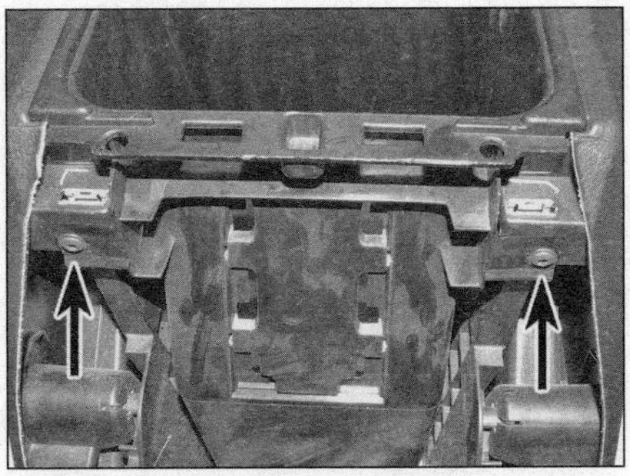

4.39a Remove the screws (arrowed) ...

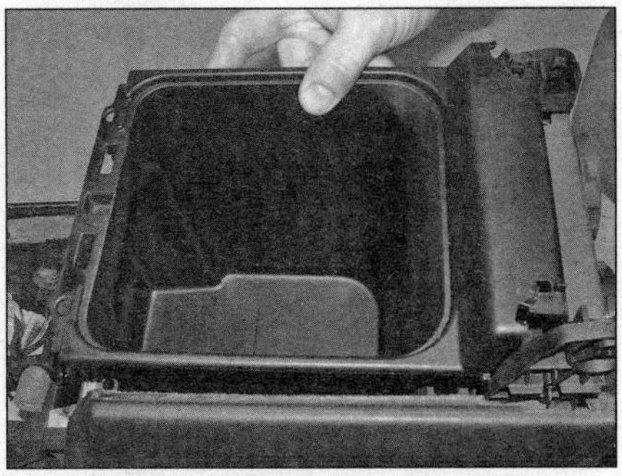

4.39b ... and pull up the insert

4.40a Undo the screw (arrowed) ...

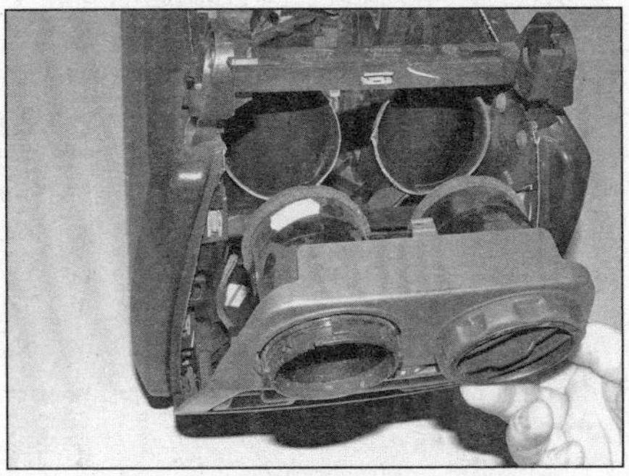

4.40b ... and unclip the rear panel

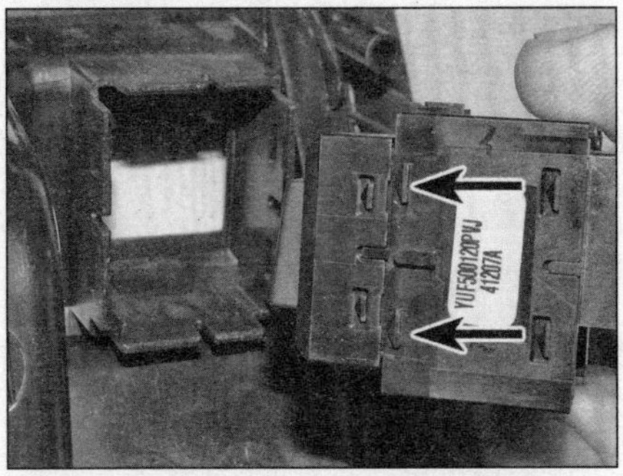

4.41 Release the clips (arrowed) each side and remove the switch

38 Undo the screw each side, slide up the hinge covers, and pull up the storage box lid **(see illustration)**.

39 Remove the 2 screws at the front and carefully pull up the plastic insert from the storage box **(see illustrations)**.

40 Undo the retaining screw and remove the rear panel from the console **(see illustrations)**. Disconnect the wiring plugs as the panel is withdrawn.

41 Depress the retaining clips and push the switch out of position **(see illustration)**.

42 Refitting is the reverse of removal.

Glovebox illumination switch

43 Open the glovebox, press the retaining struts downwards a little, and lower the glovebox lid to the 'service' position.

44 Prise out the white plastic locking element, then carefully squeeze together the ends of the clips securing the switch to the facia **(see illustrations)**. Manoeuvre the switch from place and disconnect the wiring plug.

45 Reconnect the wiring plug and refit the switch to the facia. Once the clips are engaged, press the locking element inwards to secure the switch.

Electric seat switches

46 Set the seat to its highest position, then remove it as described in Chapter 12, Section 23.

47 Trace the wiring harness back, release it from the retaining clips, disconnect the wiring plug, then undo the 2 screws, prise off the retaining clips and detach the switch from the panel.

48 Refitting is a reversal of removal.

Oil pressure warning light switch

49 Refer to Chapter 2, Section 16.

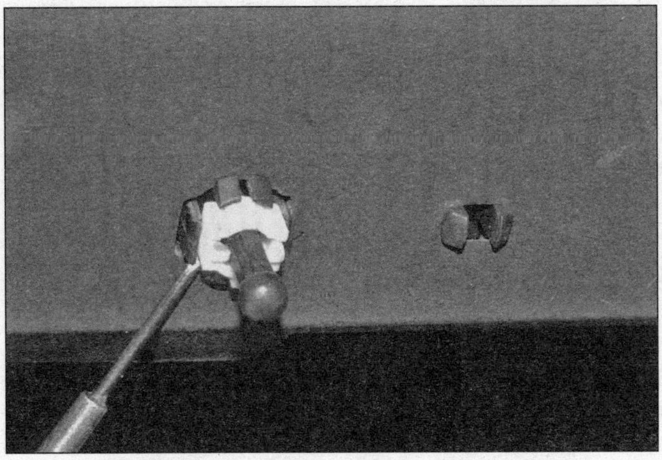

4.44a Prise out the white locking element a little ...

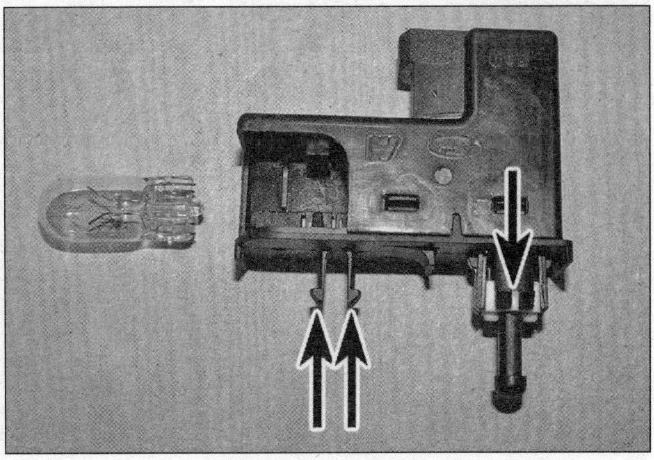

4.44b ... and squeeze together the clips (arrowed)

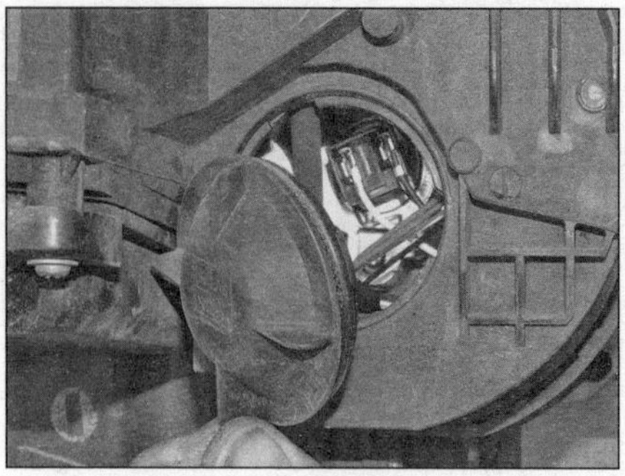

5.3 Rotate the cap anti-clockwise to remove it

5 Bulbs (exterior lights) – renewal

General

1 Whenever a bulb is renewed, note the following points:

a) Disconnect the battery negative lead before starting work. Refer to the precautions in Section 1 before proceeding.

b) Remember that if the light has just been in use, the bulb may be extremely hot.

c) Always check the bulb contacts and holder, ensuring that there is clean metal-to-metal contact between the bulb and its live(s) and earth. Clean off any corrosion or dirt before fitting a new bulb.

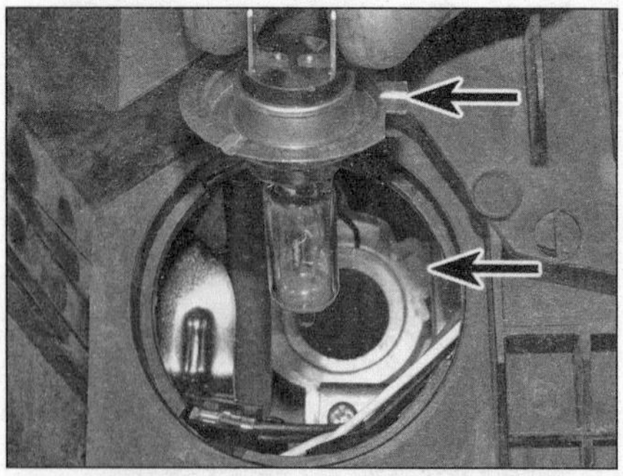

5.5 The locating tab must align with the cut-out (arrowed)

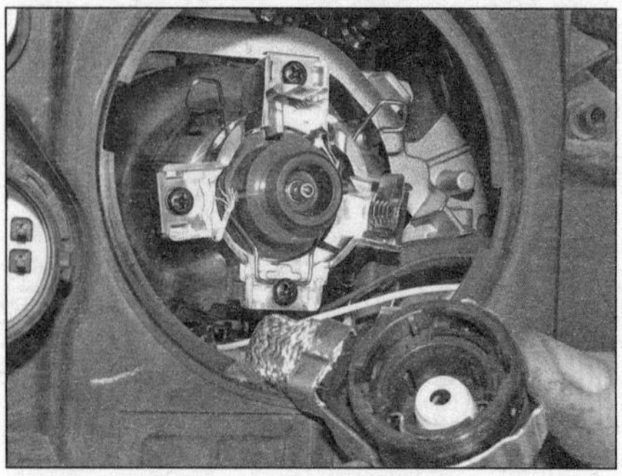

5.14 Rotate the wiring plug anti-clockwise and disconnect it

5.4a Pull the wiring plug from the bulb ...

d) Wherever bayonet-type bulbs are fitted ensure that the live contact(s) bear firmly against the bulb contact.

e) Always ensure that the new bulb is of the correct rating, and that it is completely clean before fitting it; this applies particularly to headlight bulbs (see below).

Halogen headlights

Main or dipped beam

2 Remove the headlight unit as described in Section 7.

3 Rotate the cap anti-clockwise and remove it **(see illustration)**.

4 Disconnect the wiring plug from the rear of the bulb, then release the lower edge of the retaining clip **(see illustrations)**.

5 Withdraw the bulb **(see illustration)**.

6 When handling the new bulb, use a tissue or clean cloth to avoid touching the glass with the fingers; moisture and grease from the skin can cause blackening and rapid failure of this type of bulb.

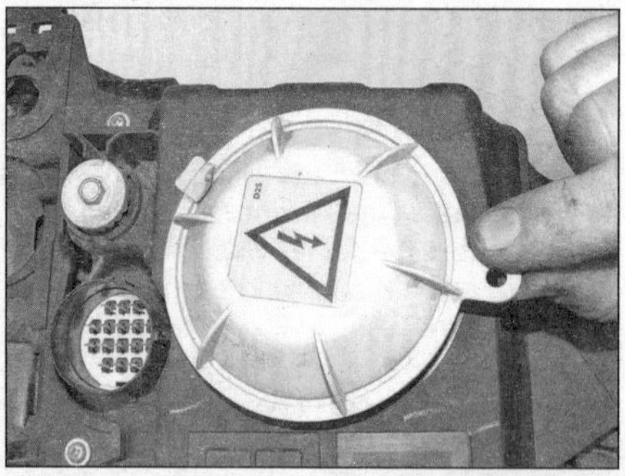

5.13 Rotate the cap anti-clockwise to remove it

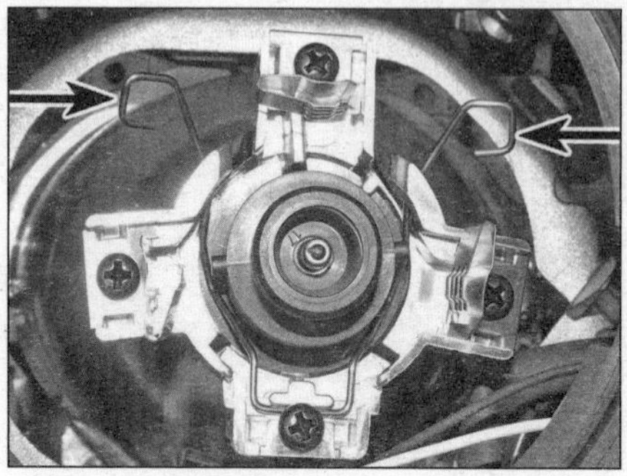

5.15a Squeeze together the ends of the clip (arrowed) and pivot it away from the bulb

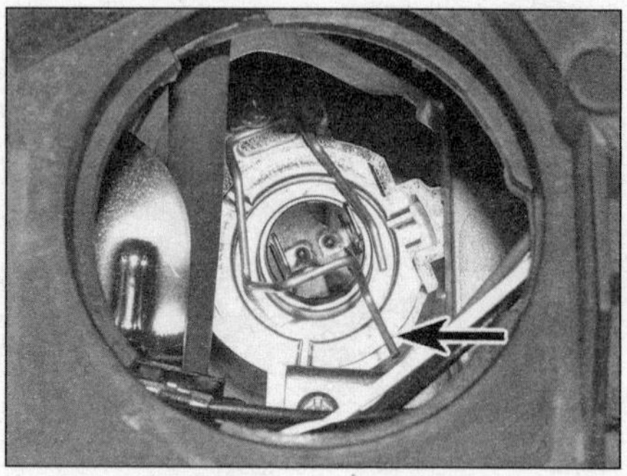

5.4b ... then release the lower edge of the retaining clip (arrowed)

7 Install the new bulb, ensuring that its locating tabs are correctly located in the light cut-outs, and secure it in position with the retaining clip.

8 Reconnect the wiring connector, and refit the cap.

9 Refit the headlight as described in Section 7.

Bi-xenon headlights

10 Although these headlights are equipped with bi-xenon bulbs which provide main and dipped beams, they are also fitted with a fixed halogen main beam bulb.

11 Remove the headlight unit as described in Section 7.

Main beam (halogen)

12 Renew the bulb as described for halogen headlights previously described in this Section.

Dipped/main beam (xenon)

13 Rotate the cap anti-clockwise and remove it **(see illustration)**.

14 Rotate the wiring plug on the rear of the bulb anti-clockwise and disconnect it **(see illustration)**.

15 Release the retaining clips and pull the bulb from the reflector **(see illustrations)**.

16 When handling the new bulb, use a tissue or clean cloth to avoid touching the glass with the fingers; moisture and grease from the skin can cause blackening and rapid failure of this type of bulb.

5.15b Pull the xenon bulb from the reflector

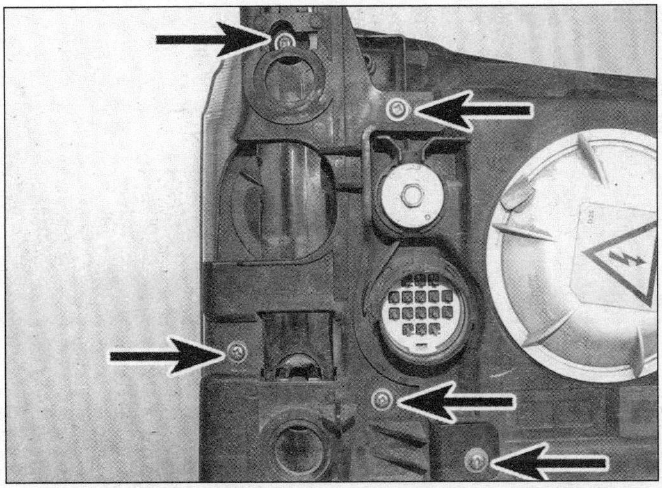

5.21 Undo the screws (arrowed) and remove the retaining frame

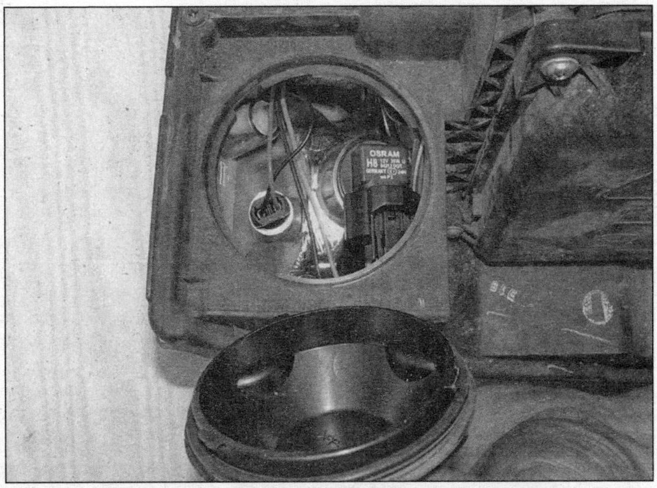

5.22 Rotate the cap anti-clockwise to remove it

17 Install the new bulb, ensuring that its locating tabs are correctly located in the light cut-outs, and secure it in position with the retaining clips.

18 Reconnect the wiring connector, and refit the cap.

19 Refit the headlight as described in Section 7.

Sidelight

20 Remove the headlight unit as described in Section 7.

21 Undo the 5 screws and remove the retaining frame assembly from the rear of the headlight **(see illustration)**.

22 Rotate the cap anti-clockwise and remove it **(see illustration)**.

23 Pull the bulbholder from the reflector, then pull the capless bulb from the holder **(see illustration)**.

24 Refitting is the reverse of the removal procedure.

Cornering/static bending bulb

25 Remove the headlight unit as described in Section 7.

26 Undo the 5 screws and remove the retaining frame assembly from the rear of the headlight **(see illustration 5.21)**.

27 Rotate the cap anti-clockwise and remove it **(see illustration 5.22)**.

28 Rotate the bulbholder clockwise (left-hand headlight) or anti-clockwise (right-hand headlight), and pull it from the reflector **(see illustration)**.

29 Squeeze together the clips and disconnect the wiring plug.

30 Refitting is the reverse of the removal procedure.

Front indicator

31 Remove the headlight unit as described in Section 7.

32 Undo the 5 screws and remove the retaining frame assembly from the rear of the headlight **(see illustration 5.21)**.

33 Rotate the cap anti-clockwise and remove it **(see illustration)**.

34 Rotate the bulbholder anti-clockwise and pull the capless bulb from the holder **(see illustration)**.

35 Refitting is the reverse of removal.

Front indicator side repeater

36 Carefully push the light unit to the front, and pull the rear edge from the wing **(see illustration)**.

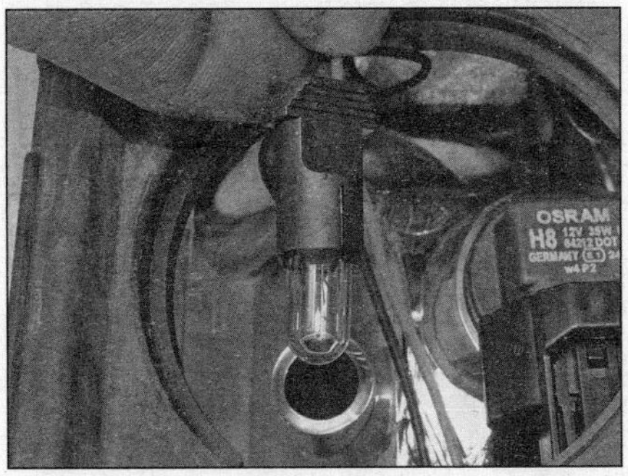

5.23 Pull the sidelight bulbholder from the reflector

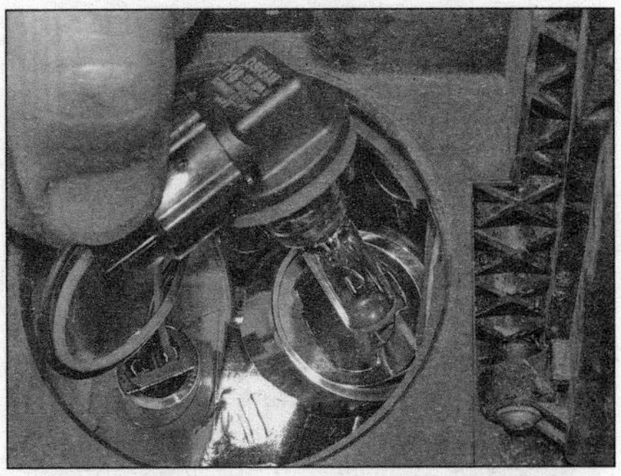

5.28 Rotate the cornering/static bulb clockwise (left-hand headlight) or anti-clockwise (right-hand headlight)

5.33 Rotate the cap anti-clockwise to remove it

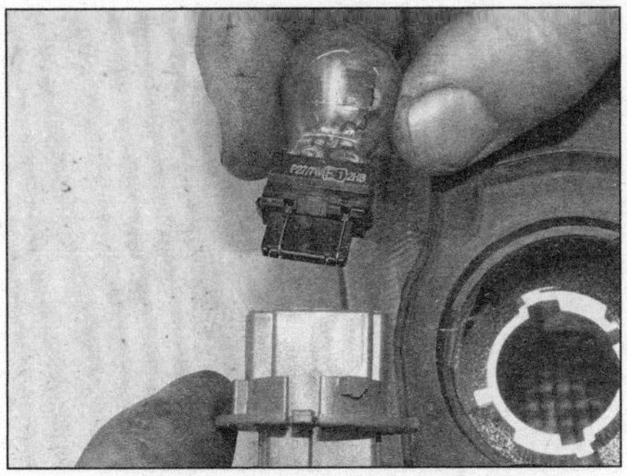

5.34 Pull the capless indicator bulb from the holder

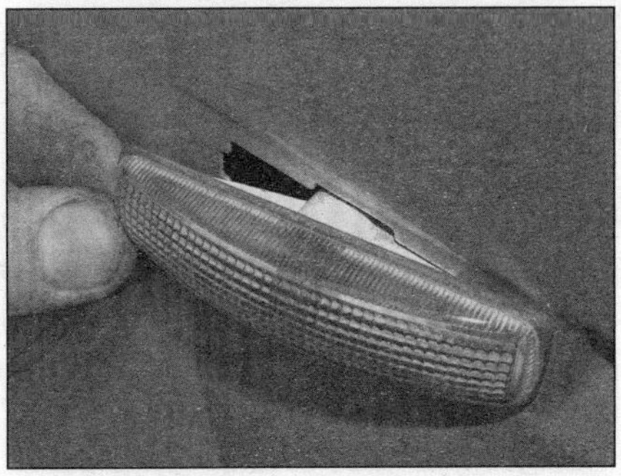

5.36 Push the side repeater forwards, and pull out the rear edge

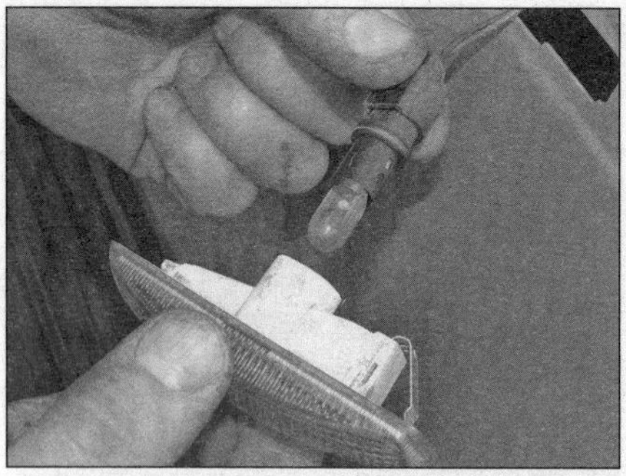
5.37 Rotate the lens anti-clockwise and pull out the bulbholder

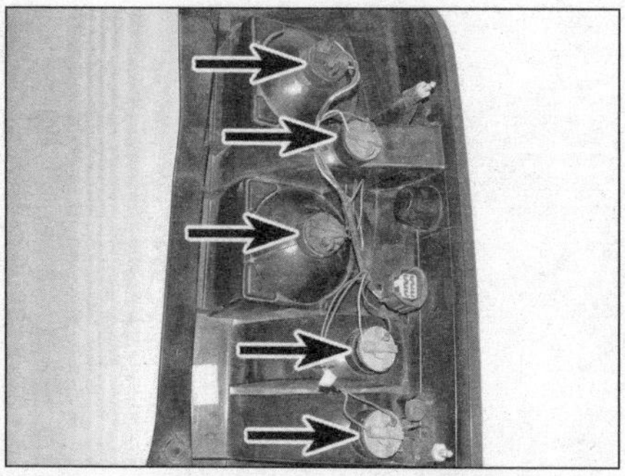
5.41 Twist the relevant bulbholder anti-clockwise (arrowed)

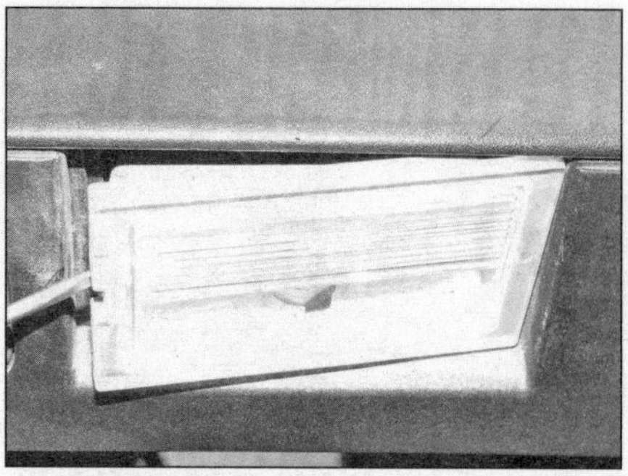
5.44 Carefully prise the number plate light from the liftgate

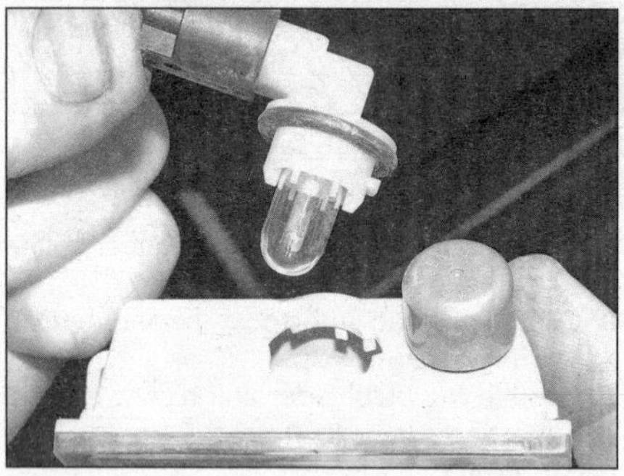
5.45 Rotate the bulbholder anti-clockwise to remove it

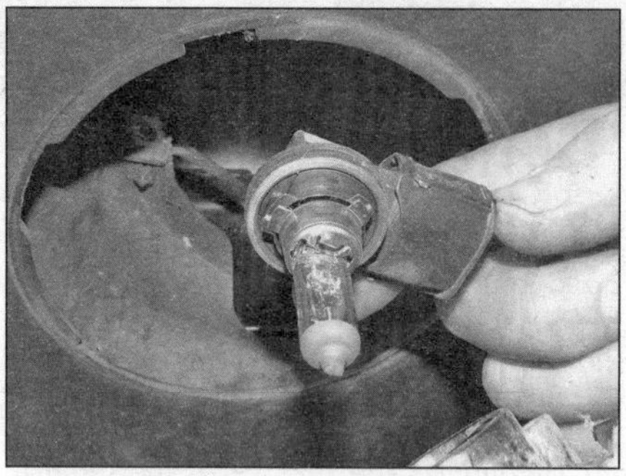
5.48 Rotate the front foglight bulbholder anti-clockwise

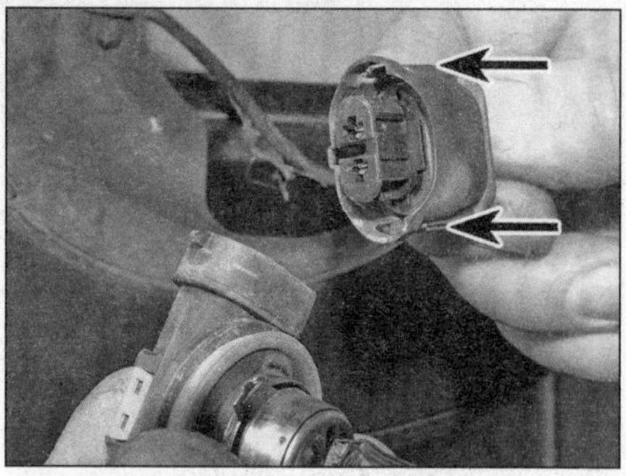
5.49 Squeeze together the clips (arrowed) and disconnect the wiring plug

37 Turn the lens unit anti-clockwise to release it, then remove it from the bulbholder **(see illustration)**.

38 The bulb is of the capless (push-fit) type, and can be removed by simply pulling it out of the bulbholder.

39 Refitting is a reverse of the removal procedure.

Rear light cluster

40 Remove the light cluster as described in Section 7.

41 Twist the relevant bulbholder anti-clockwise and remove it from the rear of the light unit **(see illustration)**. The bulbs are a bayonet fit in the holder, and can be removed by pressing them in and twisting in an anti-clockwise direction.

42 Refitting is a reverse of the removal procedure.

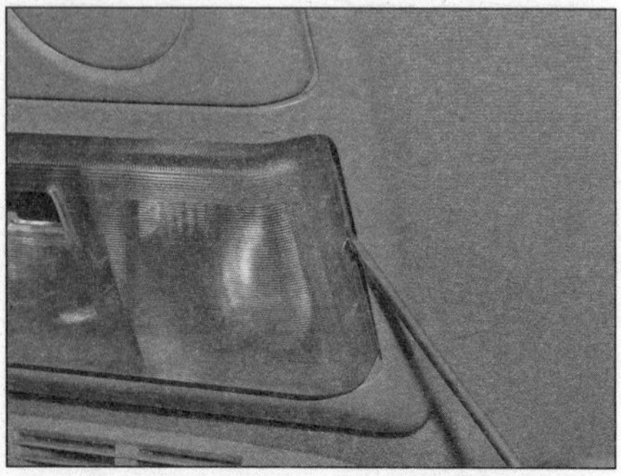
6.2a Carefully prise the lens from place ...

High-level brake light

43 The high-level brake light is illuminated by LEDs. The light unit panel is bonded into place on the liftgate. Removal of the light unit requires special tools. Entrust this task to a Land Rover dealer or suitably-equipped repairer.

Number plate light

44 Open the liftgate, and use a screwdriver to carefully prise the light unit from place **(see illustration)**.

45 Rotate the bulbholder anti-clockwise, and pull the capless bulb from place **(see illustration)**.

46 Refitting is a reversal of removal.

Front foglight

47 Remove the front foglight as described in Section 7.

6.2b ... and pull out the bulb

48 Rotate the bulb anti-clockwise, pull it from the reflector **(see illustration)**. The bulb is integral with the holder

49 Squeeze together the clips and disconnect the wiring plug **(see illustration)**.

50 Refitting is the reverse of the removal procedure.

6 Bulbs (interior lights) - renewal

General

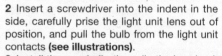

1 Refer to Section 5, paragraph 1.

Courtesy lights

2 Insert a screwdriver into the indent in the side, carefully prise the light unit lens out of position, and pull the bulb from the light unit contacts **(see illustrations)**.

3 Install the new bulb, then clip the lens back into position.

Instrument panel illumination/warning lights

4 The instrument cluster and warning lights are illuminated by a combination of LEDs (light emitting diodes) and LCD (liquid crystal display). The instrument cluster contains no user-serviceable parts. If defective, the complete cluster must be renewed – see Section 9.

Glovebox illumination light bulb

5 Open the glovebox, then press down the

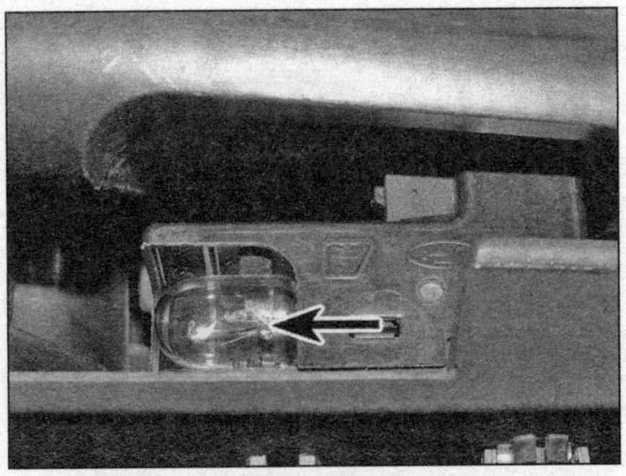
6.6 Slide the bulb (arrowed) from the switch unit

6.14 ... and pull the capless bulb (arrowed) from the contacts

supports a little and open the glovebox to the service position.

6 Using a small flat-bladed screwdriver, carefully prise the bulb from the switch unit **(see illustration)**.

7 Install the new bulb, and close the glovebox.

Heater control panel

8 The heater control panel is illuminated by LEDs. If defective the complete control panel must be renewed – see Chapter 3, Section 9.

Switch illumination bulbs

9 The switches are illuminated by non-renewable light emitting diodes (LED). If the illumination fails, the switch must be renewed.

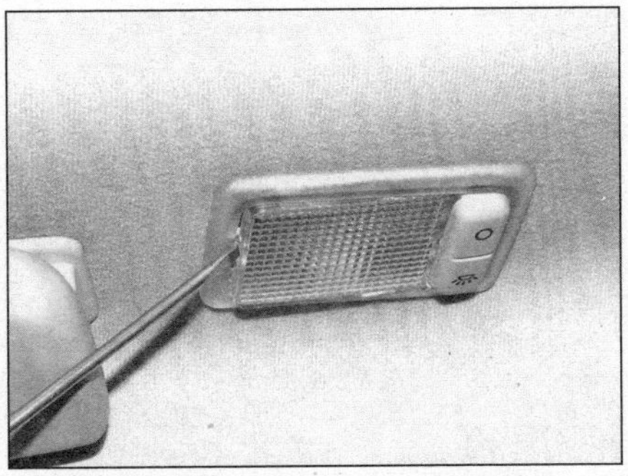
6.10 Prise out the edge of the lens

Puddle/footwell/ luggage compartment lights

10 Using a flat-bladed screwdriver, carefully prise the edge of the lens out, and remove the lamp from place **(see illustration)**.

11 Pull the capless bulb from the holder.

12 Refitting is the reverse of removal.

Vanity mirror light

13 Use a small flat-bladed screwdriver to prise the lens from place **(see illustration)**.

14 Pull the capless bulb from the contacts **(see illustration)**.

15 Refitting is a reversal of removal.

7 Exterior light units – removal and refitting

Note: *Refer to the precautions in Section 1 before proceeding.*

Headlight

1 Open the bonnet.

2 Release the 4 clips at the top edge of the grille **(see illustration)**.

3 Release the clip each side, and remove the radiator grille **(see illustrations)**.

4 Pull up the locking slides, manoeuvre the headlight forwards, depress the clip and disconnect the wiring plug **(see illustrations)**.

5 Refitting is a direct reversal of the removal procedure. On completion, check the headlight beam alignment using the information given in Section 8. Where necessary, check the operation of the headlight levelling system.

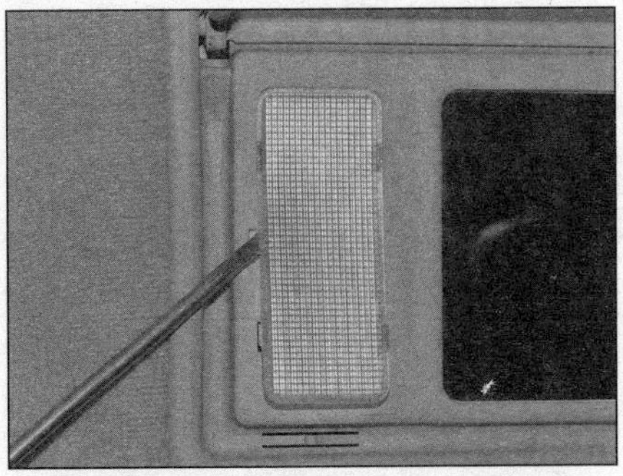
6.13 Prise out the vanity mirror light lens ...

Front indicator side repeater light

6 Carefully push the light unit to the front, and pull the rear edge from the wing **(see illustration 5.36)**.

7 Turn the lens unit anti-clockwise to release it, then remove it from the bulbholder.

8 Refitting is a reverse of the removal procedure.

Rear light cluster

9 Open the liftgate and fold down the tailgate.

10 Undo the 2 retaining screws and pull the

7.2 Press down to release the clips at the top of the radiator grille (arrowed) ...

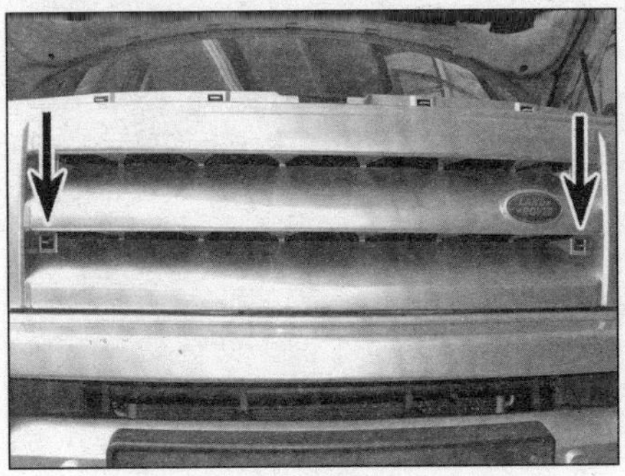
7.3 ... and each side (arrowed)

7.4a Pull up the locking slide each side (arrowed)

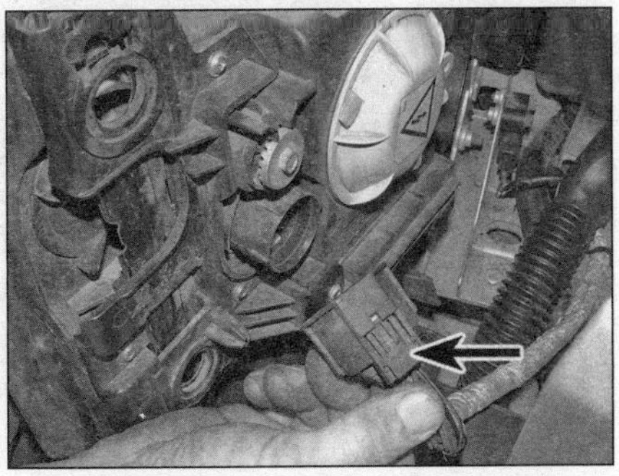
7.4b Depress the clip (arrowed) and disconnect the wiring plug

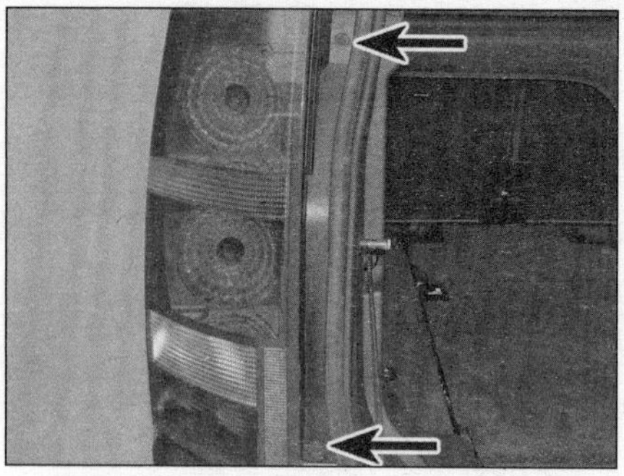

7.10a Undo the screws (arrowed) ...

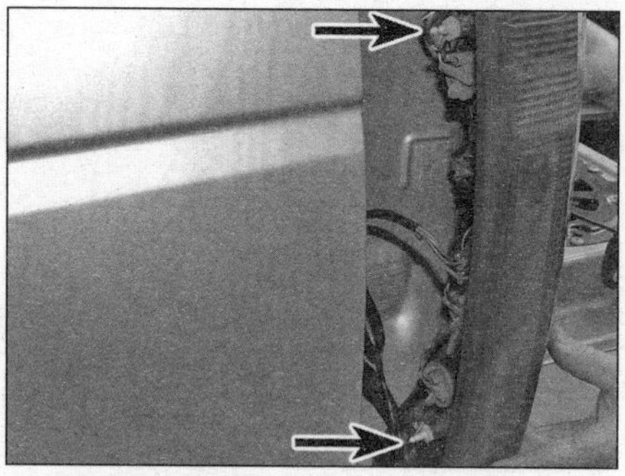

7.10b ... then pull the light unit rearwards to release the pins (arrowed)

7.15 Prise the foglight trim from the bumper

light unit rearwards from the vehicle body **(see illustrations)**.

11 Disconnect the wiring connector as the unit is removed.

12 Refitting is the reverse of removal.

High-level brake light

13 The light unit panel is bonded into place on the liftgate. Removal of the light unit requires special tools. Entrust this task to a Land Rover dealer or suitably-equipped repairer.

Number plate light

14 Refer to the bulb renewal procedure in Section 5.

Front foglight

15 Using a blunt, flat-bladed tool, carefully prise the foglight surround trim from the bumper **(see illustration)**.

16 Undo the 3 retaining screws and pull the foglight from the bumper **(see illustration)**. Disconnect the wiring plug as the light is withdrawn.

17 Refitting is a reversal of removal. The aim of light can be adjusted by means of the screw adjacent to the lens **(see illustration)**.

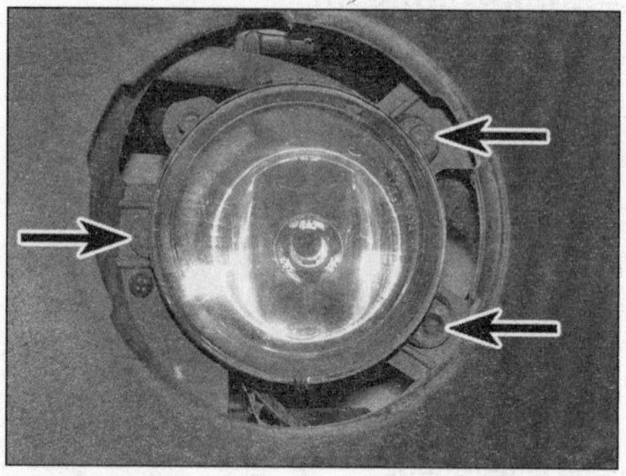

7.16 Foglight retaining screws (arrowed)

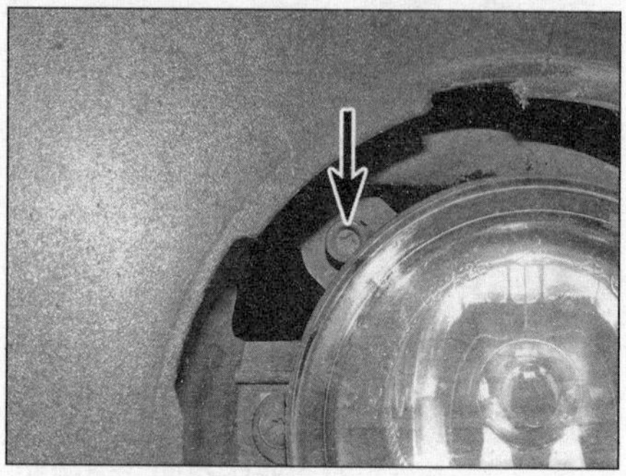

7.17 Foglight adjusting screw (arrowed)

8 Headlight beam alignment – general information

Accurate adjustment of the headlight beam is only possible using optical beam-setting equipment, and this work should therefore be carried out by a Land Rover dealer or suitably-equipped workshop.

For reference, the headlights can be adjusted using the adjuster assemblies fitted to the rear of each light unit **(see illustration)**.

9 Instrument cluster – removal and refitting

Removal

1 Remove the steering column switch assembly as described in Section 4.

2 Pull the panel beneath the steering column rearwards to release the clips **(see illustration)**.

3 Prise rearwards the trim panel

8.2 Headlight aim adjusting screws (arrowed)

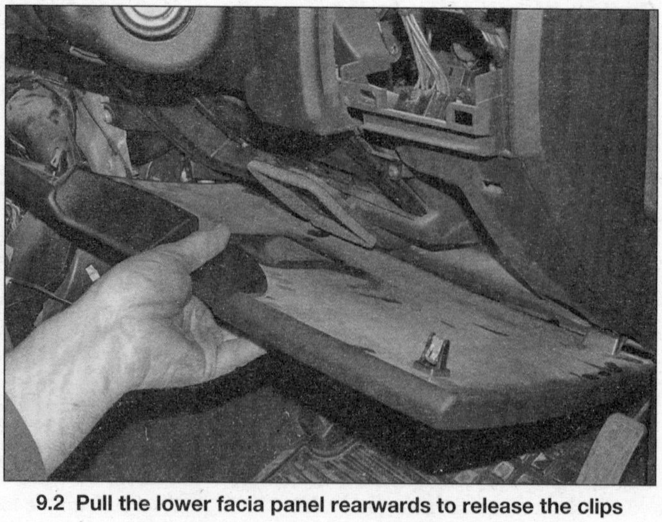

9.2 Pull the lower facia panel rearwards to release the clips

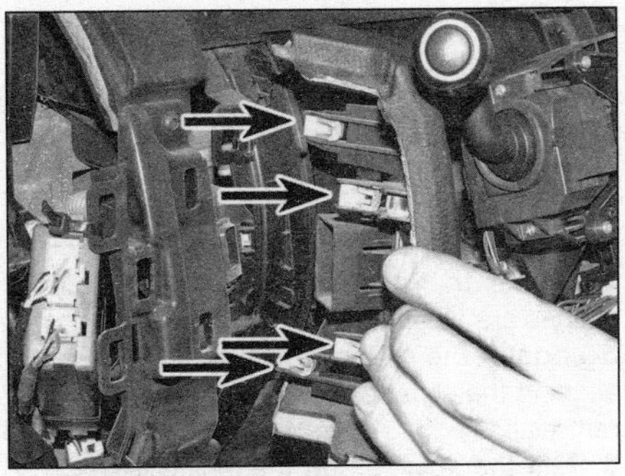
9.3 Pull the panel each side rearwards to release the clips (arrowed)

9.4a Undo the screws (arrowed) ...

9.4b ... and pull the column gaiter panel rearwards

each side of the steering column **(see illustration)**.

4 Undo the 2 screws and pull the steering column gaiter panel rearwards **(see illustrations)**.

5 Undo the 2 retaining screws at the lower edge and remove the instrument cluster. Disconnect the wiring plug as the unit is withdrawn **(see illustrations)**.

6 If required, the lens can be detached by release the clips around its edge.

Refitting

7 Refitting is a reversal of removal. Note that if a new instrument cluster has been fitted, make a note of the serial number and build date information on the reverse of the unit. The new unit must be configured using Land Rover diagnostic equipment (T4), with the information from the new unit.

10 Tyre pressure monitoring system – general information and component renewal

General information

1 The tyre pressure monitoring system comprises the following components:

a) Control module.
b) Initiators.
c) Pressure sensors.
d) Warning display in the instrument cluster.

2 Every time the vehicle is driven, the initiators transmit a signal to each pressure sensor, which then sends data to the control module, concerning the tyre pressure, sensor identification, and tyre temperature. If the control module determines that the pressure in any tyre has decreased by 25%, an amber warning symbol is displayed in the instrument cluster, whilst if the pressure drops by more than 35% a warning message is displayed.

Component renewal

Control module

3 The control module is located above the headlining.

4 The headlining is clipped to the roof, and can only be withdrawn once all fittings such as the grab handles, sunvisors, windscreen and rear quarter windows, and related trim panels have been removed, and the door, tailgate and sunroof aperture sealing strips have been prised clear.

5 Note that headlining removal requires considerable skill and experience if it is to be carried out without damage, and is therefore best entrusted to an expert.

Pressure sensors

6 The sensor is integral with the inflation valve fitted to each wheel. With the tyre removed, undo the collar and remove the sensor. Note that the valve seal and washer must be renewed.

7 Fit the sensor to the wheel and tighten the retaining collar to the specified torque. Note that if a new sensor is fitted to a 'running' wheel, the module will automatically identify the sensor. However, if a new sensor is fitted to the spare wheel, it must be calibrated using Land Rover diagnostic equipment (T4). Entrust this task to a Land Rover dealer or suitably-equipped repairer.

Initiators

8 The initiators are located behind the wheel arch liners. Release the fasteners and remove the relevant wheel arch liner.

9 Undo the 2 retaining screws and remove the initiator.

10 Refitting is a reversal of removal. Note that if a new initiator is fitted, it must be calibrated using Land Rover diagnostic equipment (T4). Entrust this task to a Land Rover dealer or suitably-equipped repairer.

9.5a Instrument cluster retaining screws (arrowed)

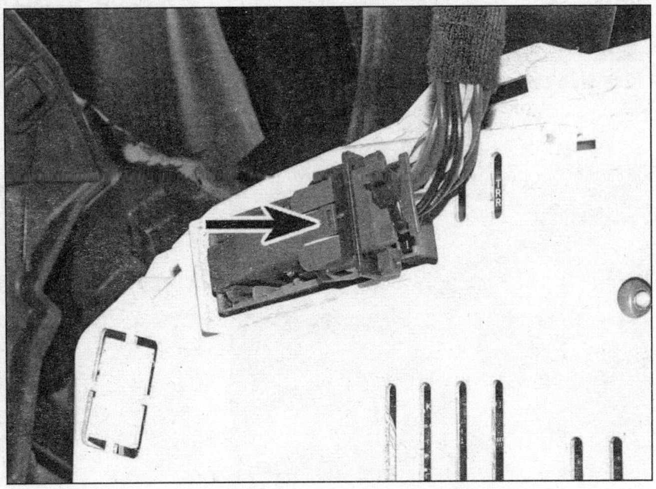
9.5b Depress the clip (arrowed), lever over the catch, and disconnect the wiring plug

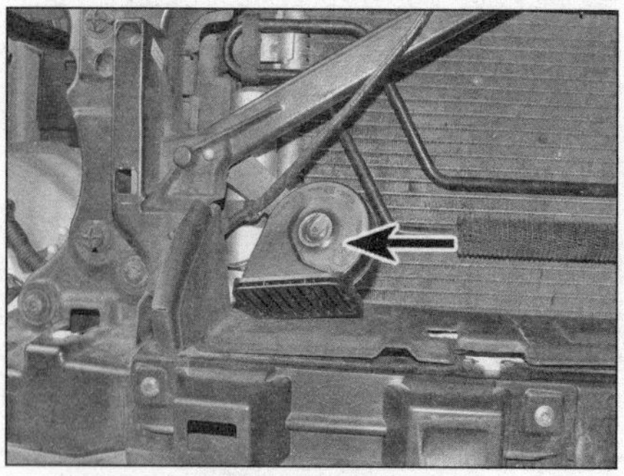

11.2a Horns may be fitted behind the radiator grille (arrowed) ...

11.2b ... or adjacent to the left-hand headlight (arrowed)

11 Horns – removal and refitting

Removal

1 Two horns may be fitted. One behind the radiator grille, and one adjacent to the left-hand headlight. Remove the radiator grille as described in Chapter 12, Section 29, or the headlight as described in Section 7 of this Chapter.

2 Disconnect the wiring connector from the relevant horn **(see illustrations)**.

3 Slacken and remove the retaining nut and washer, then remove the horn from the vehicle.

Refitting

4 Refitting is the reverse of removal.

12 Wiper arm – removal and refitting

Removal

1 Operate the wiper motor, then switch it off so that the wiper arm returns to the at rest (parked) position.

2 Stick a piece of masking tape to the windscreen along the edge of the wiper blade, to use as an alignment aid on refitting **(see illustration)**.

3 Lift up/remove (as applicable) the wiper arm spindle nut cover, then slacken and remove the spindle nut. Lift the blade off the glass, and pull the wiper arm off its spindle. If necessary, the arm can be removed using a puller **(see illustrations)**.

Refitting

4 Ensure that the wiper arm and spindle splines are clean and dry.

5 Locate the wiper arm on the spindle, aligning the wiper blade with the tape fitted on removal.

6 Refit the spindle nut, tightening it securely, and clip the nut cover back in position.

13 Windscreen wiper motor and linkage – removal and refitting

Removal

1 Open the bonnet, and pull the windscreen pillar trims each side forwards to release the clips **(see illustration)**. Discard the clips – new ones must be fitted.

2 Remove both windscreen wiper arms as described in Section 12.

3 Pull up the rubber sealing strip from the rear of the engine compartment **(see illustration)**.

4 Pull up the plenum chamber cover from the base of the windscreen to release the 8 retaining clips **(see illustration)**.

5 Undo the 2 retaining bolts, disconnect the

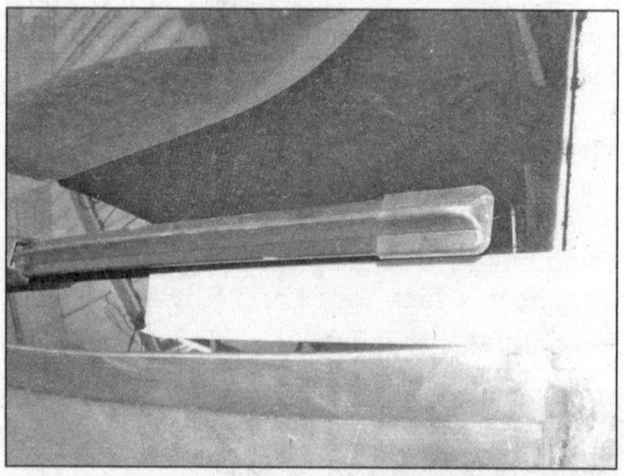

12.2 Use tape to mark the parked position of the wiper blades

12.3a Prise up the cap and undo the spindle nut

12.3b Using a puller to release a wiper arm

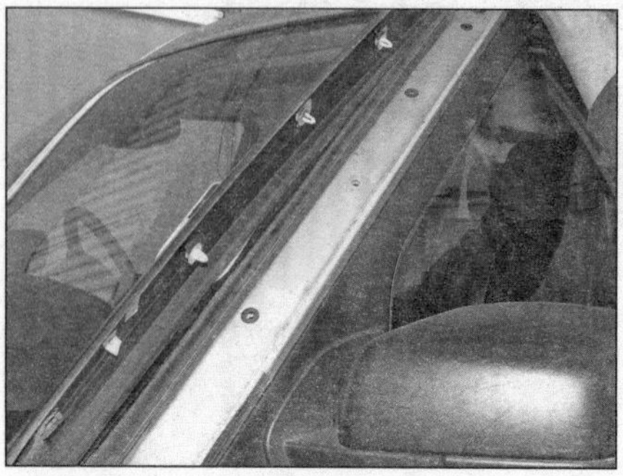

13.1 Pull the windscreen pillar trim forwards each side to release the clips

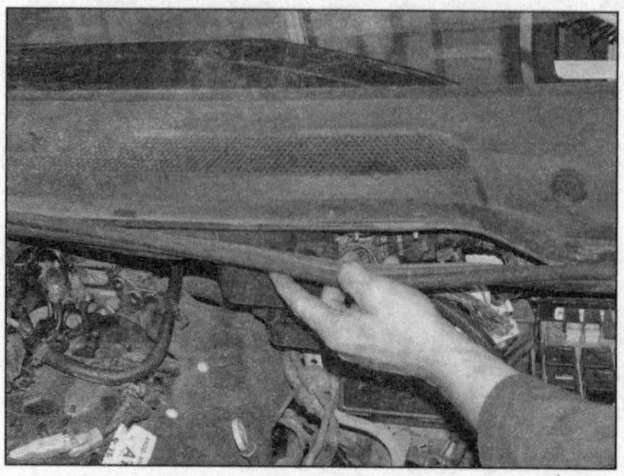

13.3 Remove the rubber sealing strip

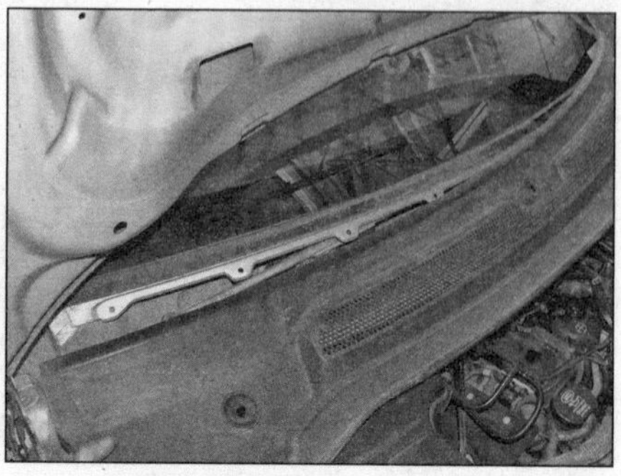

13.4 Pull up the plenum chamber cover

wiring plug and remove the wiper motor and linkage **(see illustration)**.

6 If necessary, mark the relative positions of the motor shaft and linkage arm, then unscrew the retaining nut from the motor spindle. Free the wiper linkage from the spindle, then remove the motor retaining bolts and separate the motor and linkage.

Refitting

7 Where necessary, assemble the motor and linkage, and securely tighten the motor retaining bolts. Locate the linkage arm on the motor spindle, aligning the marks made prior to removal, and securely tighten its retaining nut.

8 The remainder of refitting is a reversal of removal.

14 Liftgate wiper motor – removal and refitting

1 Remove the liftgate trim panel as described in Chapter 12, Section 16.

2 Remove the wiper arm as described in Section 12.

3 Undo the 3 retaining nuts, disconnect the wiring plug and remove the motor **(see illustration)**.

4 Refitting is a reversal of removal.

15 Windscreen/liftgate washer system components – removal and refitting

Washer system reservoir

1 Remove the front grille and bumper.

2 Unclip the reservoir filler neck from the coolant expansion tank, and detach it from the reservoir **(see illustration)**. Renew the seal if necessary.

3 Note their fitted positions, then disconnect the wiring plugs and hoses from the reservoir pumps **(see illustration)**.

4 The reservoir is retained by 4 bolts. Undo the bolts and remove the reservoir **(see illustration)**.

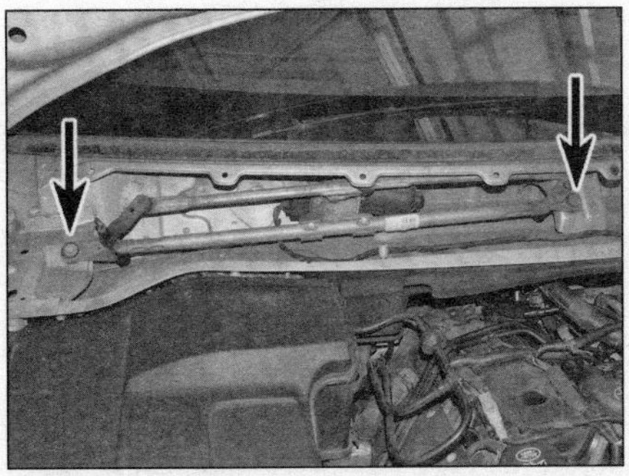

13.5 Windscreen linkage/motor assembly retaining bolts (arrowed)

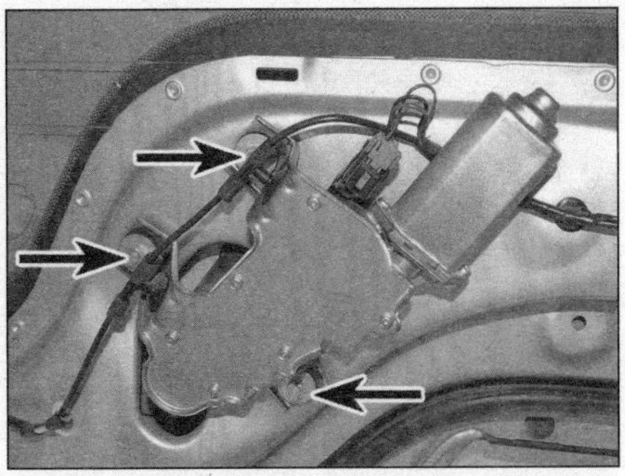

14.3 Liftgate wiper motor retaining nuts (arrowed)

5 If required, prise the pump from the reservoir.

6 Refitting is a reversal of removal.

Washer pumps

7 Remove the front grille and bumper.

8 Note their fitted positions, and disconnect the hoses and wiring plugs from the pumps **(see illustration 15.3)**.

9 Prise the pump from the reservoir. Renew the seal if necessary.

10 Refitting is the reverse of removal.

Windscreen washer jets

11 Unclip the bonnet soundproofing panel.

12 Carefully pull the hose from the base of the jet, and disconnect the wiring plug **(see illustration)**.

13 Pull the jet towards the front of the vehicle, and manoeuvre the jet up from the bonnet **(see illustration)**.

14 Refitting is a reversal of removal. If necessary, adjust the aim of the jet using a pin inserted into the nozzle.

16 Headlight washer system components – removal and refitting

Washer system reservoir

1 Refer to Section 15.

Washer pump

2 Refer to Section 15.

Headlight washer jets

3 Remove the front foglight as described in Section 7.

4 Slide out the clip on the base of the jet,

15.2 Unclip the filler neck from the coolant expansion tank

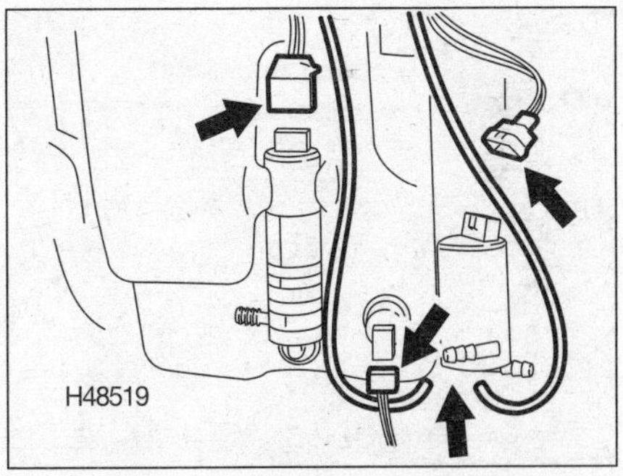

15.3 Disconnect the wiring plugs and hoses from the pump (arrowed)

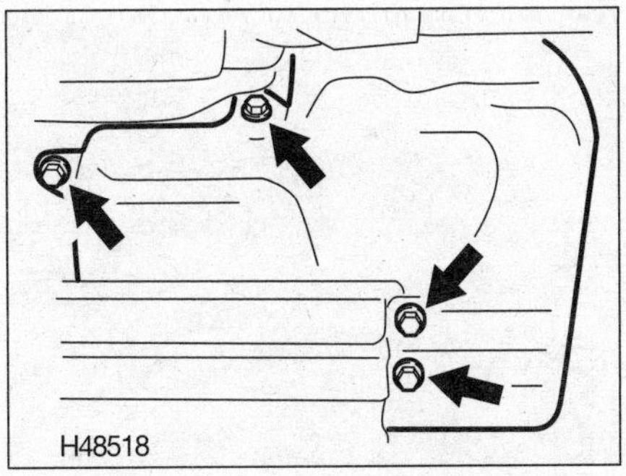

15.4 Reservoir retaining bolts (arrowed)

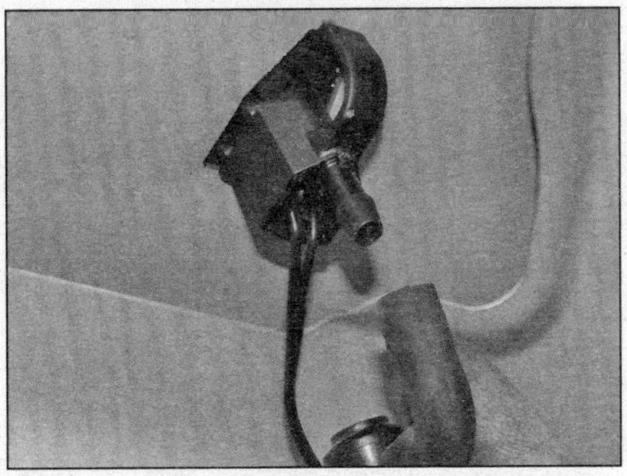

15.12 Disconnect the hose from the base of the jet

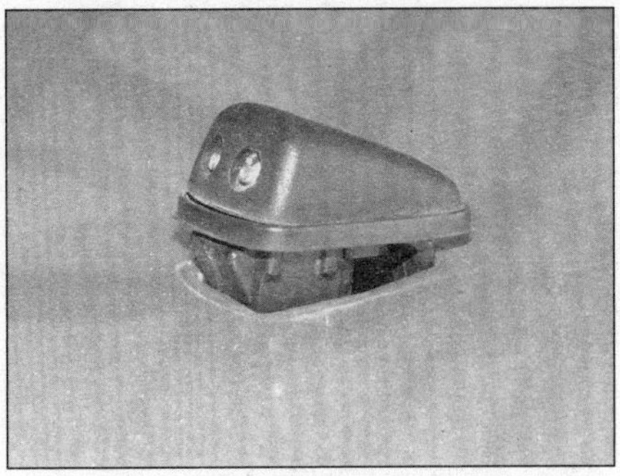

15.13 Pull the jet forwards to unhook the rear clip

16.4 Headlight washer jet retaining clip (arrowed)

and lift it from the bumper **(see illustration)**. Take great care not to damage the bonnet paintwork.

5 Disconnect the washer hose from the base of the jet.

6 On refitting, refit the washer, reconnect the washer hose, and check the operation of the jet. If necessary adjust the nozzle using a pin.

17 Infotainment systems – component removal and refitting

Note: *The following removal and refitting procedure is for the range of infotainment units which Land Rover fit as standard equipment. Removal and refitting procedures of non-standard units may differ slightly. Before removing the unit, refer to battery disconnection information in Chapter 5, Section 4.*

Audio unit

1 Carefully prise the facia centre panel rearwards to release the 4 clips **(see illustration 4.13)**.

2 Undo the 4 retaining screws and remove the heater control panel **(see illustration)**. Disconnect the wiring plug as the panel is withdrawn.

3 Undo the 4 retaining screws, and slide the unit from the facia. Disconnect the wiring plugs and the aerial lead from the rear of the unit as it's withdrawn **(see illustrations)**.

4 Refitting is a reversal of removal.

Audio amplifier

5 Remove the right-hand front seat as described in Chapter 12, Section 23.

6 Undo the 4 retaining screws and remove the amplifier **(see illustration)**. Disconnect the wiring plugs as the unit is withdrawn. **Note:** *Cover the fibre optic connectors to minimise dust/dirt ingress, and avoid bending the cables at the radius of less than 30 mm.*

7 Refitting is a reversal of removal. Note that if a new amplifier is fitted, it must be configured using Land Rover diagnostic equipment (T4). Entrust this task to a Land Rover dealer or suitably-equipped repairer.

DVD player

8 Remove the right-hand luggage compartment side trim panel as described in Chapter 12, Section 26.

9 Undo the 2 screws and release the rear quarter panel trim mounting bracket.

10 Prise out the clips and remove the panel mounting bracket.

11 Undo the 3 nuts and position the rear seat infotainment unit to one side (where fitted).

12 Undo the 4 Torx bolts and remove the DVD player. Disconnect the wiring plugs as the unit is withdrawn. **Note:** *Cover the fibre optic connectors to minimise dust/dirt ingress, and avoid bending the cables at the radius of less than 30 mm.*

13 Refitting is a reversal of removal.

DVD screen

14 Carefully prise the surround trim from the DVD screen.

15 Undo the 3 retaining screws around the screen, and manoeuvre it from position. Disconnect the wiring plug as the unit is withdrawn.

16 Refitting is a reversal of removal.

Navigation screen

17 Carefully prise the facia centre panel rearwards to release the 4 clips **(see illustration 4.13)**.

18 Undo the 4 screws and manoeuvre the screen from the facia **(see illustrations)**. Disconnect the wiring plugs as the unit is withdrawn. **Note:** *Cover the fibre optic connectors to minimise dust/dirt ingress, and avoid bending the cables at the radius of less than 30 mm.*

19 Refitting is a reversal of removal.

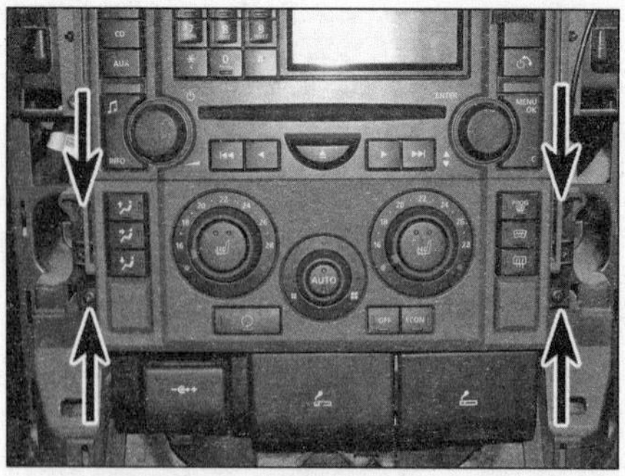

17.2 Undo the heater control panel screws (arrowed)

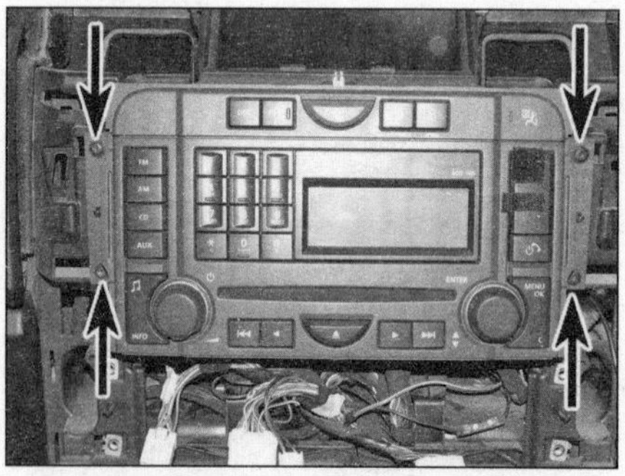

17.3a Undo the screws (arrowed) ...

17.3b ... and pull the audio unit rearwards

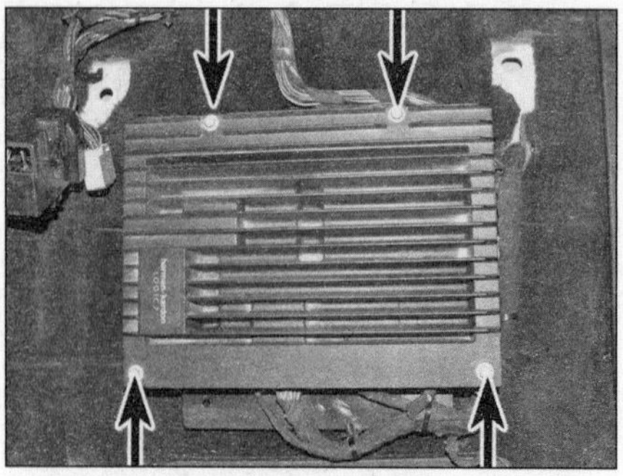

17.6 Audio amplifier retaining screws (arrowed)

17.18a Undo the retaining screws (arrowed) ...

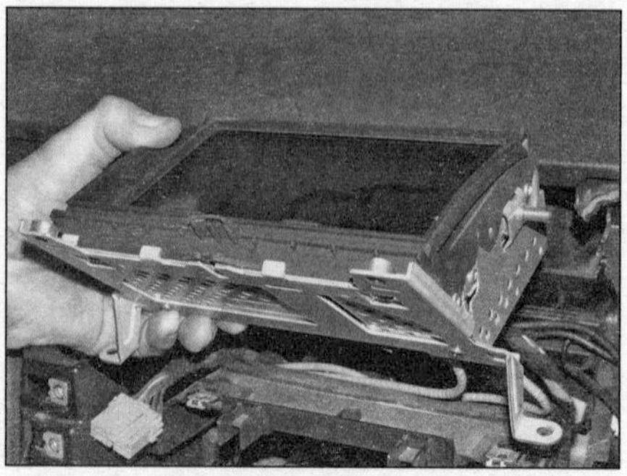

17.18b ... and manoeuvre the navigation screen from position

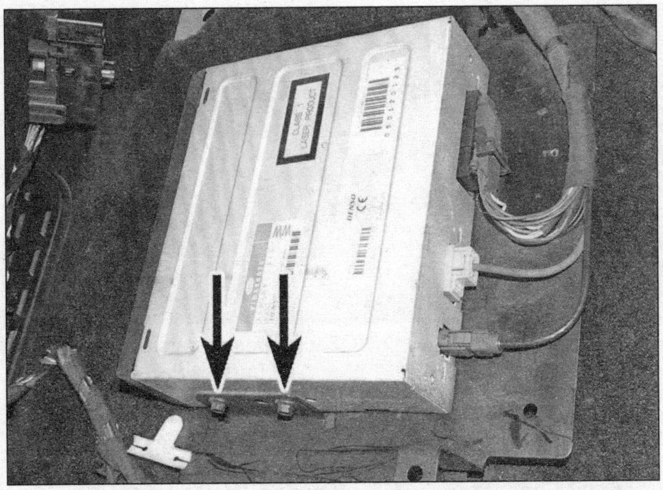

17.21 Disconnect the wiring plugs, undo the bolts each side (arrowed) and remove the CD unit

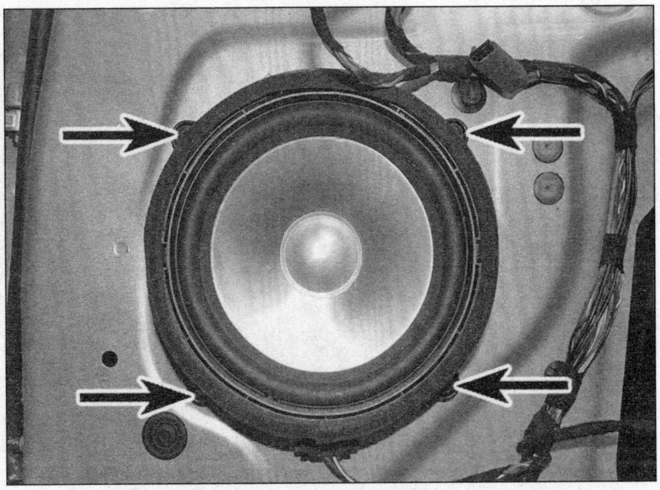

17.24 Lower speaker retaining screws (arrowed)

Navigation CD unit

20 Remove the front passenger's seat as described in Chapter 12, Section 23.

21 Undo the 4 bolts, disconnect the wiring plugs, and remove the CD unit **(see illustration)**.

22 Refitting is a reversal of removal.

Speakers removal

Lower door speaker

23 Remove the door inner trim panel as described in Chapter 12, Section 12.

24 Undo the screws securing the speaker to the door, and disconnect the wiring plug **(see illustration)**.

Upper door speaker

25 Remove the door inner trim panel as described in Chapter 12, Section 12.

26 Release the clips/screws, and detach the speaker from the door trim **(see illustrations)**.

Tailgate speaker

27 Remove the tailgate trim panel as described in Chapter 12, Section 16.

28 Undo the 10 Torx screws, and remove the speaker assembly **(see illustration)**. Disconnect the wiring plugs as the speaker is withdrawn.

29 Undo the 6 retaining screws, and detach the speaker **(see illustration)**.

D-pillar speaker

30 Remove the D-pillar trim panel as described in Chapter 12, Section 26.

31 Undo the 3 screws, and detach the speaker from the trim panel **(see illustration)**.

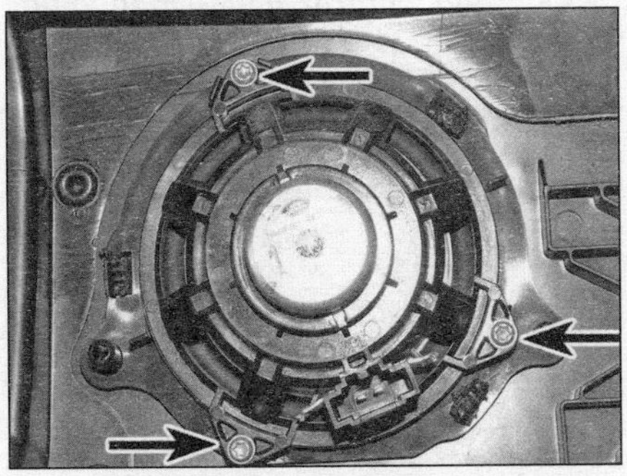

17.26a Front door mid-range speaker retaining screws (arrowed)

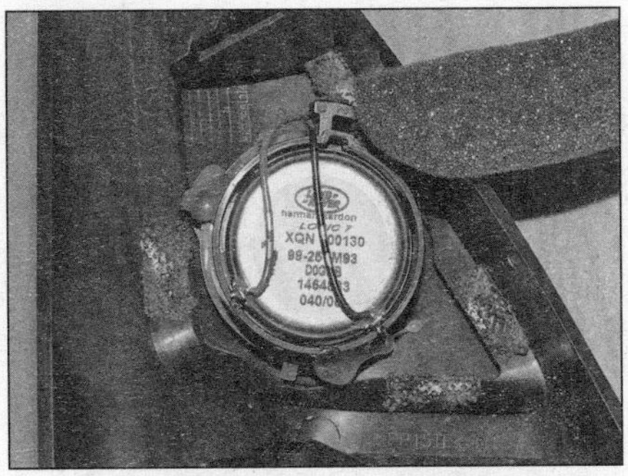

17.26b Front door tweeter

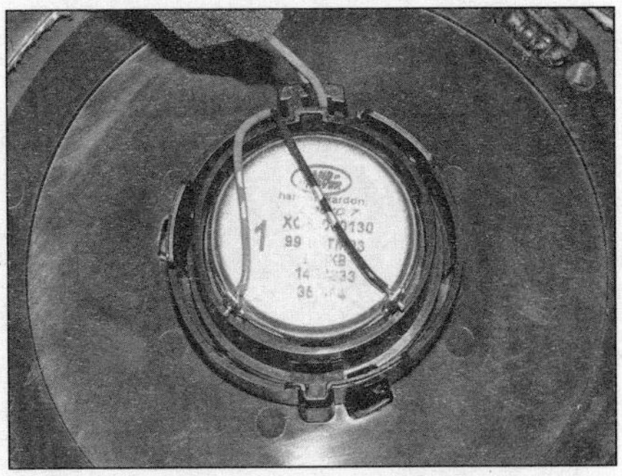

17.26c Rear door tweeter

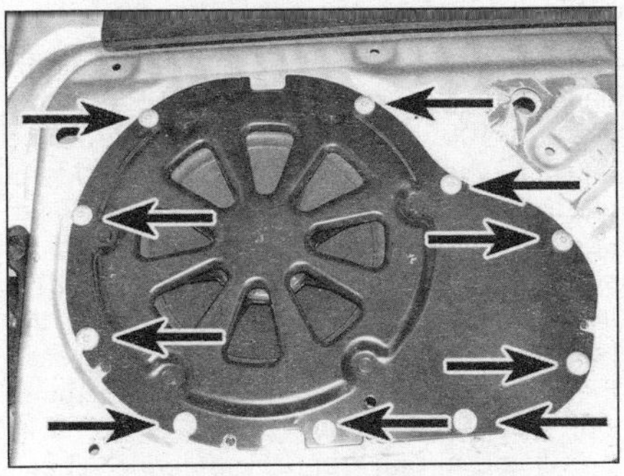

17.28 Tailgate speaker panel retaining screws (arrowed)

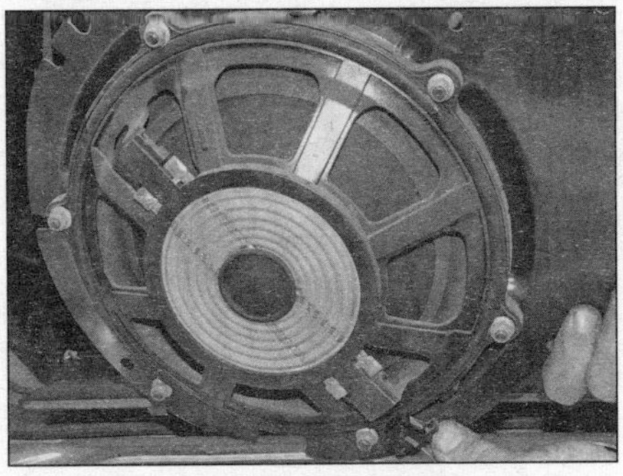

17.29 Disconnect the wiring plug and undo the retaining nuts

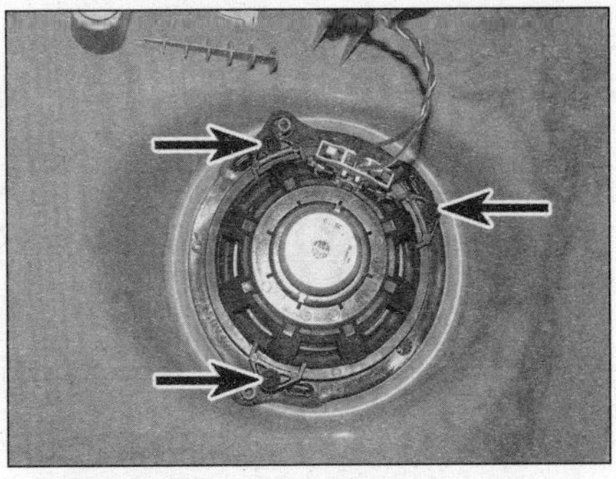

17.31 D-pillar speaker retaining screws (arrowed)

Facia speaker

32 Prise the speaker grille from the facia **(see illustration)**

33 Undo the 3 screws and remove the speaker **(see illustration)**. Disconnect the wiring plug as the speaker is withdrawn.

Speakers refitting

34 In all cases, refitting is a reversal of removal, noting the following points:

- *Tighten all fasteners securely.*
- *Ensure all harnesses are correctly routed, and secured with cable-ties – where applicable.*

18 Airbag system – general information and precautions

All models are equipped with a various airbags as standard equipment.

The driver's airbag unit is fitted to the steering wheel, the passenger's airbag unit is fitted to the top of the facia panel, the side airbags are fitted into the front seats, whilst head-height airbags are fitted to each side of the headlining. In addition to the airbag units, there is a restraints control module (RCM), impact sensors, and a warning light in the instrument panel.

The airbag system is triggered in the event of a frontal, or side impact. The airbags are inflated (by a built-in gas generator) within milliseconds, and forms a safety cushion. This prevents contact between the occupants and the vehicle body. The airbag then deflates almost immediately.

Every time the ignition is switched on, the

17.32 Prise the speaker grille from the facia

airbag control unit performs a self-test. The self-test takes between 5 and 8 seconds, and during this time the airbag warning light in the instrument panel is illuminated. After the self-test has been completed, the warning light should go out. If the warning light fails to come on, remains illuminated after the initial period, or comes on at any time when the vehicle is being driven, there is a fault in the airbag system. The vehicle should be taken to a Land Rover dealer or specialist for examination at the earliest possible opportunity.

⚠ ***Warning: Before carrying out any operations on the airbag system, disconnect the battery positive and negative terminals, and wait AT LEAST 10 minutes, to ensure that any residual electrical energy has been dissipated.***

⚠ ***Warning: Note that the airbag must not be subjected to temperatures in excess of 90°C.***

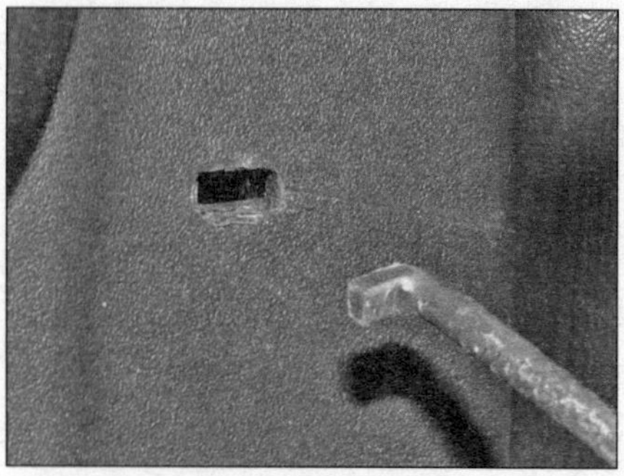

19.2a Insert a hooked tool ...

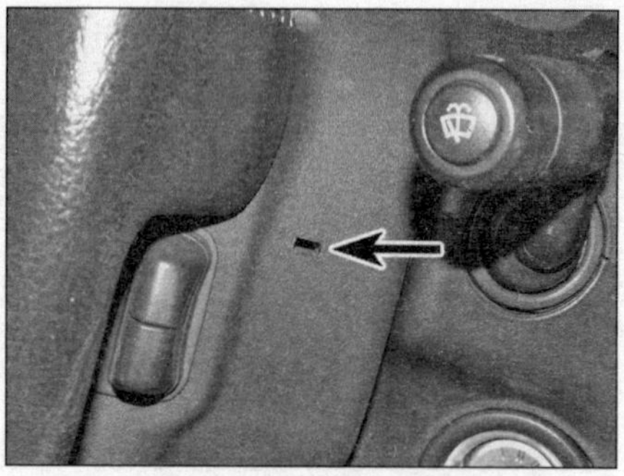

19.2b ... through the hole in the side of the steering wheel boss (arrowed) ...

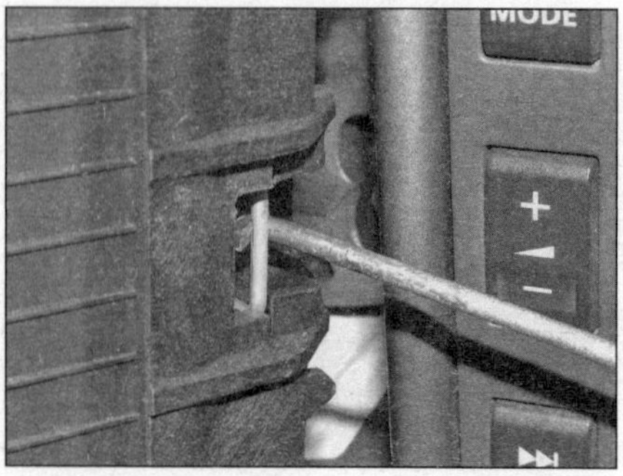

19.2c ... and pull the airbag wire clip outwards (airbag removed for clarity)

19.3 Squeeze together the clips (arrowed) and disconnect the airbag wiring plugs

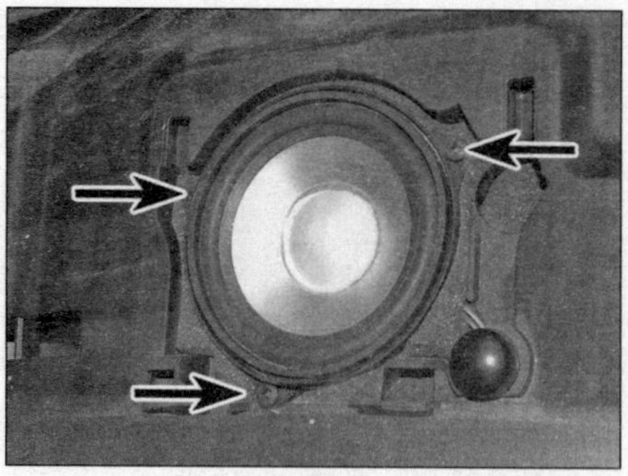

17.33 Facia speaker retaining screws (arrowed)

When the airbag is removed, ensure that it is stored the correct way up, to prevent possible inflation.

⚠ ***Warning: Do not use electrical test equipment on the airbag system components or wiring connectors, as this could lead to the system being accidentally triggered. Testing of the airbag system can only be carried out by a Land Rover dealer or specialist with access to the special electronic test equipment (T4).***

⚠ ***Warning: Do not allow any water, solvents or cleaning agents to contact the airbag unit(s). They must only be cleaned using a damp cloth.***

⚠ ***Warning: The airbag(s) and control unit are both sensitive to impact. If either is dropped or shows signs of physical damage or deterioration, they must be renewed.***

⚠ ***Warning: Disconnect the airbag(s) and control unit wiring plugs prior to using arc/mig-welding equipment on the vehicle.***

19 Airbag system components – removal and refitting

Note: *Refer to the warnings given in the previous Section before carrying out the following operations.*

1 Disconnect the battery negative then positive leads (refer to Chapter 5, Section 4), and wait at least 10 minutes before proceeding as described under the relevant sub-heading.

Driver's airbag unit

2 Ensure the wheel are in the 'straight-ahead' position, then insert Land Rover tool No. 501-106 into the hole in the side of the steering wheel boss, and release that side of the airbag. In the absence of the Land Rover special tool, use a length of welding rod (or similar), shaped as shown in the illustration. Insert the tool into the hole, and pull the retaining spring outwards slightly to release the airbag. Repeat the procedure on the other side **(see illustrations)**.

3 Pull the airbag from the steering wheel. Disconnect the wiring plugs as the airbag is withdrawn **(see illustration)**.

4 On refitting, reconnect the wiring connectors, then engage the top edge of the airbag unit, and hinge it upwards to check the wires are securely connected and not trapped behind the unit, then lower the airbag unit into the centre of the steering wheel.

5 Press the airbag firmly into place to ensure it's securely fitted.

6 Reconnect the battery leads as described in Chapter 5, Section 4.

Passenger's airbag unit

7 Remove the facia as described in Chapter 12, Section 28.

8 Undo the 4 nuts, and detach the airbag from the facia **(see illustration)**.

9 Refitting is a reversal of removal. Tighten the airbag nuts to the specified torque.

Side airbags

10 The side airbags are incorporated into the side of the front seats. Removal of the units requires the seat upholstery to be removed. This is a specialist task, which we recommend should be entrusted to a Land Rover dealer or specialist.

Head/curtain airbags

11 Renewal of the head airbags/inflatable curtain requires removal of the headlining. This is a specialist task, and should be entrusted to a Land Rover dealer or specialist.

Restraints control module

12 Remove the centre console as described in Chapter 12, Section 27.

13 Using a sharp knife, carefully cut the carpet above the control module for access.

14 Undo the 3 Torx screws, then lift the module. Disconnect the wiring plugs as the unit is withdrawn **(see illustration)**.

15 Refitting is the reverse of removal. If a new control module is fitted, it must be programmed using Land Rover diagnostic equipment (T4). Entrust this task to a Land Rover dealer or suitably-equipped specialist.

Impact sensors

Front

16 There are two impact sensors each side of the vehicle. Remove the relevant headlight as described in Section 7.

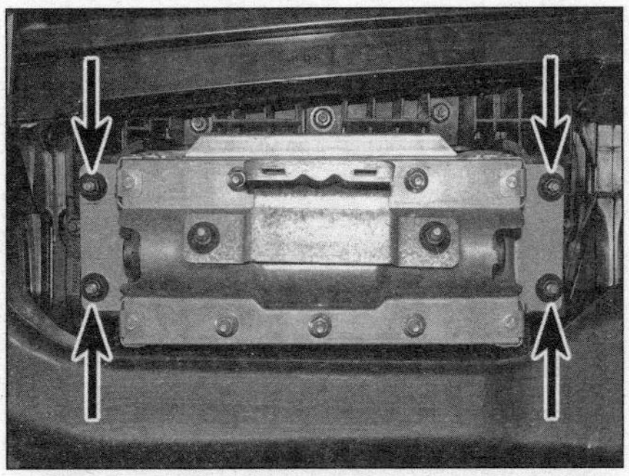

19.8 Passenger's airbag retaining nuts (arrowed)

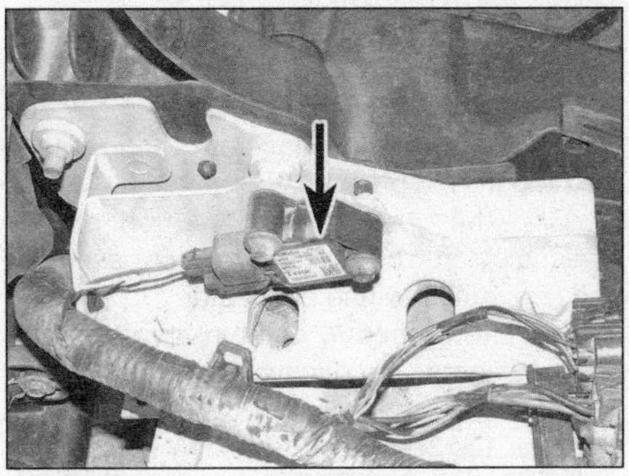

19.17 The front impact sensors are located adjacent to each headlight (arrowed)

17 Undo the 2 retaining bolts, disconnect the wiring plug and remove the sensor **(see illustration)**.

18 Refitting is a reversal of removal.

B-pillar

19 Remove the B-pillar trim panel as described in Chapter 12, Section 26.

20 Pull the sill trim panel upwards to release the retaining clips.

21 Undo the 2 retaining bolts, disconnect the wiring plug and remove the sensor **(see illustration)**.

22 Refitting is a reversal of removal.

C-pillar

23 Remove the luggage compartment side trim panel as described in Chapter 12, Section 26.

24 Undo the 2 retaining bolts, disconnect the wiring plug and remove the sensor **(see illustration)**.

25 Refitting is a reversal of removal.

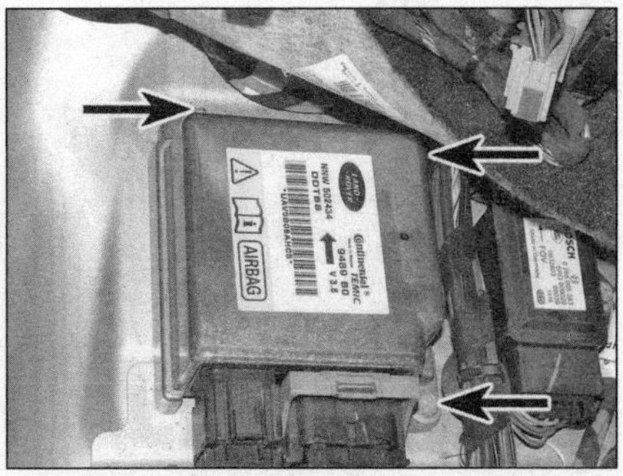

19.14 Restraint control module retaining screws (arrowed)

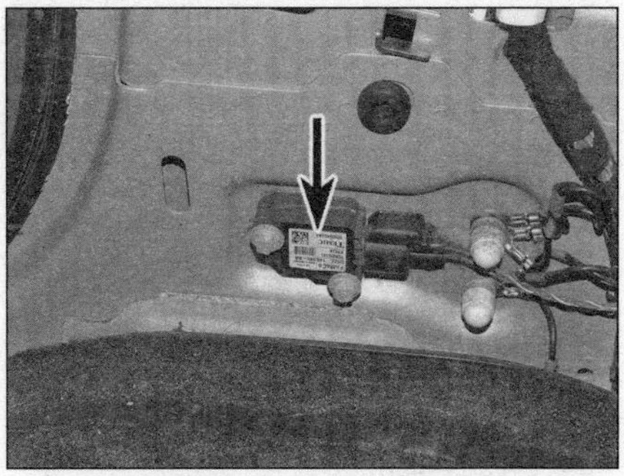

19.21 B-pillar impact sensor (arrowed)

Front door

26 Remove the door inner trim panel as described in Chapter 12, Section 12.

27 Undo the 2 retaining bolts, disconnect the wiring plug and remove the sensor **(see illustration)**.

28 Refitting is a reversal of removal.

Airbag rotary contact unit

29 Remove the steering wheel as described in Chapter 11, Section 19.

30 Carefully prise up the steering column upper shroud to release the clips **(see illustration 4.3)**.

31 Undo the 3 retaining screws, release the column adjustment lever (where fitted) and remove the steering column lower shroud **(see illustration 4.4)**.

32 Disconnect the wiring plugs, undo the 4 retaining screws and remove the contact unit from the steering column **(see illustration)**.

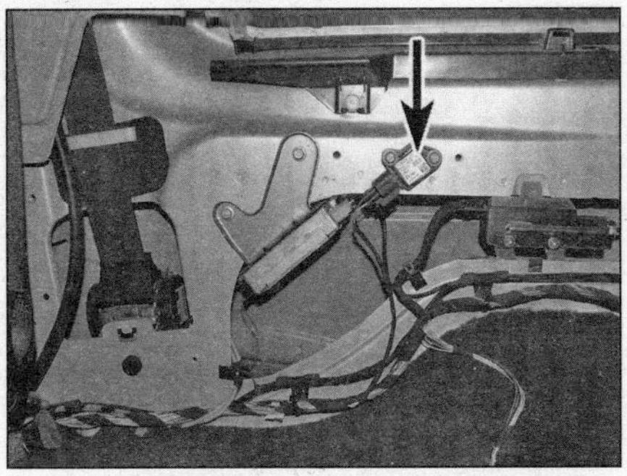

19.24 C-pillar impact sensor (arrowed)

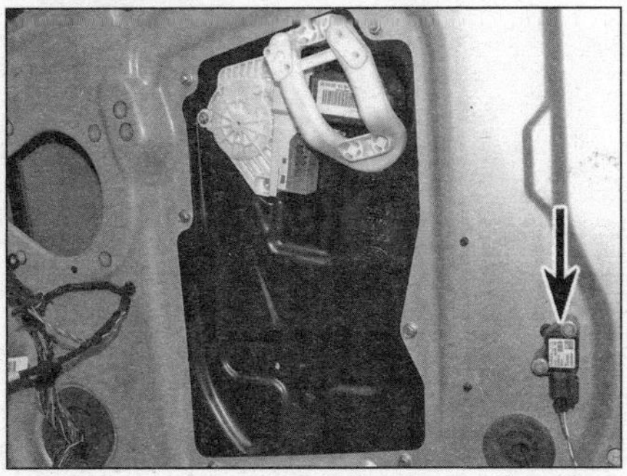

19.27 Front door impact sensor (arrowed)

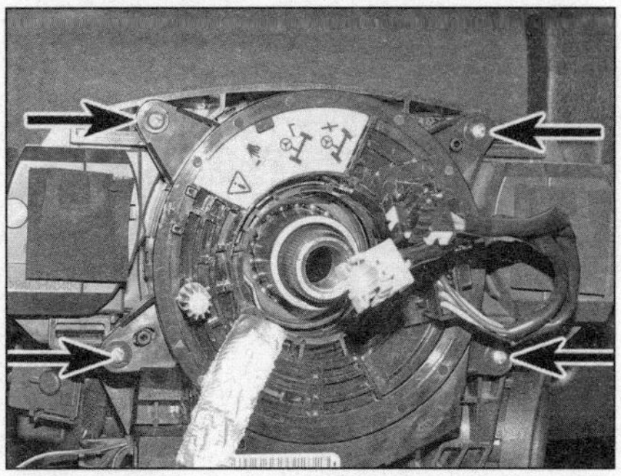

19.32 Rotary contact unit retaining screws (arrowed)

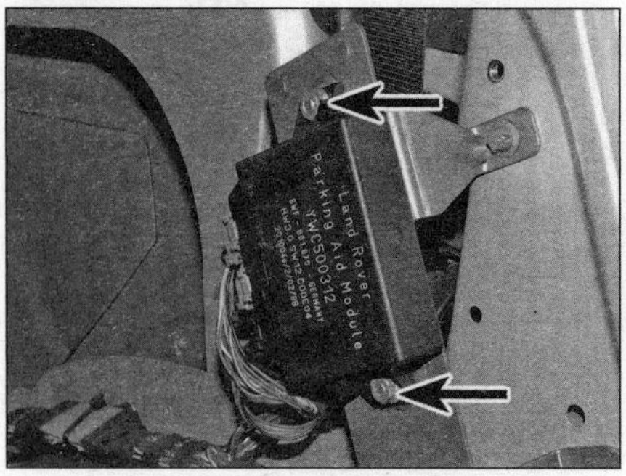

21.2 Parking distance control unit retaining nuts (arrowed)

33 Trace the wiring back from the contact unit, release the connector from the bracket and disconnect it.

34 Release the two retaining clips, then free the contact unit from the top of the combination switch assembly. If the contact unit is to be re-used, wrap adhesive tape around the unit. This will prevent unnecessary rotation of the wiring unit, and ensure that it remains correctly positioned until it is refitted.

35 If a new contact unit is being installed, ensure that the tape on the unit is unbroken. Do not install the unit if the tape has been broken.

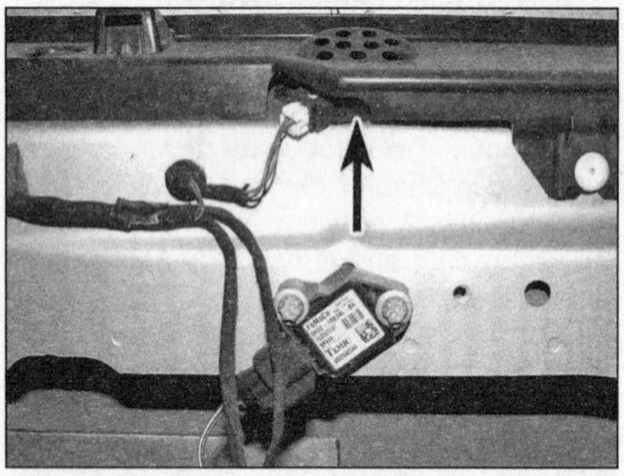

21.9 Parking distance sounder (arrowed)

21.5 Prise out the clips and remove the ultrasonic sensors

36 Ensure that the front wheels are positioned in the straight-ahead position, then remove the tape from the contact unit.

37 Clip the contact into position on the steering column combination switch assembly, and connect its wiring connector.

38 Refit the steering column shrouds, and securely tighten the retaining screws.

39 Refit the steering wheel as described in Chapter 11, Section 19, making sure that it engages correctly with the contact unit.

20 Anti-theft alarm system – general information

Note: *This information is applicable only to the anti-theft alarm system fitted by Land Rover as standard equipment.*

All models in the range are fitted with an anti-theft alarm system as standard equipment. The alarm system has ultrasonic (movement) sensing, as well as sensing opening of the doors, tailgate or bonnet. If movement is detected inside the vehicle, or if the tailgate, bonnet or any of the doors are opened whilst the alarm is set, the alarm siren will sound and the hazard warning lights will flash. The alarm also has an immobiliser function, which makes the ignition and starter circuits inoperable whilst the alarm is triggered.

Should the alarm system develop a fault, the vehicle should be taken to a Land Rover dealer or specialist for examination.

21 Parking distance control system – component removal and refitting

Electronic control unit (ECU)

1 Remove the left-hand luggage compartment side trim panel as described in Chapter 12, Section 26.

2 Undo the 2 retaining nuts, disconnect the wiring plugs and remove the ECU **(see illustration)**.

3 Refitting is a reversal of removal.

Ultrasonic sensors

4 Remove the front or rear bumper (as applicable).

5 Push the retaining clips out a little, and pull the sensor from place **(see illustration)**.

6 Refitting is a reversal of removal.

Sounder

7 Remove the left-hand luggage compartment side trim panel as described in Chapter 12, Section 26.

8 Undo the 2 screws and remove the load space trim mounting bracket.

9 Undo the 2 retaining bolts and detach the sounder **(see illustration)**. Disconnect the wiring plug as the sounder is withdrawn.

10 Refitting is a reversal of removal.

Land Rover Discovery wiring diagrams

Diagram 1

At the time of writing, certain wiring diagram technical information was unavailable. As a result these diagrams are intended as a representative set covering most major electrical systems typically encountered on this model range.

WARNING: This vehicle is fitted with a supplemental restraint system (SRS) consisting of a combination of driver (and passenger) airbag(s), side impact protection airbags and seatbelt pre-tensioners. The use of electrical test equipment on any SRS wiring systems may cause the seatbelt pre-tensioners to abruptly retract and airbags to explosively deploy, resulting in potentially severe personal injury. Extreme care should be taken to correctly identify any circuits to be tested to avoid choosing any of the SRS wiring in error.
For further information see airbag system precautions in body electrical systems chapter.
Note: The SRS wiring harness can normally be identified by yellow and/or orange harness or harness connectors.

Key to symbols

Solenoid actuator

Earth point and location (E7)

Wire colour (blue with white tracer) U/W

Dashed outline denotes part of a larger item, containing in this case an electronic or solid state device (pins 23 and 24 of connector c0582). c0582/23 c0582/24

Bulb

Switch

Fuse F26

Fusible link FL17

Resistor

Variable resistor

Variable resistor

Wire splice, soldered joint, or unspecified connector

Connecting wires

Diode

Light-emitting diode

Item number 12

Motor/pump

Heating element

Battery fusebox 2

F1	25A	Fuel pump
F2	-	Spare
F3	5A	Air suspension control unit
F4	25A	Engine management system - Diesel
F5	10A	Engine management system - petrol
F6	15A	Engine management system - petrol
F7	25A	Heated front seats
F8	25A	Heated rear seats
F9	15A	Active roll control
F10	15A	Engine management system - petrol
	15A	Engine cooling fan (Diesel)
F11	15A	Engine management system - petrol
F12	10A	Heated washer jets
F13	10A	Engine management - petrol
	10A	Engine management system - Diesel
F14	20A	Engine management system - petrol
F15	30A	Heated front screen
F16	10A	Heated door mirrors
F17	15A	Engine management system - petrol
	15A	Engine management system - Diesel
F18	30A	Heated front screen
F19	-	Spare
F20	5A	Alternator
F21	-	Spare
F22	30A	Rear heater blower
F23	25A	Dynamic stability control system
F24	20A	Brake boost pump - Petrol
F25	10A	Lighting switch
F26	20A	Air suspension control unit
F27	5A	Engine management system
F28	20A	Fuel burning heater - Diesel
F29	30A	Front wiper
F30	10A	Automatic transmission control unit

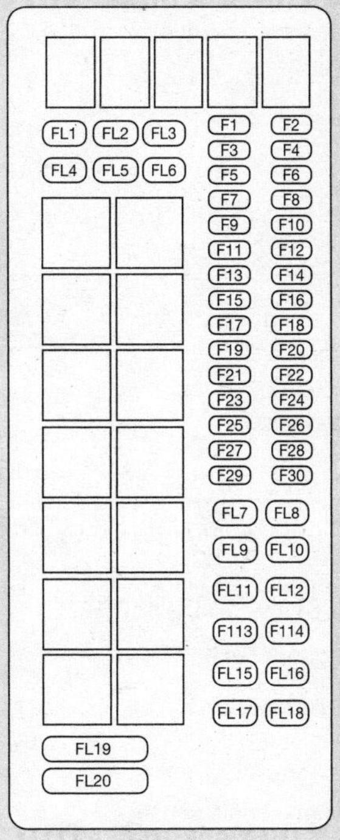

H47413

Land Rover Discovery wiring diagrams

Diagram 2

Passenger fusebox 6

F1	10A	Interior lights, glovebox light, vanity mirror light, map reading light
F2	10A	RH sidelights
F3	10A	Theatre lights
F4	10A	LH sidelights
F5	10A	Reversing lights
F6	10A	Reversing lights - trailer
F7	25A	Driver's electric window
F8	30A	Trailer pick-up (battery feed)
F9	5A	Safety restraint system
F10	-	Spare
F11	10A	Washer pump
F12	15A	Horn
F13	25A	Heated rear window
F14	10A	Sidelights - trailer
F15	15A	Stop lights
F16	10A	Folding mirrors
F17	20A	RH rear electric window
F18	5A	Rain sensor, ambient light sensor
F19	15A	Centre accessory socket
F20	15A	Sunroof
F21	25A	Passenger's electric window
F22	10A	Trailer pick-up (ignition feed)
F23	-	Spare
F24	5A	Transfer box - centre diff, terrain response
F25	5A	Engine control unit
F26	5A	Battery back-up sounder
F27	10A	Adaptive front lighting/headlight levelling
F28	5A	Battery fusebox, ignition
F29	30A	Passenger's electric seat
F30	-	Spare
F31	20A	LH rear electric window
F32	15A	Rear fog light
F33	5A	Electric mirrors, passenger's electric seat, auto. transmission selector
F34	15A	Front accessory socket
F35	5A	Air suspension control unit
F36	5A	Tyre pressure monitor, park distance control
F37	5A	Dynamic stability control
F38	15A	Front fog lights
F39	5A	Instrument cluster
F40	5A	Key in sense
F41	5A	Electric handbrake
F42	30A	Audio amplifier
F43	10A	RF receiver, tyre pressure monitor
F44	5A	Auto. transmission selector
F45	-	Spare
F46	30A	Driver's electric seat
F47	15A	Rear row accessory socket
F48	15A	Rear wiper
F49	30A	Central locking
F50	10A	Fuel filler flap
F51	10A	Air conditioning control unit
F52	5A	Telephone, traffic message centre
F53	15A	Media/dvd player
F54	5A	Electric seats memory
F55	15A	Cigar lighter
F56	10A	Adaptive front lighting
F57	10A	Rear seat entertainment control unit
F58	10A	Telephone, infotainment display, multi-media
F59	10A	Cool box
F60	5A	Engine management control unit
F61	10A	Adaptive front lighting
F62	5A	Headlight levelling, autolighting
F63	10A	Diagnostic connector
F64	5A	Auto. transmission
F65	-	Spare
F66	5A	Stop light switch, steering angle sensor
F67	5A	Autolighting
F68	5A	Instrument cluster
F69	5A	Interior mirror

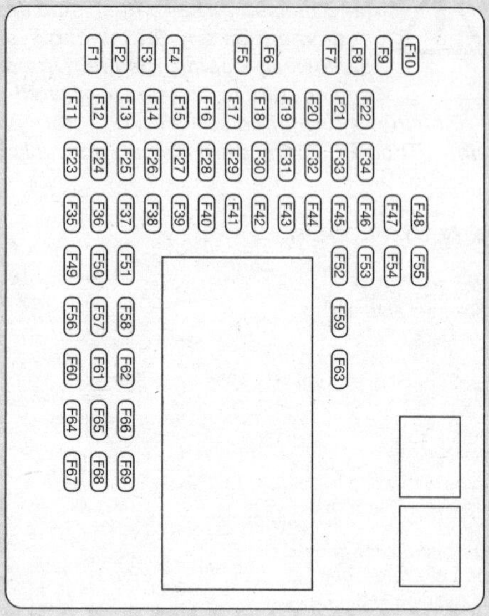

Tow bar fusebox 50

F1	7.5A	Stop lights
F2	15A	Ignition feed
F3	15A	Battery feed
F4	7.5A	Rear fog lights
F5	5A	RH tail light
F6	5A	Number plate light, LH tail light

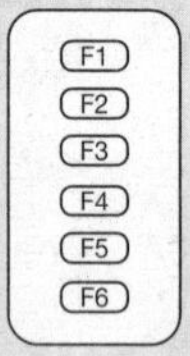

Key to circuits

Diagram 1	Key to circuits
Diagram 2	Key to circuits
Diagram 3	Starting & charging, horn, cigarette lighter & accessory sockets, sunroof
Diagram 4	Stop & reversing lights, direction indicators & hazard warning lights, fog lights, headlight levelling
Diagram 5	Headlights, side, tail & number plate lights
Diagram 6	Cornering lights, trailer wiring, cool box
Diagram 7	Interior lighting
Diagram 8	Wash/wipe
Diagram 9	Heated washer jets & heated front/rear screen, instrument cluster, heater blower
Diagram 10	Electric mirrors, audio system
Diagram 11	Central locking
Diagram 12	Electric windows

H47414

Diagram 3

Colour codes

W	White	**R**	Red
U	Blue	**K**	Pink
Y	Yellow	**G**	Green
N	Brown	**P**	Purple
B	Black	**S**	Slate
O	Orange		
T	Transparent		
LG	Light green		
LU	Light blue		

Key to items

1 Battery
2 Battery fusebox
  a = starter relay
3 Starter motor
4 Alternator
5 Ignition switch
6 Passenger fusebox
  a = generic control unit
  b = horn relay
  c = cigar lighter relay
  d = accessory socket relay
7 Instrument cluster
8 Steering wheel clock springs
9 LH horn
10 RH horn
11 Driver's airbag module
12 LH steering wheel module
  a = horn switch
13 RH steering wheel module
  a = horn
14 Cigar lighter
15 Front accessory socket
16 Centre accessory socket
17 Rear accessory socket
18 Sunroof control unit
19 Sunroof motor
20 Front interior light
  a = sunroof switch

H47415

Starting & charging

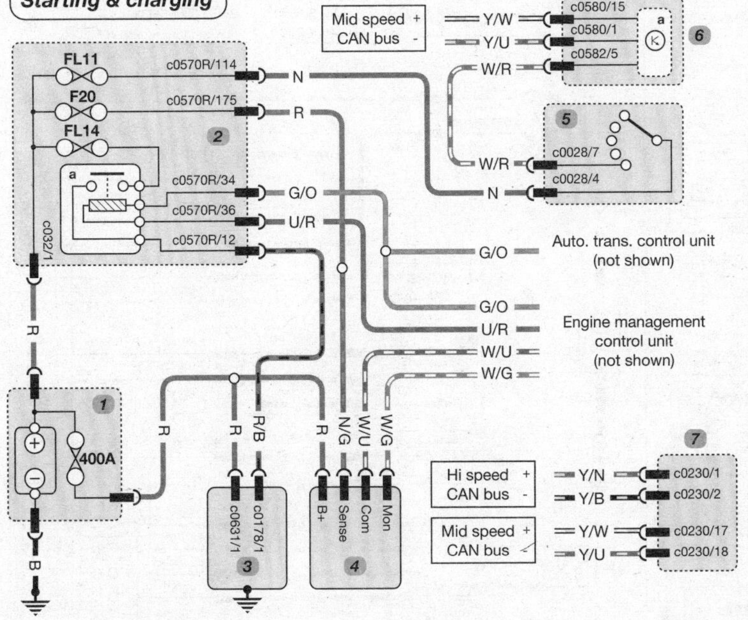

Horn

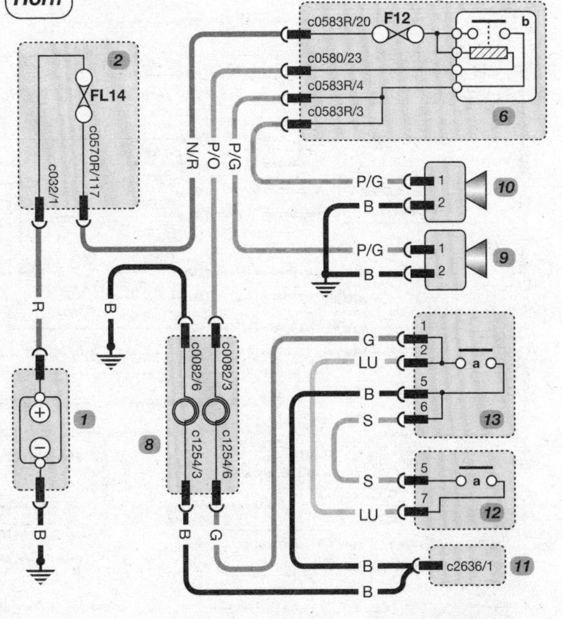

Cigarette lighter & accessory sockets

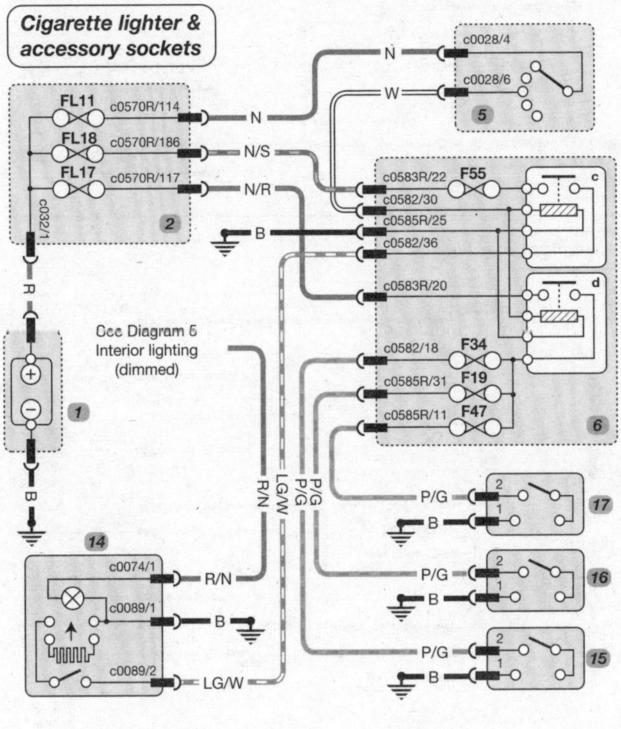

Sunroof

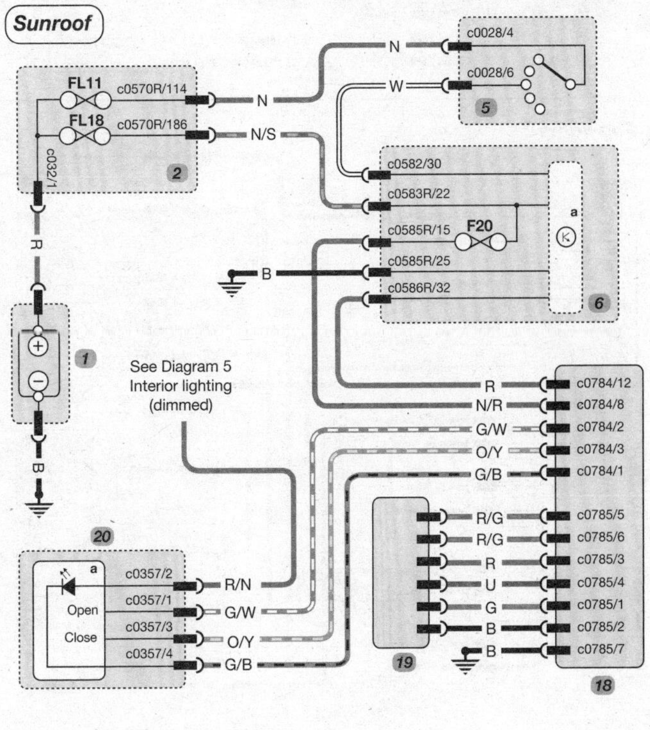

Diagram 4

Colour codes

W	White	**R**	Red
U	Blue	**K**	Pink
Y	Yellow	**G**	Green
N	Brown	**P**	Purple
B	Black	**S**	Slate
O	Orange		
T	Transparent		
LG	Light green		
LU	Light blue		

Key to items

1 Battery
2 Battery fusebox
  b = ignition relay
5 Ignition switch
6 Passenger fusebox
  a = generic control unit
  e = reversing light relay
  f = RH indicator FET
  g = LH indicator FET
7 Instrument cluster
24 Stop light switch
25 Transmission control unit
26 Gearbox position sensor
27 Transfer box control unit
28 LH rear light unit
  a = stop light
  b = reversing light
  c = fog light
  d = direction indicator
29 RH rear light unit
  (a to d as above)
30 High level stop light
31 LH front fog light
32 RH front fog light
33 Main lighting switch
  a = side/headlight
  b = fog light
  c = headlight adjuster
34 Steering column lighting switch
  a = direction indicator
35 Fascia switch
  a = hazard warning
36 LH headlight unit
  a = direction indicator
  b = headlight leveling motor
37 RH headlight unit
  (a and b as above)
38 LH indicator side repeater
39 RH indicator side repeater

H47416

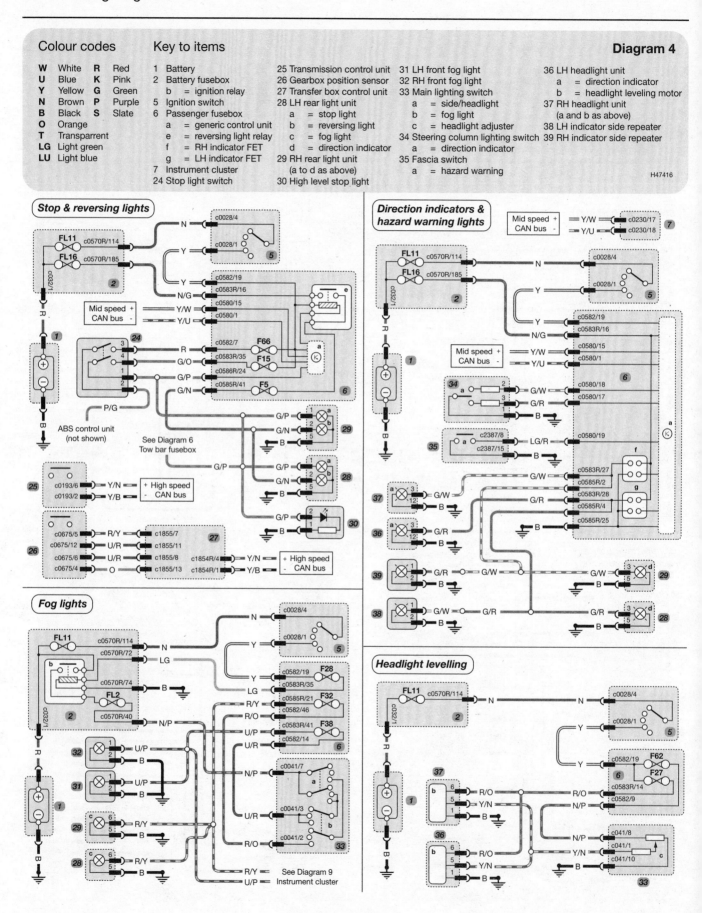

Stop & reversing lights

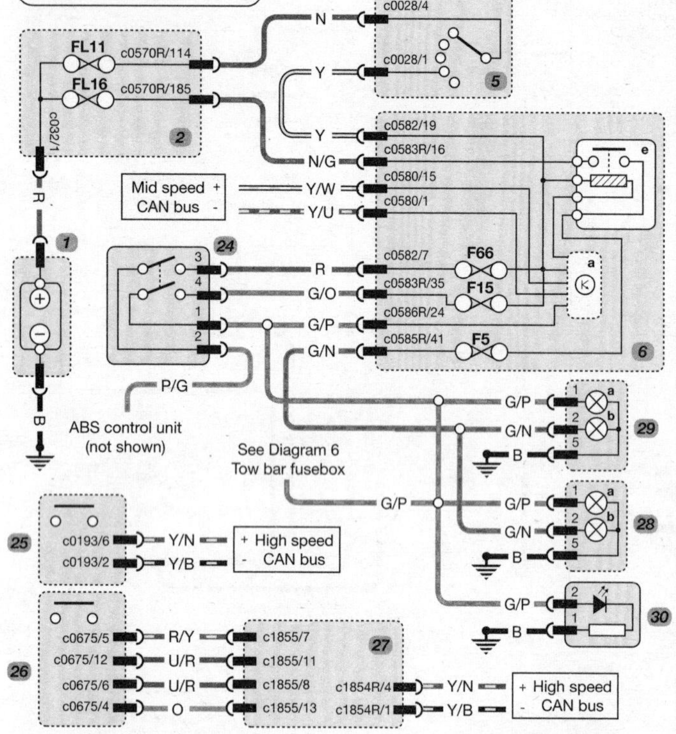

Fog lights

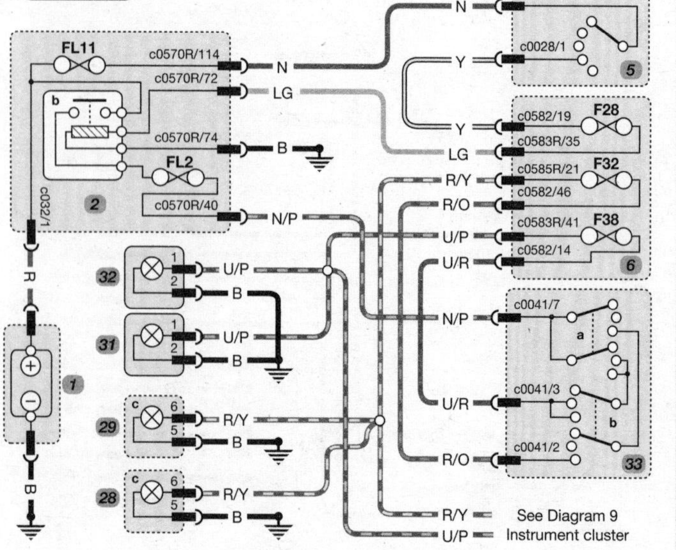

Direction indicators & hazard warning lights

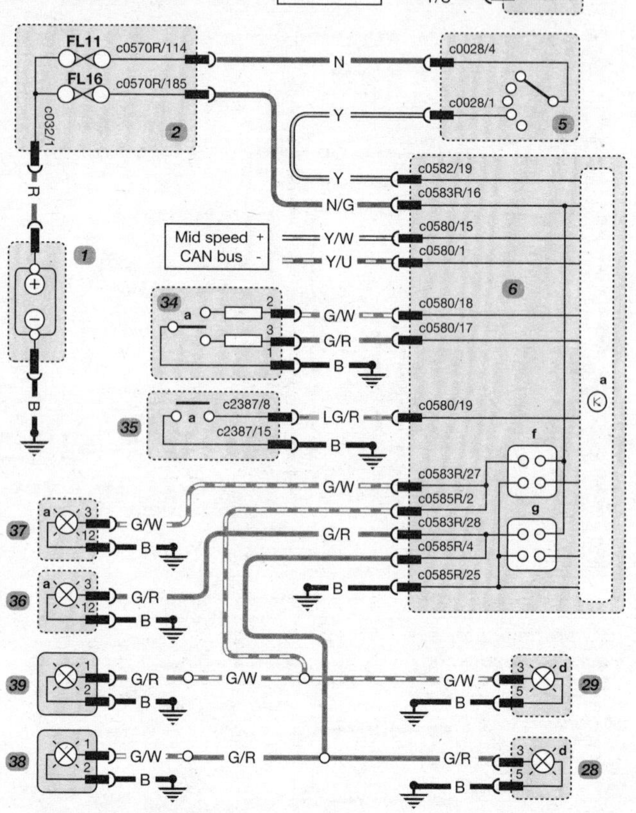

Headlight levelling

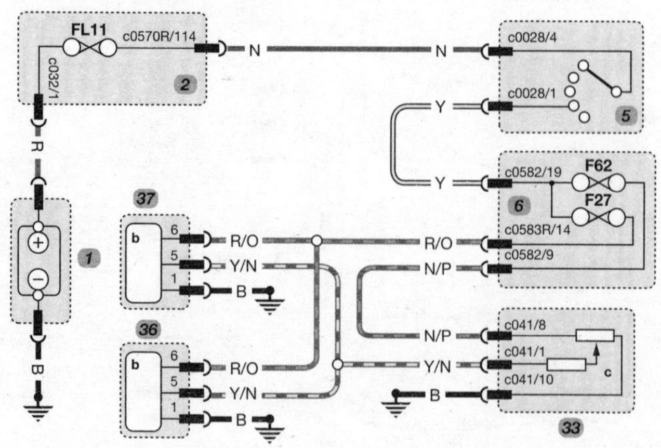

Colour codes

W	White	**R**	Red
U	Blue	**K**	Pink
Y	Yellow	**G**	Green
N	Brown	**P**	Purple
B	Black	**S**	Slate
O	Orange		
T	Transparrent		
LG	Light green		
LU	Light blue		

Key to items

Diagram 5

1 Battery
2 Battery fusebox
5 Ignition switch
6 Passenger fusebox
  a = generic control unit
  f = sidelight relay 1
  g = sidelight relay 2
  h = auto-lights relay
  i = RH dipped beam FET
  j = RH main beam FET
  k = LH dipped beam FET
  l = LH main beam FET
28 LH rear light unit
  e = tail light
  f = tail light
  g = side marker
29 RH rear light unit
  (e to g as above)
33 Main lighting switch
  a = side/headlight
  d = interior lioghting dimmer
34 Steering column lighting switch
  b = main beam/flash
36 LH headlight unit
  c = side marker light
  d = sidelight
  e = dipped beam
  f = main beam
37 RH headlight unit
  (c to f as above)
43 Number plate light/tailgate release switch
44 Rain/light sensor

H47417

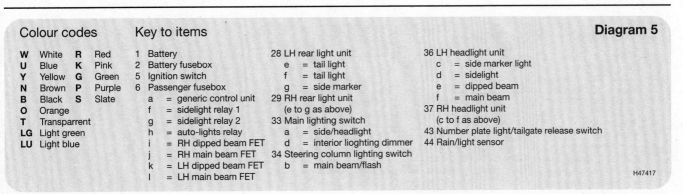

Headlights, side, tail & number plate lights

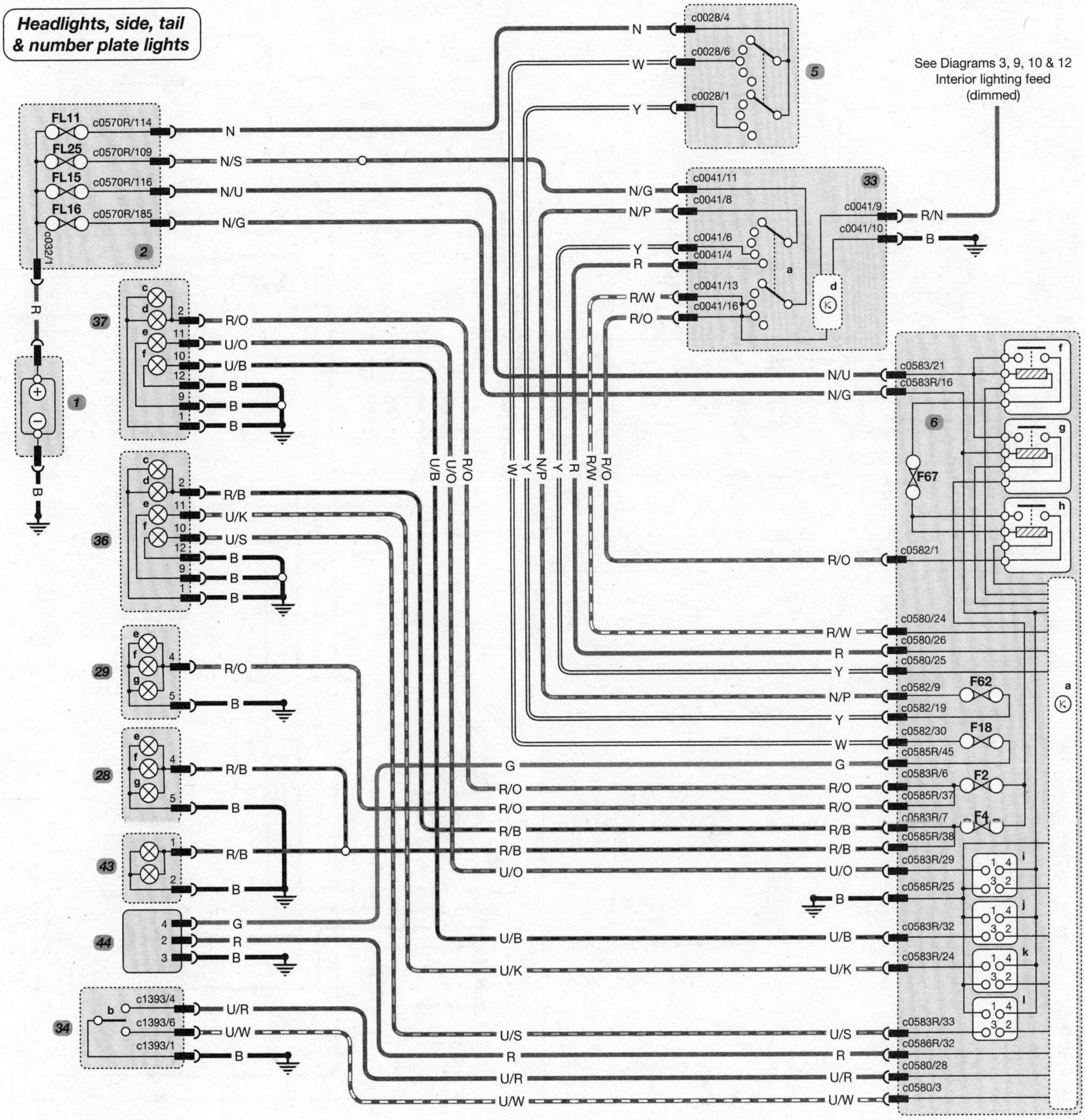

Diagram 6

Colour codes

W	White	R	Red
U	Blue	K	Pink
Y	Yellow	G	Green
N	Brown	P	Purple
B	Black	S	Slate
O	Orange		
T	Transparent		
LG	Light green		
LU	Light blue		

Key to items

1 Battery
2 Battery fusebox
5 Ignition switch
6 Passenger fusebox
 a = generic control unit
 e = reversing light relay 1
 f = sidelight relay
 m = RH cornering light FET
 n = LH cornering light FET
 o = LH trailer indicator FET
 P = RH trailer indicator FET
7 Instrument cluster
27 Transfer box control unit
33 Lighting switch
 a = side/headlight
34 Steering column lighting switch
 a = direction indicator
36 LH headlight unit
 g = cornering light
37 RH headlight unit
 g = cornering light
48 Steering angle sensor
49 ABS control unit
50 Tow bar fusebox
51 Rear wiper/trailer fusebox
 a = trailer supply relay
52 Trailer socket 1
53 Trailer socket 2
54 Cool box

H47418

Cornering lights

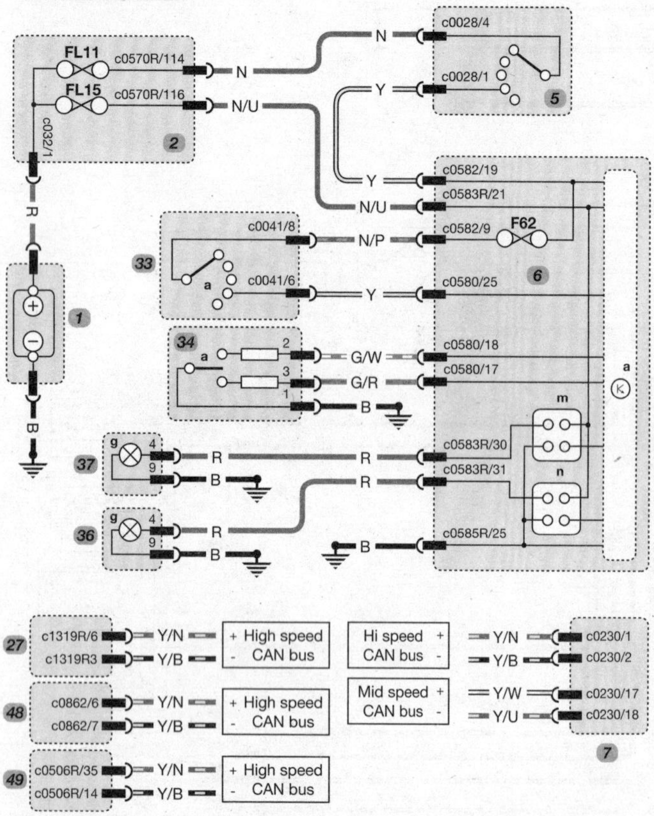

Cool box

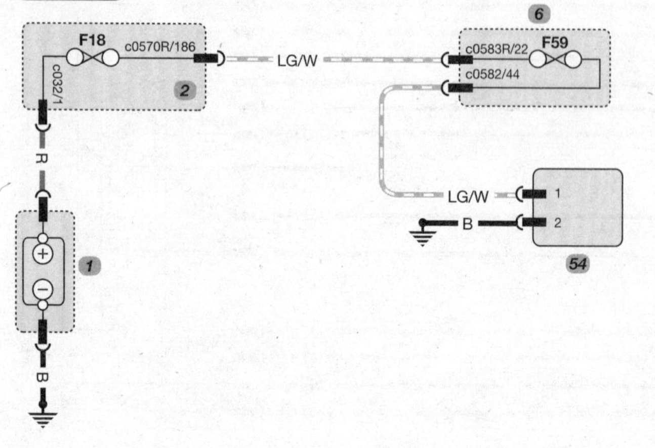

Trailer wiring

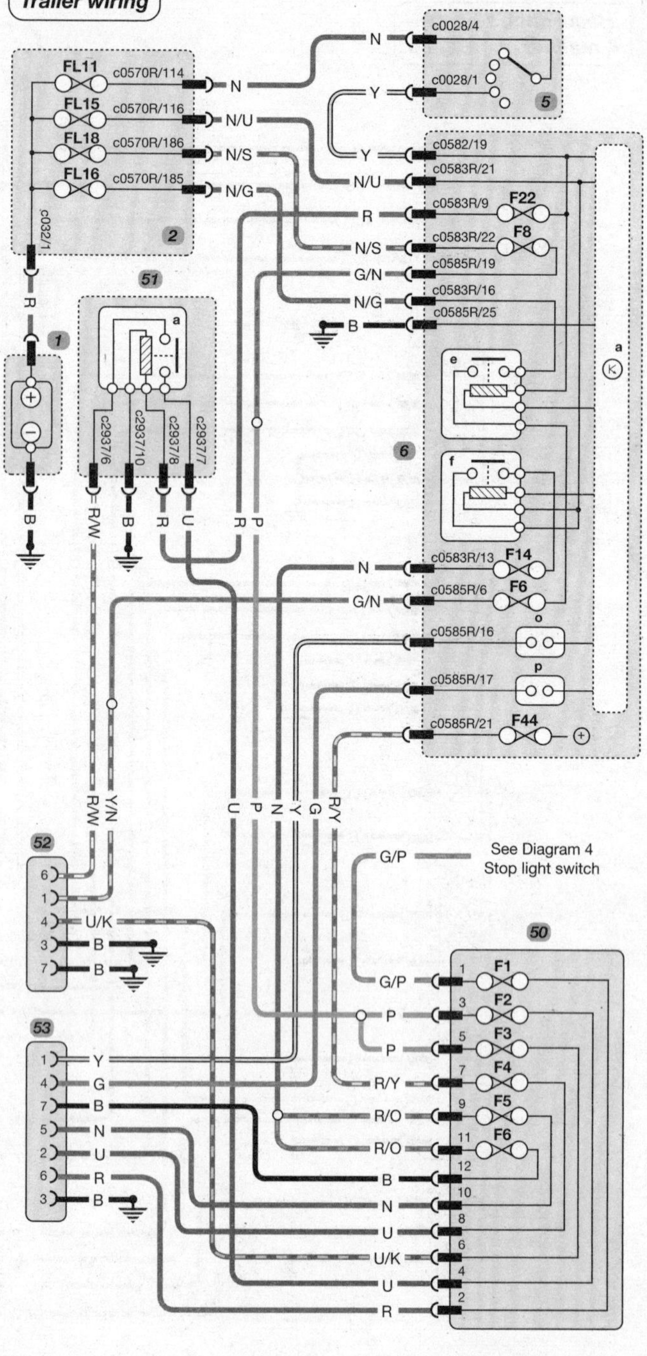

Diagram 7

Colour codes

W	White	**R**	Red
U	Blue	**K**	Pink
Y	Yellow	**G**	Green
N	Brown	**P**	Purple
B	Black	**S**	Slate
O	Orange		
T	Transparent		
LG	Light green		
LU	Light blue		

Key to items

1 Battery
2 Battery fusebox
5 Ignition switch
6 Passenger fusebox
  a = generic control unit
  q = battery saver relay
  r = interior lighting FET 1
  s = interior lighting FET 2
  t = approach light FET
57 Upper tailgate release motor/switch
58 Driver's door lock assembly
59 Passenger's door lock assembly
60 LH rear door lock assembly
61 RH rear door lock assembly
62 Glovebox light/switch
63 Load space light
64 Front interior light
65 Rear interior light
66 LH vanity mirror light
67 RH vanity mirror light
68 LH map reading light
69 RH map reading light
70 LH front puddle light
71 RH front puddle light
72 LH rear puddle light
73 RH rear puddle light
74 LH footwell light
75 RH footwell light
76 Ignition key barrel light
77 Driver's approach light
78 Passenger's approach light

H47419

Interior lighting

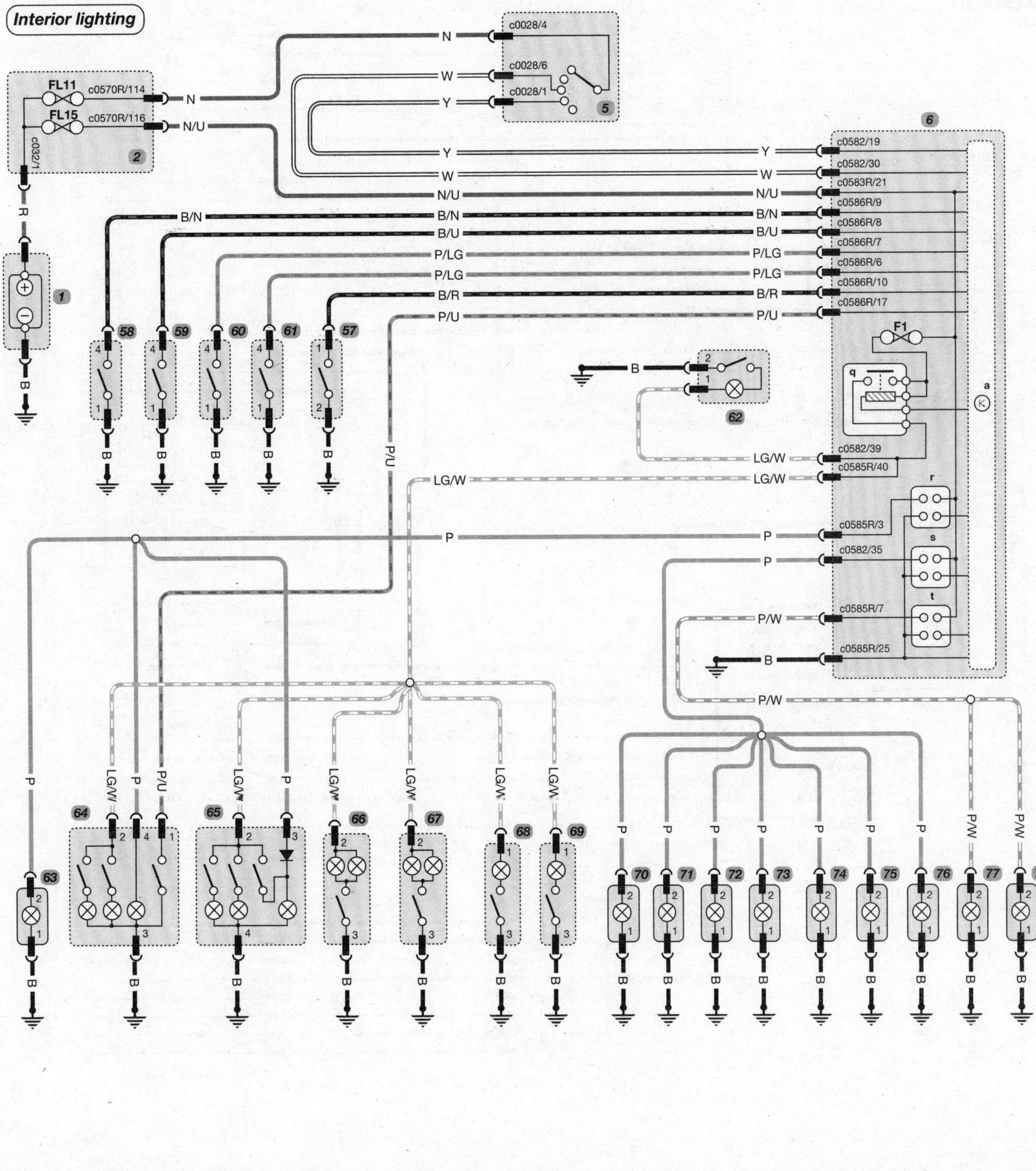

Colour codes

W	White	**R**	Red
U	Blue	**K**	Pink
Y	Yellow	**G**	Green
N	Brown	**P**	Purple
B	Black	**S**	Slate
O	Orange		
T	Transparrent		
LG	Light green		
LU	Light blue		

Key to items

1 Battery
2 Battery fusebox
  c = wiper relay 1
  d = wiper relay 2
  e = washer relay
5 Ignition switch
6 Passenger fusebox
  a = generic control unit
  t = washer pump relay
33 Main lighting switch
  a = side/headlight
44 Rain/light sensor
51 Rear wiper/trailer fusebox
  b = rear wiper relay
80 Front wiper motor
81 Rear wiper motor
82 Headlight washer pump
83 Upper tailgate lock assembly
84 Front/rear washer pump
85 Steering column wash/wipe switch
  a = front washer
  b = slow wiper
  c = flick wiper
  d = fast wiper
  e = intermittent wiper
  f = rear washer
  g = rear wiper
  h = variable delay

Diagram 8

H47420

Wash/wipe

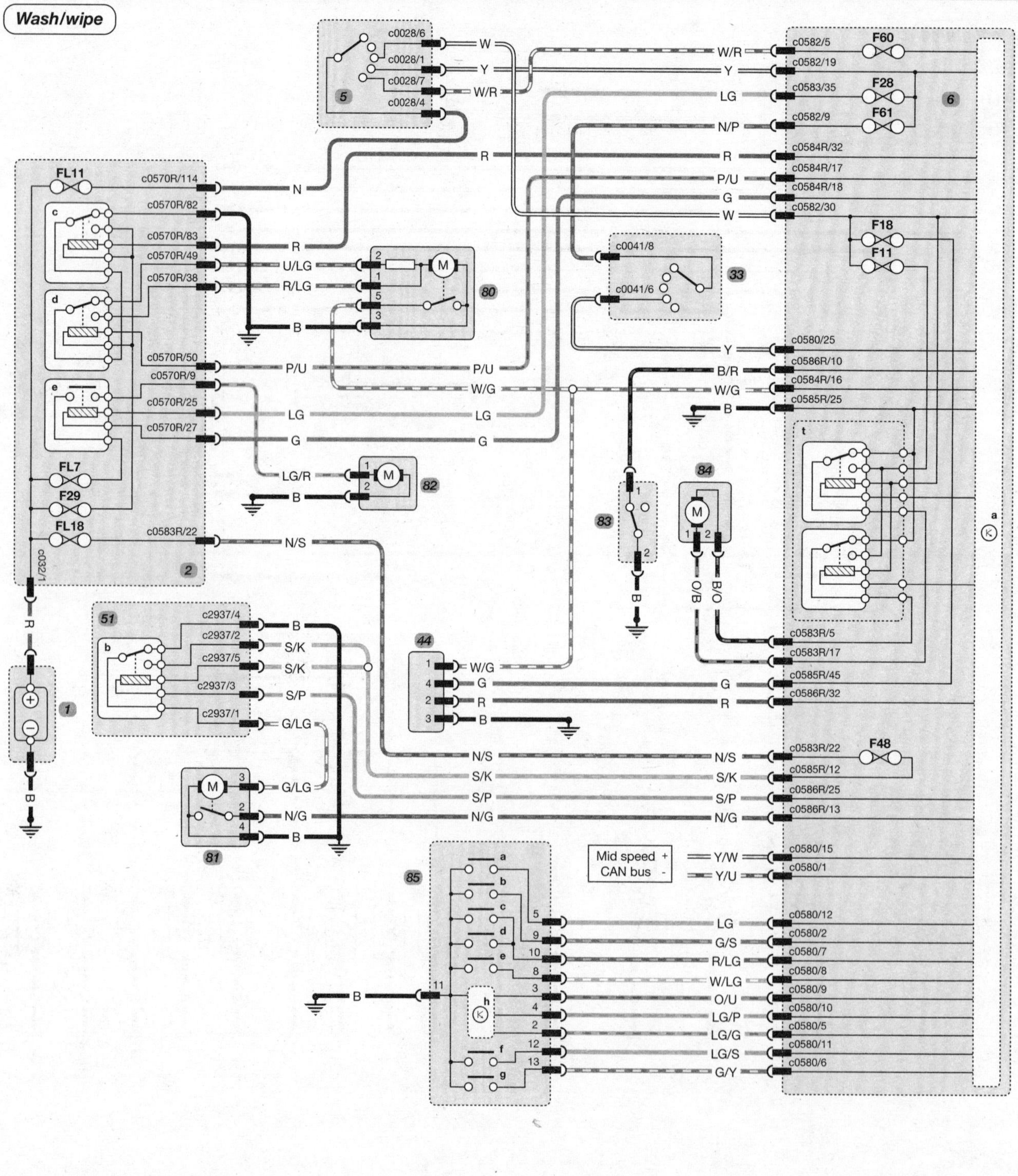

Colour codes

W	White	R	Red
U	Blue	K	Pink
Y	Yellow	G	Green
N	Brown	P	Purple
B	Black	S	Slate
O	Orange		
T	Transparent		
LG	Light green		
LU	Light blue		

Key to items

Diagram 9

1 Battery
2 Battery fusebox
  f = heated washer jet/mirror relay
  g = heated front screen relay
  h = heater blower relay
5 Ignition switch
6 Passenger fusebox
  a = generic control unit
  u = heated rear window relay
7 Ignition switch
34 Steering column lighting switch
  c = trip computer reset
85 Steering column wash/wipe switch
88 Heater control panel
89 LH heated washer jet
90 RH heated washer jet
91 Ambient air temp. sensor
92 LH heated screen element
93 RH heated screen element
94 Heated rear window element
95 Filter
96 Pad wear sensor
97 Instrument cluster
98 Fuel pump/fuel gauge sender unit
99 Parking brake control unit
100 Brake fluid switch
101 Coolant level sensor
102 Low washer fluid sensor
103 Seat belt switch
104 Oil pressure switch
105 Front heater blower motor
106 Heater blower control unit

H47421

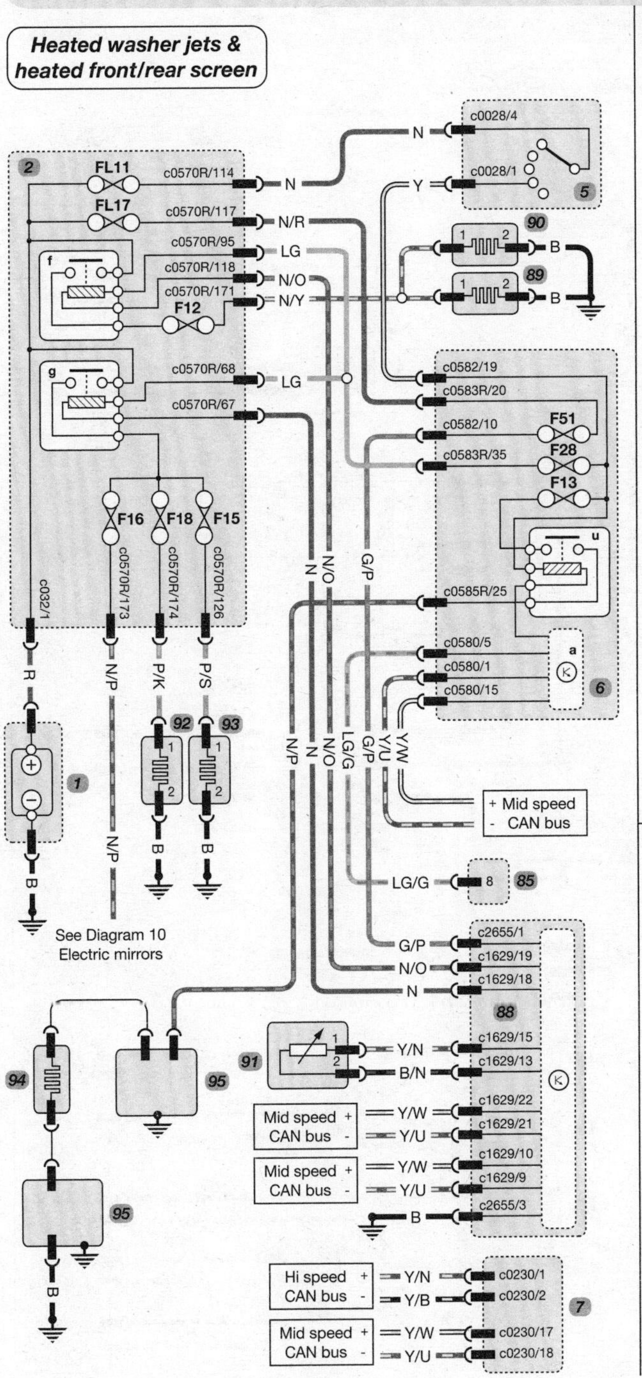

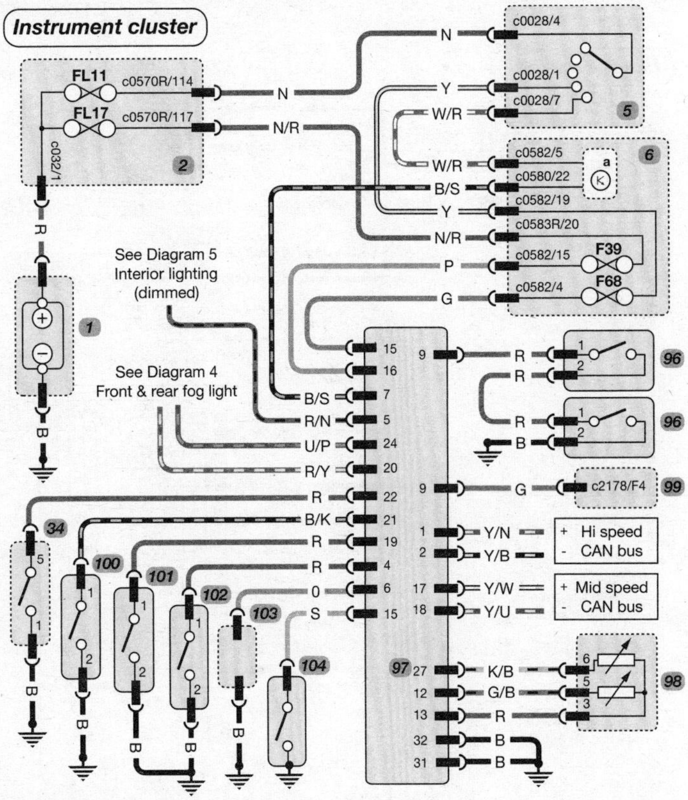

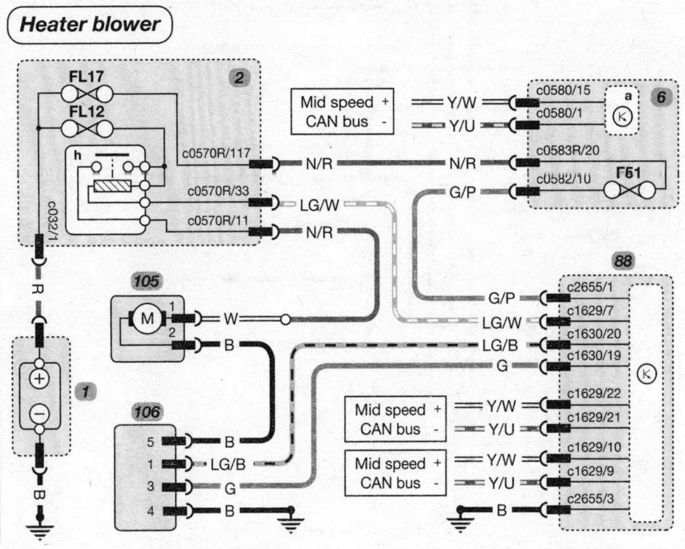

Colour codes

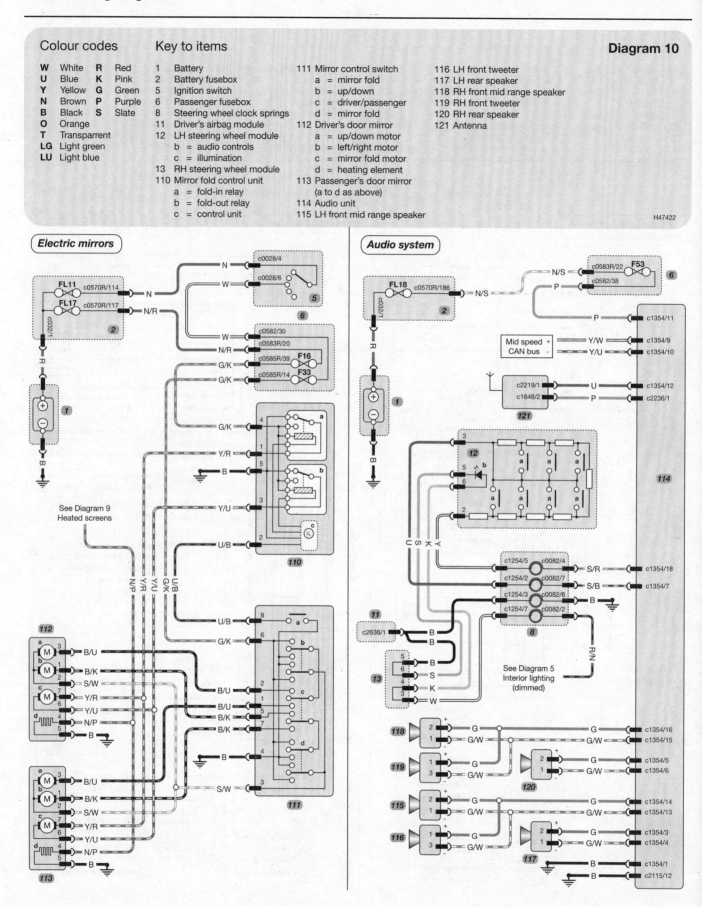

W	White	**R**	Red
U	Blue	**K**	Pink
Y	Yellow	**G**	Green
N	Brown	**P**	Purple
B	Black	**S**	Slate
O	Orange		
T	Transparrent		
LG	Light green		
LU	Light blue		

Key to items

1 Battery
2 Battery fusebox
5 Ignition switch
6 Passenger fusebox
8 Steering wheel clock springs
11 Driver's airbag module
12 LH steering wheel module
  b = audio controls
  c = illumination
13 RH steering wheel module
110 Mirror fold control unit
  a = fold-in relay
  b = fold-out relay
  c = control unit
111 Mirror control switch
  a = mirror fold
  b = up/down
  c = driver/passenger
  d = mirror fold
112 Driver's door mirror
  a = up/down motor
  b = left/right motor
  c = mirror fold motor
  d = heating element
113 Passenger's door mirror
  (a to d as above)
114 Audio unit
115 LH front mid range speaker
116 LH front tweeter
117 LH rear speaker
118 RH front mid range speaker
119 RH front tweeter
120 RH rear speaker
121 Antenna

Diagram 10

H47422

Electric mirrors

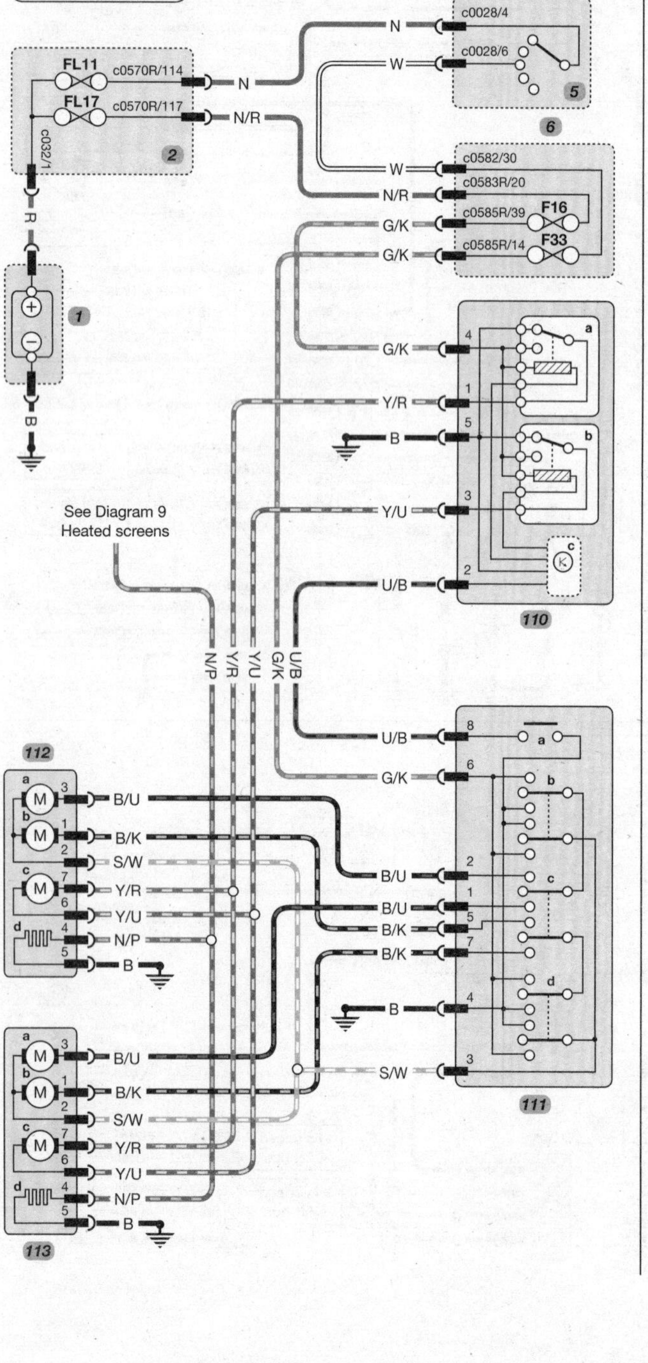

Audio system

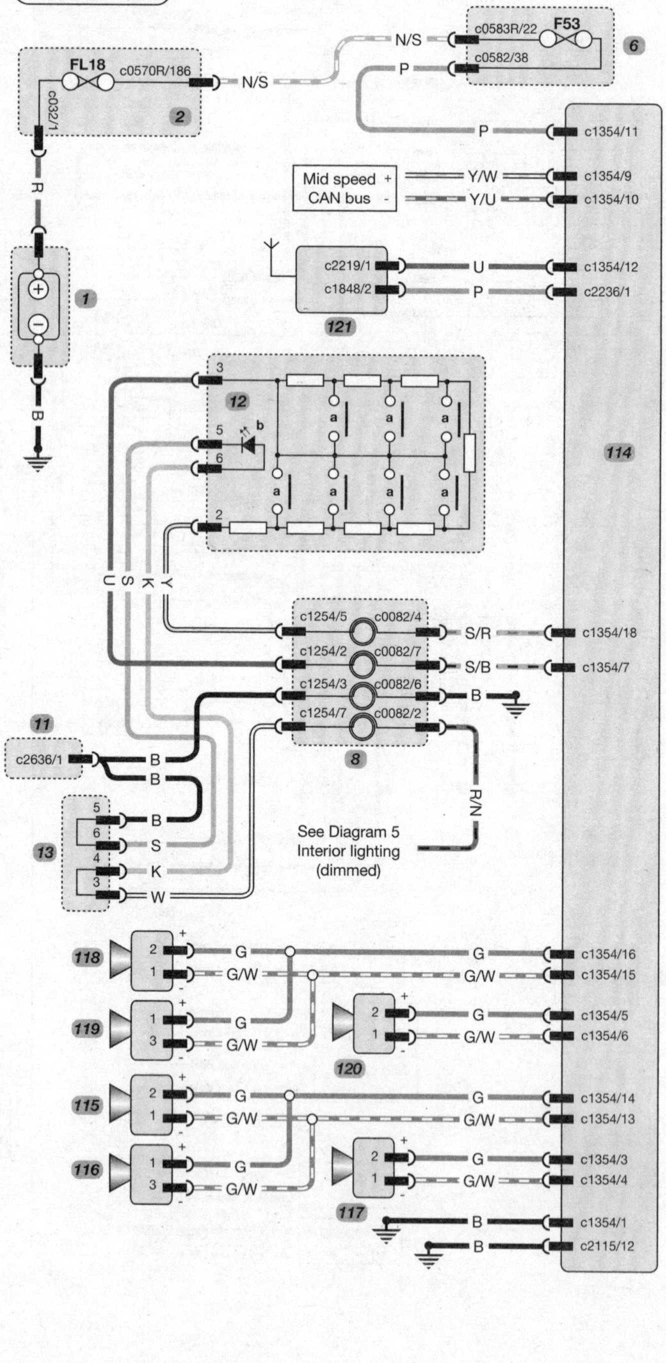

Colour codes

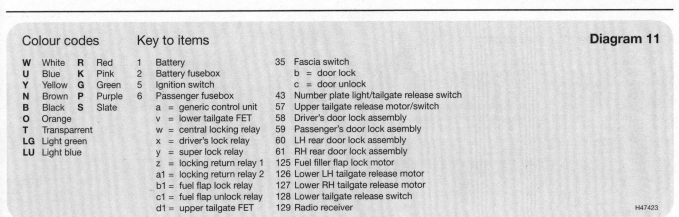

W	White	**R**	Red
U	Blue	**K**	Pink
Y	Yellow	**G**	Green
N	Brown	**P**	Purple
B	Black	**S**	Slate
O	Orange		
T	Transparrent		
LG	Light green		
LU	Light blue		

Key to items

Diagram 11

1 Battery
2 Battery fusebox
5 Ignition switch
6 Passenger fusebox
  a = generic control unit
  v = lower tailgate FET
  w = central locking relay
  x = driver's lock relay
  y = super lock relay
  z = locking return relay 1
  a1 = locking return relay 2
  b1 = fuel flap lock relay
  c1 = fuel flap unlock relay
  d1 = upper tailgate FET
35 Fascia switch
  b = door lock
  c = door unlock
43 Number plate light/tailgate release switch
57 Upper tailgate release motor/switch
58 Driver's door lock assembly
59 Passenger's door lock asembly
60 LH rear door lock assembly
61 RH rear door lock assembly
125 Fuel filler flap lock motor
126 Lower LH tailgate release motor
127 Lower RH tailgate release motor
128 Lower tailgate release switch
129 Radio receiver

H47423

Central locking

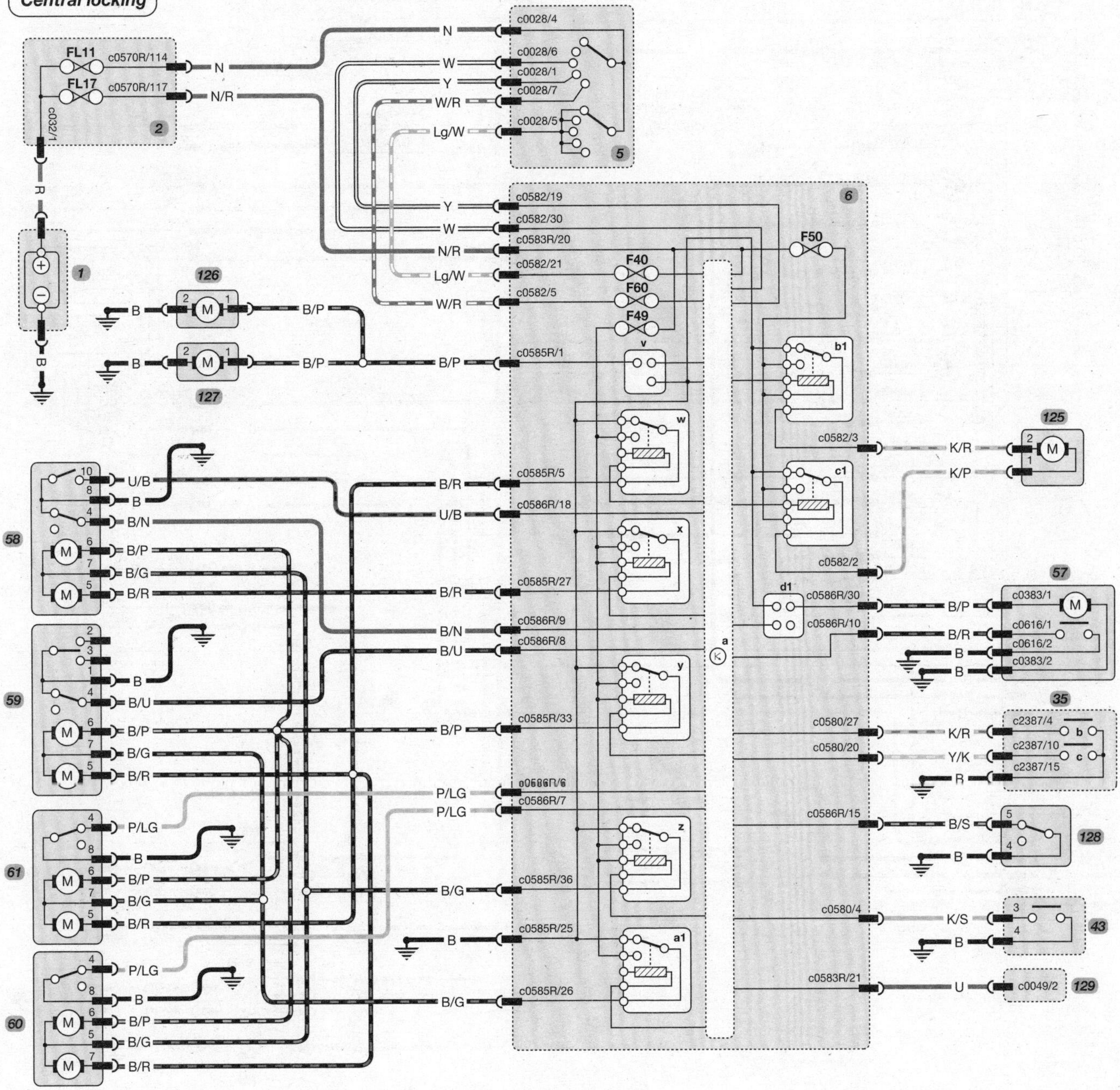

Diagram 12

Colour codes

W	White	**R**	Red
U	Blue	**K**	Pink
Y	Yellow	**G**	Green
N	Brown	**P**	Purple
B	Black	**S**	Slate
O	Orange		
T	Transparrent		
LG	Light green		
LU	Light blue		

Key to items

1 Battery
2 Battery fusebox
5 Ignition switch
6 Passenger fusebox
  a = generic control unit
  e1 = electric window relay
  f1 = open/close FET
58 Driver's door lock assembly
59 Passenger's door lock asembly
135 Driver's window door switch
  a = illumination
  b = driver's 'up'
  c = driver's 'auto-down'
  d = driver's down
  e = driver's 'auto-up'
  f = RH rear 'up'
  g = RH rear 'down'
  h = LH rear 'up'
  i = LH rear 'down'
  j = isolator switch
  k = passenger's 'up'
  l = passenger's 'down'
136 Driver's window motor
137 Passenger's window motor
138 LH rear window motor
139 RH rear window motor
140 Passenger's window switch
141 LH rear window switch
142 RH rear window switch

H47424

Electric windows

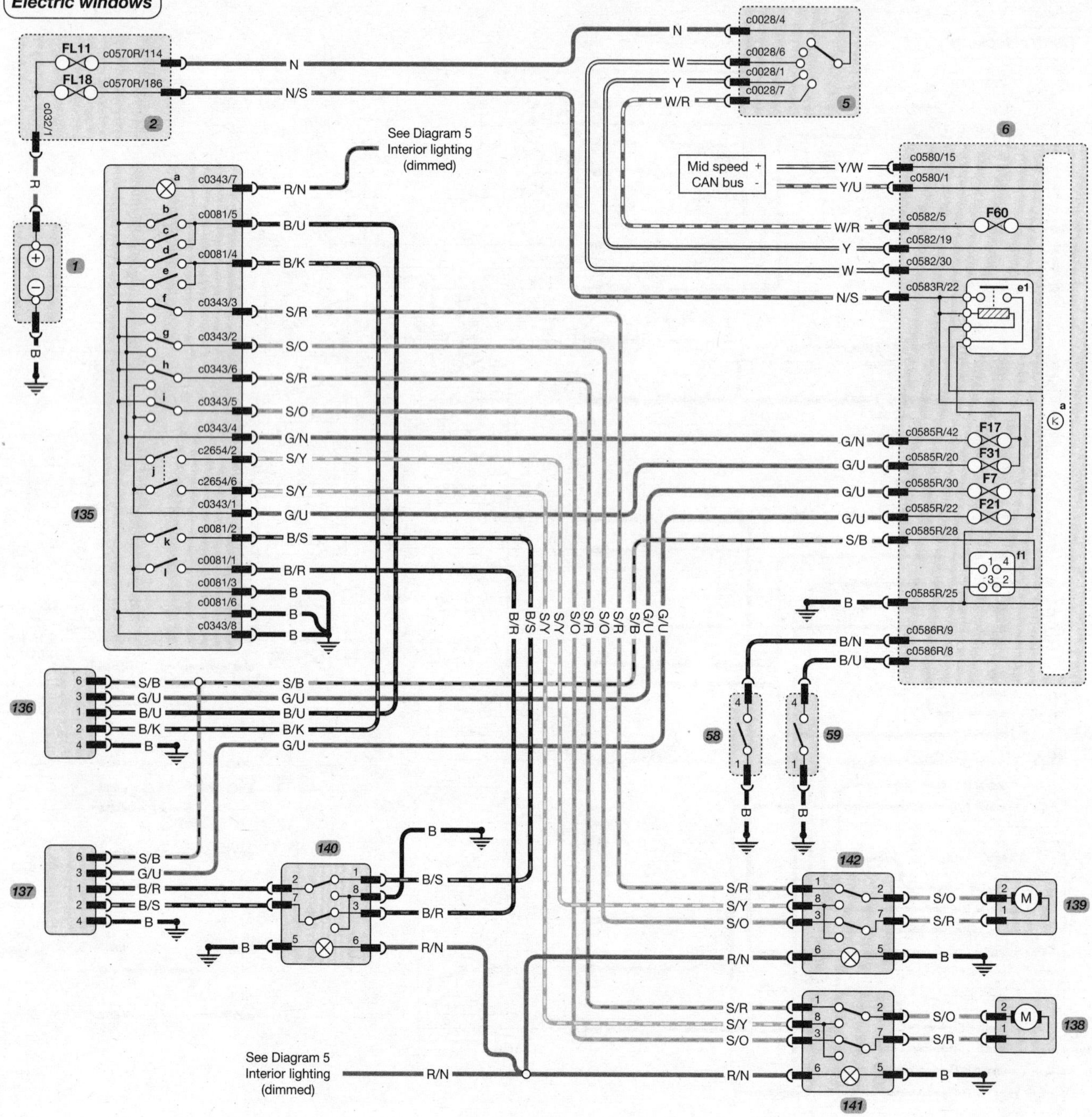

Dimensions and weights

Note: *All figures are approximate, and may vary according to model. Refer to manufacturer's data for exact figures.*

Dimensions

Overall length:	
Excluding tow hitch	4848 mm
Including tow hitch	4913 mm
Overall width (including mirrors)	2191 mm
Overall height:	
Access height	1837 mm
Standard height	1887 mm
Off-road height	1942 mm

Weights

Kerb weight (full fuel tank, excluding options)	2494 to 2704 kg
Maximum gross vehicle weight (all models)	3180 to 3230 kg
Maximum roof rack load:	
On-road	75 kg
Off-road	50 kg
Maximum trailer nose weight	150 kg
Maximum towing weight:	
Unbraked trailer:	
On-road	750 kg
Off-road	750 kg
Trailer with overrun brakes:	
On-road	3500 kg
Off-road	1000 kg

Fuel economy

Although depreciation is still the biggest part of the cost of motoring for most car owners, the cost of fuel is more immediately noticeable. These pages give some tips on how to get the best fuel economy.

Working it out

Manufacturer's figures

Car manufacturers are required by law to provide fuel consumption information on all new vehicles sold. These 'official' figures are obtained by simulating various driving conditions on a rolling road or a test track. Real life conditions are different, so the fuel consumption actually achieved may not bear much resemblance to the quoted figures.

How to calculate it

Many cars now have trip computers which will display fuel consumption, both instantaneous and average. Refer to the owner's handbook for details of how to use these.

To calculate consumption yourself (and maybe to check that the trip computer is accurate), proceed as follows.

1. Fill up with fuel and note the mileage, or zero the trip recorder.
2. Drive as usual until you need to fill up again.
3. Note the amount of fuel required to refill the tank, and the mileage covered since the previous fill-up.
4. Divide the mileage by the amount of fuel used to obtain the consumption figure.

For example:

Mileage at first fill-up (a) = 27,903
Mileage at second fill-up (b) = 28,346
Mileage covered (b - a) = 443
Fuel required at second fill-up = 48.6 litres

The half-completed changeover to metric units in the UK means that we buy our fuel in litres, measure distances in miles and talk about fuel consumption in miles per gallon. There are two ways round this: the first is to convert the litres to gallons before doing the calculation (by dividing by 4.546, or see Table 1). So in the example:

48.6 litres ÷ 4.546 = 10.69 gallons
443 miles ÷ 10.69 gallons = 41.4 mpg

The second way is to calculate the consumption in miles per litre, then multiply that figure by 4.546 (or see Table 2).

So in the example, fuel consumption is:

443 miles ÷ 48.6 litres = 9.1 mpl
9.1 mpl x 4.546 = 41.4 mpg

The rest of Europe expresses fuel consumption in litres of fuel required to travel 100 km (l/100 km). For interest, the conversions are given in Table 3. In practice it doesn't matter what units you use, provided you know what your normal consumption is and can spot if it's getting better or worse.

Table 1: conversion of litres to Imperial gallons

litres	1	2	3	4	5	10	20	30	40	50	60	70
gallons	0.22	0.44	0.66	0.88	1.10	2.24	4.49	6.73	8.98	11.22	13.47	15.71

Table 2: conversion of miles per litre to miles per gallon

miles per litre	5	6	7	8	9	10	11	12	13	14
miles per gallon	23	27	32	36	41	46	50	55	59	64

Table 3: conversion of litres per 100 km to miles per gallon

litres per 100 km	4	4.5	5	5.5	6	6.5	7	8	9	10
miles per gallon	71	63	56	51	47	43	40	35	31	28

Maintenance

A well-maintained car uses less fuel and creates less pollution. In particular:

Filters

Change air and fuel filters at the specified intervals.

Oil

Use a good quality oil of the lowest viscosity specified by the vehicle manufacturer (see *Lubricants and fluids*). Check the level often and be careful not to overfill.

Spark plugs

When applicable, renew at the specified intervals.

Tyres

Check tyre pressures regularly. Under-inflated tyres have an increased rolling resistance. It is generally safe to use the higher pressures specified for full load conditions even when not fully laden, but keep an eye on the centre band of tread for signs of wear due to over-inflation.

When buying new tyres, consider the 'fuel saving' models which most manufacturers include in their ranges.

Driving style

Acceleration

Acceleration uses more fuel than driving at a steady speed. The best technique with modern cars is to accelerate reasonably briskly to the desired speed, changing up through the gears as soon as possible without making the engine labour.

Air conditioning

Air conditioning absorbs quite a bit of energy from the engine – typically 3 kW (4 hp) or so. The effect on fuel consumption is at its worst in slow traffic. Switch it off when not required.

Anticipation

Drive smoothly and try to read the traffic flow so as to avoid unnecessary acceleration and braking.

Automatic transmission

When accelerating in an automatic, avoid depressing the throttle so far as to make the transmission hold onto lower gears at higher speeds. Don't use the 'Sport' setting, if applicable.

When stationary with the engine running, select 'N' or 'P'. When moving, keep your left foot away from the brake.

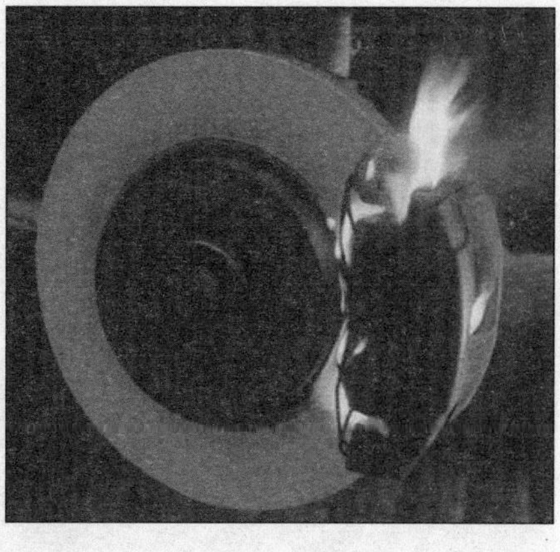

Braking

Braking converts the car's energy of motion into heat – essentially, it is wasted. Obviously some braking is always going to be necessary, but with good anticipation it is surprising how much can be avoided, especially on routes that you know well.

Carshare

Consider sharing lifts to work or to the shops. Even once a week will make a difference.

Electrical loads

Electricity is 'fuel' too; the alternator which charges the battery does so by converting some of the engine's energy of motion into electrical energy. The more electrical accessories are in use, the greater the load on the alternator. Switch off big consumers like the heated rear window when not required.

Freewheeling

Freewheeling (coasting) in neutral with the engine switched off is dangerous. The effort required to operate power-assisted brakes and steering increases when the engine is not running, with a potential lack of control in emergency situations.

In any case, modern fuel injection systems automatically cut off the engine's fuel supply on the overrun (moving and in gear, but with the accelerator pedal released).

Gadgets

Bolt-on devices claiming to save fuel have been around for nearly as long as the motor car itself. Those which worked were rapidly adopted as standard equipment by the vehicle manufacturers. Others worked only in certain situations, or saved fuel only at the expense of unacceptable effects on performance, driveability or the life of engine components.

The most effective fuel saving gadget is the driver's right foot.

Journey planning

Combine (eg) a trip to the supermarket with a visit to the recycling centre and the DIY store, rather than making separate journeys.

When possible choose a travelling time outside rush hours.

Load

The more heavily a car is laden, the greater the energy required to accelerate it to a given speed. Remove heavy items which you don't need to carry.

One load which is often overlooked is the contents of the fuel tank. A tankful of fuel (55 litres / 12 gallons) weighs 45 kg (100 lb) or so. Just half filling it may be worthwhile.

Lost?

At the risk of stating the obvious, if you're going somewhere new, have details of the route to hand. There's not much point in achieving record mpg if you also go miles out of your way.

Parking

If possible, carry out any reversing or turning manoeuvres when you arrive at a parking space so that you can drive straight out when you leave. Manoeuvering when the engine is cold uses a lot more fuel.

Driving around looking for free on-street parking may cost more in fuel than buying a car park ticket.

Premium fuel

Most major oil companies (and some supermarkets) have premium grades of fuel which are several pence a litre dearer than the standard grades. Reports vary, but the consensus seems to be that if these fuels improve economy at all, they do not do so by enough to justify their extra cost.

Roof rack

When loading a roof rack, try to produce a wedge shape with the narrow end at the front. Any cover should be securely fastened – if it flaps it's creating turbulence and absorbing energy.

Remove roof racks and boxes when not in use – they increase air resistance and can create a surprising amount of noise.

Short journeys

The engine is at its least efficient, and wear is highest, during the first few miles after a cold start. Consider walking, cycling or using public transport.

Speed

The engine is at its most efficient when running at a steady speed and load at the rpm where it develops maximum torque. (You can find this figure in the car's handbook.) For most cars this corresponds to between 55 and 65 mph in top gear.

Above the optimum cruising speed, fuel consumption starts to rise quite sharply. A car travelling at 80 mph will typically be using 30% more fuel than at 60 mph.

Supermarket fuel

It may be cheap but is it any good? In the UK all supermarket fuel must meet the relevant British Standard. The major oil companies will say that their branded fuels have better additive packages which may stop carbon and other deposits building up. A reasonable compromise might be to use one tank of branded fuel to three or four from the supermarket.

Switch off when stationary

Switch off the engine if you look like being stationary for more than 30 seconds or so. This is good for the environment as well as for your pocket. Be aware though that frequent restarts are hard on the battery and the starter motor.

Windows

Driving with the windows open increases air turbulence around the vehicle. Closing the windows promotes smooth airflow and reduced resistance. The faster you go, the more significant this is.

And finally . . .

Driving techniques associated with good fuel economy tend to involve moderate acceleration and low top speeds. Be considerate to the needs of other road users who may need to make brisker progress; even if you do not agree with them this is not an excuse to be obstructive.

Safety must always take precedence over economy, whether it is a question of accelerating hard to complete an overtaking manoeuvre, killing your speed when confronted with a potential hazard or switching the lights on when it starts to get dark.

Conversion factors

Length (distance)

Inches (in)	x 25.4	= Millimetres (mm)	x 0.0394	= Inches (in)
Feet (ft)	x 0.305	= Metres (m)	x 3.281	= Feet (ft)
Miles	x 1.609	= Kilometres (km)	x 0.621	= Miles

Volume (capacity)

Cubic inches (cu in; in^3)	x 16.387	= Cubic centimetres (cc; cm^3)	x 0.061	= Cubic inches (cu in; in^3)
Imperial pints (Imp pt)	x 0.568	= Litres (l)	x 1.76	= Imperial pints (Imp pt)
Imperial quarts (Imp qt)	x 1.137	= Litres (l)	x 0.88	= Imperial quarts (Imp qt)
Imperial quarts (Imp qt)	x 1.201	= US quarts (US qt)	x 0.833	= Imperial quarts (Imp qt)
US quarts (US qt)	x 0.946	= Litres (l)	x 1.057	= US quarts (US qt)
Imperial gallons (Imp gal)	x 4.546	= Litres (l)	x 0.22	= Imperial gallons (Imp gal)
Imperial gallons (Imp gal)	x 1.201	= US gallons (US gal)	x 0.833	= Imperial gallons (Imp gal)
US gallons (US gal)	x 3.785	= Litres (l)	x 0.264	= US gallons (US gal)

Mass (weight)

Ounces (oz)	x 28.35	= Grams (g)	x 0.035	= Ounces (oz)
Pounds (lb)	x 0.454	= Kilograms (kg)	x 2.205	= Pounds (lb)

Force

Ounces-force (ozf; oz)	x 0.278	= Newtons (N)	x 3.6	= Ounces-force (ozf; oz)
Pounds-force (lbf; lb)	x 4.448	= Newtons (N)	x 0.225	= Pounds-force (lbf; lb)
Newtons (N)	x 0.1	= Kilograms-force (kgf; kg)	x 9.81	= Newtons (N)

Pressure

Pounds-force per square inch (psi; lbf/in^2; lb/in^2)	x 0.070	= Kilograms-force per square centimetre (kgf/cm^2; kg/cm^2)	x 14.223	= Pounds-force per square inch (psi; lbf/in^2; lb/in^2)
Pounds-force per square inch (psi; lbf/in^2; lb/in^2)	x 0.068	= Atmospheres (atm)	x 14.696	= Pounds-force per square inch (psi; lbf/in^2; lb/in^2)
Pounds-force per square inch (psi; lbf/in^2; lb/in^2)	x 0.069	= Bars	x 14.5	= Pounds-force per square inch (psi; lbf/in^2; lb/in^2).
Pounds-force per square inch (psi; lbf/in^2; lb/in^2)	x 6.895	= Kilopascals (kPa)	x 0.145	= Pounds-force per square inch (psi; lbf/in^2; lb/in^2)
Kilopascals (kPa)	x 0.01	= Kilograms-force per square centimetre (kgf/cm^2; kg/cm^2)	x 98.1	= Kilopascals (kPa)
Millibar (mbar)	x 100	= Pascals (Pa)	x 0.01	= Millibar (mbar)
Millibar (mbar)	x 0.0145	= Pounds-force per square inch (psi; lbf/in^2; lb/in^2)	x 68.947	= Millibar (mbar)
Millibar (mbar)	x 0.75	= Millimetres of mercury (mmHg)	x 1.333	= Millibar (mbar)
Millibar (mbar)	x 0.401	= Inches of water (inH_2O)	x 2.491	= Millibar (mbar)
Millimetres of mercury (mmHg)	x 0.535	= Inches of water (inH_2O)	x 1.868	= Millimetres of mercury (mmHg)
Inches of water (inH_2O)	x 0.036	= Pounds-force per square inch (psi; lbf/in^2; lb/in^2)	x 27.68	= Inches of water (inH_2O)

Torque (moment of force)

Pounds-force inches (lbf in; lb in)	x 1.152	= Kilograms-force centimetre (kgf cm; kg cm)	x 0.868	= Pounds-force inches (lbf in; lb in)
Pounds-force inches (lbf in; lb in)	x 0.113	= Newton metres (Nm)	x 8.85	= Pounds-force inches (lbf in; lb in)
Pounds-force inches (lbf in; lb in)	x 0.083	= Pounds-force feet (lbf ft; lb ft)	x 12	= Pounds-force inches (lbf in; lb in)
Pounds-force feet (lbf ft; lb ft)	x 0.138	= Kilograms-force metres (kgf m; kg m)	x 7.233	= Pounds-force feet (lbf ft; lb ft)
Pounds-force feet (lbf ft; lb ft)	x 1.356	= Newton metres (Nm)	x 0.738	= Pounds-force feet (lbf ft; lb ft)
Newton metres (Nm)	x 0.102	= Kilograms-force metres (kgf m; kg m)	x 9.804	= Newton metres (Nm)

Power

Horsepower (hp)	x 745.7	= Watts (W)	x 0.0013	= Horsepower (hp)

Velocity (speed)

Miles per hour (miles/hr; mph)	x 1.609	= Kilometres per hour (km/hr; kph)	x 0.621	= Miles per hour (miles/hr; mph)

Fuel consumption*

Miles per gallon, Imperial (mpg)	x 0.354	= Kilometres per litre (km/l)	x 2.825	= Miles per gallon, Imperial (mpg)
Miles per gallon, US (mpg)	x 0.425	= Kilometres per litre (km/l)	x 2.352	= Miles per gallon, US (mpg)

Temperature

Degrees Fahrenheit = (°C x 1.8) + 32

Degrees Celsius (Degrees Centigrade; °C) = (°F - 32) x 0.56

** It is common practice to convert from miles per gallon (mpg) to litres/100 kilometres (l/100km), where mpg x l/100 km = 282*

Spare parts are available from many sources, including maker's appointed garages, accessory shops, and motor factors. To be sure of obtaining the correct parts, it will sometimes be necessary to quote the vehicle identification number. If possible, it can also be useful to take the old parts along for positive identification. Items such as starter motors and alternators may be available under a service exchange scheme – any parts returned should be clean.

Our advice regarding spare parts is as follows.

Officially appointed garages

This is the best source of parts which are peculiar to your car, and which are not otherwise generally available (eg, badges, interior trim, certain body panels, etc). It is also the only place at which you should buy parts if the car is still under warranty.

Accessory shops

These are very good places to buy materials and components needed for the maintenance of your car (oil, air and fuel filters, light bulbs, drivebelts, greases, brake pads, touch-up paint, etc). Components of this nature sold by a reputable shop are usually of the same standard as those used by the car manufacturer.

Besides components, these shops also sell tools and general accessories, usually have convenient opening hours, charge lower prices, and can often be found close to home. Some accessory shops have parts counters where components needed for almost any repair job can be purchased or ordered.

Motor factors

Good factors will stock all the more important components which wear out comparatively quickly, and can sometimes supply individual components needed for the overhaul of a larger assembly (eg, brake seals and hydraulic parts, bearing shells, pistons, valves). They may also handle work such as cylinder block reboring, crankshaft regrinding, etc.

Engine reconditioners

These specialise in engine overhaul and can also supply components. It is recommended that the establishment is a member of the Federation of Engine Re-Manufacturers, or a similar society.

Tyre and exhaust specialists

These outlets may be independent, or members of a local or national chain. They frequently offer competitive prices when compared with a main dealer or local garage, but it will pay to obtain several quotes before making a decision. When researching prices, also ask what extras may be added – for instance fitting a new valve, balancing the wheel and tyre disposal all both commonly charged on top of the price of a new tyre.

Other sources

Beware of parts or materials obtained from market stalls, car boot sales, on-line auctions or similar outlets. Such items are not invariably sub-standard, but there is little chance of compensation if they do prove unsatisfactory. In the case of safety-critical components such as brake pads, there is the risk not only of financial loss, but also of an accident causing injury or death.

Second-hand components or assemblies obtained from a car breaker can be a good buy in some circumstances, but this sort of purchase is best made by the experienced DIY mechanic.

Vehicle identification numbers

Modifications are a continuing and unpublicised process in vehicle manufacture, quite apart from major model changes. Spare parts manuals and lists are compiled upon a numerical basis, the individual vehicle identification numbers being essential to correct identification of the component concerned.

When ordering spare parts, always give as much information as possible. Quote the vehicle model, year of manufacture, body and engine numbers as appropriate.

The *Vehicle Identification Number (VIN) plate* is riveted to the top of the body front panel, and can be viewed once the bonnet is open **(see illustration)**. The plate carries the VIN number, vehicle weight information and paint and trim colour codes. The VIN number is also repeated on a plate fixed to the facia, visible through the lower left-hand corner of the windscreen, and also stamped on the right-hand longitudinal chassis member beneath the driver's door **(see illustration)**.

The *engine number* is stamped into the cylinder block, on the right-hand side of the cylinder block, just below the joint with the cylinder head.

The *transmission identification number* is stamped into a flat on the bottom right-hand side of the transmission casing.

The *transfer gearbox identification number* is stamped into the lower left-hand side of the gearbox casing.

The VIN is stamped onto a plate on the bonnet slam panel (arrowed) ...

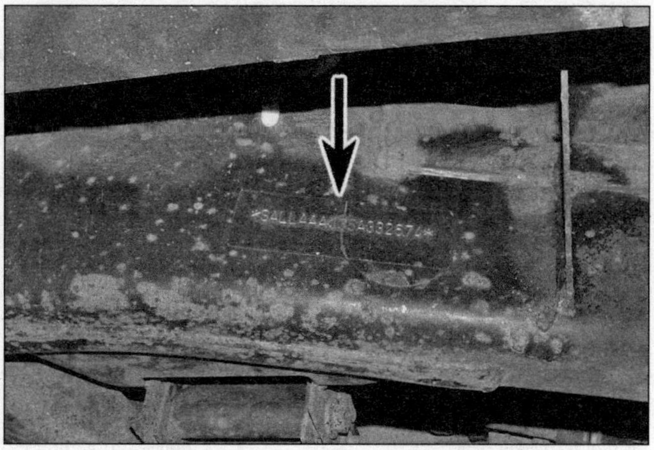

... and the right-hand chassis member (arrowed)

Whenever servicing, repair or overhaul work is carried out on the car or its components, observe the following procedures and instructions. This will assist in carrying out the operation efficiently and to a professional standard of workmanship.

Joint mating faces and gaskets

When separating components at their mating faces, never insert screwdrivers or similar implements into the joint between the faces in order to prise them apart. This can cause severe damage which results in oil leaks, coolant leaks, etc upon reassembly. Separation is usually achieved by tapping along the joint with a soft-faced hammer in order to break the seal. However, note that this method may not be suitable where dowels are used for component location.

Where a gasket is used between the mating faces of two components, a new one must be fitted on reassembly; fit it dry unless otherwise stated in the repair procedure. Make sure that the mating faces are clean and dry, with all traces of old gasket removed. When cleaning a joint face, use a tool which is unlikely to score or damage the face, and remove any burrs or nicks with an oilstone or fine file.

Make sure that tapped holes are cleaned with a pipe cleaner, and keep them free of jointing compound, if this is being used, unless specifically instructed otherwise.

Ensure that all orifices, channels or pipes are clear, and blow through them, preferably using compressed air.

Oil seals

Oil seals can be removed by levering them out with a wide flat-bladed screwdriver or similar implement. Alternatively, a number of self-tapping screws may be screwed into the seal, and these used as a purchase for pliers or some similar device in order to pull the seal free.

Whenever an oil seal is removed from its working location, either individually or as part of an assembly, it should be renewed.

The very fine sealing lip of the seal is easily damaged, and will not seal if the surface it contacts is not completely clean and free from scratches, nicks or grooves. If the original sealing surface of the component cannot be restored, and the manufacturer has not made provision for slight relocation of the seal relative to the sealing surface, the component should be renewed.

Protect the lips of the seal from any surface which may damage them in the course of fitting. Use tape or a conical sleeve where possible. Where indicated, lubricate the seal lips with oil before fitting and, on dual-lipped seals, fill the space between the lips with grease.

Unless otherwise stated, oil seals must be fitted with their sealing lips toward the lubricant to be sealed.

Use a tubular drift or block of wood of the appropriate size to install the seal and, if the seal housing is shouldered, drive the seal down to the shoulder. If the seal housing is unshouldered, the seal should be fitted with its face flush with the housing top face (unless otherwise instructed).

Screw threads and fastenings

Seized nuts, bolts and screws are quite a common occurrence where corrosion has set in, and the use of penetrating oil or releasing fluid will often overcome this problem if the offending item is soaked for a while before attempting to release it. The use of an impact driver may also provide a means of releasing such stubborn fastening devices, when used in conjunction with the appropriate screwdriver bit or socket. If none of these methods works, it may be necessary to resort to the careful application of heat, or the use of a hacksaw or nut splitter device. Before resorting to extreme methods, check that you are not dealing with a left-hand thread!

Studs are usually removed by locking two nuts together on the threaded part, and then using a spanner on the lower nut to unscrew the stud. Studs or bolts which have broken off below the surface of the component in which they are mounted can sometimes be removed using a stud extractor.

Always ensure that a blind tapped hole is completely free from oil, grease, water or other fluid before installing the bolt or stud. Failure to do this could cause the housing to crack due to the hydraulic action of the bolt or stud as it is screwed in.

For some screw fastenings, notably cylinder head bolts or nuts, torque wrench settings are no longer specified for the latter stages of tightening, "angle-tightening" being called up instead. Typically, a fairly low torque wrench setting will be applied to the bolts/nuts in the correct sequence, followed by one or more stages of tightening through specified angles.

When checking or retightening a nut or bolt to a specified torque setting, slacken the nut or bolt by a quarter of a turn, and then retighten to the specified setting. However, this should not be attempted where angular tightening has been used.

Locknuts, locktabs and washers

Any fastening which will rotate against a component or housing during tightening should always have a washer between it and the relevant component or housing.

Spring or split washers should always be renewed when they are used to lock a critical component such as a big-end bearing retaining bolt or nut. Locktabs which are folded over to retain a nut or bolt should always be renewed.

Self-locking nuts can be re-used in non-critical areas, providing resistance can be felt when the locking portion passes over the bolt or stud thread. However, it should be noted that self-locking stiffnuts tend to lose their effectiveness after long periods of use, and should then be renewed as a matter of course.

Split pins must always be replaced with new ones of the correct size for the hole.

When thread-locking compound is found on the threads of a fastener which is to be re-used, it should be cleaned off with a wire brush and solvent, and fresh compound applied on reassembly.

Special tools

Some repair procedures in this manual entail the use of special tools such as a press, two or three-legged pullers, spring compressors, etc. Wherever possible, suitable readily-available alternatives to the manufacturer's special tools are described, and are shown in use. In some instances, where no alternative is possible, it has been necessary to resort to the use of a manufacturer's tool, and this has been done for reasons of safety as well as the efficient completion of the repair operation. Unless you are highly-skilled and have a thorough understanding of the procedures described, never attempt to bypass the use of any special tool when the procedure described specifies its use. Not only is there a very great risk of personal injury, but expensive damage could be caused to the components involved.

Environmental considerations

When disposing of used engine oil, brake fluid, antifreeze, etc, give due consideration to any detrimental environmental effects. Do not, for instance, pour any of the above liquids down drains into the general sewage system, or onto the ground to soak away. Many local council refuse tips provide a facility for waste oil disposal, as do some garages. You can find your nearest disposal point by calling the Environment Agency on 08708 506 506 or by visiting www.oilbankline.org.uk.

OIL CARE

FOLLOW THE CODE

Note: It is illegal and anti-social to dump oil down the drain. To find the location of your local oil recycling bank, call 08708 506 506 or visit www.oilbankline.org.uk.

Warning: *The parking brake acts on the transmission, not the rear wheels, and may not hold the vehicle stationary when jacking. If one front wheel and one rear wheel are raised, no vehicle holding or braking effect is possible using the parking brake, therefore the wheels must always be chocked (using the chock supplied in the tool kit). If the vehicle is coupled to a trailer, disconnect the trailer from the vehicle before commencing jacking. This is to prevent the trailer pulling the vehicle off the jack and causing personal injury.*

Using the vehicle jack

The jack supplied with the vehicle tool kit should only be used for changing the roadwheels, as described in *Wheel changing* at the front of this Manual.

When jacking up a wheel, only slide the jack into position from the side of the vehicle. Position the jack head so that when raised, it will engage with the notch in the radius arm (steel coil spring suspension) or the locating hole in the chassis (air suspension) **(see illustration)**.

Using a hydraulic (trolley) jack and axle stands

Note: *To raise the vehicle, a hydraulic jack with a minimum load capacity of 1500 kg must be used.* **Never** *work under a vehicle supported solely by a hydraulic jack, as even a hydraulic jack could fail under load – always supplement the jack with axle stands. Do not use piles of bricks or wooden blocks for supporting – the Discovery is a heavy vehicle, and makeshift methods should not be used.*

When carrying out any other kind of work, raise the vehicle using a hydraulic jack, and always supplement the jack with axle stands positioned under the axles or the chassis side members. **Do not** jack the vehicle, or position axle stands under any of the following components:

a) Body structure.
b) Bumpers.
c) Underbody pipes and hoses.
d) Gearbox/transmission/transfer gearbox housings.
e) Engine sump.
f) Fuel tank.

Only ever jack the vehicle up on a solid, level surface. If there is even a slight slope, take great care that the vehicle cannot move as the wheels are lifted off the ground. Jacking up on an uneven or gravelled surface is not recommended, as the weight of the vehicle will not be evenly distributed, and the jack may slip as the vehicle is raised.

As far as possible, do not leave the vehicle unattended once it has been raised, particularly if children are playing nearby.

To raise the front of the vehicle, chock the rear roadwheels, then position the jack head under the centre of the recess in the engine undershield **(see illustration)**. If the undershield has been removed, position the jack head under the centre of the front crossmember. Raise the jack, position axle stands at the front of the longitudinal chassis members as shown **(see illustration)**, then lower the jack until the vehicle rests securely on the axle stands.

To raise the rear of the vehicle, chock the front roadwheels, then position the jack head under the centre of the rear crossmember **(see illustration)**. Raise the jack, position axle stands under the rear of the longitudinal chassis members as shown, then lower the jack until the vehicle rests securely on the axle stands.

Wheel fitting

When refitting a roadwheel, ensure the hub and wheel mating surfaces are clean and free from debris. Where alloy wheels are fitted, apply a little anti-seize compound to the mating surfaces to prevent the wheels sticking in future. If this is not practical at the time, fit the roadwheel, but remove it later to apply the compound. Take care not to allow any of the compound to come into contact with the brake friction surfaces.

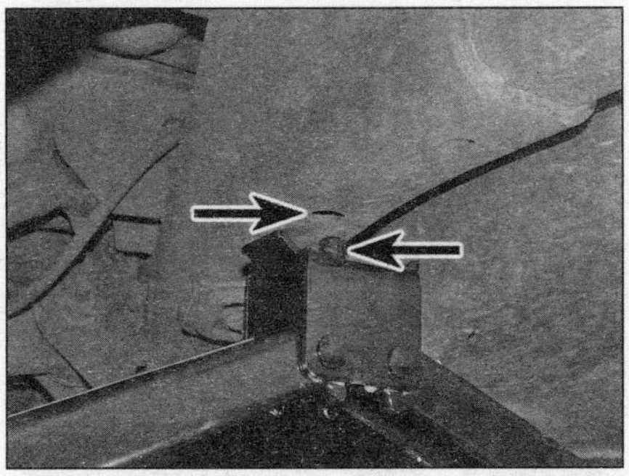

The pin on the top of the jack must engage with the hole in the chassis member (arrowed)

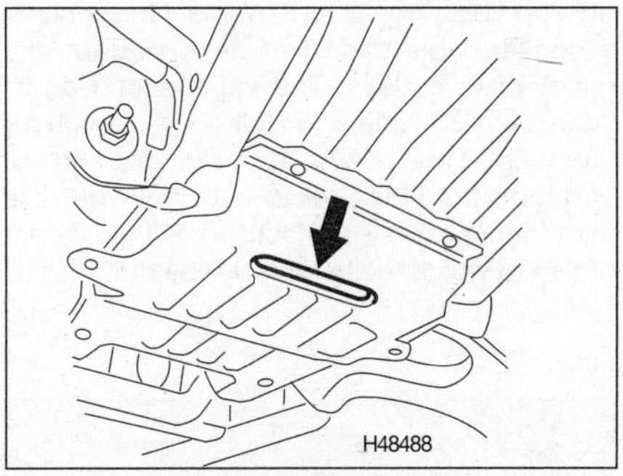

Position the jack head under the recess in the engine undershield (beneath the crossmember)

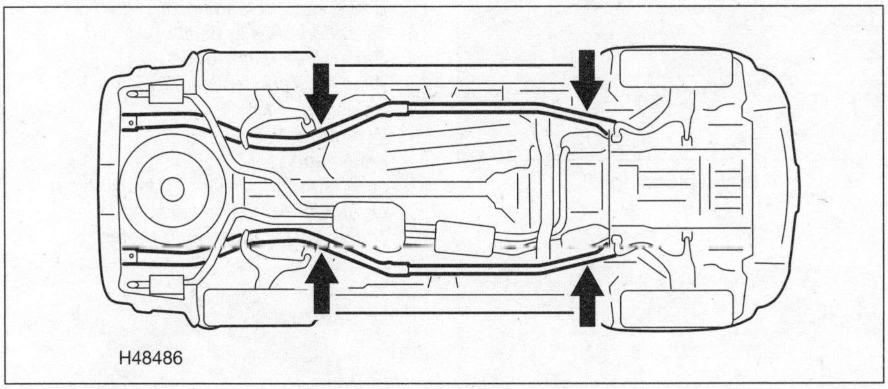

Front and rear axle stand positions

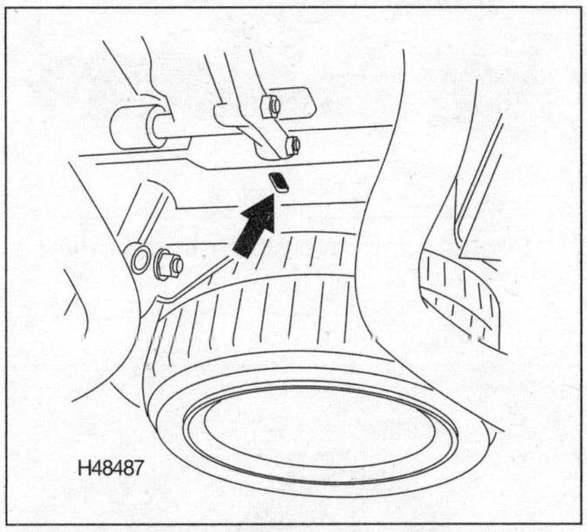

Position the jack head under the rear crossmember (arrowed)

Introduction

A selection of good tools is a fundamental requirement for anyone contemplating the maintenance and repair of a motor vehicle. For the owner who does not possess any, their purchase will prove a considerable expense, offsetting some of the savings made by doing-it-yourself. However, provided that the tools purchased meet the relevant national safety standards and are of good quality, they will last for many years and prove an extremely worthwhile investment.

To help the average owner to decide which tools are needed to carry out the various tasks detailed in this manual, we have compiled three lists of tools under the following headings: *Maintenance and minor repair*, *Repair and overhaul*, and *Special*. Newcomers to practical mechanics should start off with the *Maintenance and minor repair* tool kit, and confine themselves to the simpler jobs around the vehicle. Then, as confidence and experience grow, more difficult tasks can be undertaken, with extra tools being purchased as, and when, they are needed. In this way, a *Maintenance and minor repair* tool kit can be built up into a *Repair and overhaul* tool kit over a considerable period of time, without any major cash outlays. The experienced do-it-yourselfer will have a tool kit good enough for most repair and overhaul procedures, and will add tools from the *Special* category when it is felt that the expense is justified by the amount of use to which these tools will be put.

Maintenance and minor repair tool kit

The tools given in this list should be considered as a minimum requirement if routine maintenance, servicing and minor repair operations are to be undertaken. We recommend the purchase of combination spanners (ring one end, open-ended the other); although more expensive than open-ended ones, they do give the advantages of both types of spanner.

- ☐ *Combination spanners:*
  Metric - 8 to 19 mm inclusive
- ☐ *Adjustable spanner - 35 mm jaw (approx.)*
- ☐ *Spark plug spanner (with rubber insert) - petrol models*
- ☐ *Spark plug gap adjustment tool - petrol models*
- ☐ *Set of feeler gauges*
- ☐ *Brake bleed nipple spanner*
- ☐ *Screwdrivers:*
  Flat blade - 100 mm long x 6 mm dia
  Cross blade - 100 mm long x 6 mm dia
  Torx - various sizes (not all vehicles)
- ☐ *Combination pliers*
- ☐ *Hacksaw (junior)*
- ☐ *Tyre pump*
- ☐ *Tyre pressure gauge*
- ☐ *Oil can*
- ☐ *Oil filter removal tool (if applicable)*
- ☐ *Fine emery cloth*
- ☐ *Wire brush (small)*
- ☐ *Funnel (medium size)*
- ☐ *Sump drain plug key (not all vehicles)*

Repair and overhaul tool kit

These tools are virtually essential for anyone undertaking any major repairs to a motor vehicle, and are additional to those given in the *Maintenance and minor repair* list. Included in this list is a comprehensive set of sockets. Although these are expensive, they will be found invaluable as they are so versatile - particularly if various drives are included in the set. We recommend the half-inch square-drive type, as this can be used with most proprietary torque wrenches.

The tools in this list will sometimes need to be supplemented by tools from the *Special* list:

- ☐ *Sockets to cover range in previous list (including Torx sockets)*
- ☐ *Reversible ratchet drive (for use with sockets)*
- ☐ *Extension piece, 250 mm (for use with sockets)*
- ☐ *Universal joint (for use with sockets)*
- ☐ *Flexible handle or sliding T "breaker bar" (for use with sockets)*
- ☐ *Torque wrench (for use with sockets)*
- ☐ *Self-locking grips*
- ☐ *Ball pein hammer*
- ☐ *Soft-faced mallet (plastic or rubber)*
- ☐ *Screwdrivers:*
  Flat blade - long & sturdy, short (chubby), and narrow (electrician's) types
  Cross blade – long & sturdy, and short (chubby) types
- ☐ *Pliers:*
  Long-nosed
  Side cutters (electrician's)
  Circlip (internal and external)
- ☐ *Cold chisel - 25 mm*
- ☐ *Scriber*
- ☐ *Scraper*
- ☐ *Centre-punch*
- ☐ *Pin punch*
- ☐ *Hacksaw*
- ☐ *Brake hose clamp*
- ☐ *Brake/clutch bleeding kit*
- ☐ *Selection of twist drills*
- ☐ *Steel rule/straight-edge*
- ☐ *Allen keys (inc. splined/Torx type)*
- ☐ *Selection of files*
- ☐ *Wire brush*
- ☐ *Axle stands*
- ☐ *Jack (strong trolley or hydraulic type)*
- ☐ *Light with extension lead*
- ☐ *Universal electrical multi-meter*

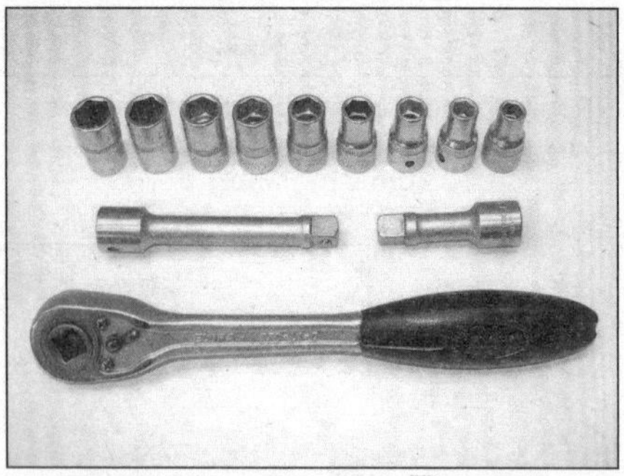

Sockets and reversible ratchet drive

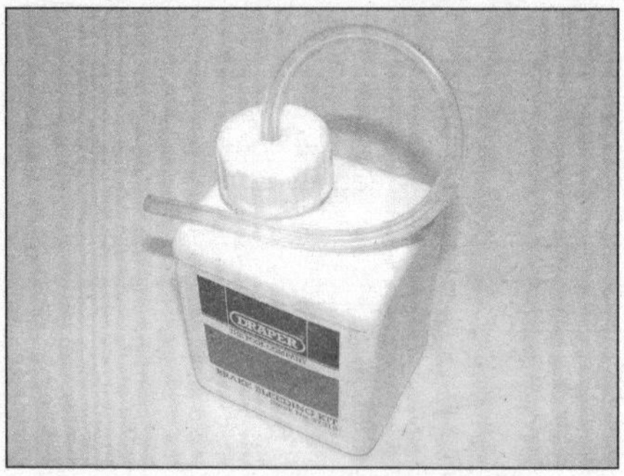

Brake bleeding kit

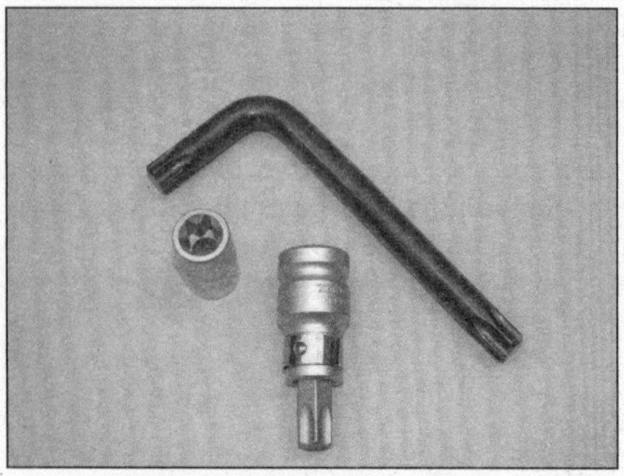

Torx key, socket and bit

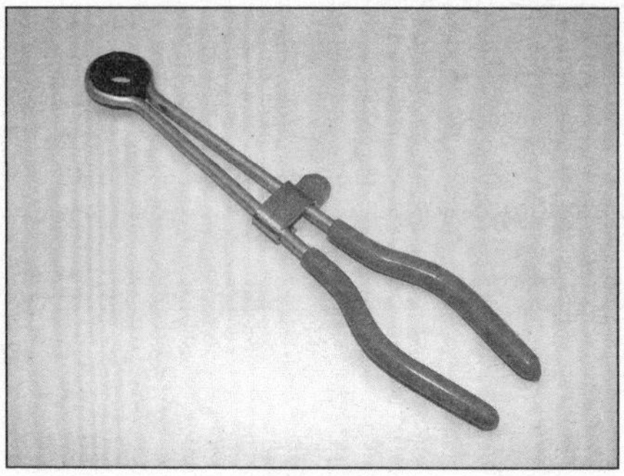

Hose clamp

Angular-tightening gauge

Special tools

The tools in this list are those which are not used regularly, are expensive to buy, or which need to be used in accordance with their manufacturers' instructions. Unless relatively difficult mechanical jobs are undertaken frequently, it will not be economic to buy many of these tools. Where this is the case, you could consider clubbing together with friends (or joining a motorists' club) to make a joint purchase, or borrowing the tools against a deposit from a local garage or tool hire specialist.

The following list contains only those tools and instruments freely available to the public, and not those special tools produced by the vehicle manufacturer specifically for its dealer network. You will find occasional references to these manufacturers' special tools in the text of this manual. Generally, an alternative method of doing the job without the vehicle manufacturers' special tool is given. However, sometimes there is no alternative to using them. Where this is the case and the relevant tool cannot be bought or borrowed, you will have to entrust the work to a dealer.

- ☐ *Angular-tightening gauge*
- ☐ *Valve spring compressor*
- ☐ *Valve grinding tool*
- ☐ *Piston ring compressor*
- ☐ *Piston ring removal/installation tool*
- ☐ *Cylinder bore hone*
- ☐ *Balljoint separator*
- ☐ *Coil spring compressors (where applicable)*
- ☐ *Two/three-legged hub and bearing puller*
- ☐ *Impact screwdriver*
- ☐ *Micrometer and/or vernier calipers*
- ☐ *Dial gauge*
- ☐ *Tachometer*
- ☐ *Fault code reader*
- ☐ *Cylinder compression gauge*
- ☐ *Hand-operated vacuum pump and gauge*
- ☐ *Clutch plate alignment set*
- ☐ *Brake shoe steady spring cup removal tool*
- ☐ *Bush and bearing removal/installation set*
- ☐ *Stud extractors*
- ☐ *Tap and die set*
- ☐ *Lifting tackle*

Buying tools

Reputable motor accessory shops and superstores often offer excellent quality tools at discount prices, so it pays to shop around.

Remember, you don't have to buy the most expensive items on the shelf, but it is always advisable to steer clear of the very cheap tools. Beware of 'bargains' offered on market stalls, on-line or at car boot sales. There are plenty of good tools around at reasonable prices, but always aim to purchase items which meet the relevant national safety standards. If in doubt, ask the proprietor or manager of the shop for advice before making a purchase.

Care and maintenance of tools

Having purchased a reasonable tool kit, it is necessary to keep the tools in a clean and serviceable condition. After use, always wipe off any dirt, grease and metal particles using a clean, dry cloth, before putting the tools away. Never leave them lying around after they have been used. A simple tool rack on the garage or workshop wall for items such as screwdrivers and pliers is a good idea. Store all normal spanners and sockets in a metal box. Any measuring instruments, gauges, meters, etc, must be carefully stored where they cannot be damaged or become rusty.

Take a little care when tools are used. Hammer heads inevitably become marked, and screwdrivers lose the keen edge on their blades from time to time. A little timely attention with emery cloth or a file will soon restore items like this to a good finish.

Working facilities

Not to be forgotten when discussing tools is the workshop itself. If anything more than routine maintenance is to be carried out, a suitable working area becomes essential.

It is appreciated that many an owner-mechanic is forced by circumstances to remove an engine or similar item without the benefit of a garage or workshop. Having done this, any repairs should always be done under the cover of a roof.

Wherever possible, any dismantling should be done on a clean, flat workbench or table at a suitable working height.

Any workbench needs a vice; one with a jaw opening of 100 mm is suitable for most jobs. As mentioned previously, some clean dry storage space is also required for tools, as well as for any lubricants, cleaning fluids, touch-up paints etc, which become necessary.

Another item which may be required, and which has a much more general usage, is an electric drill with a chuck capacity of at least 8 mm. This, together with a good range of twist drills, is virtually essential for fitting accessories.

Last, but not least, always keep a supply of old newspapers and clean, lint-free rags available, and try to keep any working area as clean as possible.

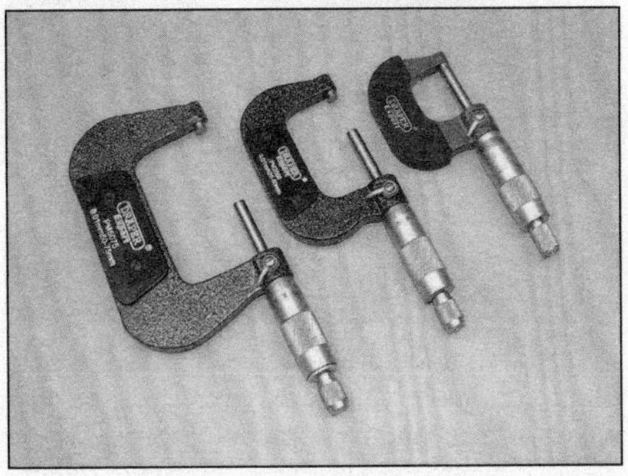

Micrometers

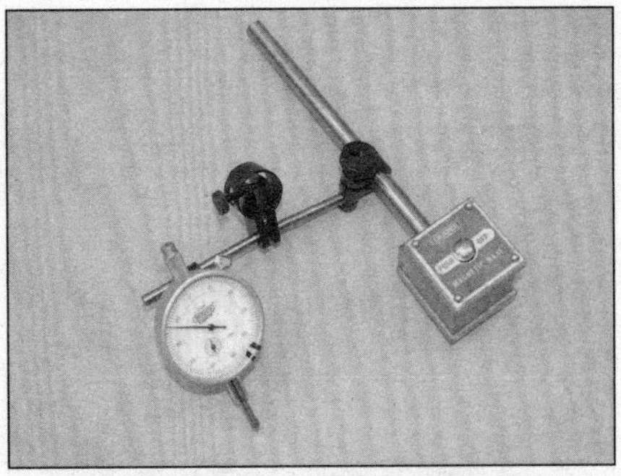

Dial test indicator ("dial gauge")

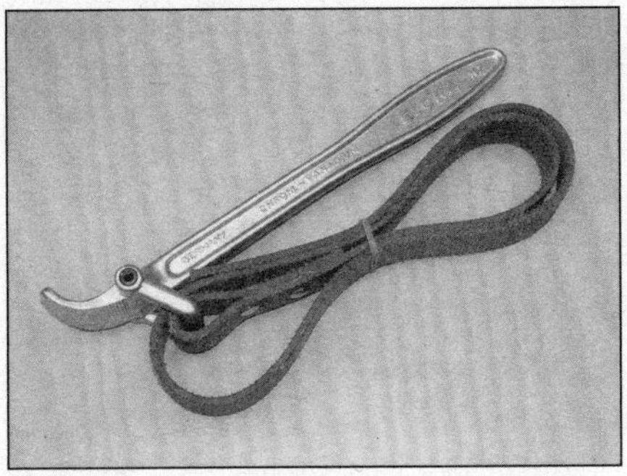

Oil filter removal tool (strap wrench type)

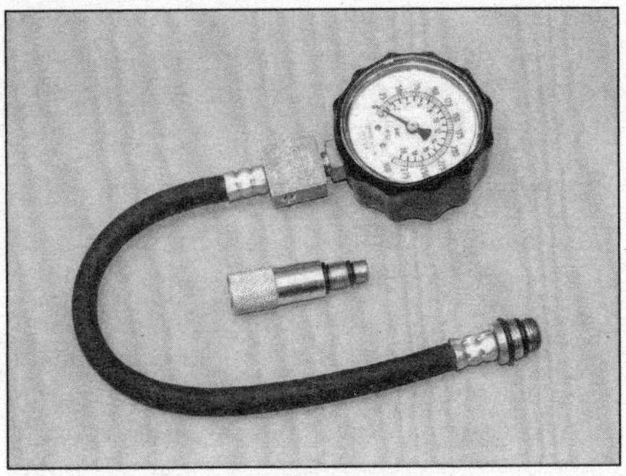

Compression tester

Bearing puller

MOT test checks

This is a guide to getting your vehicle through the MOT test. Obviously it will not be possible to examine the vehicle to the same standard as the professional MOT tester. However, working through the following checks will enable you to identify any problem areas before submitting the vehicle for the test.

It has only been possible to summarise the test requirements here, based on the regulations in force at the time of printing. Test standards are becoming increasingly stringent, although there are some exemptions for older vehicles.

An assistant will be needed to help carry out some of these checks.

The checks have been sub-divided into four categories, as follows:

1 Checks carried out **FROM THE DRIVER'S SEAT**

2 Checks carried out **WITH THE VEHICLE ON THE GROUND**

3 Checks carried out **WITH THE VEHICLE RAISED AND THE WHEELS FREE TO TURN**

4 Checks carried out on **YOUR VEHICLE'S EXHAUST EMISSION SYSTEM**

1 Checks carried out FROM THE DRIVER'S SEAT

Handbrake (parking brake)

☐Test the operation of the handbrake. Excessive travel (too many clicks) indicates incorrect brake or cable adjustment.

☐Check that the handbrake cannot be released by tapping the lever sideways. Check the security of the lever mountings.

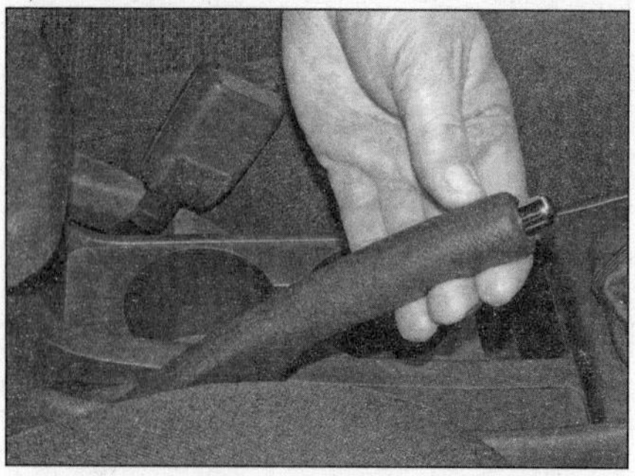

☐If the parking brake is foot-operated, check that the pedal is secure and without excessive travel, and that the release mechanism operates correctly.

☐Where applicable, test the operation of the electronic handbrake. The brake should engage and disengage without excessive delay. If the warning light does not extinguish when the brake is disengaged, this could indicate a fault which will need further investigation.

Footbrake

☐Depress the brake pedal and check that it does not creep down to the floor, indicating a master cylinder fault. Release the pedal, wait a few seconds, then depress it again. If the pedal travels nearly to the floor before firm resistance is felt, brake adjustment or repair is necessary. If the pedal feels spongy, there is air in the hydraulic system which must be removed by bleeding.

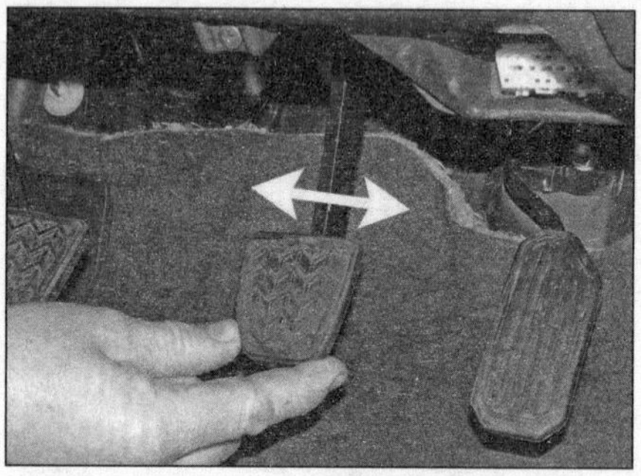

☐Check that the brake pedal is secure and in good condition. Check also for signs of fluid leaks on the pedal, floor or carpets, which would indicate failed seals in the brake master cylinder.

☐Check the servo unit (when applicable) by operating the brake pedal several times, then keeping the pedal depressed and starting the engine. As the engine starts, the pedal will move down slightly. If not, the vacuum hose or the servo itself may be faulty.

Steering wheel and column

☐Examine the steering wheel for fractures or looseness of the hub, spokes or rim.

☐Move the steering wheel from side to side and then up and down. Check that the steering wheel is not loose on the column, indicating wear or a loose retaining nut. Continue moving the steering wheel as before, but also turn it slightly from left to right.

☐Check that the steering wheel is not loose on the column, and that there is no abnormal movement of the steering wheel, indicating wear in the column support bearings or couplings.

☐Check that the ignition lock (where fitted) engages and disengages correctly.

☐Steering column adjustment mechanisms (where fitted) must be able to lock the column securely in place with no play evident.

Windscreen, mirrors and sunvisor

☐The windscreen must be free of cracks or other significant damage within the driver's field of view. (Small stone chips are acceptable.) Rear view mirrors must be secure, intact, and capable of being adjusted.

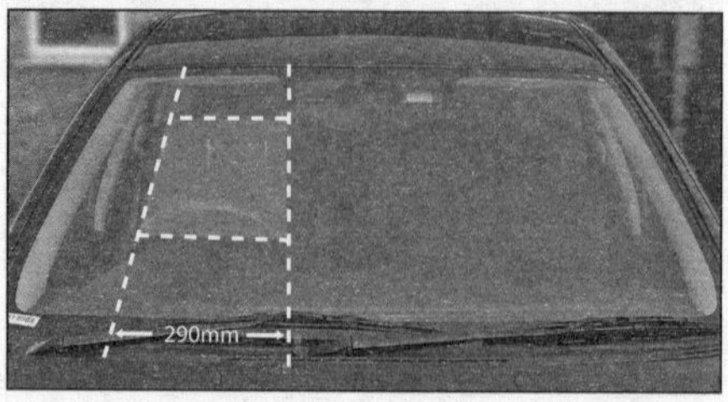

☐ The driver's sunvisor must be capable of being stored in the "up" position.

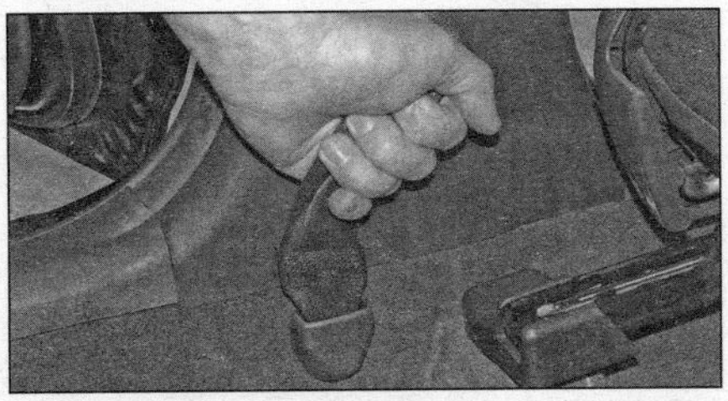

Seat belts and seats

Note: *The following checks are applicable to all seat belts, front and rear.*

☐ Examine the webbing of all the belts (including rear belts if fitted) for cuts, serious fraying or deterioration. Fasten and unfasten each belt to check the buckles. If applicable, check the retracting mechanism. Check the security of all seat belt mountings accessible from inside the vehicle, ensuring any height adjustable mountings lock securely in place.

☐ Seat belts with pre-tensioners, once activated, have a "flag" or similar showing on the seat belt stalk. This, in itself, is not a reason for test failure.

☐ The front seats themselves must be securely attached and the backrests must lock in the upright position.

Doors

☐ Both front doors must be able to be opened and closed from outside and inside, and must latch securely when closed.

Bonnet and boot/tailgate

☐ The bonnet and boot/tailgate must latch securely when closed.

2 Checks carried out WITH THE VEHICLE ON THE GROUND

Vehicle identification

☐ Number plates must be in good condition, secure and legible, with letters and numbers correctly spaced – spacing at (A) should be 33 mm and at (B) 11 mm. At the front, digits must be black on a white background and at the rear black on a yellow background. Other background designs (such as honeycomb) are not permitted.

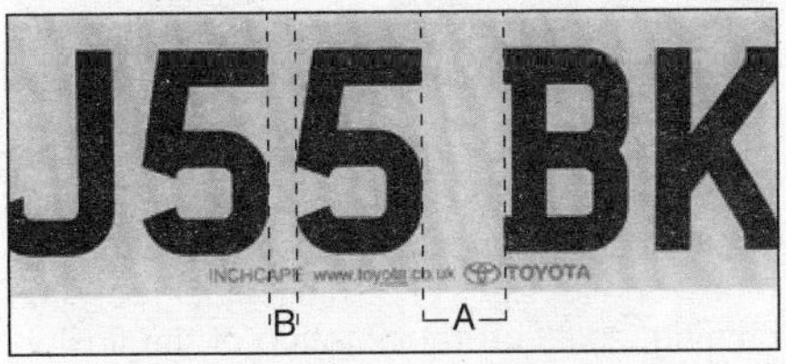

☐ The VIN plate and/or homologation plate must be permanently displayed and legible.

Electrical equipment

☐ Switch on the ignition and check the operation of the horn.

☐ Check the windscreen washers and wipers, examining the wiper blades; renew damaged or perished blades. Also check the operation of the stop-lights.

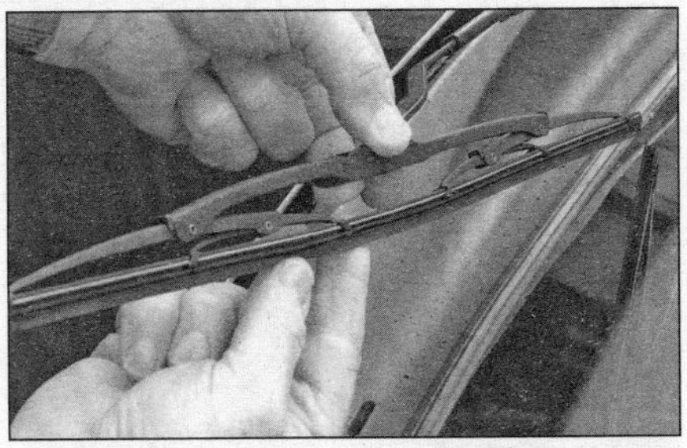

☐ Check the operation of the sidelights and number plate lights. The lenses and reflectors must be secure, clean and undamaged.

☐ Check the operation and alignment of the headlights. The headlight reflectors must not be tarnished and the lenses must be undamaged.

☐ Switch on the ignition and check the operation of the direction indicators (including the instrument panel tell-tale) and the hazard warning lights. Operation of the sidelights and stop-lights must not affect the indicators - if it does, the cause is usually a bad earth at the rear light cluster. Indicators should flash at a rate of between 60 and 120 times per minute – faster or slower than this could indicate a fault with the flasher unit or a bad earth at one of the light units.

☐ Check the operation of the rear foglight(s), including the warning light on the instrument panel or in the switch.

☐ The warning lights must illuminate in accordance with the manufacturer's design. For most vehicles, the ABS and other warning lights should illuminate when the ignition is switched on, and (if the system is operating properly) extinguish after a few seconds. Refer to the owner's handbook.

Footbrake

☐ Examine the master cylinder, brake pipes and servo unit for leaks, loose mountings, corrosion or other damage. If ABS is fitted, this unit should also be examined for signs of leaks or corrosion.

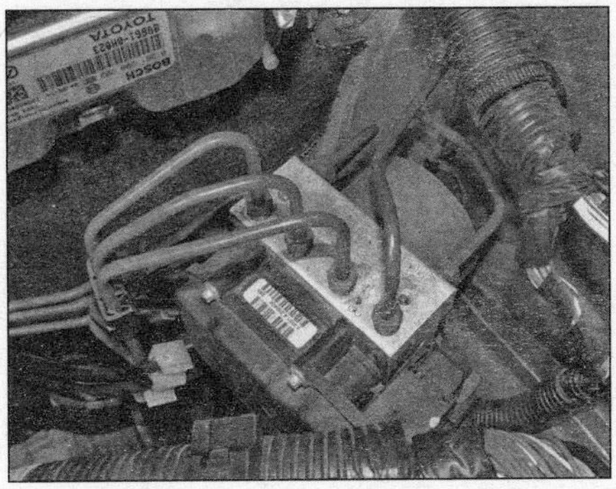

☐ The fluid reservoir must be secure and the fluid level must be between the upper (**A**) and lower (**B**) markings.

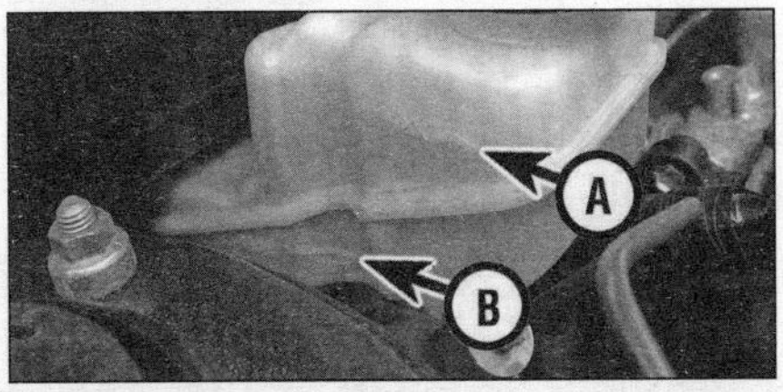

☐ Inspect both front brake flexible hoses for cracks or deterioration of the rubber. Turn the steering from lock to lock, and ensure that the hoses do not contact the wheel, tyre, or any part of the steering or suspension mechanism. With the brake pedal firmly depressed, check the hoses for bulges or leaks under pressure.

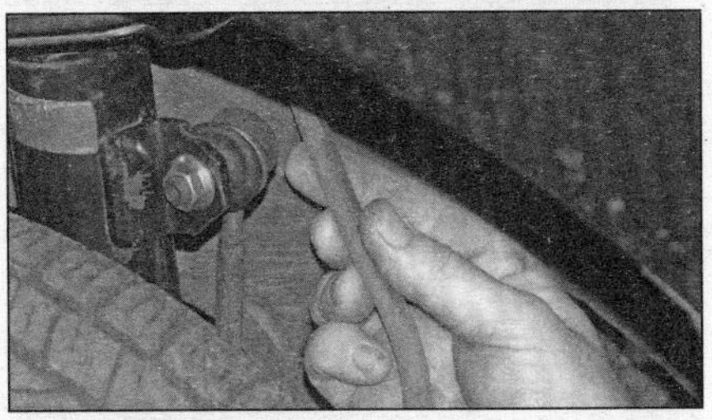

Steering and suspension

☐ Have your assistant turn the steering wheel from side to side slightly, up to the point where the steering gear just begins to transmit this movement to the roadwheels. Check for excessive free play between the steering wheel and the steering gear, indicating wear or insecurity of the steering column joints, the column-to-steering gear coupling, or the steering gear itself.

☐ Have your assistant turn the steering wheel more vigorously in each direction, so that the roadwheels just begin to turn. As this is done, examine all the steering joints, linkages, fittings and attachments. Renew any component that shows signs of wear or damage. On vehicles with power steering, check the security and condition of the steering pump, drivebelt and hoses.

☐ Check that the vehicle is standing level, and at approximately the correct ride height.

Shock absorbers

☐ Depress each corner of the vehicle in turn, then release it. The vehicle should rise and then settle in its normal position. If the vehicle continues to rise and fall, the shock absorber is defective. A shock absorber which has seized will also cause the vehicle to fail.

Exhaust system

☐ Start the engine. With your assistant holding a rag over the tailpipe, check the entire system for leaks. Repair or renew leaking sections.

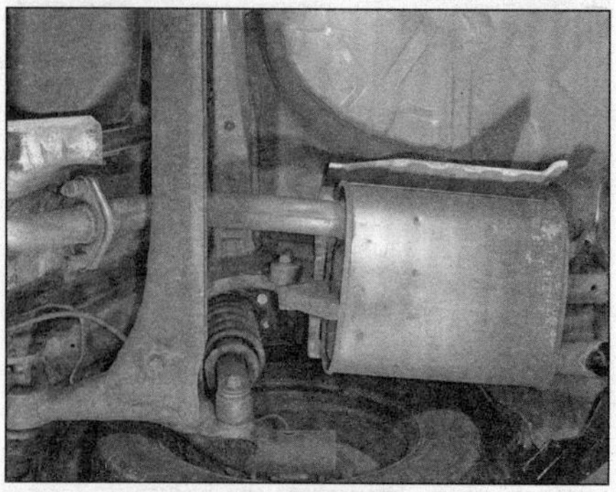

3 Checks carried out **WITH THE VEHICLE RAISED AND THE WHEELS FREE TO TURN**

Jack up the front and rear of the vehicle, and securely support it on axle stands. Position the stands clear of the suspension assemblies. Ensure that the wheels are clear of the ground and that the steering can be turned from lock to lock.

Steering mechanism

☐ Have your assistant turn the steering from lock to lock. Check that the steering turns smoothly, and that no part of the steering mechanism, including a wheel or tyre, fouls any brake hose or pipe or any part of the body structure.

☐ Examine the steering rack rubber gaiters for damage or insecurity of the retaining clips. If power steering is fitted, check for signs of damage or leakage of the fluid hoses, pipes or connections. Also check for excessive stiffness or binding of the steering, a missing split pin or locking device, or severe corrosion of the body structure within 30 cm of any steering component attachment point.

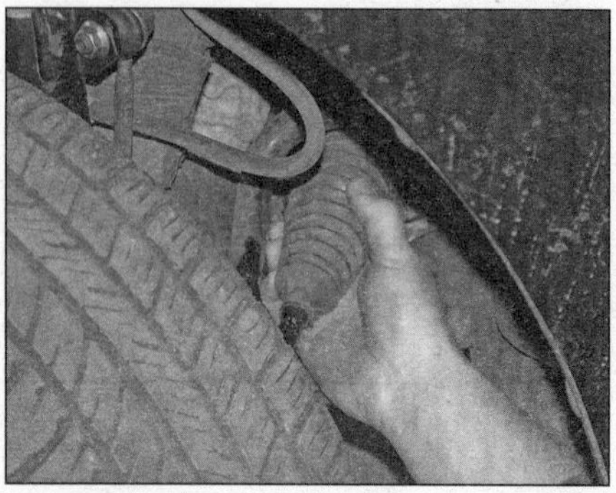

Front and rear suspension and wheel bearings

☐ Starting at the front right-hand side, grasp the roadwheel at the 3 o'clock and 9 o'clock positions and rock gently but firmly. Check for free play or insecurity at the wheel bearings, suspension balljoints, or suspension mount-ings, pivots and attachments.

☐ Now grasp the wheel at the 12 o'clock and 6 o'clock positions and repeat the previous inspection. Spin the wheel, and check for roughness or tightness of the front wheel bearing.

☐ If excess free play is suspected at a component pivot point, this can be confirmed by using a large screwdriver or similar tool and levering between the mounting and the component attachment. This will confirm whether the wear is in the pivot bush, its retaining bolt, or in the mounting itself (the bolt holes can often become elongated).

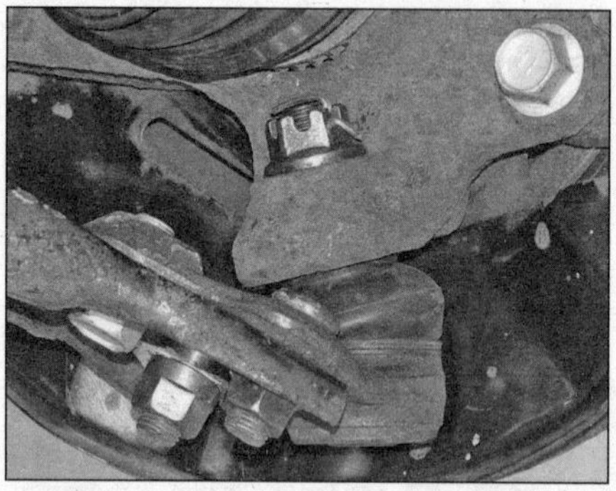

☐ Carry out all the above checks at the other front wheel, and then at both rear wheels.

Springs and shock absorbers

☐ Examine the suspension struts (when applicable) for serious fluid leakage, corrosion, or damage to the casing. Also check the security of the mounting points.

☐ If coil springs are fitted, check that the spring ends locate in their seats, and that the spring is not corroded, cracked or broken.

☐ If leaf springs are fitted, check that all leaves are intact, that the axle is securely attached to each spring, and that there is no deterioration of the spring eye mountings, bushes, and shackles.

☐ The same general checks apply to vehicles fitted with other suspension types, such as torsion bars, hydraulic displacer units, etc. Ensure that all mountings and attachments are secure, that there are no signs of excessive wear, corrosion or damage, and (on hydraulic types) that there are no fluid leaks or damaged pipes.

☐ Inspect the shock absorbers for signs of serious fluid leakage. Check for wear of the mounting bushes or attachments, or damage to the body of the unit.

Driveshafts (fwd vehicles only)

☐ Rotate each front wheel in turn and inspect the constant velocity joint gaiters for splits or damage. Also check that each driveshaft is straight and undamaged.

Braking system

☐ If possible without dismantling, check brake pad wear and disc condition. Ensure that the friction lining material has not worn excessively, (A) and that the discs are not fractured, pitted, scored or badly worn (B).

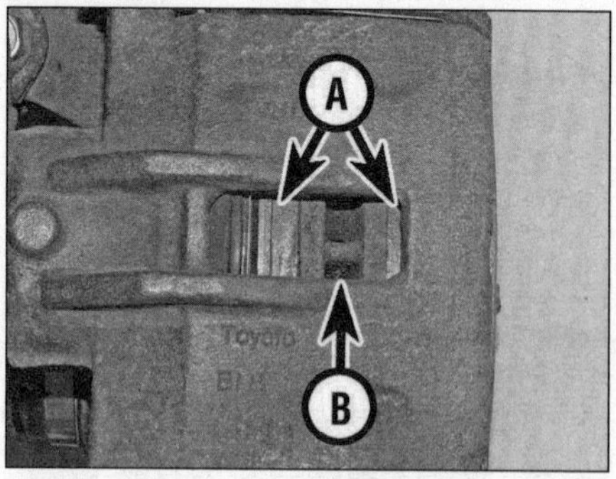

☐ Examine all the rigid brake pipes underneath the vehicle, and the flexible hose(s) at the rear. Look for corrosion, chafing or insecurity of the pipes, and for signs of bulging under pressure, chafing, splits or deterioration of the flexible hoses.

☐ Look for signs of fluid leaks at the brake calipers or on the brake backplates. Repair or renew leaking components.

☐ Slowly spin each wheel, while your assistant depresses and releases the footbrake. Ensure that each brake is operating and does not bind when the pedal is released.

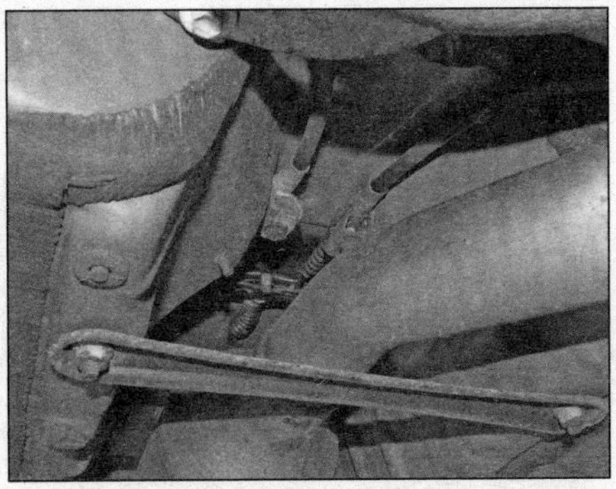

☐Examine the handbrake mechanism, checking for frayed or broken cables, excessive corrosion, or wear or insecurity of the linkage. Check that the mechanism works on each relevant wheel, and releases fully, without binding.

☐It is not possible to test brake efficiency without special equipment, but a road test can be carried out later to check that the vehicle pulls up in a straight line.

Fuel and exhaust systems

☐Inspect the fuel tank (including the filler cap), fuel pipes, hoses and unions. All components must be secure and free from leaks. Locking fuel caps must lock securely and the key must be provided for the MOT test.

☐Examine the exhaust system over its entire length, checking for any damaged, broken or missing mountings, security of the retaining clamps and rust or corrosion.

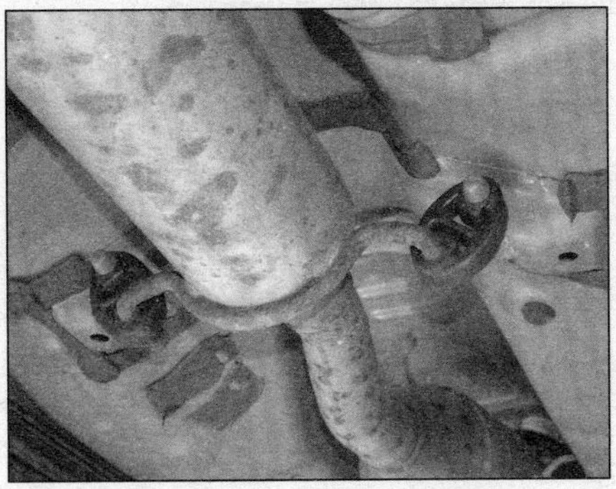

Wheels and tyres

☐Examine the sidewalls and tread area of each tyre in turn. Check for cuts, tears, lumps, bulges, separation of the tread, and exposure of the ply or cord due to wear or damage. Check that the tyre bead is correctly seated on the wheel rim, that the valve is sound and properly seated, and that the wheel is not distorted or damaged.

☐Check that the tyres are of the correct size for the vehicle, that they are of the same size and type on each axle, and that the pressures are correct.

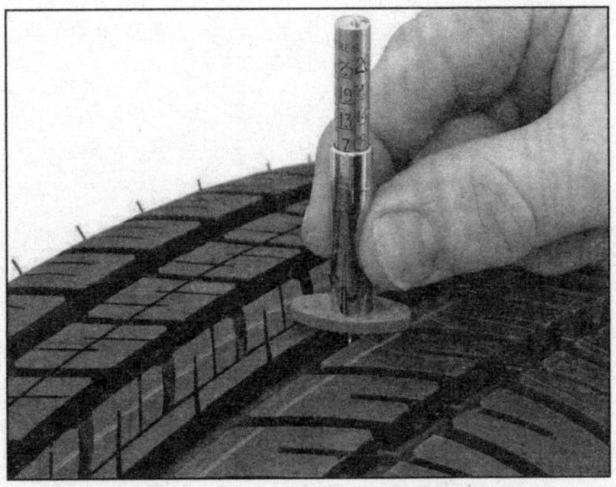

☐Check the tyre tread depth. The legal minimum at the time of writing is 1.6 mm over the central three-quarters of the tread width. Abnormal tread wear may indicate incorrect front wheel alignment or wear in steering or suspension components.

☐If the spare wheel is fitted externally or in a separate carrier beneath the vehicle, check that mountings are secure and free of excessive corrosion.

Body corrosion

☐Check the condition of the entire vehicle structure for signs of corrosion in load-bearing areas. (These include chassis box sections, side sills, cross-members, pillars, and all suspension, steering, braking system and seat belt mountings and anchorages.) Any corrosion which has seriously reduced the thickness of a load-bearing area (or is within 30 cm of safety-related components such as steering or suspension) is likely to cause the vehicle to fail. In this case professional repairs are likely to be needed.

☐Damage or corrosion which causes sharp or otherwise dangerous edges to be exposed will also cause the vehicle to fail.

Towbars

☐Check the condition of mounting points (both beneath the vehicle and within boot/hatchback areas) for signs of corrosion, ensuring that all fixings are secure and not worn or damaged. There must be no excessive play in detachable tow ball arms or quick-release mechanisms.

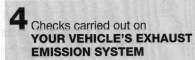

4 Checks carried out on YOUR VEHICLE'S EXHAUST EMISSION SYSTEM

Petrol models

☐The engine should be warmed up, and running well (ignition system in good order, air filter element clean, etc).

☐Before testing, run the engine at around 2500 rpm for 20 seconds. Let the engine drop to idle, and watch for smoke from the exhaust. If the idle speed is too high, or if dense blue or black smoke emerges for more than 5 seconds, the vehicle will fail. Typically, blue smoke signifies oil burning (engine wear); black smoke means unburnt fuel (dirty air cleaner element, or other fuel system fault).

☐An exhaust gas analyser for measuring carbon monoxide (CO) and hydrocarbons (HC) is now needed. If one cannot be hired or borrowed, have a local garage perform the check.

CO emissions (mixture)

☐The MOT tester has access to the CO limits for all vehicles. The CO level is measured at idle speed, and at 'fast idle' (2500 to 3000 rpm). The following limits are given as a general guide:

At idle speed – Less than 0.5% CO
At 'fast idle' – Less than 0.3% CO
Lambda reading – 0.97 to 1.03

☐If the CO level is too high, this may point to poor maintenance, a fuel injection system problem, faulty lambda (oxygen) sensor or catalytic converter. Try an injector cleaning treatment, and check the vehicle's ECU for fault codes.

HC emissions

☐The MOT tester has access to HC limits for all vehicles. The HC level is measured at 'fast idle' (2500 to 3000 rpm). The following limits are given as a general guide:

At 'fast idle' – Less then 200 ppm

☐Excessive HC emissions are typically caused by oil being burnt (worn engine), or by a blocked crankcase ventilation system ('breather'). If the engine oil is old and thin, an oil change may help. If the engine is running badly, check the vehicle's ECU for fault codes.

Diesel models

☐The only emission test for diesel engines is measuring exhaust smoke density, using a calibrated smoke meter. The test involves accelerating the engine at least 3 times to its maximum unloaded speed.

Note: *On engines with a timing belt, it is VITAL that the belt is in good condition before the test is carried out.*

☐With the engine warmed up, it is first purged by running at around 2500 rpm for 20 seconds. A governor check is then carried out, by slowly accelerating the engine to its maximum speed. After this, the smoke meter is connected, and the engine is accelerated quickly to maximum speed three times. If the smoke density is less than the limits given below, the vehicle will pass:

Non-turbo vehicles: 2.5m-1
Turbocharged vehicles: 3.0m-1

☐If excess smoke is produced, try fitting a new air cleaner element, or using an injector cleaning treatment. If the engine is running badly, where applicable, check the vehicle's ECU for fault codes. Also check the vehicle's EGR system, where applicable. At high mileages, the injectors may require professional attention.

Engine
- ☐ Engine fails to rotate when attempting to start
- ☐ Starter motor turns engine slowly
- ☐ Starter motor spins without turning engine
- ☐ Starter motor noisy or excessively-rough in engagement
- ☐ Engine rotates but will not start
- ☐ Engine fires but will not run
- ☐ Engine difficult to start when cold
- ☐ Engine difficult to start when hot
- ☐ Engine idles erratically
- ☐ Engine misfires at idle speed
- ☐ Engine misfires throughout the driving speed range
- ☐ Engine stalls
- ☐ Engine lacks power
- ☐ Oil pressure warning light illuminated with engine running
- ☐ Engine runs-on after switching off
- ☐ Engine noises

Cooling system
- ☐ Overheating
- ☐ Overcooling
- ☐ External coolant leakage
- ☐ Internal coolant leakage
- ☐ Corrosion

Fuel and exhaust systems
- ☐ Excessive fuel consumption
- ☐ Fuel leakage and/or fuel odour
- ☐ Excessive noise or fumes from exhaust system

Clutch
- ☐ Pedal travels to floor – no pressure or very little resistance
- ☐ Clutch fails to disengage (unable to select gears)
- ☐ Clutch slips (engine speed increases, with no increase in vehicle speed)
- ☐ Judder as clutch is engaged
- ☐ Noise when depressing or releasing clutch pedal

Manual gearbox
- ☐ Noisy in neutral with engine running
- ☐ Noisy in one particular gear
- ☐ Difficulty engaging gears
- ☐ Jumps out of gear
- ☐ Vibration
- ☐ Lubricant leaks

Automatic transmission
- ☐ Fluid leakage
- ☐ Transmission fluid brown, or has burned smell
- ☐ General gear selection problems
- ☐ Transmission will not downshift (kickdown) with accelerator fully depressed
- ☐ Engine will not start in any gear, or starts in gears other than Park or Neutral
- ☐ Transmission slips, shifts roughly, is noisy, or has no drive in forward or reverse gears

Transfer gearbox
- ☐ Noisy in neutral with engine running
- ☐ Noisy in Low or High positions
- ☐ Difficulty engaging ranges
- ☐ Jumps out of gear
- ☐ Vibration
- ☐ Lubricant leaks

Propeller shafts
- ☐ Knock or clunk when taking up drive
- ☐ Oil leak where propeller shaft enters transfer gearbox
- ☐ Oil leak where propeller shaft enters axle
- ☐ Metallic grating sound consistent with vehicle speed
- ☐ Scraping noise
- ☐ Vibration

Front and rear final drives
- ☐ Noise on drive and overrun
- ☐ Noise consistent with road speed
- ☐ Knock or clunk when taking up drive
- ☐ Oil leakage

Driveshafts
- ☐ Vibration when accelerating or decelerating
- ☐ Clicking or knocking noise on turns (at slow speed on full-lock)

Braking system
- ☐ Vehicle pulls to one side under braking
- ☐ Noise (grinding or high-pitched squeal) when brakes applied
- ☐ Excessive brake pedal travel
- ☐ Brake pedal feels spongy when depressed
- ☐ Excessive brake pedal effort required to stop vehicle
- ☐ Judder felt through brake pedal or steering wheel when braking
- ☐ Brakes binding
- ☐ Rear wheels locking under normal braking

Suspension and steering
- ☐ Vehicle pulls to one side
- ☐ Wheel wobble and vibration
- ☐ Excessive pitching and/or rolling around corners, or during braking
- ☐ Wandering or general instability
- ☐ Excessively-stiff steering
- ☐ Excessive play in steering
- ☐ Lack of power assistance
- ☐ Tyre wear excessive

Electrical system
- ☐ Battery will not hold a charge for more than a few days
- ☐ Ignition/no-charge warning light remains illuminated with engine running
- ☐ Ignition/no-charge warning light fails to come on
- ☐ Lights inoperative
- ☐ Instrument readings inaccurate or erratic
- ☐ Horn inoperative, or unsatisfactory in operation
- ☐ Windscreen/tailgate wipers inoperative, or unsatisfactory in operation
- ☐ Windscreen/tailgate washers inoperative, or unsatisfactory in operation
- ☐ Electric windows inoperative, or unsatisfactory in operation
- ☐ Central locking system inoperative, or unsatisfactory in operation

Introduction

The vehicle owner who does his or her own maintenance according to the recommended service schedules should not have to use this section of the manual very often. Modern component reliability is such that, provided those items subject to wear or deterioration are inspected or renewed at the specified intervals, sudden failure is comparatively rare. Faults do not usually just happen as a result of sudden failure, but develop over a period of time. Major mechanical failures in particular are usually preceded by characteristic symptoms over hundreds or even thousands of miles. Those components which do occasionally fail without warning are often small and easily carried in the vehicle.

With any fault-finding, the first step is to decide where to begin investigations. Sometimes this is obvious, but on other occasions, a little detective work will be necessary. The owner who makes half a dozen haphazard adjustments or replacements may be successful in curing a fault (or its symptoms), but will be none the wiser if the fault recurs, and ultimately may have spent more time and money than was necessary. A calm and logical approach will be found to be more satisfactory in the long run. Always take into account any warning signs or abnormalities that may have been noticed in the period preceding the fault – power loss, high or low gauge readings, unusual smells, etc – and remember that failure of components such as fuses or relays may only be pointers to some underlying fault.

The pages which follow provide an easy reference guide to the more common problems which may occur during the operation of the vehicle. These problems and their possible causes are grouped under headings denoting various components or systems, such as Engine, Cooling system, etc. The Chapter and/or Section which deals with the problem is also shown in brackets. Whatever the fault, certain basic principles apply. These are as follows:

Verify the fault. This is simply a matter of being sure that you know what the symptoms are before starting work. This is particularly important if you are investigating a fault for someone else, who may not have described it very accurately.

Don't overlook the obvious. For example, if the vehicle won't start, is there fuel in the tank? (Don't take anyone else's word on this particular point, and don't trust the fuel gauge either!) If an electrical fault is indicated, look for loose or broken wires before digging out the test gear.

Cure the disease, not the symptom. Substituting a flat battery with a fully-charged one will get you off the hard shoulder, but if the underlying cause is not attended to, the new battery will go the same way.

Don't take anything for granted. Particularly, don't forget that a 'new' component may itself be defective (especially if it's been rattling around in the boot for months), and don't leave components out of a fault diagnosis sequence just because they are new or recently fitted.

When you do finally diagnose a difficult fault, you'll probably realise that all the evidence was there from the start.

Diesel engine fault finding

The majority of starting problems on small diesel engines are electrical in origin. The mechanic who is familiar with petrol engines but less so with diesel may be inclined to view the diesel's injectors and pump in the same light as the spark plugs and distributor, but this is generally a mistake.

When investigating complaints of difficult starting for someone else, make sure that the correct starting procedure is understood and is being followed. Some drivers are unaware of the significance of the preheating warning light – many modern engines are sufficiently forgiving for this not to matter in mild weather, but with the onset of winter, problems begin. Glow plugs in particular are often neglected – just one faulty plug will make cold-weather starting very difficult.

As a rule of thumb, if the engine is difficult to start but runs well when it has finally got going, the problem is electrical (battery, starter motor or preheating system). If poor performance is combined with difficult starting, the problem is likely to be in the fuel system. The low-pressure (supply) side of the fuel system should be checked before suspecting the injectors and high-pressure pump. The most common fuel supply problem is air getting into the system, and any pipe from the fuel tank forwards must be scrutinised if air leakage is suspected.

Engine

Engine fails to rotate when attempting to start

- ☐ Battery terminal connections loose or corroded (*Weekly checks*).
- ☐ Battery discharged or faulty (Chapter 5).
- ☐ Broken, loose or disconnected wiring in the starting circuit (Chapter 5).
- ☐ Automatic transmission not in P or N (Chapter 7B)
- ☐ Defective starter solenoid or switch (Chapter 5).
- ☐ Defective starter motor (Chapter 5).
- ☐ Starter pinion or flywheel ring gear teeth loose or broken (Chapters 2 and 5).
- ☐ Engine earth strap broken or disconnected (Chapter 5 and 13).

Engine rotates, but will not start

- ☐ Fuel tank empty.
- ☐ Battery discharged (engine rotates slowly) (Chapter 5).
- ☐ Battery terminal connections loose or corroded (*Weekly checks*).
- ☐ Immobiliser fault (Chapter 13).
- ☐ Preheating system faulty (Chapter 5).
- ☐ Air in fuel system (Chapter 4A).
- ☐ Major mechanical failure (eg. timing belt) (Chapter 2).

Engine difficult to start when cold

- ☐ Battery discharged (Chapter 5).
- ☐ Battery terminal connections loose or corroded (*Weekly checks*).
- ☐ Preheating system faulty (Chapter 5).
- ☐ Wax formed in fuel (in very cold weather).
- ☐ Low cylinder compressions (Chapter 2).

Engine difficult to start when hot

- ☐ Air filter element dirty or clogged (Chapter 1).
- ☐ Low cylinder compressions (Chapter 2).

Starter motor noisy or excessively-rough in engagement

- ☐ Starter pinion or flywheel ring gear teeth loose or broken (Chapters 2 and 5).
- ☐ Starter motor mounting bolts loose or missing (Chapter 5).
- ☐ Starter motor internal components worn or damaged (Chapter 5).

Engine starts, but stops immediately

- ☐ Fuel lines restricted (Chapter 4A).
- ☐ Air in fuel system (Chapter 4A).
- ☐ Wax formed in fuel (in very cold weather).

Engine idles erratically

- ☐ Air filter element clogged (Chapter 1).
- ☐ Vacuum leak at the intake manifold or associated hoses (Chapter 4A).
- ☐ Uneven or low cylinder compressions (Chapter 2).
- ☐ Camshaft lobes worn (Chapter 2).
- ☐ Faulty injector(s) (Chapter 4A).
- ☐ Wax formed in fuel (in very cold weather).

Engine (continued)

Engine misfires at idle speed

- ☐ Vacuum leak at the intake manifold or associated hoses (Chapter 4A).
- ☐ Faulty injector(s) (Chapter 4A).
- ☐ Uneven or low cylinder compressions (Chapter 2).
- ☐ Disconnected, leaking, or perished crankcase ventilation hoses (Chapter 4B).

Engine misfires throughout the driving speed range

- ☐ Fuel filter choked (Chapter 1).
- ☐ Fuel pump faulty, or delivery pressure low (Chapter 4A).
- ☐ Fuel tank vent blocked, or fuel pipes restricted (Chapter 4A).
- ☐ Vacuum leak at the intake manifold or associated hoses (Chapter 4A).
- ☐ Faulty injector(s) (Chapter 4A).
- ☐ Uneven or low cylinder compressions (Chapter 2).

Engine hesitates on acceleration

- ☐ Vacuum leak at the intake manifold or associated hoses (Chapter 4A).
- ☐ Faulty injector(s) (Chapter 4A).

Engine stalls

- ☐ Vacuum leak at the intake manifold or associated hoses (Chapter 4A).
- ☐ Fuel filter choked (Chapter 1).
- ☐ Fuel pump faulty, or delivery pressure low (Chapter 4A).
- ☐ Fuel tank vent blocked, or fuel pipes restricted (Chapter 4A).
- ☐ Faulty injector(s) (Chapter 4A).
- ☐ Wax formed in fuel (in very cold weather).

Engine lacks power

- ☐ Timing belt incorrectly fitted or tensioned (Chapter 2).
- ☐ Fuel filter choked (Chapter 1).
- ☐ Fuel pump faulty, or delivery pressure low (Chapter 4A).
- ☐ Fuel lines leaking or restricted (Chapter 4A).
- ☐ Uneven or low cylinder compressions (Chapter 2).
- ☐ Vacuum leak at the intake manifold or associated hoses (Chapter 4A).
- ☐ Faulty injector(s) (Chapter 4A).
- ☐ Wax formed in fuel (in very cold weather).
- ☐ Brakes binding (Chapters 1 and 10).
- ☐ Clutch slipping (Chapter 6).

Engine backfires

- ☐ Timing belt incorrectly fitted or tensioned (Chapter 2).
- ☐ Vacuum leak at the intake manifold or associated hoses (Chapter 4A).

Oil pressure warning light illuminated with engine running

- ☐ Low oil level, or incorrect oil grade (*Weekly checks*).
- ☐ Worn engine bearings and/or oil pump (Chapter 2).
- ☐ High engine operating temperature (Chapter 3).
- ☐ Oil pressure relief valve defective (Chapter 2).
- ☐ Oil pick-up strainer clogged (Chapter 2).

Engine runs-on after switching off

- ☐ Excessive carbon build-up in engine (Chapter 2).
- ☐ High engine operating temperature (Chapter 3).

Engine noises

Note: *To inexperienced ears, a diesel engine can sound alarming even when there is nothing wrong with it, so it may be prudent to have an unusual noise expertly diagnosed before making renewals or repairs.*

Pre-ignition (pinking) or knocking during acceleration or under load

- ☐ Incorrect grade of fuel.
- ☐ Vacuum leak at the intake manifold or associated hoses (Chapter 4A).
- ☐ Excessive carbon build-up in engine (Chapter 2).
- ☐ Overheating (Refer to *Cooling system* of Fault finding).

Whistling or wheezing noises

- ☐ Leaking intake manifold gasket (Chapter 4A).
- ☐ Leaking exhaust manifold gasket or pipe-to-manifold joint (Chapter 4A).
- ☐ Leaking vacuum hose (Chapter 4).
- ☐ Blowing cylinder head gasket (Chapter 2).

Tapping or rattling noises

- ☐ Insufficient oil reaching hydraulic tappets – check oil level, or change oil (*Weekly checks* or Chapter 1).
- ☐ Worn hydraulic tappet or camshaft (Chapter 2).
- ☐ Worn camshaft (Chapter 2).
- ☐ Ancillary component fault (water pump, alternator, etc) (Chapters 3, 5, etc).

Knocking or thumping noises

- ☐ Worn big-end bearings (regular heavy knocking, perhaps less under load) (Chapter 2).
- ☐ Worn main bearings (rumbling and knocking, perhaps worsening under load) (Chapter 2).
- ☐ Piston slap (indicating piston and/or bore wear – most noticeable when cold) (Chapter 2).
- ☐ Ancillary component fault (water pump, alternator, etc) (Chapters 3, 5, etc).

Cooling system

Overheating

- ☐ Insufficient coolant in system (*Weekly checks*).
- ☐ Auxiliary drivebelt broken or drivebelt tensioner faulty (Chapter 1)
- ☐ Thermostat faulty (Chapter 3).
- ☐ Radiator core blocked, or grille restricted (Chapter 3).
- ☐ Cooling fan viscous coupling faulty (Chapter 3).
- ☐ Pressure cap faulty (Chapter 3).
- ☐ Inaccurate coolant temperature sensor (Chapter 3).
- ☐ Airlock in cooling system (Chapter 1).

Overcooling

- ☐ Thermostat faulty (Chapter 3).
- ☐ Cooling fan viscous coupling faulty (Chapter 3).
- ☐ Inaccurate coolant temperature sensor (Chapter 3).

External coolant leakage

- ☐ Deteriorated or damaged hoses or hose clips (Chapter 1).
- ☐ Radiator core or heater matrix leaking (Chapter 3).
- ☐ Pressure cap faulty (Chapter 3).
- ☐ Water pump seal leaking (Chapter 3).
- ☐ Boiling due to overheating (Chapter 3).
- ☐ Core plug leaking.

Internal coolant leakage

- ☐ Leaking cylinder head gasket (Chapter 2).
- ☐ Cracked cylinder head or cylinder bore (Chapter 2).

Corrosion

- ☐ Infrequent draining and flushing (Chapter 1).
- ☐ Incorrect coolant mixture or inappropriate coolant type (Chapter 1).

Fuel and exhaust systems

Excessive fuel consumption

- ☐ Air filter element dirty or clogged (Chapter 1).
- ☐ Faulty injector(s) (Chapter 4A).
- ☐ Fuel tank/lines damaged or leaking, or fuel return line restricted (Chapter 4A).
- ☐ Tyres under-inflated (*Weekly checks*).
- ☐ Brakes binding (Chapter 10).

Fuel leakage and/or fuel odour

- ☐ Damaged or corroded fuel tank, pipes or connections (Chapter 4).

Excessive noise or fumes from exhaust system

- ☐ Leaking exhaust system or manifold joints (Chapters 1 and 4).
- ☐ Leaking, corroded or damaged silencers or pipe (Chapters 1 and 4).
- ☐ Broken mountings causing body or suspension contact (Chapter 1).

Clutch

Judder as clutch is engaged

- ☐ Clutch disc linings contaminated with oil or grease (Chapter 6).
- ☐ Clutch disc linings excessively worn (Chapter 6).
- ☐ Faulty or distorted pressure plate or diaphragm spring (Chapter 6).
- ☐ Worn or loose engine/transmission mountings (Chapter 2).
- ☐ Faulty dual mass flywheel (Chapter 2).
- ☐ Clutch disc hub or gearbox input shaft splines worn (Chapter 6).

Clutch fails to disengage (unable to select gears)

- ☐ Leak in clutch hydraulic system (Chapter 6).
- ☐ Faulty hydraulic master or slave cylinder (Chapter 6).
- ☐ Clutch disc sticking on gearbox input shaft splines (Chapter 6).
- ☐ Clutch disc sticking to flywheel or pressure plate (Chapter 6).
- ☐ Faulty pressure plate assembly (Chapter 6).
- ☐ Clutch release mechanism worn or incorrectly assembled (Chapter 6).

Clutch slips (engine speed increases, with no increase in vehicle speed)

- ☐ Clutch disc linings excessively worn (Chapter 6).
- ☐ Clutch disc linings contaminated with oil or grease (Chapter 6).
- ☐ Faulty pressure plate or weak diaphragm spring (Chapter 6).

Pedal travels to floor – no pressure or very little resistance

- ☐ Leak in clutch hydraulic system (Chapter 6).
- ☐ Faulty hydraulic master or slave cylinder (Chapter 6).
- ☐ Broken clutch release bearing (Chapter 6).
- ☐ Broken diaphragm spring in clutch pressure plate (Chapter 6).

Noise when depressing or releasing clutch pedal

- ☐ Worn clutch release bearing (Chapter 6).
- ☐ Worn or dry clutch pedal bushes (Chapter 6).
- ☐ Faulty pressure plate assembly (Chapter 6).
- ☐ Pressure plate diaphragm spring broken (Chapter 6).
- ☐ Broken clutch disc cushioning springs (Chapter 6).

Manual transmission

Difficulty engaging gears

- ☐ Clutch fault (Chapter 6).
- ☐ Worn or damaged gear linkage (Chapter 7A).
- ☐ Faulty dual mass flywheel (Chapter 3).
- ☐ Worn synchroniser units (Chapter 7A).*

Jumps out of gear

- ☐ Worn or damaged gear linkage (Chapter 7A).
- ☐ Incorrectly-adjusted gear linkage (Chapter 7A).
- ☐ Worn synchroniser units (Chapter 7A).*
- ☐ Worn selector forks (Chapter 7A).*

Vibration

- ☐ Lack of oil (Chapter 1).
- ☐ Worn bearings (Chapter 7A).*

Noisy in one particular gear

- ☐ Worn, damaged or chipped gear teeth (Chapter 7A).*

Noisy in neutral with engine running

- ☐ Input shaft and/or mainshaft bearings worn (noise apparent with clutch pedal released, but not when depressed) (Chapter 7A).*
- ☐ Clutch release bearing worn (noise apparent with clutch pedal depressed, possibly less when released) (Chapter 6).

Lubricant leaks

- ☐ Leaking oil seal (Chapter 7A).
- ☐ Leaking housing joint (Chapter 7A).*

**Although the corrective action necessary to remedy the symptoms described is beyond the scope of the home mechanic, the above information should be helpful in isolating the cause of the condition, so that the owner can communicate clearly with a professional mechanic.*

Automatic transmission

Note: *Due to the complexity of the automatic transmission, it is difficult for the home mechanic to properly diagnose and service this unit. For problems other than the following, the vehicle should be taken to a dealer service department or automatic transmission specialist.*

Fluid leakage

- ☐ Automatic transmission fluid is usually deep red in colour. Fluid leaks should not be confused with engine oil, which can easily be blown onto the transmission by air flow.
- ☐ To determine the source of a leak, first remove all built-up dirt and grime from the transmission housing and surrounding areas, using a degreasing agent or by steam-cleaning. Drive the vehicle at low speed, so that air flow will not blow the leak far from its source. Raise and support the vehicle, and determine where the leak is coming from. The following are common areas of leakage.
  - *a) Fluid pan (transmission sump).*
  - *b) Dipstick tube (Chapter 1).*
  - *c) Transmission-to-fluid cooler fluid pipes/unions (Chapter 7B).*

Transmission fluid brown, or has burned smell

- ☐ Transmission fluid level low, or fluid in need of renewal (Chapter 1).

Transmission will not downshift (kickdown) with accelerator pedal fully depressed

- ☐ Low transmission fluid level (Chapter 1).

General gear selection problems

- ☐ The most likely cause of gear selection problems is a faulty or poorly-adjusted gear selector mechanism. The following are common problems associated with a faulty selector mechanism:
  - *a) Engine starting in gears other than Park or Neutral.*
  - *b) Indicator on gear selector lever pointing to a gear other than the one actually being used.*
  - *c) Vehicle moves when in Park or Neutral.*
  - *d) Poor gear shift quality, or erratic gear changes.*
- ☐ Refer any problems to a Land Rover dealer, or an automatic transmission specialist.

Engine will not start in any gear, or starts in gears other than Park or Neutral

- ☐ Faulty gear position sensor or TCM (Chapter 7B).

Transmission slips, shifts roughly, is noisy, or has no drive in forward or reverse gears

- ☐ There are many probable causes for the above problems, but the home mechanic should be concerned with only one possibility – fluid level. Before taking the vehicle to a dealer or transmission specialist, check the fluid level and condition of the fluid as described in Chapter 1. Correct the fluid level as necessary, or change the fluid and filter if needed. If the problem persists, professional help will be necessary.

Transfer gearbox

Noisy in neutral with engine running

- ☐ Worn mainshaft or output shaft bearings (Chapter 7C).*

Noisy in Low or High positions

- ☐ Worn, damaged or chipped gear teeth (Chapter 7C).*

Jumps out of gear

- ☐ Worn or damaged gear linkage (Chapter 7C).*
- ☐ Worn selector fork (Chapter 7C).*

Vibration

- ☐ Lack of oil (Chapter 1).
- ☐ Worn bearings (Chapter 7C).*

Difficulty engaging ranges

- ☐ Clutch fault (Chapter 6).
- ☐ Main transmission fault (Chapter 7A or 7B).
- ☐ Worn selector fork (Chapter 7C).*

Lubricant leaks

- ☐ Leaking oil seal (Chapter 7C).*
- ☐ Leaking housing joint (Chapter 7C).*

**Although the corrective action necessary to remedy the symptoms described is beyond the scope of the home mechanic, the above information should be helpful in isolating the cause of the condition, so that the owner can communicate clearly with a professional mechanic.*

Propeller shafts

Knock or clunk when taking up drive

- ☐ Worn universal joint bearings (Chapter 8).
- ☐ Worn axle drive pinion splines (Chapter 9).
- ☐ Loose drive flange bolts (Chapter 8).
- ☐ Excessive backlash in axle gears (Chapter 9).

Metallic grating sound, consistent with vehicle speed

- ☐ Severe wear in universal/constant velocity joint bearings (Chapter 8).

Vibration

- ☐ Wear in sliding sleeve splines (Chapter 8).
- ☐ Worn universal joint bearings (Chapter 8).
- ☐ Worn constant velocity joints (Chapter 8).
- ☐ Propeller shaft out of balance (Chapter 8).

Front and rear final drives

Noise on drive and overrun

- ☐ Worn crownwheel and pinion gears (Chapter 9).
- ☐ Worn differential bearings (Chapter 9).
- ☐ Main transmission or transfer gearbox fault (Chapter 7).

Noise consistent with road speed

- ☐ Worn hub bearings (Chapter 9).
- ☐ Worn differential bearings (Chapter 9).
- ☐ Main transmission or transfer gearbox fault (Chapter 7).

Knock or clunk when taking up drive

- ☐ Excessive crownwheel and pinion backlash (Chapter 9).
- ☐ Worn driveshaft joints (Chapters 8 and 9).
- ☐ Worn driveshaft splines (Chapter 9).
- ☐ Driveshaft nut or roadwheel nuts loose (Chapter 9).
- ☐ Broken, damaged, or worn suspension components or final drive mountings (Chapters 11 and 9).
- ☐ Main transmission or transfer gearbox fault (Chapter 7).

Oil leakage

- ☐ Faulty differential pinion or halfshaft oil seals (Chapter 9).
- ☐ Damaged driveshaft oil seal (Chapter 9).

Driveshafts

Vibration when accelerating or decelerating

- ☐ Worn inner constant velocity joint (Chapter 9).
- ☐ Bent or distorted driveshaft (Chapter 9).

Clicking or knocking noise on turns (at slow speed on full-lock)

- ☐ Worn outer constant velocity joint (Chapter 9).
- ☐ Lack of constant velocity joint lubricant, possibly due to damaged gaiter (Chapter 9).

Braking system

Note: *Before assuming that a brake problem exists, make sure that the tyres are in good condition and correctly inflated, the front wheel alignment is correct, and the vehicle is not loaded with weight in an unequal manner. Apart from checking the condition of all pipe and hose connections, any faults occurring on the anti-lock braking system should be referred to a Land Rover dealer for diagnosis.*

Vehicle pulls to one side under braking

- ☐ Worn, defective, damaged or contaminated front or rear brake pads on one side (Chapter 10).
- ☐ Seized or partially-seized front or rear brake caliper piston (Chapter 10).
- ☐ A mixture of brake pad lining materials fitted between sides (Chapter 10).
- ☐ Brake caliper mounting bolts loose (Chapter 10).
- ☐ Worn or damaged steering or suspension components (Chapter 11).

Noise (grinding or high-pitched squeal) when brakes applied

- ☐ Brake pad friction lining material worn down to metal backing (Chapter 10).
- ☐ Brake pads incorrectly fitted, or pad backing plates dry (Chapter 10).
- ☐ Excessive corrosion of brake disc – may be apparent after the vehicle has been standing for some time (Chapter 10).

Excessive brake pedal travel

- ☐ Faulty master cylinder (Chapter 10).
- ☐ Air in hydraulic system (Chapter 10).
- ☐ Faulty vacuum servo unit (Chapter 10).
- ☐ Faulty brake vacuum pump (Chapter 10).

Brake pedal feels spongy when depressed

- ☐ Air in hydraulic system (Chapter 10).
- ☐ Deteriorated flexible rubber brake hoses (Chapter 10).
- ☐ Master cylinder mountings loose (Chapter 10).
- ☐ Faulty master cylinder (Chapter 10).

Excessive brake pedal effort required to stop vehicle

- ☐ Faulty vacuum servo unit (Chapter 10).
- ☐ Disconnected, damaged or insecure brake servo vacuum hose (Chapters 1 and 10).
- ☐ Faulty brake vacuum pump (Chapter 10).
- ☐ Primary or secondary hydraulic circuit failure (Chapter 10).
- ☐ Seized brake caliper piston(s) (Chapter 10).
- ☐ Brake pads incorrectly fitted (Chapter 10).
- ☐ Incorrect grade of brake pads fitted (Chapter 10).
- ☐ Brake pads contaminated (Chapter 10).

Judder felt through brake pedal or steering wheel when braking

Note: *Under heavy braking, models equipped with ABS may exhibit a 'pulsing' sensation felt through the brake pedal. This is a normal feature of ABS operation, and does not necessarily indicate a fault.*

- ☐ Excessive run-out or distortion of brake disc(s) (Chapter 10).
- ☐ Brake pad linings worn (Chapter 10).
- ☐ Brake caliper mounting bolts loose (Chapter 10).
- ☐ Wear in suspension or steering components or mountings (Chapter 11).

Brakes binding

- ☐ Seized brake caliper piston(s) (Chapter 10).
- ☐ Faulty master cylinder (Chapter 10).

Suspension and steering

Note: *Before diagnosing suspension or steering faults, be sure that the trouble is not due to incorrect tyre pressures, mixtures of tyre types or binding brakes.*

Vehicle pulls to one side

- ☐ Defective tyre (*Weekly checks*).
- ☐ Excessive wear in suspension or steering components (Chapter 11).
- ☐ Incorrect front wheel alignment (Chapter 11).
- ☐ Accident damage to steering or suspension components (Chapter 11).

Wheel wobble and vibration

- ☐ Front roadwheels out of balance – vibration felt mainly through the steering wheel (Chapter 11).
- ☐ Rear roadwheels out of balance – vibration felt throughout the vehicle (Chapter 11).
- ☐ Roadwheels damaged or distorted (*Weekly checks*).
- ☐ Faulty or damaged tyre (*Weekly checks*).
- ☐ Worn steering or suspension joints, bushes or components (Chapter 11).
- ☐ Wheel nuts loose (*Wheel changing*).

Excessive pitching and/or rolling around corners or during braking

- ☐ Defective shock absorbers (Chapter 11).
- ☐ Broken or weak coil spring and/or suspension component (Chapter 11).
- ☐ Worn or damaged anti-roll bar or mountings (Chapter 11).

Wandering or general instability

- ☐ Incorrect front wheel alignment (Chapter 11).
- ☐ Worn steering or suspension joints, bushes or components (Chapter 11).
- ☐ Roadwheels out of balance (*Weekly checks*).
- ☐ Faulty or damaged tyre (*Weekly checks*).
- ☐ Wheel nuts loose (*Wheel changing*).
- ☐ Defective shock absorbers (Chapter 11).

Excessively-stiff steering

- ☐ Lack of steering gear lubricant (Chapter 11).
- ☐ Seized track-rod end balljoint (Chapter 11).
- ☐ Lack of power steering fluid (Chapter 1).
- ☐ Incorrect front wheel alignment (Chapter 11).
- ☐ Steering rack or column damaged (Chapter 11).
- ☐ Power steering pump fault (Chapter 11).

Excessive play in steering

- ☐ Worn steering column universal joint(s) or intermediate coupling (Chapter 11).
- ☐ Worn steering track-rod end balljoints (Chapter 11).
- ☐ Worn steering rack (Chapter 11).
- ☐ Worn steering or suspension joints, bushes or components (Chapter 11).

Lack of power assistance

- ☐ Broken or power steering pump drivebelt (Chapter 1).
- ☐ Incorrect power steering fluid level (*Weekly checks*).
- ☐ Restriction in power steering fluid hoses (Chapter 1).
- ☐ Faulty power steering pump (Chapter 11).
- ☐ Faulty steering rack (Chapter 11).

Tyre wear excessive

Tyres worn on inside or outside edges

- ☐ Tyres under-inflated (wear on both edges) (*Weekly checks*).
- ☐ Incorrect camber or castor angles (wear on one edge only) (Chapter 11).
- ☐ Worn steering or suspension joints, bushes or components (Chapter 11).
- ☐ Excessively hard cornering.
- ☐ Accident damage.

Tyre treads exhibit feathered edges

- ☐ Incorrect toe setting (Chapter 11).

Tyres worn in centre of tread

- ☐ Tyres over-inflated (*Weekly checks*).

Tyres worn on inside and outside edges

- ☐ Tyres under-inflated (*Weekly checks*).

Tyres worn unevenly

- ☐ Tyres out of balance (*Weekly checks*).
- ☐ Faulty tyre (*Weekly checks*).
- ☐ Excessive wheel or tyre run-out (*Weekly checks*).
- ☐ Worn shock absorbers (Chapter 11).

Electrical system

Note: *For problems associated with the starting system, refer to the faults listed under Engine earlier in this Section.*

Battery will not hold a charge for more than a few days

- ☐ Battery defective internally (Chapter 5).
- ☐ Battery electrolyte level low – where applicable (Chapter 1).
- ☐ Battery terminal connections loose or corroded (*Weekly checks*).
- ☐ Alternator drivebelt worn or incorrectly adjusted (Chapter 1).
- ☐ Alternator not charging at correct output (Chapter 5).
- ☐ Alternator or voltage regulator faulty (Chapter 5).
- ☐ Short-circuit causing continual battery drain (Chapter 5 or 13).

Ignition/no-charge warning light remains illuminated with engine running

- ☐ Alternator drivebelt broken, worn, or incorrectly adjusted (Chapter 1).
- ☐ Alternator brushes worn, sticking, or dirty (Chapter 5).
- ☐ Alternator brush springs weak or broken (Chapter 5).
- ☐ Internal fault in alternator or voltage regulator (Chapter 5).
- ☐ Broken, disconnected, or loose wiring in charging circuit (Chapter 5).

Ignition/no-charge warning light fails to come on

- ☐ Broken, disconnected, or loose wiring in warning light circuit (Chapter 13).
- ☐ Alternator faulty (Chapter 5).

Electrical system (continued)

Lights inoperative

- ☐ Bulb blown (*Weekly checks* or Chapter 13).
- ☐ Corrosion of bulb or bulbholder contacts (Chapter 13).
- ☐ Blown fuse (*Weekly checks* or Chapter 13).
- ☐ Faulty relay (Chapter 13).
- ☐ Broken, loose, or disconnected wiring (Chapter 13).
- ☐ Faulty switch (Chapter 13).

Instrument readings inaccurate or erratic

Instrument readings increase with engine speed

- ☐ Faulty instrument cluster (Chapter 13).

Fuel or temperature gauge give no reading

- ☐ Faulty sensor (Chapters 3 or 4).
- ☐ Wiring open-circuit (Chapter 13).
- ☐ Faulty gauge (Chapter 13).

Fuel or temperature gauges give continuous maximum reading

- ☐ Faulty sensor (Chapters 3 or 4).
- ☐ Wiring short-circuit (Chapter 13).
- ☐ Faulty gauge (Chapter 13).

Horns inoperative, or unsatisfactory in operation

Horns operates all the time

- ☐ Horn push either earthed or stuck down (Chapter 13).
- ☐ Horn cable to horn push earthed (Chapter 13).

Horns fails to operate

- ☐ Blown fuse (*Weekly checks* or Chapter 13).
- ☐ Cable or cable connections loose, broken or disconnected (Chapter 13).
- ☐ Faulty horns (Chapter 13).

Horns emits intermittent or unsatisfactory sound

- ☐ Cable connections loose (Chapter 13).
- ☐ Horns mountings loose (Chapter 13).
- ☐ Faulty horns (Chapter 13).

Windscreen/tailgate wipers inoperative, or unsatisfactory in operation

Wipers fail to operate, or operate very slowly

- ☐ Wiper blades stuck to screen, or linkage seized or binding (Chapters 1 and 13).
- ☐ Blown fuse (*Weekly checks* or Chapter 13).
- ☐ Cable or cable connections loose, broken or disconnected (Chapter 13).
- ☐ Faulty relay (Chapter 13).
- ☐ Faulty wiper motor (Chapter 13).

Wiper blades sweep over too large or too small an area of the glass

- ☐ Wiper arms incorrectly positioned on spindles (Chapter 13).
- ☐ Excessive wear of wiper linkage (Chapter 13).
- ☐ Wiper motor or linkage mountings loose or insecure (Chapter 13).

Wiper blades fail to clean the glass effectively

- ☐ Wiper blade rubbers worn or perished (*Weekly checks*).
- ☐ Wiper arm tension springs broken, or arm pivots seized (Chapter 13).
- ☐ Insufficient windscreen washer additive to adequately remove road film (*Weekly checks*).

Windscreen/tailgate washers inoperative, or unsatisfactory in operation

One or more washer jets inoperative

- ☐ Blocked washer jet (Chapter 13).
- ☐ Disconnected, kinked or restricted fluid hose (Chapter 13).
- ☐ Insufficient fluid in washer reservoir (*Weekly checks*).

Washer pump fails to operate

- ☐ Broken or disconnected wiring or connections (Chapter 13).
- ☐ Blown fuse (*Weekly checks* or Chapter 13).
- ☐ Faulty washer switch (Chapter 13).
- ☐ Faulty washer pump (Chapter 13).

Electric windows inoperative, or unsatisfactory in operation

Window glass will only move in one direction

- ☐ Faulty switch (Chapter 12).
- ☐ Faulty motor (Chapter 12).

Window glass slow to move

- ☐ Regulator seized or damaged, or in need of lubrication (Chapter 12).
- ☐ Door internal components or trim fouling regulator (Chapter 12).
- ☐ Faulty motor (Chapter 12).

Window glass fails to move

- ☐ Blown fuse (*Weekly checks* or Chapter 13).
- ☐ Faulty relay (Chapter 13).
- ☐ Broken or disconnected wiring or connections (Chapter 13).
- ☐ Faulty motor (Chapter 12).

Central locking system inoperative, or unsatisfactory in operation

Complete system failure

- ☐ Blown fuse (*Weekly checks* or Chapter 13).
- ☐ Faulty relay (Chapter 13).
- ☐ Broken or disconnected wiring or connections (Chapter 13).

Latch locks but will not unlock, or unlocks but will not lock

- ☐ Faulty switch (Chapter 13).
- ☐ Broken or disconnected latch operating rods or levers (Chapter 12).
- ☐ Faulty relay (Chapter 13).

One solenoid/motor fails to operate

- ☐ Broken or disconnected wiring or connections (Chapter 13).
- ☐ Faulty solenoid/motor (Chapter 12).
- ☐ Broken, binding or disconnected latch operating rods or levers (Chapter 12).
- ☐ Fault in door latch (Chapter 12).

Glossary of technical terms

A

ABS (Anti-lock brake system) A system, usually electronically controlled, that senses incipient wheel lockup during braking and relieves hydraulic pressure at wheels that are about to skid.
Air bag An inflatable bag hidden in the steering wheel (driver's side) or the dash or glovebox (passenger side). In a head-on collision, the bags inflate, preventing the driver and front passenger from being thrown forward into the steering wheel or windscreen.
Air cleaner A metal or plastic housing, containing a filter element, which removes dust and dirt from the air being drawn into the engine.
Air filter element The actual filter in an air cleaner system, usually manufactured from pleated paper and requiring renewal at regular intervals.

Air filter

Allen key A hexagonal wrench which fits into a recessed hexagonal hole.
Alligator clip A long-nosed spring-loaded metal clip with meshing teeth. Used to make temporary electrical connections.
Alternator A component in the electrical system which converts mechanical energy from a drivebelt into electrical energy to charge the battery and to operate the starting system, ignition system and electrical accessories.
Ampere (amp) A unit of measurement for the flow of electric current. One amp is the amount of current produced by one volt acting through a resistance of one ohm.
Anaerobic sealer A substance used to prevent bolts and screws from loosening. Anaerobic means that it does not require oxygen for activation. The Loctite brand is widely used.
Antifreeze A substance (usually ethylene glycol) mixed with water, and added to a vehicle's cooling system, to prevent freezing of the coolant in winter. Antifreeze also contains chemicals to inhibit corrosion and the formation of rust and other deposits that would tend to clog the radiator and coolant passages and reduce cooling efficiency.
Anti-seize compound A coating that reduces the risk of seizing on fasteners that are subjected to high temperatures, such as exhaust manifold bolts and nuts.
Asbestos A natural fibrous mineral with great heat resistance, commonly used in the composition of brake friction materials. Asbestos is a health hazard and the dust created by brake systems should never be inhaled or ingested.
Axle A shaft on which a wheel revolves, or which revolves with a wheel. Also, a solid beam that connects the two wheels at one end of the vehicle. An axle which also transmits power to the wheels is known as a live axle.
Axleshaft A single rotating shaft, on either side of the differential, which delivers power from the final drive assembly to the drive wheels. Also called a driveshaft or a halfshaft.

B

Ball bearing An anti-friction bearing consisting of a hardened inner and outer race with hardened steel balls between two races.
Bearing The curved surface on a shaft or in a bore, or the part assembled into either, that permits relative motion between them with minimum wear and friction.

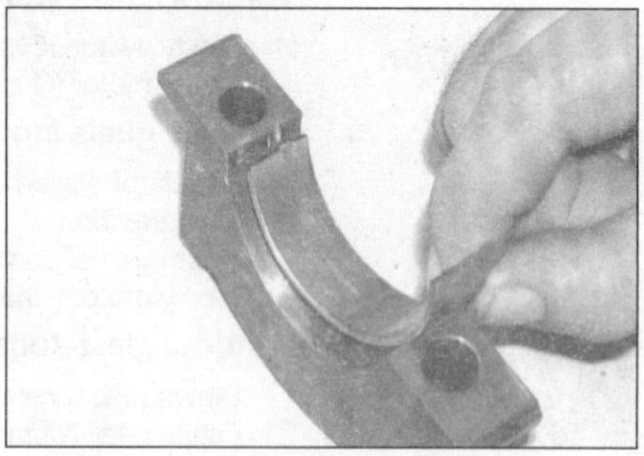

Bearing

Big-end bearing The bearing in the end of the connecting rod that's attached to the crankshaft.
Bleed nipple A valve on a brake wheel cylinder, caliper or other hydraulic component that is opened to purge the hydraulic system of air. Also called a bleed screw.
Brake bleeding Procedure for removing air from lines of a hydraulic brake system.

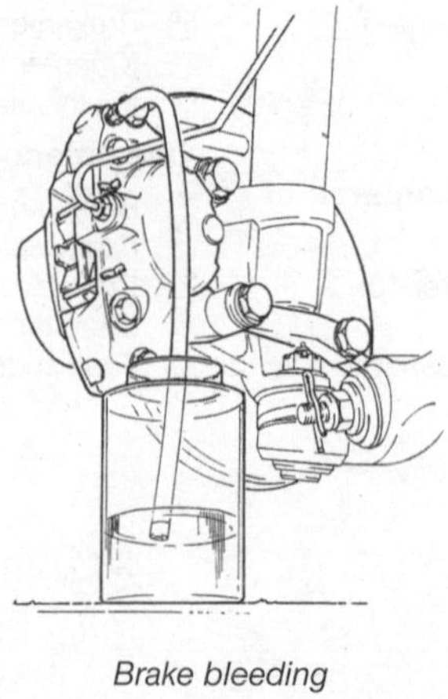

Brake bleeding

Brake disc The component of a disc brake that rotates with the wheels.
Brake drum The component of a drum brake that rotates with the wheels.
Brake linings The friction material which contacts the brake disc or drum to retard the vehicle's speed. The linings are bonded or riveted to the brake pads or shoes.
Brake pads The replaceable friction pads that pinch the brake disc when the brakes are applied. Brake pads consist of a friction material bonded or riveted to a rigid backing plate.
Brake shoe The crescent-shaped carrier to which the brake linings are mounted and which forces the lining against the rotating drum during braking.
Braking systems For more information on braking systems, consult the *Haynes Automotive Brake Manual*.
Breaker bar A long socket wrench handle providing greater leverage.
Bulkhead The insulated partition between the engine and the passenger compartment.

C

Caliper The non-rotating part of a disc-brake assembly that straddles the disc and carries the brake pads. The caliper also contains the hydraulic components that cause the pads to pinch the disc when the brakes are applied. A caliper is also a measuring tool that can be set to measure inside or outside dimensions of an object.
Camshaft A rotating shaft on which a series of cam lobes operate the valve mechanisms. The camshaft may be driven by gears, by sprockets and chain or by sprockets and a belt.
Canister A container in an evaporative emission control system; contains activated charcoal granules to trap vapours from the fuel system.

Canister

Carburettor A device which mixes fuel with air in the proper proportions to provide a desired power output from a spark ignition internal combustion engine.
Castellated Resembling the parapets along the top of a castle wall. For example, a castellated balljoint stud nut.
Castor In wheel alignment, the backward or forward tilt of the steering axis. Castor is positive when the steering axis is inclined rearward at the top.

Catalytic converter A silencer-like device in the exhaust system which converts certain pollutants in the exhaust gases into less harmful substances.

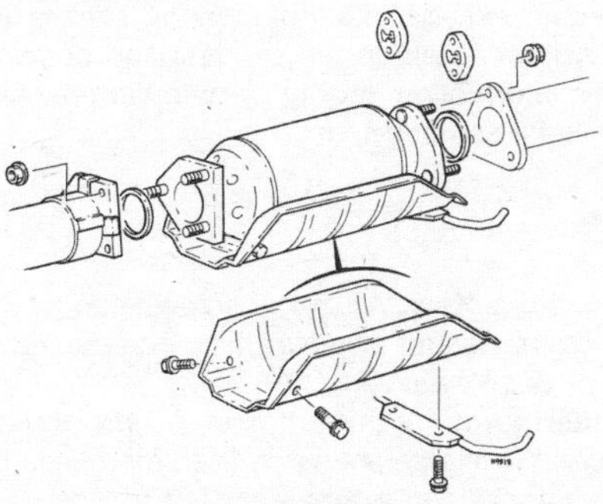

Catalytic converter

Circlip A ring-shaped clip used to prevent endwise movement of cylindrical parts and shafts. An internal circlip is installed in a groove in a housing; an external circlip fits into a groove on the outside of a cylindrical piece such as a shaft.

Clearance The amount of space between two parts. For example, between a piston and a cylinder, between a bearing and a journal, etc.

Coil spring A spiral of elastic steel found in various sizes throughout a vehicle, for example as a springing medium in the suspension and in the valve train.

Compression Reduction in volume, and increase in pressure and temperature, of a gas, caused by squeezing it into a smaller space.

Compression ratio The relationship between cylinder volume when the piston is at top dead centre and cylinder volume when the piston is at bottom dead centre.

Constant velocity (CV) joint A type of universal joint that cancels out vibrations caused by driving power being transmitted through an angle.

Core plug A disc or cup-shaped metal device inserted in a hole in a casting through which core was removed when the casting was formed. Also known as a freeze plug or expansion plug.

Crankcase The lower part of the engine block in which the crankshaft rotates.

Crankshaft The main rotating member, or shaft, running the length of the crankcase, with offset "throws" to which the connecting rods are attached.

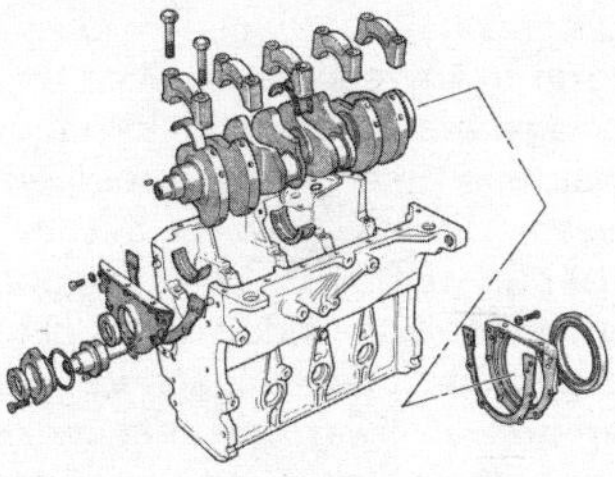

Crankshaft assembly

Crocodile clip See Alligator clip

D

Diagnostic code Code numbers obtained by accessing the diagnostic mode of an engine management computer. This code can be used to determine the area in the system where a malfunction may be located.

Disc brake A brake design incorporating a rotating disc onto which brake pads are squeezed. The resulting friction converts the energy of a moving vehicle into heat.

Double-overhead cam (DOHC) An engine that uses two overhead camshafts, usually one for the intake valves and one for the exhaust valves.

Drivebelt(s) The belt(s) used to drive accessories such as the alternator, water pump, power steering pump, air conditioning compressor, etc. off the crankshaft pulley.

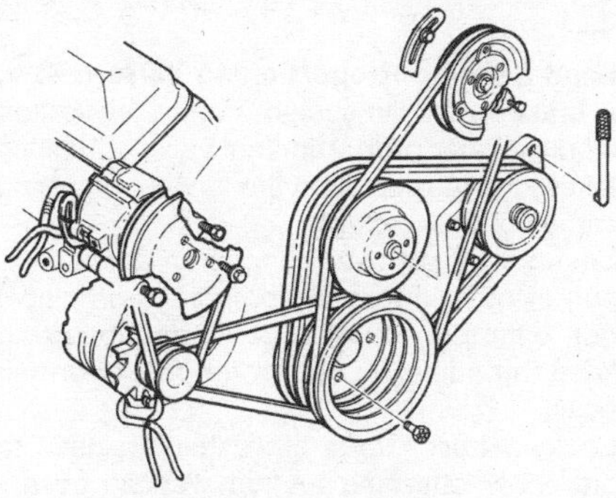

Accessory drivebelts

Driveshaft Any shaft used to transmit motion. Commonly used when referring to the axleshafts on a front wheel drive vehicle.

Drum brake A type of brake using a drum-shaped metal cylinder attached to the inner surface of the wheel. When the brake pedal is pressed, curved brake shoes with friction linings press against the inside of the drum to slow or stop the vehicle.

E

EGR valve A valve used to introduce exhaust gases into the intake air stream.

Electronic control unit (ECU) A computer which controls (for instance) ignition and fuel injection systems, or an anti-lock braking system. For more information refer to the *Haynes Automotive Electrical and Electronic Systems Manual*.

Electronic Fuel Injection (EFI) A computer controlled fuel system that distributes fuel through an injector located in each intake port of the engine.

Emergency brake A braking system, independent of the main hydraulic system, that can be used to slow or stop the vehicle if the primary brakes fail, or to hold the vehicle stationary even though the brake pedal isn't depressed. It usually consists of a hand lever that actuates either front or rear brakes mechanically through a series of cables and linkages. Also known as a handbrake or parking brake.

Endfloat The amount of lengthwise movement between two parts. As applied to a crankshaft, the distance that the crankshaft can move forward and back in the cylinder block.

Engine management system (EMS) A computer controlled system which manages the fuel injection and the ignition systems in an integrated fashion.

Exhaust manifold A part with several passages through which exhaust gases leave the engine combustion chambers and enter the exhaust pipe.

F

Fan clutch A viscous (fluid) drive coupling device which permits variable engine fan speeds in relation to engine speeds.

Feeler blade A thin strip or blade of hardened steel, ground to an exact thickness, used to check or measure clearances between parts.

Feeler blade

Firing order The order in which the engine cylinders fire, or deliver their power strokes, beginning with the number one cylinder.

Flywheel A heavy spinning wheel in which energy is absorbed and stored by means of momentum. On cars, the flywheel is attached to the crankshaft to smooth out firing impulses.

Free play The amount of travel before any action takes place. The "looseness" in a linkage, or an assembly of parts, between the initial application of force and actual movement. For example, the distance the brake pedal moves before the pistons in the master cylinder are actuated.

Fuse An electrical device which protects a circuit against accidental overload. The typical fuse contains a soft piece of metal which is calibrated to melt at a predetermined current flow (expressed as amps) and break the circuit.

Fusible link A circuit protection device consisting of a conductor surrounded by heat-resistant insulation. The conductor is smaller than the wire it protects, so it acts as the weakest link in the circuit. Unlike a blown fuse, a failed fusible link must frequently be cut from the wire for replacement.

G

Gap The distance the spark must travel in jumping from the centre electrode to the side electrode in a spark plug. Also refers to the spacing between the points in a contact breaker assembly in a conventional points-type ignition, or to the distance between the reluctor or rotor and the pickup coil in an electronic ignition.

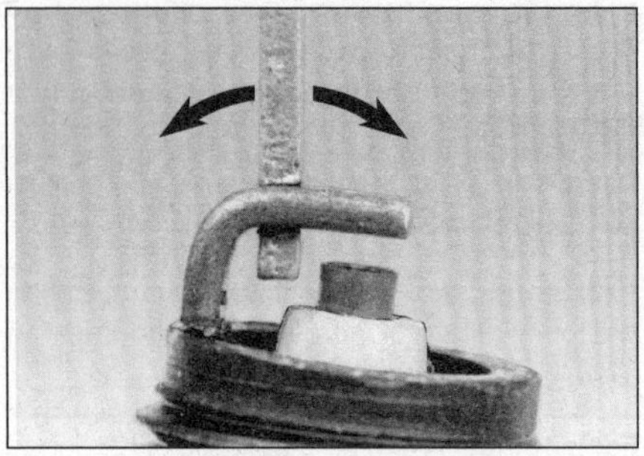

Adjusting spark plug gap

Gasket Any thin, soft material - usually cork, cardboard, asbestos or soft metal - installed between two metal surfaces to ensure a good seal. For instance, the cylinder head gasket seals the joint between the block and the cylinder head.

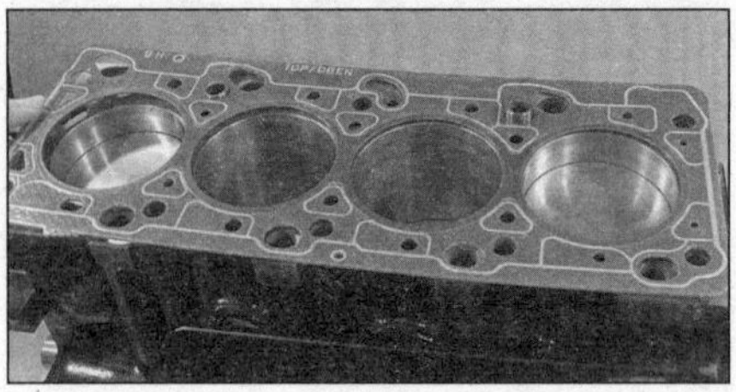

Gasket

Gauge An instrument panel display used to monitor engine conditions. A gauge with a movable pointer on a dial or a fixed scale is an analogue gauge. A gauge with a numerical readout is called a digital gauge.

H

Halfshaft A rotating shaft that transmits power from the final drive unit to a drive wheel, usually when referring to a live rear axle.

Harmonic balancer A device designed to reduce torsion or twisting vibration in the crankshaft. May be incorporated in the crankshaft pulley. Also known as a vibration damper.

Hone An abrasive tool for correcting small irregularities or differences in diameter in an engine cylinder, brake cylinder, etc.

Hydraulic tappet A tappet that utilises hydraulic pressure from the engine's lubrication system to maintain zero clearance (constant contact with both camshaft and valve stem). Automatically adjusts to variation in valve stem length. Hydraulic tappets also reduce valve noise.

I

Ignition timing The moment at which the spark plug fires, usually expressed in the number of crankshaft degrees before the piston reaches the top of its stroke.

Inlet manifold A tube or housing with passages through which flows the air-fuel mixture (carburettor vehicles and vehicles with throttle body injection) or air only (port fuel-injected vehicles) to the port openings in the cylinder head.

J

Jump start Starting the engine of a vehicle with a discharged or weak battery by attaching jump leads from the weak battery to a charged or helper battery.

L

Load Sensing Proportioning Valve (LSPV) A brake hydraulic system control valve that works like a proportioning valve, but also takes into consideration the amount of weight carried by the rear axle.

Locknut A nut used to lock an adjustment nut, or other threaded component, in place. For example, a locknut is employed to keep the adjusting nut on the rocker arm in position.

Lockwasher A form of washer designed to prevent an attaching nut from working loose.

M

MacPherson strut A type of front suspension system devised by Earle MacPherson at Ford of England. In its original form, a simple lateral link with the anti-roll bar creates the lower control arm. A long strut - an integral coil spring and shock absorber - is mounted between the body and the steering knuckle. Many modern so-called MacPherson strut systems use a conventional lower A-arm and don't rely on the anti-roll bar for location.

Multimeter An electrical test instrument with the capability to measure voltage, current and resistance.

N

NOx Oxides of Nitrogen. A common toxic pollutant emitted by petrol and diesel engines at higher temperatures.

O

Ohm The unit of electrical resistance. One volt applied to a resistance of one ohm will produce a current of one amp.

Ohmmeter An instrument for measuring electrical resistance.

O-ring A type of sealing ring made of a special rubber-like material; in use, the O-ring is compressed into a groove to provide the sealing action.

Overhead cam (ohc) engine An engine with the camshaft(s) located on top of the cylinder head(s).

Overhead valve (ohv) engine An engine with the valves located in the cylinder head, but with the camshaft located in the engine block.

Oxygen sensor A device installed in the engine exhaust manifold, which senses the oxygen content in the exhaust and converts this information into an electric current. Also called a Lambda sensor.

P

Phillips screw A type of screw head having a cross instead of a slot for a corresponding type of screwdriver.

Plastigage A thin strip of plastic thread, available in different sizes, used for measuring clearances. For example, a strip of Plastigage is laid across a bearing journal. The parts are assembled and dismantled; the width of the crushed strip indicates the clearance between journal and bearing.

Plastigage

Propeller shaft The long hollow tube with universal joints at both ends that carries power from the transmission to the differential on front-engined rear wheel drive vehicles.

Proportioning valve A hydraulic control valve which limits the amount of pressure to the rear brakes during panic stops to prevent wheel lock-up.

R

Rack-and-pinion steering A steering system with a pinion gear on the end of the steering shaft that mates with a rack (think of a geared wheel opened up and laid flat). When the steering wheel is turned, the pinion turns, moving the rack to the left or right. This movement is transmitted through the track rods to the steering arms at the wheels.

Radiator A liquid-to-air heat transfer device designed to reduce the temperature of the coolant in an internal combustion engine cooling system.

Refrigerant Any substance used as a heat transfer agent in an air-conditioning system. R-12 has been the principle refrigerant for many years; recently, however, manufacturers have begun using R-134a, a non-CFC substance that is considered less harmful to the ozone in the upper atmosphere.

Rocker arm A lever arm that rocks on a shaft or pivots on a stud. In an overhead valve engine, the rocker arm converts the upward movement of the pushrod into a downward movement to open a valve.

Rotor In a distributor, the rotating device inside the cap that connects the centre electrode and the outer terminals as it turns, distributing the high voltage from the coil secondary winding to the proper spark plug. Also, that part of an alternator which rotates inside the stator. Also, the rotating assembly of a turbocharger, including the compressor wheel, shaft and turbine wheel.

Runout The amount of wobble (in-and-out movement) of a gear or wheel as it's rotated. The amount a shaft rotates "out-of-true." The out-of-round condition of a rotating part.

S

Sealant A liquid or paste used to prevent leakage at a joint. Sometimes used in conjunction with a gasket.

Sealed beam lamp An older headlight design which integrates the reflector, lens and filaments into a hermetically-sealed one-piece unit. When a filament burns out or the lens cracks, the entire unit is simply replaced.

Serpentine drivebelt A single, long, wide accessory drivebelt that's used on some newer vehicles to drive all the accessories, instead of a series of smaller, shorter belts. Serpentine drivebelts are usually tensioned by an automatic tensioner.

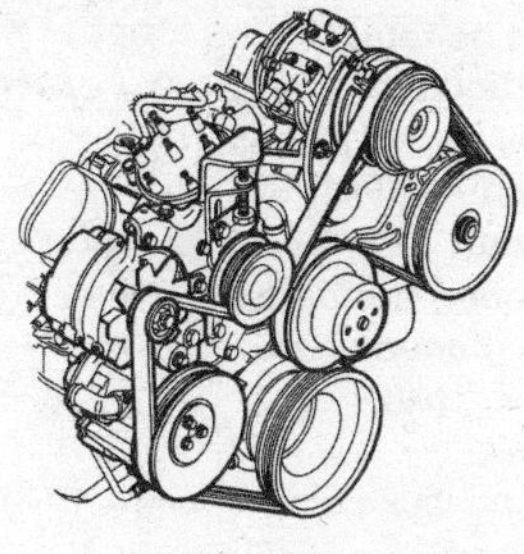

Serpentine drivebelt

Shim Thin spacer, commonly used to adjust the clearance or relative positions between two parts. For example, shims inserted into or under bucket tappets control valve clearances. Clearance is adjusted by changing the thickness of the shim.

Slide hammer A special puller that screws into or hooks onto a component such as a shaft or bearing; a heavy sliding handle on the shaft bottoms against the end of the shaft to knock the component free.

Sprocket A tooth or projection on the periphery of a wheel, shaped to engage with a chain or drivebelt. Commonly used to refer to the sprocket wheel itself.

Starter inhibitor switch On vehicles with an automatic transmission, a switch that prevents starting if the vehicle is not in Neutral or Park.

Strut See MacPherson strut.

T

Tappet A cylindrical component which transmits motion from the cam to the valve stem, either directly or via a pushrod and rocker arm. Also called a cam follower.

Thermostat A heat-controlled valve that regulates the flow of coolant between the cylinder block and the radiator, so maintaining optimum engine operating temperature. A thermostat is also used in some air cleaners in which the temperature is regulated.

Thrust bearing The bearing in the clutch assembly that is moved in to the release levers by clutch pedal action to disengage the clutch. Also referred to as a release bearing.

Timing belt A toothed belt which drives the camshaft. Serious engine damage may result if it breaks in service.

Timing chain A chain which drives the camshaft.

Toe-in The amount the front wheels are closer together at the front than at the rear. On rear wheel drive vehicles, a slight amount of toe-in is usually specified to keep the front wheels running parallel on the road by offsetting other forces that tend to spread the wheels apart.

Toe-out The amount the front wheels are closer together at the rear than at the front. On front wheel drive vehicles, a slight amount of toe-out is usually specified.

Tools For full information on choosing and using tools, refer to the *Haynes Automotive Tools Manual*.

Tracer A stripe of a second colour applied to a wire insulator to distinguish that wire from another one with the same colour insulator.

Tune-up A process of accurate and careful adjustments and parts replacement to obtain the best possible engine performance.

Turbocharger A centrifugal device, driven by exhaust gases, that pressurises the intake air. Normally used to increase the power output from a given engine displacement, but can also be used primarily to reduce exhaust emissions (as on VW's "Umwelt" Diesel engine).

U

Universal joint or U-joint A double-pivoted connection for transmitting power from a driving to a driven shaft through an angle. A U-joint consists of two Y-shaped yokes and a cross-shaped member called the spider.

V

Valve A device through which the flow of liquid, gas, vacuum, or loose material in bulk may be started, stopped, or regulated by a movable part that opens, shuts, or partially obstructs one or more ports or passageways. A valve is also the movable part of such a device.

Valve clearance The clearance between the valve tip (the end of the valve stem) and the rocker arm or tappet. The valve clearance is measured when the valve is closed.

Vernier caliper A precision measuring instrument that measures inside and outside dimensions. Not quite as accurate as a micrometer, but more convenient.

Viscosity The thickness of a liquid or its resistance to flow.

Volt A unit for expressing electrical "pressure" in a circuit. One volt that will produce a current of one ampere through a resistance of one ohm.

W

Welding Various processes used to join metal items by heating the areas to be joined to a molten state and fusing them together. For more information refer to the *Haynes Automotive Welding Manual*.

Wiring diagram A drawing portraying the components and wires in a vehicle's electrical system, using standardised symbols. For more information refer to the *Haynes Automotive Electrical and Electronic Systems Manual*.

Note: *References throughout this index are in the form* **"Chapter number" • "Page number"**. *So, for example, 2C•15 refers to page 15 of Chapter 2C.*

Note: *References throughout this index are in the form* **"Chapter number" • "Page number"**. *So, for example, 2C•15 refers to page 15 of Chapter 2C.*

Note: *References throughout this index are in the form* **"Chapter number" • "Page number"**. *So, for example, 2C•15 refers to page 15 of Chapter 2C.*

Note: *References throughout this index are in the form* **"Chapter number" • "Page number"**. *So, for example, 2C•15 refers to page 15 of Chapter 2C.*

Preserving Our Motoring Heritage

The Model J Duesenberg Derham Tourster. Only eight of these magnificent cars were ever built – this is the only example to be found outside the United States of America

Almost every car you've ever loved, loathed or desired is gathered under one roof at the Haynes Motor Museum. Over 300 immaculately presented cars and motorbikes represent every aspect of our motoring heritage, from elegant reminders of bygone days, such as the superb Model J Duesenberg to curiosities like the bug-eyed BMW Isetta. There are also many old friends and flames. Perhaps you remember the 1959 Ford Popular that you did your courting in? The magnificent 'Red Collection' is a spectacle of classic sports cars including AC, Alfa Romeo, Austin Healey, Ferrari, Lamborghini, Maserati, MG, Riley, Porsche and Triumph.

A Perfect Day Out

Each and every vehicle at the Haynes Motor Museum has played its part in the history and culture of Motoring. Today, they make a wonderful spectacle and a great day out for all the family. Bring the kids, bring Mum and Dad, but above all bring your camera to capture those golden memories for ever. You will also find an impressive array of motoring memorabilia, a comfortable 70 seat video cinema and one of the most extensive transport book shops in Britain. The Pit Stop Cafe serves everything from a cup of tea to wholesome, home-made meals or, if you prefer, you can enjoy the large picnic area nestled in the beautiful rural surroundings of Somerset.

John Haynes O.B.E., Founder and Chairman of the museum at the wheel of a Haynes Light 12.

Graham Hill's Lola Cosworth Formula 1 car next to a 1934 Riley Sports.

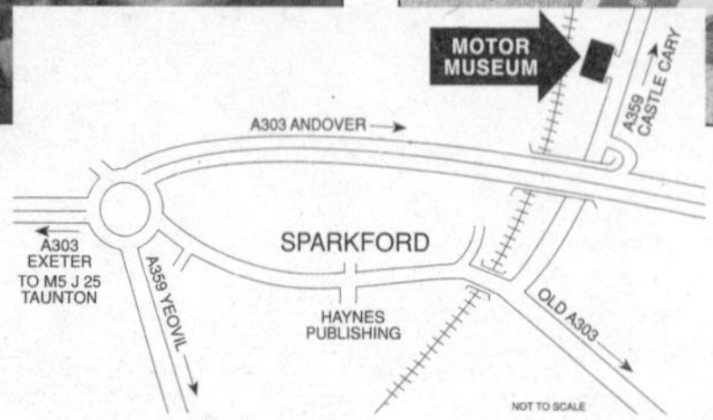

The Museum is situated on the A359 Yeovil to Frome road at Sparkford, just off the A303 in Somerset. It is about 40 miles south of Bristol, and 25 minutes drive from the M5 intersection at Taunton.

Open 9.30am - 5.30pm (10.00am - 4.00pm Winter) 7 days a week, *except Christmas Day, Boxing Day and New Years Day*

Special rates available for schools, coach parties and outings Charitable Trust No. 292048